GLOBAL EMPLOYEE PRIVACY AND DATA SECURITY LAW

Related Titles from BNA Books

Privacy in Employment Law, Second Edition

International Labor and Employment Laws, Third Edition

Canadian Labour and Employment Law for the U.S. Practitioner, Second Edition

Global Employee Privacy and Data Security Law

Morrison & Foerster LLP

Editors

Miriam H. Wugmeister
Morrison & Foerster
New York, NY

Christine E. Lyon
Morrison & Foerster
Palo Alto, CA

BNA Books, *A Division of BNA*, Arlington, VA

Library of Congress Cataloging-in-Publication Data

Global employee privacy and data security law / Morrison & Foerster LLP ; editors Miriam H. Wugmeister [and] Christine E. Lyon.
p. cm.
Includes index.
ISBN 978-1-57018-805-3
1. Data protection-- Law and legislation. 2. Privacy, Right of. 3. Employee rights. I. Wugmeister, Miriam. II. Lyon, Christine E. III. Morrison & Foerster.
KF3264.C65G578 2009
342. 08 ‘ 58--dc22

2009018792

Published by BNA Books
1801 S. Bell Street, Arlington, VA 22202
bnabooks.com

ISBN 978-1-57018-805-3
Printed in the United States of America

PREFACE

More than 65 countries now have some type of law that regulates the collection, use, and disclosure of personal information. As the workplace becomes more global, employers must recognize and comply with a myriad of privacy and data security laws (also known as "data protection" laws) that affect employees and other workers. Employers who fail to address workplace privacy and data security issues may find that they are precluded from sharing information with affiliated entities, subject to fines and scrutiny by data protection regulators, and the object of negative publicity.

Companies operating in multiple jurisdictions often struggle to try to find a method of complying with the complex and sometimes conflicting obligations imposed by data protection laws while running their businesses in a cost-effective manner. There is a tension between a desire to provide a safe and secure work environment and at the same time respect the privacy of individual employees. Global employers seek the right balance between ensuring that employees are free from sexual harassment and inappropriate conduct on the one hand and respecting legal restrictions on monitoring of Internet or email use on the other hand. Similarly, employers are seeking to streamline processes and save money by centralizing the human resources function, while at the same time limiting access to employees' personal information on a need-to-know basis. The first step to working through any of these issues is to understand the questions that must be asked and then to develop a method of examining the issues to find solutions that are practical for each particular organization. There is no "right" answer and no magic bullet to global privacy and data security compliance. Each organization must find a solution that works within its culture and based on the resources available to it.

The Purpose of This Book

This book is designed to help employers understand the legal landscape related to workplace privacy and data security, and begin to ask the necessary questions to make the key decisions. As more and more personal information is available, laws and regulations are being adopted to enhance an individual's right to make decisions about his or her personal information. The contours of these protections vary from state to state and from country to country. The varied social, cultural, and legal regimes that influence the development of privacy laws are significant. Human resources professionals are often surprised to learn that, in many countries, basic details such as an employee's work email address or employee ID number are considered personal information and subject to the same protections and restrictions as an employee's home address. Lawyers are surprised to learn that the same limitations apply to disclosing personal information to an affiliate as to disclosing information to an unaffiliated third party. The purpose of this book is to limit those "surprises" and to help professionals prepare for and implement cogent privacy and data security policies and programs.

How This Book Is Organized

Unlike other books on the subject, this book is organized not by the particular law or country; rather, it is organized based on the manner in which human resources professionals, privacy and compliance professionals, and lawyers think about privacy issues in the employment context. We begin with an overview of the legal landscape in the United States, European Union (EU), Japan and other key jurisdictions, while each of the remaining chapters analyzes an important topic across jurisdictions to raise awareness about the conflicts among and variation of the laws. For example, we have examined the issues confronted by human resources personnel when they wish to monitor an employee's Internet use or email across a variety of U.S. federal and state laws, the EU Member State laws, and selected countries in Asia. Similarly we have compared the laws relating to the collection, use, and disclosure of medical information across a variety of countries.

Professionals working in this area know that having a different process or procedure for each country or state in which an organization operates is quickly becoming impractical and cost prohibitive. By understanding the key differences among the various jurisdictions for the most vexing privacy issues, organizations can begin to formulate policies and practices that balance compliance obligations with practical considerations. By organizing the book along substantive lines and then comparing the laws and regulations across countries (within the same substantive area), professionals working in this area will be able to identify the key issues, ask the right questions, and find the solutions that are practical and tailored to each organization.

Chapter Outline

Chapter 1, "Overview of Privacy and Data Security," provides a comprehensive overview of the legal framework applied to workplace privacy issues in key jurisdictions, such as the United States, Canada, the European Union, Japan, and a number of other countries. While each chapter of this book provides a stand-alone discussion—for instance, employers interested in Internet monitoring can go directly to Chapter 3—Chapter 1 will help to provide a greater understanding of the "big picture" approach to workplace privacy in the various jurisdictions. Additional information about EU standard clauses for cross-border transfers of personal information, which are discussed in section III.D of this chapter, is provided in Appendix B.

Chapter 2, "Background Checks and Investigations," addresses the first topic that an employer is likely to encounter when it expands its operations to another country. The rules governing criminal background checks, credit checks, and other background inquiries vary significantly by jurisdiction, and even within the U.S. These laws also limit the information that an employer may lawfully consider in making hiring or other employment decisions.

Chapter 3, "Email and Internet Monitoring/Video and Physical Surveillance," explains the increasingly complex restrictions on electronic monitoring in the workplace. This chapter includes employer monitoring of work email and Internet use, as well as the use of video and audio surveillance in the workplace.

Chapter 4, "Employees' Off-Duty Conduct," addresses limitations on an employer's ability to monitor or take action based on an employee's off-duty conduct. It covers topics such as union and political activities, religious observances, fraternization and romantic relationships with coworkers or others in the workplace, and "moonlighting" or outside employment.

Chapter 5, "Confidentiality of Health Information," describes the legal protections for employees' health information, including data security and confidentiality obligations that apply to medical and health information. This is followed by a separate discussion of medical examinations conducted by employers, in Chapter 6.

Chapter 6, "Medical Examinations and Drug Testing of Applicants and Employees," analyzes the highly regulated areas of medical examination and drug testing, including the applicable procedural requirements. This chapter also discusses other types of physical or mental testing, such as personality tests, fingerprinting, polygraph testing, and genetic testing.

Chapter 7, "Personnel Records," describes the use and disclosure of personnel records, including employee access rights. It also explains some of the potential negative consequences arising from a misuse or improper disclosure of personnel records.

Chapter 8, "Use of Government Identifiers and Social Security Numbers," discusses the expanding restrictions on the use of Social Security Numbers (SSNs) and other government identification numbers by employers. This is a particular focus in the U.S., due to the widespread use of the SSN for financial and credit purposes.

Chapter 9, "Security Breach Notification Requirements," explains notification obligations that may be triggered by a breach of the security of employees' SSNs or various other types of personal information. This chapter also describes the growing number of countries adopting security breach notification laws.

Chapter 10, "Data Security: Maintaining an Information Security Program," provides guidelines for developing an effective program to protect employee data, as well as other personal information. This chapter describes the process for creating an effective program, from the initial risk assessment through policy development and employee training. It also identifies specific measures for such a program, such as document classification, access controls, technical measures such as encryption, and vendor monitoring.

Each chapter begins with a discussion of the applicable privacy and data security issues under U.S. federal and state laws. This U.S. section may serve as a refresher for U.S.-based employers, or as a primer for professionals trained in non-U.S. jurisdictions as they launch operations in the U.S. Following the U.S. section, we provide a detailed explanation of the relevant data protection issues in Europe and the Asia Pacific region, using a variety of representative countries. This book does not seek to be an encyclopedia that covers each and every country. Instead, it is intended to provide a more global perspective on workplace issues, by helping employers understand the differing approaches to workplace privacy by region and jurisdiction. Additional countries may be added to this book over time, as privacy and data security laws continue to expand.

Additional Resources

This book includes references to a variety of statutes, regulations, cases, and other legal guidance. Readers interested in reviewing these source materials can find links to online copies of many of these documents through Morrison & Foerster's online Privacy Library, available at www.mofoprivacy.com. The Privacy Library is organized by jurisdiction, allowing easy retrieval of privacy laws for a certain country (or, within the U.S., by state). Additionally, the Privacy Library includes a "Legal Updates and News" page, which provides articles and news alerts written by Morrison & Foerster's Privacy and Data Security Practice. Further information on the Privacy Library is provided in Appendix A. Detailed analysis of virtually every data protection law is also available on a subscription basis through Summit Privacy Resources. For more information see www.summitprivacy.com. BNA also provides information on new developments in this area in its *Privacy and Security Law Report* (www.bna.com/products/corplaw/pvln.htm) and publishes *Privacy in Employment Law*, a companion volume focused on U.S. law.

About the Editors and Authors

This book was written by an international team of attorneys in the Privacy and Data Security Practice of Morrison & Foerster LLP, a global law firm with more than 1,000 lawyers in 17 offices around the world. Today, the firm has more than 60 attorneys in our global offices addressing privacy issues, several of whom were instrumental in the drafting of key pieces of legislation in the field, as well as litigating cutting-edge privacy and data security issues. Information on the individual editors and authors is provided in the "About the Editors and Authors" section following this Preface.

Morrison & Foerster advises and represents clients on a wide range of privacy issues both in and outside of the U.S., including data security and regulatory compliance; employee privacy; Web site and online privacy issues; data security, security breach notification, industry-specific privacy issues facing sectors such as financial services and health care; and international data protection. Clients include financial institutions (including banks, insurance companies, and securities firms), hardware and software companies, health care providers and health plans, payment systems providers, retailers, telecommunications networks, medical device companies, entertainment companies, and content providers.

We hope that you find this book a useful tool as you seek to find solutions to what will only become a more interesting and complicated area in the years to come.

MIRIAM H. WUGMEISTER
Editor
New York, NY

CHRISTINE E. LYON
Editor
Palo Alto, CA

April 2009

ABOUT THE EDITORS AND AUTHORS

The Firm

Morrison & Foerster LLP offers clients comprehensive global legal services in business and litigation through more than 1,000 lawyers in 17 offices around the world. Its cross-disciplinary Privacy and Data Security Practice Group includes more than 60 attorneys internationally. Group members have a wide range of expertise in disciplines such as corporate practice, financial services, labor, technology, and litigation, providing clients a broad and global perspective on privacy matters.

The Editors

Miriam Wugmeister is a partner in the New York office of Morrison & Foerster and is head of the Firm's Privacy and Data Security Practice Group. She counsels clients regarding the collection, use, and transfer of personal information as organizations seek to comply with U.S. and non-U.S. data protection laws. She regularly advises global companies on multinational privacy compliance efforts. Ms. Wugmeister also has had significant experience in all areas of employment and labor law.

Christine Lyon is a partner in Morrison & Foerster's Palo Alto office, where her practice concentrates on employment and privacy law. She works extensively in the Firm's Privacy and Data Security Practice Group, with respect to both U.S. and international privacy issues. She has published articles and lectured on privacy, data security, and anti-spam legislation; assists clients in developing compliance strategies and internal governance policies; and advises clients in the areas of data protection and employee privacy.

Senior Editor and Contributing Author

Cynthia Rich is a senior international policy analyst in Morrison & Foerster's Washington, D.C., office, where she advises clients on privacy and transborder data transfers. Prior to joining the firm, Ms. Rich served as a senior international policy advisor at the U.S. Department of Commerce, where she worked to develop the groundbreaking safe harbor privacy arrangement between the U.S. and the European Union (EU).

Contributing Authors

Amina Adam is an associate in Morrison & Foerster's London office. She represents clients on privacy and employment matters in a wide range of industries on both contentious and noncontentious matters. She is a very experienced advocate, having been called to the Bar in 1996.

Teresa Basile is an associate in Morrison & Foerster's Brussels office, where she advises multinational companies on the different aspects of EU competition law and on data protection, privacy law, and e-commerce, at both EU and national levels.

Joyita Basu is an associate in Morrison & Foerster's Washington, D.C., office. She has experience advising on a wide range of issues related to privacy and data security under the Gramm-Leach-Bliley Act, the Fair Credit Reporting Act, the Fair and Accurate Credit Transactions Act, and state privacy and data security laws. She also handles a broad range of transactional and regulatory matters for financial institutions.

Ann Bevitt is a partner in the London office of Morrison & Foerster and head of the office's EU Privacy and Employment & Labor Groups. She has extensive expertise advising clients on international data protection and privacy issues. Her practice area covers all aspects of employment law and privacy-related matters, both contentious and noncontentious, with a focus on outsourcing (information technology, best practices, and human resources), international reorganizations, and mergers and acquisitions.

Cindy Chiu is an associate in the Hong Kong office of Morrison & Foerster. She has a broad-ranging practice and advises on general corporate matters. Ms. Chiu is admitted to practice in Hong Kong and is fluent in English, Cantonese, and Mandarin.

Suzanne Horne is an associate in Morrison & Foerster's London office, where she advises a wide range of clients on all aspects of employment law, data protection and privacy, and strategic human resources issues.

Michiko Ito Crampe is a partner in the New York office and is involved in international privacy issues, particularly with respect to Japan, including advising U.S. multinational corporations on how to comply with Japan's laws concerning the protection of personal information. She was the first lawyer admitted to practice law in both Japan and the United States when she was admitted to the State Bar of New York in 1976.

Charles Kennedy is Of Counsel in Morrison & Foerster's Washington, D.C., office and his practice focuses on privacy, data protection, e-commerce, and telecommunications. He is an adjunct professor of law at Catholic University of America, where he teaches cyberlaw and telecommunications regulation. He also has written four books on communications law and has testified before Congress as an expert on cyberlaw.

Gordon Milner is a partner in Morrison & Foerster's Hong Kong office, where he specializes in providing advice on information technology law, privacy and data security, and outsourcing. Mr. Milner has particular expertise in respect of Asian cross-border projects. Mr. Milner has been resident in Hong Kong since 2001, having previously practiced in London.

Karin Retzer is Of Counsel in Morrison & Foerster's Brussels office, where she focuses on the legal aspects of electronic e-commerce and data protection, technology licensing, and intellectual property law. She assists on worldwide privacy and data security projects and has advised clients on global data processing, data retention obligations, direct marketing, and employee monitoring.

Thomas Scanlon is Of Counsel in the Washington, D.C., office of Morrison & Foerster. He focuses on helping clients manage information about consumers and develop solutions to comply with complex privacy and data security laws. Mr. Scanlon's work in these emerging areas of the law, informed by his work for the

Federal Reserve Board, enables him to provide practical advice to address novel regulatory issues.

Toshihiro So is Of Counsel in the Tokyo office of Morrison & Foerster. He represents both Japanese and non-Japanese clients on a wide range of general corporate, labor, privacy, civil litigation, real estate, and securities-related matters. From 1990 to 1998, Mr. So was employed by Fuji Electric Co., Ltd., in the Legal Department. He graduated from the Legal Training and Research Institute of the Supreme Court of Japan and was admitted to practice in Japan in 2000.

Nathan Taylor is an associate in Morrison & Foerster's Washington, D.C., office. His practice focuses on consumer financial services and the regulation of financial institutions, in particular in relation to privacy and data security issues, including compliance with the Fair Credit Reporting Act, the Gramm-Leach-Bliley Act privacy and security requirements, and state security breach notification and security freeze statutes.

Timothy Verrall is Of Counsel with Morrison & Foerster's Northern Virginia office, where he advises a broad range of clients on the tax, labor, and securities aspects of employee benefit programs. He also has substantial experience dealing with issues arising under the Consolidated Omnibus Budget Reconciliation Act (COBRA) and the Health Insurance Portability and Accountability Act (HIPAA), including the HIPAA privacy, security, and transaction standards rules.

Marian Waldmann is an associate in Morrison & Foerster's New York office. Her practice focuses on the areas of privacy and data security and labor and employment. She received her J.D. from the University of Pennsylvania Law School in 2004, where she was a senior editor of the Journal of International Economic Law.

Other Contributors

Olivier Angotti is an associate in the firm of JeantetAssociés in Paris. On a regular basis, he advises international clients on data protection issues, with a focus on their criminal law aspects, from a French employment law perspective. Mr. Angotti also represents both French and foreign firms in litigation arising from noncompliance with employees' and employee representatives' privacy rights and data protection regulations.

Isabelle Pontal is a senior associate in the firm of JeantetAssociés in Paris. With more than 15 years of practice in employment law, she has extensive expertise in advising clients on issues arising from company restructurings, with a focus on collective redundancy exercises, compliance issues, and employees' data protection. Mrs. Pontal assists both French and foreign firms with due diligence exercises and subsequent negotiation over employment-related issues in the merger and acquisition context.

Dr. Jyn Schultze-Melling LL.M. is a senior privacy professional in the Munich office of Noerr Stiefenhofer Lutz, one of Germany's biggest independent law firms, which has 13 offices in Germany and Central and Eastern Europe. Dr. Schultze-Melling's practice focuses on setting up global privacy compliance schemes, preparing cross-border data transfers, and developing sound strategies in regard to corporate information security management.

Acknowledgements

The Firm greatly acknowledges the contributions of the following individuals who contributed in a variety of ways to the success of this book:

Oliver Bisazza
Sara Brin
Mary Jo Ellingson
Ivan J. Flores
Kimberly Harbin
Saori Horikawa
Leonard Lipsztein
Guy McPherson
Fraser Mendel
Katharine Pauley
Janelle Sahouria
Charles Shaw

SUMMARY TABLE OF CONTENTS

Preface		v
About the Editors and Authors		xvii
Detailed Table of Contents		xix
Chapter 1	Overview of Privacy and Data Security	1
Chapter 2	Background Checks and Investigations	117
Chapter 3	Email and Internet Monitoring/ Video and Physical Survellance	197
Chapter 4	Employees' Off-Duty Conduct	297
Chapter 5	Confidentiality of Health Information	329
Chapter 6	Medical Examinations and Drug Testing of Applicants and Employees	415
Chapter 7	Personnel Records	467
Chapter 8	Use of Government Identifiers and Social Security Numbers	501
Chapter 9	Security Breach Notification Requirements	531
Chapter 10	Data Security: Maintaining an Information Security Program	595
Appendix A	About Morrison & Foerster's Privacy Library	625
Appendix B	EU Standard Clauses for Cross-Border Transfers of Personal Information	627
Index		667

DETAILED TABLE OF CONTENTS

Preface v

About the Editors and Authors xi

Summary Table of Contents xvii

Chapter 1 Overview of Privacy and Data Security 1

I. The United States 5
  A. Overview 5
  B. Federal Law and Regulation 7
    1. Sectoral Regulations 8
      a. Financial Information 8
        i. Financial Privacy Rule 9
        ii. Safeguards Rule 9
      b. Health Information 10
        i. The Health Insurance Portability and Accountability Act of 1996 10
          (a) Standards for Privacy of Individually Identifiable Health Information (Privacy Rule) 10
          (b) Security Standards (Security Rule) 11
        ii. The Americans With Disabilities Act 11
        iii. Genetic Information 11
      c. Consumer Report Information 12
        i. Fair Credit Reporting Act 12
        ii. The Fair and Accurate Credit Transactions Act 12
      d. Children's Information 13
    2. Regulatory Focus on Electronic Data 13
      a. Computer Fraud and Abuse Act 13

b. Electronic Communications Privacy Act...... 14
3. Regulatory Focus on Misrepresentation and Unfairness 14
a. Federal Trade Commission Act 14
C. State Laws 16
1. State Constitutions 17
2. State Laws and Regulations 17
a. Financial Information 17
b. Health Information 18
c. Consumer Report Information 19
3. Misuse of Information 19
a. Procedures and Practices 19
b. Security Breach Notification 21
c. Social Security Number Laws 21
d. Employee Monitoring 22
4. Unfair or Deceptive Acts or Practices 22
II. Countries Other Than the United States—Global Overview 23
Exhibit 1.1 Countries With Data Privacy Laws 25
III. Europe 27
A. Introduction 27
B. Legislative Framework 29
C. Requirements for Processing of Information Within the EU 31
1. Legal Basis 31
2. Sensitive Data 33
3. Notice Requirements 34
4. Access Rights 35
5. Right to Object 36
6. Contracts With Data Processors 36
7. Registration Obligations 37
D. Cross-Border Restrictions 39
1. Transfers to Countries Providing "Adequate Data Protection" 39
2. The U.S. Safe Harbor Framework 39
Exhibit 1.2 The Safe Harbor Privacy Principles 40
3. Adequate Safeguards: Contracts or Binding Corporate Rules 45
4. Other Options 49
E. Employer Policy Formulation 50

IV. Asia and Asia Pacific 53
A. Australia 54
1. Overview 54
2. The Privacy Act—Employee Records Exemption 55
3. Obligations Under the Privacy Act When the Employee Records Exemption Does Not Apply 57
4. Penalties 59
5. Health Information 59
6. Workplace Monitoring and Surveillance 59
B. Hong Kong 59
1. Notice 60
2. Consent 61
3. Access and Correction Requirements 61
4. Accuracy Requirements 61
5. Retention of Employment-Related Data 62
6. Disclosure or Transfer of Employment-Related Data 62
7. Transfer of Employment-Related Data Outside Hong Kong 63
8. Providing Job References 63
9. Sensitive Information 63
a. Medical and Health Data 63
b. Identity Card Numbers 64
10. Security Requirements 64
11. Monitoring of Employees 65
12. Penalties 65
C. Japan 65
1. Notice 67
2. Breach Notice 68
3. Notice to Labor Unions 69
4. Consent 69
5. Third-Party Sharing of Employee Information 69
6. Supervision of Service Providers 70
7. Security 71
8. Sensitive Information 72
9. Access and Correction Rights 72
10. Monitoring of Employees 73
D. Korea 73
1. Notice 74
2. Privacy Policy 74

3. Consent 74
4. Access and Correction Rights 75
5. Cross-Border Requirements 75
6. Security 75
7. Supervision of Service Providers 77
8. Data Retention 77
9. Breach Notification 77
10. Penalties 78
11. Surveillance/Monitoring of Employees 78

E. New Zealand 78
1. Collection and Use Limitations 79
2. Notice 79
3. Security and Data Retention 79
4. Access and Correction 80
5. Data Accuracy 80
6. Data Retention 80
7. Unique Identifiers 80

F. Taiwan 80
1. License/Database Registration 81
2. Consent 82
3. Use Limitations 82
4. Limits on Data Transfers; Cross-Border Limitations 83
5. Access Rights 83
6. Accuracy/Right to Correct/Cease Use 83
7. Data Retention 84
8. Monitoring of Employees 84
9. Security 85
10. Penalties 85

V. Americas 86

A. Argentina 86
1. Notice/Privacy Policy 87
2. Consent/Use Limitations 87
3. Access and Correction 88
4. Security/Data Retention 88
5. Database Registration 90
6. Cross-Border Transfers 90
7. Onward Transfer Agreements 90
8. Dispute Resolution 91

B. Canada 91
1. Federal Regulation 91

2. PIPEDA Requirements 93
   a. Notice 93
   b. Consent 93
   c. Database Registration 94
   d. Data Processing Contracts 94
   e. Designation of a Privacy Officer 94
   f. Implementation of Policies and Practices; Audit 94
   g. Access 94
   h. Cross-Border Transfers 94
   i. Complaint Handling 94
   j. Security 95
   k. Data Retention 95
3. Provincial Privacy Laws 95
   a. British Columbia 95
   b. Ontario 96
   c. Quebec 96

C. Chile 96
1. Notice 97
2. Privacy Policy 97
3. Consent; Limitations on Collection, Use, and Disclosure 97
4. Access and Correction 98
5. Security; Data Retention 98
6. Database Registration 98
7. Cross-Border Limitations 98
8. Onward Transfer Agreements 98
9. Dispute Resolution 98

Exhibit 1.3 EU Member State Implementation Legislation for Data Privacy and Security 99

CHAPTER 2 BACKGROUND CHECKS AND INVESTIGATIONS 117

I. Overview 121
II. Americas 122
A. United States 122
1. Application of the FCRA to Background Check Reports 123
   a. What Is a Consumer Reporting Agency? 123
   b. What Is a Consumer Report? 124

2. Notice and Consent Requirements Under the FCRA ... 125
   a. Notice and Consent Requirements to Obtain Reports ... 125
      Exhibit 2.1 U.S.: Sample Authorization Under the Fair Credit Reporting Act ... 126
      i. Additional Notice Requirements for Investigative Reports ... 127
      ii. Additional State Notice Requirements to Obtain Reports ... 128
   b. Notice Requirements for Adverse Action Based on Report ... 129
      i. Pre-Adverse Action Notice Requirements ... 129
         Exhibit 2.2 U.S.: Sample Pre-Adverse Action Notice Under the Fair Credit Reporting Act ... 130
      ii. Adverse Action Notice Requirements ... 133
         Exhibit 2.3 U.S.: Sample Adverse Action Notice Under the Fair Credit Reporting Act ... 134
   c. Certain Misconduct Investigations Exempt From the FCRA ... 135
3. Limitations on Content of Background Check Reports ... 136
4. Access and Correction Rights ... 137
   Exhibit 2.4 U.S.: Sample Background Check Process ... 138
5. Potential Liability for Violations of the FCRA and Similar State Laws ... 140
6. State Law Rules Relating to Background Checks by Vendors ... 140
   a. California ... 141
   b. New York ... 142
7. Background Checks and Investigations Conducted In-House by Employers ... 143
8. Limitations on Direct Inquiries by Employers ... 144
   a. Arrests and Sealed or Expunged Convictions ... 144
   b. Convictions ... 145
      i. Access Rights ... 146

ii. Exceptions ... 147
iii. Employer Liability ... 148
c. Fingerprinting ... 148
d. Bankruptcy Act ... 149
9. Hiring and Payment of OFAC-Designated Nationals in the Post-9/11 Environment ... 149
10. Disposal of Background Information ... 151
a. Disposal Rules Under Federal Law ... 151
b. Disposal Rules Under State Law ... 153
B. Brazil ... 154
1. Background Checks ... 154
2. Responding to Employment Verification Requests ... 155
C. Canada ... 155
1. Background Checks ... 155
2. Responding to Employment Verification Requests ... 156
D. Mexico ... 156
1. Background Checks ... 156
2. Responding to Employment Verification Requests ... 157
III. Europe ... 157
Exhibit 2.5 EU: Background Checks—United Kingdom, Germany, and France ... 158
A. Belgium ... 158
1. Background Checks ... 158
2. Responding to Employment Verification Requests ... 159
B. France ... 159
1. Applicable Statutes ... 159
2. General Requirements ... 160
3. Sensitive Data ... 161
4. Notice Requirements ... 161
5. Access and Correction ... 162
6. Use Restrictions ... 162
7. Guidance on Specific Background Checks ... 163
a. Credit ... 163
b. Criminal Records ... 163
c. Work History ... 163
d. References ... 164
e. General Reputation/Character ... 164
C. Germany ... 164

1. Applicable Statutes 164
2. General Requirements.. 165
3. Sensitive Data 167
4. Notice Requirements.. 168
5. Access and Correction Rights............................ 168
6. Use Restrictions 168
7. Guidance on Specific Background Checks......... 169
a. Credit 169
b. Criminal Records.. 170
c. Work History 171
d. References 172
e. General Reputation/Character 172

D. Italy 172
1. Background Checks 172
2. Responding to Employment Verification Requests 173

E. United Kingdom 173
1. Applicable Statutes 173
2. General Requirements.. 174
3. Sensitive Data 178
4. Notice Requirements.. 179
5. Access and Correction 179
6. Use Restrictions 179
7. Guidance on Specific Background Checks......... 180
a. Credit 180
b. Criminal Records.. 180
Exhibit 2.6 "Spent Conviction" Time Periods 181
c. Work History 182
d. References 182
e. General Reputation/Character 183

IV. Asia 184
A. China... 184
1. Background Checks Generally 184
2. Guidance on Specific Background Checks in China 185
a. Credit 185
b. Criminal Records.. 185
c. Work History 185

B. Hong Kong 185
1. Applicable Laws 185

2. General Requirements—Employment Candidates 186
3. General Requirements—Existing Employees 187
4. Access 187
5. Guidance on Specific Background Checks 187
a. Credit 187
b. Criminal Records 188
c. Work History 188
d. References 188
C. Japan 189
1. Background Checks During the Recruitment Period 189
a. General Restrictions Based on the Personal Information Protection Law 190
b. Special Restrictions Based on the Employment Security Law 191
c. Seeking References From the Former Workplace of the Job Applicant 191
d. Acquisition of Information After Employment 192
e. Prohibition or Limitation on the Collection of Sensitive Data 193
D. Korea 194
1. Background Checks 194
2. Responding to Employment Verification Requests 195

CHAPTER 3 EMAIL AND INTERNET MONITORING/ VIDEO AND PHYSICAL SURVELLANCE 197

I. Overview 200
II. Americas 202
A. United States 202
1. Surveillance of Employees' Electronic Communications 202
2. Surveillance of Employees' Telephone Conversations 203
3. Surveillance of Telephone Calls Under the ECPA 205
a. Prohibited Surveillance Under the ECPA 205

b. Permitted Surveillance Under the ECPA...... 207
i. Interceptions With Prior Consent 207
ii. Business Extension Exception............ 209
c. Surveillance to Protect the Employer's Rights or Property 211
4. Surveillance of Telephone Calls Under California Law 212
5. Surveillance of Telephone Calls Under New York Law.. 214
6. Surveillance of Employees' Email..................... 216
a. Email Monitoring Under Federal Law 216
b. Email Monitoring Under California Law 219
c. Email Monitoring Under Connecticut Law 219
d. Email Monitoring Under Delaware Law...... 220
e. Email Monitoring Under New York Law 220
7. Monitoring of Employees' Use of Employers' Computers 221
8. Do Employers Have a Duty to Monitor? 223
9. Surveillance by Government: ECPA, FISA, USA PATRIOT Act, and State Wiretap Laws.. 226
10. Physical Surveillance and Workplace Searches 228
11. Visual and Auditory Surveillance in the Workplace 228
12. Location-Based Restrictions on Surveillance..... 229
13. Use of Amplifying or Recording Devices.......... 230
14. Undercover Investigators 231
15. Invasion of Privacy Claims 232
a. Elements of Privacy Claim.......................... 233
b. Effect of Providing Notice of Surveillance.. 234
16. Additional Restrictions on Surveillance in Public-Sector Employment 236
17. Video Surveillance Viewed by Courts as Highly Intrusive 236
18. An Employee's Reasonable Expectation of Privacy Varies Based on the Type of Area Under Surveillance.. 237

19. Title III of the Omnibus Crime Control and Safe Streets Act May Also Provide a Source of Protection for Public Employees 238
20. Additional U.S. Restrictions on Surveillance in a Unionized Workplace 239
21. Restrictions on Surveillance of Union Activities 239
22. Restrictions on Video Surveillance in a Unionized Facility 240
23. Private-Sector Employers 241
a. Elements of an Invasion of Privacy Claim 241
i. Legally Protected Privacy Interest 241
ii. Reasonable Expectation of Privacy 242
iii. Serious Invasion of Privacy Interests ... 242
b. Employer's "Competing Nonprivacy Interests" Defense 243
24. Public-Sector Employers 244
a. Expectations of Privacy in the Public-Sector Workplace.. 244
b. Balancing of Public Employer's Legitimate Interests 245
25. Postal Mail Received by Employees at the Workplace 246
26. Setting Reasonable Workplace Privacy Expectations.. 247
27. Limiting the Intrusiveness of Workplace Searches 248
III. Europe 249
A. The European Union Approach 249
1. Email and Internet Monitoring 249
2. Monitoring of Employee Telephone Calls 252
3. Video Surveillance 252
4. Works Councils Role in Monitoring 253
B. Finland 255
1. Email and Internet Monitoring 255
2. Monitoring of Employee Telephone Calls 258
3. Video Surveillance 258
C. France 259
1. Email and Internet Monitoring 259
2. Monitoring of Employee Telephone Calls 263

3. Video Surveillance 264
D. Germany 267
1. Email and Internet Monitoring 267
2. Monitoring of Employee Telephone Calls 271
3. Video Surveillance 271
E. United Kingdom 273
1. Email and Internet Monitoring 273
2. Monitoring of Employee Telephone Calls 278
3. Video Surveillance 279
IV. Asia and Asia Pacific 280
A. Australia 280
1. General Requirements for Monitoring 280
2. Monitoring of Employee Email 281
3. Video Surveillance and Other Surveillance 282
B. China 284
1. General Requirements for Monitoring 284
C. Hong Kong 285
1. Monitoring Guidelines 285
2. Video Surveillance 287
D. Japan 288
1. General Requirements for Monitoring 288
2. Monitoring of Computer Use 289
E. Korea 290
1. Monitoring of Employee Email 290
2. Video Surveillance 291
F. New Zealand 292
1. Monitoring of Employee Email 292
2. Video Surveillance 292
G. Taiwan 293
1. General Requirements for Monitoring 293
2. Monitoring of Employee Email 293
V. What to Consider Before Monitoring Employees 294

CHAPTER 4 EMPLOYEES' OFF-DUTY CONDUCT 297

I. Overview 298
II. Americas 299
A. United States 299
1. Union Membership or Affiliation 300
a. Off-Duty Union Activities Outside Employer's Premises 300

b. Off-Duty Union Activities on Employer's Premises 301
2. Political Activities 302
a. Participation in Political Campaigns 302
b. Freedom of Political Activities and Affiliations 303
3. Religious Activities 305
4. Fraternization/Romantic Relationships 305
a. Relationships Between Managers and Nonmanagers 306
b. Relationships Between Co-Workers 306
c. Relationships With Nonemployees 308
5. "Moonlighting" or Outside Employment 308
6. Off-Duty Use of Tobacco, Alcohol, or Other Legal Substances 309
a. Off-Duty Use of Lawful "Consumable Products" 309
b. Laws Protecting Off-Duty Smoking and Tobacco Use 310
c. Off-Duty Use of Medical Marijuana 310
7. Participation in Alcohol or Drug Rehabilitation Programs 312
8. Participation in Literacy Programs 312
9. Other Lawful Off-Duty Activities 313
Exhibit 4.1 U.S.: Examples of Off-Duty Conduct That May Be Legally Protected 314
III. Europe 315
A. Overview 315
B. United Kingdom 316
1. Union Membership 316
2. Political Activities 317
3. Religious Activities 319
4. Fraternization/Romantic Relationships 319
5. "Moonlighting" or Outside Employment 320
IV. Asia 320
A. China 320
1. "Moonlighting" or Outside Employment 320
2. Union Membership or Affiliation 320
B. Hong Kong 321
1. "Moonlighting" or Outside Employment 321
2. Union Membership or Affiliation 321

C. Japan 322
1. "Moonlighting" or Outside Employment 322
2. Union Membership or Affiliation 323
3. Political Activities in the Workplace 325
4. Political Activities Outside the Workplace 326

CHAPTER 5 CONFIDENTIALITY OF HEALTH INFORMATION ... 329

I. Overview 333
II. Americas 334
A. United States 334
1. Health Insurance Portability and Accountability Act of 1996 334
a. Business Associates 334
b. Covered Entities 335
i. Health Care Providers 335
ii. Health Plans 335
iii. Group Health Plans 336
c. Health Care 336
d. Health Care Operations 337
e. Health Information 337
f. Individually Identifiable Health Information 338
g. Payment 338
h. Protected Health Information 339
i. Treatment 339
j. Summary of the Privacy Rules 339
k. Compliance Issues for Employers 340
i. Initial Compliance Issues 340
(a) Distinction Between Health Plan and Employer/Sponsor 340
(b) Identification and Classification of Health Plans 341
(c) Scope of Compliance Responsibitities 341
ii. Common Operational Issues Involving Health Information 343
(a) Benefit Plan Administration 343
(b) Information Sharing 344
(c) Participant Advocacy 344
iii. Specific Health Plan Compliance Requirements 345

iv. Administrative Safeguards 346
(a) Appointment of a Privacy Official and Contact Person 346
(b) Privacy Training for Plan's Workforce 347
(c) Implementation of Procedural Safeguards 347
(d) "Minimum Necessary" Policies 348
(e) Complaint Procedures 349
(f) Sanctions for Members of the Workforce Who Violate HIPAA Privacy Rules 349
(g) Duty to Mitigate Harmful Effects of Improper Uses or Disclosures... 350
(h) Prohibitions on Retaliation and Waiver 350
(i) Policies, Procedures, and Documentation 350
(j) Notice of Privacy Practices 351
v. Plan Amendment Requirements 353
vi. Individual Rights 355
vii. Business Associate Issues 355
(a) Business Associate Agreements 356
(b) Violation of Business Associate Agreements 357
viii. Implementation Deadlines 358
ix. De-Identification of Health Information 358
x. Health Information Relating to Deceased Individuals 359
xi. Disclosures to Family Members and Friends 359
xii. Disclosures Relating to Minors 360
xiii. Other Disclosures Required or Permitted by the Privacy Rules 360
(a) Response to a Complaint 360
(b) Reporting of Crimes 361
xiv. Consents to Disclosure 361
xv. Authorizations 361
(a) Psychotherapy Notes 363
(b) Marketing 363

xvi. Impact of State Medical Privacy Laws 364
l. Individual Privacy Rights 364
i. Right of Access 365
ii. Right to Request Amendment/ Correction 367
iii. Right to Accounting of Nonroutine Disclosures 369
(a) Notice of Privacy Practices 370
(b) Voluntary Restrictions on Disclosure of Health Information 371
(c) Confidential Communications 371
(d) Complaints to HHS 371
m. Enforcement 372
i. Responsibility for Enforcement 372
ii. Compliance Investigations by HHS 372
iii. Sanctions 373
iv. Private Enforcement Rights 374
v. HHS Approach to Enforcement 375
n. HIPAA Security Rules 375
i. Employer Compliance Issues 378
ii. Individual Rights Relating to the Security Rules 378
2. Other U.S. Federal Rules Relating to Confidentiality of Health Information 378
a. Americans With Disabilities Act 379
3. State Rules in the United States Relating to Confidentiality of Medical Information 379
a. California 379
i. Summary of Key Statutory Provisions 380
ii. Employer Compliance Responsibilities 381
(a) Adoption of Procedural Safeguards 381
(b) Prohibition on Discrimination 381
(c) Disclosure of Medical Information 382
(d) Authorized Disclosures 383
(e) Receipt of Medical Information 384
(f) Effects on Vendor Relationships 385

(g) Document Destruction Requirements ... 386
(h) Health Care Providers Acting as Employers ... 386
(i) Improper Use or Disclosure of Medical Information ... 387
(j) Disclosure of Genetic Data ... 387
(k) HIV/AIDS Status ... 388
(l) Prohibition on Waivers ... 388
(m) Right of Access ... 388
(n) Enforcement of Rights ... 389
iii. Additional California Medical Privacy Laws ... 390
b. New York ... 390
i. Access to Patient Information ... 391
(a) Confidentiality of Records Received Under Section 18 ... 391
(b) Violations of Section 18 ... 392
ii. On-Site Medical Facilities and Patient Health Records ... 392
(a) Conflicts Between Medical Ethics and Employer Instructions ... 393
(b) Employee Access to Information ... 394
iii. Privacy Rights of Government Employees ... 394
iv. New York Workers' Compensation Law ... 395
v. Laws Regarding Confidentiality of HIV/AIDS Information ... 396
(a) Confidentiality Required ... 396
(b) Enforcement Provisions ... 396
III. Europe ... 397
A. France ... 397
1. Subject Access Requests by Individual Employees ... 398
2. Applicable Fee and Consultation Terms ... 399
3. Denial of Subject Access Requests ... 399
B. Germany ... 400
C. United Kingdom ... 401
IV. Asia and Asia Pacific ... 404
A. Australia ... 404

1. NSW Health Records and Information Privacy Act 2002 ... 404
2. ACT Health Records (Privacy and Access) Act 1997 ... 406
3. Victoria Health Records Act 2001 ... 406
B. China ... 407
C. Hong Kong ... 407
1. Employment Candidates ... 408
2. Existing Employees ... 408
D. Japan ... 410
1. Mental Health Information ... 412
2. Additional Guidance ... 413
E. New Zealand ... 413

CHAPTER 6 MEDICAL EXAMINATIONS AND DRUG TESTING OF APPLICANTS AND EMPLOYEES ... 415

I. Overview ... 417
II. Americas ... 418
A. United States ... 418
1. Medical Examinations ... 418
Exhibit 6.1 U.S.: Timing of Inquiries Under the ADA ... 419
a. What Is a Medical Examination? ... 420
i. Psychological Examinations ... 420
ii.. Personality Assessments ... 421
iii. Physical Agility Tests ... 422
b. Medical Examinations of Job Applicants ... 423
i. Prior to Job Offer ... 423
ii. After Conditional Job Offer, Prior to Employment ... 423
(a) Standards for Conditional Job Offer ... 424
(b) Scope of Medical Examinations Pursuant to a Conditional Job Offer ... 425
c. Medical Examinations of Employees ... 426
i. EEOC Standards ... 426
ii. Standards Defined by Courts ... 426
iii. Fitness for Duty Evaluations ... 427
d. Standing to Bring Claim for Unlawful Medical Examinations Under the ADA ... 429

2. Other Inquiries Related to Physical or Mental Condition 429
  a. Examples of Permissible Job-Related Inquiries........ 429
  b. Examples of Impermissible Disability-Related Inquiries 430
  c. Inquiries Following Voluntary Disclosure of Disability........ 431
3. Drug Testing........ 432
  a. Inquiries About Current Illegal Drug Use 432
  b. Inquiries About Past Drug or Alcohol Use... 433
  c. State Laws Regulating Drug Testing........ 434
    i. California........ 434
    ii. Connecticut........ 435
    iii. Iowa 435
    iv. Minnesota and Maine 436
    v. Oklahoma........ 436
    vi. Vermont 436
4. Additional Limitations on Physical or Mental Testing of Applicants 436
  Exhibit 6.2 U.S.: Examples of Other Legally Restricted Inquiries........ 437
  a. Genetic Information Nondiscrimination Act of 2008........ 437
    i. Restrictions on Collecting Genetic Information 438
    ii. Protection Against Discrimination Based on Genetic Information........ 440
    iii. Confidentiality of Genetic Information 441
  b. State Laws Restricting Genetic Testing........ 444
  c. HIV/AIDS Testing........ 445
  d. Lie Detector and Polygraph Examinations........ 445
    i. Employee Polygraph Protection Act.... 446
    ii. State Restrictions on Lie Detector and Polygraph Tests........ 447
B. Brazil 449
  1. Medical Examinations 449
  2. Drug Testing........ 449
C. Canada........ 450
  1. Medical Examinations 450

2. Drug Testing ... 450
D. Mexico ... 450
1. Medical Examinations ... 450
2. Drug Testing ... 450
III. Europe ... 451
A. Belgium ... 451
1. Medical Examinations ... 451
2. Drug Testing ... 451
B. France ... 452
C. Germany ... 454
D. Italy ... 456
1. Medical Examinations ... 456
2. Drug Testing ... 456
E. United Kingdom ... 457
IV. Asia ... 460
A. China ... 460
B. Hong Kong ... 461
1. Medical Examinations ... 461
2. Drug and Genetic Testing ... 462
C. Japan ... 462
1. Health Examinations ... 462
2. Generally Prohibited Tests ... 464
D. Korea ... 465
1. Medical Examinations ... 465
2. Drug Testing ... 465

CHAPTER 7 PERSONNEL RECORDS ... 467

I. Overview ... 468
II. Americas ... 468
A. United States ... 468
1. Employee Rights to Personnel Records ... 468
a. Definition of "Personnel Records" ... 469
2. Occupational Health and Safety Records ... 471
3. Employee's Addition of Explanatory Statement ... 472
4 Laws Requiring Employee's Consent for Disclosure to Third Parties ... 472
5. Laws Requiring Notice to Employee of Subpoena for Personnel Records ... 473
6. Potential Consequences of Improper Disclosure of Employee Information ... 474

7. Restrictions on Use and Printing of Social Security Numbers 474
8. Security Breach Notification Issues Related to Personnel Data 474
9. Confidentiality of Medical Information 475
10. Defamation and Other Legal Claims 475

III. Europe 478
A. European Union 478
B. France 480
1. Subject Access Requests by Individual Employees 480
2. Applicable Fee 481
3. Denial of Subject Access Requests 481
C. Germany 482
1. Subject Access Requests by Individual Employees 482
2. Applicable Fee 483
3. Denial of Subject Access Requests 483
D. United Kingdom 483
1. Subject Access Requests by Individual Employees 483
2. Applicable Fee 485
3. Denial of Subject Access Requests 486

IV. Asia 489
A. China 489
B. Hong Kong 489
1. Access Requests 490
2. Relevant Process Exemption 491
3. Personal References Exemption 492
4. General Exemptions 492
5. Costs and Fees 493
C. Japan 493
1. Access Requests 494
2. Requests for Correction 495
3. Requests to Cease Use 496
4. Disclosure of Personal Records to Third Parties 497

CHAPTER 8 USE OF GOVERNMENT IDENTIFIERS AND SOCIAL SECURITY NUMBERS 501

I. Overview 502

II. Americas 503
A. United States 503
Exhibit 8.1 U.S.: Summary of State Social Security Number Disclosure Laws 504
1. Application to Employers 503
2. Types of Information Covered 506
3. Prohibited Activities 507
a. Method of Mailing Documents Containing SSNs 508
b. Electronic or Facsimile Transmission of SSNs 508
c. Sale of SSNs 508
d. Use of SSNs as Account Numbers 509
e. Collection of SSNs 509
f. Disclosure of Employee's Personal Identifying Information 509
4. Exceptions 510
a. Court Filings 510
b. Verifications and Investigations 511
c. Maintenance and Reporting of Employment Records 512
d. Other Exemptions 512
5. Privacy Policy Requirements 513
a. SSN Policy Laws Requiring Internal Policies 513
i. Michigan 513
ii. New Mexico 514
iii. New York 514
b. SSN Policy Laws Requiring External Policies 515
i. Connecticut 515
ii. Texas 515
6. Additional Requirements 516
7. Enforcement and Administration 517
8. Compliance Issues for Employers 519
B. Brazil 522
C. Canada 522
D. Mexico 523
III. Europe 523
A. Belgium 523
B. Germany 523

C. Italy 523
D. United Kingdom 524
IV. Asia and Asia Pacific 524
A. Australia 524
B. Hong Kong 525
1. Employment Candidates 526
2. Existing Employees 527
C. Japan 528
D. Korea 529
E. New Zealand 529

CHAPTER 9 SECURITY BREACH NOTIFICATION REQUIREMENTS 531

I. Overview 532
II. Americas 533
A. United States 533
Exhibit 9.1 U.S.: Summary of State Security Breach Notification Laws 534
1. State Notification Laws 536
2. Scope and Coverage 539
a. Information Brokers and Other Species of Covered Entities 540
b. Paper Records 542
3. Covered Information 542
a. Exceptions for Publicly Available Information 546
4. Notification Triggers 547
a. Unauthorized Acquisition 547
b. Risk-Based Triggers for Notification 548
c. Employee Exception to Notification Obligation 553
5. Timing Requirements 555
a. Generally 555
b. Delay for Law Enforcement Investigation 557
6. Notice to Specified State Authorities 559
7. Notification Methods 559
a. Thresholds for Providing Substitute Notice 562
b. Methods of Providing Substitute Notice 565

8. Notice Contents 568
a. Coordination With Consumer Reporting Agencies 570
9. Safe Harbors 572
a. Other Exemptions 575
B. Canada 578
1. Personal Information Covered 579
2. Risk Assessment 579
3. Timing and Content of the Notice 580
4. Prevention of Future Breaches 581
5. Ontario Personal Health Information Privacy Act, 2004 (PHIPA) 582
III. Europe 583
A. European Union 583
B. Norway 584
C. United Kingdom 585
IV. Middle East 587
A. United Arab Emirates 587
V. Asia Pacific 588
A. Australia 588
1. Personal Information Covered 588
2. Risk Assessment 589
3. Timing and Content of the Notice 589
B. Japan 590
C. New Zealand 592
1. Personal Information Covered 592
2. Risk Assessment 592
3. Timing and Content of the Notice 593

CHAPTER 10 DATA SECURITY: MAINTAINING AN INFORMATION SECURITY PROGRAM 595

I. Introduction 595
II. Overview of Data Security Laws and Regulations 598
III. Creating an Information Security Program 600
Exhibit 10.1 Selected Domestic and International Data Security Requirements 601
A. Personal Information 600
B. Written Security Program 603
C. Risk Assessment 605

D. Security Program Coordinator 608
E. Employee Training and Awareness 609
F. Access Controls 612
G. Physical Access Controls 614
H. Technical Security Controls 615
I. Data Destruction/Retention Limits 618
J. Documentation of Security Breach Responses 620
K. Oversight of Service Providers 621
L. Internal Audits/Reviews 623

APPENDIX A ABOUT MORRISON & FOERSTER'S PRIVACY LIBRARY 625

APPENDIX B EU STANDARD CLAUSES FOR CROSS-BORDER TRANSFERS OF PERSONAL INFORMATION 627

INDEX 667

CHAPTER 1

OVERVIEW OF PRIVACY AND DATA SECURITY

I. The United States ... 5
  A. Overview ... 5
  B. Federal Law and Regulation ... 7
    1. Sectoral Regulations ... 8
      a. Financial Information ... 8
        i. Financial Privacy Rule ... 9
        ii. Safeguards Rule ... 9
      b. Health Information ... 10
        i. The Health Insurance Portability and Accountability Act of 1996 ... 10
          (a) Standards for Privacy of Individually Identifiable Health Information (Privacy Rule) ... 10
          (b) Security Standards (Security Rule) ... 11
        ii. The Americans With Disabilities Act ... 11
        iii. Genetic Information ... 11
      c. Consumer Report Information ... 12
        i. Fair Credit Reporting Act ... 12
        ii. The Fair and Accurate Credit Transactions Act ... 12
      d. Children's Information ... 13
    2. Regulatory Focus on Electronic Data ... 13
      a. Computer Fraud and Abuse Act ... 13
      b. Electronic Communications Privacy Act ... 14
    3. Regulatory Focus on Misrepresentation and Unfairness ... 14
      a. Federal Trade Commission Act ... 14
  C. State Laws ... 16

1. State Constitutions 17
2. State Laws and Regulations 17
    a. Financial Information 17
    b. Health Information 18
    c. Consumer Report Information 19
3. Misuse of Information 19
    a. Procedures and Practices 19
    b. Security Breach Notification 21
    c. Social Security Number Laws 21
    d. Employee Monitoring 22
4. Unfair or Deceptive Acts or Practices 22

II. Countries Other Than the United States—Global Overview 23
Exhibit 1.1 Countries With Data Privacy Laws 25

III. Europe 27
A. Introduction 27
B. Legislative Framework 29
C. Requirements for Processing of Information Within the EU 31
1. Legal Basis 31
2. Sensitive Data 33
3. Notice Requirements 34
4. Access Rights 35
5. Right to Object 36
6. Contracts With Data Processors 36
7. Registration Obligations 37
D. Cross-Border Restrictions 39
1. Transfers to Countries Providing "Adequate Data Protection" 39
2. The U.S. Safe Harbor Framework 39
Exhibit 1.2 The Safe Harbor Privacy Principles 40
3. Adequate Safeguards: Contracts or Binding Corporate Rules 45
4. Other Options 49
E. Employer Policy Formulation 50

IV. Asia and Asia Pacific 53
A. Australia 54
1. Overview 54
2. The Privacy Act—Employee Records Exemption 55

3. Obligations Under the Privacy Act When the Employee Records Exemption Does Not Apply ... 57
4. Penalties ... 59
5. Health Information ... 59
6. Workplace Monitoring and Surveillance ... 59

B. Hong Kong ... 59
1. Notice ... 60
2. Consent ... 61
3. Access and Correction Requirements ... 61
4. Accuracy Requirements ... 61
5. Retention of Employment-Related Data ... 62
6. Disclosure or Transfer of Employment-Related Data ... 62
7. Transfer of Employment-Related Data Outside Hong Kong ... 63
8. Providing Job References ... 63
9. Sensitive Information ... 63
a. Medical and Health Data ... 63
b. Identity Card Numbers ... 64
10. Security Requirements ... 64
11. Monitoring of Employees ... 65
12. Penalties ... 65

C. Japan ... 65
1. Notice ... 67
2. Breach Notice ... 68
3. Notice to Labor Unions ... 69
4. Consent ... 69
5. Third-Party Sharing of Employee Information ... 69
6. Supervision of Service Providers ... 70
7. Security ... 71
8. Sensitive Information ... 72
9. Access and Correction Rights ... 72
10. Monitoring of Employees ... 73

D. Korea ... 73
1. Notice ... 74
2. Privacy Policy ... 74
3. Consent ... 74
4. Access and Correction Rights ... 75
5. Cross-Border Requirements ... 75

6. Security 75
7. Supervision of Service Providers 77
8. Data Retention 77
9. Breach Notification 77
10. Penalties 78
11. Surveillance/Monitoring of Employees 78

E. New Zealand 78
1. Collection and Use Limitations 79
2. Notice 79
3. Security and Data Retention 79
4. Access and Correction 80
5. Data Accuracy 80
6. Data Retention 80
7. Unique Identifiers 80

F. Taiwan 80
1. License/Database Registration 81
2. Consent 82
3. Use Limitations 82
4. Limits on Data Transfers; Cross-Border Limitations 83
5. Access Rights 83
6. Accuracy/Right to Correct/Cease Use 83
7. Data Retention 84
8. Monitoring of Employees 84
9. Security 85
10. Penalties 85

V. Americas 86

A. Argentina 86
1. Notice/Privacy Policy 87
2. Consent/Use Limitations 87
3. Access and Correction 88
4. Security/Data Retention 88
5. Database Registration 90
6. Cross-Border Transfers 90
7. Onward Transfer Agreements 90
8. Dispute Resolution 91

B. Canada 91
1. Federal Regulation 91
2. PIPEDA Requirements 93
a. Notice 93

b. Consent 93
c. Database Registration.................................. 94
d. Data Processing Contracts........................... 94
e. Designation of a Privacy Officer 94
f. Implementation of Policies and Practices; Audit 94
g. Access 94
h. Cross-Border Transfers 94
i. Complaint Handling.................................... 94
j. Security 95
k. Data Retention... 95
3. Provincial Privacy Laws 95
a. British Columbia... 95
b. Ontario 96
c. Quebec 96
C. Chile 96
1. Notice... 97
2. Privacy Policy 97
3. Consent; Limitations on Collection, Use, and Disclosure 97
4. Access and Correction 98
5. Security; Data Retention..................................... 98
6. Database Registration 98
7. Cross-Border Limitations 98
8. Onward Transfer Agreements 98
9. Dispute Resolution... 98
Exhibit 1.3 EU Member State Implementation Legislation for Data Privacy and Security 99

I. THE UNITED STATES

A. Overview

This chapter begins with an overview of the U.S. approach to privacy, followed by an introduction to the privacy regimes of the European Union (EU) and other key jurisdictions around the world. We conclude this chapter with examples of privacy regimes in other countries in the Americas, which highlight the significant variations from country to country.[1]

Over the years, the United States has adopted a myriad of federal and state privacy laws that give protections to individuals, including employees, regarding the collection and use of personal information by both the public and private sectors. These laws are carefully targeted to address specific instances of abuse or perceived market failures, or to protect particularly sensitive information, such as health information, and groups deemed worthy of special protections, such as children. The U.S. approach stands in sharp contrast to the approach found in Europe and other countries around the world that have adopted omnibus privacy laws. Those countries do not focus on particular harms to individuals or types of data that may be particularly sensitive; rather those laws regulate the collection and use of all personal information across all sectors of the economy.

Legal and historical reasons largely account for the differences in privacy approaches. Although the U.S. Constitution establishes certain privacy protections for individuals, such as the right to be free from warrantless searches by the government, it does not explicitly protect information privacy or actions by private entities. The U.S. approach to the regulation of information as a general matter relies on the "marketplace of ideas." Reflected in the First Amendment to the Constitution, the U.S. has a long history of rectifying inaccurate and inappropriate speech with more speech rather than less. Understanding this history and faith in the free exchange of ideas and information is central to understanding the U.S. approach to privacy protection.

As a result of these legal traditions, the United States focuses on the misuse of information rather than prohibiting or strictly regulating the collection or use of personal information. In contrast to the privacy regimes in the EU, whether an individual can

---

[1]In general, the remaining chapters are organized by region, covering the United States/Americas, Europe, and the Asia and Asia Pacific regions. This chapter follows a different path by departing from the U.S. to the EU and Asia, before returning to visit other countries in the Americas. The privacy regimes of countries such as Canada and Argentina have been influenced by the approaches taken in the EU and Asia. Thus, we will conclude with these examples of the considerable differences among privacy approaches within the Americas.

be harmed by the misuse of personal information about him is the focus of any privacy inquiry in the US. The premise under U.S. law is not that the mere collection of personal information is improper and must be justified; rather, under U.S. law an organization can collect any information it desires, but it may not misuse that information or use it to commit fraud. In addition, there is a belief in the United States that information privacy issues differ from one industry sector to another and, consequently, "a one size fits all" legislative approach would lack the necessary precision to avoid interfering with the benefits resulting from the free flow of information. Similarly, the U.S. states, rather than the federal government, often pass their own versions of sectoral laws and enact legislation aimed at correcting specific issues of misuse or preventing harm in limited situations.

B. Federal Law and Regulation

The United States has a federal system in which laws are enacted at the levels of local government (e.g., cities and counties), state government, and national government. In general, privacy and data security laws are enacted at the state and national levels of government, but certain workplace rules that could regulate privacy and data security issues may be enacted by cities or counties, depending on the legal systems of the states in which those government units are located.

The legal traditions of the U.S. are based, in part, on the understanding that a state government is authorized to broadly enforce its "police powers" for the benefit of its residents, particularly in the areas of employment or consumer protection. By contrast, the U.S. Constitution customarily is described as granting to the national government limited powers to govern the states and residents of the U.S. under the grants of authority (given by the states) to Congress and to the President under Articles I and II of the U.S. Constitution. In particular, Congress and the President are authorized to enact laws governing matters of interstate commerce, as opposed to those matters that could be characterized as "internal" to each state and subject to its police powers. Nevertheless, the national government has increasingly expanded the scope of its authority to occupy many facets of interstate commerce; thus, a wide range of organizations conducting various commercial activities are currently subject to detailed national laws and regulations, including matters that continue to be regulated by the states. For example, the national government in the U.S. has enacted detailed privacy and data security rules that apply to financial institutions for information about individual consumers, even though the states are still authorized to regulate these same entities (with certain exceptions) with respect to the same information. As a result, an organization that is subject to the laws of the state in which the organization is located, as well as potentially subject to the laws of other states in which the organization conducts activity, is subject to all of those state laws and the federal laws regulating those activities. Moreover, state laws continue to be enforceable even if a national law regulates the same conduct, unless certain conflicts between the laws cannot be reconciled under certain principles of Constitutional law. However, the national law prevails over, or "preempts," the state or local law.

1. *Sectoral Regulations*

Regulation in the United States focuses on information viewed as particularly sensitive on a sectoral basis, such as financial information, health information, consumer report information, and information about children.[2]

a. *Financial Information*

The Gramm-Leach-Bliley Act (1999) (GLBA) regulates disclosures of nonpublic personal information about consumers by financial institutions to nonaffiliated third parties. The GLBA also prescribes data security standards that apply to the customer records and information. In general, the GLBA requires a financial institution to provide to a consumer an initial privacy notice when establishing a customer relationship, as well as an annual privacy notice throughout the duration of the relationship, that describes the institution's policies and practices relating to the treatment of "nonpublic personal information." In addition, prior to disclos-

---

[2]It is interesting to note that omnibus privacy laws outside of the U.S. often do not treat financial information or information about children as sensitive information.

ing nonpublic personal information about a consumer to a nonaffiliated third party, the institution must provide a consumer with a privacy notice that describes the consumer's right to prevent, or "opt out" of, the disclosure, unless the disclosure is permitted by an exception in the GLBA. Pursuant to the GLBA, the Comptroller of the Currency, the Federal Reserve Board, the Federal Deposit Insurance Corporation, the Office of Thrift Supervision, the National Credit Union Administration, the Commodity Futures Trading Commission, the Securities and Exchange Commission, and the Federal Trade Commission (FTC) have promulgated regulations (Financial Privacy Rule) that govern the privacy practices of institutions and activities within their respective jurisdictions.[3]

i. Financial Privacy Rule

The Financial Privacy Rule requires a financial institution to give privacy notices to their customers and prescribes requirements relating to the timing and methods of delivering the notices. In addition, the Rule contains requirements regarding the contents of a privacy notice, including a notice that must be provided to allow the consumer to opt out of disclosures to nonaffiliated third parties. Finally, the Rule places limitations on the ability of a financial institution, or other person, that receives nonpublic personal information from a financial institution to re-disclose and re-use the information.

ii. Safeguards Rule

The GLBA requires the FTC and other federal agencies to set standards regarding the administrative, technical, and physical safeguards for customer information (Safeguards Rule). Each agency is charged with issuing its own Safeguards Rule that imposes specific security requirements on institutions subject to its jurisdiction, but these rules are similar in many respects. For example, the FTC's Safeguards Rule directs all covered financial institutions to "develop, implement, and maintain a comprehensive

---

[3]*See, e.g.*, the Joint Guidelines issued by the Office of the Comptroller of the Currency, Federal Reserve Board, Federal Deposit Insurance Corporation, and Office of Thrift Supervision, 66 Fed. Reg. 8616 (Jan. 17, 2001) (codified at 12 C.F.R. pt. 30 (OCC); 12 C.F.R. pts. 208, 225, & 263 (FRB); 12 C.F.R. pts. 308 & 364 (FDIC); 12 C.F.R. pts. 568 & 570 (OTS)).

information security program that is written in one or more readily accessible parts and contains administrative, technical, and physical safeguards that are appropriate to your size and complexity, the nature and scope of your activities, and the sensitivity of any customer information at issue." The Safeguards Rule requires a financial institution to conduct a risk assessment of the reasonably foreseeable internal and external threats to the security, confidentiality, and integrity of customer information; implement a comprehensive, written information security program appropriate to the institution's size and complexity, the nature and scope of its activities, and the sensitivity of the customer information that it handles; designate employee(s) to coordinate the program; train employees; contractually require service providers to safeguard personally identifiable information about customers; and periodically update the information security program.

b. Health Information

i. The Health Insurance Portability and Accountability Act of 1996

The Health Insurance Portability and Accountability Act of 1996 (HIPAA)[4] and the rules issued pursuant to HIPAA by the U.S. Department of Health and Human Services impose obligations on covered entities, which are defined as health plans, health care clearinghouses, and health care providers. HIPAA regulates the use of patient health information (PHI). The HIPAA Rules prohibit these covered entities from using or disclosing identifiable health information, except with opt-in consent by the patient or as explicitly permitted by the regulations.

(a) Standards for Privacy of Individually Identifiable Health Information[5] (Privacy Rule)

The Privacy Rule requires covered entities to implement standards to protect and guard against the misuse of PHI, which

---

[4]Health Insurance Portability and Accountability Act of 1996, Pub. L. No. 104-191, 110 Stat. 1936.

[5]45 C.F.R. §160.103.

includes all "individually identifiable health information" held or transmitted by a covered entity or its business associate in any form, whether electronic, paper, or oral.

(b) Security Standards (Security Rule)[6]

The Security Rule under HIPAA is more detailed than the GLBA Safeguards Rule, but it is more limited in application, applying only to electronic protected health information. For example, the Security Rule requires covered entities to institute access controls and technical security measures to guard against unauthorized access and recommends encrypting personal health information, both in storage and in transmission, designating this as "addressable" but not the required method of accomplishing this goal. In addition, the Security Rule requires that covered entities adopt reasonable and appropriate safeguards on business associates (third-party service providers) who handle covered information, including by entering into written agreements imposing the same restrictions on business associate behavior that is required of the covered entity.

ii. The Americans With Disabilities Act

The Americans With Disabilities Act (ADA) strongly affects the ability of employers to acquire and disclose medical information concerning job applicants and employees.[7] Specifically, the ADA prohibits employers from requiring medical examinations or making medical inquiries concerning a prospective employee before an offer of employment is made.[8]

iii. Genetic Information

The Genetic Information Nondiscrimination Act (2008) (GINA) prohibits both employers and group health plans from

---

[6]The HIPAA Security Rule: Health Insurance Reform: Security Standards, 68 Fed. Reg. 8334 (Feb. 20, 2003).

[7]Americans With Disabilities Act, Pub. L. 101-136, 103 Stat. 783, 42 U.S.C. §§12101–12213.

[8]ADA §102(d)(2)(A), 42 U.S.C. §12112(d)(2)(A). An employer may, however, inquire generally at this stage as to the applicant's ability to perform job-related functions.

discriminating on the basis of genetic information relating to employees (including family medical histories). GINA also places significant limits on the ability of employers and group health plans to collect genetic information or use any such information once collected. GINA adopts a broad definition of "genetic information" that encompasses not only genetic test results relating to an individual and his or her family members (including both blood relatives and adoptive relatives to the fourth degree of relation) but also to any manifestation of disease or disorder in any individual within the covered class.

c. *Consumer Report Information*

i. *Fair Credit Reporting Act*

The Fair Credit Reporting Act (FCRA)[9] regulates the use and disclosure of certain personal information—namely, "consumer reports"—compiled and furnished by consumer reporting agencies. The FCRA and counterpart state laws restrict the ability of employers, in particular, to use consumer reports and investigative reports in connection with pre-employment screening and internal investigations. See Chapter 2 for more information.

ii. *The Fair and Accurate Credit Transactions Act*

The Fair and Accurate Credit Transactions Act of 2003 (FACTA)[10] amends the FCRA and, among other provisions, requires "any person that maintains or otherwise possesses consumer information, or any compilation of consumer information, derived from consumer reports for a business purpose[,] [to] properly dispose of any such information or compilation." The FTC Disposal Rule, which implements this provision of the FACTA, requires large and small organizations that use consumer reports, including employers, to implement reasonable and appropriate disposal procedures to prevent unauthorized access to or use of con-

---

[9]Fair Credit Reporting Act, 15 U.S.C. §§1681–1681x.

[10]Fair and Accurate Credit Transactions Act of 2003, Pub. L. No. 108-159, 117 Stat. 1952.

sumer report information.[11] FACTA and the Disposal Rule were drafted in response to the growing practice of dumpster diving as a method of gaining access to personal information and committing identity theft. See Chapter 2 for more information.

d. Children's Information

The Children's Online Privacy Protection Act of 1998 (COPPA) applies to operators of Web site or online services that collect information from children under the age of 13. Such operators must provide certain online disclosures regarding the collection and use of information collected from children. Collection and use of a child's information, in most instances, requires the opt-in consent of the child's parent or legal guardian. Interestingly, the COPPA rules also apply to foreign Web sites that collect information from children in the United States.

2. *Regulatory Focus on Electronic Data*

The United States regulates the misuse of information by focusing on data stored electronically because there is a perception that such data can be misused more easily and can cause greater problems. Other countries with omnibus laws tend not to distinguish among the forms in which data are maintained.

a. Computer Fraud and Abuse Act

The Computer Fraud and Abuse Act[12] (CFAA) imposes criminal and civil liability on any individual who (1) accesses data without authorization or exceeds any such authorization; (2) obtains information from any protected computer; and (3) engages in conduct that affects interstate or foreign commerce. Employers have used the CFAA as one method of recovery in actions against departing employees believed to have misappropriated company information and tampered with company computer equipment.

---

[11] FTC, Disposal of Consumer Report Information and Records, 16 C.F.R. pt. 682.

[12] 18 U.S.C. §1030.

Most provisions of the CFAA require that plaintiffs show damages of at least $5,000 in any one-year period.[13]

b. Electronic Communications Privacy Act

The Electronic Communications Privacy Act of 1986[14] (ECPA) prohibits the interception of wire, oral, and electronic communication. However, certain exceptions allow employers to monitor employee communications. For example, the ECPA does not apply if the employer can establish that either (1) it intercepted the e-mail in the ordinary course of business or (2) one of the parties consented to the interception. See Chapter 3 for more information.

3. *Regulatory Focus on Misrepresentation and Unfairness*

U.S. laws also regulate against misrepresentation. The FTC has been granted the authority over all of the companies except those listed in Section 5 of the FTC Act (i.e., telecommunications providers) and organizations regulated by other government regulators that have the authority to exert similar powers in various sectors (i.e., banks that are supervised by the financial regulators). Thus the FTC has broad regulatory authority. In addition, the FTC has relied on its powers to regulate false and deceptive trade practices under Section 5 of the Federal Trade Commission Act to prosecute entities that make public statements regarding their privacy protections and practices with which they fail to comply.

a. Federal Trade Commission Act

Section 5 of the Federal Trade Commission Act (FTC Act) makes "[u]nfair methods of competition in or affecting commerce, and unfair or deceptive acts or practices in or affecting commerce" unlawful and grants the FTC the authority to prosecute such unlawful activity in all companies except those listed

---

[13] 18 U.S.C. §1030(e). Recent cases have found that damages may include lost revenue associated with an interruption of service and the company's cost of investigating the violation.

[14] 18 U.S.C. §§22510 et seq.

by the section.[15] The FTC has relied heavily upon this section in recent years to bring actions against companies that have either not followed stated privacy practices or engaged in practices that are "deceptive." For example, a company's failure to abide by its own privacy policy may be deemed a deceptive practice. In addition, even if a company follows its privacy policy, its practice may be deemed "unfair" if the FTC determines that the actions are inherently unfair or insufficient. Penalties of up to $11,000 per violation may be imposed.

In 2004, the FTC announced that Gateway Learning Corporation (Gateway) had agreed to settle charges of unfair and deceptive practices with respect to its privacy policy. The Gateway Web site privacy policy had stated that they would "not sell, rent, or loan any personally identifiable information regarding our consumers with any third party . . . [without the] customer's explicit consent." Gateway indicated that it would inform consumers and provide the opportunity to "opt out" if the policy changed. According to the FTC, Gateway began renting consumers' personal information to target marketers for use in mailings and telemarketing calls. A revised privacy policy appeared on the Gateway Web site stating that they would "from time to time" provide consumers' personal information to third parties. The FTC charged Gateway with violating Section 5 of the FTC Act for unfair and deceptive practices, including continuing to rent information collected under the original policy, failing to contact consumers about the revised privacy policy, and neglecting to highlight the privacy policy change on its Web site. The settlement bars misrepresentations about how Gateway uses data it collects from consumers, prohibits sharing any personal information collected from consumers on its Web site under earlier privacy policy without consumers' affirmative consent, and prohibits future material changes to its privacy policy retroactively without consumers' consent.

---

[15] 15 U.S.C. §45. Section 5 excludes banks, savings and loan institutions, federal credit unions, common carriers subject to the acts to regulate commerce, certain domestic and foreign air carriers, and most persons, partnerships, or corporations subject to the Packers and Stockyards Act of 1921. *Id.*

In 2005, the FTC accused BJ's Wholesale Club, Inc. (BJ's) of engaging in "unfair" practices prohibited by Section 5(a) of the FTC Act. The FTC charged BJ's with failing to take appropriate security measures to protect consumers' sensitive information. This is the first time the FTC acted against a company that gave no assurances to the public concerning its handling of customer information. The Final Consent Order required BJ's to establish, implement, and maintain a comprehensive security program that included key elements required under the GLBA Safeguards Rule. BJ's was obligated to: (1) obtain a security risk assessment by an independent third-party expert; (2) submit reports on the specific administrative, technical, and physical safeguards that it will implement and maintain during the reporting period; and (3) file those reports with the FTC biennially for 20 years. This case is significant for applying the Safeguards Rule to a nonfinancial institution.

Interestingly, it remains unclear whether the FTC Act gives the FTC jurisdiction over false and deceptive acts aimed at employees. It is possible that the FTC may consider employees to be "consumers" for purposes of the FTC Act and thus would assert jurisdiction if an organization were to make false statements to or failed to appropriately protect personal information relating to its employees. The view that the FTC has jurisdiction over information relating to employees is supported by the fact that U.S. organizations can certify compliance with the Safe Harbor Principles relating to human resources data, which the FTC has authority to enforce.[16] To date, however, the FTC has not brought a case in which the "consumers" were employees.

C. State Laws

Many states in the United States also have passed privacy laws. These state privacy laws may include constitutional privacy rights, but many also focus on regulating sensitive information in certain sectors, misuse of information, and the misrepresentation of how information may be used or protected.

---

[16]See Section III.D.2 for further discussion relating to the Safe Harbor.

1. State Constitutions

Several states guarantee the right to privacy in their state constitutions. For example, California's state constitution includes an explicit right to privacy[17] and the New Jersey Supreme Court has recognized that "[w]ith its declaration of the right to life, liberty and the pursuit of happiness, *Article I, §1 of the New Jersey Constitution* encompasses the right to privacy."[18] This right is often interpreted to apply to employee information. The result is that employees in many of these states have a reasonable expectation of privacy in their personnel files (i.e., evaluations/performance appraisals and disciplinary memos). See Chapter 7 for more information.

2. State Laws and Regulations

States also have implemented laws and regulations to protect sensitive information on a sectoral basis along the same lines as the federal government, but sometimes providing more robust and detailed laws than the federal law.

a. Financial Information

The privacy provisions of GLBA do not preempt state laws that offer stronger consumer protections, and a number of states continue to enact and enforce their own privacy statutes. The California Financial Information Privacy Act, for example, imposes more detailed protections, including a requirement that financial institutions obtain affirmative "opt-in" consent to the sharing of consumers' nonpublic personal information with nonaffiliated third parties, rather than the "opt-out" approval permitted by GLBA.[19] Similarly, Vermont has adopted a financial privacy regulation ("Vermont Rule") that limits a financial institution from disclosing nonpublic personal information about a resident customer to any nonaffiliated third party unless the customer has

---

[17]CAL. CONST. art. 1, §1.

[18]Burnett v. County of Bergen, 954 A.2d 483, 491 (N.J. Super. Ct. App. Div. 2008).

[19]California Financial Information Privacy Act, CAL. FIN. CODE §4051.5(a)(3).

been provided with a notice and an opportunity to authorize, or "opt in" to, the disclosure, and the consumer opts in.[20]

The financial privacy laws of California and Vermont are enforced against financial institutions that disclose nonpublic information in a way that is inconsistent with applicable requirements. However, neither California nor Vermont provides a private right of action with respect to a violation of its financial privacy law. The California law authorizes an action for civil money penalties to be brought by the Attorney General or the Department of Corporations with respect to an "investment broker or dealer" or "investment advisor" subject to the jurisdiction of the agency.[21] The California law authorizes a civil money penalty to be imposed regardless of whether any consumer suffers actual damages, but the amount of the penalty is subject to limitations per violation and per institution, which may vary depending on specified aggravating or mitigating factors such as whether the disclosure results in identity theft of a consumer.[22] Similarly, the Vermont Rule authorizes the Commissioner of the Department of Banking, Insurance, Securities and Health Care Administration to impose injunctive remedies (such as an order to cease and desist) and civil money penalties that are limited per violation.[23]

b. Health Information

A number of states have medical privacy laws. These laws are not preempted by HIPAA to the extent that they provide greater protections. California, for example, prohibits the disclosure of human immunodeficiency virus (HIV) test results to third parties, limits the disclosure of genetic test results, and requires "each employer who receives medical information [to] establish appropriate procedures to ensure the confidentiality and protec-

---

[20]VT. STAT. ANN. tit. 8, §§10201–10205. The Vermont Department of Banking, Insurance, Securities, and Health Care Administration promulgated a privacy rule that implements the Vermont law. 21-101-016 VT. CODE R. §§1–26.

[21]CAL. FIN. CODE §4057(e)(2)(A).

[22]CAL. FIN. CODE §4057(a)–(c).

[23]21-010-016 VT. CODE R. §24.

tion from unauthorized disclosure and use of that information."[24] See Chapter 5 for more information.

c. Consumer Report Information

The FCRA is not the exclusive source of restrictions on employers' use of information gathered by consumer reporting agencies. State laws also may apply and in some cases may be more restrictive than the FCRA. California, for example, has two applicable statutes: the Investigative Consumer Reporting Agencies Act[25] (ICRAA) and the Consumer Credit Reporting Agencies Act[26] (CCRAA). California's ICRAA regulates internal investigations by the employer's own staff, which the federal FCRA does not cover, and also defines certain key terms in ways that overlap with, but are confusingly different from, their approximate counterparts in the FCRA. See Chapter 2 for more information.

3. Misuse of Information

State legislatures also have passed laws regulating against misuse of information. These laws often cover a greater number of areas and contain broader requirements than comparable federal laws against misuse.

a. Procedures and Practices

The California Security Safeguard Act[27] applies to any company that owns or licenses unencrypted "personal information" about California residents. The Security Safeguard Act requires these companies to implement and maintain "reasonable security procedures and practices" to protect such data. Texas and Rhode Island[28] followed with similar laws. These laws apply to a

---

[24]CAL. HEALTH AND SAFETY CODE §120975 et seq. (HIV testing); CAL. CIV. CODE §56.17 (genetic testing); *id.* §§56.20–56.245 (employer disclosure of employee medical information). The Genetic Information Nondiscrimination Act (2008) supplements the existing California limitations on the use of genetic information by employers and group health plans.

[25]CAL. CIV. CODE §§1786–1786.60.

[26]CAL. CIV. CODE §§1785.1–1785.36.

[27]CAL. CIV. CODE §1798.81.5(b).

[28]R.I. GEN. LAWS §11-49.2-2(2); TEX. BUS. & COM. CODE §48.102(a).

business that maintains unencrypted personal information about its employees.

Nevada enacted a data security law, effective October 1, 2008, that mandates encryption for the transmission of personal information.[29] Specifically, the Nevada encryption statute prohibits a business in Nevada from transferring "any personal information of a customer through an electronic transmission," except via facsimile, "unless the business uses encryption to ensure the security of electronic transmission."[30] The "personal information" covered by the Nevada encryption law is the same information that is subject to that state's security breach notification law, namely: "a natural person's first name or first initial and last name in combination with any one or more of the following . . . : (1) Social Security number[;] (2) driver's license number or identification card number[; or] (3) account number, credit card number or debit card number, in combination with any required security code, access code or password that would permit access to the person's financial account."[31] Although the Nevada encryption law does not define a "customer," and the law does not otherwise appear to be limited to Nevada residents, the law could be interpreted as applying to a covered entity's transmission of "any personal information of a customer," regardless of where the customer resides. Moreover, the Nevada encryption law does not define the scope of a "business in this state" that is subject to the law.

The Massachusetts Office of Consumer Affairs and Business Regulations has adopted a rule that requires "[e]very person that owns, licenses, stores or maintains personal information about a [Massachusetts] resident [to] develop, implement, maintain and monitor a comprehensive, written information security program applicable to any records containing such personal information" (hereinafter, Massachusetts Program Rule).[32] The Massachusetts Program Rule requires a covered entity to implement, maintain, and update from time to time a risk-based security program that is appropriate to the size, complexity, and nature and scope of the

---

[29] NEV. REV. STAT. §597.970.

[30] *Id.*

[31] NEV. REV. STAT. §603A.040.

[32] 201 MASS. REGS. CODE §17.03(1).

activities of the particular entity. However, the Massachusetts Program Rule prescribes particular requirements that must be included in an organization's risk-based security program, such as "[t]aking reasonable steps to verify that third-party service providers with access to personal information have the capacity to protect such personal information," including "contractually requiring services providers to maintain such safeguards."[33] In addition, the Massachusetts Program Rule prescribes several specific elements of a company's comprehensive information security program that must address its computer systems, including any wireless system.[34]

b. Security Breach Notification

California was the first state to enact a security breach notification act in 2003,[35] and more than 40 other states, the District of Columbia, and Puerto Rico have followed suit. These laws generally require an organization to expeditiously notify individuals when unencrypted computerized personal information has been, or is reasonably believed to have been, accessed or acquired by an unauthorized person. In addition, several of these laws also apply to security breach incidents affecting personal information stored in any medium, including paper records, rather than only computerized records. Some of these notification laws also require that state regulators be informed about a data security incident. Congress has considered, but not passed, many similar bills that would enact national requirements to notify individuals about a breach of security. See Chapter 9 for more information.

c. Social Security Number Laws

More than 30 states have passed laws restricting the use of Social Security Numbers. Many of these laws prohibit a person or entity from (1) publicly posting or publicly displaying in any manner an individual's Social Security Number; (2) printing an individual's Social Security Number on any card required for the individual to receive products or services provided by the person or entity; (3) requiring the use of an individual's Social Security

---

[33] 201 MASS. REGS. CODE §17.03(2)-6.b.
[34] 201 MASS. REGS. CODE §17.04.
[35] CAL. CIV. CODE §1798.29.

Number to access an Internet Web site, unless a password or other authentication device is also required; (4) requiring an individual transfer the Social Security Number over the Internet unless the connection is secure or the number is encrypted; and (5) printing a number known to be the individual's Social Security Number on materials that are mailed to the individual unless required by federal or state law. Some states, such as Connecticut, Massachusetts, Michigan, New Mexico, New York, and Texas also require that an organization adopt a policy designed to ensure that Social Security Numbers are properly safeguarded. See Chapter 8 for more information.

d. Employee Monitoring

Businesses that intend to engage in surveillance of employee communications also must be aware of state law. The ECPA does not preempt state wiretap statutes that offer privacy protections greater than those available under federal law, and many states restrict surveillance activities. For example, California as well as Connecticut, Delaware, Florida, Illinois, Maryland, Massachusetts, Michigan, Montana, Nevada, New Hampshire, Pennsylvania, and Washington require both parties' consent before a conversation may be overheard, intercepted, or recorded in real time.[36] In addition to state wiretap laws, many states also prohibit video surveillance in certain circumstances. Video surveillance laws differ substantially in their terms, but may apply to employee surveillance. Unlike many non-U.S. countries in which notice to monitor employees is essential, only two states, Connecticut and Delaware, have implemented laws that govern e-mail monitoring, requiring employers to notify employees if they are being monitored.[37] See Chapter 3 for more information.

4. *Unfair or Deceptive Acts or Practices*

Similar to the federal approach to regulating the misrepresentation of information, many states have adopted laws that regulate

---

[36]CAL. PENAL CODE §631; CONN. GEN STAT. §52-570(d); DEL. CODE ANN. tit. 11, §2402; FLA. STAT. §934.03; 720 ILL. COMP. STAT. 5/14-2, 5/14-3; MD. CODE ANN., CTS. & JUD. PROC. §10-402; MASS. GEN. LAWS ch. 272, §99; MICH. COMP. LAWS §750.539 et seq; MONT. CODE ANN. §45-8-213; NEV. REV. STAT. §§200.620–650; N.H. REV. STAT. ANN. §570-A:2; 18 PA. CONS. STAT. §§5703–5704; WASH. REV. CODE §9.73.030.

[37]CONN. GEN. STAT. §31-48(d); DEL. CODE tit. 19, §705.

unfair or deceptive acts or practices (UDAP). Some of these are modeled after Section 5 of the FTC Act and are often referred to as "Mini-FTC Acts." Other states have modeled their UDAP laws after the FTC's model law. States have used these laws to bring enforcement actions against companies, alleging failure to protect the security of customer information. Ohio's Attorney General relied on that state's UDAP law to bring a complaint against DSW, Inc. (DSW), a large shoe retailer, after it experienced a security breach affecting customers' personal information and failed to identify and notify all affected customers. The Attorney General claimed that DSW's conduct was both deceptive and unfair, although the complaint made no allegation that DSW had made any commitments to consumers regarding the disclosure of data security incidents and, at the time, Ohio did not have a security breach notification law in force.[38]

II. Countries Other Than the United States—Global Overview

Most privacy laws outside the United States are broader than U.S. law, typically covering any personally identifiable information pertaining to customers, consumers, employees, and in some instances legal entities. These laws can cover both public and private sector collection, use, disclosure, and storage of personal information, as well as the transfer of such information across national borders. Countries that now have such comprehensive privacy statutes include Australia,[39] Hong Kong,[40] Japan,[41] New Zealand,[42] South Korea,[43] and Taiwan[44] in Asia; the Euro-

[38]State of Ohio v. DSW, Inc., Case No. 05CV06-6128 (Ct. of Common Pleas, Franklin County, Ohio, June 6, 2005) (complaint for declaratory judgment).

[39]Privacy Act of 1988 (amended 2001).

[40]Personal Data (Privacy) Ordinance of 1996.

[41]Personal Information Protection Law (2003).

[42]Privacy Act (1993).

[43]The 1999 Act on Promotion of Information and Communications Network Utilization and Data Protection (PICNU).

[44]The Computer Processed Personal Data Protection Act (1995).

pean Union (EU) Member States,[45] Norway,[46] Switzerland,[47] and Israel[48] in Europe and the Middle East; and Argentina,[49] Canada,[50] Chile,[51] Paraguay,[52] Peru,[53] and Uruguay[54] in North and South America. Moreover, many other countries are debating or considering privacy legislation, including Barbados, Bolivia, Brazil, China, Costa Rica, Ecuador, India, Jordan, Lebanon, Malaysia, Mexico, Morocco, Pakistan, Panama, Singapore, South Africa, Sri Lanka, Tanzania, Thailand, Trinidad and Tobago, Turkey, Ukraine, and Venezuela. See Exhibit 1.1.

---

[45]The 25 EU Member States and their respective data protection acts are: Austria—Federal Act Concerning the Protection of Personal Data 2000; Belgium—Privacy Protection in Relation to the Processing of Personal Data 1992 (amended 1998); Bulgaria—Personal Data Protection Act 2002; Cyprus—The Processing of Personal Data (Protection of the Individual) Law of 2001 (amended in 2003); Czech Republic—Personal Data Protection Act 2002; Denmark—The Act on Processing of Personal Data 2000; Estonia—Personal Data Protection Act of 1996 (amended in 2003); Finland—Personal Data Act (523/1999); France—The Act of 6 January 1978 relative to computers, files, and liberties; Germany—Federal Data Protection Act 1990 (amended 2001); Greece—Law 2472/1997 on the Protection of Individuals with regard to the Processing of Personal Data (as amended by Laws 2819/2000 and 2915/2001); Hungary—Act No. LXIII of 1992 on Protection of Personal Data and Disclosure of Data of Public Interest (amended in 1999); Ireland—Data Protection (Amendment) Act 2003; Italy—Law n. 675 of December 31, 1996 on the protection of personal data (amended 1999); Latvia—Personal Data Protection Law of 2000 (amended in 2002); Lithuania—Law on Legal Protection of Personal Data 2004; Luxembourg—Law of 2 August 2002 on the Protection of Persons with Regard to the Processing of Personal Data; Malta—Data Protection Act 2001; Netherlands—Personal Data Protection Act 2000; Poland—The Act of 29 August 1997 on the Protection of Personal Data; Portugal—1998 Act on the Protection of Personal Data; Romania—Protection of Persons Concerning the Processing of Personal Data and Free Circulation of Such Data; Slovakia—Act No. 428 of 3 July 2002 on personal data protection; Slovenia—Personal Data Protection Act of 1999; Spain—Law on the Protection of Personal Data 1999; Sweden—Personal Data Act 1998; and United Kingdom—Data Protection Act 1998.

[46]Personal Data Act of 2000.

[47]Federal Act of Data Protection of 19 June 1992.

[48]The Protection of Privacy Law (Amendment) 5745-1985.

[49]Personal Data Protection Act No. 25 and the Regulation approved by Decree No. 1558/2001.

[50]Personal Information Protection and Electronic Documents Act, 2001.

[51]Privacy Protection Act, 1999 (Law No. 19628).

[52]Law 1682 Regulating Personal Data (2000).

[53]Law No. 27489, Centrales Privadas de Información de Riesgo (CEPIRS).

[54]Law 17.838, Proteccion De Datos Personales Para Ser Utilizados En Informes Comerciales Y Accion De Habeas Data.

EXHIBIT 1.1

Countries With Data Privacy Laws
(As of 11/07/08)

Data Privacy Legislation Enacted (66 Countries)		Laws With Limited Data Privacy Provisions (14 Countries)	Data Privacy Legislation Pending/Under Development (12 Countries)
Albania Andorra Argentina Armenia Australia Austria Bahamas Belgium Bosnia & Herzegovina Bulgaria Canada Chile Croatia Cyprus Czech Republic Denmark Estonia Faroe Islands Finland France Germany Gibraltar Greece Greenland Guam Guernsey Hong Kong Hungary Iceland Ireland Isle of Man Israel Italy	Japan Jersey Korea, Republic of Latvia Liechtenstein Lithuania Luxembourg Macau Macedonia Malta Moldova Monaco Netherlands New Zealand Norway Poland Portugal Puerto Rico Romania Russian Federation San Marino Slovakia Slovenia Spain Sweden Switzerland Taiwan Tunisia Ukraine United Arab Emirates (DIFC) United Kingdom United States Uruguay[i]	Azerbaijan Bolivia* Brazil* Colombia* Egypt Kazakhstan Mexico* Mongolia Panama Paraguay Peru* Singapore Thailand Venezuela	Barbados Belarus China Costa Rica Malaysia Montenegro Pakistan Philippines South Africa Sri Lanka Turkey Vietnam*

[i]New Uruguayan data privacy law enacted in August 2008 that abrogates existing data protection law (Law No. 17,838). Databases have one year to come into compliance. Regulations are to be issued within 180 days of enactment of the Law.

*Denotes that additional legislation is under development or pending before the legislature.

Generally, these laws require that the collection of personal information, in a database for example, be disclosed and that the databases be registered with the government or with an independent data protection authority (DPA). They also require that individuals whose personal information is maintained in these databases be given notice of, and in certain circumstances consent to, the collection, use, and transfer of their personal information, as well as the right to access and correct the information held about them. In most of these countries "transparency" or notice is paramount. Individuals have the right to know what personal information is collected, how it is used, and with whom it is shared. The laws of some of these countries also require the permission of a DPA to "export" the personal information.[55] The DPA may refuse permission if the data protection laws of the receiving country are not considered to be as strong as those of the home country or if the DPA believes that the contemplated uses of the personal information are excessive.

Security also is increasingly a key consideration. For example, some countries, such as Argentina,[56] Denmark,[57] Italy,[58] Japan, and Spain,[59] have enacted regulations that set forth in great detail the particular technical and organizational security measures that must be implemented. In addition, the Organization for Economic

[55]*See, e.g.*, Personal Data Act 2002 (Nor.), ch. VIII, §42.

[56]*See* DNPDP N° 11/06—Implementación Medidas de Seguridad en Bases Privada.

[57]*See* Act on Processing of Personal Data—Act No. 429 of 31 May 2000. Title IV, Part 11 concerns "security of processing." Technical and organizational security measures have been adopted concerning the processing of personal data by public authorities and courts (Sikkerhedsbekendtgørelsen (Bkg. nr. 528 af 15. juni 2000 som ændret ved bkg. nr. 201 af 22. marts 2001)—7/8/2001; Sikkerhedsforanstaltninger til beskyttelse af personoplysninger, som behandles for domstolene (Bek. nr. 535 af 15. juni 2000)—25/9/2000).

[58]*See* Personal Data Protection Code—Legislative Decree no. 196 of 30 June 2003. Title V concerns "Data and System Security." Annex B of the Code lays down "technical specifications concerning minimum security measures."

[59]*See* Organic Law 15/1999 of 13 December on the Protection of Personal Data. Article 9 concerns "data security." Technical and organizational security measures have been laid down by the "Royal Decree 994/1999" of 11 June, which approves the Regulation on Mandatory Security Measures for the Computer Files that contain Personal Data.

Cooperation and Development (OECD) has adopted Guidelines for the Security of Information Systems and Networks.[60]

III. Europe

A. Introduction

Virtually every organization collecting and using information about its employees in the European Union (EU)[61] is subject to EU data privacy laws.[62] These laws regulate the online and offline processing of personal information and apply equally to the public and private sector.

The term "personal information" covers all details relating to an identified or identifiable individual, including sound and image data such as voice mail, photographs, and video recordings. Processing is very broadly defined to encompass any collection, recording, storage, transmission, or use of personal information including the sharing of such information with affiliated entities, for example, the sharing of payroll data with the corporate headquarters in the United States. As a result, any use of information such as employees' contact details at work, terms of employment, appraisals, next of kin data, e-mail or telephone use, and e-mail and Internet logs may be governed by EU privacy laws.

Unlike U.S. law, there is no diminished expectation of privacy at the workplace, and employees cannot be asked to waive their expectation of privacy at the workplace at the inception of employment or at any other time during the working relationship. Rather, employees are considered a vulnerable class by many, and EU privacy regulators and trade unions argue more protection is needed in the employment context than current privacy law

[60]OECD Guidelines for the Security on Information Systems and Networks: Towards a Culture of Security (2002). See also Exhibit 1.1 of this chapter.

[61]The 27 Member States of the European Union currently are Austria, Belgium, Bulgaria, Cyprus, Czech Republic, Denmark, Estonia, Finland, France, Germany, Greece, Hungary, Ireland, Italy, Latvia, Lithuania, Luxembourg, Malta, the Netherlands, Poland, Portugal, Romania, Slovakia, Slovenia, Spain, Sweden, and the United Kingdom.

[62]In the EU, the terms "privacy legislation" and "data protection legislation" are used interchangeably.

provides, because of the perceived imbalance of power between employers and employees. For example, Finland enacted the Act on Data Protection in Working Life to require employers to justify the collection and use of any information about their employees.[63] The privacy regulator in the United Kingdom, the Information Commissioner, has adopted an Employment Practices Code (Code) for employee personal information handling. Although compliance with the Code is ostensibly voluntary, failure to comply could draw the scrutiny of the Commissioner. Also, France's highest appellate court held that employers do not have the right to read their employees' e-mails or other personal computer files. The ruling involved a French organization that had terminated an engineer's employment after a search of his e-mail and word processing files revealed that he was performing unauthorized freelance work during organization hours. The engineer sued the organization, saying his rights to workplace privacy and secrecy of correspondence were violated. The high court agreed, holding that an employer cannot read an employee's e-mail, even if the company prohibits personal use of company computers.[64]

In brief, failure to comply with EU Member State privacy laws can affect organizations with operations in the EU in five distinct respects:

- EU privacy regulators may suspend or block transfers of information from EU subsidiaries or branch offices, such as the sharing of payroll information and employee performance reviews with operations outside the EU, if privacy requirements are not met.
- Privacy regulators and law enforcement agencies may impose administrative, civil, and even criminal penalties. The Spanish privacy regulator, for example, has imposed fines of €840,000 (approximately US$900,000) for sharing customer records with affiliated entities.
- EU Member State law grants employees substantial privacy rights that every employer must respect, and individuals

---

[63] Act on Protection of Privacy in Working Life, 477/2001.

[64] Société Nikon France SA v. M. Onof 99-42.942, No. 416, Cour de Cassation Chambre Sociale.

generally have a private right of action to recover damages arising from violations of their privacy rights.

- Organizations may face wrongful termination suits if they terminate employees based on information improperly obtained, such as the content of personal e-mails under certain circumstances.
- Failure to comply with EU Member State privacy laws may result in loss of reputation; employee morale, retention, and recruitment; and goodwill of employees and customers.

It is important, therefore, that all organizations operating in the EU—not just the Fortune 1000—review information processing practices and adopt appropriate policies on how to handle employee data. With the globalization of the economy and the growing regulatory reach of the EU, even moderately sized organizations are learning that they need to understand the implications of having overseas employees.

This chapter outlines key facets of the requirements imposed by EU Member State data privacy laws. More detail about specific aspects of employee privacy such as monitoring and video surveillance, background checks, and health information is provided in the following chapters of this book.

B. Legislative Framework

The general principles of EU privacy laws are set forth in the Directive 95/46/EC of the European Parliament and of the Council of 24 October 1995 on the protection of individuals with regard to the processing of personal information and the free movement of such data (Directive).[65] The Directive provides the framework and requires each Member State to enact implementing legislation.[66] Unlike federal law in the U.S., the Directive is not directly applicable to any individual or organization. Rather, a Directive requires each Member State of the EU to adopt a law that

---

[65]Published in the Official Journal on 23 November 1995, L 281/31.

[66]A Directive is fully effective only when implemented by Member States in national law. With respect to the Directive, Member States were obliged to ensure implementation before October 25, 1998.

implements the Directive into its countries laws. A directive sets the floor for the Member State legislation, and in some instances it may also set a ceiling. It does not, however, prohibit divergences among Member State laws, and, indeed, great differences exist in both the interpretation and application of implementing laws in the Member States.

Accordingly, in order to accommodate these local differences, an organization processing employee information in multiple EU Member States may need to modify its practices to accommodate local requirements. In many instances the requirements will be the same but there may be jurisdictional variations. Details on Member States' regulators and laws implementing the Directive can be found in Exhibit 1.3 at the end of this chapter.

As for the territorial reach of EU privacy law, Article 4(1)(a) of the Directive provides that each EU Member State's law applies to processing of personal information that is "carried out in the context of the activities of an establishment of the controller on the territory of the Member State."[67] An "establishment" generally refers to a presence in the territory of a Member State, "the effective and real exercise of activity through stable arrangements, whereas the legal form of such an establishment [ ] is not the determining factor in this respect."[68] Thus, most processing (i.e., collection, use, storage) of employee data in an EU country will trigger the application of that Member State's data protection law.[69] Put another way, if an organization employs people in a particular Member State, it is likely that that Member State law will apply to the personal information of those employees.

[67]*See* Art. 4(1)(a) of the Directive.

[68]*See* Recital 19 of the Directive.

[69]The Directive also attempts to regulate the activities of parties that are not established in the EU. Article 4(1)(c) stipulates that EU law applies to an organization that is not established on EU territory but *"for purposes of processing personal information makes use of equipment, automated or otherwise, situated on the territory"* of a Member State (unless the equipment is used solely for the transit of data through the country). As yet, the scope of Article 4(1)(c) is uncertain. With respect to employee information, Article 4(1)(c) is, however, of limited relevance as employing staff in the EU will create a permanent establishment under the Directive, and thus, virtually any processing of data relating to staff employed in the EU will trigger the application of Article 4(1)(a).

C. Requirements for Processing of Information Within the EU

The Directive's purposes are twofold:

- To protect individuals and impose restrictions on the processing of personal information within the EU; and
- To generally prohibit transfers of personal information outside the EU unless the information is afforded "adequate" protection.

This section outlines the key requirements for processing of personal information within the EU; the following section addresses the transfer restrictions imposed by EU privacy laws.

1. Legal Basis

Unlike the U.S., the basic concept under EU privacy law is that any processing of personal information is to be avoided; put another way, the mere collection of information is considered a "bad thing." Thus, if an organization wishes to collect or use or share personal information with a parent organization or service provider it must have a "good reason" or a legal basis for that processing activity. If, for example, an organization with operations in the United Kingdom provides information regarding individual employees to its head operations in the United States, that organization must have a justification sufficient under English data protection law.

The following legal bases may be relevant for information processing in the employment context:

- *Contractual necessity.* Information may be processed if the processing is necessary for the performance of the labor contract. In some countries, such as Germany, when relying on this legal ground, "necessary" means "indispensable."[70] Thus, only information truly needed to perform the agreement between the (local) employer and employee could be

---

[70] *See* Wolfgang Däubler, *Internet und Arbeitsrecht*, 2001, p 143.

processed under this legal ground. It is unlikely, for example, that disclosure to other affiliates would be found to be required for the performance of the labor contract with the employee (unless the employee is reporting to a line manager based elsewhere).

- *Compliance with legal obligations.* This basis applies only to situations in which processing is required to ensure compliance with EU legal obligations. Reporting requirements under U.S. or other non-EU laws such as the Sarbanes-Oxley Act generally are deemed insufficient.
- *Balance between the legitimate interests of the organization processing the information and the legitimate interests of the individual.* Under this legal basis, organizations are expected to balance the organization's interests against the privacy interests of the individual. Much of the information collected by employers might be able to be justified under this legal basis, but it is unlikely that this exemption would provide a legitimate basis for the processing of all the employee information typically collected by an organization. In particular, as currently interpreted in some Member States, this legal basis does not seem to cover transfers to non-EU countries, even where there is an adequacy finding (see below).[71] Also, to date, Spain has yet to implement the balance of interest as a legal basis.
- *Consent.* This basis may provide a safe ground for the processing of employee information. Under German law, however, consent has to be in writing (i.e., pen on paper). Fax copies are not sufficient. This may be rather burdensome from an administrative point of view. In addition, the Working Party has issued an opinion that employees do not always have the necessary freedom to consent meaningfully to the processing of information because of their

---

[71]Commission Decision 2000/520/EC of 26 July 2000 pursuant to Directive 95/46/EC of the European Parliament and of the Council on the adequacy of the protection provided by the Safe Harbor privacy principles and related frequently asked questions issued by the U.S. Department of Commerce, published in the Official Journal L, 215/7 of 25 August 2000.

inherent dependence on their employers.[72] Under this view, employee consent could be invalid and would not suffice as a legal ground for information processing. Several Member State authorities including the French and German have adopted similar positions.[73]

2. *Sensitive Data*

"Sensitive data," defined as data revealing racial or ethnic origin, political opinions, religious or philosophical beliefs, trade union membership, or health information or data on sexual preferences and sex life in general, are subject to even more stringent protection.[74] Generally, sensitive data cannot be processed unless the individual gives explicit (opt-in) consent. The only possibility for employers to process sensitive data without obtaining consent is if the processing of such data is necessary for carrying out their obligations and specific rights in the field of employment law *"in so far as authorized by national law providing for adequate safeguards."*[75] Under this basis, some Member States allow the processing of sick leave data, which is considered medical information and hence sensitive data, without obtaining consent from employees. However, this possibility does not extend to sharing the information with corporate affiliates, and all information must be deleted after payroll processing is completed.

In addition, sensitive data may be processed without consent when necessary for establishing legal claims unless the employee has an "overriding privacy interest." For example, the processing of data on the affiliation with a church may qualify for this

---

[72]See Article 29 Data Protection Working Party Opinion 8/2001 on the processing of personal information in the employment context, 13 September 2001.

[73]See German position in Recommendation on Data Protection Measures for Private Enterprises of January 12, 1994 (Hinweise zum Datenschutz für die private Wirtschaft (Nr. 32) vom 12. Januar 1994"). The French view is set forth in the Practical Guide for Employers and Employees published November 12, 2008 ("Guide pratique pour les employeurs et las salariés 17/11/2008"). The U.K. position is set forth in the Employment Practices Data Protection Code published by the Information Commissioner's Office.

[74]*See* Article 8 of the Directive.

[75]*See* Article 8(2)(b) of the Directive.

exemption in Germany because that information is required in Germany for complying with tax obligations.

The processing of sensitive data frequently requires prior approval from national data protection authorities. For example, in Italy, sensitive data other than sick leave records may be processed only with the authorization of the privacy regulator, the Garante, unless narrow exemptions are met.[76]

Furthermore, in some countries, the processing of sensitive data requires organizations to adopt enhanced security standards. In Italy, a detailed security policy document is required, and specific technical requirements must be met. Spain also imposes security requirements that must be met when sensitive data are processed, and specific security policies must be established.[77]

3. *Notice Requirements*

Organizations must also provide individuals with details about their information processing activities, including:

- The information collected (unless the data are provided directly by the individual);
- The purpose(s) for which information is collected, used, transferred, etc.;

---

[76]These exemptions are issued by the Garante in the form of "general authorizations." See, for instance, General Authorization no. 1/2008 for the processing of sensitive data in the employment context ("Autorizzazione n.1/2008 al trattamento dei dati sensibili nei rapporti di lavaoro") and General Authorization no. 4/2008 for the processing of sensitive data by self-employed professionals ("Autorizzazione n. 4/2008 al trattamento dei dati sensibili da parte dei liberi professionisti"). See also General Authorization no. 2/2008 for the processing of data disclosing health and sexual life ("Autorizzazion n. 2/2008 al trattamento dei dati idonei a rivelare lo stato di salute e la vita sessuale"), General Authorization no. 3/2008 for the processing of sensitive data carried out by associations and foundations ("Autorizzazione n. 3/2008 al trattamento dei dati sensibili da parte degli organismi di tipo associativo e delle fondazioni"), General Authorization no. 5/2008 for the processing of sensitive data carried out by different categories of data controllers (Autorizzazione n. 5/2008 al trattamento dei dati sensibili da parte di diverse categorie di titolari), and General Authorization no. 6/2008 for the processing of sensitive data carried out by private detectives ("Autorizzazione n. 6/2008 al trattamento dei dati sensibili da parte degli inestigatori private").

[77]See Guidance from the Spanish privacy regulator on data security measures, which includes a sample of the security document ("Guía de Seguridad de Datos").

- The identity of the entity(ies) controlling the information processing activities;
- The processing and disclosure(s) of personal information within EU countries;
- The processing and transfer(s) of information to non-EU countries and the degree of protection provided by the entity importing the data;
- The categories of individuals who will have access to the data;[78]
- Whether the provision of data is obligatory or voluntary;
- The right to access and to correct the information processed;
- The right to object to any processing, and in particular any processing for marketing purposes;[79] and
- If applicable, the fact that cookies are set; the data collected, stored, or transmitted through cookies; the purpose for which those data are used; and the right to refuse the setting of cookies "easily and free of charge."

In most Member States notice may be provided electronically, such as through a privacy policy, provided a link to the privacy policy is prominently placed in the upper part of the home page and on any site where personal information is collected. Also, the text of the privacy policy should be accessible to the user at any time, for example, by offering to download the text, and the user has to be able to print the full text of the privacy policy.

4. *Access Rights*

The Directive provides employees with rights of access and correction.[80] That means that an employee may request and must be given access to information held by the employer about him and the employee must be able to correct inaccurate or incomplete

[78]Some countries distinguish between service providers and entities that may independently use the information. The former may be identified by type (e.g., payroll agency), whereas the latter must be named.

[79]Note that in the United Kingdom, there is no obligation to inform employees about the right to object.

[80]*See* Article 12 of the Directive.

personal information. An employer may refuse to comply with the request only if the same employee previously made a similar or identical request and a reasonable time interval has not yet elapsed between compliance with the previous request and the making of the current request. There are also some limited exemptions available under national laws, including circumstances in which the personal information is protected by legal privilege, or the information relates to third parties. These exemptions vary from Member State to Member State, however. In some Member States, compliance with access requests may be made subject to a handling fee. Details on access requests are provided in Chapter 5.

5. *Right to Object*

Individuals have the right to object to any information processing *"on compelling legitimate grounds"* by the employer of data relating to him or her, except where otherwise provided by national legislation.[81] Rights to object vary greatly from Member State to Member State.

6. *Contracts With Data Processors*

Organizations are required to enter into (written) contracts with all data processors or agents processing personal information on their behalf.[82] Data processors may include such entities as payroll agencies and IT (information technology) service providers, but the view on which service providers qualify as data processors varies from country to country; the German view on what constitutes a data processor, for example, is far narrower than the view in the United Kingdom.

At a minimum, the processing contract must stipulate (1) the conditions under which information may be processed; (2) an explicit obligation on the data processor to implement appropriate technical and organizational measures to protect the security and confidentiality of the information; and (3) some mechanism or provision that will enable the organization to ensure that the processor complies with the contractual obligations.

---

[81] *See* Article 14 of the Directive.
[82] *See* Article 17 of the Directive.

7. *Registration Obligations*

The Directive establishes an obligation to file registrations with national DPAs prior to the processing of personal information.[83] The Directive allows Member States to:

- Exempt from this obligation certain categories of processing;
- Substitute registration for the appointment of a data protection official (DPO) in charge of ensuring compliance with the national provisions; or
- Request that a record of the processing be kept internally within the organization.

Member States that have implemented the Directive's registration provisions and corresponding exemptions have done so in different ways. In Denmark, Finland, Ireland, and Italy, for example, registration with the DPA is the exception rather than the rule.

In Sweden, there generally is no obligation to file a registration if, for example, the employee gives unambiguous consent to the information processing. When collecting the employee's consent, it is important to specify clearly the purposes of the information processing and the information that is processed, and to set these out in a way that is easy for the employee to read and understand.

The data protection laws of France, the Netherlands, and Sweden allow a choice between registering with the DPA or appointing a DPO. In Sweden, however, if a DPO is appointed, the privacy regulator must be notified of such appointment. In France, when information is transferred outside the EU, prior approval from the privacy regulator is required irrespective of the appointment of a DPO. In other words, appointing a DPO alleviates the need for obtaining the privacy regulator's approval only if information is not available outside the EU. In practice, most multinationals, therefore, will not benefit from the exemption when appointing a DPO in France.

---

[83] *See* Article 18 of the Directive.

In Germany, by contrast, the appointment of a DPO is mandatory for most organizations, and appointing a DPO eliminates the need to file a registration.[84]

The registration procedure normally involves the use of standard forms with standard descriptions. Some DPAs allow these forms to be filled in online. Although there are slight differences among Member States, generally speaking, all the registration procedures will require the following information to be provided:

- The name and contact details of the responsible party;
- The purposes of the processing;
- A description of the individuals concerned and the data or categories of data relating to them;
- The recipients or categories of recipients to whom the data may be supplied; and
- The planned transfer of information data to countries outside the EU.

Some regulators do, however, require extensive details to be provided. These regulators, however, are unlikely to make the full registration file publicly available (as does the Information Commissioner, the privacy regulator in the United Kingdom who requests basic information only for registration purposes).

---

[84]For most organizations other than direct marketers, the appointment of a DPO is mandatory in Germany when more than nine staff members are employed who are continually occupied with the automatic processing or use of personal information. The DPO is responsible, in particular, for ensuring the internal application of data protection laws in an independent manner; he must also keep a register of the processing operations (*Verfahrensverzeichnis*), which must be made available to everybody upon request. The register should contain information on:

- The full legal name, address, and legal officers of the entity controlling the data;
- The purposes for which personal data are collected, processed, and/or used;
- The types of personal data retained;
- The types of individuals to whom the data relate;
- The recipients or categories of recipients to whom personal data are disclosed;
- Data retention periods;
- Transfers to non-EU countries; and
- A general description of the technical and organizational security measures.

Note that generally both the organization and the DPO can be held liable for noncompliance with data privacy laws.

Also, any changes to the above information must be provided to the DPA. In most countries, it is not required to renew registration, but rather to provide updates of any material changes. In some countries, however, registration expires after a certain period of time (e.g., in the United Kingdom, the registration period is one year). After being informed of the information processing, the DPA is required to check those that are likely to present specific risks to the rights and freedom of employees.

D. Cross-Border Restrictions

1. Transfers to Countries Providing "Adequate Data Protection"

Transfer of personal information is considered to be legitimate under the Directive only if it is within the boundaries of the EU (as well as Iceland, Liechtenstein, and Norway, the three other Member States of the European Economic Area) or if the transfer is to other countries or national bodies providing "adequate" data protection. To date, the European Commission has deemed adequate the laws of Argentina,[85] Canada,[86] Guernsey,[87] the Isle of Man,[88] and Switzerland[89] as well as the U.S. Safe Harbor Framework.[90] Important trading partners such as Australia, China, India, Japan, and, to a lesser extent, as discussed below, the United States have yet to be found to provide adequate data protection.

2. The U.S. Safe Harbor Framework

To facilitate the sharing of information between the EU and the U.S. in light of these restrictions, the Department of Commerce (DOC), in consultation with the European Commission, developed the Safe Harbor Framework to provide U.S. organizations with a streamlined means of satisfying the "adequacy"

[85] *See* Commission decision of 30 June 2003.
[86] *See* Commission decision of 20 December 2001.
[87] *See* Commission decision of 21 November 2003.
[88] *See* Commission decision of 28 April 2004.
[89] *See* Commission decision of 26 July 2000.
[90] *See id.*

requirement under the Directive. U.S. organizations that certify to the Safe Harbor are deemed to be adequate.

The Safe Harbor Framework consists of seven Safe Harbor Principles (which are set forth in Exhibit 1.2), 15 frequently asked questions and answers (FAQs), the European Commission's ade-

EXHIBIT 1.2

U.S. Department of Commerce Safe Harbor Privacy Principles Developed in Cooperation With the European Union

The seven Safe Harbor Principles require the following:

Notice: The organization must provide information about: (i) the purposes for which the organization collects and uses information about individuals; (ii) how such individuals can contact the organization with any inquiries or complaints; (iii) the types of third parties to which the organization discloses the information; and (iv) the choices and means the organization offers for limiting use and disclosure.

Choice: The organization must give individuals the opportunity to choose (opt out) whether their personal information will be disclosed to a third party or used for a purpose incompatible with the purpose for which it was originally collected or subsequently authorized by the Individual.

Onward Transfer (Transfers to Third Parties): To disclose information to a third party, organizations must apply the notice and choice principles. Where an organization wishes to transfer information to a third party that is acting as an agent, it may do so if it makes sure that the third party subscribes to the Safe Harbor Principles or is subject to the Directive or another adequacy finding. As an alternative, the organization can enter into a written agreement with such third party requiring that the third party provide at least the same level of privacy protection as is required by the relevant principles. The notice and consent principles do not apply to transfers to agents. The Safe Harbor Principles are silent, however, about whether an agreement is necessary between a third party that is not acting as an agent (e.g., making decisions regarding how the personal information is processed or how it will be used) and the organization. In addition, the Safe Harbor Principles do not define third parties and, in particular, whether an affiliated organization constitutes a third party. Conse-

Exhibit 1.2—*cont'd*

quently, there is no explicit requirement to establish written agreements with third parties that are not acting as agents and/or affiliated organizations.

Access: Individuals must be given access to personal information about them that the organization holds and be able to correct, amend or delete that information where it is inaccurate.

Security: The organization must take reasonable precautions to protect personal information from loss, misuse and unauthorized access, disclosure, alteration and destruction.

Data Integrity: The organization should take reasonable steps to ensure that data is reliable for its intended use, is accurate, complete and current.

Enforcement: The organization must: (a) have enforcement in place in order that each Individual's complaints and disputes can be investigated, resolved and damages awarded, where appropriate; (b) have procedures for verifying that the commitments the organization makes to adhere to the Safe Harbor Principles have been implemented; and (c) remain obligated to remedy problems arising out of a failure to comply with the principles.

---

quacy decision, the exchange of letters between the DOC and the European Commission, and letters from the Department of Transportation (DOT) and Federal Trade Commission (FTC) on their enforcement powers.[91] The Safe Harbor can, but does not have to, apply to all personal information transferred from the EU, whether

[91] U.S. Safe Harbor Documents include: Cover letter from Acting Under Secretary of Commerce Robert S. LaRussa to U.S. organizations, dated July 21, 2000; Safe Harbor Privacy Principles issued by the U.S. Department of Commerce on July 21, 2000; Frequently Asked Questions; Letter from U.S. Department of Commerce to European Commission Services transmitting the Safe Harbor Privacy Principles and FAQs, etc., dated July 17, 2000; Safe Harbor Enforcement Overview, dated July 14, 2000; Department of Commerce Memorandum on Damages for Breaches of Privacy, Legal Authorizations and Mergers and Takeovers in U.S. Law, dated July 14, 2000; Letter from the Federal Trade Commission concerning its jurisdiction over consumer privacy issues, dated July 14, 2000; Letter from the Department of Transportation concerning its authority in protecting the privacy of consumers with respect to information provided to airlines, dated July 14, 2000.

collected online or offline. The decisions by a U.S. organization to enter the Safe Harbor are entirely voluntary.

For a U.S. organization to be eligible for the Safe Harbor, it must be subject to the jurisdiction of a "government body which is empowered to investigate complaints and to obtain relief against unfair and deceptive practices... in case of noncompliance with the [Safe Harbor] Principles."[92] At present, only the FTC (under Section 5 of the FTC Act) and the DOT (under 49 U.S.C. §41712, which covers air carriers) satisfy this requirement. Therefore, only organizations subject to the jurisdiction of either of those two agencies are eligible to join the Safe Harbor.[93]

The Safe Harbor provides one privacy regime for all EU personal information that is transferred to the United States. It eliminates the need for prior approvals or makes them automatic. As a result, the Safe Harbor can provide a streamlined approach for data transfers from the EU and can make those transfers less expensive and less onerous.

To comply with the Safe Harbor, organizations must undertake specific actions with respect to the personal data received from the EU. These actions include the following:

- Providing notice to individuals when the personal information transferred to the organization is used for a different purpose or disclosed to a third party;
- Providing individuals with the opportunity to opt out of third-party disclosures or uses that are incompatible with the purpose(s) for which their personal information was originally collected; or in the case of sensitive data, obtaining opt-in consent to use the data for a different purpose or disclose it to third parties;

---

[92]See Article 1(2)(b) of the Commission Decision of 26 July 2000 pursuant to Directive 95/46/EC of the European Parliament and of the Council on the adequacy of the protection provided by the Safe Harbor privacy principles and related FAQs issued by the U.S. Department of Commerce.

[93]Financial services institutions that are subject to the jurisdiction of the banking regulatory agencies and telecommunications common carriers (which are subject to the jurisdiction of the Federal Communications Commission) are not eligible for the Safe Harbor at this time.

- Executing onward transfer agreements (to govern transfers to third parties);
- Providing individuals with access to relevant information;
- Undertaking security precautions to protect the data;
- Ensuring data integrity (i.e., reliable for intended use and accurate, complete, and current); and
- Establishing enforcement mechanisms.

In addition, personnel who input, access, or disclose personal information should receive training on how to handle the data in accordance with the Safe Harbor requirements. Human resources or other personnel in the EU and the United States who receive complaints or access requests should know how to respond to such requests in accordance with the Safe Harbor requirements.

The organizations also will need to provide individuals with an independent third-party dispute resolution mechanism in the event that they feel their privacy may have been violated based on the Safe Harbor privacy principles (possibly in addition to an internal resolution mechanism). For this, organizations may either join a private sector dispute resolution program[94] or formally agree to cooperate with the European DPAs. For human resources data, however, organizations must agree to cooperate with the European DPAs for handling complaints.[95] Private sector dispute resolution as an alternative is not an option.

The organization will need to establish procedures for verifying annual compliance, either by using a self-assessment or an

---

[94]Third-party dispute resolution programs such as BBBOnline, TRUSTe, AICPA WebTrust, and the Direct Marketing Association have developed privacy programs that allow organizations to comply with the Safe Harbor Principles on enforcement. Other programs such as an outside arbitration and mediation service (e.g., JAMS or the American Arbitration Association) also may be used, as long as every complaint is heard in compliance with the enforcement principle and FAQ 11. The costs of using these dispute resolution bodies vary and often will depend on the volume of data processed, number of employees, revenue, etc.

[95]Organizations that agree to cooperate with the EU DPAs for dispute resolution are required to comply with the procedures outlined in FAQ 5 in the event of a complaint from the individual and pay an annual $50 fee. This fee is payable to the United States Council for International Organization, which has agreed to act as a trusted third party for this purpose.

outside/third-party assessment program. The method of verification selected, however, should be identified in the privacy policy.

- Under the self-assessment approach, an organization must verify that its published Safe Harbor privacy policy is accurate, comprehensive, prominently displayed, completely implemented, and accessible and conforms to the Safe Harbor Principles. It must also verify that it has in place appropriate employee training and internal procedures for periodically conducting objective reviews of compliance. A statement verifying the self-assessment should be signed by a corporate officer or other authorized representative of the organization at least once a year.
- If an organization has chosen external compliance review (e.g., by outside consultants), the review needs to demonstrate that its privacy policy regarding personal information received from the EU conforms to the Safe Harbor Principles, that it is in compliance, and that individuals are advised about how they may pursue complaints. The methods of review may include auditing, random reviews, use of "decoys," or use of technology tools. A statement verifying that an outside compliance review has been successfully completed should be signed either by the reviewer or by the corporate officer or other authorized representative of the organization at least once a year.

The organization must state that it adheres to the Safe Harbor in a publicly available privacy policy (e.g., on its corporate Web site).

Lastly, to be included on the Safe Harbor list, the organization must formally notify the DOC that it adheres to the Safe Harbor Principles either (1) by letter signed by a corporate officer or (2) by having a corporate officer register on the DOC's Web site http://export.gov/safeharbor.[96] As notification is effective for only a 12-month period, the organization will need to annually recertify its continued adherence to the Safe Harbor Principles.

---

[96]The certification form can be completed and submitted online or can be printed directly from the Safe Harbor Web site: www.export.gov/safeharbor.

3. *Adequate Safeguards: Contracts or Binding Corporate Rules*

Alternatively, an organization may transfer personal information to a recipient country that does not provide "adequate protection" if it ensures that "adequate safeguards" are in place when the information is to be transferred. Traditionally, contracts have been established between the entity exporting the data ("the exporter") and the importing entity ("the importer"). Approval of most Member State DPAs are required if individually negotiated contacts (ad hoc contracts) are used. Contracts that incorporate certain standard contractual clauses approved by the European Commission (Standard Clauses)[97] do not require DPA approval.

When Standard Clauses were introduced, it was hoped that because they provided one form contract useable in all EU Member States and required no approval by individual DPAs, they would create workable and substantially more streamlined international data transfers. Unfortunately, however, it appears that the drawbacks of Standard Clauses may outweigh their advantages. Besides entailing burdensome compliance requirements, Standard Clauses require that employees be made third-party beneficiaries of the agreement, providing employees with a direct cause of action, and impose liabilities on both the exporter and the importer. Further, an importer may generally provide the information to third parties only if those third parties are subject to an adequacy finding or execute Standard Clauses, or if consent is obtained by each and every employee. Only in environments in which the data flow is stable and fairly limited would such limitations work.

---

[97]See Commission Decision 2001/497/EC of 15 June 2001 on standard contractual clauses for the transfer of personal information to third countries, under Directive 95/46/EC, OJ (L181/19) of 4 July 2001 available at http://europa.eu.int/comm/internal_market/en/dataprot/news/1539en.pdf. The European Commission also has adopted standard contractual clauses for the transfer of personal information to third countries from a data controller to a data processor. See Commission Decision 2002/16/EC of 27 December 2001 on standard contractual clauses for the transfer of personal information to data processors established in third countries, under Directive 95/46/EC, OJ (L006/52) of 10 January 2002. In 2004 the European Commission amended its 2001 Decision and added a new set of standard contractual clauses. Commission Decision 2004/915/EC of 27 December 2004 amending Decision 2001/497/EC as regards the introduction of an alternative set of standard contractual clauses for the transfer of personal information to third countries, OJ 2004 L385/74.

In addition, both ad hoc contracts and Standard Clauses can be very difficult to administer. Data flows do not follow neat or well-established paths, but travel along multiple paths through a multitude of channels, through e-mail exchange, databases, and intranets. Global organizations have complex organizational structures that can change frequently. Unless regularly revised—at considerable expense—contracts are unlikely to reflect the changes in usage of information in organizations, as required under the contract regime.

Alternatively, the organization may adopt codes of conduct or binding corporate rules (BCRs). Under BCRs, an organization would establish its own internal set of rules for the treatment of employee information. BCRs could cover all or only some of the organization's data processing activities. BCRs appear to be particularly suitable for multinationals with offices inside and outside the EU/European Economic Area (EEA), and comprise the main alternative to the Safe Harbor for transfers outside the EU/EEA.

The Working Party has published a wealth of materials, giving detailed instructions on the elements required for BCRs authorization:[98] Especially to newer documents raise the spectre of possibility.

In order to comply with the Working Party guidance, BCRs must be: (1) binding on and enforceable against all corporate affiliates (internally binding) (e.g., through contracts or unilateral undertakings); (2) enforceable by all individuals concerned (externally binding) (e.g., as third-party beneficiaries); and (3) effective (e.g., through staff training, audit, compliance and supervisions, and adequate complaint handling procedures).

---

[98]"Working Document: Transfer of personal data to third countries: Applying Article 26(2) of the EU Data Protection Directive to Binding Corporate Rules for International Data Transfers," WP 74. "Model Checklist: Application for approval of Binding Corporate Rules," WP 102. "Working Document Setting Forth a Co-Operation Procedure for Issuing Common Opinions on Adequate Safeguards Resulting From "Binding Corporate Rules," WP107. "Recommendation 1/2007 on the Standard Application of Binding Corporate Rules for the Transfer of Personal Data," WP 133. "Working Document setting up a table with the elements and principles to be found in Binding Corporate Rules," WP 153. "Working Document Setting up a framework for the structure of Binding Corporate Rules," WP 154. "Working Document on Frequently Asked Questions (FAQ) related to Binding Corporate Rules," WP 155.

Most EU DPAs do require prior approval for BCRs, and there is no one-stop approval process. Rather, an organization seeking to establish pan-European BCRs would select and contact a "lead authority" that would interact with all the relevant EU authorities to produce a consolidated draft. In theory, the process should take as little as three to four months, but many organizations have spent three to four years obtaining approval for pan-European BCRs.

The draft BCR has to be presented in English as well as the language of the "lead authority." However, no single Member State can approve the rules for other Member States, and each privacy regulator has the right to demand that certain provisions be added or altered. Thus, each DPA has the opportunity to assess the content of a particular BCR when deciding whether the transfer to a third country is legitimate.

The documents presented to the "lead authority" should address the following:

- Scope, including list of entities covered
- Purpose limitations
- Details on legal basis
- Commitment to adhere to data protection principles: data quality and proportionality, transparency, security, and confidentiality
- Commitment to comply with local data protection standards where higher
- Grant of individual rights of access, rectification, erasure, and blocking
- Automated decisions
- Relationship with processors (both internal and external)
- Onward transfer limitations
- Staff training
- Regular audit, internal compliance, and supervision (DPO)
- Internal complaint handling procedures
- Cooperation by EU entities with DPAs (including obligation to consult with DPA if compliance with BCRs will be prevented due to applicable legislation); notification of significant changes
- Third-party beneficiary rights
- Acceptance of liability by EU entity

- Miscellaneous (list of definitions, effective date, transitional issues)

In October 2008, a group of nine DPAs, namely France, Germany, Ireland, Italy, Latvia, Luxembourg, the Netherlands, Spain, and the United Kingdom, committed to "Mutual Recognition." However, this is a policy commitment to aim at faster approval procedures rather than a legal change. Also, some countries remain opposed to "Mutual Recognition."

While BCRs may be limited to particular sets of information, it would have to apply throughout the entire organization with respect to that information. BCRs, therefore, would be appropriate if an organization is prepared to have a common set of standards around the world (i.e., provide some of the rights granted to information collected in the EU or Japan to individuals in the United States and other countries where there is currently no privacy regime, such as China, India, and Mexico). As a result, employees in those countries would be entitled to rely on the guarantees made in the BCRs to the extent that they rely on similar promises made in employee handbooks or in work rules and if applicable may file claims under their local regimes. This could expose organizations to additional liability from such claims.

The Working Party also requires that one legal entity be named as the guarantor of actions for all of the other affiliated entities in order for the BCRs to be effective. An entity established within the EU would be responsible for compliance with EU data protection laws. For non-EU headquartered entities, an EU affiliate would need to be designated as the entity responsible for compliance with the BCR, for remedying acts of affiliates including entities established outside the EU, and for paying compensation for damages resulting from any violation of the rules by other corporate entities bound by the BCR. The organization would need to give evidence that the delegated EU affiliate has sufficient assets to cover payments of compensation for breaches of the rules, or that other measures have been taken to ensure it would be able to meet such claims, for example, by obtaining sufficient insurance coverage.

4. *Other Options*

If neither an adequacy decision nor adequate safeguards are in place, the Directive provides for certain exemptions under which employee information may be transferred, but these are very narrow in scope and do not cover the broad range of uses for data, as in the following:

- The employee has given his unambiguous consent;
- The transfer is necessary for the performance of the contract with the individual, or concluded in the interest of the individual; or
- The transfer is necessary for the defense of a legal claim.

The Working Party has issued an opinion paper elaborating on the scope of these exemptions, stressing the limited application of these exemptions and that the exemptions should not *"become the rule.*"[99]

In particular, the Working Party stated that for consent to be valid, it must be *"a clear and unambiguous indication of the wishes of the individual.*" Consent must be specific (for the particular transfer or a particular set of transfers) and informed (implying that the individual must be properly informed in advance of the specific circumstances of the transfer such as, for instance, the purpose of the transfer and the identity and details of the recipient). Consent will be valid only if employees have a real opportunity to withhold their consent without suffering any penalty. Failure to consent cannot therefore result in sanctions. Also, because of the perceived imbalance of power and the potential inability of employees to withhold consent, the Working Party casts serious doubts on the validity of employee consent for most standard processing of employee data.

With respect to the contractual necessity exemption that allows the transfer when necessary for the conclusion of performance of a contract between the individual and the data controller,

---

[99]Working document on a common interpretation of Article 26(1) of Directive 95/46/EC of 24 October 1995, WP 114.

the Working Party states that there must be a *"close and substantial connection between the individual and the purposes of the contract."* In particular, the Working Party expressly stated that there was no contractual necessity where international groups wanted to transfer employee information from a subsidiary to the parent company (e.g., to centralize the group's payment and human resources management functions). Furthermore, although transfers are generally permissible when necessary for the conclusion or performance of a contract made with a third party, in the interest of the employee, the Working Party stated that this does not justify the transfer of employee data to service providers based outside the EU (e.g., to outsource payroll management, as outsourcing was not in the interest of employees).

With respect to the permissibility of transfers for the defense of a legal claim, the Working Party stated that data relating to an employee working for a European subsidiary can be transferred to the parent company only if there is an actual claim and not because there is the possibility that such legal proceedings might be brought against the parent company.

In summary, despite the fact that the Directive provides multiple means for transferring information, the narrow scope of the exemptions, the inadequacies of contracts or BCRs, and the divergent implementations and interpretations of the Directive among Member States make it difficult for organizations to select a single safeguard to protect the employee data they transfer out of the EU. To date, no truly viable transfer solution exists for global organizations that wish to comply with all applicable privacy laws. The European Commission acknowledged this difficulty in its first report on the implementation of the Directive, and stated *"more work is needed on the simplification of the conditions for international transfers."*[100]

E. Employer Policy Formulation

Given these complexities of EU privacy laws, the divergences between Member States regulations, and the substantial penalties

---

[100]First report on the implementation of the Data Protection Directive (95/46/EC) of 15 May 2003, COM (2003) 265 final.

that they impose, how does an organization formulate a policy that will apply to all the countries in which it is likely to operate? Organizations often find themselves making a choice between the lesser of two evils, formulating a single policy for all employees or having as many policies as are needed to fully comply with the laws of the countries in which they operate. Most organizations would prefer a single policy for all employees and operations. Having varying policies and operational requirements is anathema to most organizations owing to the difficulties they create for management. Having different policies for different employees, depending on where they reside, can also create resentment and tensions among the work force. Given these facts, organizations often attempt to forge a single policy that will meet the requirements of all the countries in which they operate.

In any event, organizations with EU operations can reduce the risk of regulatory actions by taking the following steps to safeguard employee privacy, based on the Directive's requirements and common elements among Member State implementation:

- The first task is to understand what personal information an organization collects, how this information is processed, to whom it is disclosed, and whether it will be transferred internationally. Special attention should be paid to sensitive data (e.g., health information, data on ethnicity, and trade union status) because it requires special handling. The organization should consider whether all the information collected and retained serves a purpose, or whether some of the information is unnecessary and merely increases costs in terms of technical infrastructure and staff resources, as well as regulatory compliance.
- Security issues are closely tied to privacy, and while an organization is examining its internal information flows, it also may wish to assess how it is protecting proprietary and sensitive information.
- Generally, organizations should issue privacy policies that give employees notice about what information is collected, how it will be used, and with whom it will be shared. Privacy policies also should clarify whether monitoring will occur, the reasons for it, and what privileges, if any,

an employee has to access Internet and telephone facilities for personal use. Member States may, however, restrict employee monitoring even if a privacy policy reserves the right to monitor.

- Employees' consent to personal information handling should be obtained, in particular, for (a) processing of sensitive data; (b) transfers from or disclosures to third parties; (c) direct marketing; and (d) transfers of personal information outside the EU. Nonetheless, EU privacy regulators may challenge the validity of an employee's consent if the circumstances appear coercive, and in certain cases, employee consent will be per se invalid.
- Any organization transferring personal information from the EU to other countries should examine the various methods for transferring personal information in compliance with the Directive, such as joining the Safe Harbor Framework.
- Contracts with service suppliers and any other recipients of information should be reviewed to ensure appropriate contractual warranties.
- Organizations should determine whether employees' representatives or trade unions have a right of consultation in the development of the privacy policy. In addition, organizations should consider whether negotiations with employees' representatives concerning privacy would be beneficial.
- Organizations should determine whether Member State law requires the filing of a registration with the privacy regulators, or prior approval.
- When receiving an access request, an organization should, if necessary, verify the identity of the person requesting access to the data to ensure that personal information is disclosed only to the person to whom the information relates, inform the person making the application whether a fee is payable, and promptly provide the person requesting access with the information to which he is entitled.
- Organizations should ensure that files and databases containing employee information are secure and handled only by personnel trained in their company's security policy.

- Organizations must make sure their privacy policy is enforced.
- Finally, given the evolving discussion on privacy requirements, organizations should routinely monitor new developments and adjust their compliance measures accordingly. Particular attention should be paid to "hotspots" among employee privacy issues, such as video surveillance, monitoring of employee communications, and limits on the background checks employers may perform on applicants and employees.

IV. ASIA AND ASIA PACIFIC

Unlike in Europe, the data privacy laws in Asia vary more widely from country to country, particularly with respect to the processing of employee data, cross-border transfers, and database registration. Australia, for example, exempts much of employee data from requirements of its Act; Taiwan covers employee data but only for selected sectors of the economy. Taiwan also requires covered sectors to register their data processing activities before transferring personal information outside the country. Australia has no database registration requirements but restricts cross-border data transfers by organizations to recipients in foreign countries that are subject to a "substantially similar" privacy regime; however, organizations must determine for themselves what constitutes "substantially similar." In contrast, the law in Japan does not distinguish between cross-border and domestic transfers to third parties. It applies the same rules to all third parties regardless of their location. In addition, the law requires organizations to remain accountable for protecting personal information transferred to third parties by establishing contracts with delegates and other third parties that contain specific data security provisions.

Nonetheless, all these laws impose substantive local compliance obligations such as requiring that:

- Notices be given to individuals about what personal information is being collected, the purposes for which it will be used, and the identity and location of the organization collecting and using the information;

- Individuals be given choices and means to limit the use and disclosure of their personal information;
- Organizations provide individuals with the right to access and correct their personal information; and
- Organizations protect personal information from loss; misuse; and unauthorized access, disclosure, alteration, and destruction.

A. Australia

1. Overview

The *Privacy Act 1988* (Cth) (the Privacy Act)[101] regulates the collection and use of personal information by private sector organizations, requiring organizations to comply with ten National Privacy Principles (NPPs). With the exception of certain acts or practices discussed below in relation to employee records, an organization must take reasonable steps to make individuals aware that it is collecting personal information about them, the purposes for which it is collecting the information, and to whom it might disclose the information. There are some restrictions on what an organization can do with the personal information it collects and when it can disclose personal information or transfer it overseas. Except for some special circumstances, individuals have a right to access personal information that an organization holds about them and to have the information corrected or amended if the information is incorrect, out of date, or incomplete. Individuals also can file a complaint if they think information about them is not being handled properly.

In addition to the Privacy Act, there are state and territory laws in the Australian Capital Territory (ACT), New South Wales (NSW), and Victoria that regulate the handling of personal health information in the private sector and surveillance of the workplace. The laws applicable to the collection, use, and disclosure of health information are discussed in Chapter 5; the laws applicable

---

[101] *See* the Privacy Act 1988.

to workplace monitoring and surveillance are discussed in Chapter 3.

A comprehensive review of Australian privacy regulations was completed in 2008 by the Australian Law Reform Commission (ALRC). The ALRC, tasked by the Office of the Attorney General to conduct the review, issued its final recommendations in August 2008[102] and recommended that there be a major overhaul of Australia's privacy laws. In particular, the ALRC recommended that the Privacy Act be revised to focus on a single set of privacy principles that would apply to all sectors at both the provincial and national levels. In addition, the ALRC recommended that the employee records exemption be eliminated and that the Act be supplemented by regulations dealing with specific areas such as health privacy, credit reporting, and breach notification.

In response, the government announced that it would focus first on the recommendations relating to the unified privacy principles, health information, and credit reporting regulations and respond to those recommendations within 12–18 months from the public release of the report. After that, it will consider the other recommendations such as those pertaining to data breach notices and the employee records exemption.

2. *The Privacy Act—Employee Records Exemption*

The Privacy Act exempts from its coverage "acts or practices in relation to employee records of an individual if the act or practice directly relates to a current or former employment relationship between the employer and the individual" (Employee Records Exemption).[103] An "employee record" is defined as a record of personal information relating to the employment of an employee and includes health information[104] about the employee and personal information about all or any of the following:

---

[102]*See* ALRC Report 108, "For Your Information: Australian Privacy Law and Practice."

[103]*See* 7(B)(3) of the Privacy Act.

[104]Health information is defined in Section 6 of the Privacy Act as follows:

a. information or an opinion about:
   i. the health or a disability (at any time) of an individual; or
   ii. an individual's expressed wishes about the future provision of health services to him or her; or

(a) the engagement, training, disciplining, or resignation of the employee;
(b) the termination of the employment of the employee;
(c) the terms and conditions of employment of the employee;
(d) the employee's personal and emergency contact details;
(e) the employee's performance or conduct;
(f) the employee's hours of employment;
(g) the employee's salary or wages;
(h) the employee's membership of a professional or trade association;
(i) the employee's trade union membership;
(j) the employee's recreation, long service, sick, personal, maternity, paternity, or other leave;
(k) the employee's taxation, banking, or superannuation affairs.[105]

Although the Employee Records Exemption is likely to cover the majority of personal information that an organization will collect, use, or disclose about an employee, it does not apply to the records of workers who are not employees such as independent contractors or temporary agents of an organization or to files of job applicants before they become employees or files of unsuccessful job applicants.[106] In addition, except for health or trade union membership information, which is included in the definition of an employee record, the Employee Records Exemption does not apply to most kinds of sensitive information.[107] Furthermore, if the employing

---

iii. a health service provided, or to be provided, to an individual; that is also personal information; or

b. other personal information collected to provide, or in providing, a health service; or

c. other personal information about an individual collected in connection with the donation, or intended donation, by the individual of his or her body parts, organs or body substances.

[105] *See* Information Sheet 12-2001 Coverage of and Exemptions from the Private Sector Provisions issued by the Office the Privacy Commissioner.

[106] Once a job applicant becomes an employee, however, the records the employer holds relating to that individual's pre-employment checks become exempt.

[107] Sensitive information is defined in the Privacy Act to include information or an opinion about an individual's racial or ethnic origin, political opinions, membership of a political association, religious beliefs or affiliations, philosophical beliefs, membership of a professional or trade association, membership of a trade union, sexual preferences or practices, or health information about an individual. Sensitive information about an individual may be collected only in certain circumstances, including those in which the individual has consented or collection is authorized by law.

organization is part of a multinational enterprise and transfers its employee records to other subsidiaries or the parent organization for enterprise-wide use, the Employee Records Exemption will not apply to such uses.

3. Obligations Under the Privacy Act When the Employee Records Exemption Does Not Apply

When personal information that is collected, used, and disclosed by organizations is not covered by the Employee Records Exemption, organizations will need to comply with the NPPs. The NPPs require the following:

- *Notice.* Notice must be provided at or before the time of collection unless an exemption, such as the Employee Records Exemption, applies. Individuals should be notified about the identity of the organization and how to contact it, the purposes of collection, the types of third parties to whom it will be disclosed, the individual's right to access, and the consequences, if any, for the individual if all or part of the information is not provided.
- *Privacy policy.* Under NPP 5 (Openness), an organization must have a document that describes its policies on its management of personal information and make that document available upon request. Although the organization would not need to have in place a privacy policy for its current and former employees, it would need to have one for prospective employees and all other workers such as contract workers.
- *Consent/limitations on collection, use, and disclosure.* An organization must not collect personal information unless the information is necessary for one or more of its functions or activities. Personal information must be collected by lawful and fair means and not in an "unreasonably intrusive" way. Consent is not required when the use and disclosure of personal information is for the primary purpose of collection or for a related purpose. Otherwise, consent (opt-in or opt-out) is required. In the case of sensitive information, however, such information may be collected only

if the individual has consented or collection is authorized by law. Once consent has been obtained for the collection of sensitive information, the sensitive information may be used or disclosed only for the primary purpose of collection or a directly related secondary purpose unless further consent has been obtained to use the information for other purposes.

- *Access and correction.* Unless the information is covered by the employee records exemption, individuals have the right to access and correct their personal information.
- *Security/data retention.* Reasonable steps must be taken to protect personal information from misuse, loss, unauthorized access, modification, or disclosure. Reasonable steps must be taken to destroy or permanently de-identify personal information that is no longer needed.
- *Database registration.* There are no database registration obligations in Australia.
- *Cross-border limitations.* Unless the information is covered by the Employee Records Exemption, there are restrictions on cross-border transfers of personal information where the recipient is not bound by privacy rules substantially similar to the Australian NPPs. If the recipient is not subject to a law, binding scheme, or contract that provides substantially similar protection, then, with some exceptions, cross-border transfer agreements or individual consent is required to transfer the personal information.
- *Onward transfer agreements.* Onward transfer agreements with third parties in Australia not covered by the Privacy Act are not required but recommended by the Australian Privacy Commissioner.
- *Dispute resolution.* Although not required, it is recommended that an organization have an effective complaint handling process.
- *Identifiers.* See Chapter 8 for information regarding the rules applicable to the use of government identity numbers.

4. *Penalties*

Failure to comply with decisions or requests by the Privacy Commissioner, or for obstruction of the Commissioner's performance of its functions, can result in administrative sanctions. Penalties include fines up to AUD 2,000 (approx. US$1,400) for individuals and AUD 1,000 (approx. US$700) for corporate entities or imprisonment for 12 months or both. The Privacy Commissioner also can make a determination that privacy has been interfered with and that compensation should be paid for loss. Additional remedies also may apply at the provincial level with respect to health information.

5. *Health Information*

Australia has federal, state, and territory laws that regulate the collection and use of personal health information in the private sector. The rules applicable to health information are discussed in Chapter 5.

6. *Workplace Monitoring and Surveillance*

Workplace monitoring and surveillance activities are broadly covered by the Privacy Act. In addition to the federal Privacy Act, there is currently only one state law in NSW that regulates private sector workplace monitoring and surveillance. The rules applicable to workplace monitoring and surveillance are discussed in Chapter 3.

B. Hong Kong

Hong Kong was one of the first countries in Asia to enact a comprehensive data protection law in 1995. The Personal Data (Privacy) Ordinance (the PDPO)[108] covers any data relating directly or indirectly to a living individual, from which it is practicable to

---

[108]Cap. 486, Laws of Hong Kong.

ascertain the identity of the individual and which are in a form in which access or processing is practicable. The Ordinance applies to any person who controls the collection, holding, processing, or use of personal data.

The Code of Practice on Human Resource Management (HR Code)[109] offers guidance on the application of the PDPO in the employment context. There are also separate guidelines regarding the monitoring and privacy of employees in the workplace, called Privacy Guidelines: Monitoring and Personal Data Privacy at Work (Employee Monitoring Guidelines),[110] which are discussed in Chapter 3. In addition, privacy issues in relation to identity cards are addressed in the Code of Practice on the Identity Card Number and Other Personal Identifiers (the ID Code), which is discussed in Chapter 8.

It should be noted that the provisions of these codes and guidelines are not legally binding. A breach of the codes and guidelines by a data user, however, will give rise to a presumption against the data user in any legal proceedings under the PDPO.

To comply with the PDPO, organizations must undertake the actions described in the following sections.

1. Notice

When an employer collects personal data from a job applicant or employee, the employer should take all practicable steps to explicitly inform the individual, on or before collecting the data, the purpose for which the data are to be used, the classes of persons to whom the data may be transferred, and whether it is obligatory or voluntary for the individual to supply the data unless it is obvious from the circumstances.[111] Before using the data, an employer should notify the job applicant or employee of the rights of the individual to request access or correct personal data, and to whom such requests should be made.

---

[109]The Code of Practice on Human Resource Management, Office of the Privacy Commissioner for Personal Data (Hong Kong), September 2000.

[110]Guide to Preparing On-Line Personal Information Collection (PIC) Statements and Privacy Policy Statements, Office of the Privacy Commissioner for Personal Data (Hong Kong), December 1998.

[111]HR Code §1.2.1.

The HR Code states that such notice requirements should be complied with by means of a written Personal Information Collection Statement (PICS). A PICS can be attached to or printed as a part of standard employment forms, such as job application forms.

2. *Consent*

Opt-out consent is required when the use of the information is limited to the purposes for which the information is collected or directly related to those purposes or where the information is disclosed to third parties for such purposes. Opt-in consent is required whenever there is a change in purpose that is not related to the purposes for which the information is collected or the information is disclosed to third parties for such purposes.

3. *Access and Correction Requirements*

Employees are entitled to be given a copy of the personal data held by their employer, and to request that the employer correct any data they consider to be inaccurate. Unless exempted from doing so under the PDPO, employers must provide a copy of the data or corrected data no later than 40 days after receiving a data access or data correction request. If an employer is unable to do so, it must communicate that fact before the end of that period and provide a copy as soon as possible thereafter. If the employer, pursuant to permitted circumstances under the PDPO, refuses to make the necessary correction, the employer should inform the requester in writing of the refusal and the reasons for such refusal.

4. *Accuracy Requirements*

Employers must take steps to ensure that the employee personal data are accurate with respect to the purpose for which the data are used. If the employer has reason to believe that the personal data are not accurate, the employer cannot use the data or must delete the data. If the employer had disclosed inaccurate data to a third party, the employer must notify such third party of the inaccuracy and provide the third party with the necessary information to correct the personal data.

5. *Retention of Employment-Related Data*

An employer should implement a written data retention policy that specifies a retention period of no longer than two years from the date of rejection with respect to recruitment-related data held about a job applicant who was not hired, and no longer than seven years with respect to employment-related data held about an employee from the date the employee leaves employment. Exceptions to such data retention requirements should be allowed if the individual gave express consent for a longer retention period, or if there is a subsisting reason that obliges the employer to keep the data for a longer period.

Also, the Employment Ordinance requires an employer to retain wage and employment records of employees covering the period of their employment during the preceding six months. The HR Code states that such records should be kept for six months after an employee ceases employment.[112]

In terms of retired employees, an employer may retain relevant personal data of retired employees, or their family members, as long as there is an obligation on the part of the employer to administer any affairs relating to the retirement plan of employees.[113]

6. *Disclosure or Transfer of Employment-Related Data*

Provided that the requisite notice was given to the employees at the time of collection about the classes of persons to which their data might be transferred, such transfers do not require consent.[114] The HR Code provides that an employer who seeks professional services of third parties on matters that involve the disclosure or transfer of employment-related data should ensure that the data are limited to those required for the specific services that they are to provide.[115] The HR Code also provides that when an employer outsources or contracts out its human resource processing to an external agency, the employer should take all practicable steps to ensure that the processing agency protects the employment-related

---

[112]HR Code §4.1.3.
[113]HR Code §4.8.1.
[114]HR Code §1.2.3.
[115]HR Code §3.11.1.

data against unauthorized or accidental access or disclosure, such as by making sure the outsourcing agreement contains security provisions to protect the data.[116]

7. *Transfer of Employment-Related Data Outside Hong Kong*

Section 33 of the PDPO prohibits the transfer of personal data outside Hong Kong unless it is to a jurisdiction that has in place a law that is substantially similar to the PDPO, or the individual consents to the transfer, or another exception applies. Section 33, however, has not yet entered into force and there is currently no timetable for its implementation.

In terms of international transfers of personal data within an organization, Sections 3.11.5 and 3.11.6 of the HR Code provide that employment-related personal data may be transferred to a related office of the organization outside Hong Kong provided that such transfer is for a purpose directly related to employment of employees and the data are adequate but not excessive in relation to that purpose.

8. *Providing Job References*

An employer should not provide a reference concerning an employee or former employee to a third party without the employee's prescribed consent unless the employer is satisfied that the third party requesting the reference has obtained the prior consent of the employee concerned.

9. *Sensitive Information*

a. *Medical and Health Data*

Employers may collect personal data relating to the health of a potential employee or an employee. For a potential employee, the data should be limited to that required to confirm the suitability of the candidate with respect to the inherent requirements of the position and should be collected only after the employer has

[116]HR Code §3.11.2.

made a conditional offer of employment to the candidate.[117] For a current employee, the collection has to be for a purpose that is directly related to the assessment of the suitability of the employee's continuance in employment or directly related to the employer's administration of medical or other benefits or compensation provided to the employee.

The HR Code states that employers should ensure that such personal data are kept secure owing to the sensitive nature of the data. Suggested security measures include secure terminals, access protocols, audit trail software, logging, and compliance checks.

Pursuant to Section 59 of the PDPO, personal data related to the physical or mental health of the employee are exempt from certain access rights under the PDPO, if the application of these provisions would be likely to cause serious harm to the physical or mental health of the employee or any other individual.

b. Identity Card Numbers

Pursuant to the ID Code, the employer may collect and use the identity card or number of job applicants and employees under certain conditions and subject to certain requirements as discussed in Chapter 8.

10. Security Requirements

The PDPO requires that data users implement and maintain security measures based on the kind of data they hold and the harm that could result if the data were accidentally disclosed, consider and implement appropriate security measures based on where the data are stored, secure transmission of data, and ensure that the individuals who have access to the data are properly trained.

The Hong Kong Privacy Commissioner's office also recently issued security guidelines for IT practitioners. The guidelines, entitled "Recommended Procedures for IT Practitioners on Personal Data Handling,"[118] outline the procedures to be followed in circumstances in which personal data collected by a data user

---

[117]Code of Practice on Human Resource Management—Compliance Guide for Employers and HRM Practitioners.

[118]"Recommended Procedures for IT Practitioners on Personal Data Handling," October 2006.

are accessed or processed by an IT contractor or subcontractor appointed to work on some aspect of the system. Employers, IT practitioners, and system administrators are being encouraged to implement the guidelines and work to ensure their effective implementation.

11. Monitoring of Employees

The PDPO broadly applies to monitoring and surveillance in the workplace. The Employee Monitoring Guidelines provide guidance to employers on the steps they can take in assessing whether employee monitoring is appropriate, and how they can develop compliant practices in the management of personal data obtained from employee monitoring. The rules applicable to electronic monitoring and surveillance are discussed in Chapter 3.

12. Penalties

In the event that an employer fails to comply with requirements of the PDPO, it could be subject to an investigation by the Privacy Commissioner, who may then issue a recommendation for compliance or an Enforcement Notice directing the employer to take certain steps. Contravention of an Enforcement Notice is punishable by a fine of HK$50,000 and up to two years' imprisonment, and in the case of a continuing offense, a daily penalty of HK$1,000.[119] Any act done or practice engaged in by a person in the course of his employment shall be treated as done or engaged in by his employer as well as by him, whether or not it was done or engaged in with the employer's knowledge or approval.[120]

C. Japan

The Protection of Personal Information Law[121] (PIPL), which regulates the acquisition and dissemination of personal information for commercial use, is the primary statute with which employers must comply with respect to their handling of employee personal

[119]§64 of the Ordinance.

[120]§65 of the Ordinance.

[121]Protection of Personal Information Law (Law No. 57 of 2003) (hereinafter PIPL).

data. Organizations are subject to the PIPL if they "use personal information databases in their business operations" and such databases contain the information on 5,000 or more individuals on any day in the past six months.[122] Both customer and employee databases, as well as any other databases that contain personal information (such as e-mail address books stored by e-mail software), are counted together to determine whether an organization is subject to the PIPL. Organizations subject to the law must provide notice about the purposes for which they collect and use information, adopt security control measures, respond to access and correction requests from individuals, and establish a complaint handling system. Unlike the EU Directive, the PIPL does not impose additional requirements on cross-border data transfers.

Much like other Japanese laws, the PIPL is framework legislation and gives discretion to national administrative agencies and local governments to develop implementing regulations, supervise, and enforce the PIPL. At the national level, competent Ministries include the Ministry of Economy, Trade, and Industry (METI); the Ministry of Internal Affairs and Communications (MIC) (formerly the Ministry of Public Management, Home Affairs, Posts and Telecommunication); the Ministry of Finance (FSA); the Ministry of Health, Labor, and Welfare (MHLW); and the Ministry of Land, Infrastructure and Transport (MLIT). These Ministries have promulgated guidelines that detail specific obligations and recommendations. As a result, organizations operating in Japan must carefully examine the guidelines issued by the competent Ministries under whose jurisdiction they operate. For example, an organization may be subject to multiple guidelines depending on the scope of its business operations, and the provisions of such guidelines may not be the same; in fact, they may actually conflict.

The handling of personal information in the employment context is addressed in several guidelines and commentary issued

---

[122] "Personal information" is defined broadly as information that relates to a living individual, which can be used to identify specific individuals by name, date of birth, or other description (including information that can be easily compared with other information to identify a specific individual, and includes those in electronic and nonelectronic forms).

by the MHLW: the "Guidelines for the Appropriate Handling of Personal Information in Employment Management" (MHLW Guidelines), the "Commentary to the Guidelines" (Commentary), and the "Points to Consider when Handling Health Information in Employment Management" (Health Points).[123] When the MHLW Guidelines and Commentary state that something "must" be done and businesses do not comply with such a mandatory provision, the MHLW may judge it to be a violation of the PIPL Concerning the Protection of Personal Information.

In addition, as mentioned above, organizations subject to the PIPL also will be subject to the MHLW Guidelines for their respective business areas, such as financial services, health care, and transportation. General businesses will be subject to the Guidelines issued by METI (the METI Guidelines). The METI Guidelines also contain provisions that apply to the handling of personal information in the employment context, such as when an employer decides to monitor the activities of its employees.

The main obligations under the PIPL, MHLW Guidelines, Commentary, and METI Guidelines applicable to personal information in the employment context are as described in the following sections.

1. *Notice*

Employers must specify to the extent possible the purpose of use of all of the personal information that they hold, and provide notice to the employees regarding such purpose of use or inform the employees concerning where such purpose of use can easily be found.[124] Notices regarding purpose of use must be specific and detailed enough so that the employees can reasonably foresee the final use of their personal information.[125] Any changes in purpose

---

[123]Guidelines for the Appropriate Handling of Personal Information in Employment Management, Announcement No. 259 of 2004 by the Ministry of Health, Labour and Welfare; the Commentary to the Guidelines and the Points to Consider when Handling Health Information in Employment Management, Ministry of Health, Labor, and Welfare (MHLW), Notice No. 1029009 dated October 29, 2004 from the Head of Labor Standards Bureau of the Ministry of Health, Labor, and Welfare to the head of the Prefectural Labor Standards Office.

[124]PIPL, Articles 15, 24.

[125]MHLW Guidelines and Commentary.

of use that are not foreseeable to the individual must be notified or publicly announced.[126]

If an employer intends to share information with third parties pursuant to the joint use or opt-out exceptions (discussed in the third-party sharings section below), then the notice must include the following additional information:

- *Opt-out notice.* Opt-out notice must contain the purpose of use of such sharing, items of personal information to be provided, means and methods of providing the data to third parties, and assurance that the provision of personal information will cease upon request.
- *Joint use notice.* Notice must be given regarding joint use, specifying the items of personal data to be used jointly, the range of joint users, the purpose of joint use, and the name of the entity responsible for the management of the jointly used data. Joint users may include corporate affiliates or unaffiliated entities with whom the business may be engaged in joint marketing activities.

The notice also must provide the name of the entity and contact information and procedures for submitting access, correction requests, and complaints.[127]

2. *Breach Notice*

If there has been a leak of personal information, the METI Guidelines state that the following notices should be given:[128]

- Leakage should be reported to the appropriate Minister.
- A public announcement should be made of relevant facts to the extent possible.

---

[126]PIPL, Article 18.3.

[127]PIPL, Article 24.

[128]The language of the METI Guidelines suggests that providing notices is not mandatory but is included as METI's example of how to comply with the mandatory requirement to take appropriate measures in the event of a leakage of personal information.

- Individuals should be notified regarding the relevant facts of the leakage. See Chapter 10 for more detail.

3. *Notice to Labor Unions*

The MHLW Guidelines state that employers should notify and, if necessary, consult with labor unions in deciding important matters relating to disclosure and handling of personal information (such as when requests for disclosure by employees should be denied, etc.), and when important matters have been decided, they should be made publicly known to the employees.

4. *Consent*

When employers want to use personal information of employees beyond the specified purpose of use or when employers want to transfer personal information to third parties (see Section 1.IV.C.4., below), employers generally need to obtain the opt-in consent of the individuals. The MHLW Commentary states that oral and written confirmation of consent, clicking on a Web site button, receipt of e-mail from the individual communicating consent, and receipt of a signed consent form are all examples of obtaining consent.

5. *Third-Party Sharing of Employee Information*

Sharing employee personal information with third parties must be pursuant to opt-in consent; pursuant to an applicable exception, such as joint use, delegation, or opt-out; or pursuant to a merger and acquisition transaction (M&A). To use the joint use and opt-out exceptions, the necessary notices need to be made (see Section 1.IV.C.1., above). The government ministries have indicated that joint users would be jointly liable for any leaks, deletions, divulgences, or alterations to personal information.

In terms of the M&A exception, the ministries have indicated that the exception is not applicable in the due diligence context, so that entities cannot rely on a Confidentiality Agreement for the protection of personal information. Entities that want to share employee information for due diligence purposes in the M&A context must take care to either make the personal information anonymous or obtain consent (both costly and impractical solutions).

The METI Guidelines provide that when employee personal information, such as personnel ratings, is provided to third parties pursuant to consent (and not pursuant to any of the exceptions such as joint use, opt-out, etc.), such as when an employee is seconded to a subsidiary or if a worker is dispatched, employers should "pay attention to" the following matters (the language used suggests that these provisions are not mandatory):

- The party being provided data has established that the personal information learned with regard to the employee in the handling of the corresponding personal data must not be divulged or misused.
- The third party has confirmed that it will not leak or divulge the personal information or use it for another purpose.
- The prior written approval of the business is to be obtained when engaging in a subsequent provision of the personal data.
- The copying and duplication of personal data (excluding that required for backup purposes under security control) are prohibited for the party being provided the data.
- The party being provided the data will clarify the retention term.
- After achieving the purpose of use, the personal data will be returned, destroyed, deleted, or handled by the combination thereof, and the party that was provided the data will provide confirmation of the same.

6. *Supervision of Service Providers*

Employers that provide personal data to service providers pursuant to the delegation exception are required to supervise their service providers (delegates).[129] The MHLW Guidelines and Commentary instruct organizations to "pay attention to" the following matters (the language used suggests that these provisions are not mandatory):

---

[129] PIPL, Article 22.

1. Appropriate standards should be set for the selection of a company that is taking sufficient measures to protect personal information.
2. The Delegation Agreement should detail measures to be taken by the delegatee to protect the personal information to be handled by the delegatee. Specific provisions for such an agreement should cover the following:
   a. The delegatee shall prohibit its employees from divulging or misappropriating personal information;
   b. The delegatee shall give written notice to delegator if such delegate will subdelegate handling of such personal information;
   c. The term of delegation shall be explicitly set in the Delegation Agreement;
   d. After the purpose of use is achieved, the personal information shall be returned or destroyed or deleted by the delegatee;
   e. The delegatee shall prohibit or limit processing beyond the scope of outsourcing agreement;
   f. The delegatee shall prohibit the reproduction of personal information (excluding that necessary for backup);
   g. The delegatee shall have the duty to report to the delegator any leakage, divulgence, damage, or alteration of personal information, and the delegate should have set liability in case of such divulgence, etc.

7. Security

Pursuant to Article 20 of the PIPL, organizations must adopt organizational, personnel, and technological security measures to prevent divulgence, loss, or damage of personal information. Organizations will be subject to the security requirements provided in the METI Guidelines, as well as the security guidelines provided in the MHLW Guidelines and Commentary specifically applicable to personal information related to employment management. The MHLW Guidelines and Commentary provide that an organization "shall exert efforts to" take measures in order to:

- Clarify the authority of those employees who will be handling personal information related to employment management, such as by defining their roles in internal security regulations;
- Ensure that only those employees who have been given the authority to handle such personal information related to employment management shall handle it only to the extent necessary to conduct business;
- Ensure that personal information will be handled only to the extent necessary, and employees shall not recklessly inform any third party of the content of any personal data or use for an unjustifiable purpose (even after such employees have left duties relating to such operations), such as through the use of confidentiality agreements;
- Appoint a Personal Information Manager from among those who are recognized to have the necessary knowledge and experience to manage the personal information relating to employment management pursuant to these Guidelines;
- Conduct the necessary training to make sure employees handling personal information relating to employment management understand the importance of their responsibilities and to make sure they know the security regulations.

8. Sensitive Information

While the PIPL does not define sensitive information, MHLW has issued guidelines or other guidance that imposes restrictions on the use of health information of employees. The rules applicable to employee health information are discussed in Chapter 5.

9. Access and Correction Rights

Organizations must promptly respond to access and correction requests in writing, unless (1) there is a risk that the life, health, property, or other rights of the individual or other third party would be infringed; (2) the proper operation of the business would be significantly obstructed; or (3) if other laws would be violated. (Articles 25 and 26 of the PIPL.) If a request is denied, notice must be provided and the business must "make best efforts" to provide reasons for denial.

The MHLW Guidelines provide that organizations should make efforts to consult with labor unions to set rules about what kinds of held personal data will likely not be disclosed because there is a risk that the organization will suffer extreme obstruction by the disclosure of some or all of such information, and such rules should be made known to the employees. In addition, organizations should give consideration regarding viewing times/places so that requests by employees will be carried out as smoothly as possible.

10. Monitoring of Employees

The rules applicable to workplace monitoring are discussed in Chapter 3.

D. Korea

In South Korea (officially, the Republic of Korea), there is an information protection law applicable to the private sector, called the Act on Promotion of Information and Communications Network Utilization and Information Protection (the APICNU). The Act was originally intended to apply specifically to information and communication providers, but the Act has been applied more broadly to the activities of any entity, including an employer, using and transmitting personal information over information and communications networks. Efforts to enact comprehensive privacy legislation have been underway for a few years but it is unclear if and when new legislation would be enacted.

In addition to APICNU, the Korean Constitution provides a constitutional right to privacy.[130] In addition, there are sectoral laws that have provisions regarding the protection of personal information, such as the Protection of Communications Secret Law of 1993, the Telecommunications Business Act of 1991, the Medical Service Act of 1973, the Use and Protection of Credit Information Act of 1995, the Pharmaceutical Affairs Act of 1967, and the

---

[130] Article 17 of the Korean Constitution protects "the privacy of a citizen"; Article 18 protects "the privacy of correspondence of a citizen."

Act on Financial Transactions with Real Name and Guarantee of Secrecy of 1997, that may be applicable to employers.

The key privacy obligations on employers, however, are largely found in APICNU and include the following. (*Note:* An entity subject to the APICNU will be referred to herein as "Provider.")

1. Notice

Notice must be given if consent is to be requested. Notice must give information regarding:

- The name, department, position, telephone number, and other communications means of the person in charge of managing the personal information;
- The purpose of collection and use;
- The third parties to whom the information will be disclosed, the purpose of disclosure, and the information or categories of information to be disclosed; and
- The rights of the individual to withdraw consent, access, and correct information;
- The information on installation and operation of any device that automatically collects personal information such as Internet access data and the refusal thereof;
- The categories of information to be collected; and
- The duration of retention and use.

2. Privacy Policy

Privacy policies are not specifically required under the APICNU, but are strongly recommended. The notice and consents required under the APICNU may be achieved through the use of a privacy policy.

3. Consent

Consent is required to collect, use, and disclose personal information over communications networks. In particular, opt-in consent is required to collect, use, and disclose sensitive information[131] and personal credit information. Opt-in consent is required to transfer personal information outside Korea. Consent may be withdrawn at any time.

4. *Access and Correction Rights*

Users have the right to request to review their personal information and receive details regarding the use of and any third-party transfers of such information. If a user's personal information is incorrect, the user may request the correction of such information. When a Provider receives a request to correct a user's personal information, the Provider may not use or provide incorrect personal information to a third party. (Article 30.)

5. *Cross-Border Requirements*

Providers of information and communications services may not enter into any international contract that violates the provisions of APICNU with respect to the personal information of users. As mentioned above, Providers are required to (1) obtain opt-in consent from the users after notifying the purpose and method of transfer, description of information to be transferred, recipient country, name of recipient, contact details of the person in charge of personal information protection, etc.; and (2) take necessary security measures (including technical and administrative measures to protect personal information and procedures to handle complaints and disputes). Cross-border agreements to transfer personal information to third parties outside Korea are not required, however.

6. *Security*

Under Article 28, Providers are required to take technical and administrative measures necessary to ensure the safety of the

[131] Sensitive information is information that relates to racial or ethnic origin or opinions, religion or other beliefs, and health, as well as trade union membership, and may not be collected, except if the individual consents to such collection or collection is required by other laws. (Article 23.)

personal information in order to keep personal information from being lost, stolen, leaked out, changed, or damaged. Article 32 of the Enforcement Decree of the APICNU states that technical and administrative measures mentioned in Article 28 should include the following:

- Establishment and implementation of an internal plan to safeguard personal information;
- Installation and implementation of an access control system to block unauthorized access;
- Establishment of measures necessary to prevent falsification or alteration of access records;
- Establishment of security measures, including encryption technologies, to safely store and transmit personal information;
- Installation and implementation of a computer antivirus program; and
- Establishment of other protective measures deemed by the Minister of Information and Communications to be necessary to ensure the security of personal information.

Providers of nationwide information and communications connection services, operators of agglomerated information and communications facilities, and the providers of information and communications services that meet certain standards set by the Ordinance of the Ministry of Information and Communication (MIC) with respect to the sales amount, facility size, etc. (collectively, the "major providers of information and communications services") must (1) conduct an annual security audit by external security consultants and (2) take security measures in accordance with the Enforcement Regulations of APICNU.[132] Any leaks or infringements must be reported.

---

[132]Such providers would include multinational corporations that maintain a worldwide communications network for the purpose of conducting business with their customers and communicating with their affiliates and employees around the world if they provide their services on a nationwide basis in Korea or meet the sales or number of subscribers/users requirements set by the MIC. The MIC eligibility criteria are (1) having at least KRW 10 billion in sales as of the last fiscal year; or (2) having at least 1 million daily average subscribers/users for the three months at the end of the last fiscal year.

Providers of information and communications services, operators of agglomerated information and communications facilities, and other operators of information and communications network as prescribed by the Enforcement Decree of APICNU must report any leaks or infringements to the MIC or KISA.

7. *Supervision of Service Providers*

There is a requirement to supervise service providers. Providers and recipients of personal information remain fully accountable for any damages caused by service providers with respect to the handling of personal information. Third parties must use the information only for the purposes for which they were provided. The use of onward transfer (confidentiality) agreements with such service providers are not specifically required but strongly recommended.

8. *Data Retention*

Providers must promptly dispose of personal information after the specified retention period has expired or the objective of use has been achieved, unless retention is required under other law (e.g., businesses need to keep personal information relating to e-commerce for five years and keep records about customer complaints and resolution for three years).

Employers must be particularly aware of the Labor Standards Act (LSA), whereby an employer with five or more employees is required to retain certain documents for three years from specified dates. (Article 41 of the LSA, Article 17 of the Presidential Decree of LSA.)

9. *Breach Notification*

Breaches or suspected breaches must be reported immediately to the Minister of Information and Communications or the Korean Information Security Agency.[133]

---

[133]Under APICNU, a breach is referred to as an infringement event. An "infringement event" is defined as an "event occurring as a result of attack on an information and communication network or related information system through hacking, computer virus, logic bomb, mail bomb, service rejection, high power electromagnetic waves, etc."

10. Penalties

The APICNU provides for criminal and administrative penalties for various offenses including, but not limited to, the following: imprisonment of not more than five years and/or a fine not exceeding 50 million KRW (South Korean won) for persons who use or transfer such information to third parties beyond the scope of notification, or damages or leaks information learned while handling the information. (Article 62.)

Under Article 32, if an individual suffers any damage due to a Provider's violations of the APICNU, the individual may claim the compensation for such damages against the Provider.

11. Surveillance/Monitoring of Employees

In Korea, the monitoring of work e-mails of employees is covered by the APICNU and the Protection of Communications Secret Law of 1993 (the Secrecy Act). In addition, there are also nonbinding guidelines on video surveillance issued recently by the Ministry of Information and Communication. The rules applicable to workplace monitoring and surveillance are discussed in Chapter 3.

E. New Zealand

The Privacy Act 1993[134] applies with few exceptions to both the public and private sectors. The Act contains 12 information privacy principles that pertain to the collection, use, storage, and disclosure of personal information and the assignment of unique identifiers. The principles also give individuals including employees the right to access personal information and to request correction of that information. The principles do not override other laws that govern the collection, use, or disclosure of personal information.[135]

The Privacy Act gives the Privacy Commissioner the power to issue codes of practice that become part of the law. These codes are designed to address the requirements of specific industries,

---

[134]The Privacy Act 1993.

[135]*See* Fact Sheet No. 2 Information Privacy Principles.

sectors, activities, or types of personal information. To date, the Privacy Commissioner has issued codes on credit reporting, health information privacy, and telecommunications information privacy. As in Australia, the government is currently conducting a full scale review of its Privacy Act; however, unlike Australia, the government's focus is on the changes to the law that would enable New Zealand to satisfy the EU adequacy requirements. In particular, the government is considering adopting EU-style restrictions on cross-border transfers.

Obligations applicable to employers under the Privacy Act are described in the following sections.

1. Collection and Use Limitations

Personal information must be collected directly from the individual concerned unless otherwise authorized by the individual. The collection must be for a lawful purpose connected with the function or activity of the organization collecting the information. Personal information obtained in connection with one purpose must not be used for another purpose unless consented to by the individual or authorized by the Privacy Commissioner.

2. Notice

The organization must provide notice either before or as soon as possible after the information is collected. The notice should provide information about the fact that personal information is being collected, the purpose of use, the intended recipients, the names and addresses of who is collecting and storing the information, any specific law governing provision of the information and whether provision is voluntary or mandatory, the consequences if all or any part of the requested information is not provided, and the individual's rights of access to and correction of personal information.

3. Security and Data Retention

An organization must ensure there are reasonable safeguards against loss, misuse, and disclosure. If the information is to be disclosed to another person, then the business must do everything reasonable to prevent unauthorized use and unauthorized disclosure of the information.

4. Access and Correction

Subject to some exceptions, individuals are entitled to obtain confirmation of whether the information is held and to have access to information about them. Frivolous or vexatious requests for access can be denied. Individuals have the right to request correction of their personal information and to request that if it is not corrected, a statement is attached to the original information saying what correction was sought but not made.

5. Data Accuracy

An agency must not use or disclose personal information without taking reasonable steps to check that it is accurate, complete, relevant, up to date, and not misleading.

6. Data Retention

Data must not be kept for longer than needed for the purpose for which the business collected it.

7. Unique Identifiers

See Chapter 8 for information on the rules applicable to the use of government identifiers.

F. Taiwan

In the Republic of China (Taiwan), there is a constitutional right to privacy. Article 12 of the Constitution of the Republic of China (the ROC Constitution) provides that "[t]he people shall have freedom of privacy of correspondence."[136] In addition, Taiwan's Computer Processed Personal Data Protection Act (the Act) governs the collection, computerized processing, utilization, and transfer of personal data, including employee data by public institutions and certain private entities. Private entities that are

---

[136] Article 12 of the Constitution of the Republic of China.

subject to this Act (hereinafter referred to as Businesses) are as follows:

1. Any credit investigation business or organization or individual whose principal business is to make the collection or computerized processing of personal data;
2. Any hospital, school, telecommunication business, financial business, securities business, insurance business, and mass media; and
3. Other enterprises, organizations, or individuals designated by Ministry of Justice and the central government authorities in charge of concerned end enterprises.

If an employer is subject to the Act, it will be subject to the following key obligations under the Act.

1. License/Database Registration

Before Businesses in Taiwan start collecting, processing, transferring, or using personal data, they must register with the Ministry of Justice by submitting an application for registration and obtain a license.[137] Registration applications must contain the following information:

1. Name of Business, principal office, branch office(s) or business operation office(s), and its representative's or administrator's name, place of residence, or domicile;
2. Name of the personal data file;
3. Specific purposes for personal data file;
4. Classification of personal information;
5. Scope of personal information;
6. Period to maintain a personal data file;
7. Collection method of personal data;
8. Scope of use;
9. Direct recipients of international transmission of personal information;

---

[137]Computer Processed Personal Data Protection Act, Article 19.

10. Name of person responsible for preserving personal data file; and
11. Security Control Plan for personal data file.

Upon approval of registration, information in the application pertaining to items 1 through 10 above must be published in an official gazette and local newspapers.[138] The publication shall run for at least two days.[139]

2. Consent

A Business may collect or process personal data of employees upon the written consent of the employees. In practice, it is quite common to build in a provision in the employment contract to obtain a general consent for the collection, computer processing, transfer, and use of employee personal data.

3. Use Limitations

Use of personal data must be limited to the specific purpose of collection. More than 100 purposes under the Act have been identified by the Ministry of Justice. Such permissible purposes include personnel management, compliance auditing, customer management, statistics investigation and analysis, and credit check.[140]

Use beyond a permitted specified purpose may be made under the following exceptions:

1. To enhance the public interest;
2. To avoid imminent danger to life, body, freedom, or property of a concerned party;
3. To prevent grave damages to the rights and interest of others, when necessary; and
4. Pursuant to the written consent of a concerned party.

---

[138] *Id.*, Article 21.

[139] Enforcement Rules of the Labor Inspection Law, Article 38.

[140] "Standard Purposes under the Data Protection Law."

4. *Limits on Data Transfers; Cross-Border Limitations*

Transfers of personal data to third parties are limited to a permissible specific purpose. To transfer personal data to entities located outside Taiwan, a Business subject to the Act must list in its registration application the intended recipients of international data transfer. In addition, pursuant to Article 24 of the Act, the government authorities may restrict international transmission and use of personal information under the following circumstances:

1. If it involves the greater interest of Taiwan;
2. If it is specially provided for in an international treaty or agreement;
3. If the receiving country lacks proper laws and ordinances to adequately protect personal data and where there is risk of injury to the rights and interests of concerned parties; and
4. If by indirectly transmitting personal information to a third country or using personal information in a third country the business is evading control of the Act.

5. *Access Rights*

The Act requires Businesses to reply to access inquiries, enable individuals to review their data files, and make duplicates of the files, except if it is likely to cause interference with business functions or likely to undermine the greater interest of a third party. Employers are not required to provide access to information relating to personnel, daily duties, salary, sanitation, or welfare. If it is permissible for the Business to deny access, it does not have to notify employees about the denial.

6. *Accuracy/Right to Correct/Cease Use*

Businesses are required to maintain the accuracy of personal information, and make timely amendments or supplements ex officio or upon request by a concerned party. If there is a dispute about the accuracy of personal information, the Business shall cease the processing and use of such personal information ex officio or upon request by the concerned party, except when it is necessary to use such information to carry out a duty and the dispute is noted, or with the consent of the concerned party.

The right of the individual to request a cessation of computerized processing, use, and deletion of his personal data cannot be contracted away.

7. *Data Retention*

Pursuant to the local labor law, an employer is required to maintain comprehensive records for his employees, including name, sex, birth date and birthplace, address, educational background, identification card number, date of reporting for duty, wages, labor insurance starting date, merits and demerits, injury and disease, and other significant facts of his employees. Such records must be maintained for five years after termination of the employment. The labor authority may conduct compliance inspections on the employee records and documents at the employer's office from time to time.

Under the Act, a Business must delete or cease computerized processing of personal information when the specific purpose of computerized processing of personal information no longer exists or the time limit thereof expires, ex officio or upon request by the concerned party. An exception is made if the information is required to carry out official duties, a change of purpose is made, or the written consent of the concerned party has been obtained.

8. *Monitoring of Employees*

The ROC Constitution protects privacy of communications of the people. Privacy is also a protected right under the Civil Code, and infringement of privacy may be subject to civil liabilities. Within the legal and academic communities, the current thinking is that the ability of an employer to monitor the activities and speech of its employees depends on whether or not an employee has been given a "reasonable expectation" of privacy in the activities or speech that is to be monitored. The monitoring of employees is discussed in Chapter 3.

9. Security

Businesses subject to the Act must prepare and submit a safety maintenance plan for the personal data file and register it with the authorities. Article 17 of the Act requires the business to "appoint a full time employee to handle matters relevant to the security and maintenance of said files to prevent personal data from being stolen, altered without authorization, damaged, lost or disclosed."

10. Penalties

The Act sets forth various criminal penalties for the violation of its provisions:

- *Search and seizure of personal data.* A government authority may dispatch officials to conduct inspections. If any data violating this Act is found, the data may be seized.[141]
- *Compensation for damages.* Businesses violating the Act and causing damages to individuals shall be liable for compensation for damages unless they can prove that there was no intention or fault.[142] The burden of proof is on the defendant, which makes it much easier for an injured plaintiff to establish his claim.
- *Criminal and administrative penalties.* Criminal and administrative penalties are imposed on various types of violations (see Chapter 3). The responsible person of such a violating entity may be held personally liable. The highest penalty is imprisonment for up to three years. The highest fine is NT$100,000, which could be imposed consecutively until the violation is ceased or corrected.

---

[141] Computer Processed Personal Data Protection Act, Article 25.
[142] *Id.*, Article 28.

V. AMERICAS OTHER THAN UNITED STATES

A. Argentina

Of all the countries in Latin America, Argentina has the most developed framework for the protection of personal information that includes habeas data provisions enacted in 1994 and a comprehensive, EU-style data protection law enacted in 2000. The habeas data provisions in Article 43 of the Constitution enable any person to obtain information on the data held in files or databases about himself or herself and the purposes of use and request the suppression, rectification, confidentiality, or updating of that data when they are false or discriminatory. The Personal Data Protection Law (PDPL)[143] regulates the collection, use, and disclosure of all personal information contained in databases that are shared.

Like the EU Data Protection Directive, the PDPL and its implementing regulations[144] require database registration and limit cross-border transfers to countries that provide "adequate" data protection unless the individual consents to the transfer. The consent, onward transfer, and access requirements, however, go beyond those found in the EU Directive. In 2002, the EU granted an adequacy finding to Argentina—the first (and only) country in South America to receive one.

To ensure compliance with the law, a data protection authority, the Dirección Nacional de Protección de Datos Personales (DNPDP), was established within the Ministry of Justice. The DNPDP has the power to impose sanctions such as warnings, suspensions, fines, and even cancellation of data files, registers, or databanks for each breach of the PDPL. For example, the collection of personal data on data subjects without providing them with the information set out in the PDPL is punishable by a fine ranging from 1,000 to 3,000 pesos (approximately US$342 to US$1,025). Failure to comply with the duty of information laid down in the PDPL when data have been obtained from a person other than the data subject is punishable by a fine of up to 50,000 pesos (approxi-

---

[143] Act 25,326, Personal Data Protection Law.

[144] *See* Decree 1558/2001.

mately US$17,000); systematic failure to comply with the duty to notify the inclusion of personal data in a file is punishable by a fine of up to 100,000 pesos (approximately US$34,000).

Summarized below are the key requirements under the PDPL, implementing regulations, and related decrees.

1. Notice/Privacy Policy

Individuals must be notified in advance regarding the collection of their personal information, including information collected from third parties. In particular, the individual must be notified regarding:

1. The purposes of information collection, use, storage, and disclosure;
2. The recipients or type of recipients;
3. The existence of the relevant data file(s) or database(s);
4. The identity and address of the data controller;
5. The compulsory or discretionary nature of the information collected, particularly with respect to sensitive information;
6. The consequences of providing or refusing to provide personal data or providing inaccurate data; and
7. The access and correction rights.

In the event that there is a change in purpose that has not been previously identified by the company, the company must issue a new notice and obtain the individual's consent. Because consent must be drafted in a way that is understandable, notices and consent requests, therefore, by implication, should be provided in the local language.

2. Consent/Use Limitations

Consent is not required to collect, use, and disclose personal information that is required for a contractual relationship (i.e., employment relationship). Otherwise, written consent is required to process any personal information or to share information with affiliated companies. There are some exceptions for direct marketing and some selected information (e.g., individual's name, identification numbers, employment, birth date, and domicile). Consent may be revoked at any time.

Collection of sensitive information is permitted only where authorized by law or for statistical or scientific purposes provided that individuals cannot be identified. There is an exception, though, for health-related data that allows public and private health institutions to collect and process health-related data. Otherwise, express consent is required to collect, use, and disclose sensitive personal information.

3. *Access and Correction*

Individuals have the right to access their personal information and to have their personal information corrected or updated every six months free of charge. The employing organization has a general obligation to maintain accurate, updated information and to remove, substitute, and complete untruthful or incomplete information.

4. *Security/Data Retention*

Under the PDPL, the employer must adopt appropriate safeguards to protect the security and confidentiality of databases containing personal information in order to protect against loss, unauthorized access or processing, or adulteration. All personal information must be destroyed when it is no longer necessary or relevant to the purposes of collection.

In September 2006, the DNPDP issued the "Security Measures for the Treatment and Preservation of Personal Data Contained in Non-governmental Public Archives, Registries, Data Banks and Data Bases" (the Security Measures).[145] The Security Measures, which provide for three security levels for the treatment and preservation (protection) of personal information, required compliance within 12 months from September 22, 2006, for basic level protections, 24 months for the medium level protections, and 36 months for the critical level protections. However, in September 2008, the DNPDP extended by one year the timetables for

---

[145] *See* DNPDP N° 11/06—Implementación Medidas de Seguridad en bases privada.

implementation of the medium and critical level protections.[146] Implementation of basic security measures was not postponed.

For each of those security levels, there are certain security measures and requirements, which were based on the need to guarantee the confidentiality and integrity of the data contained in the corresponding data bank; the nature of the data; and the appropriate management of the risks related thereto.

All organizations that maintain archives, registries, databases, and data banks (collectively, the Databases) that contain data of a personal nature must have implemented the basic level security measures by September 2007. In particular, these organizations should have a Personal Data Security Document, specifying the security measures and procedures that must be followed.[147] Such Personal Data Security Document should be updated and revised when any changes in the information system occur. The DPA also has published a template to implement the Security and Privacy Policy that data controllers are required to have in place.[148]

Private companies that provide public services, as well as entities that comply with a public or private purpose and that are bound by law to maintain personal data secret (e.g., banking secret), must comply with both basic and medium level security requirements. Medium level requires such organizations to identify the person or corporate body responsible for security and perform audits (internal and external) and verify compliance with the proceedings and instructions applicable to personal data security.

Organizations that maintain databases containing sensitive data must comply with the requirements of all three levels of security. The critical level of security requires that sensitive data be encrypted, access records or logs, indicating when the data was accessed and the type of access, be maintained, and additional backup copies be kept offsite.

---

[146]*See* DNPDP N° 9/2008—Medidas de Seguridad para el Tratamiento y Conservación de los Datos Personales Contenidos en Archivos, Registros, Bancos y Bases de Datos Públicos no estatales y Privados. Prorrógase el plazo establecido por la Disposición N° 11/2006.

[147]*See* Regulation 11/2006.

[148]*See* Regulation 9/2008.

5. *Database Registration*

Database registration is required under the PDPL. In February 2005, the Argentine DPA officially enacted its registry of private databases. Organizations were required to register all databases containing personal information with the DPA by January 31, 2006. In late 2005, the Argentine DPA created an official registry of privacy law offenders, identifying those who have been found to be in violation of the privacy law.

6. *Cross-Border Transfers*

Contract or consent of the individual is required if the transfer of information is to a country that does not provide adequate protection. To date, however, no countries have been formally deemed to provide adequate protection, so the adequacy of a particular country would need to be proven by the company seeking to transfer the data. (The presumption is, however, that countries deemed adequate by the EU would also be found adequate by Argentina.)

To obtain a valid consent to transfer the personal information to a country that is not deemed to provide adequate protection, the individual must be notified of the country to which the information will be transferred and the consequences and risks of that transfer. Nonresidents of Argentina are not subject to the same data protection rights as residents of Argentina. Accordingly, their personal information may be transferred outside Argentina, even to a country that is deemed to provide inadequate protection, without obtaining their written consent.

In addition, the Argentine data protection agency is purportedly developing model contractual clauses for cross-border data transfers; however, the timetable for their completion is unclear.

7. *Onward Transfer Agreements*

Agreements must include provisions requiring joint and several liability and subjecting the third-party recipient to the same security obligations as the company that controls the personal information. For purposes of Argentina's data protection law, affiliates are considered third parties.

8. *Dispute Resolution*

There is no requirement to establish an internal dispute resolution or complaint handling program. Complaints can be filed with the DPA. A private right of action is possible under the law.

B. Canada

1. *Federal Regulation*

In Canada, private sector use of personal information is regulated at the federal level by the Personal Information Protection and Electronic Documents Act (PIPEDA).[149] PIPEDA, enacted on January 1, 2001, sets out ground rules for how private sector organizations may collect, use, or disclose personal information in the course of commercial activities. As of January 1, 2004, PIPEDA applies to all businesses and organizations to which a "substantially similar" provincial law does not apply. "Substantially similar" means that provincial privacy legislation must incorporate the 10 principles of PIPEDA; provide for an effective oversight and redress mechanism; and contain a reasonable purpose test. At present, Alberta, British Columbia, and Quebec are the only provinces that have legislation that has been deemed substantially similar.

With respect to employee data, PIPEDA applies only to personal information about employees of an organization that falls within the legislative authority of the Parliament of Canada, which includes the following sectors:

- Telecommunications
- Broadcasting
- Interprovincial or international trucking, shipping, railways, or other transportation

[149]Bill C-6, Personal Information Protection and Electronic Documents Act.

- Aviation
- Banking
- Nuclear energy
- Activities related to maritime navigation and shipping (including, for example, ports and longshoring)
- Local businesses in Yukon, Nunavut, and the Territories (where all private sector activity is in federal jurisdiction)

For those organizations that are subject to the law, PIPEDA defines personal information as "information about an identifiable individual" that includes any factual or subjective information, recorded or not, in any form. This would include, for example, name, address, telephone number, gender identification numbers, income, blood type, credit records, loan records, existence of a dispute between a consumer and a merchant, and intentions to acquire goods or services. Unlike other privacy laws such as the EU Directive, however, personal information would not include the name, business title, business address, or business telephone of any employee (i.e., information on a business card). Like the EU Directive, though, PIPEDA covers sensitive personal information, which may include health or medical history, racial or ethnic origin, political opinions, religious beliefs, trade union membership, financial information, and sexual preferences.

In addition to the exclusion for business contact information, another important difference between PIPEDA and the Directive is that PIPEDA does not explicitly restrict cross-border transfers. In fact, the same notice and consent rules apply for cross-border transfers as for disclosures to any third party. Information about the location of transferee or the adequacy of the privacy laws in the jurisdiction in which the transferee is located is not specifically required. Despite these differences, the European Commission has found PIPEDA to be adequate under the Directive.

Modifications to PIPEDA, however, are expected in the coming year. The government is currently drafting proposed amendments to PIPEDA as a result of a legally mandated review of the law, which began in 2006. A Parliamentary committee, tasked with conducting the review, issued a report[150] in May 2007 that recommended amendments to PIPEDA in a number of areas including security breach notification. The government issued its formal response to the Parliamentary report in November 2007 and then launched a public consultation on its proposed changes. As of December 2008, however, the government has yet to submit to Parliament its proposed legislative amendments.

2. *PIPEDA Requirements*

Employers subject to PIPEDA must comply with the requirements set out in the following sections.

a. Notice

Individuals must be informed about the information to be collected and the purposes for which it will be collected, used, and disclosed. Depending on the way in which the information is collected, notice may be provided orally or in writing. When personal information that has been collected is to be used for a purpose not previously identified, the new purpose must be identified prior to use. All purposes must be documented.

b. Consent

Consent is required to collect and use personal information. Consent may be express or implied. The form of the consent obtained will depend on the circumstances, reasonable expectations of the individual, and the type or sensitivity of the information collected. Generally, express consent should be obtained when the information is likely to be considered sensitive. Implied consent is generally appropriate when the information is less sensitive.

An individual has the right to withdraw consent at any time, subject to legal or contractual restrictions and reasonable notice. The organization must inform the individual of the implications

---

[150]*See* Recommendations 23, 24, and 25, Statutory Review of the Personal Information Protection and Electronic Documents Act (PIPEDA), Fourth Report of the Standing Committee on Access to Information, Privacy, and Ethics, May 2007, 39th Parliament, 1st Session.

of such withdrawal. Individuals should be given the right to opt out of the use of personal information for secondary marketing purposes.

c. Database Registration

No database registration is required.

d. Data Processing Contracts

The company should enter into written data processing contracts with all data processors.

e. Designation of a Privacy Officer

An individual responsible for compliance with PIPEDA must be appointed.

f. Implementation of Policies and Practices; Audit

Written policies regarding the protection of personal information must be developed and made available on request. There is no requirement related to audit, although this is recommended.

g. Access

Access must be provided on request and personal information must be corrected or amended if its accuracy and completeness is challenged and found to be deficient. The company must respond to requests as quickly as possible and no later than 30 days from receipt of the request.

h. Cross-Border Transfers

Although there are no restrictions on cross-border data transfers, a business retains accountability for the protection of personal information it collects and transfers to third parties regardless of where those third parties are located.

i. Complaint Handling

The company must develop complaint handling procedures, inform complainants of their avenues of recourse, investigate all complaints, and take appropriate measures to correct deficient information handling practices and policies.

j. Security

The company must have appropriate organizational and technical security safeguards in place.

k. Data Retention

The company should develop retention guidelines and implement procedures regarding retention and destruction of personal information.

3. Provincial Privacy Laws

In addition to PIPEDA, some of the provinces (Alberta, British Columbia, and Quebec) have privacy laws that pertain to private sector collection and use of personal information; Ontario has a privacy law that pertains only to private sector collection, use, and disclosure of personal health information. So, while an employer may not be subject to PIPEDA for the collection and use of its employee data, it may need to comply with the private sector privacy laws in the provinces in which it operates with respect to the processing of employee data.

a. British Columbia

For example, British Columbia's Personal Information Protection Act (PIPA) applies to employee personal information but does not apply to contact information or work product information. Employee personal information is defined as "personal information about an individual that is collected, used, and disclosed solely for the purposes reasonably required to establish, manage, or terminate an employment relationship between the organization and that individual, but does not include personal information that is not about an individual's employment." Guidance provided by the Privacy Commissioner's office suggests that personal information of contractors and consultants would not be considered to fall within the definition of employee personal information. Personal information of prospective, current, and former employees would be covered, however.

b. Ontario

Ontario's Personal Health Information Protection Act applies to personal health information that is collected, used, and disclosed by health information custodians and personal health information that is used and disclosed by persons such as employers who receive personal health information from health information custodians. Health information custodians include health care practitioners, long-term care service providers, community care access corporations, hospitals, laboratories, pharmacies, medical officers of health or a board of health, and the Ministry of Health and Long-Term Care. Personal health information includes oral or written information about the individual if the information relates to the individual's physical or mental health, the provision of health care, including the identification of persons providing care, a plan of service for individuals requiring long-term care, the payment or eligibility for health care, and the individual's health number.

c. Quebec

Quebec's Act Respecting the Protection of Personal Information in the Private Sector does not treat personal information about employees as a distinct category of personal information subject to special provisions, so employers would need to comply with the Quebec law for the processing of its employee data.

C. Chile

Chile was the first Latin American country to enact a data protection law, the "Law for the Protection of Private Life," Act No. 19628, in 1999. The law regulates the processing and use of personal data by the public and private sectors and gives individuals rights to access and correct their personal data. The law contains provisions that pertain to the use of financial, commercial, and banking data, and creates rules for the use of information by government agencies. Only government databases must be registered. There is no data protection authority and enforcement of the law is done individually by each affected person.

In November 2008, the Chilean government introduced new data privacy legislation intended to strengthen the country's existing data privacy law, by, among other things, establishing an autonomous data protection authority and prohibiting transfers of personal data to countries "that do not provide an adequate level of protection" unless the transfer is approved by the regulator. The government's move to strengthen the country's privacy law comes after a massive data breach in May 2008 that resulted in the online publication of personal details of six million Chileans, including names, government identification numbers, telephone numbers, addresses, and e-mail addresses.

1. Notice

Notice must be provided regarding the purposes of collection and use, possible disclosures to third parties, and whether the collection is mandatory or voluntary. There are no exceptions to the notice requirement for public information (see discussion under Section 3, below).

2. Privacy Policy

There are no requirements to have a privacy policy.

3. Consent; Limitations on Collection, Use, and Disclosure

Written consent is required to collect, use, and disclose personal information that is not available to the public or publicly known. Such information can be used only for the purposes for which it was collected, as established in the notice. Consent may be revoked at any time. Personal information that is public or publicly known is not subject to any specific limitations or consent obligations. Personal information that is necessary to complete the contract between the individual (employee) and the company is deemed public information; however, it is unlikely that all of a business's human resources data would be considered public information.

Written or express consent is required to collect, use, and disclose any sensitive information.

Consent is required to disclose nonpublic personal information to third parties.

4. *Access and Correction*

Access must be provided free of charge. Personal information must be corrected when it is erroneous, inexact, misleading, or incomplete.

5. *Security; Data Retention*

There is a general obligation to keep personal information secret and confidential. The business must eliminate personal information that has no reason to be kept or is not updated. If the information cannot be eliminated, the business must block access to inaccurate or out-of-date information.

6. *Database Registration*

Database registration is not required.

7. *Cross-Border Limitations*

There are no restrictions or limitations on the transfer of personal information outside Chile.

8. *Onward Transfer Agreements*

Businesses must have a confidentiality agreement in place to transfer nonpublic information.

9. *Dispute Resolution*

Dispute resolution is handled through the civil courts.

EXHIBIT 1.3
EU Member State Implementation Legislation for Data Privacy and Security

Listed below are the EU Member State data privacy and security statutes and guidance papers issued by the national data protection authorities. We also include contact details for the local data protection authorities.

MEMBER STATE	DATA PROTECTION AUTHORITY	STATUTE
AUSTRIA	Austrian Data Protection Commission *(Österreichische Datenschutzkommission)* Ballhausplatz 1 A-Wien Austria Tel: +43 1 531 15 / 2525 Fax: +43 1 531 15 / 2690 Email: dsk@dsk.gv.at Web site: http://www.dsk.gv.at/	Federal Law on the Protection of Personal Data *(Datenschutzgesetz 2000—DSG 2000)*
BELGIUM	Data Protection Commission (Commission de la protection de la vie privée —French)) (Commissie voor de berscherming van de persoonlijke levenssfeer—Dutch)) Rue Haute 139 B-1000 Brussels Belgium Tel: +32 2 213 85 40 Fax: +32 2 213 85 65 Email: commission@privacycommission.be Web site: http://www.privacycommission.be/	Consolidated text of the Belgian Law of December 8, 1992, on Privacy Protection in Relation to the Processing of Personal Data as Modified by Law of December 11, 1998, Implementing Directive 95/46/EC *(Version coordonnée de la loi relative à la protection des données à caractère personel du 8 décembre 1992 (janvier 2006—French text) (Wet van 8 december 1992 tot bescherming van de persoonlijke levenssfeer ten opzichte van de verwerking van persoonsgegevens. Gecoördineerde versie (januari 2006—Dutch text)*

MEMBER STATE	DATA PROTECTION AUTHORITY	STATUTE
BELGIUM—*cont'd*		Common Agreement on Regulating Electronic Surveillance of Workers' Computers in the Workplace of June 29, 2002 *(Arrêté royal rendant obligatoire la Convention Collective de Travail no. 81 du 26 avril 2002, conclue au sein du Conseil National du travail, relative à la protection de la vie privée des travailleurs à l'égard du contrôle des données de communication électroniques en réseau, Moniteur belge, 29489-29501—French text) (Koninklijk besluit waarbij algemeen verbindend wordt verklaard de collectieve arbeidsovereenkomst nr. 81 van 26 april 2002, gesloten in de Nationale Arbeidsraad, tot berscherming van de persoonlijke levenssfeer van de werknemers ten opzichte van de controle op de elektronische on-linecommunicatiegegevens —Dutch text)* Collective Bargaining Agreement N° 81 of the National Labor Council of April 26, 2002, on the Protection of the Private Lives of Employees With Respect to Controls on Electronic Online Communications Data *(Convention collective de travail No. 81 du 26 avril relative à la protection de la vie privée des travailleurs à l'égard du contrôle des données de communication*

MEMBER STATE	DATA PROTECTION AUTHORITY	STATUTE
BELGIUM—*cont'd*		*électroniques réseau—French text) (Collectieve arbeidsovereenkomst nr. 81 van 26 april 2002 tot bescherming van de persoonlijke levenssfeer van de werknemers ten opzichte van de controle op de elektronische on-linecommunicatiegegevens—Dutch text)*
		Recommendation Relating to Internal Whistleblowing Systems of November 29, 2006 *(Recommandation relative à la compatibilité des systèmes d'alerte interne professionnelle avec la loi du 8 décembre 1992 relative à la protection de la vie privée à l'égard des traitements de données à caractère personnel—French text)*
		(Aanbeveling betreffende de verenigbaarheid van meldsystemen (klokkenluidersystemen) met de wet van 8 december 1992 tot bescherming van de persoonlijke levenssfeer ten opzichte van de verwerking van persoonsgegevens—Dutch text)
		Law on Certain Legal Aspects of the Information Society of March 11, 2003 *(Loi sur certains aspects juridiques des services de la société de l'information—French text) (Wet betreffende bepaalde juridische aspecten van de diensten van de informatiemaatschappij—Dutch text)*

MEMBER STATE	DATA PROTECTION AUTHORITY	STATUTE
BULGARIA	Bulgarian Commission for Personal Data Protection 76 Vassil Levski Blvd, Apt. 3 Sofia 1142 Bulgaria Tel/Fax: +359 2 988 5062 Email: office@aip-bg.org Web site: http://www.cpdp.bg/	Data Protection Act of December 21, 2001
CYPRUS	Office of the Commissioner for Personal Data Protection *(Γραφείου Επιτρόπου Προστασίας Δεδομένων Προσωπικού Χαρακτήρα)* 40, Themistokli Dervi str. Natassa Court, 3rd floor 1066 Nicosia Cyprus Tel: +2 28 184 56 Fax: +2 23 045 65 Email: commissioner@dataprotection.gov.cy Web site: http://www.dataprotection.gov.cy/	The Processing of Personal Data (Protection of the Individual) Law of 2001, as amended in 2003 *(Οδηγία που εκδίδεται από την Επίτροπο Προστασίας Δεδομένων Προσωπικού Χαρακτήρα βάσει του Άρθρου 23(ι) του περί Επεξεργασίας Δεδομένων Προσωπικού Χαρακτήρα (Προστασία του Ατόμου) Νόμου 138(I)/2001)* The Regulation of Electronic Communications and Postal Services Law of 2004 112(I)/2004 *(Ο Περί Ρυθμίσεως Ηλεκτρονικών Επικοινωνιών και Ταχυδρομικών Υπηρεσιών Νόμος του 2004, 112(I)/2004)* Processing of Data (Permits and Fees) Regulations of 2002 of November 8, 2002

MEMBER STATE	DATA PROTECTION AUTHORITY	STATUTE
CZECH REPUBLIC	Office for Personal Data Protection (Urad pro ochranu osobnich udaju) Pplk. Sochora 27 170 00 Praha 7 Czech Republic Tel: +420 234 665 111 Fax: +420 234 665 444 Email: info@uoou.cz Web site: http://www.uoou.cz/	Act No.101 of April 4, 2000 on the Protection of Personal Data and on Amendments to Some Related Acts *(Zákon č. 101/2000 Sb., o ochraně osobních údajů (úplné znění)* Position No. 1/2005—Activities of Insurance Intermediaries and the Notification Obligation Position No. 3/2004—Personal Data Processing in the Context of Clinical Testing of Drugs and Other Medical Substances Act 480/2004 on Certain Information Society Services and on the Amendment to Certain Other Acts (Certain Information Society Services Act)
DENMARK	Danish Data Protection Agency Datatilsynet Borgergade 28, 5 DK-1300 Copenhagen Denmark Tel: +45 33 19 3200 Fax: +45 33 19 3218 Email: dt@datatilsynet.dk Web site: http://www.datatilsynet.dk/	The Act on Processing of Personal Data (Act No. 429 of 31 May 2000) *(Lov nr. 429 af 31. maj 2000 som ændret ved lov nr. 280 af 25. april 2001)* The Marketing Practices Act (Act No. 1389 of December 21, 2005) (*Lov om markedsføring (LOV nr 1389 af 21/12/2005)*
ESTONIA	Estonian Data Protection Inspectorate (Andmekaitse Inspektsioon) Väike-Ameerika 19 10129 Tallinn Estonia Tel: +72 627 4135 Fax: +372 627 4137 Email: info@dp.gov.ee Web site: http://www.dp.gov.ee/	Personal Data Act of February 12, 2003 Information Society Services Act of April 14, 2004

MEMBER STATE	DATA PROTECTION AUTHORITY	STATUTE
FINLAND	Office of the Data Protection Ombudsman *(Tietosuojalautakunta)* Albertinkatu 25 A, 3rd floor P.O. Box 315 FIN-00181 Helsinki Finland Tel: +358 10 36 66700 Fax: +358 10 36 66735 Email: tietosuojaltk@om.fi Web site: http://www.tietosuoja.fi/	Personal Data Act 523/1999 *(Henkilötietolaki 22.4.1999/523)* Act on the Amendment of the Personal Data Act (986/2000) *(Annettu Helsingissä 24 päivänä marraskuuta 2000—muutetaan 22 päivänä huhtikuuta 1999 annetun henkilötietolain (523/1999) 23 §:n johdantokappale sekä 6 ja 7 kohta sekä—lisätään lakiin uusi 22 a § ja 23 §:ään uusi 8 kohta seuraavasti)* Act on the Protection of Privacy in Electronic Communications (516/2004) *(Sähköisen viestinnän tietosuojalaki (516/2004))* Act on the Protection of Privacy in Working Life (729/2004) *(Laki yksityisyyden suojasta työelämässä (759/2004))* Consumer Protection Act (38/1978) (includes amendments up to 29/2005) *(Kuluttajansuojalaki 20.1.1978/38)*
FRANCE	French Data Protection Authority *(Commission Nationale de l'Informatique et des Libertés)* 8 rue Vivienne CS 30223 F-75083 Paris Cedex 02 France Tel: +33 1 53 73 22 22 Fax: +33 1 53 73 22 00 Web site: http://www.cnil.fr/	Act No. 78-17 of January 6, 1978 on Data Processing, Data Files and Individual Liberties (Amended by the Act of August 6, 2004 Relating to the Protection of Individuals With Regard to the Processing of Personal Data) *(Loi n° 78-17 du 6 Janvier 1978 relative à l'informatique, aux fichiers et aux libertés)*

MEMBER STATE	DATA PROTECTION AUTHORITY	STATUTE
FRANCE—*cont'd*		Act n° 2004-575 21 June 2004 on Confidence for the Digital Economy *(Loi n° 2004-575 du 21 juin 2004 pour la confiance dans l'économie numérique)*
GERMANY	The Federal Commissioner for Data Protection and Freedom of Information (Der Bundesbeauftragte für den Datenschutz und die Informationsfreiheit) Husarenstraße 30 D-53117 Bonn Germany Tel: +49 1888 7799 0 Fax: +49 1888 7799 550 Email: poststelle@bfdi.bund.de Web site: http://www.bfdi.bund.de/	Federal Data Protection Act *(Bundesdatenschutzgesetz)* Works Council Act *(Betriebsverfassungsgesetz)* Sect. 7 of the Act on Unfair Competition Act of July 3, 2004 *(Gesetz gegen den unlauteren Wettbewerb)* Sect. 88 et seq. Telecommunications Act of June 22, 2004 *(Telekommunikationsgesetz)* Teleservices Data Protection Act of July 22, 1997 *(Teledienstedatenschutzgesetz)*
GREECE	Hellenic Data Protection Authority Kifisias Av. 1-3, PC 11523 Ampelokipi Athens Greece Tel: +30 1 33 52 600 10 Fax: +30 1 33 52 617 Email: kkosm@dpa.gr Web site: http://www.dpa.gr/	Law 2472/1997 on the Protection of Individuals With Regard to the Processing of Personal Data (as amended) Telecoms Data Protection Act (Law No.2774/1999) Consumer Protection Act (Law no.2251/1994) (See Article 9 para. 10 and Article 14 para. 6) Presidential Decree 131/2003 of May 16, 2003 (Transposes Directive 2000/31 of the European Parliament and the Council on Certain Legal Aspects of Information Society Services, in particular electronic commerce, in the Internal Market (Directive on electronic commerce))

MEMBER STATE	DATA PROTECTION AUTHORITY	STATUTE
HUNGARY	Office of the Parliamentary Commissioner for Data Protection and Freedom of Information (Adatvédelmi Biztos) Nádor u. 22 1051 Budapest Hungary Tel: +36 1 475 71 86 Fax: +36 1 269 35 41 Email: adatved@obh.hu Web site: http://abiweb.obh.hu/dpc/index.htm	ACT LXIII OF 1992 ON THE PROTECTION OF PERSONAL DATA AND PUBLIC ACCESS TO DATA OF PUBLIC INTEREST (*1992. ÉVI LXIII. TÖRVÉNY A SZEMÉLYES ADATOK VÉDELMÉRŐL ÉS A KÖZÉRDEKŰ ADATOK NYILVÁNOSSÁGÁRÓL)* Electronic Communications Act (Act C of 2003) *(Évi C 2003 törvény az elektronikus hírközlésröl)* Act on Insurance Institutes and Insurance Activities (Act XCVI of 1995) *(1995. évi XCVI. Törvény a biztosítóintézetekről és a biztosítási tevékenységről)* Act CXIX of 1995 on the Use of Name and Address Information Serving the Purposes of Research and Direct Marketing *(Az adatvédelmi biztos tájékoztatója a kutatási és közvetlen üzletszerzési (direkt marketing) célú adatok kezeléséről)* Act CVIII of 2001 on Certain Aspects of Electronic Communications Services and Information Society Services (as amended by Act No. XCVII of 2003) *(2001 vi CVIII. Törvény az elektronikus kereskedelmi szolgáltatások, valamint az információs társadalommal összefüggő szolgáltatások egyes kérdéseiről)*

MEMBER STATE	DATA PROTECTION AUTHORITY	STATUTE
IRELAND	Office of the Data Protection Commissioner Canal House Station Road Portarlington Co. Laois Ireland Tel: +353 57 868 4800 Fax: +353 57 868 4757 Email: info@ dataprotection.ie Web site: http://www. dataprotection.ie	Data Protection Act 1998 and Data Protection (Amendment) Act 2003 European Communities (Electronic Communications Networks and Services) (Data Protection and Privacy) Regulations 2003—Statutory instrument 535/2003
ITALY	Italian Data Protection Authority (Garante per la protezione dei dati personali) Piazza di Monte Citorio, 121 I-00186 Rome Italy Tel: +39 06 696 771 Fax: +39 06 696 77 15 Email: garante@ garanteprivacy.it Web site: http://www. garanteprivacy.it	Legislative Decree No. 196 of June 30, 2003 *(Codice in material di protezione dei dati personali)* Law 300/1970 (the "Workers' Statute") *(Legge 20 maggio 1970 n. 300 Statuto dei Lavoratori)* Legislative Decree No. 259 of August 1, 2003 (the "Electronic Communications Code") and Related Annexes *(Decreto legislativo recante il "Codice delle comunicazioni elettroniche)* Legislative Decree No. 171 of May 13, 1998 (as modified by Legislative Decree 467/2001 Concerning the Protection of Private Life in the Telecommunication and Journalistic Sectors) *(Decreto legislativo n. 171 del 05/13/1998—Disposizioni in materia di tutela della vita privata nel settore delle telecomunicazioni, in attuazione della direttiva*

MEMBER STATE	DATA PROTECTION AUTHORITY	STATUTE
ITALY— *cont'd*		*97/66/CE del Parlamento europeo e del Consiglio, ed in tema di attività giornalistica (modificato dal d.lg. 467/2001))*
LATVIA	Data State Inspection (Datu Valsts Inspecija) Kr. Barona 5-4 Riga LV-1050 Latvia Tel: +371 72 23 131 Fax: +371 72 23 556 Email: info@dvi.gov.lv Web site: http://www.dvi.gov.lv	Personal Data Protection Law Amended by Law of October 24, 2002 *(Fizisko personu datu aizsardzības likums)* Electronic Communications Law (October 28, 2004) Law on Information Society Services (November 4, 2004) (*see* Section 9)
LITHUANIA	State Data Protection Inspectorate (*Valstybine duomenu Apsaugos Inspekcija)* Gedimino ave. 27/2 LT-01104 Vilnius Lithuania Tel: +370 5 279 1445 Fax: +370 5 261 9494 Email: ada@ada.lt Web site: http://www.ada.lt/	Law on Legal Protection of Personal Data of January 21, 2003, No. IX-1296, with amendments of April 13, 2004 Law on Electronic Communications (April 15, 2004) (Article 68)
LUXEMBOURG	National Data Protection Authority (Commission nationale pour la protection des données) 68 rue de Luxembourg L-4221 Esch-sur-Alzette Luxembourg Tel: +352 26 106 020 Fax: +352 26 106 029 Email: info@cnpd.lu Web site: http://www.cnpd.lu/fr/	Law of August 2, 2002, on the Protection of Persons With Regard to the Processing of Personal Data *(Loi du 2 août 2002 relative à la protection des personnes à l'égard du traitement des données à caractère personnel)* Act of November 27, 2004, on the Protection of Personal Information (*Règlement grand-ducal du 27 novembre 2004 (chargés de la protection des données))*

MEMBER STATE	DATA PROTECTION AUTHORITY	STATUTE
LUXEMBOURG—*cont'd*		Law of May 30, 2005, on Networks and Services of Electronic Communications (*Loi du 30 mai 2005 sur les réseaux et les services de communications électroniques)*
MALTA	Office of the Data Protection Commissioner 2 Airways House, High Street Sliema SLM 16 Malta Tel: +356 2328 7100 Fax: +356 23287198 Email: commissioner.dataprotection@gov.mt Web site: http://www.dataprotection.gov.mt/	Data Protection Act 2001 (Act XXVI of 2001 as amended by Act XXXI of 2002) (*L-Att XXVI ta' l-2001, kif emendat bl-Att XXXI ta' l-2002*) Notification and Fees (Data Protection Act) Regulations Legal Notice 154/2003 *(Regolamenti ta' 154 L-2003 dwar in-Notifika u t-Tariff fl- Att dwar il-Protezzjoni u l-Privatezza tad-Data)* as amended by Legal Notice 162/2004 *(Regolamenti ta' 162 L-2004 li jemendaw ir-Regolamenti dwar in-Notifika u t-Tariff fl-Att dwar il-Protezzjoni u L-Privatezza tad-Data)* Data Protection (Processing of Personal Data in the Police Sector) Regulations Legal Notice 142/2004 *(Regolamenti ta' 142 L-2004 dwar il-Protezzjoni u L-privatezza tad-Data (Proċessar ta' data fis-settur tal-Pulizija))* Telecommunications (Personal Data Protection of Privacy) Regulations of 2003 *(Regolamenti ta' 19 L-2003 dwar Data Personali u Protezzjoni tal-Privatezza)*

MEMBER STATE	DATA PROTECTION AUTHORITY	STATUTE
MALTA— *cont'd*		Processing of Personal Data (Telecommunications Sector) Regulations Legal Notice 16/2003 *(Regolamenti 16 L-2003 dwar l-Ipproċessar ta' Data Personali fis-settur tat-Telekomunikazzjonijiet)* as amended by Legal Notice 153/2003) *(Regolamenti ta' 153 L-2003 li jemendaw ir-Regolamenti dwar l-Ipproċessar ta' Data Personali fis-settur tat-Telekomunikazzjonijiet)* Legal Notice 522/2004 *(Regolamenti ta' 522 L-2004 li jemendaw ir-Regolamenti dwar l-Ipprocessar ta' Data Personali fis-settur tat-Telekomunikazzjonijiet),* and Legal Notice 109/2005 *(Regolamenti ta' 109 L-2005 li jemendaw ir-Regolamenti dwar l-Ipproċessar ta' Data Personali fis-settur tat-Komunikazzjonijiet Elettroniċi)*
NETHERLANDS	Dutch Data Protection Authority (College bescherming persoonsgegevens (CBP)) Postbus 93374 2509 AJ Den Haag The Netherlands Tel: +31 70 888 85 00 Fax: +31 70 888 85 01 Email: info@cbpweb.nl Web site: http://www.cbpweb.nl/	Personal Data Protection Act of July 6, 2000 *(Wet van 6 juli 2000, houdende regels inzake de bescherming van persoonsgegevens (Wet bescherming persoonsgegevens))* Telecommunications Act of October 19, 1998 (as amended May 19, 2004) Article 11.7 *(Wet van 19 oktober 1998 houdende regels inzake de telecommunicatie)*

MEMBER STATE	DATA PROTECTION AUTHORITY	STATUTE
POLAND	The Bureau of the Inspector General for the Protection of Personal Data (Biuro Generalnego Inspektora Ochrony Danych Osobowych) ul. Stawki 2 PO-0193 Warsaw Poland Tel: +48 22 860 70 81 Fax: +48 22 860 70 90 Email: sekretariat@giodo.gov.pl Web site: http://www.giodo.gov.pl/	The Act of August 29, 1997, on the Protection of Personal Data with amendments *(Zmiany ustawy o ochronie danych osobowych z dnia 29 serpnia 1997 r.)* Act of July 16, 2004, Telecommunications Law (Official Journal No 171, Item 1800 of August 3, 2004) (See article 169) *(Ustawa z dnia 16 lipca 2004 r. Prawo telekomunikacyjne)* Act of July 18, 2002, on Providing Services by Electronic Means (Article 10) *(Ustawa z dnia 18 lipca 2002 r. o świadczeniu usług drogą elektroniczną)* Law of April 16, 1993, on Combating Unfair Competition (Official Journal No 47, Item 211 as amended) *(Ustawa z dnia 16 kwietnia 1993 r. o zwalczaniu nieuczciwej konkurencji)*
PORTUGAL	National Data Protection Commission (Comissão Nacional de Protecção de Dados) Rua de São Bento, 148, 3° 1200-821 Lisboa Portugal Tel: +351 21 392 84 00 Fax: +351 21 397 68 32 Email: geral@cnpd.pt Web site: http://www.cnpd.pt/	Data Protection Act No.67 of 26 October 1998 *(Lei n.º 67/98 de 26 de Outubro Lei da protecção de dados pessoais)* Law 41/2004 of August 18, 2004, Implementing EC Directive 2002/58 on Privacy and Electronic Communication *(Lei nº 69/98 de 28 de Outubro regula o tratemento dos dados pessoias e a protecção da privacidade no sector das telecommuncações)*

MEMBER STATE	DATA PROTECTION AUTHORITY	STATUTE
PORTUGAL— *cont'd*		Decree-Law 7/2004 of January 7, 2004, on Privacy and Electronic Communications With Regard to the Use of Unsolicited Communications for Direct Marketing Purposes *(Decreto-Lei n.º 7/2004, de 7 de Janeiro Transpõe para a ordem jurídica nacional a Directiva 2000/31/CE, do Parlamento Europeu e do Conselho, de 8 de Junho de 2000, relativa a certos aspectos legais dos serviços da sociedade da informação, em especial do comércio electrónico, no mercado interno)*
ROMANIA	National Supervisory Authority for Personal Data Processing *(Directia Pentru Protectia Persoanelor cu Privire la Prelucrarea Datelor cu Caracter)* Eugen Carada Street, no. 3 Sector 3 Bucuresti Romania Tel: +40 21 312 49 34 Fax: +40 21312 71 02 Email: basarabescu@avp.ro Web site: http://www.avp.ro/	Law no. 677/2001 for the Protection of Persons Concerning the Processing of Personal Data and Free Circulation of Such Data *(Legea nr. 677/2001 din 21 noiembre 2001 pentru protectia persoanelor cu privire la prelucrare datelor cu character personal)* Law n°102/2005 Regarding the Setting Up, Organization and Functioning of the National Supervisory Authority of Personal Data *(Lege nr. 102 din 3 mai 2005 privind înfiinţarea, organizarea şi funcţtionarea Autorităţii Nationale de Supraveghere a Prelucrării Datelor du Caracter Personal)*

MEMBER STATE	DATA PROTECTION AUTHORITY	STATUTE
ROMANIA— *cont'd*		Law n° 506/2004 on the Processing of Personal Data and the Protection of Privacy in the Electronics Communications Sector *(Lege nr. 506 din 17 noiembre 2004 privind prelucrarea datelor cu character personal şi protecţia vieţii private în sectorul communicaţiilor electronice*)
SLOVAKIA	Office for Personal Data Protection *(Úrad na ochranu osobných údajov)* Odborárske námestie č. 3 817 60 Bratislava 15 Slovak Republic Tel: +421 2 502 39 418 Fax: +421 2 502 39 441 Email: statny.dozor@pdp.gov.sk Web site: http://www.dataprotection.gov.sk/	Act No. 428/2002 Coll. on Protection of Personal Data, as amended by Act No. 602/2003 Coll., Act No. 576/2004 Coll., and Act No. 90/2005 Coll. *(Zákon č. 428/2002 Z.z. o ochrane osobnych údajov v znení zákona č. 602/2003 Z.z. zákona č. 576/2004 Z.z. a zákona č. 90/2002 Z.z.)* Act No. 610/2003 of 3 December 2003, on Electronic Communications (Section 65) *(Všeobecne záväzné právne predpisy k zákonu č. 610/2003 Z.z. o elektronických komunikáciách)*
SLOVENIA	Information Commissioner (*Informacijski Pooblaščsenec)* Vošnjakova 1 SI-1000 Ljubljana Slovenia Tel: +386 1 230 97 30 Fax: +386 1 230 97 78 Email: gp.ip@ip-rs.si Web site: http://www.ip-rs.si	Personal Data Protection Act as amended in July 2004 (*Zakon o varstvu osebnih podatkov (ZVOP))*

MEMBER STATE	DATA PROTECTION AUTHORITY	STATUTE
SPAIN	Data Protection Agency (Agencia de Protección de Datos) C/Jorge Juan, 6 E-28001 Madrid Spain Tel: +34 901 100 099 Fax: +34 91445 5699 Email: internacional@agpd.es Web site: https://www.agpd.es/index.php	Organic Law 15/1999 of December 13, 1999, on the Protection of Personal Data *(Ley Orgánica 15/1999, de 13 de diciembre, de Protección de Datos de Carácter Personal)* Royal Decree 1736/1998 of July 31, 1998, Implementing the General Telecommunication Act *(Real Decreto 1736/1998, de 31 de julio, por el que se aprueba el Reglamento por el que se desarrolla el Título III de la Ley General de Telecomunicaciones)* Law 34/2002 on Information Society Services and Electronic Commerce *(Ley 34/2002, de 11 de julio, de servicios de la sociedad de la información y de comercio electrónico)* as amended by Law 32/2003 on General Telecommunications *(Ley 32/2003, de 3 de noviembre, General de Telecomunicaciones)*
SWEDEN	Data Inspection Board (Datainspektionen) Fleminggatan 14, 9th floor Box 8114 SE-104 20 Stockholm Sweden Tel: +46 8 657 6100 Fax +46 8 652 8652 Email: datainspektionen@datainspektionen.se Web site: http://www.datainspektionen.se/	Personal Data Act 204/1998 *(Personuppgiftslag (1998:204))* The Personal Data Ordinance (1998:1191) of 3 September 1998 *(Personuppgiftsförordning (1998:1191))* The Electronic Communications Act (2003:389) *(Lag (2003:389) om elektronisk kommunikation)* The Marketing Act (1995:450) (Section 13b) *(Marknadsföringslag (1995:450))*

MEMBER STATE	DATA PROTECTION AUTHORITY	STATUTE
UNITED KINGDOM	Information Commissioner's Office Wycliffe House, Water Lane Wilmslow Cheshire SK9 5AF United Kingdom Tel: +44 1625 545 700 Fax: +44 1625 545 748 Email: mail@ico.gsi.gov.uk Web site: http://www.ico.gov.uk/	Data Protection Act 1998 Data Protection (Processing of Sensitive Personal Data) Order 2000 of February 17, 2000 The Privacy and Electronic Communications (EC Directive) Regulations 2003 as amended by the Privacy and Electronic Communications (EC Directive) (Amendment) Regulations 2004

CHAPTER 2

BACKGROUND CHECKS AND INVESTIGATIONS

I. Overview ... 121

II. Americas ... 122

A. United States ... 122

1. Application of the FCRA to Background Check Reports ... 123

a. What Is a Consumer Reporting Agency? ... 123

b. What Is a Consumer Report? ... 124

2. Notice and Consent Requirements Under the FCRA ... 125

a. Notice and Consent Requirements to Obtain Reports ... 125

Exhibit 2.1 U.S.: Sample Authorization Under the Fair Credit Reporting Act ... 126

i. Additional Notice Requirements for Investigative Reports ... 127

ii. Additional State Notice Requirements to Obtain Reports ... 128

b. Notice Requirements for Adverse Action Based on Report ... 129

i. Pre-Adverse Action Notice Requirements ... 129

Exhibit 2.2 U.S.: Sample Pre-Adverse Action Notice Under the Fair Credit Reporting Act ... 130

ii. Adverse Action Notice Requirements ... 133

Exhibit 2.3 U.S.: Sample Adverse Action Notice Under the Fair Credit Reporting Act ... 134

c. Certain Misconduct Investigations Exempt From the FCRA ... 135

3. Limitations on Content of Background Check Reports ... 136
4. Access and Correction Rights ... 137
Exhibit 2.4 U.S.: Sample Background Check Process ... 138
5. Potential Liability for Violations of the FCRA and Similar State Laws ... 140
6. State Law Rules Relating to Background Checks by Vendors ... 140
a. California ... 141
b. New York ... 142
7. Background Checks and Investigations Conducted In-House by Employers ... 143
8. Limitations on Direct Inquiries by Employers ... 144
a. Arrests and Sealed or Expunged Convictions ... 144
b. Convictions ... 145
i. Access Rights ... 146
ii. Exceptions ... 147
iii. Employer Liability ... 148
c. Fingerprinting ... 148
d. Bankruptcy Act ... 149
9. Hiring and Payment of OFAC-Designated Nationals in the Post-9/11 Environment ... 149
10. Disposal of Background Information ... 151
a. Disposal Rules Under Federal Law ... 151
b. Disposal Rules Under State Law ... 153
B. Brazil ... 154
1. Background Checks ... 154
2. Responding to Employment Verification Requests ... 155
C. Canada ... 155
1. Background Checks ... 155
2. Responding to Employment Verification Requests ... 156
D. Mexico ... 156
1. Background Checks ... 156
2. Responding to Employment Verification Requests ... 157
III. Europe ... 157
Exhibit 2.5 EU: Background Checks—United Kingdom, Germany, and France ... 158

A. Belgium 158
1. Background Checks 158
2. Responding to Employment Verification Requests 159
B. France 159
1. Applicable Statutes 159
2. General Requirements 160
3. Sensitive Data 161
4. Notice Requirements 161
5. Access and Correction 162
6. Use Restrictions 162
7. Guidance on Specific Background Checks 163
a. Credit 163
b. Criminal Records 163
c. Work History 163
d. References 164
e. General Reputation/Character 164
C. Germany 164
1. Applicable Statutes 164
2. General Requirements 165
3. Sensitive Data 167
4. Notice Requirements 168
5. Access and Correction Rights 168
6. Use Restrictions 168
7. Guidance on Specific Background Checks 169
a. Credit 169
b. Criminal Records 170
c. Work History 171
d. References 172
e. General Reputation/Character 172
D. Italy 172
1. Background Checks 172
2. Responding to Employment Verification Requests 173
E. United Kingdom 173
1. Applicable Statutes 173
2. General Requirements 174
3. Sensitive Data 178
4. Notice Requirements 179
5. Access and Correction 179
6. Use Restrictions 179
7. Guidance on Specific Background Checks 180

a. Credit ... 180
b. Criminal Records ... 180
Exhibit 2.6 "Spent Conviction" Time Periods ... 181
c. Work History ... 182
d. References ... 182
e. General Reputation/Character ... 183
IV. Asia ... 184
A. China ... 184
1. Background Checks Generally ... 184
2. Guidance on Specific Background Checks in China ... 185
a. Credit ... 185
b. Criminal Records ... 185
c. Work History ... 185
B. Hong Kong ... 185
1. Applicable Laws ... 185
2. General Requirements—Employment Candidates ... 186
3. General Requirements—Existing Employees ... 187
4. Access ... 187
5. Guidance on Specific Background Checks ... 187
a. Credit ... 187
b. Criminal Records ... 188
c. Work History ... 188
d. References ... 188
C. Japan ... 189
1. Background Checks During the Recruitment Period ... 189
a. General Restrictions Based on the Personal Information Protection Law ... 190
b. Special Restrictions Based on the Employment Security Law ... 191
c. Seeking References From the Former Workplace of the Job Applicant ... 191
d. Acquisition of Information After Employment ... 192
e. Prohibition or Limitation on the Collection of Sensitive Data ... 193
D. Korea ... 194
1. Background Checks ... 194
2. Responding to Employment Verification Requests ... 195

I. OVERVIEW

Employers use background checks to assess and verify the qualifications and qualities of applicants and employees. In the U.S. and in those countries that are destinations for outsourcing services, the use of background checks by employers has increased in recent years as employers are more concerned about liability resulting from hiring or retaining individuals in instances in which the employer should have known that the employee had a history of inappropriate behavior or activity. Increasingly, employers retain specialized vendors to conduct background checks in order to supplement the information available from a candidate's resume, references, and interviews. However, employers must take care to follow all applicable laws when obtaining and using these reports.

In many countries, an employer must notify an applicant or employee prior to conducting a background check. The employer may need to obtain the individual's consent, as well. For instance, U.S. law imposes notice and consent requirements when obtaining a background check report from a consumer reporting agency, if that report will be used for employment purposes. In comparison, some of the European Union (EU) Member States, Japan, Hong Kong, and other countries with data protection laws typically require notice and consent for any type of background check, regardless of the source of the data. If an employer fails to comply with applicable notice or consent requirements, the employer may be precluded from taking action based on the information received from the background check report.

In many countries, employers are restricted in the types of information they can seek about applicants or employees, even with the individual's consent. Employment and privacy laws directly prohibit employers from requesting certain types of information and indirectly penalize employers for collecting other legally sensitive information, through heightened exposure to discrimination claims.

This chapter begins with a detailed discussion of U.S. legal requirements relating to the use of background check reports provided by vendors, as well as the restrictions that apply directly to employers conducting their own in-house background checks.

From there, the chapter proceeds to discuss the broader approach to background checks in countries such as the United Kingdom (UK), France, Germany, Japan, Hong Kong, and China. All employers should be familiar with these rules, regardless of whether they currently create their own in-house reports or obtain background check reports from third-party vendors.

II. AMERICAS

A. United States

In the United States, the Fair Credit Reporting Act (FCRA) is the primary federal law governing the use of a background check report provided by a vendor, which acts as a "consumer reporting agency" (agency).[1] In addition, many states have statutes that are equivalent to or augment the FCRA. Among other objectives, the FCRA is a consumer protection law that seeks to ensure that consumer reporting agencies provide fair and accurate information about the "creditworthiness, credit standing, credit capacity, character, and general reputation of consumers,"[2] as well as to protect a "consumer's right to privacy."[3] The information provided by consumer reporting agencies not only affects an individual's ability to obtain employment, but also may prevent that individual from securing credit, insurance, or other benefits. The FCRA mainly regulates consumer credit reporting agencies,[4] but also imposes obligations on employers and other parties that seek to obtain consumer reports from such agencies.

---

[1]15 U.S.C. §1681.

[2]In enacting the FCRA, Congress observed that "[a]n elaborate mechanism has been developed for investigating and evaluating the creditworthiness, credit standing, credit capacity, character, and general reputation of consumers," and that "[c]onsumer reporting agencies have assumed a vital role in assembling and evaluating consumer credit and other information on consumers." In light of those circumstances, Congress asserted that "[t]here is a need to insure that consumer reporting agencies exercise their grave responsibilities with fairness, impartiality and respect for the consumer's right to privacy." 15 U.S.C. §1681(a)2–4.

[3]15 U.S.C. §1681(a)(4).

[4]15 U.S.C. §1681(b) ("It is the purpose of this subchapter to require that consumer reporting agencies adopt reasonable procedures for meeting the needs of commerce for consumer credit, personnel, insurance, and other information in a manner which is fair and equitable to the consumer, with regard to the confidentiality, accuracy, relevancy, and proper utilization of such information.").

As a general principle, the FCRA applies to any background check report prepared by an agency for employment-related purposes.[5] The FCRA establishes baseline requirements for all U.S. employers, but state laws may impose more stringent notice requirements.[6] This section explains the standard federal requirements, and addresses key additional requirements under U.S. state law. The common elements of these federal and state laws are notice, consent, access, and correction rights, as well as data security.

1. *Application of the FCRA to Background Check Reports*

a. *What Is a Consumer Reporting Agency?*

The FCRA covers consumer reports, such as background check reports, about individuals to third parties, such as employers. Although the term "consumer reporting agency" leads many people to think of a credit bureau, the statutory definition is broader and encompasses "any person or entity" that, in general, regularly assembles and evaluates information about consumers for the purpose of furnishing "consumer reports" to third parties—whether for monetary fees, dues, or on a cooperative nonprofit basis—as long as the person or entity uses any "means or facility of interstate commerce" to prepare or distribute the consumer reports.[7] Merely using the telephone or U.S. mail may be considered a "means or facility of interstate commerce" for this purpose.[8] Given the

---

[5] 15 U.S.C. §1681a(d)(1)(B).

[6] Subject to certain exceptions, the FCRA does not preempt state laws "with respect to the collection, distribution, or use of any information on consumers." 15 U.S.C. §1681t(a). *See also* Credit Data of Ariz., Inc. v. State of Ariz., 602 F.2d 195, 198 (1979) (concluding that the FCRA allows a state "to go further than the [FCRA] does to protect consumers so long as [state law] is not inconsistent with the [FCRA]"). However, the FCRA does prevent states from imposing differing obligations with respect to taking adverse action based on the consumer reports, and other specified matters. 15 U.S.C. §1681t(b)(1)(C). Arizona, California, Maine, Massachusetts, Minnesota, Montana, New Hampshire, New Jersey, New Mexico, New York, and Oklahoma are among the states that have adopted laws regulating background check reports. ARIZ. REV. STAT. §44-1691; CAL. CIV. CODE §1785.20.5(a); 10 ME. REV. STAT. §1314; MASS. GEN. LAWS ch. 93, §53(a)(1); MINN. STAT. §13C.02; MONT. CODE ANN. §31-3-113; N.H. REV. STAT. §359-B; N.J. STAT. §56:11-33(a)(1); N.M. STAT. ANN. §56-3-1; N.Y. GEN. BUS. LAW §380-c(b)(2); and 24 OKLA. STAT. §148.

[7] 15 U.S.C. §1681a(f).

[8] *See* Colletti v. Credit Bureau Servs., Inc., 644 F.2d 1148 (5th Cir. 1981) ("It is undisputed that CBS [defendant] is a 'consumer reporting agency' within the purposes of [FCRA]; CBS uses the mail and telephone in interstate commerce for the

breadth of this definition, employers should assume that any vendor retained to provide a background check report is an agency that is regulated under the FCRA.[9] As a result, an employer that obtains a report from a vendor—that is, an agency—also is subject to certain requirements under the FCRA and must, for example, take precautions in using and disposing of the report.

b. What Is a Consumer Report?

The FCRA also broadly defines a "consumer report." In fact, the definition is so broad that at least one federal court concluded that a consumer report is "virtually any information communicated by a 'consumer reporting agency' for ... employment purposes."[10] For ease of reference, this chapter will refer to the various types of consumer reports covered by the FCRA and analogous state laws by the more familiar term of "background check reports."

Officially, a "consumer report" under the FCRA is "any written, oral, or other communication of any information by a consumer reporting agency bearing on a consumer's creditworthiness, credit standing, character, general reputation, personal characteristics, or mode of living which is used or expected to be used or collected in whole or in part for the purpose of serving as a factor in establishing, the consumer's eligibility for...employment purposes."[11] Note that, in this context, "employment purposes" is defined to include "evaluating a consumer for employment, promotion, reassignment, or retention as an employee,"[12] and, therefore, extends

---

purpose of preparing or furnishing consumer reports to third parties for monetary consideration.").

[9]However, a person or entity that rarely engages in consumer reporting may be exempt from FCRA. For example, in *Johnson v. Federal Express Corp.*, 147 F. Supp. 2d 1268 (M.D. Ala. 2001), the court concluded that a handwriting expert retained to analyze whether an employee wrote a threatening letter was not a "consumer reporting agency," because he rarely evaluated consumer information for reporting purposes. *Id.* at 1276.

[10]Hoke v. Retail Credit Corp., 521 F.2d 1079, 1081 (4th Cir. 1975) (concluding that "employment purposes" are not "restricted to the situation in which information is sought by an actual or prospective employer."). In *Hoke,* the background report was obtained by the Texas Board of Medical Examiners, in assessing a doctor's application for a state medical license. *Id.* The court concluded that this constituted an "employment purpose" under FCRA because it related to his ability to obtain a medical license, which would determine his ability to work as a doctor in Texas. *Id.* at 1082.

[11]15 U.S.C. §1681a(d)(1).

[12]15 U.S.C. §1681a(h).

beyond initial hiring decisions. A "consumer" under the FCRA simply means an individual, so both applicants for employment and current employees are consumers covered by the FCRA.[13] For simplicity, this chapter will use the term "applicant" to encompass both employees and applicants.

Within this general category of consumer reports, the FCRA and state law recognize a narrower category of "investigative consumer reports." An "investigative consumer report" is a consumer report that includes information obtained through personal interviews with neighbors, friends, or associates of the applicant.[14]

2. *Notice and Consent Requirements Under the FCRA*

a. *Notice and Consent Requirements to Obtain Reports*

Under the FCRA, an employer must give applicants "clear and conspicuous" written notice that the company may procure a background check report for employment purposes and obtain the applicant's written consent before requesting such a report from the agency.[15] This notice must be a stand-alone document, rather than part of another document.[16] A notice that is included in the same document used as an employment application, for example, would not satisfy the notice requirement under the FCRA.[17]

The FCRA allows an agency to provide a background check report for employment purposes only if the employer has certified that the employer: (1) has provided the required notice to the applicant; (2) has obtained the applicant's authorization to procure the report; (3) will comply with the FCRA's requirements prior to taking adverse action based in whole or in part on the report; and (4) will not use the information from the report in violation of any equal employment opportunity law or regulation.[18] (A sample authorization appears in Exhibit 2.1.)

---

[13] 15 U.S.C. §1681a(c).

[14] More specifically, an investigative consumer report is defined as "a consumer report, or portion of a consumer report, provided by a consumer reporting agency, in which information on a consumer's character, general reputation, personal characteristics, or mode of living is obtained through personal interviews with the consumer's neighbors, friends, or associates, or with others who may have knowledge concerning any such items of information." 15 U.S.C. §1681a(e).

[15] 15 U.S.C. §1681b(b)(2)(A)(i)–(ii).

[16] *Id. See also* Medine-Coffey, Fed. Trade Comm'n Letter, Feb. 11, 1998.

[17] 15 U.S.C. §1681b(b)(2)(A)(i)–(ii).

[18] 15 U.S.C. §1681b(b)(1)(A)–(B).

EXHIBIT 2.1
U.S.: Sample Authorization Under the Fair Credit Reporting Act

This sample authorization form addresses the requirements of the U.S. federal Fair Credit Reporting Act. Additional provisions may be required under state law, as discussed in this chapter. Please consult with your legal counsel prior to using this or any form, as legal requirements may change from time to time.

As a condition of employment, transfer, or promotion by **[Name of Company]** (the "Company"), I acknowledge and agree that the Company or its authorized representatives may obtain consumer [and investigative][a] reports about me before and during employment. These reports may include written, oral, or other information about my character, general reputation, personal characteristics, mode of living, and creditworthiness. [In addition, investigative consumer reports may include such information obtained through personal interviews of past or present employers, business or personal acquaintances, or others who may have knowledge concerning this information.]

I understand that the Company will use the information contained in these reports as a factor in determining my eligibility for employment and, if I become an employee, for other employment purposes. If I become employed by the Company, this document will provide ongoing authorization for the Company to procure consumer [and investigative] reports about me at any time during my employment with the Company.

In connection with "investigative consumer reports" obtained by the Company, I understand that the Company will, upon my written request made within a reasonable period of time after my receipt of this document, make a complete and accurate disclosure to me of the nature and scope of the investigation requested. I also acknowledge that I have received the accompanying document entitled "A Summary of Your Rights Under the Fair Credit Reporting Act."

Authorization

I hereby voluntarily authorize the Company to obtain, and any consumer-reporting agency or investigative consumer-reporting agency to provide to the Company, consumer [and investigative] reports about me before and during employment. I understand that the Company will use these reports as a factor in determining my eligibility for employment and, if I become an employee, for other employment purposes.
I have read and fully understand this Authorization.

Applicant's/Employee's Signature Date

Print Name

---

[a]As discussed in Section 2.II.A.2.a.i, the additional disclosures for investigative consumer reports may be provided in a separate document after this authorization has been submitted. 15 U.S.C. §1681d(a)(1)(A). Alternatively, the employer may simply include these additional disclosures in the authorization form, as illustrated in the bracketed language of this sample form.

i. Additional Notice Requirements for Investigative Reports

If the background check report will contain information based on personal interviews, the written notice also must clearly inform an applicant that an investigative consumer report may be requested and that this report may include information about the applicant's "character, general reputation, personal characteristics, and mode of living."[19] Additionally, this notice must include: (1) a statement informing the applicant that he is entitled to request additional disclosure of the nature and scope of the investigation requested; and (2) a written summary of the employee's or applicant's rights under the FCRA.[20] The notice must be in writing and mailed or delivered to the applicant no later than three business days after the employer requests the investigative consumer report.[21] The employer also must certify to the agency that it has complied with these notice requirements.[22] The agency may not prepare or provide the investigative consumer report until it has received this certification from the employer.[23]

If the applicant submits a written request for these additional disclosures, the employer must provide "a complete and accurate disclosure of the nature and scope of the investigation requested."[24] This disclosure must be provided in writing and mailed or otherwise delivered within five days after the later of the following: (1) the date the employer receives the consumer's request; or (2) the date that the report was first requested.[25]

---

[19] 15 U.S.C. §1681d(a)(1).

[20] *Id.* The form and content of this summary are provided by the Federal Trade Commission (FTC) and can be obtained by contacting the FTC.

[21] For convenience, the employer may choose to provide these additional disclosures *prior to* requesting the investigative consumer report, along with the standard disclosures required for all consumer reports. *See* Haynes-Hawkley, Fed. Trade Comm'n Letter, Dec. 18, 1997.

[22] 15 U.S.C. §1681d(a)(2).

[23] 15 U.S.C. §1681d(d)(1).

[24] 15 U.S.C. §1681d(b).

[25] *Id.*

ii. *Additional State Notice Requirements to Obtain Reports*

State laws impose a variety of additional requirements for background checks. For example, if the background check report qualifies as an "investigative consumer report," Massachusetts and New Jersey laws require the employer to notify the applicant of "the precise nature and scope of the investigation requested."[26] California's Investigative Consumer Reporting Act (ICRAA) also requires the employer to notify the applicant of the nature and scope of investigation requested, as well as the name, address, and telephone number of the investigative consumer-reporting agency conducting the investigation.[27] These requirements differ from the FCRA, which simply requires such information to be provided upon the applicant's request.[28]

Additionally, state laws may confer greater rights for applicants to receive a copy of the background check report. Under the FCRA, an employer is required to give the applicant a copy of the background check report only if the employer plans to take adverse action based on that report.[29] In contrast, if an employer obtains an investigative consumer report about an applicant, California, Minnesota, and Oklahoma laws require the employer to include a box on the written notice that the applicant may check to receive a copy of that report regardless of the employer's plans with respect to the use of the report.[30] Similarly, if the report contains credit information, California requires that employers include a box on the written notice that the applicant may check off to receive a copy of the credit report, and the third-party vendor must provide that report to the employer and the employee at the same time.[31]

Practice Pointer. Many states have recently adopted laws allowing consumers to freeze all reporting of their credit reports.[32]

---

[26]MASS. ANN. LAWS ch. 93, §53(a)(1); N.J. STAT. §56:11-33(a)(1).

[27]CAL. CIV. CODE §1786.16(3).

[28]15 U.S.C. §1681d(b).

[29]15 U.S.C. §1681b(b)(3)(A).

[30]CAL. CIV. CODE §1785.205(a); MINN. STAT. §13C.02; 24 OKLA. STAT. §148.

[31]CAL. CIV. CODE §1785.20.5(a).

[32]*See, e.g.*, CAL. CIV. CODE §1785.12; COLO. REV. STAT. 12-14.3-102; CONN. GEN. STAT. §36a-701a; DEL. CODE ANN. tit. 6, §§2201–2204; FLA. STAT. §501.005; HAW.

If an applicant has placed a freeze on his credit reports, it may be necessary to obtain a further authorization from the applicant for release of credit-related information. If an employer wishes to obtain a background check, the employer should consider conditioning an offer of employment on successful completion of the background check, including the temporary lifting of any security freeze, in order to secure the applicant's cooperation in this process.

b. Notice Requirements for Adverse Action Based on Report

Under the FCRA, an "adverse action" includes the denial of employment or any other employment-related decision that adversely affects a current or prospective employee.[33] The FCRA requires an employer to provide supplemental notice to the applicant before and after taking adverse action based, whether in whole or in part, on the contents of a background check report.

i. Pre-Adverse Action Notice Requirements

Prior to taking any adverse action based on the contents of a background check report, the employer must give the applicant a copy of the report and another copy of the summary of rights under the FCRA. This "pre-adverse action notice" is intended to allow the applicant to review the report and contact the agency to seek correction of any disputed information. (A sample pre-adverse action notice appears in Exhibit 2.2.)

After providing the pre-adverse action notice, the employer is not required to wait for any specified time period before taking the adverse action. The Federal Trade Commission (FTC) advises

---

REV. STAT. ANN. §§489P-3 to 489P-5 for victims of identity theft only; 815 ILL. COMP. STAT. 505/2 MM; KAN. STAT. ANN. §§50-702, 50-723 to 50-724; KY. REV. STAT. ANN. §§367.363–.365; LA. STAT. ANN. §9.3571(H)–(Y); ME. REV. STAT. ANN. tit. 10, §§1313-C to 1313-E; MINN. STAT. §13C.016; NEV. REV. STAT. §§598C.105, 598C.300–.390; N.H. REV. STAT. ANN. §359B:23; N.J. STAT. ANN. §56:11-46; N.Y. GEN. BUS. LAW §§380-a(k)–(n), 380-t; OKLA. STAT. tit. 24 §§149–159; 73 PA. CONS. STAT. §§2501–2510; R.I. GEN. LAWS §§6-48-1 to 6-48-7, 6-48-9; S.D. CODIFIED LAWS 54-15-1 et seq.; TEX. BUS. & COM. CODE ANN. §§20.031–.039 for identity theft victims; UTAH CODE ANN. §§13-45-102, 13-45-201 et seq.; VT. STAT. ANN. tit. 9 §§2480a–2480j; WASH. REV. CODE §§19.182.170–.200 for identity theft victims; and WIS. STAT. §100.54.

[33] 15 U.S.C. §1681a(k).

EXHIBIT 2.2
U.S.: Sample Pre-Adverse Action Notice Under the Fair Credit Reporting Act

This sample pre-adverse action notice addresses the requirements of the U.S. federal Fair Credit Reporting Act. Additional provisions may be required under state law, as discussed in this chapter. Please consult with your legal counsel prior to using this or any form, as legal requirements may change from time to time.

[Date]

[Candidate Name]
[Address]
[City, State, Zip Code]

Dear **[Candidate Name]**:

In connection with your application for employment, you authorized us to obtain background check reports about you. I am enclosing a copy of a background check report that we received about you, which was issued by:

[Consumer Reporting Agency]
[Address]
[City, State, Zip Code]
[Toll-free number]

Please review this report carefully, along with the enclosed summary of your rights under the Fair Credit Reporting Act. If we decide not to employ you based on information contained in this report, we will notify you that our decision was affected by the contents of this report. Please note that any inquiry concerning the contents of this report must be submitted directly to the consumer reporting agency listed above. We cannot answer any inquiries or requests regarding the contents of this report.

Thank you for your interest in our company.

Sincerely,

[Name]
[Title]

Enclosures: Copy of background check report
Summary of Your Rights Under the Fair Credit Reporting Act

Para informacion en espanol, visite www.ftc.gov/credit o escribe a la FTC Consumer Response Center, Room 130-A 600 Pennsylvania Ave. N.W., Washington, D.C. 20580.

A Summary of Your Rights Under the Fair Credit Reporting Act

The federal Fair Credit Reporting Act (FCRA) promotes the accuracy, fairness, and privacy of information in the files of consumer reporting agencies. There are many

Exhibit 2.2—*cont'd*

types of consumer-reporting agencies, including credit bureaus and specialty agencies (such as agencies that sell information about check-writing histories, medical records, and rental history records). Here is a summary of your major rights under the FCRA. For more information, including information about additional rights, go to *www.ftc.gov/credit* or write to: Consumer Response Center, Room 130-A, Federal Trade Commission, 600 Pennsylvania Ave. N.W., Washington, D.C. 20580.

You must be told if information in your file has been used against you. Anyone who uses a credit report or another type of consumer report to deny your application for credit, insurance, or employment—or to take another adverse action against you—must tell you, and must give you the name, address, and phone number of the agency that provided the information.

You have the right to know what is in your file. You may request and obtain all the information about you in the files of a consumer reporting agency (your "file disclosure"). You will be required to provide proper identification, which may include your Social Security number. In many cases, the disclosure will be free. You are entitled to a free file disclosure if:

- a person has taken adverse action against you because of information in your credit report;
- you are the victim of identity theft and place a fraud alert in your file;
- your file contains inaccurate information as a result of fraud;
- you are on public assistance; or
- you are unemployed but expect to apply for employment within 60 days.

In addition, by September 2005 all consumers will be entitled to one free disclosure every 12 months upon request from each nationwide credit bureau and from nationwide specialty consumer reporting agencies. See *www.ftc.gov/credit* for additional information.

You have the right to ask for a credit score. Credit scores are numerical summaries of your creditworthiness based on information from credit bureaus. You may request a credit score from consumer reporting agencies that create scores or distribute scores used in residential real property loans, but you will have to pay for it. In some mortgage transactions, you will receive credit score information for free from the mortgage lender.

You have the right to dispute incomplete or inaccurate information. If you identify information in your file that is incomplete or inaccurate, and report it to the consumer reporting agency, the agency must investigate unless your dispute is frivolous. See *www.ftc.gov/credit* for an explanation of dispute procedures.

Consumer-reporting agencies must correct or delete inaccurate, incomplete, or unverifiable information. Inaccurate, incomplete, or unverifiable information must be removed or corrected, usually within 30 days. However, a consumer reporting agency may continue to report information it has verified as accurate.

Consumer-reporting agencies may not report outdated negative information. In most cases, a consumer reporting agency may not report negative information that is more than seven years old, or bankruptcies that are more than ten years old.

Exhibit 2.2—*cont'd*

Access to your file is limited. A consumer reporting agency may provide information about you only to people with a valid need—usually to consider an application with a creditor, insurer, employer, landlord, or other business. The FCRA specifies those with a valid need for access.

You must give your consent for reports to be provided to employers. A consumer reporting agency may not give out information about you to your employer, or a potential employer, without your written consent given to the employer. Written consent generally is not required in the trucking industry. For more information, go to *www.ftc.gov/credit.*

You may limit "pre-screened" offers of credit and insurance you get based on information in your credit report. Unsolicited "pre-screened" offers for credit and insurance must include a toll-free phone number you can call if you choose to remove your name and address from the lists these offers are based on. You may opt-out with the nationwide credit bureaus at 1-888-5-OPTOUT (1-888-567-8688).

You may seek damages from violators. If a consumer-reporting agency, or, in some cases, a user of consumer reports or a furnisher of information to a consumer-reporting agency violates the FCRA, you may be able to sue in state or federal court.

Identity theft victims and active duty military personnel have additional rights. For more information, visit *www.ftc.gov/credit.*

States may enforce the FCRA, and many states have their own consumer reporting laws. In some cases, you may have more rights under state law. For more information, contact your state or local consumer protection agency or your state Attorney General. Federal enforcers are listed here:

TYPE OF BUSINESS:	CONTACT:
Consumer reporting agencies, creditors, and others not listed below	Federal Trade Commission: Consumer Response Center—FCRA Washington, DC 20580 877-382-4357
National banks, federal branches/agencies of foreign banks (word "National" or initials "N.A." appear in or after bank's name)	Office of the Comptroller of the Currency Compliance Management, Mail Stop 6-S Washington, DC 20219 800-613-6743
Federal Reserve System member banks (except national banks, and federal branches/agencies of foreign banks)	Federal Reserve Board Division of Consumer & Community Affairs Washington, DC 20551 202-452-3693

Exhibit 2.2—*cont'd*

TYPE OF BUSINESS:	CONTACT:
Savings associations and federally chartered savings banks (word "Federal" or initials "F.S.B." appear in federal institution's name)	Office of Thrift Supervision Consumer Complaints Washington, DC 20552 800-342-6929
Federal credit unions (words "Federal Credit Union" appear in institution's name)	National Credit Union Administration 1775 Duke Street Alexandria, VA 22314 703-519-4600
State-chartered banks that are not members of the Federal Reserve System	Federal Deposit Insurance Corporation Consumer Response Center 2345 Grand Avenue, Suite 100 Kansas City, MO 64108-2633 877-275-3342
Air, surface, or rail common carriers regulated by former Civil Aeronautics Board of Interstate Commerce Commission	Department of Transportation Office of Financial Management Washington, DC 20590 202-366-1306
Activities subject to the Packers and Stockyards Act 1921	Department of Agriculture Office of Deputy Administrator—GIPSA Washington, DC 20250 202-720-7051

that an employer should wait a reasonable amount of time after providing this notice before it takes the adverse action.[34] What is considered reasonable depends on the facts of the particular situation, but the FTC has found five days to be reasonable.[35]

ii. Adverse Action Notice Requirements

When the employer proceeds to take the adverse action, it must notify the applicant of the adverse action and the fact that this decision was based, in part or in full, on information contained in the background check. (A sample adverse action notice appears in Exhibit 2.3.) Specifically, the employer is required to provide to the consumer the following:

[34] Brinckerhoff-Weisberg, Fed. Trade Comm'n Letter, June 27, 1997.
[35] *Id.*

EXHIBIT 2.3
U.S.: Sample Adverse Action Notice Under the Fair Credit Reporting Act

This sample adverse action notice addresses the requirements of the U.S. federal Fair Credit Reporting Act. Additional provisions may be required under state law, as discussed in this chapter. Please consult with your legal counsel prior to using this or any form, as legal requirements may change from time to time.

[Date]

[Candidate Name]
[Address]
[City, State, Zip Code]

Dear **[Candidate Name]**:

We previously sent you a copy of a background check report that you authorized US to obtain in connection with your application for employment. I am sending you this letter to inform you that we have decided not to employ you, and that the information contained in that report affected the Company's decision.

As explained in our prior letter, this report was issued by:

[Consumer Reporting Agency]
[Address]
[City, State, Zip Code]
[Toll-free number]

[Consumer-Reporting Agency] (the "Agency") did not make the decision regarding your application for employment, and is not able to explain to you why the decision was made.

However, you are entitled to contact the Agency to dispute the accuracy or completeness of any of the information contained in this report. You also may obtain a free duplicate copy of this report from the Agency, if you make a written request directly to the Agency within sixty (60) days after receiving this letter. Additionally, you may request a free copy of the report from any other consumer credit reporting agency that compiles and maintains files on consumers on a nationwide basis, if you make a written request directly to the consumer-reporting agency within sixty (60) days after receiving this letter. We are enclosing a duplicate copy of the summary of your rights under the Fair Credit Reporting Act, which accompanied the copy of the report you previously received.

Please note that any inquiry concerning the contents of this report must be submitted directly to the Agency at the address and telephone number listed above. We do not have authority to handle any inquiries or requests regarding the contents of this report.

Thank you.

[Name]
[Title]

Enclosure: Summary of Your Rights Under the Fair Credit Reporting Act

(aa) Oral, written, or electronic notice of the adverse action;

(bb) Oral, written, or electronic notice of the name, address, and telephone number of the consumer reporting agency that furnished the report (including a toll-free number established by the agency if the agency compiles and maintains files on consumers on a nationwide basis);

(cc) A statement that the consumer reporting agency did not make the decision to take the adverse action and is unable to provide the consumer with specific reasons why the adverse action was taken; and

(dd) Oral, written, or electronic notice of the consumer's right to obtain a free copy of his consumer report from the consumer reporting agency within 60 days and to dispute with a consumer reporting agency the accuracy or completeness of any information in a consumer report furnished by the agency.[36]

c. Certain Misconduct Investigations Exempt From the FCRA

The FCRA's notice and consent requirements do not apply to consumer reports obtained in connection with an investigation of suspected employment-related misconduct.[37] In such a case, the employer is not required to notify or obtain consent from the employee who is subject of the misconduct investigation. Instead, if the employer takes adverse action based in whole or in part on the report, the employer need only disclose a paraphrased "summary containing the nature and substance of the communication upon which the adverse action is based."[38] Note that this exception allows the employer to provide a summary, rather than the full report, and the employer need not disclose any information about the report before taking the adverse action.[39]

---

[36] 15 U.S.C. §1681m.

[37] Under FCRA, misconduct is defined as a violation of federal, state, or local laws or regulations; a violation of any of the employer's pre-existing written policies; and/or noncompliance with the rules of a self-regulatory agency.

[38] 15 U.S.C. §1681a(x)(2).

[39] *Id.*

These rules apply to investigations that involve "suspected misconduct relating to employment."[40] To qualify for this exception, the investigation results may be provided only to the employer or the employer's agent and certain types of governmental agencies.[41]

This amendment to the FCRA, passed in 2003, allows employers to act more swiftly and confidentially to investigate misconduct. It also settled a controversy under which the FTC suggested that investigators or attorneys conducting misconduct investigations were subject to the FCRA notice requirements, jeopardizing attorney-client privilege.[42] This exception allows employers to maintain the confidentiality of the misconduct investigation, until such time as the employer takes adverse action based on a report that otherwise would be subject to FCRA.

3. *Limitations on Content of Background Check Reports*

The FCRA prohibits consumer reporting agencies from including any of the following types of information in background check reports, unless the subject of the report would be employed at an annual salary of at least $75,000:[43]

- Bankruptcy cases more than ten years old;
- Civil suits, civil judgments, and arrest records that predate the report by seven years or the expiration of the applicable statute of limitations, whichever is the longer period;
- Paid tax liens more than seven years old;
- Accounts placed for collection or charged to profit and loss more than seven years old; and
- Any other "adverse item of information," other than records of criminal convictions, which are more than seven years old.[44]

---

[40] 15 U.S.C. §1681a(x)(1)(B), defining misconduct as "suspected misconduct relating to employment . . . or . . . compliance with Federal, State or local laws and regulations, the rules of a self-regulatory organization, or any pre-existing written policies of the employer."

[41] 15 U.S.C. §1681a(x)(D).

[42] Vail, Fed. Trade Comm'n Op. Letter, April 5, 1999.

[43] 15 U.S.C. §1681c(b)(3).

[44] 15 U.S.C. §1681c(a).

The FCRA also strictly limits the agency's ability to disclose medical information related to the applicant, unless the applicant specifically consents to the disclosure of medical information as part of the report.[45] (A sample background check process appears in Exhibit 2.4.)

Note that state laws impose additional restrictions on the information that may be contained in a background check report. In California, for instance, background check reports cannot include information about criminal convictions more than seven years old.[46] A California consumer credit report also may not include information about arrests or indictments that did not result in a conviction, unless the criminal proceeding remains pending.[47] Moreover, California law typically does not permit the report to include other adverse information that predates the report by more than seven years.[48]

Practice Pointer. Employers should exercise caution in making employment decisions based on the contents of a background check report, as federal or state law may not allow an employer to act upon all of the information contained in that report. For example, the FCRA allows background check reports to contain information about personal bankruptcies during the past ten years, while the federal Bankruptcy Act prohibits discrimination against individuals who have filed for bankruptcy.[49] Similarly several state laws put limits on the use of "old" or unrelated convictions when making employment decisions.

4. *Access and Correction Rights*

If the applicant disputes the accuracy of information contained in the report, the FCRA provides a mechanism for the applicant to ask the agency to correct this information. The applicant initiates this process by giving the agency written notice of the information in the report that is alleged to be incorrect.[50] Within 30 days

[45] 15 U.S.C. §1681b(g).
[46] CAL. CIV. CODE §§1785.13(6), 1786.18(a).
[47] CAL. CIV. CODE §§1785.13(6), 1786.18(a)(7).
[48] CAL. CIV. CODE §§1785.13(a)(8), 1786.18(8).
[49] 11 U.S.C. §525(b).
[50] 15 U.S.C. §1681i(a)(1)(A).

EXHIBIT 2.4
U.S.: Sample Background Check Process

<table>
<tr><th colspan="6">SAMPLE BACKGROUND CHECK PROCESS</th></tr>
<tr><td colspan="6">Step 1: Employer provides FCRA authorization to job applicant</td></tr>
<tr><td colspan="5">Applicant signs FCRA authorization</td><td>Applicant declines to sign FCRA authorization— End of process</td></tr>
<tr><td colspan="5">Step 2: Employer requests background check report from consumer-reporting agency (“CRA”) and provides certification</td><td rowspan="3"></td></tr>
<tr><td colspan="5">Step 3: Employer receives background check report</td></tr>
<tr><td colspan="4">Report contains information that may adversely affect employment decision</td><td>Report does not contain adverse information; employer makes hiring decision— End of process</td></tr>
<tr><td colspan="4">Step 4: Employer sends pre-adverse action notice, Summary of Rights, and copy of background check report</td><td colspan="2" rowspan="3"></td></tr>
<tr><td colspan="2">Applicant does not dispute adverse information</td><td colspan="2">Applicant disputes adverse information with CRA</td></tr>
<tr><td>Step 5: Employer decides not to hire applicant and sends adverse action notice— End of process</td><td>Employer decides to hire applicant despite adverse information— End of process</td><td>Applicant fails to resolve alleged discrepancy with CRA within reasonable period allowed by employer</td><td>Applicant successfully resolves alleged discrepancy with CRA within reasonable period allowed by employer; employer hires applicant— End of process</td></tr>
</table>

Exhibit 2.4—*cont'd*

SAMPLE BACKGROUND CHECK PROCESS		
	Step 5: Employer decides not to hire applicant and sends adverse action notice—End of process	

after receiving such a complaint, the agency must reinvestigate the disputed information, free of charge to the applicant, and update or delete that information from the file.[51] This 30-day period may be extended up to 15 days, if the applicant subsequently provides additional information that is relevant to the reinvestigation.[52] The agency must notify the applicant of the outcome of the reinvestigation within five business days after completing that reinvestigation.[53] Even if the disputed information is not removed from the file, the applicant may add a statement to the consumer file, disputing the accuracy or completeness of that information.[54]

Within five business days after receiving the applicant's complaint, the agency must also notify the source of the disputed information about the applicant's complaint.[55] If the agency determines that the disputed information is inaccurate or unverifiable, the agency must delete or modify that information accordingly and notify the source of the information that it has done so.[56]

---

[51] *Id.*
[52] 15 U.S.C. §1681i(a)(1)(B).
[53] 15 U.S.C. §1681i(6).
[54] 15 U.S.C. §1681i(6)(B)(iv).
[55] 15 U.S.C. §1681i(a)(2).
[56] 15 U.S.C. §1681i(a)(5)(A).

5. *Potential Liability for Violations of the FCRA and Similar State Laws*

The FCRA provides sanctions that potentially apply to an employer depending on the nature of the violation. Employers can be liable for both civil and criminal penalties for failure to comply with the requirements of the FCRA.[57] Civil remedies include actual damages up to $1,000, punitive damages, and attorneys' fees.[58] Employers can be criminally liable if they attempt to obtain consumer reports under false pretenses.[59] The FTC is authorized to investigate violations of the FCRA.

Any person who knowingly and willfully obtains information on a consumer from an agency under false pretenses may be fined, imprisoned for up to two years, or both.[60]

State law may offer remedies to applicants, including injunctive relief, and relief for invasion of privacy or defamation.[61] For example, California law provides remedies that are similar to those under the FCRA, but with increased thresholds for damages, from $2,500 to $5,000, plus attorneys' fees and costs.[62]

6. *State Law Rules Relating to Background Checks by Vendors*

Employers must take care to follow both state and federal laws when conducting background checks. Many states have their own laws that apply to background checks conducted by third parties, and some of these laws can be quite extensive. Employers should know that they may need to adjust their consent forms to comply with state laws. This section will focus on some of the special requirements in California and New York as examples of state laws relating to background checks that are different from the federal law.

---

[57] 15 U.S.C. §1681n(a), 15 U.S.C. §1681w.

[58] 15 U.S.C. §1681o, 15 U.S.C. §1681p.

[59] 15 U.S.C. §1681q.

[60] *Id.*

[61] CAL. CIV. CODE §1786.52.

[62] CAL. CIV. CODE §§1785.19, 1785.31.

a. California

California has two laws that provide regulations in addition to those imposed by FCRA. The first law, California's Consumer Credit Reporting Agencies Act (CCRAA), requires employers to provide additional notice and disclosure when requesting and using background checks that contain consumer credit information.[63] FCRA requires employers to seek advance consent before procuring background checks, but CCRAA additionally requires employers to also provide a check box that allows an employee to request a copy of the credit report at the same time the employer receives it.[64] Employers who plan to take adverse action based upon a background check containing credit information must provide notice to the agency providing the report.[65]

The second law, California's Investigative Consumer Reporting Agency Act (ICRAA) requires employers to affirmatively provide the employee with information about the nature and scope of investigation requested, including a summary of the provisions of ICRAA's Section 1786.22 describing the employee's rights, as well as the name, address, and telephone number of the investigative consumer reporting agency conducting the investigation when seeking investigative consumer reports.[66] In contrast, the FCRA requires employers to provide this information only when the employee requests it.[67] The employer also must provide the employee with the opportunity to check a box to request a copy of the report procured.[68] An employer must provide requested credit reports contemporaneously, but it has three days after it receives the investigative reports to provide copies of the reports to the employee.[69] If the employer plans to take adverse action based on the investigative background check, the employer must provide the employee with the name, address, and telephone number of the company conducting the background check.[70]

---

[63] CAL. CIV. CODE §1785 et seq.

[64] CAL. CIV. CODE §1785.20.5(a).

[65] CAL. CIV. CODE §1785.20.5(b).

[66] CAL. CIV. CODE §1786.12(2)(b)(v).

[67] 15 U.S.C. §1681d(b).

[68] CAL. CIV. CODE §1786.16(b)(1).

[69] CAL. CIV. CODE §1786.16(b)(1), 15 U.S.C. §1785.20.5(a).

[70] CAL. CIV. CODE §1786.40(a).

California's ICRAA, like FCRA, exempts from these requirements any investigative consumer report requested to research suspected wrongdoing or misconduct on the part of the subject of the investigation.[71]

The ICRAA also provides some unique regulations that apply to background checks that are conducted by employers, rather than by third-party vendors.[72] A discussion of these requirements is contained in Section 2.II.A.7.

b. New York

New York's FCRA also requires employers to notify the applicant and get the applicant's authorization before seeking a background check.[73] The applicant has the right to inspect and receive a copy of the report.[74] In addition, upon request, the applicant has the right to be informed of whether a credit report was requested and, if requested, the name and address of the consumer reporting agency that furnished the report.[75]

Starting February 1, 2009, a new law amending New York's General Business and Labor Laws will affect a New York employer's obligations when conducting background checks. An employer must:

> 1) post a copy of Article 23-A of New York Corrections Law ("Article 23-A")[76] and any regulations promulgated pursuant to Article 23-A in a conspicuous manner in a place accessible to employees;[77]

---

[71] CAL. CIV. CODE §1786.16(b)(2)(c).

[72] CAL. CIV. CODE §1786.53(b)(2).

[73] N.Y. GEN. BUS. LAW §§380–380t.

[74] N.Y. GEN. BUS. LAW §380-c.

[75] N.Y. GEN. BUS. LAW §380-b.

[76] Article 23-A applies to any applicant with a prior criminal conviction who applies for a license or employment with either public agencies or private employers. For the purpose of Article 23-A, a private employer has ten or more employees. Article 23-A does not apply to situations where it is illegal to employ such applicant. Article 23-A is discussed more fully below in Section 2.II.A.8.b.

[77] N.Y. LAB. LAW §201-f.

2) provide a copy of Article 23-A to all job applicants undergoing a background check when the individual is informed that the background check may be requested;[78] and

3) provide applicants with an additional copy of Article 23-A if a criminal record is found from the background check.[79]

Further. if a public agency or private employer denies the application of an individual convicted of a criminal offense, it must provide, within 30 days of a request, a written statement of the reasons for denial.

The new law is enforceable against public agencies pursuant to Article 78 of the New York Civil Practice Law and Rules and against private employers by the New York Division of Human Rights pursuant to Article 15 of New York Executive Law. They also may be enforced concurrently against private employers by the New York City Commission on Human Rights.

7. *Background Checks and Investigations Conducted In-House by Employers*

Rather than retaining a third-party agency, employers may assign their own in-house employees to perform background checks. Common types of in-house background checks conducted by employers include:

- An HR manager calling an applicant's references;
- An employer going to the courthouse to check public criminal records;
- An HR manager interviewing employees regarding alleged workplace misconduct; and
- A manager conducting an Internet search about an applicant.

As a general principle, the FCRA does not apply when an employer conducts its own in-house background checks.[80] Employers must still observe certain other federal and state laws that

---

[78]N.Y. GEN. BUS. LAW §380-c(2)(b).
[79]N.Y. GEN. BUS. LAW §380-g(d).
[80]15 U.S.C. §1681a(f).

apply to in-house background checks. For example, if a California employer collects "public records" about an applicant or employee for employment purposes, it must give the applicant or employee a copy of those records within seven days after receiving them.[81] "Public records" are defined as "records documenting an arrest, indictment, conviction, civil judicial action, tax lien, or outstanding judgment."[82] If the employer collected the public records in connection with an investigation of suspected wrongdoing by that individual, however, this disclosure can be postponed until the completion of the investigation.[83]

8. *Limitations on Direct Inquiries by Employers*

Section 2.II.A.3 of this chapter discussed categories of background information that cannot be included in a background check report created by a third-party agency. Separate and apart from those limitations, however, employers are directly prohibited from seeking or using certain types of information about an applicant's background, even when the employer collects the information without the assistance of a third-party agency. This section describes several key examples of laws that regulate in-house background checks conducted by employers.

a. *Arrests and Sealed or Expunged Convictions*

Many states restrict an employer's ability to inquire about arrests that did not result in a conviction, or about criminal convictions that have been sealed or expunged. These states include California, Colorado, Massachusetts, New York, and Oregon.[84] California law also prohibits an employer from asking an applicant to disclose minor marijuana-related misdemeanor convictions that are more than two years old.[85]

---

[81]CAL. CIV. CODE §1786.53(b)(2). The statute allows employers to include a box on the job application form that the applicant may check to waive his or her right to receive a copy of such public records collected by the employer. *Id.* However, even if the applicant or employee agrees to such a waiver, the employer must provide a copy of any public records upon which it takes adverse action against the individual. CAL. CIV. CODE §1876.53(b)(4).

[82]CAL. CIV. CODE §1786.53(a)(3).

[83]CAL. CIV. CODE §1786.53(b)(3).

[84]CAL. LAB. CODE §432.7; COLO. REV. STAT. §24-72-308(f); MASS. ANN. LAWS ch. 276 §100A; N.Y. EXEC. LAW §296.16; OR. REV. STAT. §659A-030.

[85]CAL. LAB. CODE §432.8.

Under California law, an employer may not ask an applicant for employment to disclose, either verbally or in writing: (1) information concerning an arrest or detention that did not result in a conviction; (2) participation in any pre-trial or post-trial diversion program; or (3) certain misdemeanor marijuana convictions that are more than two years old.[86] Also, an employer cannot use such information as a factor in determining a condition of employment, such as hiring, promotion, termination, or any apprenticeship training program or any other training program leading to employment. A conviction is defined as a plea, verdict, or finding of guilt, regardless of whether a sentence is imposed.[87] An employer may, however, ask an employee or applicant about an arrest for which he is out on bail or on his or her own recognizance pending trial.[88]

b. Convictions

New York law allows employers to inquire into prior convictions,[89] but new amendments to the New York Corrections Law, Article 23-A, prohibits public agencies and private employers from denying or taking adverse action upon any application for any license or employment based on: (1) the existence of a prior criminal conviction; or (2) "a finding of lack of 'good moral character'" as a result of prior criminal conviction(s) unless one of the following exceptions applies:[90]

---

[86]CAL. LAB. CODE §§432.7(a), 432.8.

[87]CAL. LAB. CODE §432.7(a).

[88]*Id.*

[89]In assessing whether an employer has a right to inquire into a potential employee's criminal convictions or to terminate an employee because of such convictions, New York courts point out that a "crime" in this context refers only to felonies and misdemeanors. Minor violations are not included in the definition of crime as taken from Penal Law §10.00(6). *See* State Div. of Human Rights v. Sorrento Cheese Co., 115 A.D.2d 323 (N.Y. App. Div. 1985) (plaintiff was terminated for lying about a conviction of "disorderly conduct" on his application and court found that this did not come within the definition of a crime and therefore did not constitute a dishonest answer).

[90]Article 23-A applies to any applicant with a prior criminal conviction who applies for a license or employment with either public agencies or private employers. For the purpose of Article 23-A, a private employer has ten or more employees. Article 23-A does not apply to situations where it is illegal to employ such applicant.

- there is a direct relationship between the criminal offenses and the specific license or employment; or
- a grant or continuation of the license or employment would involve an unreasonable risk to property, safety, or welfare of specific individuals or the general public.

Public agencies and private employers making a decision about an applicant with a prior criminal conviction must weigh the following factors:

- New York state public policy to encourage the licensure and employment of persons with criminal convictions;
- the specific duties and responsibilities necessarily related to the license or employment;
- any bearing the criminal offense(s) will have on the applicant's fitness or ability to perform his duties or responsibilities;
- the time elapsed since the criminal offense(s) occurred;
- the applicant's age at the time the criminal offense(s) occurred;
- the seriousness of the offense(s);
- any information produced regarding either the applicant's rehabilitation or good conduct;
- the public agency's or private employer's legitimate interest in protecting the property, safety, and welfare of specific individuals or the general public; and
- any certificate of relief from disabilities or a certificate of good conduct issued to the applicant in deciding on the application. Such certificates create a presumption of rehabilitation regarding the offense(s) specified on the certificate.

i. Access Rights

If an applicant with one or more criminal convictions requests a written statement setting forth the reason for which his application was denied,[91] the agency or private employer must provide a written statement setting forth the reasons for the denial

[91] N.Y. CORRECT. LAW §754.

within 30 days.[92] Failure to give the requested information or failure to comply with any other provision of the article may result in an enforcement proceeding. For public agencies, enforcement is brought pursuant to Article 78 of the Civil Practice Laws and Rules.[93] For private employers, these provisions are enforceable by the New York State Division of Human Rights and the New York City Commission on Human Rights.[94] These agencies may receive complaints against employers, institute investigations, hold hearings, and impose damages.[95]

ii. Exceptions

New York cases tend to interpret the "directly related" exception fairly broadly, allowing for an adverse action if the offense was in any way connected to the job responsibilities of the applicant or employee. The New York Supreme Court found that a landfill owner's two prior federal tax-related crimes were "directly related" to the duties inherent in the license he sought to expand his landfill.[96] Courts will not always use the "directly related" wording and instead will often speak of the "nature of the conduct" for which the conviction occurred.[97]

The second exception to the prohibition on adverse employment action based upon a conviction relates to whether the potential or current employee poses an unreasonable risk to property,

---

[92]*Id. See also* 12 U.S.C. §1829 (federal statute that requires insured banks to obtain written consent of the Federal Deposit Insurance Corporation before employing any individual convicted of a criminal offense involving dishonesty or a breach of trust).

[93]N.Y. CORRECT. LAW §755.

[94]*Id.*

[95]N.Y. EXEC. LAW §295; N.Y. COMP. CODES R. & REGS. tit. 8, §8-105.

[96]Al Turi Landfill, Inc. v. N.Y. State Dep't of Envtl. Conservation, 98 N.Y.2d 758, 761–62 (N.Y. 2002) (affirming that "the elements inherent in the criminal conduct... dishonesty, lack of integrity in conducting business, and a willingness to mislead the government have a direct relationship to the duties and responsibilities of the license sought").

[97]Pisano v. McKenna, 466 N.Y.S.2d 231, 233 (N.Y. App. Div. 1983) (court finds that the nature of a fireman's convictions for state tax crime was sufficient grounds for dismissal as he was a "quite visible public employee (and) the public trust placed in such an employee has been sufficiently violated...").

safety, or health.[98] This exception, too, has been interpreted fairly broadly by New York courts.[99]

iii. Employer Liability

Recent New York decisions suggest that an employer can be held liable for negligently hiring an employee who then commits a wrongful act if the employer knew or should have known of the employee's propensity to commit injury.[100] These decisions have stressed the importance of an employer using the factors and exceptions set forth in New York Law when assessing whether a nexus exists between a conviction and the position of employment sought by the applicant.[101]

c. Fingerprinting

State laws often restrict the use of fingerprinting as part of background checks. For example, New York law prohibits a private employer from requiring fingerprinting as a condition of employment, with the exception of a narrow group of employers.[102] This prohibition does not apply to state or municipal workers, legally incorporated hospitals, or employees of medical colleges affiliated with such hospitals.[103] Similarly, California allows employers to collect fingerprints for internal use, but providing the prints to a law enforcement agency or other third party that could cause a detriment to the employer is a misdemeanor.[104] Therefore, functionally, California employers in most professions cannot use fingerprints for background checks. A few exceptions on this prohibition exist for financial institutions, certain financial manage-

---

[98]N.Y. EXEC. LAW §296.16.

[99]Grafer v. N.Y. City Civ. Serv. Comm'n, 581 N.Y.S.2d 337 (N.Y. App. Div. 1992) (plaintiff's application to be a fireman was rejected, due in part to his previous conviction for drunk driving).

[100]*See* T.W. v. City of New York, 729 N.Y.S.2d 96 (N.Y. App. Div. 2001) (holding an employer liable when a community center employee who had notified his employers of a prior conviction was found guilty of sexually assaulting a child at the center); *see also* Adorno v. Correctional Servs. Corp., 312 F. Supp. 2d 505 (S.D.N.Y. 2004) (citing *T.W.* in reference to an employer's failure to do an adequate background check on an employee who later assaulted tenants in a halfway house).

[101]*Id.*

[102]N.Y. LAB. LAW §201-a.

[103]*Id.*

[104]CAL. LAB. CODE §1051.

ment companies, securities brokers and dealers, and licensed child care providers.[105]

d. Bankruptcy Act

The federal Bankruptcy Act prohibits an employer from discriminating against an employee or applicant solely because the individual has filed for bankruptcy.[106] Employers who obtain bankruptcy information in the process of procuring a consumer report under the FCRA, or a comparable state statute, could risk liability for violation of the Bankruptcy Act if they rely upon that information to make employment decisions. This is true whether the employer finds the information through its own investigation or through the use of a consumer reporting agency.

Accordingly, employers should avoid considering an applicant's bankruptcy as a factor in employment-related decisions. Instead, employment decisions should be based on legitimate business reasons independent of the bankruptcy.[107]

9. *Hiring and Payment of OFAC-Designated Nationals in the Post-9/11 Environment*

U.S. employers should be aware of the U.S. trade sanctions and economic embargoes as set forth in the regulations of the Office of Foreign Assets Control (OFAC) of the U.S. Department of the Treasury, which implements statutory sanctions against transactions with various foreign countries, and specially designated nationals and blocked persons (SDNs).[108] Although these programs were in place and actively enforced before the attacks

---

[105] CAL. FIN. CODE §§6525(a), 1057, 15 U.S.C. §78q(f)(2); CAL. HEALTH & SAFETY CODE §1596.871.

[106] 11 U.S.C. §525(b).

[107] Stockhouse v. Hines Motor Supply, Inc., 75 BR 83, 85 (D. Wyo. 1987) ("An essential element of a claim under [the Bankruptcy Act] is that the employee's insolvency, the filing of bankruptcy or the discharge of his debts is the sole reason for discriminatory treatment by an employer."). *See also* Laracuente v. Chase Manhattan Bank, 891 F.2d 17 (1st Cir. 1989) (confirming that "a fundamental element of a [discrimination claim under the Bankruptcy Act] is that the insolvency, the filing of bankruptcy, or the discharge of a debt is the sole reason for discriminatory treatment by an employer").

[108] The OFAC regulations are set forth at 31 C.F.R. pts. 500–598. *See* United States Department of the Treasury, Office of Foreign Assets Control, Mission, at http://www.treas.gov/offices/enforcement/ofac.

of September 11, 2001, their enforcement has acquired greater urgency in the post-9/11 environment.

For purposes of U.S. employers, the most important of these regulations involve the SDN lists. These lists are published on the OFAC Web site and also may be found in the Code of Federal Regulations and the Federal Register.[109] The persons whose names appear on those lists may be referred to as "blocked persons," "specially designated nationals," or other categories of persons with whom a U.S. person's dealings are prohibited without a specific OFAC license.

Although the trade bans and sanctions implemented by OFAC are complex and vary according to the countries and activities at which they are aimed, they generally restrict "transactions" with or "transfers" to blocked and designated individuals.[110] As a general matter, employing and/or paying compensation to a blocked or designated individual is considered by OFAC as a prohibited transaction or transfer. Therefore, U.S. employers may take the precaution of checking the names of prospective employees against the SDN lists, and some employers consult the lists periodically to determine if any current employees' names have been added.

As a practical matter, an employer might reasonably weigh the cost of consulting the SDN lists against the real-world risk of hiring or employing a blocked or designated individual. The likelihood that a person who can document his identity and eligibility for employment in the United States also appears on an OFAC list, or appears there under the same name that he gives to the employer, is slight. However, the most conservative approach

---

[109] *See* 31 C.F.R. ch. V app. A, "Alphabetical Listing of Blocked Persons, Specially Designated Nationals, Specially Designated Terrorists, Specially Designated Global Terrorists, Foreign Terrorist Organizations, and Specially Designated Narcotics Traffickers." An electronic version of the SDN list is available at the Web site cited in note 108.

[110] For example, the Cuban Assets Control Regulations define a "transaction" to include "any payment or transfer to such designated foreign country or national thereof . . . ," a definition that would appear to include salaries or other compensation to employees. 31 C.F.R. §515.309(a). Regulations aimed at other countries and activities may not define the terms "transaction" or "transfer" or may define them differently. *See, e.g.*, Iranian Transactions Regulations, 31 C.F.R. pt. 560.

is to check the lists at the time of hiring and at some appropriate interval thereafter.[111]

10. Disposal of Background Information

Background check reports typically contain highly sensitive information. Employers must take care to appropriately handle and store background check reports so that the reports will be used only for the permissible purpose for which the reports were furnished, such as an initial employment decision.[112] In addition, while an employer has the background information in its possession and when the employer no longer has a need for the information, the employer must protect the information from inadvertent disclosure and properly dispose of it.[113] Given that many background check applications and reports contain an individual's name plus Social Security number or driver's license number, the inadvertent disclosure of the background check applications or reports can trigger the various U.S. state breach notification rules. See Chapter 9 regarding breach notification.

a. Disposal Rules Under Federal Law

Employers must take care when discarding background check reports.[114] In particular, the Disposal Rule, adopted by the FTC under the FCRA, requires businesses to take reasonable measures against the unauthorized disclosure of a background check report when disposing of the report.[115]

---

[111]The application of OFAC screening obligations to foreign subsidiaries of U.S. corporations also varies according to the specific regulatory scheme. *See* 31 C.F.R. §515.329, Cuban Assets Control Regulations, which defines the entities subject to those regulations to include any "corporation, partnership, or association, whether organized or doing business, that is owned or controlled by [U.S. citizens, U.S. residents, and corporations organized under the laws of the United States or any of its states, territories, possessions or district]."

[112]*See generally* 15 U.S.C. §1681b.

[113]If the employer that requests the background check report intends to resell the report or any of its contents, that employer must comply with the FCRA's special requirements for resellers. *See* 15 U.S.C. §1681e(e). These requirements include notifying the agency of the intended end-user of the report and the purposes for which it would be used, as well as obtaining specified certifications from the end-user. *See* 15 U.S.C. §1681e(e)(1)–(2).

[114]15 U.S.C. §1681w.

[115]16 C.F.R. pt. 682. The Disposal Rule became effective on June 1, 2005.

The Disposal Rule regulates the handling of "consumer information," which is generally defined as any record containing information derived from a consumer report.[116] Any person who maintains or otherwise possesses consumer information for a business purpose "must properly dispose of such information by taking reasonable measures to protect against unauthorized access to or use of the information in connection with its disposal."[117]

Reasonable disposal measures include, but are not limited to, the following examples:

1. Implementing and monitoring compliance with policies and procedures that require the burning, pulverizing, or shredding of papers containing consumer information so that the information cannot practicably be read or reconstructed.
2. Implementing and monitoring compliance with policies and procedures that require the destruction or erasure of electronic media containing consumer information so that the information cannot practicably be read or reconstructed.
3. After due diligence, entering into and monitoring compliance with a contract involving another party engaged in the business of record destruction to dispose of material, specifically identified as consumer information, in a manner consistent with this rule. In this context, due diligence could include reviewing an independent audit of the disposal company's operations and its compliance with this rule; obtaining information about the disposal company from several references or other reliable sources; requiring that the disposal company be certified by a recognized trade association or similar third party; reviewing and evaluating the disposal company's information security policies or procedures; or taking other appropriate measures to determine the competency and integrity of the potential disposal company.[118]

---

[116] 16 C.F.R. §682.1(b).
[117] 16 C.F.R. §682.3(a).
[118] 16 C.F.R. §682.3(b).

One of the most difficult types of data to dispose of is data stored electronically. Because the rules relating to pulverizing or shredding apply equally to consumer information stored on hard drives of computers, employers should erase or destroy electronic media so that the information cannot be read or reconstructed.[119]

Even if an employer outsources data disposal services, the employer remains responsible for ensuring that the service provider disposes of this information in accordance with the Disposal Rule.[120]

Practice Pointer. Employers should pay particular attention to background check reports, as well as other types of consumer reports, sent over e-mail to be sure that they are not forwarded to unauthorized sources, and that the reports are deleted from e-mail boxes. Because of the practical difficulties of deleting this information from e-mail boxes, employers may wish to refrain from sending consumer reports via e-mail.

b. Disposal Rules Under State Law

Like the federal Disposal Rule, several state laws require the proper disposal of sensitive personal information. For example, California and Texas have enacted statutes that specifically require a business to implement policies and procedures to properly dispose of customer records containing personal information about an individual.[121] Accordingly, under these state laws, an employer must implement and maintain reasonable procedures to properly dispose of background check records containing personal information.

The Texas law, for example, defines "sensitive personal information" as an individual's name in combination with one or more specified data elements, including a Social Security Number and driver's license number.[122] Employers that obtain background check reports that include an individual's Social Security Number or driver's license number should be mindful that these data elements, if left unredacted or unencrypted, would be covered under

---

[119] 16 C.F.R. §682.3(b)(2).

[120] 16 C.F.R. §682.3(b)(3).

[121] CAL. CIV. CODE §1798.81; TEX. BUS. & COM. CODE ANN. §48.102(b).

[122] TEX. BUS. & COM. CODE ANN. §48.002(2).

the Texas law. As a result, employers must use procedures to protect that information, particularly when disposing of that information. Under the Texas law, a business must "destroy or arrange for the destruction of customer records containing sensitive personal information within the business's custody or control that are not to be retained by the business."[123] In addition, the Texas law specifies three methods of destroying sensitive personal information, namely: "(1) shredding; (2) erasing; or (3) otherwise modifying the sensitive personal information in the records to make the information unreadable or undecipherable through any means."[124]

B. Brazil

1. Background Checks

Brazilian law places nonstatutory restrictions on an employer's ability to seek background checks, including criminal record checks, personal credit checks, or driving record checks. Denial of employment based on information contained in a background check, however, is warranted only if that information suggests the candidate's working capacity, safety, or reliability would be materially impaired. Otherwise, the employer faces liability for discrimination. The candidate must consent to undergo a background check. For example, an offer letter stating that employment is contingent upon the successful completion of a background check, signed by the applicant, would indicate his consent. An applicant who refuses to consent to a medical examination may lawfully be denied employment. The individual right of intimacy guaranteed by the Brazilian Constitution obligates employers to safeguard the confidentiality of all records relating to background checks.[125] On account of the statute of limitations for labor-related actions, employers should retain such records for five years, or for two years after the termination of the employee's employment, whichever is longer.

---

[123]TEX. BUS. & COM. CODE ANN. §48.102(b).

[124]TEX. BUS. & COM. CODE ANN. §48.102(b)(1)–(3).

[125]Brazilian Federal Constitution, Article 5, subsection X.

2. *Responding to Employment Verification Requests*

There are no formal requirements governing procedure or records maintenance policies for employment verification requests. However, obtaining the written consent of the employee who is the subject of the request will minimize the risk of subsequent claims concerning improper dissemination of employee personal information.

C. Canada

1. *Background Checks*

Canadian employers may in some circumstances condition employment upon clearance of a criminal background check or credit check. However, privacy legislation in Quebec, Alberta, and British Columbia requires that such inquiries are reasonable in scope given the nature of the position sought.[126] An employer may request to conduct a background check either before or after an offer is extended. The applicant must complete and sign a consent form before submitting to a criminal background check or credit record check.

An employer may refuse to hire a candidate who fails to consent to a background check. However, in British Columbia and Quebec, refusal to hire an applicant for a criminal background unrelated to the position in question constitutes discrimination. Additionally, it is unlawful for employers in Ontario and Quebec to deny employment based solely on a criminal offense for which a pardon has been granted. Moreover, denying employment to an applicant who refuses to submit to a credit check is permissible only if a credit check is a reasonable request in light of the nature of the vacant position.

---

[126]In Canada, the collection, use, and disclosure of personal information is regulated by the Personal Information and Protection and Electronic Documents Act (PIPEDA). PIPEDA's requirements are supplemented by provincial data protection laws, which may impose greater (but not lesser) obligations. Quebec, Alberta, and British Columbia are among the provinces that have adopted provincial data protection legislation: respectively, Quebec's Act Respecting the Protection of Personal Information in the Private Sector 1993, Alberta's Personal Information Act 2003, and British Columbia's Personal Information Protection Act 2003.

Canadian employers may condition employment upon a satisfactory driving record only where driving is an essential job responsibility. In this case, the applicant must complete a separate consent form that will be provided by the employer to the Ministry of Transportation, unless the prospective employer permits the applicant to obtain and turn over his own driving record personally. In general, failure to consent to a driving record check provides adequate grounds for denying employment. However, a rejected candidate may have recourse through the Privacy Commission in British Columbia, Alberta, or Quebec, or the Human Rights Commission in Ontario, if the driving record check is deemed unnecessary for employment.

In British Columbia, records supporting any employment "decision that directly affects the individual," including those related to background checks, must be retained for a period of at least one year to ensure that the screened individual has a reasonable opportunity to access that information.[127]

2. *Responding to Employment Verification Requests*

An employer may respond to inquiries verifying that an individual is or was an employee, as well as his or her job title, without that individual's consent. However, an individual's written, signed consent is necessary for the disclosure of other job-related personal information, such as the employee's income.

D. Mexico

1. *Background Checks*

Prospective employees may be required to consent to background checks, including inquiries about their criminal background, credit history, and driving records, as a condition of employment. When such consent is not provided, an employer may lawfully refuse to hire an otherwise-qualified applicant. An employer must request background checks of a candidate, if at all, prior to extending an offer of employment. The candidate must furnish consent to undergo a background check. Proof of consent

---

[127] Personal Information Protection Act, Chapter 6, Part 9, Section 35(1).

must be found invalid if it lacks specific language indicating that the candidate agrees to the background check. Records pertaining to employee background checks are highly confidential and must be retained by the employer for a period of at least five years.

2. *Responding to Employment Verification Requests*

Mexican law obligates employers to respond to employment verification requests by providing an employee's termination date, his or her level of seniority, and the terms and conditions of his or her employment. While the employee's consent is required, either verbal or written consent of the employee who is the subject of the request shall be sufficient.

III. EUROPE

Employers who use background checks in the European Union (EU) in order to assess and verify the qualifications of applicants and employees must comply with the local laws applicable in the relevant Member State. Although the general principles are set forth in the Directive 95/46/EC of the European Parliament and of the Council of 24 October 1995 on the protection of individuals with regard to the processing of personal information and on the free movement of such data (Directive),[128] the main legal instrument of EU data protection law, the details are ultimately governed by the laws of the Member States implementing the Directive.

The basic concept is that employers must obtain the employee's consent or another justification (appropriate "legal grounds") to collect, use, or disclose personal information. All Member States define personal information broadly to include any details relating to an identified or identifiable individual. As a result, all information relating to applicants or employees gathered through background checks will qualify as personal information.

Background check reports typically also contain information that would be considered as "sensitive" data (e.g., criminal records, information on the candidate's or employee's health or

[128]Published in the Official Journal on Nov. 23, 1995, L 281/31.

ethnic origin, or data on trade union membership). Sensitive data are subject to particularly strict requirements.

Many Member States have enacted additional regulations on background checks, in particular with respect to the collection of criminal records. Local labor and employment laws impose additional obligations or restraints.

Accordingly, in order to accommodate local differences, the background-checking process may need to be modified from Member State to Member State. (See Exhibit 2.5.) This chapter discusses the principal legal requirements in various EU Member States relating to the use of such background checks. These restrictions apply to reports provided by vendors as well as to employers conducting their own in-house background checks.

EXHIBIT 2.5
EU: Background Checks—United Kingdom, Germany, and France

Subject	UK	Germany	France
Credit	Limited yes	Limited yes	As a general rule no, but limited to justified circumstances
Criminal Records	Limited yes	No, can only ask for certificate of good standing	Can only ask for a criminal record provided by the candidate
Work History	Yes	Yes	Yes
References	Yes	Yes	Professional only
General Reputation/Character	Only in exceptional circumstances	No	No

A. Belgium

1. Background Checks

Employers generally may not conduct criminal background checks or driving record checks on prospective employees because Belgian law strictly limits access to data pertaining to an individual's criminal background, which includes driving records.[129] Specific statutory exceptions to this policy exist, for example, for jobs providing access to classified information. For qualifying exceptions, the scope of the background check is limited to convictions for offenses related to the applicable position. Also, in those cases, employment may be denied if the applicant refuses to submit to a criminal background check.

In Belgium, an applicant's personal credit is widely viewed as irrelevant to his suitability for employment; thus, while technically permissible, it may be problematic for an employer to condition employment upon a favorable credit check. Positions requiring high levels of trust in an employee, however, may warrant an exception.

When an applicant is not hired, any records pertaining to background checks should be destroyed by the employer within a reasonable period of time.

2. *Responding to Employment Verification Requests*

Belgium has no formal legal requirements regarding employment verification requests. However, the requesting party is advised to obtain the employee's written consent to the request.

B. France

1. *Applicable Statutes*

French privacy law restricts employers from inquiring about or considering a number of issues which may not necessarily seem private in nature to employers located in other countries. An employer must take into account the potential impact of the following French laws:

- Article 9 of the French Civil Code, which states that each person is entitled to respect for his/her private life;[130]

---

[129]Belgium's data protection law is the Law of December 8, 1992 on Privacy Protection in relation to the Processing of Personal Data (Loi relative a protection de la vie Privee a legard ees traitements de donnees a caractere personnel).

[130]Article 9 of the French Civil Code.

- Article L. 120-2 of the French Labor Code, which states that no restriction on individual and collective liberties can be imposed unless it is justified by the nature of the task to be accomplished and proportionate to the goal sought to be achieved;[131]
- Article L. 122-45 of the French Labor Code and L. 225-1 of the French Criminal Code,[132] which prohibit, during the recruiting process, questions relating to national or ethnic origin, sex, "morals" (moeurs), sexual orientation, age, family situation, genetic characteristics, ethnic group, nationality, race, political opinions, labor union activities, religious beliefs, physical appearance, state of health, handicap, or pregnancy;[133] and
- The French Data Protection Bill: Act No. 78-17 of 6 January 1978 on data processing, data files, and individual liberties.[134]

The French Data Protection Authority's (hereinafter the CNIL) recommendation regarding the collection and the processing of personal information in recruitment procedures gives precise indications as to what data may be collected.[135]

2. *General Requirements*

In summary, an employer can seek information related only to the applicant's ability to perform a particular position and the information requested from the applicant must have a direct and necessary connection with the candidate's professional skills or the requirements for the job.[136] Recruitment tests or interviews are lawful only if:

---

[131]Code du Travail, Article L. 120-2.

[132]Code Pénal, Article L. 225-1.

[133]Code du Travail, Article L. 122-45.

[134]French Data Protection Act No. 87-17 of 6 January 1978.

[135]Délibération n°02/017 du 21 mars 2002 portant adoption d'une recommendation relative à la collecte et au traitement d'informations nominatives lors d'opérations de recrutement.

[136]Article L. 121-6 of the French Labor Code.

- An applicant is informed beforehand;
- The results are not disclosed to third parties;
- The recruitment method or recruitment test is relevant to the job and reliable;[137] and
- The Works Council has been informed prior to the implementation of the recruiting method, including testing.[138]

3. *Sensitive Data*

"Sensitive" data (such as medical information, union membership, nationality of origin, date of entry into France, and ethnicity) may be collected only with the individual's explicit consent, and the applicant must be notified of the information to be checked or supplemented as well as the references or agencies that are asked to provide the information. Further, according to the CNIL's recommendation,[139] this sensitive personal information may be collected only if justified by the nature of the job or if there are specific legal requirements to collect this information in a foreign country.

4. *Notice Requirements*

According to Article 6 of the French Data Protection Bill,[140] illicit or fraudulent collection of personal information is prohibited. Therefore, the candidate will need to be expressly, fully, and directly informed of any data that are collected, and the purpose of the collection prior to this collection. According to Article 32 of this Bill, the candidates will need to be informed as to whether answering certain questions is mandatory, whether there could be consequences if they were not to answer these questions, the identity of persons or companies who will have access to this information, and their right of access and correction to the data.

---

[137] Article L. 121-7 of the French Labor Code.

[138] Article L. 432-2-1 of the French Labor Code.

[139] Délibération n°02/017 du 21 mars 2002 portant adoption d'une recommendation relative à la collecte et au traitement d'informations nominatives lors d'opérations de recrutement.

[140] Article 6 of the French Data Protection Bill.

5. *Access and Correction*

Every candidate must be able to access his or her personal data that have been collected in the course of a recruitment process.[141] The candidate must be adequately informed about the modalities of his or her access right in order to be able to obtain any information upon request, including any recruitment test or analysis results that the candidate took. This access right applies to information given by the candidate, given by third parties, and obtained through recruitment tests and analysis results. The CNIL recommends that this information should be provided in writing to the candidate.

6. *Use Restrictions*

The French Data Protection Bill[142] prohibits a recruiter from selecting a candidate purely on results of automatic processing of data intended to define the profile of the candidate or to assess some aspects of his personality. Hence, an application should never be rejected by an employer on the sole grounds of an automatic processing. An employer also will have to humanely judge the candidate.

In application of Article 34 of the French Data Protection Bill, the persons in charge of the recruitment process need to assure the candidate that all security and confidentiality measures have been taken regarding the candidate's personal information. This confidentiality obligation prohibits third parties to the procedure to have direct or indirect access to this information.

Practice Pointer. In practice, employers must inform the candidate that his personal information will be collected and the purpose of this collection. However, the law does not impose a specific form of notice. The only obligation is that the candidate should know which information is being collected and the objective of the collection. The candidate should, for example, be able to determine whether the employer is seeking certain personal

[141] Article 39 of the French Data Protection Bill and Article L. 121-7 of the French Labor Code.

[142] Article 10 §2 of the French Data Protection Bill.

information beyond the information that is usually necessary for a recruitment procedure.

7. *Guidance on Specific Background Checks*

a. Credit

Employers or recruitment agencies are prohibited from asking about financial/credit history if this has no connection with an applicant's ability to carry out the tasks relating to a position. Under French law, asking for such information would be considered a violation of the applicant's privacy rights. There is, however, an exception to this rule, namely, when an employer recruits for a specific job that necessitates the collection of this particular information and the employer obtains the candidate's prior consent. In practice, it can be difficult for an employer to justify getting this information, and the candidate should be fully informed of the purpose of the collection of such personal information.

b. Criminal Records

Employers may not ask about the applicant's criminal record unless the employer can establish that information on a criminal background is required for the specific job.[143] A criminal background check may be considered relevant for certain regulated jobs or jobs in the banking, auditing, or defense sectors. An applicant is not obligated to volunteer information relating to his criminal record to a potential employer. However, certain employers in the foregoing sectors may ask for previous criminal records that the candidate can provide after consenting to it. The candidate will then be the one providing the employer with a copy of his criminal record.

c. Work History

Generally, it is permissible for employers to confirm information on the candidate's work history. Background checks in France, in practice, are done by the company that is recruiting or by the

---

[143]Délibération n°02/017 du 21 mars 2002 portant adoption d'une recommendation relative à la collecte et au traitement d'informations nominatives lors d'opérations de recrutement.

recruitment agency acting on behalf of the recruiting company. The candidate must, prior to his work history being investigated, provide reference contacts. The candidate must always be informed that the recruiting company will contact previous employers or colleagues; it would be considered a breach of privacy if the candidate were not informed of these practices by recruiters.

d. References

According to French jurisprudence and guidance given by the French Data Protection Authority,[144] professional references are authorized if the candidate has given his consent or has been informed of this procedure. Further, collection of "personal" references that go beyond the scope of previous employers, colleagues, clients, or suppliers, in view of carrying out a "morality investigation" of the candidate, are illegal.

e. General Reputation/Character

The French Labor Code, along with the recommendations and decisions of the French Data Protection Authority, prohibit discrimination in recruitment procedures. Discrimination on the grounds of sex, family situation, or pregnancy is prohibited by Article L.123-1 of the French Labor Code and discrimination on the grounds of age, race, political opinions, union membership, and religious beliefs is also prohibited by the French Labor and Criminal Codes. Any questions about general reputation and character insofar as they relate to such matters could lead to claims of unlawful discrimination if this information is collected without the consent of the candidate or if it is unjustifiably collected.

C. Germany

1. Applicable Statutes

In Germany, any collection of personal information is subject to the restrictions imposed by a number of different statutes, in particular the following:

---

[144]The French Data Protection Guide to Employers (*Les Guides de la CNIL: Guide pratique pour les employeurs*).

- The Federal Data Protection Act;[145]
- The Central Registry Act;[146]
- The Criminal Procedure Code;[147]
- Section 611 et seq. of the Civil Code;[148]
- The General Act on Equal Treatment;[149] and
- Articles 1 and 9 of the Basic Act.[150]

2. *General Requirements*

The primary purpose of the law governing background checks in Germany, the Federal Data Protection Act (BDSG), is to ensure, among other things, that personal information is collected directly from the applicant or employee rather than from third parties such as third-party vendors, consumer-reporting agencies, former employers, referees, the courts, or the Internet. The BDSG permits the collection of information via third parties only where the "nature of the business purpose" necessitates the collection from third parties and there is "no overriding legitimate interest" of the individual to whom the data relate to.[151] In other words, employers may seek information from third parties only where the particular position requires certain information to be confirmed and supplemented through background checks. Commentary suggests that background checks are permitted only where the trustworthiness of an applicant or employee is particularly relevant, such as for positions in financial services institutions, for positions involving child care, or where certain qualifications are essential for the employment decision.[152]

---

[145]Bundesdatenschutzgesetz (BDSG), as amended on May 18, 2001.

[146]Gesetz über das Zentralregister und das Erziehungsregister, as amended on December 17, 2006.

[147]Strafprozessordnung, as amended on December 17, 2006.

[148]Bürgerliches Gesetzbuch, as amended January 1, 2002.

[149]Allgemeines Gleichbehandlungsgesetz, as amended on December 12, 2006.

[150]Grundgesetz, adopted on May 23, 1949, and amended on March 19, 2009.

[151]BDSG §4(2). The BDSG also allows the collection of personal information from third-party sources where expressly required by statute, or where the collection from the individual would involve unreasonable efforts. These provisions do not apply to background checks effected by employers other than security agencies or public sector employers.

[152]Gola/Wronka: *Handbuch zum Arbeitnehmerdatenschutz*, Rdn. 221.

In addition, all inquiries have to be approved via the written consent of the individual concerned, unless the employer obtains another justification (appropriate legal grounds). Legal grounds that may alleviate the need for obtaining consent for background checks are as follows:

- Information may be collected and confirmed if required in order to comply with (German) statutory obligations.[153] As a result, financial institutions, security agencies, and public sector employers are allowed to inquire into prior convictions relevant for specific duties and responsibilities related to the employment without prior consent as there are statutory obligations to confirm the trustworthiness of their personnel.
- The collection of information is allowed where it is in the "legitimate interests of the data controller or third parties collecting (or using) the data and there is no overriding privacy interest of the candidate."[154] In other words, information also may be collected when required to preserve the justified interests of the employer and there is no reason to assume that "protection-worthy" privacy interests of the individual override the employer's interests. The exact scope of this provision is unclear, and to date there is no case law clarifying the types of information that may be collected if there is a legitimate interest of the employer. However, commentary states that only information directly relevant for the employment relationship may be collected based on this legal ground.
- The collection and use of information from the Internet or other public sources may be justified if there are no overriding privacy interests of the (prospective) employee.[155] Note, however, that it is not permissible to transfer and share the information with another party; for example, a third-party vendor may not transmit the details to the (prospective) employer, and it is not permissible to share the information

---

[153] BDSG §4.
[154] BDSG §§28(1)2 & 29(1)1.
[155] BDSG §§28(1)3 & 29(1)2.

with corporate affiliates. Therefore, the practical application of this provision is limited.

- The creation of in-house reports may be justified by contractual necessity;[156] that is, personal information may be collected if necessary for the performance of the labor contract. For example, employers may collect information about the professional qualifications required for the position. Verification of that information through third parties is permitted only if so required.

In light of the narrow scope of these legal grounds and the uncertainties in interpreting them, most employers will therefore need to obtain consent when performing background checks. Consent has to be explicit (i.e., opt-in) and in writing, meaning pen on paper or via qualified electronic signature. Verbal consent over the phone or by ticking a box online, although common practice, does not suffice. Also, the consent form must be a stand-alone document, rather than part of another document. A consent that is included in the same document used as an employment application, for example, would not satisfy the consent requirement under the BDSG.[157] In addition, consent must be given voluntarily, which implies that employers may not put pressure on applicants or employees to provide consent.

3. Sensitive Data

"Sensitive" data contained in background checks (such as medical information, union membership, or ethnicity) may be collected only with the individual's specific consent, and the applicant must be notified of the information to be checked or supplemented as well as the references or agencies that are asked to provide the information.

Also, employers are prohibited from using medical information unless directly relevant for the position; for example, certain allergies or disabilities that may impede the applicant from performing his duties of employment.[158] There is dispute as to

---

[156]BDSG §28(1)1.

[157]BDSG §3a.

[158]Gola/Wronka: *Handbuch zum Arbeitnehmerdatenschutz*, Rdn. 213.

whether human immunodeficiency virus (HIV) infection may be tested and verified. Guidance suggests that HIV infection may be tested only for personnel in the health sector (e.g., nurses, doctors), where the infection otherwise impedes the (prospective) employee's abilities to perform his work duties, or where there is a general risk of infecting co-workers or customers (e.g., for personnel at food manufacturers).[159]

4. *Notice Requirements*

In addition, candidates must be provided with fair and accurate information about the information included in the report, the purposes for which the data are used, the names of all recipients (other than data processing agents), the source of the information, and the individual's right to access and correct the data. Also, prospective employees must be informed about the fact that service providers may collect, access, or use the information.

5. *Access and Correction Rights*

Applicants or employees may request access to the information collected and may dispute the accuracy of information contained in the report. The employer then must correct this information. More detailed information on access to personnel files and correction rights is contained in Chapter 7.

6. *Use Restrictions*

Employers should also be aware that certain questions and the way in which such questions are asked or such checks are conducted could infringe labor law obligations or the General Act on Equal Treatment (AGG). For example, it is generally not permitted to ask applicants for information on sexual orientation, and if the interviewer does, the applicant has the right to lie. Background checks may therefore not be performed in order to verify this information.

Even when employers are able to justify the carrying out of background checks, employers must be careful not to use background checks to discriminate. The AGG applies to the recruit-

---

[159]Richardi NZA 1988, 75.

ment process and may be infringed by certain types of background checks or the way in which such checks are conducted. In particular, any discrimination for age, gender, religion, union membership, disabilities, and sexual preferences is prohibited, and information collected on these items may not be used. Also, if an employer asks questions that suggest a tendency to discriminate (e.g., whether a female candidate was pregnant), an employment tribunal could infer that discrimination has occurred.

Practice Pointer. Background checks to supplement information available from a candidate's resume and interview are not very common in Germany. There are severe restrictions on the scope of information to be obtained in order to protect the individual's privacy and right of self-determination. If employers do create or obtain background check reports, they should provide detailed information on the background check, and ensure the applicant's cooperation in the process.

7. *Guidance on Specific Background Checks*

a. Credit

Although credit data are not regarded as sensitive data per se, financial institutions are generally not permitted under the BDSG to share information on an individual's creditworthiness or credit standing with employers or third-party vendors. In order to facilitate credit decisions by financial institutions, SCHUFA, a private organization, has been established and hosts a database to facilitate the sharing of credit data. Financial institutions associated with SCHUFA provide credit data to the system, update the data, and receive data in return. Although employers or third-party vendors are not permitted to access the information contained in the SCHUFA database, employers or third-party vendors may ask candidates to provide a self-declaration (*Eigenauskunft*) authorized by SCHUFA. The candidate is able to request a certificate from SCHUFA, and SCHUFA then prepares a standard report, which can be provided to the potential employer.

Again, this is permissible only if such information is relevant for the position for which the applicant is applying, where the trustworthiness and reliability in financial matters is of particular importance (personnel working in the banking and financial services sectors, accountants, etc.).[160] Also, the content of the SCHUFA self-declaration is highly regulated, and contains only "hard" credit-standing data, such as the opening of a bankruptcy proceeding or the affidavit of the debtor.

Credit scoring, meaning the generation of a score value from a database containing credit history and other relevant information by using mathematical and statistical procedures, is generally not permitted under the BDSG.

Practice Pointer. Employers should exercise caution in requesting information on credit standing, etc. When required for the employment relationship in question, employers may ask the applicant to provide a SCHUFA self-declaration.

b. Criminal Records

Employers can ask applicants to list any convictions that they may have on their application form. However, employers should request information about an applicant's criminal convictions only if that information can be justified in terms of the role offered (e.g., the previous conviction of an accountant for fraud, a driver for a road traffic offense, or a teacher for a sexual offense involving children). For most positions, employers are not entitled to ask whether an applicant has a criminal record.

However, employers may inquire if the applicant is likely to be sentenced to imprisonment to the extent the investigations or the imprisonment prevent the applicant from taking up the position for which he or she is applying.

Even where the employer is permitted to require information on criminal convictions, background checks in order to verify records are virtually impossible in Germany. Law enforcement agencies or courts are generally prohibited from sharing such information with employers or third-party vendors.[161] Rather, the

---

[160] Gola/Wronka: *Handbuch zum Arbeitnehmerdatenschutz*, Rdn. 216.

[161] Courts may, however, provide access to current records on criminal convictions if a legitimate interest is evidenced in writing by the employer or third-party vendor, and there is no overriding privacy interest of the individual concerned. *See* §475 of the Criminal Procedure Code (StPO). Commentary suggests that the provision must be interpreted narrowly, and generally, only permitted attorneys or insurance providers have access to the information. Note, however, that courts are obliged to transfer the information to the Central Registry in due course after the closure of the case, and must delete the information thereafter.

information is governed by the Central Registry Act (ZRG). It is contained in the Central Registry held by public authorities, and may be provided only to public entities.

Applicants may, however, be asked to provide a certificate of good standing to be issued by the Registry Office (*Führungszeugnis*).[162] This certificate will not contain all convictions, as there are strict rules on what may or may not be contained in the Central Registry. In general, there is no information about the following:

- Criminal convictions more than five years old;
- Criminal convictions resulting in imprisonment not exceeding a term of three months or penalties not exceeding the amount equivalent to 90 days' income (unless there are no other entries in the Central Registry);
- Criminal convictions resulting in imprisonment not exceeding two years when on provisional discharge for certain drug-related crimes (unless there are no other entries in the Central Registry);
- Imprisonment or detention of a young offender (i.e., younger than 21 years);
- Information about arrests or indictments that did not result in a conviction; and
- Civil suits, civil judgments.

Practice Pointer. Employers should exercise caution in making employment decisions based on the contents of a background check report.

c. Work History

Generally, it is permissible for employers to confirm information on the candidate's employment history. It is not permissible to inquire into the applicant's previous salary unless the candidate has revealed the figures and used the information to negotiate his new salary.

---

[162]ZRG §30. Note that the employer's right to ask for the certificate (which contains any convictions, including convictions not relevant for particular positions) is not undisputed, but generally accepted.

d. References

It is generally permissible to contact an applicant's references when prior consent is obtained.

e. General Reputation/Character

Checking an applicant's character and general reputation is generally not permitted as this information is considered irrelevant for employment decisions.

D. Italy

1. Background Checks

In Italy, criminal background checks may be imposed as a pre-employment condition only if such information is related to the position in question.[163] Checks of a candidate's driving record are allowed only if driving is a primary job responsibility, and personal credit checks of prospective employees generally are not permitted.

Inquiries into a candidate's criminal and driving records must be requested in advance of an offer of employment. An employer may deny employment based on refusal to consent to a background check when the information sought is relevant to the applicant's qualifications for a position. Similarly, employment may be denied based on the information provided in a criminal background check, insofar as the conviction or record is relevant to the job responsibilities of the position in question. Access to records relating to background checks must be limited to interested parties and employees responsible for maintaining such records. There is no requirement to retain these records.

---

[163]In Italy, the processing of sensitive data by employers is regulated by the Authorisation no. 1/2005 Concerning Processing of Sensitive Data in the Employment Context (Authorizzazione n. 1/2005 al trattamento dei dati sensibili nei rapporti di lavoro – 21 dicembre 2005).

2. *Responding to Employment Verification Requests*

While Italian law does not restrict the scope of or procedures for employment verification requests, the express, written authorization of the employee is advised.

E. United Kingdom[164]

1. *Applicable Statutes*

The legal rules that restrict an employer's freedom to conduct background checks are not contained in one statute. Rather, an employer must take into account the potential impact of a number of different laws, including:

- Data Protection Act 1998;[165]
- Human Rights Act 1998;[166]
- Rehabilitation of Offenders Act 1974;[167]
- Sex Discrimination Act 1975;[168]
- Race Relations Act 1976;[169]
- Disability Discrimination Act 1995;[170]
- Employment Equality (Sexual Orientation) Regulations 2003;[171]
- Employment Equality (Religion or Belief) Regulations 2003;[172] and
- Employment Equality (Age) Regulations 2006.[173] (Discrimination Legislation)

---

[164]The laws listed apply to England and Wales. The applicable laws in Northern Ireland and Scotland differ in some respects.

[165]1998 c29.

[166]1998 c42.

[167]1974 c53.

[168]1975 c65.

[169]1976 c74.

[170]1995 c50.

[171]SI 2003/1661.

[172]SI 2003/1660.

[173]SI 2006/1031.

2. *General Requirements*

The Human Rights Act (HRA) requires courts in the United Kingdom (UK) to take account of the judgments of the European Court of Human Rights and the European Commission of Human Rights in deciding issues concerning the Convention and, if possible, to interpret legislation in a manner compatible with the Convention.

Article 8 of the HRA protects respect for private life and may therefore affect an employer's ability to conduct background checks. However, the right to respect for private life is not absolute and interference with that right is allowed if "in accordance with the law and . . . necessary in a democratic society in the interests of national security, public safety or the economic well-being of the country, for the prevention of disorder or crime, for the protection of health or morals, or for the protection of the rights and freedoms of others."

Accordingly, an employer may be able to justify conducting background checks that collect information about a (prospective) employee's private life.

In addition, if an employer collects personal information about a (prospective) employee that has the person as its focus or is otherwise biographical in nature, and if the data are either in electronic form or in "a relevant filing system" (i.e., manual information that is part of a structured manual system), the employer must comply with the Data Protection Act 1998 (DPA).

The Information Commissioner (the United Kingdom's Data Protection Authority) has published two very user-friendly documents that give employers helpful guidance on how to comply with the DPA when conducting background checks: the Employment Practices Code (Code) and the Employment Practices Code Supplementary Guidance (Supplementary Guidance).

As a general comment, under the Code, background checks are divided into two categories: "verification" and "vetting." Verification is the process of checking whether details supplied by applicants are accurate and complete. Vetting is more intrusive and involves actively making enquiries with third parties as to an applicant's background and circumstances. As it is less intrusive to obtain relevant information directly from the applicant and to then verify it than it is to obtain information about the applicant directly from third parties, the Code recommends that the former approach should be adopted wherever practicable.

The Code and Supplementary Guidance give both general guidance and specific advice on certain forms of background checks. The general guidance is summarized immediately below and the specific guidance on particular background checks follow in Section 2.III.E.7.

In summary, the Code advises employers to:

- Use vetting only where there are particular and significant risks involved for the employer, clients, customers, or others, and where there is no less intrusive and reasonably practicable alternative;
- Carry out pre-employment vetting on an applicant at as late a stage as is practicable in the recruitment process;
- Make it clear early in the recruitment process that vetting will take place and how it will be conducted;
- Use vetting only as a means of obtaining specific information, not as a means of general intelligence gathering;
- Seek information only from sources where it is likely that relevant information will be revealed and approach the applicant's family or close associates only in exceptional cases;
- Not rely on information collected from possibly unreliable sources and allow the applicant to make representations regarding information that will affect the decision to finally appoint;
- Ensure, as much as practicable, that affected parties are informed when information is collected about a person other than the applicant that affects that other person's privacy;
- Obtain a signed consent from the applicant if it is necessary to secure the release of documents or information from a third party; and
- Destroy information obtained by a vetting exercise as soon as possible or in any case within six months, although a record of the result of vetting or verification may be retained.

The Supplementary Guidance recommends that employers as a general rule do not routinely vet all applicants and do not subject all short-listed applicants to more than basic written checks and the taking up of references. Checks should be proportionate to the risks faced by an employer and be likely to reveal information that would have a significant bearing on the employment decision. The risks are likely to involve aspects of the security of the employer or of others. They could range from the risk of breaches of national security, or the risk of employing unsuitable individuals to work with children through to the risk of theft or the disclosure of trade secrets or other commercially confidential information. Sometimes a customer for a supplier's products or services may seek to impose a condition requiring the supplier to carry out pre-employment vetting of its prospective employees. For example, a contractor working in a defense establishment may be required to vet prospective employees taken on to work on the relevant contract. If this vetting involves processing personal information about the prospective employees, it will not be justified simply because it is a condition of business. Such a condition cannot override the employer's obligation to comply with the Act. Vetting of prospective employees by the supplier or contractor must be based on the outcome of its own assessment, although this does not stop the supplier or contractor being guided by any assessment for its products or services that the customer might have undertaken for himself.

Accordingly, regarding vetting, the Code advises employers to:

- Find out for which jobs, if any, pre-employment vetting takes place;
- Consider whether pre-employment vetting is justified for each of these jobs and whether the information could be obtained in a less intrusive way;
- Obtain relevant information directly from the applicant wherever practicable and, if necessary, verify it rather than undertake pre-employment vetting; and
- Not vet prospective employees just because a customer imposes a condition requiring the employer to do so unless it can satisfy itself that the condition is justified.

When determining how to carry out pre-employment vetting on an applicant at as late a stage as is practicable in the recruitment process, the Code recommends that employers:

- Ascertain at which point pre-employment vetting takes place and who is subject to it;
- Eliminate any comprehensive pre-employment vetting that takes place for all short-listed applicants (only the people selected for the job should be submitted to comprehensive pre-employment vetting);
- Make it clear early in the recruitment process that vetting will take place and explain how it will be conducted;
- Provide information about any vetting that might take place on application forms or other recruitment material. This should explain the nature, extent, and range of sources to be used to carry out the vetting; and
- Make clear the extent to which information about the applicant will be released to the sources the employer uses.

To ensure that vetting is used only as a means of obtaining specific information, not as a means of general intelligence gathering, the Code advises employers to:

- Ensure that the extent and nature of information sought is justified;
- Ensure that there are clearly stated objectives in any vetting process;
- Consider the extent and nature of information that is sought in light of these objectives; and
- Eliminate any vetting that consists of general intelligence gathering and ensure that they seek only clearly focused information that will have a significant bearing on the employment decision.

The Supplementary Guidance advises employers to use all reasonable means to ensure that any external sources used as part of the vetting process are reliable. Where the vetting results in the recording of adverse information about an applicant, the applicant should be made aware of this and should be given the opportunity to represent himself, either in writing or face to face. The Code further advises employers to:

- Ensure that information that has been collected from a vetting process is evaluated in the light of the reliability of the sources;
- Ensure that no recruitment decision is made solely on the basis of information obtained from a source that may be unreliable; and
- Put in place a mechanism for the applicant to provide feedback, allowing them to respond and obliging those involved in the recruitment decision to take this response into account.

To ensure the destruction of information obtained by a vetting exercise as soon as possible, or in any case within six months, the Code advises employers to:

- Check who retains information from vetting and ensure that vetting records are destroyed after six months. Manual records should be shredded and electronic files permanently deleted from the system; and
- Inform those responsible for the destruction of this information that they may keep a record that vetting was carried out, the result, and the recruitment decision taken.

3. Sensitive Data

The Code also requires an employer that is collecting sensitive personal information to establish that the benefits gained from the processing justify the privacy intrusion or any other adverse impact on the employee and recommends impact assessments as a tool for determining and documenting that the collection and processing of such data is justified. The impact assessment needs to consider the purpose of the processing; any adverse impact from collecting the information; what alternatives are available; the obligations that arise; and whether the collection is justified.

4. *Notice Requirements*

In addition, the employer will need to comply with the "fair processing code." Personal data will not be treated as processed fairly unless an employer provides the applicant or employee with its identity or the identity of any contractor to which the employer has outsourced its human resources management or the background check process, the purpose for which the data is used, and any further information that is necessary in all the circumstances to enable the processing to be fair such as the length of time that the data will be held. This information does not actually need to be set out in writing and given to the applicants or employees, but considering that not all applicants or employees will have ready access to the company notice board or the intranet, it is best to have a separate notice that forms part of the wider hiring or promotion process documents.

5. *Access and Correction*

Applicants or employees may request access and correction of the information collected. More detailed information on access and correction rights is contained in Chapter 7.

6. *Use Restrictions*

Although an employer may be able to justify the conducting of background checks, employers must be careful not to use background checks to discriminate. The Discrimination Legislation applies to the recruitment process and may be infringed by certain types of background checks or the way in which such checks are conducted. For example, checking criminal records of applicants of only certain nationalities will constitute direct race discrimination. Also, if an employer asks questions that suggest a tendency to discriminate, an employment tribunal could infer that discrimination has occurred. For example, an employer should avoid asking female candidates only who will look after their children while they are at work.

Practice Pointer. It is common to conduct some background checks for most types of employment in the UK. The types of checks conducted will depend on the nature of the position but, at a minimum, references from previous employers will usually be taken.

7. Guidance on Specific Background Checks

a. Credit

Background credit checks are common for certain types and levels of jobs. However, they should not be used as a means of general intelligence gathering about a prospective employee's finances; rather, they should be used to obtain specific information such as whether the prospective employee has any County Court judgments against him, if such information is relevant to the position. Accordingly, any limits on the credit checks that can be conducted are usually dictated by the type and levels of the jobs rather than to specific legislation.

b. Criminal Records

Employers can (and sometimes do) ask applicants to list any convictions that they may have on their application form. However, employers should request information about an applicant's criminal convictions only if that information can be justified in terms of the role offered. Even if the collection of the information is justified, the employer must make clear that "spent" convictions do not have to be declared, unless the job being filled is covered by the Exceptions Order.[174]

Under the Rehabilitation of Offenders Act 1974, it is illegal for an employer to discriminate against an ex-offender on the grounds of a "spent" conviction (i.e., a conviction that no longer has to be legally disclosed), unless the position for which the ex-offender is applying is exempt by law.[175] Exempt posts include posts involving contact with children and vulnerable adults, some professionals, those working in the banking and financial services sectors, and

---

[174]*See* Rehabilitation of Offenders Act 1974 (Exceptions) Order 1975, SI 1975/1023.

[175]*Id.*

law enforcers (judges, police officers, and traffic wardens). Most convictions become spent after the lapse of a period of time, as set out in Exhibit 2.6.

EXHIBIT 2.6.
UK "Spent Conviction" Time Periods

Sentence	*Rehabilitation Period*
Imprisonment, custody, or detention for life or detention at her Majesty's pleasure	Never
Imprisonment, youth custody, detention in a young offender institution, or corrective training for a term exceeding 30 months	Never
Imprisonment, youth custody, detention in a young offender institution, or corrective training for between 6 and 30 months	10 years/5 years (if under 18 when convicted)
Imprisonment or youth custody for 6 months or less	7 years/3 years (if under 18 when convicted)
Probation (for convictions on/after February 3, 1995), fines	5 years/2 years (if under 18 when convicted)
Probation (for convictions before February 3, 1995), conditional discharge, binding over, care or supervision order	1 year or the duration of the order/bond, if longer
Absolute discharge	6 months
Disqualification from driving	Period of disqualification

A person whose conviction is "spent" must be treated as a person who has not committed or been charged with or convicted of the offense in question and must not be prejudiced in any way by virtue of that conviction or its nondisclosure. Accordingly, a spent conviction, or the failure to disclose such a conviction, is not a ground for rejecting an applicant.

Furthermore, the information requested should be relevant to the job being filled and should be limited to only what is actually needed, such as, "Do you have any criminal convictions in the last five years involving dishonesty?" Information regarding convictions is sensitive personal information[176] and, as such, unless such

[176] *See* §2 of the DPA.

information is required by law, an employer will need a prospective employee's consent to collect such information.

An employer can verify any information on criminal convictions volunteered by an applicant through the Criminal Records Bureau (CRB). The function of the CRB is to issue "disclosures," of which there are three different levels: basic disclosure, standard disclosure, and enhanced disclosure.

Basic disclosure covers information relating to convictions held on the National Police Computer, other than "spent" convictions. Basic disclosure is not yet currently available. However, when it does become available, it will be issued on request only to individuals, subject to confirmation of identity.

Standard disclosure and enhanced disclosure make information available for a fee directly to recruiting employers and provide a greater level of detail. They are issued to the individual and the employer (or employer's organization) making the application (who must be registered and have signed up to the CRB Code). However, they can be obtained in respect to only a certain, limited number of roles (e.g., positions of trust and positions where an individual is working with children or providing care to vulnerable adults). Standard disclosure contains details of "spent" and unspent convictions, as well as cautions, reprimands, and final warnings held on central police records. Enhanced disclosure, applying to posts involving significant contact with children or vulnerable adults, contains the same information as standard disclosure together with information from local police records if relevant.

c. Work History

It is common for an employer to request, and a prospective employee to provide, such information that can then be verified by the employer.

d. References

It is very common for references to be taken, and employers may check them by directly contacting the referee. Employment is regularly made conditional on receipt of satisfactory references. Regarding securing the release of documents or information from a third party, the Code advises employers to obtain a signed consent from the applicant and points out that if an employer is asking a previous employer to disclose confidential personal information, the third party will need the applicant's permission before doing so and it may be easier for the employer to obtain this permission from the applicant and pass it on to the third party than for the third party to obtain permission directly.

e. General Reputation/Character

This sort of check could be highly intrusive and should be limited to occasions in which there are particular and significant risks. Such checks therefore should be conducted only in limited circumstances. The Code recommends that employers:

- Ensure that those who will seek the information are briefed about which sources to use, ensuring that those sources are likely to produce relevant information;
- Ensure that if family members or close associates are approached it can be justified by the special nature of the job; and
- Approach the applicant's family or close associates only in exceptional cases.

If information is collected about a person other than the applicant that affects the other person's privacy, to ensure as much as practicable that the other person is made aware of this, the Code recommends that employers:

- Ensure that those conducting a vetting process are briefed to avoid discovering information about other people unnecessarily; and
- Ensure there is a process in place to inform the other person of this and how the information will be used if substantial personal information has been collected about another person and is to be retained.

The Supplementary Guidance points out that it is only in exceptional cases that an employer might be justified in collecting information about members of the family or close associates of the applicant. This is most likely to arise in connection with the recruitment of police or prison officers. When information about a third party (e.g., an applicant's partner) that affects the third party's privacy is to be recorded, the collection must be fair and lawful in respect to the third party. An employer will not be obliged to inform third parties that information about them has been obtained and of the purposes for which it will be processed, if it would not be practicable to do so or would involve disproportionate effort, for example, if the employer does not have contact details for the third party or the information will be kept in an identifiable form for only a very short period.

IV. ASIA

A. China

1. Background Checks Generally

There are no specific statutory limitations under Chinese law regarding background checks on job applicants. Under the PRC Labor Law, an applicant's misrepresentation on an employment application is grounds for immediate termination of the employment relationship.[177]

Employers will typically ask employees to answer pre-employment questionnaires. Although personnel at a foreign-invested enterprise are not permitted to view a PRC government-maintained personnel file, they are permitted to make inquiries to the organization maintaining the employee's personnel file to seek confirmation of information contained in that file.[178]

When an employer seeks to collect personal information from a credit agency, this must be done with the consent of the individual.[179]

---

[177]PRC Labor Law, Art. 18; Labor Contract Law, Art. 26; Regulation on the Implementation of the Employment Contract Law, Art. 19.

[178]Law of the People's Republic of China Governing Personnel Files, Law of the People's Republic of China for Maintenance of Confidentiality, and Regulations for the Administration of Personnel Files of Enterprise Employees.

[179]The Administrative Measures of Shanghai Municipality on Personal Credit Information Collecting (for Trial Implementation), Art. 14; Shenzhen City, Administration of Personal Credit Information Collection and Credit Rating Procedures, Art. 12.

2. *Guidance on Specific Background Checks in China*

a. Credit

An employer must obtain consent from an employee in order to obtain credit data.

b. Criminal Records

Criminal records are not available in China for background checks.

c. Work History

It is common for an employer to request, and a prospective employee to provide, such information, which can then be verified by the employer.

B. Hong Kong

1. *Applicable Laws*

When assessing its freedom to conduct background checks in Hong Kong, an employer must take into account the potential impact of a number of different statutes, including:

- Personal Data (Privacy) Ordinance[180] (the PDPO)
- Rehabilitation of Offenders Ordinance[181]
- Disability Discrimination Ordinance[182]
- Sex Discrimination Ordinance[183]
- Family Status Discrimination Ordinance[184]

The Hong Kong Privacy Commissioner has issued a Code of Practice on Human Resource Management (the HR Code), which seeks to provide more detailed guidance to complement the high-level data privacy principles set out in the PDPO.

---

[180]Cap. 486, Laws of Hong Kong.
[181]Cap. 297, Laws of Hong Kong.
[182]Cap. 487, Laws of Hong Kong.
[183]Cap. 480, Laws of Hong Kong.
[184]Cap. 527, Laws of Hong Kong.

It should be noted that the provisions of the HR Code are not legally binding. A breach of the HR Code by a data user, however, will give rise to a presumption against the data user in any legal proceedings under the PDPO.

2. General Requirements—Employment Candidates

The general principle is that an employer can compile information about a job candidate from other sources such as background checks to supplement data provided by the candidate in order to assess the suitability of the candidate for the job, provided that:

- On or before the collection of any personal data, the employer should notify the candidate of (i) the purpose for which the data are to be used; (ii) the classes of persons to whom the data may be transferred; (iii) whether it is obligatory or voluntary to supply the data; and (iv) the candidate's right to request access and corrections to personal data held. This is typically effected by means of a Personal Information Collection Statement (PICS).[185] As a matter of good practice the employer also should inform the candidate of the background check's relevance to the selection process and the types of personal data that will be collected.
- The purpose for which the data are to be used is lawful. It would be unlawful to discriminate against a candidate on the grounds of disability, family status, sex, marital status, and pregnancy (unless such a certain status is a genuine occupational qualification for the job).[186]
- The employer does not collect personal data that are excessive in relation to the purpose of recruitment.[187] Rather, the employer should collect only that data that the employer can demonstrate are directly relevant to the identification of suitable candidates, such as information on the candidate's

---

[185] *See* Chapter 1.
[186] Data Protection Principles (DPP), Schedule 1 of PDPO, 1(a).
[187] Data Protection Principles (DPP), Schedule 1 of PDPO, 4(d).

skills, good character, competencies, or abilities related to the nature of the job in question.[188]

Personal data regarding unsuccessful candidates should not be retained for longer than two years unless the candidate has given consent, or a subsisting reason (e.g., potential legal proceedings) exists.

3. *General Requirements—Existing Employees*

In addition to the requirements for candidates set out above, when conducting background checks with respect to current employees, the HR Code requires that:

- The data be important to the employer in relation to the inherent nature of the employee's job; and
- The employer has in place a policy covering such background checks that has previously been brought to the attention of the employee concerned.

4. *Access*

Both candidates and existing employees have the right to request access of the information collected. More detailed information on access rights is contained in Chapter 7.

5. *Guidance on Specific Background Checks*

a. *Credit*

The collection of credit data will need to be relevant to the position, and the employer should not collect more than is necessary in order to be lawful. Generally it will not be difficult to justify the collection of data with respect to bankruptcy of the individual, and this is publicly available from the official receiver's office. Likewise, it is possible to undertake a search of the Hong Kong court records to ascertain whether there are any judgments against the prospective employee.

---

[188] HR Code §2.7.1.

However, as a matter of practice, the Privacy Commissioner's office advises employers against seeking to obtain credit information on a candidate or employee from a credit reference agency and is of the view that it is extremely unlikely that an employer will be able to prove that such information serves any relevant purpose for the employment.

b. Criminal Records

As a matter of practice, criminal records are not available in Hong Kong for the purpose of background checks.

Any request made to the candidate or employee for information regarding previous criminal convictions cannot be excessive and must be justified in terms of the requirements of the role offered. Under the Rehabilitation of Offenders Ordinance, it is unlawful to dismiss or exclude an individual, or to prejudice him from employment, by virtue of a criminal conviction or failure to disclose such a conviction, if (1) the individual was sentenced to no more than three months of imprisonment and fined no more than HK$10,000 (US$1,282); (2) the individual had no previous record of conviction in Hong Kong prior to that time; and (3) a period of at least three years have elapsed since the conviction. Note, however, that this restriction does not apply to certain posts, for example, solicitor, barrister, accountant or controller, director, or chief executive of an authorized financial institution.

c. Work History

It is common for an employer to request, and a prospective employee to provide, information about work history that can then be verified by the employer. Generally such background checks will be considered relevant and not excessive.

d. References

Employers wishing to obtain references from a candidate's current or former employers or other sources should ensure that such references are provided with the consent of the candidate, which can be given orally or in writing. The HR Code advises that the prospective employer should seek consent from the candidate prior to approaching the candidate's current or former employer for a reference. When requesting a reference, the employer should notify the sources that the potential candidate has consented to the provision of the reference. Conversely, an employer should not provide reference concerning an employee or former employee to a third party without the employee's prescribed consent unless the employer is satisfied that the third party requesting the reference has obtained the prior consent of the employee concerned.[189]

C. Japan

1. Background Checks During the Recruitment Period

Until quite recently, businesses had the right, under Japanese case law, to undertake background checks on job applicants. Unless the scope of investigation was extremely unreasonable, or clearly unnecessary, and could be recognized as an invasion of privacy, job applicants had the obligation to respond truthfully to questions posed by their potential employers.[190] The use of detective agencies to conduct background checks was quite common.

This practice, however, has been limited greatly in the past several years by the enactment of a new provision in the Employment Security Law in 1999, the "Action Guide regarding to the Protection of Personal Information of Workers" (Action Guide) issued by the Ministry of Health, Labour and Welfare (MHLW) in 2000, the Personal Information Protection Law of 2004 (PIPL), and the various ministry guidelines issued for various business areas that contain specific measures for businesses to take under the PIPL.[191]

---

[189]HR Code §§2.8 & 3.7.

[190]It must be noted, however, that litigation is very rare in Japan, and because most cases are settled before they reach the courthouse, there is not much case law; as a result, the opinions of scholars and other experts tend to have much more influence and weight.

[191]The guidelines applicable to employees include the "Guidelines Regarding the Protection of Personal Information Law in the Economic and Industrial Areas" (METI Guidelines) and the "Guidelines Relating to the Measures for the Appropriate Handling of Personal Information in Employment Management" (Employment Management Guidelines). Rules regarding the handling of employee health information are addressed in MHLW guidelines on "Matters to Consider when Handling Health Information in Employment Management" (Health Information Guidelines).

a. General Restrictions Based on the Personal Information Protection Law

Under the PIPL, when acquiring personal information directly from the individual in writing, businesses must clearly indicate the purpose for the use of such personal information prior to its acquisition.[192] On the other hand, if obtaining personal information in other ways, such as from the individual verbally or from a credit agency or other third parties, the business must notify the individual or publicly announce the purpose for the use of this information promptly thereafter, if this was not publicly announced in advance.[193]

Such notice or public announcement is not necessary, however, if such notice may threaten the life, person, or property or other rights of the individual or a third party or may infringe the rights of the business handling personal information, or when the purpose is clear from the circumstances of acquisition.[194]

In addition, in terms of the method of acquisition of personal information, obtaining personal information by "fraudulent means" is prohibited because of the high likelihood that the rights and interests of the individual will be infringed.[195] "Fraudulent means" include methods or procedures that are illegal or inappropriate. For example, acquiring personal information by violating other laws, being managed by others without authority, or by deception would be included.

In terms of businesses that are recruiting workers, the purpose of use of personal information is clear, so it could be said that it is not necessary to provide notice or public announcement regarding such purpose of use. However, if the personal information acquired during the recruiting process may be used for other purposes after employment, notice or public announcement of such purposes of use is required.

---

[192] PIPL Article 18.2.
[193] PIPL Article 18.1.
[194] PIPL Article 18.4.
[195] PIPL Article 17.

b. Special Restrictions Based on the Employment Security Law

The Employment Security Law, recently added in 1999, and guidelines relating to such article, imposes stricter regulations regarding background checks and the acquisition of personal information from job applicants than the PIPL.[196]

The Employment Security Law provides that, except if a business has obtained the consent of the principal or if there are other proper reasons, "the collection of personal information of job applicants must be within the range necessary to achieve the business purpose, and the storage and use of such information must be within the range of the purpose of collection," and that "necessary measures must be taken to appropriately manage the personal information of job applicants."

The guidelines pertaining to this article provide specific rules regarding the collection, storage, and use of personal information by recruiting businesses. In order to eradicate discriminatory hiring practices in background checks and other job application processes, the collection of personal information that may cause social discrimination (so-called sensitive information) is generally prohibited. The guidelines also provide that when personal information is to be "collected indirectly from third parties" (such as from credit agencies), this must be done with the consent of the individual, and by using certain specified forms.

Of course, acts that violate the above rules may be considered acquisition of personal information through "fraudulent means," and violate Article 17 of the PIPL.

c. Seeking References From the Former Workplace of the Job Applicant

Obtaining references from the former workplace of the job applicant is an "indirect acquisition from a third party," and, pursuant to the guidelines regarding the Employment Security Law, it is necessary to obtain the prior consent of the individual. In addition, from the point of view of the former workplace of the job applicant responding to such inquiry, providing such information

[196]Employment Security Law Article 5.4.

is a provision of personal information to a third party limited under Article 23 of the PIPL and may also be a use beyond the range of purpose of use limited under Article 16 of the PIPL, and it will be necessary to obtain the consent of the former worker before responding to such inquiry.

d. Acquisition of Information After Employment

In terms of the acquisition of personal information of workers by employers, there are no special laws such as the Employment Security Law other than the PIPL, but the Action Guide issued by the MHLW in 2000 provides detailed rules for the handling of personal information of workers, and encourages the self-regulation of businesses. Although the Action Guide does not have the force of law, it is generally regarded by businesses as an agency rule that should be followed.

Whereas the PIPL distinguishes between direct and indirect acquisition of personal information, and no special restrictions are placed on indirect acquisition as long as the individual is notified of the purpose of use, the Action Guide provides that the general rule should be to collect information directly from the principal.

Information about workers may be obtained from sources other than the worker only if:

1. Consent has been obtained from the worker after providing notice regarding the source of information, purpose, and items of information to be obtained;
2. Pursuant to law;
3. Necessary in emergency situations for the protection of the worker's life, body, or property;
4. Due to the nature of the business, obtaining information from the worker directly would hinder the proper execution of collection and achievement of the purpose; or
5. There is an appropriate reason for collecting information from sources other than the worker him- or herself.

In supervising their employees, businesses must collect personal information regarding how a worker is carrying out his duties from a wide range of sources, such as from the supervisors or colleagues of such worker, and these kinds of collections are of course deemed lawful.

The Health Information Guidelines provide that when it is necessary to collect health information from medical institutions or health insurance associations and the like, it is desirable for businesses to obtain the consent of the worker after providing notice regarding the purpose of collection and, if necessary, to obtain such information from the worker himself directly.

e. *Prohibition or Limitation on the Collection of Sensitive Data*

According to the Action Guide, certain types of "sensitive data" should not be collected, due to the risk that such data may be used for unjust discriminatory purposes. These restrictions apply to data such as: (1) race, ethnicity, social class, lineage, domicile, place of origin, etc.; and (2) philosophy, faith, religion.

In addition, the collection of personal information regarding membership in labor unions or participation in labor union activities is prohibited where it is against the will of the worker or the labor union, unless there is a particular provision of law or labor agreement that permits such collection, or it is necessary to fulfill obligations of law or labor agreements.

In terms of health information, the Action Guide seeks to balance the privacy of this sensitive information with the employer's obligations to fulfill its duties under the Occupational Health and Safety Law as well as other safety obligations under labor contracts. The Action Guide states that such health information may be collected if it is pursuant to law, there are confidentiality obligations imposed on workers handling health information, and if it is: (1) a necessity for a certain type of work (such as to confirm the vision of a driver at a transportation company); (2) to implement measures for occupational health and safety or protection of mothers (measures taken pursuant to law); or (3) clear that it will be for the benefit of the worker, and it is recognized that there is a justifiable reason for the collection of such health information (for example, if a worker requests to take a leave of absence or change in position due to health reasons, and the business requests a medical certificate).

The Health Information Guidelines also provide that employers should not obtain information regarding infectious diseases that are unlikely to infect others in the office such as HIV status and hepatitis B or genetic information such as abnormal color sensation unless there is a particular need in business operations.

D. Korea

1. Background Checks

Employers may investigate an applicant's criminal background by seeking a criminal background certificate from the National Police Academy before or after extending a job offer. However, because Korean law restricts the release of actual criminal records for reasons unrelated to a criminal case, such as employment-related requests, employers are not able to verify the accuracy of the certificate or any information provided by the applicant. The prospective employee's consent is required to obtain a criminal background certificate. An offer letter, signed by the applicant, stating that obtaining such a certificate is a condition of hire should provide adequate proof of consent. Under the National Human Rights Commission Act, when an applicant has a criminal record but has completed all criminal sentences, refusing to hire such a candidate based on his criminal record is presumed to be discriminatory.

Employment offers may also be conditioned upon either satisfactory completion of a driving test or a driving record check. There are no restrictions on when such a request must be made, and an offer letter stating this requirement, signed by the candidate, would indicate the required consent to the driving test or driving record check.

Korean law permits a job applicant's personal credit information to be used as a factor in hiring decisions. The Use and Protection of Credit Information Act prohibits release of personal credit information without the individual's written consent. If the applicant wishes not to provide consent to a credit check for this purpose, he or she may offer to respond personally to the employer's credit-related questions. However, an employer may lawfully refuse to hire a candidate based on his failure to consent to a credit check.

2. *Responding to Employment Verification Requests*

Former employees may obtain verification of their past employment by seeking a "factually correct certificate" from former employers.[197] A former employer need respond only to specific requests, which may include such information as duration of employment, title, wage or salary history, and scope of employee duties. Pursuant to the Labor Standards Act, former employers must retain these certificates for three years.

---

[197] Labor Standards Act, Art. 39, ¶(1).

CHAPTER 3

EMAIL AND INTERNET MONITORING/ VIDEO AND PHYSICAL SURVEILLANCE

I. Overview 200
II. Americas 202
  A. United States 202
    1. Surveillance of Employees' Electronic Communications 202
    2. Surveillance of Employees' Telephone Conversations 203
    3. Surveillance of Telephone Calls Under the ECPA 205
      a. Prohibited Surveillance Under the ECPA 205
      b. Permitted Surveillance Under the ECPA 207
        i. Interceptions With Prior Consent 207
        ii. Business Extension Exception 209
      c. Surveillance to Protect the Employer's Rights or Property 211
    4. Surveillance of Telephone Calls Under California Law 212
    5. Surveillance of Telephone Calls Under New York Law 214
    6. Surveillance of Employees' Email 216
      a. Email Monitoring Under Federal Law 216
      b. Email Monitoring Under California Law 219
      c. Email Monitoring Under Connecticut Law 219
      d. Email Monitoring Under Delaware Law 220
      e. Email Monitoring Under New York Law 220
    7. Monitoring of Employees' Use of Employers' Computers 221

8. Do Employers Have a Duty to Monitor? 223
9. Surveillance by Government: ECPA, FISA, USA PATRIOT Act, and State Wiretap Laws 226
10. Physical Surveillance and Workplace Searches 228
11. Visual and Auditory Surveillance in the Workplace 228
12. Location-Based Restrictions on Surveillance 229
13. Use of Amplifying or Recording Devices 230
14. Undercover Investigators 231
15. Invasion of Privacy Claims 232
    a. Elements of Privacy Claim 233
    b. Effect of Providing Notice of Surveillance 234
16. Additional Restrictions on Surveillance in Public-Sector Employment 236
17. Video Surveillance Viewed by Courts as Highly Intrusive 236
18. An Employee's Reasonable Expectation of Privacy Varies Based on the Type of Area Under Surveillance 237
19. Title III of the Omnibus Crime Control and Safe Streets Act May Also Provide a Source of Protection for Public Employees 238
20. Additional U.S. Restrictions on Surveillance in a Unionized Workplace 239
21. Restrictions on Surveillance of Union Activities 239
22. Restrictions on Video Surveillance in a Unionized Facility 240
23. Private-Sector Employers 241
    a. Elements of an Invasion of Privacy Claim 241
        i. Legally Protected Privacy Interest 241
        ii. Reasonable Expectation of Privacy 242
        iii. Serious Invasion of Privacy Interests 242
    b. Employer's "Competing Nonprivacy Interests" Defense 243

24. Public-Sector Employers 244
 a. Expectations of Privacy in the Public-Sector Workplace 244
 b. Balancing of Public Employer's Legitimate Interests 245
25. Postal Mail Received by Employees at the Workplace 246
26. Setting Reasonable Workplace Privacy Expectations 247
27. Limiting the Intrusiveness of Workplace Searches 248

III. Europe 249
 A. The European Union Approach 249
  1. Email and Internet Monitoring 249
  2. Monitoring of Employee Telephone Calls 252
  3. Video Surveillance 252
  4. Works Councils Role in Monitoring 253
 B. Finland 255
  1. Email and Internet Monitoring 255
  2. Monitoring of Employee Telephone Calls 258
  3. Video Surveillance 258
 C. France 259
  1. Email and Internet Monitoring 259
  2. Monitoring of Employee Telephone Calls 263
  3. Video Surveillance 264
 D. Germany 267
  1. Email and Internet Monitoring 267
  2. Monitoring of Employee Telephone Calls 271
  3. Video Surveillance 271
 E. United Kingdom 273
  1. Email and Internet Monitoring 273
  2. Monitoring of Employee Telephone Calls 278
  3. Video Surveillance 279

IV. Asia and Asia Pacific 280
 A. Australia 280
  1. General Requirements for Monitoring 280
  2. Monitoring of Employee Email 281
  3. Video Surveillance and Other Surveillance 282
 B. China 284

1. General Requirements for Monitoring 284
C. Hong Kong 285
1. Monitoring Guidelines 285
2. Video Surveillance 287
D. Japan 288
1. General Requirements for Monitoring 288
2. Monitoring of Computer Use 289
E. Korea 290
1. Monitoring of Employee Email 290
2. Video Surveillance 291
F. New Zealand 292
1. Monitoring of Employee Email 292
2. Video Surveillance 292
G. Taiwan 293
1. General Requirements for Monitoring 293
2. Monitoring of Employee Email 293
V. What to Consider Before Monitoring Employees 294

I. OVERVIEW

Technology offers myriad and ever-changing ways for employers to monitor the workplace activities of their employees, detect and prevent misuse of company resources, and investigate potential misconduct. U.S. employers assume that employees have no expectation of privacy at work, and that an employer has the unfettered right to review any email messages or other communications created or sent using company property. Such assumptions are likely to be unfounded, however. Privacy rights are independent of property rights: as a general matter, an employer's ownership of telephone or computer equipment does not confer an absolute right to monitor all use of such equipment. Consequently, employers must be aware of restrictions that exist in the U.S., as well as internationally, concerning the right to monitor employees' activities.

For purposes of this discussion, the term "monitoring" is broadly used to refer to any electronic surveillance of employees, such as reading or collection of electronic communications (whether in transit or storage), or video or audio surveillance. Monitoring can occur passively as well as actively. Thus, copying email for the purpose of making a backup or scanning email to detect viruses are both forms of monitoring. In many countries, an employer's ability to monitor employee communications turns on whether individuals are allowed to use company-provided systems for personal use and whether the purposes for which the employer seeks to monitor are deemed legitimate. As noted above, the fact that the computer equipment is provided by the employer or that the employee is sending the electronic communications during work hours on that equipment is usually not relevant.

In the U.S., employees do not have an inherent right to privacy at work. Instead, monitoring activities become unlawful only if: (1) they are prohibited by a specific law; or (2) the employee had a reasonable expectation of privacy under the circumstances. U.S. employers typically seek to prevent or remove any reasonable expectation of privacy by distributing a written policy explaining the monitoring practices and explicitly retaining the right to monitor employee activity. This approach can be effective in the U.S. and in certain other countries, such as Japan, that apply a balancing-test approach to workplace privacy. However, this approach is insufficient in the European Union (EU) Member States or Korea, as well as in other jurisdictions that treat employees as having inherent privacy rights even while at work. Thus, a multinational employer cannot simply forward a U.S.-style workplace monitoring policy to all of its employees globally, figuring this will remove any privacy rights and permit the employer to monitor employees globally. The employer must instead consider applicable limitations and requirements in the countries in which it operates. Some of these limitations and restrictions are described below.

II. AMERICAS

A. United States

1. Surveillance of Employees' Electronic Communications

Most employers furnish their employees with the means to make work-related telephone calls, send and receive electronic mail (email) and wireless text messages, and search the Internet. As with other on-the-job activities, the misuse of these services can be used to harm the interests of the employer, fellow employees, or third parties. Failure to prevent and investigate the misuse of company resources may even, in some cases, expose the employer to liability to injured third parties.[1] Accordingly, monitoring of employees' electronic communications over employer-provided facilities, conducted within the limits of the law, is a legitimate function of responsible management.

The privacy of employees within the workplace is protected by a wide variety of statutes and case law. In the private sector, workplace surveillance and searches are regulated by state statutes and common-law theories. Public employers face the added concern of Fourth Amendment claims involving illegal searches. In addition, federal statutes such as the National Labor Relations Act (NLRA) and Labor Management Relations Act (LMRA) place substantial limitations on employer monitoring of union organizing activities and union employees in the workplace. Employers may take steps to maximize their ability to conduct workplace surveillance and searches through careful planning and compliance with these legal restrictions.

Employer surveillance of employee communications is governed primarily by the federal wiretapping statute, known as the Electronic Communications Privacy Act (ECPA), by the federal Stored Communications Act (SCA), and by the wiretapping and eavesdropping statutes of the various states. Those wiretapping statutes clearly apply to telephone calls and email messages (includ-

---

[1]*See* Doe v. XYC Corp., 382 N.J. Super. 122 (App. Div. 2005) (finding that employer could be liable to victim for failure to investigate employee's viewing of child pornography over company-provided Internet access service).

ing wireless text messages) and may, in some circumstances, apply to Internet usage as well.[2]

This section reviews in detail the provisions of the ECPA and the wiretapping and eavesdropping statutes of two of the largest states—California and New York—as they affect the right of employers to monitor telephone calls, emails, and Internet usage. It also presents the impact of federal and state law generally upon the rights of employers to monitor employees' Internet use and other uses of employer-provided computer systems.

As the following discussion makes clear, the employer's best protection against liability for surveillance of employee communications is the employee's knowledge of those monitoring activities. Accordingly, employers should, as a matter of routine, give their personnel express notice that all of their workplace electronic communications may be monitored for any purpose, at the employer's sole discretion.

2. *Surveillance of Employees' Telephone Conversations*

Under both state and federal law, employers generally may listen to or record employee telephone conversations with the employee's prior consent. For this purpose, consent may be demonstrated by the employee's acknowledgment that he has received and understood a written policy that gives the employer the right to engage in such monitoring. Other forms of notice, such as posting of a surveillance policy in the employee's work area, also might constitute evidence that the employee's use of business telephones is done with consent to the employer's monitoring of those activities.

---

[2]It should be noted that challenges to interceptions of telephone calls and email sometimes are based upon constitutional grounds (chiefly the Fourth Amendment) and tort theories such as invasion of privacy. *See, e.g.*, Quon v. Arch Wireless Operating Co., 529 F.3d 892 (9th Cir. 2008); Smyth v. Pillsbury, 914 F. Supp. 97 (E.D. Pa. 1996); Bohach v. City of Reno, 932 F. Supp. 1232 (D. Nev. 1996). However, these theories usually are relied upon as supplements to claims under wiretapping and eavesdropping laws, and are generally more difficult to establish than the wiretapping and eavesdropping claims. Also, Fourth Amendment and other constitutional causes of action are good only against governmental bodies, including employers that happen to be governmental agencies.

Even when employee consent has not been obtained, employers are permitted by federal law (and some state laws) to monitor employee conversations as necessary to protect the employer's interests, or to listen to those conversations for business reasons by means of an extension telephone or similar device. These grounds for monitoring, however, should not be relied upon in place of employee consent when such consent can be obtained.

Also, so-called "two-party consent" states permit telephone conversations to be monitored only with the consent of all parties to those conversations. When a call is monitored in such a state or involves a nonemployee resident of such a state, it may be necessary for the employer to give notice to nonemployee parties to the conversation that the call is being recorded or otherwise monitored.[3]

Finally, some recent court decisions suggest that an employer may be found to be negligent, under certain circumstances, for failure to monitor the communications of an employee that engages in harmful conduct, where such monitoring might have prevented that conduct. Although the scope of any obligation to monitor is unclear, these cases underscore the importance of advising employees of the employer's surveillance policy and obtaining consent to that policy.

Surveillance of employee telephone calls is governed primarily by the various state and federal wiretap laws, and especially by the federal ECPA, which evolved from Title III of the Omnibus Crime Control and Safe Streets Act of 1968.[4]

Although many state wiretap laws are modeled on the ECPA and set out essentially the same requirements for employers as federal law, a number of state laws contain prohibitions and exceptions that differ from those of the ECPA. Accordingly, employers planning to monitor employee telephone calls should consult not only federal law but also the laws of the states in which those acts of monitoring will take place.

---

[3]At this writing, the two-party consent states are California, Connecticut, Florida, Illinois, Maryland, Massachusetts, Michigan, Montana, Nevada, New Hampshire, Pennsylvania, and Washington.

[4]Omnibus Crime Control and Safe Streets Act of 1968, Pub. L. No. 90-351, 82 Stat. 197 (1968) (codified at 18 U.S.C. §§2510–2521), reprinted in 1968 U.S.C.CAN 237.

The following describes the requirements of the ECPA and, as examples of state law approaches, the wiretapping/eavesdropping laws of California and New York as they affect the right of employers to listen to or record employees' telephone calls.

3. Surveillance of Telephone Calls Under the ECPA

Subject to certain exceptions, Title I of the ECPA prohibits any person, including an employer, from "intercepting" any telephone call or other "wire communication."[5] Title I also prohibits a number of interception-related activities, including disclosure and use of the contents of an unlawfully intercepted telephone call.[6]

The application of Title I in any particular case, however, requires a careful reading of all relevant portions of the statute, including the definitions and exceptions. The following sections describe the principal elements of a Title I violation, then discuss the circumstances under which employers may intercept employee telephone calls *without* violating Title I.

a. Prohibited Surveillance Under the ECPA

Not all interceptions of telephone calls are prohibited by Title I of the ECPA. Prohibited interceptions include the following elements:

- The interception must be intentional.[7] The statute does not require proof of specific intent to violate the law, but inadvertent interceptions are not unlawful;

---

[5] 18 U.S.C. §2511. The ECPA defines "wire communication" as "any aural transfer made in whole or in part through the use of facilities for the transmission of communications by the aid of wire, cable, or other like connection between the point of origin and the point of reception (including the use of such connection in a switching station) furnished or operated by any person engaged in providing or operating such facilities for the transmission of interstate or foreign communications or communication affecting interstate or foreign commerce." *Id.* "Aural transfer" is defined in the statute as "a transfer containing the human voice at any point between and including the point of origin and the point of reception." 18 U.S.C. §2510(18). This definition encompasses all wireline and wireless telephone conversations, including those carried by "Voice over Internet Protocol" services.

[6] 18 U.S.C. §2511(1)(b)–(e).

[7] 18 U.S.C. §2511(1).

- The interception must involve the acquisition of the *contents* of a communication.[8] Acquisition of information concerning the time, place, parties to, or other circumstances of a communication is not an acquisition of the communication's contents and does not violate Title I;[9]
- The interception must be made with the aid of an "electronic, mechanical, or other device."[10] The ECPA defines such devices expansively, but extension telephones and hearing aids, for example, do not fall within the definition, and interceptions made with those devices are not prohibited by the ECPA; and
- The interceptions involve the acquisition of the contents of communications in *real time*, that is, when those communications are in process of transmission. Once a communication is retained in electronic storage—even if that storage is temporary—acquisition of the contents of that communication is governed by the Stored Communications Act (discussed below) rather than the ECPA.[11]

As these elements show, employers that acquire the contents of their employees' telephone conversations, while those communications are in the process of transmission, may have violated the ECPA by acquiring the contents of a wire communication. Such "acquisition" may be accomplished by listening in on the conversation or recording the conversation.

A number of provisions of Title I of the ECPA, however, recognize circumstances under which such employer interceptions

[8] 18 U.S.C. §2510(4).

[9] 18 U.S.C. §2510(8). The ECPA does not define "acquisition" as that term is used in the definition of "interception," but the courts treat both listening to conversations and recording those conversations as "acquisitions" for purposes of the ECPA.

[10] 18 U.S.C. §2510(4).

[11] *See* Quon v. Arch Wireless Operating Co., 529 F.3d 892 (9th Cir. 2008); Theofel v. Farey-Jones, 359 F.3d 1066 (9th Cir. 2004); Fraser v. Nationwide Mut. Ins. Co., 352 F.3d 107 (3d Cir. 2003); United States v. Steiger, 318 F.3d 1039 (11th Cir.), *cert. denied*, 538 U.S. 1051 (2003); Konop v. Hawaiian Airlines, 302 F.3d 868 (9th Cir. 2002), *cert. denied*, 537 U.S. 1193 (2003); Steve Jackson Games, Inc. v. United States Secret Serv., 36 F.3d 457 (5th Cir. 1994); *but see* United States v. Councilman, 418 F.3d 67 (1st Cir. 2005). The Stored Communications Act is discussed below at Section II.A.6.a.

will be entirely lawful. These circumstances are discussed in the following section.

b. *Permitted Surveillance Under the ECPA*

i. *Interceptions With Prior Consent*

It is not unlawful, under the ECPA, to intercept a communication when "one of the parties to the communication has given prior consent."[12] Under this exception, an employer may listen to or record a conversation between an employee and a third party with only the employee's consent. However, the ECPA does not define the circumstances that will satisfy the "prior consent" requirement, and employers intending to rely on this exception should obtain and document their employees' consent in the clearest possible terms.

In this connection, the strongest form of consent is *express* consent—that is, consent affirmatively expressed or acknowledged by the employee. For example, an employee's signature on a written statement to the effect that he has been advised of the employer's right to monitor conversations; an employee checking a box on an email form and submitting the form acknowledging the receipt of the notice; or a signature or electronic response on a statement acknowledging receipt of a personnel handbook that clearly gives the employer such rights, constitutes stronger evidence of prior consent than simply making notices or policy statements available to employees without requiring their acknowledgment of receipt and understanding of those materials.

However, even if an employee's express consent is not obtained, implied consent to monitoring may be inferred from an employee's decision to use the employer's telephones after receiving notice that monitoring will occur. In order to establish implied consent, the employer should be able to demonstrate that notices were in plain language and actually communicated to affected employees.

---

[12] 18 U.S.C. §2511(d). Some state laws require the consent of both parties to an intercepted communication, and employers should familiarize themselves with the laws of the states in which the parties to a call reside before deciding to intercept that call in reliance on the one-party consent exception. *See, e.g.*, Kearney v. Solomon Smith Barney, Inc., 137 P.3d 914 (Cal. 2006).

Whether consent is express or implied, judicial decisions interpreting the one-party consent exception underscore the importance of stating the employer's policy in the clearest possible terms. Notably, in *Deal v. Spears*, the employer had told an employee that he "might be forced to monitor calls or restrict telephone privileges if [the employee's] abuse of the store's telephone for personal calls continued."[13] The court found that the employee's continued use of the employer-provided telephone, after receiving this nonspecific warning, did not constitute consent to monitor the employee's conversations. Similarly, in *Watkins v. L. M. Berry & Co.*, an employer's stated policy of monitoring sales calls but not personal calls created only a limited employee consent that did not extend to the employer's interception of a personal conversation.[14] As these decisions suggest, courts will interpret any lack of clarity or limitation in an employer's surveillance policy in the employee's favor. Accordingly, such policies must give the employer the broadest possible rights to monitor employee communications by any means and for any lawful reason.

Employers also must be careful not to make statements or take actions, or permit supervisory employees to make statements or take actions, that might be construed as withdrawing a prior notice to employees that their communications would be monitored. For example, in a case involving a governmental employer's monitoring of employees' text messages, the U.S. Court of Appeals for the Ninth Circuit found that the employer's written monitoring policy was undermined by a supervisor's assurances that text pager communications would not be audited as long as employees paid for overage charges attributable to their usage.[15] This assurance, and the fact that the employer's practices were consistent with that assurance, created an "operational reality"

---

[13]Deal v. Spears, 980 F.2d 1153, 1156–57 (8th Cir. 1992).

[14]Watkins v. L.M. Berry & Co., 704 F.2d 577 (11th Cir. 1983). The employer's policy stated that personal employee calls would be monitored only long enough to establish that they were of a personal nature. The employee's implied consent, therefore, extended only as far as a "scheme of limited monitoring." *Id. See also* Williams v. Poulos, 11 F.3d 271 (1st Cir. 1993).

[15]Quon v. Arch Wireless Operating Co., 529 F.3d 892 (9th Cir. 2008).

that gave employees a reasonable expectation of privacy in their text communications.[16]

ii. Business Extension Exception

One important gap in the ECPA's interception restrictions is known popularly as the "business extension" exception. Specifically, a call is not intercepted for purposes of the ECPA if the device by which the contents of a conversation are acquired is:

> any telephone or telegraph instrument, equipment or facility, or any component thereof . . . furnished to the subscriber or user by a provider of wire or electronic communication service in the ordinary course of its business and being used by the subscriber or user in the ordinary course of its business or furnished by such subscriber or user for connection to the facilities of such service and used in the ordinary course of its business.[17]

This language is generally interpreted to mean that an employer acting in the ordinary course of its business, and using an extension telephone or other device provided by the telephone company or other communications service provider, may listen to—and perhaps even record—employee conversations that take place on the employer's business premises.

However, the business extension exception is not absolute. Notably, not every recording or interception device an employer might use will qualify as a permitted telephone "instrument, equipment or facility" under the business extension exception.

As a general rule, employers are more likely to qualify for the exception if they monitor employee communications by means of extension telephones or other equipment historically provided by telephone companies, rather than specialized surveillance and

---

[16]*Id.* at 907. The court's finding of a reasonable expectation of privacy in *Quon* was based upon a Fourth Amendment claim, rather than a claim under the ECPA, SCA, or a state wiretapping law. As noted earlier, such constitutional theories are available to public employees but generally are not available to private employees. However, the rationale of *Quon* is not necessarily confined to Fourth Amendment claims. A court in a future case might find that a private employer's consent defense to an ECPA, SCA, or state wiretap complaint was vitiated by acts or statements that nullified the employee's consent and restored his or her expectation of privacy.

[17]18 U.S.C. §2510(5)(a).

recording equipment.[18] In *Williams v. Poulos*, for example, the First Circuit Court of Appeals found that alligator clips placed on a telephone line on the employer's premises were not devices of the kind contemplated by the business extension exception.[19] Similarly, in *Deal v. Spears*, the Eighth Circuit Court of Appeals found that a recording device connected to the employer's extension telephone did not qualify for the exception.[20] However, in *Epps v. St. Mary's Hospital, Inc.*, the Eleventh Circuit Court of Appeals held that an employer's use of a double-reeled tape recorder, attached to an ambulance dispatch console on which emergency telephone calls were terminated, qualified under the exception.[21]

An employer relying on the business extension exception also must demonstrate that its use of listening or recording equipment was "in the ordinary course of its business."[22] In interpreting this language, the courts distinguish employees' business calls, which may be extensively monitored if necessary to serve the employer's business purpose, and personal calls, which ordinarily may be monitored only to the extent necessary to ascertain that those calls are, in fact, personal.[23] In *Ali v. Douglas Cable Communications*, for example, the district court found that an employer that listened in extensively on its sales representatives' business conversations in order to "monitor [representatives] in the use of proper skills and to assist the [representatives] with difficult customers" acted

---

[18]The ECPA's "business extension exception" language is badly in need of updating. The ECPA's reference to facilities and equipment furnished by a service provider dates from the time when telephones and associated equipment still were leased to customers at tariffed rates by monopoly telephone companies. In that environment, there was a sharp distinction between extension telephones, private branch exchanges, and other equipment leased to customers by telephone companies under tariff, and tape recorders and other devices not obtainable from the monopoly carrier. Since the telephone industry was deregulated, all customer premises telephone equipment is acquired by the customer. Accordingly, the distinction between equipment furnished by a service provider and equipment not furnished by a service provider is no longer meaningful. Accordingly, the best an employer wishing to rely on this exception can do is use extension telephones and similar devices traditionally associated with monopoly-provided equipment.

[19]Williams v. Poulos, 11 F.3d 271, 280–81 (1st Cir. 1993).

[20]Deal v. Spears, 980 F.2d 1153, 1158 (8th Cir. 1992).

[21]Epps v. St. Mary's Hosp., Inc., 802 F.2d 412, 415 (11th Cir. 1986).

[22]18 U.S.C. §2510(5)(a).

[23]*See* Watkins v. L.M. Berry & Co., 704 F.2d 577, 581 (11th Cir. 1983).

in the ordinary course of business within the exception.[24] In *Deal v. Spears*, however, the Eighth Circuit Court of Appeals found that an employer's interest in preventing use of its telephones for personal calls might justify limited monitoring, but did not support "record[ing] twenty-two hours of calls" and listening to all of them.[25] Similarly, in *United States v. Harpel*, the Tenth Circuit Court of Appeals found "as a matter of law that a telephone extension used without authorization or consent to surreptitiously record a private telephone conversation is not used in the ordinary course of business."[26]

c. *Surveillance to Protect the Employer's Rights or Property*

The ECPA also permits "an operator of a switchboard, or an officer, employee, or agent of a provider of wire or electronic communication service, whose facilities are used in the transmission of a wire or electronic communication, to intercept, disclose, or use that communication in the normal course of his employment while engaged in any activity which is a necessary incident to the rendition of his service or to the protection of the rights or property of the provider of that service...."[27]

At the time the statute was first enacted, this "rights or property" exception was intended to permit telephone companies to monitor the calls of subscribers or third parties who were suspected of stealing service.[28] More recently, however, courts have recognized that employers providing telephone facilities for their employees' use also are providers of wire communication service and may engage in acts of monitoring that are necessary incidents to the protection of their rights or property.[29]

---

[24]Ali v. Douglas Cable Commc'ns, 929 F. Supp. 1362, 1373 (D. Kan. 1996).

[25]*Deal*, 980 F.2d at 1158.

[26]United States v. Harpel, 493 F.2d 346, 351 (10th Cir. 1974).

[27]18 U.S.C. §2511(2)(a)(i).

[28]*See* Campiti v. Walonis, 453 F. Supp. 819 (Mass. Dist. Ct. 1978), *aff'd*, 611 F.2d 387 (1st Cir. 1979).

[29]*See* United States v. McLaren, 957 F. Supp. 215 (M.D. Fla. 1997); United States v. Christman, 375 F. Supp. 1354 (N.D. Cal. 1974).

Reliance on the "rights or property" exception, however, can be complicated by the need to show that the challenged actions were a *necessary* incident to the protection of legitimate rights or property of the employer. Again, the employer's best defense against claims of unlawful surveillance is the prior consent of the affected employees, rather than reliance upon the "rights or property" defense or other exceptions.

4. *Surveillance of Telephone Calls Under California Law*

California's laws, which do not recognize the same exceptions to liability (one-party consent, extension telephone, protection of rights or property) as the ECPA, are a compelling example of the need to consult both state and federal law before adopting an employee surveillance program.

California has two statutes that affect the ability of employers to monitor employees' telephone calls. The California Wiretap statute provides that anyone who "willfully and without the consent of all parties to the communication, or in any unauthorized manner, reads, or attempts to read, or to learn the contents or meaning of any message, report, or communications when the same is in transit or passing over any wire, line, or cable, or is being sent from, or received at any place within this state" has committed a criminal offense and may be sued for damages by an aggrieved party.[30] The California Eavesdropping statute, which applies only to "confidential" communications, prohibits anyone who does not have the consent of all parties to a "confidential communication" from eavesdropping upon or recording that communication by means of "any electronic amplifying or recording device."[31]

For an employer's purposes, the most important features of these California statutes are the following:

- California does not permit an employee's calls with nonemployees to be monitored with the consent of the employee alone. Because California is a "two-party consent" state,

[30] CAL. PENAL CODE §631.
[31] CAL. PENAL CODE §632.

customers and other California third parties that engage in conversations with employees must have notice that the employer will listen to or record those conversations;

- California has no "business extension" exception for employers. Although the Wiretap Statute permits surveillance by means of "any instrument, equipment, facility, or service furnished and used pursuant to the tariffs of a public utility," a California court has held that this exception cannot immunize the use of telephone equipment for purposes of surveillance;[32]
- California has no "rights or property" exception. Unlike the ECPA, California law does not permit an employer, acting as a provider of communications service to its employees, to monitor employees' communications for the purpose of protecting the employer's rights or property;
- Like federal courts interpreting the ECPA, California courts interpreting California law require notice of surveillance policies to be express and unambiguous; and[33]
- California will assert jurisdiction over, and will apply its laws to, monitoring of calls that originate or terminate outside the state. As long as the act of monitoring takes place in California, or a party to the call is located in California, aggrieved persons will be able to bring lawsuits in California and have the legality of the challenged monitoring decided under California law.[34]

Finally, California law raises a question that confronts an employer whenever an employee talks over the telephone with a resident of a two-party consent state: that is, what constitutes prior consent by a person who, before the call is made, is not aware of and has not previously agreed to the employer's policy of monitoring employees' calls?

Unfortunately, the statutes of the two-party consent states do not endorse specific methods of obtaining consent, leaving

[32]Ribas v. Clark, 38 Cal. 3d 355, 212 Cal. Rptr. 143, 696 P.2d 637 (Cal. 1985).

[33]*See* People v. Jiang, 131 Cal. Rptr. 3d 184, 205 (Cal. Ct. App. 2005); *see also* Fischl v. New Horizons Learning Ctrs., Inc., B167509, 2005 Cal. App. Unpub. LEXIS 1495 at *21 (Cal. Ct. App. Feb. 22, 2005) (unpublished opinion).

[34]*See* Kearney v. Salomon Smith Barney, Inc., 45 Cal. Rptr. 3d 730 (Cal. 2006).

employers with the need to choose, at their own legal risk, a method of satisfying this requirement. Faced with this dilemma, employers that operate customer service centers and other operations that engage in high volumes of calls with third parties have generally chosen to play a prerecorded announcement at the start of the call. Those announcements typically state that the call "may be recorded or monitored for quality control purposes." The rationale for this approach is that a party's decision to proceed with the conversation after hearing this announcement constitutes that party's implied consent to the employer's monitoring of the call.

Although there is no guarantee that a court will not find that a stronger form of prior consent than the prerecorded announcement should have been used, this method seems the most practical and effective of the available alternatives. No court has held, and no reasonable court is likely to hold, that monitoring of customer service or other calls should be prohibited until a party's signature on a written waiver, or other form of express consent, has been obtained. Accordingly, if an organization's employees will be speaking with customers or other persons located in two-party consent states, clear announcements of the employer's monitoring policy should be provided at the start of the call.

5. Surveillance of Telephone Calls Under New York Law

Unlike California's wiretapping and eavesdropping statutes, New York law recognizes the one-party consent exception to liability for surveillance of employees' telephone calls. New York does not, however, recognize the "rights or property" or business extension exceptions.

Surveillance of telephone calls in New York is governed by New York's prohibition on eavesdropping, which is committed when a person "unlawfully engages in wiretapping, mechanical overhearing of a conversation, or intercepting or accessing of an electronic communication."[35] For purposes of this offense, wiretapping is defined as "the intentional overhearing or recording of a telephonic or telegraphic communication by a person other than a sender or receiver thereof, without the consent of either the

---

[35]N.Y. PENAL LAW §250.05.

sender or receiver, by means of any instrument, device or equipment."[36] Intercepting or accessing of an electronic communication is defined as "the intentional acquiring, receiving, collecting, overhearing, or recording of an electronic communication, without the consent of the sender or intended receiver thereof, by means of any instrument, device or equipment. . . ."[37] Mechanical overhearing of a conversation is defined as "the intentional overhearing or recording of a conversation or discussion, without the consent of at least one party thereto, by means of any instrument, device or equipment."[38] Under these definitions, listening to or recording an employee's telephone conversation without the consent of one party is most appropriately classified as eavesdropping by means of wiretapping.

New York courts have found that the one-party consent requirement is satisfied when employees use employer-provided telephones after receiving notice of a monitoring policy. In *Curley v. Board of Trustees*, for example, a police officer sued for violations of his rights arising from the taping, by the police department, of a conversation with another officer.[39] The officer's claim was rejected on the ground that it was "uncontroverted that the plaintiff knew that the police telephone lines were monitored." Similarly, New York courts have refused to suppress the use of recordings of telephone conversations made with the consent of police informants and other parties to the conversations that were intercepted and recorded.[40]

Because one-party consent is the only applicable statutory defense to the offense of eavesdropping in New York, employers who monitor telephone conversations involving persons in New York should ensure that their employees are effectively notified of the employer's surveillance policy.

---

[36]N.Y. PENAL LAW §250.001.

[37]N.Y. PENAL LAW §250.006. An electronic communication is "any transfer of signs, signals, writing, images, sounds, data, or intelligence of any nature transmitted in whole or in part by a wire, radio, electromagnetic, photoelectronic or photo-optical system, but does not include . . . any telephonic or telegraphic communication. . . ." N.Y. PENAL LAW §250.005.

[38]N.Y. PENAL LAW §250.002.

[39]Curley v. Board of Supervisors, 213 A.D.2d 583 (N.Y. App. Div. 1995).

[40]*See* People v. Lasher, 447 N.E.2d 70 (N.Y. 1983); People v. Brannaka, 46 App. Div. 2d 929, 361 N.Y.S.2d 434 (N.Y. App. Div. 1974).

6. *Surveillance of Employees' Email*

Most wiretapping and eavesdropping statutes predate the invention of email and wireless text messaging, but have either been amended to take those technologies into account or contain definitions of the affected communications that can be read to include them without amendment.[41] Accordingly, employers will find, in most jurisdictions, that monitoring of emails is subject to substantially the same rules that apply to telephone conversations. (This rule of thumb should not, of course, be applied without consulting the specific language of states that might have jurisdiction over the monitored messages. See, for example, the discussion of state law, in Sections 3.II.A.b–e, below.)

a. Email Monitoring Under Federal Law

The federal ECPA is one of the statutes that was specifically amended to cover email communications, which come within the definition of "electronic communication" adopted by Congress in 1986.[42] Electronic communications, like wire communications, may be intercepted with the consent of one party to the communication, or by a service provider (including an employer who furnishes email capability to an employee) as necessarily incident to the provision of the service or to the protection of the rights or property of the service provider.[43] As discussed in connection with interceptions of telephone calls under the ECPA, employers are well advised to obtain express or implied employee consent to monitoring of employees' emails, rather than relying upon the "rights or property" exception.

Employers who wish to monitor their employees' email communications also should be aware of the legal advantages of obtaining those messages while they are in storage, rather than in

---

[41]For convenience, email and wireless text messaging are referred to collectively as "email" unless it is necessary to distinguish them.

[42]18 U.S.C. §2510(12). An electronic communication is any "transfer of signs, signals, writing, images, sounds, data, or intelligence of any nature transmitted in whole or in part by wire, radio [or other electronic means] that affects interstate or foreign commerce."

[43]Of the three principal exceptions noted in connection with interception of telephone calls (i.e., wire communications) under the ECPA, only the "business extension" exception appears not to apply to emails.

the process of transmission. Interceptions of this kind are subject to Title II of the ECPA, also known as the Stored Communications Act (SCA), which protects the privacy of communications while those communications are in electronic storage.[44] The SCA makes it generally unlawful for anyone intentionally to access, without authorization, a facility through which an electronic communication service is provided (or intentionally to exceed an authorization to access that facility) and through such access to obtain, alter, or prevent authorized access to a wire or electronic communication while it is in electronic storage. However, the SCA has a strong "service provider" exception, according to which anyone may access stored communications, and thereby obtain, alter, or prevent authorized access to those communications, if such conduct is authorized by the service provider. The advantage of this exception over the counterpart "rights or property" exception of the ECPA Title I provisions is that the SCA exception permits the service provider to acquire the contents of stored communications for *any* lawful reason.[45]

In the case of a communications service, such as an email account, furnished to an employee by his employer, the employer can persuasively argue that it is the provider of the service and therefore is entitled to retrieve and review the employee's communication for any purpose. The courts generally have agreed with this interpretation of the SCA.[46]

In fact, the principal controversy concerning the ability of employers to read stored email, on a server or network provided by the employer, involves those facts that will be found to constitute "electronic storage" of a message. Specifically, courts have

---

[44]18 U.S.C. §§2701 et seq.

[45]"[The SCA] allows service providers to do as they wish when it comes to accessing communications in electronic storage." Bohach v. Reno, 932 F. Supp. 1232, 1236 (D. Nev. 1996). However, as the U.S. Court of Appeals for the Ninth Circuit found in *Quon,* a third-party provider of a communications service is not permitted to disclose the contents of employee's communications, stored on the service provider's system, without the employee's consent. Quon v. Arch Wireless Operating Co., 529 F.3d 892, 903 (9th Cir. 2008). Accordingly, if an employer does not furnish its own email service to employees and does not store employee emails on its own server, it should consider obtaining express consent from employees to the disclosure of the contents of their communications by the employer's email service vendor.

[46]*See, e.g., Bohach*, 932 F. Supp. 1232.

been asked to determine when a message has been intercepted for purposes of Title I of the ECPA and when the message has merely been acquired from storage under the SCA. According to the ECPA, "electronic storage" is "any temporary, intermediate storage of a wire or electronic communication incidental to the electronic transmission thereof... and any storage of such communication by an electronic communications service for purposes of backup protection of such communication."[47] But, how does this definition apply to communications acquired by capturing a video display of the communication on a monitor, or acquired during the milliseconds when they are held for pre-delivery inspection of routing information?[48] In other words, how long must an email be stored, and for what purpose, in order to ensure that an employer's acquisition of that message is covered by the more lenient SCA provisions rather than the interception provisions of Title I?

As a dissenting opinion in the case of *United States v. Councilman* correctly points out, the courts generally have resolved these questions by finding that the ECPA's "prohibition on intercepting electronic communications does not apply when they are contained in electronic storage, whether such storage occurs pre- or post-delivery, and even if storage only lasts a few milli-seconds."[49] However, as the majority's decision in *Councilman* shows, some courts are prepared to find that an interruption along an email's transmission path, during which that email is intercepted or copied, is too brief to constitute electronic storage. Accordingly, employers are well advised to retrieve, copy, or read employees' emails only when they are in fairly long-term storage, such as when they

[47] 18 U.S.C. §2510(17).

[48] *See, e.g.*, O'Brien v. O'Brien, 899 So. 2d 1133 (Fla. Dist. Ct. App. 2005); United States v. Councilman, 418 F.3d 67 (1st Cir. 2005).

[49] *Councilman*, 418 F.3d at 87 (citing Theofel v. Farey-Jones, 359 F.3d 1066, 1077–78 (9th Cir. 2004)); Fraser v. Nationwide Mut. Ins. Co., 352 F.3d 107, 113–14 (3d Cir. 2003); United States v. Steiger, 318 F.3d 1039, 1048–49 (11th Cir.), *cert. denied*, 538 U.S. 1051 (2003); Konop v. Hawaiian Airlines, 302 F.3d 868, 878–79 (9th Cir. 2002), *cert. denied*, 537 U.S. 1193 (2003); Bailey v. Bailey, No. 07-11672, 2008 U.S. Dist. LEXIS 8565 (E.D. Mich. Feb. 6, 2008).

are in the employee's inbox awaiting retrieval, or while they are maintained on the employer's server for backup purposes.[50]

Finally, in the case of emails, as with telephone calls, the employer's best protection is the employee's consent to all forms of monitoring of all communications, whether in the form of telephone calls, emails, or otherwise.[51]

b. Email Monitoring Under California Law

California's wiretapping and eavesdropping statutes are examples of laws that predate email technology and have not been updated to take those forms of communication into account. For this reason, a California court determined in 1991 that the state's wiretap statute did not apply to email systems.[52] As long as that decision remains good law, California employers can take the position that their interceptions of employee email are lawful under all circumstances. As with other forms of monitoring, however, surveillance of employee email should be expressly addressed in notices given to employees.

c. Email Monitoring Under Connecticut Law

Connecticut labor law directly addresses electronic monitoring by requiring that employers engaged in electronic monitoring give employees prior notice of such monitoring.[53] "Electronic monitoring" is defined as the collection of information about employees' activities or communications on the employer's premises by methods including the use of a "computer, telephone, wire,

---

[50]In *Councilman*, the employer had configured his company's email software to copy certain messages during the fraction of a second when the software was scanning the messages' addressing information for routing purposes. In a departure from the usual result in such cases, the court found that this interruption in the email's transmission was too transient to qualify as electronic storage for purposes of the SCA.

[51]The SCA is discussed primarily as it affects the monitoring of emails because emails, unlike telephone conversations, are stored and forwarded as part of the normal process of sending, routing, and receiving those messages. Stored voice communications, however, such as voicemail, sometimes are acquired from storage and might in those cases be covered by the SCA rather than Title I of the ECPA.

[52]Flanagan v. Epson Am., Inc., No. BC007036, slip op. (Cal. Sup. Ct. Jan. 4, 1991).

[53]CONN. GEN. STAT. §31-48d (2006).

radio, camera, electromagnetic or photo-optical systems."[54] Prior to engaging in one of these methods of electronic monitoring, an employer must conspicuously post a notice of the types of electronic monitoring in which the employer may engage.[55] This posting alone may satisfy the prior written notice requirement.[56]

d. Email Monitoring Under Delaware Law

Delaware labor law also explicitly requires employers to give notice before engaging in the monitoring of telephone transmission, email, and Internet usage.[57] To satisfy the notice requirement, an employer may either provide electronic notice of monitoring once each day that an employee accesses employer-provided email or Internet access services or give the employee a one-time notice in writing in an electronic record or other electronic form that has been acknowledged by the employee electronically or in writing.[58]

e. Email Monitoring Under New York Law

The New York eavesdropping law, unlike California's statute, expressly includes "intercepting or accessing an electronic communication" within the definition of eavesdropping, and defines "electronic communication" to include email messages.[59] Accordingly, as with eavesdropping on telephone conversations, New York law permits the interception of employees' emails with the consent of one party to those communications.

---

[54]CONN. GEN. STAT. §31-48d(a)(3).

[55]CONN. GEN. STAT. §31-48d(b)(1).

[56]The Connecticut law allows for certain exceptions to the prior written notice requirement, such as when the employer has "reasonable grounds to believe that employees are engaged in conduct which (i) violates the law, (ii) violates the legal rights of the employer or the employer's employees, or (iii) creates a hostile workplace environment, and . . . electronic monitoring may produce evidence of this misconduct." *Id.* §31-48d(b)(2). This law also does not apply to criminal investigations. *Id.* §31-48d(d).

[57]DEL. CODE ANN. tit. 19, §705 (2006).

[58]*Id.* This section does not apply to certain law enforcement activities; processes designed to manage the type or volume of email, voicemail, or Internet use; processes not targeted to monitor or intercept a particular individual's email, voicemail, or Internet use; and processes performed solely for the maintenance and protection of the computer system. *Id.*

[59]N.Y. PENAL LAW §§250.05, 250.005.

7. *Monitoring of Employees' Use of Employers' Computers*

Employers commonly provide their personnel with the ability to use the employers' computer networks, including the ability to access Web sites and other information on the World Wide Web, thereby giving those employees the ability to retrieve data, download text, receive audio and video files, submit communications to bulletin board services and chatrooms, and otherwise avail themselves of the Internet's resources.

Although employees' Internet usage and other usage of employer computer systems can enhance productivity, wasteful or harmful use can reduce productivity and may even expose the employer to liability for activities ranging from sexual harassment to copyright infringement.[60] In order to reduce these risks, employers must reserve the right to monitor employees' Internet use and should follow up by exercising that right, especially where the employer has reason to suspect that an employee is engaged in harmful activity. Also, in order to avoid claims by employees for invasion of privacy rights, the employer's right to monitor should be clearly expressed and effectively communicated to all personnel.

Disputes concerning the monitoring of employee Internet and computer use have arisen in a variety of contexts, and usually have required courts to inquire into the employee's expectation of privacy in his use of the employer's network.

For example, one court was asked to compel production of an employer-provided computer in response to a discovery request in a wrongful termination suit.[61] In that case, the court found that the employee had no reasonable expectation of privacy in the computer's stored data because he had acknowledged his employer's right to monitor his use of the computer.[62]

In another case, a court was asked to determine whether an employee was wrongfully discharged, in violation of his right of privacy, when his employer read employee email after declaring

---

[60] *See, e.g.,* Doe v. XYC Corp., 382 N.J. Super. 122 (App. Div. 2005); Lowry's Reports, Inc. v. Legg Mason, Inc., 271 F. Supp. 2d 737 (D. Md. 2003).

[61] TBG Ins. Servs. Corp. v. Zieminski, 117 Cal. Rptr. 2d 155 (Cal. Ct. App. 2002).

[62] *Id.*

that those communications would not be intercepted or used as the basis for termination or reprimand.[63] In this case, in spite of the employer's (quite imprudent) privacy assurances, the court found that no privacy right had been violated.

In yet another case, a trustee in bankruptcy moved to compel production of emails and documents that were claimed to be protected by attorney-client, work-product, and joint defense privileges.[64] Among other questions, the court had to consider whether the individual authors of certain emails to their personal attorneys generated them under circumstances that suggested an objectively reasonable expectation that they would be kept confidential. The answer to this question, in turn, depended in part upon whether the companies furnishing the computer system had a policy banning personal use and authorizing monitoring of communications on the system. In a decision that underscores the importance of clear, effectively communicated monitoring policies, the bankruptcy court found that "[t]he evidence is equivocal regarding the existence or notice of corporate policies banning certain uses or monitoring employee emails." Accordingly, the court could not find as a matter of law that the emails were discoverable.

Finally, in a case decided by the United States District Court for the Western District of Washington, review of the contents of an employee's employer-provided laptop's hard drive was permitted on the ground that email messages contained in the hard drive used an account provided by the employer, pursuant to a written policy reserving the right to inspect all records concerning that account without the employee's consent.[65]

Practice Pointer. Taken together, these and other cases concerning employer monitoring of Internet and computer usage demonstrate the importance of clear, effectively communicated technology use policies or notices that give the employer the right to monitor all employee communications and other activities involving employer-provided technology.

---

[63]Smyth v. Pillsbury, 914 F. Supp. 97 (E.D. Pa. 1996).

[64]Asia Global Crossing, Ltd, 322 BR 247 (Bankr. S.D.N.Y. 2005).

[65]Smith v. Lakeside Sch., No. C06-1412RSM, 2007 U.S. Dist. LEXIS 69568 (W.D. Wash. Sept. 20, 2007).

8. *Do Employers Have a Duty to Monitor?*

Recent decisions have confronted the question of an employer's possible liability for harmful acts of its employees, when monitoring of employee communications might have prevented those harmful acts. Those decisions highlight a tension in the law between the privacy rights of employees, as recognized in the ECPA and state wiretapping/eavesdropping laws, and the rights of others to be spared injuries that could be avoided by an employer's careful supervision of its personnel.

The most important of the recent decisions is that of a New Jersey appellate court in *Doe v. XYC Corporation (Doe)*.[66] In that case, an accountant's superiors and information technologies (IT) personnel became aware of the accountant's use of company facilities to access pornographic Internet sites. Although the matter was investigated by IT personnel and some of the pornographic sites visited were identified, no systematic monitoring of the accountant's online activities was undertaken. The accountant was told not to visit pornographic sites over company facilities, but there was evidence that his superior subsequently learned that the illicit Internet usage had resumed and took no action.[67]

The accountant later was arrested for possession of child pornography, including indecent photographs he had taken of his wife's young daughter and transmitted to a child pornography site from his workplace computer. The accountant's wife sued his employer, alleging that the company had both the ability and an affirmative legal duty to monitor her husband's Internet use and prevent his further exploitation of her child.

Although the trial court granted summary judgment in favor of the employer, the appellate court found that the accountant had no expectation of privacy in communications over the company's network because the company had posted a surveillance policy and required employees to sign an acknowledgment of the policy. Accordingly, the company was legally entitled to monitor the accountant's communications.[68]

---

[66]Doe v. XYC Corp., 382 N.J. Super. Ct. 122 (App. Div. 2005); *see supra* n.1.

[67]382 N.J. Super. Ct. at 128–29.

[68]*Id.* at 129–30.

The appellate court also found that the employer in this case had ample notice of the accountant's online activities, and that systematic monitoring of the accountant's communications would have disclosed "the full scope of Employee's activities," including his distribution of child pornography. The court found that under the circumstances, the employer had both a duty to monitor and a duty to act to prevent further harm to innocent third parties. The court remanded the case for further proceedings on the question of actual harm to the plaintiff's child, attributable to the accountant's conduct.[69]

The scope of the duty recognized by the New Jersey court is unclear. Lawsuits alleging a "duty to monitor" will turn on the facts of each case, including the employer's knowledge of the employee's questionable activities. No court has suggested that employers have an open-ended duty to monitor all of their employees' communications "just in case" those employees are engaged in harmful activities. However, the *Doe* case will inspire other plaintiffs to attempt to shift to employers the legal responsibility for harm caused by their employees, on the ground that the employer had notice of the employee's inclinations and failed to make the investigation called for by the circumstances.

Two other, recent decisions also have a bearing on the "duty to monitor": one of those decisions strengthens the case for the "duty to monitor" by confirming that such surveillance does not violate a rightful expectation of privacy; the other decision undermines the case for such a duty by suggesting that employers are immune from liability under a statute meant to protect Internet service providers.

In the first decision, *United States v. Ziegler*, a federal appellate court denied an employee's motion to suppress evidence obtained when his employer notified law enforcement authorities of the employee's possession of child pornography.[70] The employee claimed that the in-house investigation that uncovered his activities, and his employer's subsequent disclosure of his Internet com-

---

[69] *Id.* at 143–45.

[70] United States v. Ziegler, 456 F.3d 1138 (9th Cir. 2006), *opinion withdrawn and substituted*, 474 F.3d 1184 (9th Cir. 2007), *cert. denied*, Ziegler v. United States, 128 S. Ct. 879 (2008).

munications to the Federal Bureau of Investigation (FBI), violated his rights to be secure from unreasonable searches and seizures under the Fourth Amendment to the U.S. Constitution.

The court disagreed, finding that the employer's ownership of the computers involved and the employer's publication of a surveillance policy deprived the employee of any legitimate expectation of privacy.[71]

The second decision, in *Delfino v. Agilent Technologies, Inc.*, takes an entirely different tack from *Doe* and *Ziegler*. In *Agilent*, a recipient of threatening emails tried to hold the sender's employer responsible for the emotional distress allegedly caused by those messages, on the ground that the employer had been negligent in its supervision of its employee's use of company facilities.[72]

The appellate court turned aside this claim on a novel ground: specifically, that the defendant employer, by providing its employees with a means of accessing the Internet, was a "provider of interactive computer services" for purposes of Section 230(c) of the Communications Decency Act, which immunizes such service providers from liability as "publishers" of content provided by others.[73] In making this finding, the court extended to employers the protection of a statute that had been enacted primarily for the benefit of providers of Internet communications to the public, which could not realistically be expected to screen and censor the billions of bytes of information passing over their services.

The viability of the *Agilent* principle will almost certainly be tested in future proceedings, as employers routinely assert the Section 230(c) defense when confronted with claims of responsibility for their employees' communications. In the meantime, employers should ensure that they have removed any employee "expectation of privacy" by securing the consent of their personnel to monitoring of communications for any purpose, and should exercise that right to monitor when they become aware of employee activities that might cause harm to others.

---

[71]456 F.3d at 1145–46.

[72]Delfino v. Agilent Techs., Inc. 145 Cal. App. 4th 790 (Ct. App. 2006).

[73]*Id.* at 805–06.

9. *Surveillance by Government: ECPA, FISA, USA PATRIOT Act, and State Wiretap Laws*

Employers often are asked to cooperate with criminal investigations of their employees. Law enforcement officers conducting such investigations might approach employers with informal requests for cooperation, or might serve employers with written subpoenas, warrants, wiretap orders, or other kinds of written legal process. Although most of these investigations will be based on suspicion of routine criminal misconduct, the post-9/11 environment and the USA PATRIOT Act have brought increased scrutiny of suspected terrorist activity, including home-grown terrorism and activities directed by foreign states and extremist organizations.

Although a complete discussion of criminal investigative laws and methods is beyond the scope of this book, employers should be generally aware of their rights and obligations when asked to cooperate with law enforcement.

In some cases, state, federal, or local law enforcement will ask an employer's consent to conduct a workplace search without first serving a search warrant or other process. If the proposed search will involve only the examination and seizure of workspaces, desks, files, and other physical places and objects, an employer generally may give such consent without risk of liability. As courts have found, even if employees have a reasonable expectation of privacy in certain areas of their employer's property, that expectation is overcome by the employer's consent to a search.[74]

However, where a search and seizure will involve acquisition of the contents of an employee's electronic communications—even where those communications take place over a system or service provided by the employer—the more cautious approach is to ask law enforcement personnel to present an order rather than act on the strength of the employer's consent alone. Caution is warranted in these cases due to the possibility that the employer will

---

[74]*See* United States v. Gargiso, 456 F.2d 584 (2d Cir. 1972). In certain circumstances, even a co-worker's consent may suffice to support a search of an employee's workspace. *See* United States v. Buettner-Janusch, 646 F.2d 759 (2d Cir. 1981).

be classified as an electronic communication service provider, or a provider of remote computing services, under the ECPA.[75] Such service providers are subject to certain limitations in the communications they may provide to law enforcement voluntarily.[76]

Among the types of legal process that law enforcement might furnish to employers are the following:

- A search warrant, issued by a state or federal judge or magistrate, describing the places to be searched and the materials to be seized;
- An interception order, authorizing the real-time wiretapping or other interception of the employee's telephone calls or other communications. Such an order may be obtained under the ECPA, the Foreign Intelligence Surveillance Act (FISA), or pursuant to a state wiretap law;[77]
- A pen register or trap and trace order, authorizing the acquisition of routing, addressing, or other data associated with employees' communications.[78] Pen registers and trap and trace devices, like wiretapping and other surveillance, may be authorized under the ECPA, FISA (as amended by the USA PATRIOT Act and other post-9/11 legislation), or pursuant to state law;

[75] 18 U.S.C. §§2510–2520; 18 U.S.C. §§2701–2708. *But see* Florida v. Young, No. D06-5798, 2007 Fla. App. LEXIS 20515 (Fla. Dist. Ct. App. Dec. 26, 2007), *opinion withdrawn and substituted*, 974 So. 2d 601 (Fla. Dist. Ct. App. 2008) (finding that police officers' reliance on consent of regional church officials to search pastor's office and computer violated Fourth Amendment).

[76] *See* 18 U.S.C. §2702. *But see* United States v. Zeigler, 474 F.3d 1184 (9th Cir. 2007) (permitting a search of an employee's workplace computer with the employer's consent). Also, under the USA PATRIOT Act, an employer may authorize law enforcement to monitor the electronic communications of a so-called "computer trespasser," such as a hacker or other person who is accessing the employer's network without authorization. 18 U.S.C. §2511(2).

[77] *See* 18 U.S.C. §2518; 50 U.S.C. §§1801 et seq. Both FISA and the ECPA were substantially amended by the USA PATRIOT Act, Pub. Law No. 107-56, 115 Stat. 272 (2001), and FISA was further amended by the Intelligence Authorization Act for Fiscal Year 2002, Pub. Law No. 107-108, 115 Stat. 1394 (2001), and the Homeland Security Act of 2002, Pub. Law No. 107-296, 116 Stat. 2135 (2002).

[78] *See, e.g.*, 18 U.S.C. §3127.

- A so-called "Section 2703 Order," authorizing acquisition of the contents of stored communications;[79]
- A grand jury or investigative subpoena;
- A "computer trespasser" order, as authorized by the USA PATRIOT Act; and[80]
- A "sneak and peek" warrant.[81]

If any one of these forms of legal processes is presented, the employer is permitted to cooperate in good faith with law enforcement on the basis of that process. Although the employee might have recourse against the government for lack of probable cause or other constitutional or statutory defects in the investigatory method chosen, the employer is not liable to the employee for the government's violations of the employee's rights.

10. Physical Surveillance and Workplace Searches

Workplace surveillance and searches serve multiple purposes. They are used to detect and deter misconduct, particularly theft, and to maintain a safe and secure work environment. Federal courts, state courts, and the National Labor Relations Board (NLRB) have all examined the issue of workplace monitoring by employers. Each has essentially articulated the same principle: the balancing of the employee's reasonable expectation of privacy against the employer's legitimate interests in conducting the surveillance or search.

11. Visual and Auditory Surveillance in the Workplace

The rules governing physical surveillance of employees are found in various areas of the law, ranging from criminal laws to the NLRA. Factors that affect the privacy protections available to employees include (1) whether the employer is a private employer or the government, (2) whether the surveillance is strictly visual

---

[79] 18 U.S.C. §2703.

[80] *See* note 76, *supra*.

[81] A sneak and peek warrant may be executed without notice to the person owning or in lawful possession of the premises—effectively, by means of a government break-in. Sneak and peek warrants have been used by federal agents for many years, but were officially recognized in the USA PATRIOT Act. *See* 18 U.S.C. §3103a(b).

or contains audio content, and (3) whether the recording device is hidden or unconcealed. In general, courts have concluded that any employee conduct that can be observed by a supervisor or the general public without infringing upon that employee's reasonable expectation of privacy may also legally be observed through video surveillance.

12. Location-Based Restrictions on Surveillance

California, Connecticut, and New York are among the states that prohibit employers from recording the activities of employees in restrooms, locker rooms, or rooms designated for the changing of clothes.[82] Under New York law, the installation or maintenance of a video recording device in such a location constitutes a felony.[83]

Section 653n of the California Penal Code prohibits the installation or maintenance of two-way mirrors in any "restroom, toilet, bathroom, washroom, shower, locker room, fitting room, motel room, or hotel room."[84] This Penal Code section has been interpreted as creating "a public policy against clandestine observation"—regardless of whether it is by two-way mirror or otherwise—in the specified locations.[85] Employees have successfully used this statute to argue that the Penal Code creates a reasonable expectation of privacy when employees are using the specified locations.[86] In *Cramer*, an employer concerned about on-property drug use secretly videotaped employee restrooms through a two-way mirror. The Ninth Circuit found that the employees'

---

[82]*See, e.g.*, CAL. LAB. CODE §435(a); CAL. PENAL CODE §§647(k), 653n; CONN. GEN. STAT. ANN. §31-48b(b); N.Y. GEN. BUS. LAW §395-b(2).

[83]N.Y. GEN. BUS. LAW §395-b(5). This New York statute does not apply to premises that constitute or are part of any (1) public correctional or custodial facility, or a public or private medical facility where people are treated; (2) public or private treatment facility where people enter voluntarily or are committed or where people voluntarily receive treatment; (3) facility under the operation of any federal, state, or local law enforcement agency; or (4) a private dwelling. N.Y. GEN. BUS. LAW §395-b(3)(a).

[84]This statute exempts certain facilities such as penal or correctional institutions and public and private treatment facilities used for the treatment of confined persons. CAL. PENAL CODE §653n.

[85]*See, e.g.*, People v. Metcalf, 22 Cal. App. 3d 20, 23 (Ct. App. 1971).

[86]*See, e.g.*, Cramer v. Consolidated Freightways, Inc., 255 F.3d 683, 697 (9th Cir. 2001).

collective bargaining agreement may have permitted covert surveillance under certain circumstances, but did not destroy the employees' reasonable expectation of privacy given this statutory prohibition.[87]

Additionally, Section 647(k) of the California Penal Code generally provides that it is a misdemeanor to use a peephole, two-way mirror, camera, or other device to look into the interior of a "bathroom, changing room, fitting room, dressing room, or tanning booth, or the interior of any other area in which the occupant has a reasonable expectation of privacy, with the intent to invade the privacy of a person or persons inside."[88]

New York also prohibits the installation or use of a two-way mirror or other viewing device in certain areas of the workplace.[89] As used in this statute, a "viewing device" means a mirror, mechanical viewing device, peephole, camera, or any other instrument or method that can be used to secretly observe or record the activities of a person.[90] The owner or manager of a premise may not knowingly permit or allow the installation or maintenance of a viewing device, for the purpose of secret monitoring, inside any fitting room, restroom, toilet, bathroom, washroom, or shower.[91] As noted above, the installation or maintenance of a video recording device constitutes a felony.[92]

13. Use of Amplifying or Recording Devices

Employers are subject to general statutory restrictions on the use of electronic amplifying or recording devices to eavesdrop. For example, California's Invasion of Privacy Act provides for a fine and a prison term for anyone who "by means of any elec-

---

[87] *Id.*

[88] CAL. PENAL CODE §647(k).

[89] N.Y. GEN. BUS. LAW §395-b.

[90] N.Y. GEN. BUS. LAW §395-b(1).

[91] N.Y. GEN. BUS. LAW §395-b(2)-(2-a).

[92] N.Y. GEN. BUS. LAW §395-b(5). However, this New York law provides that an owner or manager may install a viewing device inside a fitting room if a written notice stating that a viewing device is installed for monitoring purposes is "conspicuously" posted at the fitting room's entrance. N.Y. GEN. BUS. LAW §395-b(3)(b). If the premise is located in a city with a population exceeding 1 million people, the notice must be posted in English and Spanish. *Id. See supra* note 83 for other exemptions under this New York statute.

tronic amplifying or recording device, eavesdrops upon or records [a] confidential communication."[93] By its nature, the term "eavesdropping" may imply that the surveillance must include an audio component, which suggests a stricter limitation on audio surveillance than on video surveillance alone. Nevertheless, California courts have construed Section 632 liberally and have allowed for its application in situations in which only a video component was at issue.[94]

Eavesdropping or "mechanical overhearing" is punishable as a felony under New York law.[95] Mechanical overhearing occurs when an employer intentionally overhears or records a conversation without the consent of at least one party to the conversation, by using a mechanical instrument.[96] The prohibition against mechanical overhearing "refers to the unlawful interception of a 'face to face' conversation of two or more people."[97] Under the statute, an employer may not engage in the mechanical overhearing of an employee's conversation. However, there is currently no New York case law addressing this issue.

Eavesdropping or monitoring of electronic or telephonic communications is strictly regulated by federal and state law, and separately addressed in this Chapter.

14. Undercover Investigators

Under California law, an employer that disciplines or discharges an employee based on the report of an undercover shopping investigator must first provide the employee with a copy of that report.[98] If an employee is interviewed in connection with a shopping investigation report, and the interview may result in the

---

[93]CAL. PENAL CODE §632(a).

[94]*See* People v. Gibbons, 215 Cal. App. 3d 1204, 1208–09 (Ct. App. 1989) (video recorder held to be a "recording device" within the meaning of the California Invasion of Privacy Act, although the recording contained no audio content).

[95]N.Y. PENAL LAW §250.05.

[96]N.Y. PENAL LAW §250.00(2).

[97]Sharon v. Sharon, 558 N.Y.S.2d 468, 469 (N.Y. Sup. Ct. 1990) (quoting Judge Donnino in the Practice Commentaries in the Penal Law of N.Y., Book 39, Penal Law §250.05, at 315–16).

[98]CAL. LAB. CODE §2930.

employee's termination for dishonesty, the employer must give the employee the latest copy of that report during the interview.[99]

Section 2930 defines the term "shopping investigator" as a person who

> shops in commercial, retail, and service establishments to test integrity of sales, warehouse, stockroom, and service personnel, and evaluates sales techniques and services rendered customers; reviews an establishment's policies and standards to ascertain employee performance requirements; buys merchandise, orders food, or utilizes services to evaluate sales technique and courtesy of employees, carries merchandise to check stand or sales counter and observes employees during sales transaction to detect irregularities in listing or calling prices, itemizing merchandise, or handling cash; or delivers purchases to an agency conducting shopping investigation service; and, following any one or more of the above activities, writes a report of investigations for each establishment visited.[100]

15. Invasion of Privacy Claims

Aside from these statutory restrictions, an employer's use of physical surveillance in the workplace also may be limited by common-law privacy rights. Not all states recognize a common-law right to privacy.[101] In contrast, California not only recognizes a common-law right to privacy, but also guarantees the right of privacy in its state constitution.[102] Both of these privacy rights extend to private-sector employees, as well as public-sector employees.[103] As a result, employers operating in California or other jurisdictions recognizing state privacy rights should evaluate any physical surveillance program in the context of those rights.

---

[99] *Id.*

[100] *Id.*

[101] *See, e.g.*, Dana v. Oak Park Marina, Inc., 660 N.Y.S.2d 906, 909 (App. Div. 1997) (stating that New York does not recognize a common law right to privacy).

[102] *See, e.g.*, Hill v. National Collegiate Athletic Ass'n, 7 Cal. 4th 1, 16–17 (1994).

[103] *Id.* at 20 (holding that "article I, section 1 of the California Constitution creates a right of action against private as well as government entities"). *See also* Ortiz v. Los Angeles Police Relief Ass'n, 98 Cal. App. 4th 1288, 1300 (Ct. App. 2002) (applying the right of privacy under the California Constitution to an invasion of privacy claim against a private-sector employer).

a. Elements of Privacy Claim

Within the United States, California provides among the broadest privacy rights for employees. Generally, California law allows tort liability for an invasion of privacy.[104] In order to bring such a claim, two elements must be satisfied: (1) there must be "intrusion into a private place, conversation or matter" and (2) the intrusion must occur "in a manner highly offensive to a reasonable person."[105]

With respect to the element of "intrusion," an employee must show both that the employer "penetrated some zone of physical or sensory privacy surrounding [the employee]" and that the employee had "an objectively reasonable expectation" of privacy in that zone.[106] California courts have been willing to find hidden cameras to be more intrusive than plainly visible ones. For instance, the California Supreme Court held that covert use of a video recording device could constitute an invasion of privacy even if the matters recorded are not confidential.[107] *Sanders* involved a television reporter who obtained a job as a telephone psychic (or "telepsychic") for an undercover investigative report. While on the job, she wore a small concealed video camera to record her conversations with co-workers. After the broadcast of the report, one of her co-workers (a fellow telepsychic) filed an invasion of privacy claim under California law. The defendant argued that the co-worker had no reasonable expectation of privacy in the recorded conversations because they occurred in open areas in the workplace, where they could have been overheard by others. Without deciding whether the reporter actually committed an invasion of privacy, the California Supreme Court concluded that an employee may have a reasonable expectation of privacy against the covert recording of workplace conversations, particularly by a third party. The court explained that "in the workplace, as elsewhere,

[104] *See Hill*, 7 Cal. 4th at 24–26.

[105] *See* Shulman v. Group W Prods., Inc., 18 Cal. 4th 200, 231 (1998).

[106] *See id.* at 232.

[107] *See* Sanders v. American Broad. Cos., 20 Cal. 4th 907, 915 (1999) ("neither in *Shulman* nor in any other case have we stated that an expectation of privacy, in order to be reasonable for purposes of the intrusion tort, must be of *absolute* or *complete* privacy" (emphasis in original)).

the reasonableness of a person's expectation of visual and aural privacy depends not only on who might have been able to observe the subject interaction, but on the identity of the claimed intruder and the means of intrusion."[108] Therefore, although there is clearly a lesser expectation of privacy in open and accessible areas of the workplace, employees may still retain an expectation of privacy against covert recordings of workplace conversations.[109]

In determining whether the element of "offensiveness" has been met in a common-law privacy claim, California courts consider "the degree of the intrusion, the context, conduct and circumstances surrounding the intrusion as well as the intruder's motives and objectives, the setting into which he intrudes and the expectations of those whose privacy is invaded."[110] As applied to the video surveillance of employees, such surveillance was held to be insufficiently "offensive" for a common law tort claim when it was unaccompanied by audio capabilities and the camera was located in a nonprivate office where employees had a diminished expectation of privacy.[111]

b. *Effect of Providing Notice of Surveillance*

Notifying employees about the presence of video surveillance cameras may help to avoid invasion of privacy claims, as illustrated by the First Circuit's decision in *Vega-Rodriguez v. Puerto Rico Telephone Company.*[112] The workplace surveillance in *Vega-Rodriguez* involved the use of unconcealed video cameras in open areas of a public-sector workplace.[113] Although the

---

[108] *Id.* at 923.

[109] *See id.* at 921.

[110] Hill v. National Collegiate Athletic Ass'n, 7 Cal. 4th 1, 26 (1994) (quoting Miller v. National Broad. Cos., 187 Cal. App. 3d 1463, 1483–84 (Ct. App. 1986)).

[111] Sacramento County Deputy Sheriffs' Ass'n v. County of Sacramento, 51 Cal. App. 4th 1468, 1472–73 (Ct. App. 1996) (finding that employees did not have a reasonable expectation of privacy in the release office of the county jail where a hidden camera had been installed as part of an investigation into theft of prisoner property). *See also* Marrs v. Marriott Corp., 830 F. Supp. 274, 283–84 (D. Md. 1992) (stating that an employee had no reasonable expectation of privacy against video surveillance in an open, accessible area of the office).

[112] *See* Vega-Rodriguez v. Puerto Rico Tel. Co., 110 F.3d 174 (1st Cir. 1997).

[113] The employer in *Vega-Rodriguez* was a telephone company, a quasi-public employer that was held to be subject to the Fourth Amendment's limitations on government actors. *Id.* at 178. Consequently, the invasion of privacy claim under *Vega-*

cameras were plainly visible, the employer also notified employees about the presence of the cameras and explained the cameras' field of vision. The employer took the position that the cameras merely recorded the workplace areas and activities that could be viewed by a supervisor. In response, the employees argued that the video cameras were more intrusive because "the camera, unlike the human eye, never blinks."[114] The court dismissed this argument, stating that "[w]hen all is said and done, employees must accept some circumscription of their liberty as a condition of continued employment."[115]

It should be emphasized that *Vega-Rodriguez* involved the use of unconcealed video cameras in open areas of the workplace. The court cautioned that "cases involving the covert use of clandestine cameras, or cases involving electronically-assisted eavesdropping, may be quite another story."[116] Moreover, the court emphasized that providing notice of workplace surveillance does not automatically destroy any reasonable expectation of privacy. As an illustration, the court compared workplace video surveillance to a hypothetical situation raised by the U.S. Supreme Court. In *Smith v. Maryland*,[117] the Supreme Court observed that even "'if the Government were suddenly to announce on nationwide television that all homes henceforth would be subject to warrantless entry,' individuals still might entertain an actual expectation of privacy regarding their homes, papers and effects."[118] Similarly, notice may not entirely mitigate intrusion into an employee's reasonable expectation of privacy, given the other constraints explained above.

Based on the guidance provided by these cases, employers are advised to take steps to diminish any reasonable expectation of privacy prior to installing video surveillance equipment, such as providing notice that the area is under video surveillance, and

---

Rodriguez arose under the Fourth Amendment. This case also may be illustrative of the effect of notice under state constitutional or common-law rights to privacy, as in California.

[114] *Id.* at 180.

[115] *Id.* (citing INS v. Delgado, 466 U.S. 210, 218 (1984)).

[116] *Vega-Rodriguez*, 110 F.3d at 180 n.5.

[117] Smith v. Maryland, 442 U.S. 735 (1979).

[118] *Vega-Rodriguez*, 110 F.3d at 180 n.4 (citing *Smith*, 442 U.S. at 740 n.5).

installing cameras only when and where there is a legitimate business need for surveillance, as well as avoiding surveillance of prohibited locations.

16. Additional Restrictions on Surveillance in Public-Sector Employment

Privacy protections available to public sector employees are strengthened by the applicability of the Fourth Amendment to employer surveillance of their activities. Because the U.S. Constitution protects against unreasonable government interference, some type of "state action" must be present for an individual to claim a constitutional violation. Therefore, the Fourth Amendment's protection against unreasonable searches and seizures will generally apply only to a public sector worker.[119]

17. Video Surveillance Viewed by Courts as Highly Intrusive

The Tenth Circuit has observed that "[t]he showing of necessity needed to justify the use of video surveillance is higher than the showing needed to justify other search and seizure methods, including bugging. The use of a video camera is an extraordinarily intrusive method of searching. . . . Because of the invasive nature of video surveillance, the government's showing of necessity must be very high to justify its use."[120]

The court in *Mesa-Rincon* suggested that, despite the intrusiveness of video surveillance, a showing of governmental necessity could still provide sufficient justification for its use. This sentiment has been repeated by a number of courts when public sector workplace surveillance is at issue. For example, in *Cowles v. State*, the Alaska Supreme Court found prevention of workplace theft to be a legitimate business purpose for video surveillance, while cautioning that "[l]acking a legitimate purpose, or reason-

---

[119]*See* O'Connor v. Ortega, 480 U.S. 709, 715 (1987) ("Searches and seizures by government employers . . . are subject to the restraints of the Fourth Amendment.").

[120]United States. v. Mesa-Rincon, 911 F.2d 1433, 1442 (10th Cir. 1990).

able cause, the utility of the monitoring would be diminished and a different balance might be struck."[121]

18. An Employee's Reasonable Expectation of Privacy Varies Based on the Type of Area Under Surveillance

In defining what areas of the workplace can be considered "private," courts have generally held that surveillance does not offend the Fourth Amendment if a camera is pointed at an open area.[122] In *United States v. Taketa*, the Ninth Circuit slightly expanded the area in which an employee may reasonably expect privacy.[123] The court explained that "even 'private' business offices are often subject to the legitimate visits of coworkers, supervisors, and the public, without defeating the expectation of privacy unless the office is 'so open to fellow employees or the public that no expectation of privacy is reasonable.'"[124] Thus, a key factor in

---

[121]Cowles v. State, 23 P.3d 1168, 1175 (Alaska 2001) (finding that the University of Alaska had legitimate reason to use a hidden video camera to target an employee suspected of theft). *See also* Thompson v. Johnson County Cmty. Coll., 930 F. Supp. 501, 508 (D. Kan. 1996), *aff'd mem.,* 108 F.3d 1388 (10th Cir. 1997) (holding that surveillance was not unreasonable where it was "uncontroverted that [the employer's] purpose for the video surveillance was work-related; they were investigating reports of employee misconduct in the locker area . . ."); Brannen v. Board of Educ., 144 Ohio App. 3d 620 (Ct. App. 2001) (rejecting custodians' claim of privacy in break room on the ground that it was, in fact, an all-purpose room used by teachers and other school employees, which was also open to administrative personnel).

[122]*See* Vega-Rodriguez v. Puerto Rico Tel. Co., 110 F.3d 174, 181 (1st Cir. 1997). *See also* United States v. O'Reilly, Crim. No. 91-678, 1992 U.S. Dist. LEXIS 8187 (E.D. Pa. Mar. 13, 1992) (involving the use of visible cameras, without audio recording capabilities, pointed at employee common areas). *Cf.* Plock v. Board of Educ., No. 07-C-50060, 2007 U.S. Dist. LEXIS 93141 (N.D. Ill. Dec. 18, 2007) (finding that teachers do not have an expectation of privacy in their classrooms and installing both video *and* audio surveillance equipment in a classroom, even though the classroom may contain a teacher's personal office space, is not a violation of the Fourth Amendment).

[123]United States v. Taketa, 923 F.2d 665 (9th Cir. 1991). *See also* Trujillo v. City of Ontario, 248 F. Supp. 2d 1094 (C.D. Cal. 2006) (finding that plaintiffs' Fourth Amendment rights were violated where a locker room was subject to covert video surveillance).

[124]*Taketa*, 923 F.2d at 673, 675 (quoting *O'Connor*, 480 U.S. at 717–18). *But see* Sacramento County Deputy Sheriffs' Ass'n v. County of Sacramento, 51 Cal. App. 4th 1468, 1483 n.10 (Ct. App. 1996) (noting that "*Taketa* still does not help plaintiffs, because in that case the office was exclusively assigned to someone. Here, the [videotaped area] was not exclusively assigned to any one person.").

assessing whether an employee has a reasonable expectation of privacy in a certain area of the workplace is the extent to which other individuals have regular access to that area.[125]

19. Title III of the Omnibus Crime Control and Safe Streets Act May Also Provide a Source of Protection for Public Employees

A further area in which public sector employees may find privacy protection against video surveillance is Title III of the Omnibus Crime Control and Safe Streets Act of 1968 (Title III). Title III establishes warrant requirements for intercepting wire, oral, or electronic communications during criminal investigations.[126] Although Title III is silent regarding video surveillance, some courts have applied Title III to video surveillance by law enforcement agencies, and federal courts have also held that the procedures established by Title III must be followed in determining whether video surveillance by law enforcement officials violates Fourth Amendment protections.[127] Certain cases have further held that Title III creates a private right of action for video surveillance.[128] Despite the lack of clear case law in this area, it currently appears likely that if Title III is to be applied to the workplace

---

[125]It also should be noted that video surveillance stands a much greater chance of avoiding Fourth Amendment privacy implications if it is not coupled with audio. At least one court has held that even where a reasonable expectation of privacy exists—in this instance, a break room—video surveillance that does not capture private conversations likely does not violate the Fourth Amendment. *See* Brannen v. Board of Educ., 144 Ohio App. 3d 620, 629–30 (Ct. App. 2001).

[126]Please refer to Chapter 10 for a more detailed discussion of limitations on interception of electronic communications.

[127]*See, e.g., Taketa*, 923 F.2d at 677 (warrantless video surveillance by law enforcement personnel for law enforcement purposes violated employee's Fourth Amendment rights).

[128]*See* Boddie v. American Broad. Cos., 731 F.2d 333, 336 (6th Cir. 1984) (creating a private cause of action against journalists who had used a hidden camera and microphone to record conversations); 18 U.S.C. §2520(a) ("any person whose wire, oral, or electronic communication is intercepted, disclosed, or intentionally used in violation of this chapter . . . may in a civil action recover from the person or entity, other than the United States, which engaged in that violation such relief as may be appropriate").

context, the video surveillance would need to include an audio component.[129]

20. *Additional U.S. Restrictions on Surveillance in a Unionized Workplace*

Audio and video surveillance in a union workplace brings with it added protections relating to employee privacy, including protections emanating from the NLRA and the LMRA. These acts of Congress affect not only the observation of organized labor activities, but also general video surveillance in the bargaining unit workplace.

This section addresses monitoring and surveillance in a unionized facility. Please refer to Chapter 4 concerning restrictions imposed on employer surveillance of off-duty, off-site union activities by employees.

21. *Restrictions on Surveillance of Union Activities*

Courts have held that intentional video surveillance of employees engaged in protected union activities, such as union organizing, violates the NLRA's prohibition against interfering, restraining, or coercing employees involved in these activities.[130]

---

[129]Title I of the Electronic Communications Privacy Act of 1986 (18 U.S.C. §§2510 et seq.) amended and retitled Title III of the Omnibus Crime Control and Safe Streets Act of 1968. Thompson v. Johnson County Cmty. Coll., 930 F. Supp. 501, 503 n.1 (D. Kan. 1996), *aff'd mem.,* 108 F.3d 1388 (10th Cir. 1997). *See Thompson*, 930 F. Supp. at 505 (finding that silent video surveillance does not fall within the protection of Title I of the Electronic Communications Privacy Act); United States v. Koyomejian, 970 F.2d 536, 539–40 (9th Cir. 1992) (arguing that Congress did not intend to regulate domestic silent video surveillance, stating that "if law enforcement officials were to install their own cameras and create their own closed circuit television pictures of a meeting, the capturing of the video images would not be an interception under the statute because there would be no interception of the contents of an electronic communication. Intercepting the audio portion of the meeting would be an interception of an oral communication, and the statute would apply to that portion." (quoting S. Rep. No. 541, 99th Cong., 2d Sess. 16–17, reprinted in 1986 U.S.C.CAN 3555, 3570–71)).

[130]*See* 29 U.S.C. §158(a). The concern is that such surveillance will negatively affect employees who are exercising their lawful rights to organize. *See* California Acrylic Indus., Inc. v. NLRB, 150 F.3d 1095, 1099–100 (9th Cir. 1998). *See also* National Steel & Shipbuilding Co. v. NLRB, 156 F.3d 1268, 1272 (D.C. Cir. 1998) (upholding an NLRB ruling that an employer's installation of a video camera at the

Courts have stated that surveillance of union activities is permissible only to the extent "'necessary to the furtherance of legitimate business interest.'"[131] *Parsippany Hotel* involved increased staffing of a hotel's security force during labor organizing activities. The D.C. Circuit found that the mere possibility of illegal activity or violence was insufficient justification for surveillance that was otherwise unlawful under the NLRA.[132]

State laws also restrict an employer's monitoring or surveillance of its employees' union activities. Under New York law, an employer may not conduct surveillance of or spy on employees engaged in union activities.[133] New York courts also have held that an employer may not engage an employee to conduct surveillance, either surreptitiously or in person, of employees who pass out union leaflets outside a place of business.[134] Similarly, an employer may not search an employee's locker for union literature, even if the employer has a key to the locker.[135]

22. *Restrictions on Video Surveillance in a Unionized Facility*

The NLRB has held that employers cannot unilaterally impose video surveillance upon their union employees, and has repeatedly stated that video surveillance of employees in union bargaining units is a mandatory subject of collective bargaining with their union.[136] In *Colgate-Palmolive*, the employer had placed hidden

---

location of union rallies interfered with and coerced employees who were engaged in peaceful union activity).

[131] *See* Parsippany Hotel Mgmt. Co. v. NLRB, 99 F.3d 413, 420 (D.C. Cir. 1996) (citing The Broadway, 267 NLRB 385, 401 (1983)).

[132] *See Parsipanny*, 99 F.3d at 420.

[133] N.Y. LAB. LAW §704.

[134] New York State Labor Relations Bd. v. Frank G. Shattuck Co., 20 N.Y.S.2d 949, 960 (1940).

[135] *Id.*

[136] *See, e.g.*, Colgate-Palmolive Co., 323 NLRB 515, 516 n.10 (1997) (stating that "the placing of cameras, and the extent to which they will be secret or hidden, if at all, is a proper subject of negotiations between the Respondent and the Union"). *See also* National Steel Corp. v. NLRB, 324 F.3d 928, 932–33 (7th Cir. 2003) (holding that the NLRB could determine that the use of cameras was a mandatory subject of collective bargaining, and could thus order an employer to bargain with unions over the use of cameras and the provision of information about such cameras); Brewers & Maltsters, Local Union No. 6 v. NLRB, 414 F.3d 36, 42–44 (D.C. Cir. 2005) (finding that an employer's use of hidden surveillance cameras to monitor an area where its employees occasionally worked and took breaks was a mandatory subject of bargaining).

surveillance cameras in the workplace as a means of investigating a recent increase in workplace theft. The employer subsequently refused the union's request to bargain over the installation of the cameras.[137] While recognizing that management sought to keep the installation of the cameras secret to facilitate the investigation, the Board nevertheless determined that the cameras were a mandatory subject of collective bargaining, similar to other investigatory tools such as physical examinations, drug and alcohol testing, and polygraph testing.[138]

23. *Private-Sector Employers*

As discussed in Section II.A.15, above, even private-sector employees may have a right of privacy under common law or state constitutional protections. The California Supreme Court has identified three "essential elements" of an invasion of privacy claim: (1) a "legally protected privacy interest," (2) "a reasonable expectation of privacy," and (3) a serious invasion of the privacy interest.[139] The *Hill* standards have been applied to invasion of privacy claims by employees as well.[140]

a. *Elements of an Invasion of Privacy Claim*

i. *Legally Protected Privacy Interest*

The first element of an "invasion of privacy" claim is the plaintiff's "legally protected privacy interest."[141] In *Hill*, the California Supreme Court recognized two types of privacy rights. First, the court recognized a legally protected right to "informational privacy," which applies to a person's "interests in precluding the dissemination or misuse of sensitive and confidential information."[142] Second, the court recognized an interest in "autonomy privacy," which applies to a person's "interests in making intimate personal decisions or conducting personal activities without

---

[137] *See Colgate-Palmolive*, 323 NLRB at 516.

[138] *Id.* at 515.

[139] Hill v. National Collegiate Athletic Ass'n, 7 Cal. 4th 1, 35–37 (Cal. 1994).

[140] *See, e.g.*, TBG Ins. Servs. Corp. v. Superior Court, 96 Cal. App. 4th 443, 449–52 (Ct. App. 2002) (using *Hill* factors to analyze employee's claim of invasion of privacy based on employer's monitoring of his computer use).

[141] *Hill*, 7 Cal. 4th at 35.

[142] *Id.*

observation, intrusion, or interference."[143] The *Hill* court noted that other privacy interests may be derived from social norms based on "common law development, constitutional development, statutory enactment, and the ballot arguments accompanying the Privacy Initiative."[144]

ii. Reasonable Expectation of Privacy

The second element of an invasion of privacy claim is the plaintiff's "reasonable expectation of privacy."[145] While this is a fact-specific assessment, a "reasonable expectation of privacy" depends on the facts of a plaintiff's particular situation and "broadly based and widely accepted community norms."[146] In the context of workplace searches and inspections, a plaintiff must establish that he not only believed that the location searched was not subject to employer inspection, but that this belief was reasonably held. As discussed in Section II.A.18, an employer may take measures to decrease an employee's reasonable expectations of privacy, such as notifying employees of the possibility of workplace searches.

iii. Serious Invasion of Privacy Interests

Finally, actionable invasions of privacy must be "sufficiently serious in their nature, scope, and actual or potential impact to constitute an egregious breach of the social norms underlying the privacy right."[147] A plaintiff must show that the "nature, scope, and actual or potential impact" of the defendant's intrusion into their privacy was an "egregious breach of the social norms underlying the [California Constitution's] privacy right."[148] In deciding how and when to search an employee's belongings or space, an employer should consider the degree to which the search will be a "serious" invasion of the employee's privacy before performing the search or inspections.[149]

---

[143] *Id.* at 35–36.
[144] *Id.*
[145] *Id.* at 36–37.
[146] *Id.*
[147] *Id.* at 37.
[148] *Id.*
[149] *Id.*

b. Employer's "Competing Nonprivacy Interests" Defense

In defending against an invasion of privacy claim, an employer may assert "competing interests" that may outweigh the privacy interest of the plaintiff.[150] As the California Supreme Court explained, "Invasion of a privacy interest is not a violation of the state constitutional right to privacy if the invasion is justified by a competing interest."[151] If a defendant can establish a "legitimate interest" that justifies the invasion of privacy, this may serve as a defense to liability.[152] However, the individual may challenge this justification by showing that the defendant failed to take advantage of potential safeguards and alternatives that would have avoided or minimized the invasion of privacy.[153]

In the context of workplace searches, one may observe that the same search, performed with different interests in mind, might be "justified" or an unlawful invasion of privacy. For example, consider a situation in which an employer searches an employee's purse in a locked desk drawer. If an employer conducts the search because he has reason to believe the employee has a gun in her purse and has threatened a co-worker, the courts may find that the employer's reasonable interest in workplace safety outweighed the employee's interest in keeping the contents of her purse private. In contrast, if an employer randomly searches an employee's purse in a locked desk drawer because he is curious to find out what kinds of personal items she takes to the office, the employer's justification may be too weak to outweigh the employee's privacy interest. Employers should consider the strength of their nonprivacy interests before performing searches, as discussed further in Section II.A.10. A court's assessment of a plaintiff's "invasion of privacy" claim does not end at finding a defendant's interest to be justified, however. A plaintiff may respond to the defendant's defense of a "justified" interest by showing that the defendant could have used "protective measures, safeguards, and alternatives" that would

[150] *Id.* at 37–38.
[151] *Id.*
[152] *Id.* at 38.
[153] *Id.*

have minimized or avoided the intrusion on the plaintiff's privacy interests.[154]

24. *Public-Sector Employers*

Beyond the protections of state law, government employees enjoy additional protection from workplace searches from the guarantees of the Fourth Amendment of the U.S. Constitution.[155]

a. *Expectations of Privacy in the Public-Sector Workplace*

In the case of searches by a public employer, the threshold inquiry is whether the employee had a legitimate expectation of privacy in the workplace.[156] The employee's expectation of privacy must be an expectation that society would recognize as reasonable.[157] The factors to consider are whether the employee took measures to maintain privacy, the manner in which the employee used the space or article that is the subject of the search, and whether the employee possessed the right to exclude others from the space or article that is the subject of the search.[158]

In *O'Connor v. Ortega*, a doctor brought suit when his office and desk were searched by hospital personnel following his suspension during a hospital investigation into his potential misconduct.[159] Personal items such as a greeting card and a book of poetry were seized from the doctor's desk and subsequently used as evidence against him in an administrative proceeding.[160] The U.S. Supreme Court found that the doctor had a reasonable expectation of privacy in his desk because he did not allow others to have access to its contents.[161] The hospital did not have a policy regarding its ability to search personal items in the workplace, but the Court noted that "the absence of such a policy does not [automati-

---

[154] *Id.*

[155] *See, e.g.*, O'Connor v. Ortega, 480 U.S. 709, 719 (1987).

[156] *Id.* at 715–17.

[157] People v. Holland, 591 N.Y.S.2d 744, 746 (N.Y. City Crim. Ct. 1992) (citing Katz v. United States, 389 U.S. 347, 361 (1967) (Harlan, J., concurring)).

[158] *Id.*

[159] *O'Connor*, 480 U.S. at 713.

[160] *Id.*

[161] *Id.* at 718.

cally] create an expectation of privacy" in a workplace area where an employee might store personal items.[162] At the same time, the Court cautioned that very personal items, such as a handbag or briefcase, are not part of the workplace simply because the items happen to be located in a place of employment.[163] Therefore, public sector employers must exercise caution in searching personal property brought by employees into the workplace.

An employee's expectation of privacy in the contents of his office will vary depending on the degree to which the office is generally accessible to others.[164] For example, a public employee who occupies a private office with a door; has exclusive use of a desk, filing cabinet, or computer; and does not share these spaces with other employees may have a reasonable expectation of privacy in those areas.[165] Conversely, a law clerk found no reasonable expectation of privacy in his office, desk, filing cabinet, or computer files due to the nature of judicial chambers, where an "absolute free flow of information" is necessary between a judge and his clerks.[166] As discussed in the following section, however, even an employee's reasonable expectation of privacy may still bow in relation to an employer's legitimate need to investigate work-related misconduct.[167]

b. Balancing of Public Employer's Legitimate Interests

Generally, given the "special needs" of public employers, they are allowed to conduct workplace searches that are reasonably related to an investigation of employee misconduct, thus lowering the employee's reasonable expectation of privacy.[168] A search is reasonable and justified at its inception if the employer has reasonable grounds to believe that the search will uncover employee-related work misconduct.[169] A search is also reasonable

[162] *Id.* at 719.

[163] *Id.* at 716.

[164] *Id.*

[165] Leventhal v. Knapek, 266 F.3d 64, 74 (2d Cir. 2001).

[166] Sheppard v. Beerman, 18 F.3d 147, 152 (2d Cir. 1994).

[167] *See, e.g., Leventhal*, 266 F.3d at 74.

[168] Morris v. Port Auth. of N.Y. & N.J., 736 N.Y.S.2d 324, 328 (App. Div. 2002) (quoting *Leventhal*, 266 F.3d at 73 (citing, in turn, *O'Connor*, 480 U.S. at 732 (Scalia, J., concurring))).

[169] *Id.*

and justified when conducted for a work-related reason, such as obtaining a file.[170]

To stay within the realm of reasonableness, a search must not be excessively intrusive in relation to its purpose.[171] In *Gossmeyer v. McDonald*, for example, law enforcement agents searched the office of an investigator from the child protective services agency, based on an anonymous tip that she kept child pornography in her desk. The search included the employee's locked desk, as well as a locked storage cabinet and locked filing cabinet that she had purchased at her own expense for extra storage of work-related materials. The Seventh Circuit rejected the employee's claim that the search violated her Fourth Amendment rights, concluding that she had no reasonable expectation of privacy in her office or the locked furniture. The court further concluded that the search was justified in any event, due to the nature of the reported misconduct.[172]

Law enforcement employees also have diminished expectations of privacy in the workplace, given the government's need to regulate officer conduct.[173]

25. *Postal Mail Received by Employees at the Workplace*

New York Penal Law Section 250.25 prohibits employers from tampering with the private communications of employees and provides that such tampering is punishable as a misdemeanor. Under this law, an employer may not open or read a sealed letter or other sealed private communication without the consent of the sender or of the receiver, or publish the contents of the communication without their consent.[174]

---

[170] *Id.*

[171] *Id.*

[172] Gossmeyer v. McDonald, 128 F.3d 481, 490–91 (7th Cir. 1997).

[173] *Morris* at 329. *See also* Moore v. Constantine, 594 N.Y.S.2d 395, 397 (App. Div. 1993) (finding that police officers have no reasonable expectation of privacy in their station lockers, where their personal property is stored). *Cf.* Wiley v. Department of Justice, 328 F.3d 1346, 1351 (Fed. Cir. 2003) (holding that a jail employee had no reasonable expectation of privacy against the employer's search of his car parked in the institution's lot, given that the agency maintained control over the parking lot and advised all visitors and employees that persons and property, including cars and packages, were subject to routine searches).

[174] N.Y. PENAL LAW §250.25 (Consol. 2006).

This statute has been found not to protect private communications sent to municipal employees in the care of the municipality.[175] Employees may not use the municipality as a mailing address and doing so constitutes an illegal use of public moneys.[176] In *Freedman*, the court declined to hold that a municipal employee's mail was "private" because it was sent through the care of the municipality and was not marked as being "personal and confidential."[177] The court further reasoned that even if the letter had been clearly marked for privacy, the sender and the receiver still bore the risk that the letter would be opened because the municipality was not a personal mailing address for employees.[178] Although mail sent to a municipal employee should remain confidential, the sender and receiver bear the risk that the communication may be opened even if it is marked as being personal and confidential.[179]

Practice Pointers. Because courts balance an employee's "reasonable expectation of privacy" with the employer's interests in both federal and state contexts, an employer can take steps to limit its potential liability. First, employers should inform employees that all property in the workplace is subject to search or inspection. Second, employers should perform searches only when they have a strong interest in performing the search, and conduct the search in a manner that minimizes any invasion of the employee's privacy.

26. Setting Reasonable Workplace Privacy Expectations

Employees may not have a reasonable expectation of privacy if the employer has notified employees that property in the workplace is subject to searches and inspections. For example, in *United States v. Bunkers*, a postal employee did not have a "reasonable expectation of privacy" to support her Fourth Amendment claim

[175]People v. Freedman, 386 N.Y.S.2d 306, 307 (N.Y. City Ct. 1976).
[176]*Id.*
[177]*Id.*
[178]*Id.*
[179]*Id.*

that her employer illegally searched her locker because she had been notified that her locker could be searched at any time.[180]

In contrast, employees may have a reasonable expectation of privacy in the workplace if areas of their "exclusive use" are searched and there is no policy notifying them that those areas may be searched. In *Schowengerdt v. General Dynamics Corp.*, a Navy employer searched a civilian Navy employee's locked desk drawers and used information gathered from the search to make a decision to terminate the employee.[181] The court found that the plaintiff did have a reasonable expectation of privacy in his locked desk drawers because there were "no regulations providing for searches" and his office was searched not for a legitimate government interest, but rather to inquire as to his "sexual practices."[182]

In summary, employers intending to conduct workplace searches are advised to (1) implement and publish policies informing employees that workplace searches will be conducted as required by legitimate business reasons; (2) prohibit employees from using personal locks on employer provided property; (3) maintain keys and combinations for all employer-provided locks, and advise employees that the employer has copies of all such keys; and (4) consider seeking the employee's consent prior to searching personal property such as pockets, purses, briefcases, and lunch boxes, either at the time of the search or through an acknowledgment form announcing the search policy.

27. Limiting the Intrusiveness of Workplace Searches

Employers have the strongest interest in searching their employees' workspace or belongings if their searches are work-related in nature. The U.S. Supreme Court has noted that an employer's retrieval of workplace materials, as part of their "actual office practices and procedures," does not violate employees' expecta-

---

[180]United States v. Bunkers, 521 F.2d 1217, 1221 (9th Cir. 1975). *See also* United States v. Gonzalez, 300 F.3d 1048, 1051–52 (9th Cir. 2002) (holding that an employee on a U.S. Air Force base did not have a reasonable expectation of privacy in the contents of his backpack, because he was aware of the store policy of performing random searches to prevent theft and consented to the search).

[181]Schowengerdt v. General Dynamics Corp., 823 F.2d 1328, 1331 (9th Cir. 1987).

[182]*Id.* at 1335–36.

tions of privacy.[183] The California Supreme Court has emphasized that a defendant's justification for intruding on another person's privacy must be substantial and central to the defendant's operations.[184] Thus, in the employment context, an employer's reason for searching his employee's belongings should be as close as possible to the functions of the office and running an efficient and safe workplace. Employers also should limit disclosure of the information obtained through the search to those with a legitimate need to know that information.[185]

III. EUROPE

A. The European Union Approach

1. *Email and Internet Monitoring*

As opposed to the United States, European employees can expect privacy in their communications at the workplace. In the case *Niemitz v. Germany*, the European Court of Human Rights stated:

> Respect for private life must also comprise to a certain degree the right to establish and develop relationships with other human beings. There appears, furthermore, to be no reason of principle why this understanding of the notion of private life should be taken to exclude activities of a professional or business nature since it is, after all, in the course of their working lives that the majority of people have a significant, if not the greatest, opportunity of developing relationships with the outside world. This view is supported by the fact that ... it is not always possible to distinguish clearly which of an individual's activities form part of his professional or business life and which do not.[186]

Monitoring of employee communications is highly regulated in the Member States of the EU and subject to a plethora of legal provisions and statutes. In particular, companies may be required

---

[183]O'Connor v. Ortega, 480 U.S. 709, 725–26, 732 (1987) (Scalia, J., concurring).

[184]Hill v. National Collegiate Athletic Ass'n, 7 Cal. 4th 1, 38 (Cal. 1994).

[185]*Cf. id.*

[186]ECHR, 23 November 1992, Series A No. 251/B, para. 29.

to comply with national data protection acts (DP Acts), telecommunication regulations, labor laws, constitutional provisions, criminal laws, as well as collective bargaining agreements. The Article 29 Working Party (the Working Party), comprising the representatives of the Member State Data Protection Authorities[187] (DPAs), has issued guidance relating to employee monitoring in the EU. In 2002 the Working Party adopted a working paper on the surveillance of electronic communications in the workplace (WP55)[188] that emphasizes the prevention of the misuse of company resources with means other than monitoring, which should generally be avoided unless there is a specific and important business need. In 2006, the Working Party issued further guidance on email filtering, condemning covert filtering or monitoring (WP118).[189] Even though the working papers issued by the Working Party are nonbinding and can be used only as guidance, the Member State DPAs take note of them in applying the applicable national laws. Many Member State DPAs have also issued guidance papers.

Once an employer decides to monitor employees, the Working Party suggests that the employer follow seven basic principles to ensure that the monitoring is done properly and in accordance with the right of privacy of the individual employees. These principles are:

- *Necessity.* Prior to monitoring, an employer must assess whether the monitoring in all its forms is absolutely necessary for the specified purpose. Generally, monitoring of employees' electronic communications and Internet usage is deemed unnecessary unless specific conditions are met

[187]The Working Party was established by Article 29 of Directive 95/46/EC on the protection of individuals with regard to the processing of personal data, and on the free movement of such data, Official Journal L 281, p.p31, 23 November 1995 (Directive). It is composed of representatives of national data protection authorities and the data protection unit at the European Commission acts as its secretariat.

[188]Working Party 29, WP55, surveillance of electronic communications in the workplace, adopted 19 May 2002.

[189]Working Party 29, WP118, privacy issues related to the provision of email screening services, adopted 21 February 2006.

(i.e., when proof of employee's criminal action must be obtained or when the employer's interests may be compromised). Less intrusive methods should therefore always be used if possible.

- *Finality.* Data collected through the monitoring activity must respond to a "*specified, explicit and legitimate*" purpose (i.e., the security of the system) and cannot be processed for a different purpose.
- *Transparency.* The monitoring activities must be transparent. In practice, this means that the employer must provide robust notice to employees about the monitoring. This notice should tell employees whether equipment may be used for private purposes; what the scope of the monitoring is, considering that employees' private emails enjoy a greater degree of protection and can be accessed only in exceptional circumstances (such as for the security of the system); what the surveillance measures are; what the consequences for noncompliance are; and how the employee can respond to accusations. Transparency of the monitoring also increases when employees' representatives are consulted before monitoring begins and the local DPA is notified about the processing of personal data by means of monitoring. Finally, the right of employees to access the data that an employer holds about them ensures the employees' right to transparency as they can always verify the types of data and the purposes for their processing with the DPA. Most of these requirements are compulsory under local Member State law.
- *Legitimacy.* Employers may monitor employees only to safeguard their legitimate interests and provided that they do not violate the employees' fundamental rights. Compliance with the legitimacy principle is difficult to assess in practice, especially with regard to the vague concept of "employer's legitimate interest." The Working Party considers, for example, that an employer's need to prevent the disclosure of confidential information to competitors is a legitimate interest. Importantly, monitoring cannot be

legitimate when processing employees' "sensitive data"[190] pursuant to Article 8 of the Directive 95/46/EC (the Directive), especially when those data are collected by means of monitoring.

- *Proportionality.* Personal data processed through monitoring must be adequate, relevant, and not excessive with regard to the purpose for which they are processed. For instance, the monitoring of emails should focus on the traffic data of the participants and time of the communication rather than on the content of communications.
- *Accuracy and retention of data.* Personal data captured through the monitoring activity must be updated and retained only for the period deemed necessary for the purpose to be achieved (no longer than three months).
- *Security.* The employer must adopt all appropriate technical and organizational measures to ensure that any personal data are protected from alteration, unauthorized access, and misuse.

2. *Monitoring of Employee Telephone Calls*

Employers monitoring employees' use of telephone equipment may do so only in compliance with the general requirements set forth in the Directive as implemented into Member State law. Furthermore, Member State laws place strict requirements on monitoring and intercepting of telephone calls.

3. *Video Surveillance*

The Working Party has considered video surveillance equipment and its use in daily life in different contexts. In its adopted nonbinding opinions[191, 192] the Working Party highlights a number of general principles that should be considered as part of an essen-

---

[190]Pursuant to Article 8 of the Directive, sensitive data are those data revealing racial or ethnic origin, political opinions, religious or philosophical beliefs, or trade union membership as well as data disclosing health status or sex life.

[191]Opinion No. 4/2004 on the Processing of Personal Data by means of Video Surveillance.

[192]2002 Working Document on the Processing of Personal Data by means of Video Surveillance.

tial framework for every kind of data processing, even when it is carried out through video surveillance. Although the Working Party opinions are nonbinding, the Member State DPAs consider them highly authoritative.

Video surveillance as such (including that carried out at the workplace) is caught by the general principles enshrined in the Directive.[193]

In fact, Recital 14 of the Directive establishes that it is applicable to the processing of data through "techniques used to capture, transmit, manipulate, record, store or communicate sound and image data relating to a natural person."

Furthermore, Recital 26 adds that the principles of protection of the Directive "apply to any information concerning an identified or identifiable person, [...] by taking into account of all the means likely reasonably to be used either by the controller or by any other person to identify the said person." Image and sound data are considered as information concerning an identifiable or identified person.

Lastly, Article 33 of the Directive clearly refers to video surveillance and states that the European Commission shall submit "any appropriate proposals which prove to be necessary, taking into account of developments in information technology and in the light of the state of progress in the information society."

As with email and Internet monitoring, necessity, finality, transparency, legitimacy, proportionality, accuracy, retention of data, and security are the common bases for video surveillance. Nonetheless, the Working Party points out that "*video surveillance systems aimed directly at controlling, from a remote location, quality and amount of the working activities, therefore entailing the processing of personal data in this context, should not be permitted as a rule.*"[194]

4. *Works Councils Role in Monitoring*

A particularly European element in setting up monitoring in the workplace relates to the role of the Works Councils. There

---

[193] Recital 16 of the Directive.

[194] *See* para. 8 of Opinion No. 4/2004 on the Processing of Personal Data by means of Video Surveillance.

are both EU-wide Works Councils and national Works Councils. The level of involvement of Works Councils in employee monitoring depends on the latitude given to them under national law. For example, in Austria the employer must obtain agreement from the Works Council even when employees have given their consent to monitoring. In Belgium, on the other hand, the Works Council needs only to be informed and consulted prior to adopting monitoring technologies. Finland grants its Works Councils "cooperation rights" with respect to the methods of monitoring.

Agreements between employers and Works Councils governing monitoring are seen as a way to bypass the obstacles created by the need to obtain "free and unambiguous" consent from employees. The logic here is that through appropriate agreements between employers and Works Councils, employees are adequately protected, their privacy rights are secured, and as a result, consent obtained from employees is valid.

The International Labor Organization Code of Practice on the protection of workers' personal data illustrates the role of the Works Councils in employee monitoring. In particular:

- Workers and their representatives should be kept informed of any data collection process as well as rules that govern that process and their rights in that process;
- Workers' representatives, where they exist, and in conformity with national law and practice, should be informed and consulted (1) concerning the introduction and modification of automated systems that process workers' personal data; (2) before the introduction of any electronic monitoring of workers' behavior in the workplace; and (3) about the purpose, content, and manner of administering and interpreting any questionnaires and tests concerning the personal data of the workers; and
- Employers, workers, and their representatives should cooperate in protecting personal data and in developing policies on workers' privacy consistent with the principles set forth in the Code of Practice.

Although these principles are yet to be fully implemented in the EU Member State data protection legislation (for instance, no mention of Works Councils is made in the Directive), the role and influence of Works Councils in Europe are significant. When employers want to reduce employees' expectation of privacy, Works Councils are decisive in making these actions legitimate. Before employers, even justifiably, introduce potentially intrusive technologies such as video surveillance equipment, they should involve the Works Councils in the process in addition to complying with the applicable local laws.

B. Finland

1. Email and Internet Monitoring

Unlike a number of other EU Member States, Finland has enacted a law on the protection of privacy at work, the Act on Data Protection in Working Life (the Working Life DP Act).[195] While the generally applicable DP Act also applies to personal data processed in the employment context, the Working Life DP Act purports to address the special concerns present in the workplace. "Employees" are defined in the Working Life DP Act as both existing employees and job applicants.

The Working Life DP Act applies to all forms of employee monitoring regardless of the form, as well as to other types of processing of employee personal data. The Working Life DP Act requires employers to address the following general processing requirements:

- *Necessity.* The employer may process only personal data that are necessary in the context of the employee's relationship with the employer, such as data necessary for determining employees' rights and duties, benefits, or particular job requirements. Employee's consent does not exempt the employer from the necessity requirement. For example, amassing large databases of employee Internet use would very likely run afoul of the necessity requirement.
- *The employee must be the primary source of personal data related to himself.* If an employer uses other sources of

[195]Laki Yksityisyyden Suojasta Työelämässä, 13.8.2004/759.

> personal data related to the employee, the employer must obtain the employee's consent. Recently, the Finnish DPA issued a controversial public statement according to which "googling" information about job applicants falls within this requirement. Thus, employers who "google" personal data related to applicants would be in breach of the Working Life DP Act if they do not have the applicant's consent for doing so.

The Working Life DP Act places detailed requirements on the monitoring of employee emails. Personal email accounts, as well as Internet use, are subject to more stringent requirements defined in other laws such as the Act on Data Protection in Electronic Communications.[196] Thus, the requirements mentioned here apply only to email accounts assigned to the employee by the employer for work purposes.

Employers have a duty of care with regard to the email system and therefore email messages may be monitored or opened only if the employer has in place technology whereby (1) through use of an auto-reply facility the employee may notify senders about his absence and about the person in charge of ongoing matters during the absence; (2) the employee may forward the messages either to another employee or to an acceptable external email account; or (3) the employee may consent to another employee receiving his email messages for the purpose of ascertaining whether there are messages that are necessary for the employer's business. Only if the employee does not make use of any of these available options can the employer find out whether the employee's inbox contains messages that are necessary for business purposes. Even then, identifying and opening of individual messages is subject to strict conditions.

In order to determine whether a message is necessary for business purposes and consequently not a personal message, the employer should focus on the sender and recipient identifiers and the information on the subject line of the message. If the nature of the message is not apparent based on this information, the

---

[196] Sähköisen viestinnän tietosuojalaki 16.6.2004/516.

employer may open the message only if the following conditions are present:

- The employee works independently and the employer does not have in place a system whereby the matters handled by the employee are accounted for;
- Based on the ongoing tasks of the employee it is readily apparent that business-related messages have been sent and received;
- The employee is temporarily prevented from performing his tasks and despite the facilities the employer has arranged, the employee's messages cannot be accessed; and
- The employee's consent cannot be obtained within a reasonable time and the matter is urgent.

Once a message has been identified and regardless of whether it is opened or not, the employee must be notified immediately in writing. Moreover, those participating in the identification and possible opening of the message may not disclose the identity of the sender or the recipient or the content of the message to third parties during or after their employment with the employer.

As with any other form of employee monitoring, Internet monitoring is subject to the general duty of cooperation with the employee representatives in accordance with the Act on Cooperation Within Companies.[197] Once the employer has carried out its duty to cooperate, it must define the purposes of the monitoring and the technical measures used in the monitoring; most important, it must notify the employees about the purposes of the monitoring, the timeframe for the implementation, the methods of monitoring used, and the methods of monitoring is applied to the use of email and the Internet.

In general, monitoring of employee Internet use should not target individual employees and should be carried out only for the purposes of network security and detection, prevention, and investigation of misuse.

---

[197] Laki yhteistoiminnasta yrityksissä 22.9.1978/725.

2. *Monitoring of Employee Telephone Calls*

According to the Finnish Constitution, the secrecy of correspondence, telephony, and other confidential communications is inviolable. The applicable statute, the Electronic Communications Data Protection Act (ECDP Act), further provides that the content of calls, traffic data, and location data are confidential and that these data can be processed only upon consent of the party to the communication. This means two things: First, employees must receive prior notice of phone call monitoring and the employer must obtain their consent. Second, third parties also must be notified about the monitoring. Unlawful accessing of traffic data may result in fines and, in serious cases, imprisonment. Very recently, former senior executives of a large Nordic telecommunications company received suspended sentences for violating the secrecy of communications by unlawfully obtaining traffic data for the purpose of finding out whether someone in the company was leaking confidential information.

3. *Video Surveillance*

Companies engaging in video surveillance may do so only if the following requirements of the Working Life DP Act are fulfilled:

- Video surveillance may be used only for the protection of personal safety or property, for monitoring the proper functioning of the production process, and to prevent occurrences that may pose a risk to safety, property, or production processes.
- Video surveillance may not target an individual employee or a specific group of employees. However, the surveillance may be targeted when there is a threat of violence against the employee, when there is a health risk involved, when the duties of the employee involve handling valuables such as cash or securities, or when the employee has requested surveillance. These exemptions are interpreted narrowly.
- Video surveillance may not be used in facilities intended for employees' personal use, such as restrooms, locker rooms, or other personnel facilities not intended for per-

forming work-related tasks. More important, cameras may not be placed in employees' individual offices.

- Video surveillance must be transparent. If there are less intrusive methods available, they should be utilized. Prior to commencing video surveillance, the employer must cooperate with the employees' representatives and must give employees advance notice about the video surveillance.

Data collected through surveillance can be retained only as long as they are needed and not longer than one year, unless data are needed for investigating workplace harassment claims or for establishing valid grounds for dismissal, or if there are other "particular" reasons for retaining the data.

C. France

1. Email and Internet Monitoring

France has yet to enact specific legislation on employee monitoring but more general labor,[198] civil,[199] and criminal provisions as well as the French DP Act[200] apply.

In October 2005, the French DP Authority (the CNIL[201]) adopted guidance to help employers solve some practical issues related to the detection of employees' activities at the workplace. The guidance followed some earlier reports issued by the CNIL on "cyber-surveillance at the workplace."[202]

---

[198]Articles L. 1221-9 and 1222-4 of the Labor Code, for instance, establish that "no personal information concerning an employee or a candidate for a position may be collected by a device of which the employee or the candidate would not have been informed in advance."

[199]Article 9 of the Civil Code states that: "everyone has the right to respect for his privacy. Without prejudice to compensation for the injury suffered, the court may prescribe any measure, such as sequestration, seizure and others, appropriate to prevent or put an end to a violation of a person's privacy; in case of emergency those measures may be provided for in interim proceedings."

[200]Act 1978 no. 17 of January 6, 1978, on Data Processing, Data Files and Individual Liberties.

[201]Commission nationale de l'informatique et des libertés.

[202]"La cybersurveillance des salaries dans l'entreprise," Hubert Bouchet, March 2001; "La cybersurveillance sur les lieux de travail," Humbert Bouchet, March 2004.

Transparency, proportionality, and compliance with collective bargaining agreements are key considerations for employers using monitoring technologies in France. Moreover, consultation with the Works Council is an indispensable condition for employee monitoring. According to Article L. 2323-32 of the Labor Code "*the Works Committee must be informed and consulted prior to any significant introduction of new technologies, when the technologies are likely to affect... the employees' working conditions—especially when the decisions concern means and technology allowing the control of the employees' activities.*" Importantly, the validity of any monitoring is questionable unless it is mentioned in technology use policies taking the form of internal rules (*règlement intérieur*). The establishment of these rules is subject to consultation requirements with Works Councils and employees.

In accordance with the DP Act, employers also must register the automatic processing of employees' data in the form of Internet monitoring with the CNIL. There is an exception to the obligation to register where the employer appoints a "*correspondant informatique et libertés*," an internal data protection officer (DPO). However, transfers of data outside the EU and thus any monitoring involving transfers to the United States are subject to authorization and must always be registered with the CNIL, irrespective of the appointment of a DPO. Additionally, the stored data generally cannot be retained for more than six months.

The leading Cour de Cassation (the French Supreme Court) case with respect to the monitoring of employee email is the *Nikon* case[203] in which the Court stated that

> the employee has the right, even during working hours and at his workplace to the respect of his privacy; this includes in particular the confidentiality of his correspondence; the employer cannot, without infringing this fundamental liberty, examine the personal messages sent or received by the employees on a computer tool placed at his disposal for work, and this even in the case of the employer having prohibited a non-professional use of the computer.

---

[203]Cour de Cassation chambre sociale, decision on October 2, 2001, no. 99-42.942, Nikon France.

This case emphasizes the principle that the employee has a right to privacy at work, and that an employer may not open an email that is marked "private" or "personal."

Nonetheless, more recent jurisprudence seems to indicate the adoption of a less severe approach by allowing employers to open files tagged as "personal" by employees in their presence. The employee's presence is not required when risky, exceptional circumstances are likely to occur. In a case concerning a TV channel that received threats of terrorist attacks, the Social Law Chamber of the French Supreme Court, hearing labor, workers' compensation, and social security cases, ruled on April 3, 2001, that an employer could investigate private belongings of employees in case of very serious risks.[204] On May 17, 2005, the French Supreme Court, in a case dealing with employees' personal files, stated that "save in case of a particular risk or circumstance—and the possession of pornographic photos by the employee was considered not to fall inside any of the mentioned categories—the employer cannot open the folders identified by the employee as personal on his hard drive of the computer put at his disposal except if the employee is present. [...]"[205]

The CNIL's official report of February 28, 2002, suggests that the employer can intercept emails that are marked as "private" or "personal" in exceptional circumstances, such as when there are serious reasons to believe that a criminal offense has occurred.

In summary, the conditions for lawful monitoring of employee's emails are the following:

- *Reasonableness.* The scope and the duration of workplace monitoring must be "reasonable" (i.e., the employee's fundamental rights and freedoms must be balanced against the need to protect the employer's interests).
- *Personal Communications.* Particular caution should be exercised with respect to an email that is marked "private" or "personal."

---

[204] Cour de Cassation, Chambre sociale, Pourvoi no. 98-45818, Thierry Sarrasin v. CFTD Radio-Télé.

[205] Cour de Cassation, Chambre sociale, Pourvoi no. 03-40.017 M. Klajer c/ Societe Cathnet-Science.

- *Legal Basis.* The employer must be able to establish a legal basis under the DP Act and obtain consent if required in the circumstances.
- *Notice.* The employee must have been informed about the fact that the employer stores the communication on its servers, retention periods, etc., and the conditions under which it may intercept the content.
- *Consultation with the Works Council.* The Works Council (i.e., the statutory representations of employees) must have been consulted prior to any control of the activity of employees, for example, through monitoring of email communication.[206] Such consultation requires prior written notification on the subject, and a formal meeting during which the Works Council expresses an opinion. The opinion, however, is not binding.
- *Registration with the CNIL.* If the employer controls the connections on a global basis (without identifying each user), no specific notification is required. Only the general filings with respect to the automatic treatment of employees' personal data have to be made. If the control is organized so as to identify each user, the system of control has to be filed to the CNIL.

Illegitimate monitoring may subject employers to civil and criminal sanctions. In particular, unlawful interception of employee communication may constitute "*breach of the confidentiality of personal correspondence*," and may result in imprisonment of up to one year and penalties of €35,000 (approximately US$45,000). Also, if a court decides that the monitoring was illegitimate, the employer cannot base its claim or disciplinary actions (i.e., the dismissal) on the evidence obtained through the interception. The French Supreme Court has decided that "*although the employer has the right to monitor the employee's activities during work hours, any sound or visual recording without their knowledge, for any reason, whatsoever, constitutes illegally obtained evidence.*"[207]

---

[206] *See* Article L.2323-32 of the Labor Code.

[207] Cour de Cassation, Chambre sociale, Pourvoi no. 93-44.078 M. Salingue c/ Societe Manulev.

Thus, information that is not properly obtained cannot be used in any proceeding and thus cannot be the basis for any discipline even if it shows that the employee violated company policy or the law (i.e., it will be deemed "the fruit of the poisonous tree").

2. *Monitoring of Employee Telephone Calls*

The personal use of telephones by employees is allowed, provided that it is reasonable and not abusive. To avoid abuse by employees, the CNIL recognized the admissibility of certain technical methods (e.g., by means of "*autocommutateurs*") for setting up a statistical record of incoming and outgoing calls.

When justified, the adoption of the so-called "*dispositif d'entrée en tiers*"—allowing a third party to access the phone call—must be notified to employees and a sound and image alert must be activated.

The listening to and wiretapping of phone conversations as well as the more general interception of telecommunications are prohibited under Section 226-15 of the Criminal Code and punishable by a fine of €45,000 (approximately US$60,000) as well as imprisonment of up to one year.

Exceptionally, this wide prohibition can be overcome when there is a necessity and provided that the proportionality principle is respected (e.g., wiretapping for training purposes must be limited in time). Otherwise, the employer must adopt a less intrusive method.

Section L.1121-1 of the Labor Code states that restrictions on people's rights and individual and collective freedoms cannot be imposed without them being justified in the light of the purpose to be achieved and the proportionality principle. This also applies to listening to and wiretapping of phone conversations.

Additionally, Section 6 of the DP Act establishes that data (even when collected through monitoring) must be adequate, relevant, and not excessive in relation to the purposes for which they are obtained and their further processing.

Information to be given to employees upon the installation of wiretapping systems must be comprehensive and must clearly indicate (1) the purpose of the wiretapping, (2) the addressees of the wiretapping, (3) the right to have access to the information collected by means of wiretapping, (4) the consequences employees can face if evidence of unlawful behavior is revealed, and (5) the period during which the phone calls will be subject to wiretapping. A sound and image alert should consequently be activated.

Lastly, the installation of wiretapping systems must be preceded by a registration with the CNIL.

3. *Video Surveillance*

Guidance for employers[208] issued by the representatives of the CNIL enumerates a few basic principles employers must comply with when installing a video surveillance system:

- *Finality.* Surveillance must be legitimate and used only for specific purposes (justifying the processing). For example, the installation of a system for the registration of telephone calls cannot have the object of monitoring and registering the calls made by an employee but should be justified on other grounds. The same applies to the installation of video cameras.
- *Proportionality (reflected in Article L.121-1 of the Labor Code).* A permanent system of video surveillance at a workplace cannot be installed unless specific risks for the security of the employee are highly likely and there are no alternative solutions. Employers must consider the location of the cameras, the scope of the cameras, the technical functioning of the cameras, the period of activity of the cameras, and the type of behavior subject to surveillance.
- *Retention of data.* Data collected through video surveillance cannot be retained for more than one month.
- *Security.* Security measures must be implemented in order to protect those images and sound data collected through video surveillance.
- *Transparency.* Employees must be provided with information regarding the processing of their data through video surveillance equipment, and the right to have access to

[208] "Guide pratique pour les employeurs," October 2005.

their data, oppose the processing of their data, and have their data rectified.

If there is a security need justifying the adoption of video surveillance, the system must apply to all employees and cannot be targeted at a single employee or to a specific group of employees. The adoption of a video surveillance system in violation of the proportionality principle may lead to imprisonment of up to one year and a fine of €45,000 (approximately US$60,000) (Section 226-1 of the French Criminal Code). Furthermore, the implementation of a system of video surveillance without employees' prior knowledge may expose the employer to civil liability in violation of the general obligation of loyal performance of an employment contract.

The CNIL classifies the following types of video surveillance as "illegal":

- Locating systems in facilities meant for employees' private use (toilets, shower rooms, recreation rooms);
- Using systems for the surveillance of a specific employee or a group of employees without a specific reason;
- Installing systems without the knowledge of the employees (e.g., by using miniature cameras); and
- Installing systems that register employee access to a labor union facility.

Informing employees about the adoption of a video surveillance system is mandatory under the DP Act. In particular, pursuant to Section 39 of the DP Act, the following aspects must be made "transparent" to employees and visitors when a system of video surveillance is put in place:

- Existence of the surveillance system;
- Employees subject to the surveillance; and
- Employees' right to access their visual images.

In addition, in order to be compliant with the Labor Code (Section L.2323-32), employers must consult the union representatives prior to implementing the video surveillance system.

Finally, Section L.1222 of the Labor Code states that information directly concerning a specific employee cannot be collected through a system that the concerned employee was unaware of. A video surveillance system put in place at the workplace cannot be installed without having first been registered with the CNIL.

In particular, the declaration to be submitted to the CNIL must contain the following elements:

- An explanation of the concrete necessity of a video surveillance system as well as a plan that indicates the scope and depth of the field of the camera lens;
- The type of information given to employees with regard to the equipment and the employees' right of access to their visual images captured through the visual recording;
- A description of the visual technology utilized as well as the security measures in place; and
- The exact determination of the addressees of the images (internal or eventually external) and the maximum retention period of the registered images.

A different regimen is prescribed for video surveillance systems installed in workplaces classified as "public" or "open to public."

On June 7, 2006, the French Supreme Court ruled[209] on the probative value of footage obtained by means of video surveillance at the workplace. In the case, the illegal behavior of an employee of a large company was detected by means of video surveillance, leading to the dismissal of the employee. The French Supreme Court rejected the employee's dismissal as unfounded. In particular, the Supreme Court denied any probative value to the footage and considered it to be an "illegal piece of evidence," given that the labor union had not been previously informed or consulted about the installation of the video monitoring equipment.

---

[209]Cour de Cassation, Chambre Sociale, 7 Juin 2006, No. de pourvoi 04-43.866.

D. Germany

1. *Email and Internet Monitoring*

Like France, Germany has yet to enact specific legislation on employee monitoring. Currently, monitoring is governed by provisions arising from different legislative sources, including Article 10 of the German Constitution,[210] the Federal Data Protection Act[211] (DP Act), the Works Council Act,[212] the Telecommunication Act,[213] and the Telemedia Act.[214]

The combined effect of the applicable legislation is that, generally, employers may monitor employees' email communications or Internet usage under the following rare conditions:

- *Reasonableness.* Emails may be accessed only for legitimate reasons and by means proportionate to the objectives, for example, if there is a reasonable belief of unlawful behavior, abuse, distribution of illegal content, dissemination of trade secrets, or breach of labor related duties. Automated and undifferentiated monitoring of email communication is unlikely to be permissible except when it is the "last resort." There should not be any monitoring in which any adverse impact is out of proportion to the benefits, and if comparable benefits can reasonably be achieved by another method with fewer adverse effects, this method should be adopted. Monitoring should be targeted to those areas where it is actually necessary and proportionate to achieving the legitimate purpose.
- *Personal communications.* The Telecommunication Act requires "commercial telecommunication providers" to ensure the privacy of telecommunications, including email communication. Providers intercepting communications

[210] Artikel 10 Grundgesetz für die Bundesrepublik Deutschland vom 23. Mai 1949 (BGBl. I, 1).

[211] Bundesdatenschutzgesetz vom 20. Dezember 1990 (BGBl. I 2954).

[212] Betriebsverfassungsgesetz vom 25. September 2001 (BGBl. I S. 2518).

[213] Telekommunikationsgesetz vom 22. Juni 2004 (BGBl. I 1190).

[214] Telemediengesetz vom 26. Februar 2007 (BGBl. I 179).

will be acting unlawfully unless the interception is required for law enforcement, the provision of services, billing, or combating fraud and other very limited purposes. There has been much debate as to whether the Telecommunication Act applies to communication in the workplace, but the current thinking in Germany is that if private use is permitted, the employer must respect the employee's telecommunication privacy with respect to personal communications.[215] If private and business use cannot be clearly separated, monitoring of the message content will be unlawful. If the employee uses the Internet and email for work-related purposes only, employers may monitor emails. In light of these consequences, many employers do not permit the private use of communication equipment in Germany so as to avoid the applicability of the Telecommunication Act. Any prohibition on personal use should be clearly communicated to employees and adequately enforced. In Germany it is lawful to prohibit the employee from using work equipment for private purposes.

- *Legal basis.* Review of employee communications involving the collection or processing of personal data (i.e., any information relating to an identified or identifiable natural person) falls within the scope of the DP Act. The DP Act requires a legal authorization for the collection and processing of personal data. Certain criteria (such as consent, legal requirements, contractual necessity, and balance of interest) must be met. The DP Act requires a "legal basis" for the collection and processing of personal data. In other words, collection and processing are legitimate only if a "good reason" exists. Four grounds may be relevant:

[215]The legislative materials on the Telecommunication Act expressly state that the provisions also are aimed at a company's internal communication system. Note in this respect that the Act was drafted and enacted in great haste in order to ensure the timely liberalization of the German telecommunication sector and not to put the scheduled privatization of Deutsche Telecom, the former state monopolist telecommunication operator, at any risk.

- Processing may be permitted to the extent that all employees unambiguously consent, in writing or in a qualified electronic format, to the processing of the data. A suitable consent clause may be included in the employment contract. However, this requires administrative effort, and not all employees may be willing to agree to such a clause. Also, some data protection officials do not recognize consent of an employee as a valid legal basis because employees may be under "undue pressure" to consent, and consent given by an employee would generally be void as a result. Further, email addresses may constitute personal data of the recipient or sender of the email, in other words, of those with whom the employee corresponds. It may be very difficult to obtain consent of all of these parties.
- Processing of personal data is legitimate to the extent it is necessary for compliance with legal obligations to which the data controller is subject. It is important to bear in mind that employers are under an obligation to implement appropriate technical and organizational measures to protect personal data against accidental or unlawful destruction or accidental loss, alteration, etc. Employers must install appropriate firewall and backup systems for inbound and outbound email traffic, and, in order to ensure the reliability of its communication network, it should trace data streams as such data may contain personal data such as email addresses. Collection of such data should be justified.
- Processing of personal data may be legitimate to the extent it is required for the performance of a contract with the employee. Unfortunately it is not yet clear to what extent data protection authorities allow the labor contract to serve as a basis for monitoring email communication in the workplace. In any event, processing must relate to the employer–employee relationship and must be objectively justified by an operational interest. Monitoring for the purposes of assessing the employee's performance does not appear to be allowed.

– Data processing is lawful if it is necessary to safeguard the justified interests of the employer and there is no reason to assume that the employee has an overriding legitimate interest in his data being excluded from processing or use. This exception may justify monitoring of emails, for example, during periods where the employee is absent, to check any emails directed at him. The purpose of such monitoring is to ensure the business responds properly to its customers and other contacts.

- *Notice.* Clear prior notice must be provided to the employee about the fact that his Internet use and emails will be monitored and that he has the right to access the data collected through the monitoring activity. Generally speaking, employers should provide the following information on the type of information collected: advise how the employer intends to use the information; describe to whom such personal data might be transferred; advise the employee that he may request access, correction, erasure, and blocking of his personal data.
- *Consultation with the Works Council.* Companies wishing to install monitoring technologies should first seek to consult with the Works Council pursuant to Section 87 of the German Works Council Act. The provision not only relates to intended control of employees through technical devices, but covers any and all devices that are technically designed to control and monitor employees, even if the employer does not intend to use the devices for that purpose. Consultation is required when there is a mere possibility of technical supervision and control. Collection and monitoring of email traffic might be regarded as a technical device capable of controlling personnel performance (e.g., a productivity measuring device). However, the legal position is very unclear, and the scope of application of this provision is controversial and widely discussed. The labor courts and commentators generally interpret the provision very broadly. It should be noted that Article 87 of the German Works Council Act empowers the Works Council to agree to or refuse its consent to the installation of such devices.

2. *Monitoring of Employee Telephone Calls*

Article 10 of the German Constitution (*Grundgesetz*)[216] states that "Privacy of postal service and telecommunication shall be inviolable. Restrictions may only be ordered pursuant to a legal statute...." On December 19, 1991, the Federal Constitutional Court (the Court) held that under Article 10 employers are not allowed to monitor their employees' phone calls because the fact that an employee initiates or receives the telephone call in the workplace does not limit his or her right to privacy. The Court explicitly outlawed indiscriminate review and recordings of telephone conversations. Review is possible only where the "legitimate interest of the employer" overrides the general "right of information self-determination" of the employee, but to date, no case law exists on the point.

Another important issue to consider in this respect is telecommunications law, which will be applicable as soon as the employer allows at least some degree of private calls and is thus considered a telecommunication services provider. As such, the employer has to comply with the Telecommunications Act and must safeguard the secrecy of telecommunications. A violation of this Act is considered a felony under Section 206 German Criminal Code and can be prosecuted with up to five years of imprisonment. The Telecommunications Act allows for the processing of only certain types of telecommunications data (customer data, services data, and control signal data) on very restrictive terms, for example to analyze and eliminate interruptions and malfunctions or to pursuit apparent cases of misuse of the telecommunication systems. Unless there are law enforcement reasons for doing so, listening in or recording actual conversations is unlawful.

3. *Video Surveillance*

Companies engaging in video surveillance are subject to the general requirements of the DP Act. In public places, such as showrooms and other customer or visitor areas, however, Section 6b of the DP Act sets forth specific requirements for video surveillance

---

[216] Artikel 10 Grundgesetz für die Bundesrepublik Deutschland vom 23. Mai 1949 (BGBl. I, 1).

irrespective of whether digital or analogue systems are used, whether the camera output is just monitored or also saved to data carriers of some kind, or whether the cameras used are stationary or mobile systems. Companies using video surveillance in public areas must, therefore, comply with the requirements of Section 6b of the DP Act, which states that such surveillance is allowed only in so far as it is necessary in order to:

- fulfill tasks of public administration (allowing law enforcement, for example, to monitor public places for street crime prevention or electronic pursuit of criminals);
- exercise its domestic authority on its premises (allowing, for example, supermarkets to monitor customers to prevent shopliftings); or
- pursue rightful interests for precisely defined purposes,

provided always that there are no indications that the data subjects' legitimate interests prevail. Section 6b of the DP Act also requires that the actual monitoring and the operator's identity are made discernible by appropriate means (usually by using visibly installed cameras and signs indicating the surveillance and the operator's contact details); if a person can be identified, he should be informed of this.

Generally, in terms of video monitoring their public areas, companies can often rely on their interests to prevent crime on their premises by taking appropriate preventative measures against theft, robbery, and burglary, and argue that this in fact is in the data subjects' best interest. This might, however, be more difficult in cases in which the surveillance also covers premises outside the company, for example if entrances are monitored from the outside and either willfully or accidentally cover parts of the sidewalks. If that is indeed unavoidable, the company must make sure that even pedestrians and other passers bys are properly informed about the surveillance by using visible cameras and adequately placed signs.

However, whenever video surveillance includes not only customers but also the company's employees working in such areas, the balancing of legally protected interests becomes more difficult. An employee's legitimate interests are different from those of a passer by because the employees have to bear the fact of being watched all day long and cannot really avoid it. Therefore, a considerable number of labor court decisions exist defining what kinds of video surveillance are acceptable and which cross the line and in fact violate the employees' rights. As any kind of video surveillance is always capable of assessing the employees' individual performance, consultation with an existing Works Council is necessary, too.

Violations of these statutory obligations not only can lead to proceedings being brought by data protection authorities, but also can cause the loss of labor lawsuits (in which the video footage was supposed to provide evidence and will be rejected by the court because it was gathered unlawfully), and, if the video surveillance even violates the most private aspects of life, for example by taking pictures of persons in their apartments or other protected areas such as changing cabins, it might even constitute a criminal offense under Section 201a German Criminal Code.

E. United Kingdom

1. *Email and Internet Monitoring*

Any review of employee communications implying the collection as well as the processing of personal data belonging to an identified or identifiable person is covered by the DP Act 1998.[217] Interception of emails is also governed by the Regulation of Investigatory Powers Act 2000[218] and the Telecommunications (Lawful Business Practice) Regulation 2000.[219]

- *The DP Act.* The guiding principle under the DP Act is that the processing of personal data should be carried out fairly and lawfully. In particular, with specific reference to the employment context, employees must be informed by their employers, inter alia, of the purposes for which the data must be processed. Additionally, when processing data, the employer must comply with several obligations including

[217] 1998 c29.
[218] 2000 c23.
[219] Statutory Instrument 2000 No. 2699.

the granting of individual rights to employees and the adoption of technical and security measures to protect its employees' data. As far as monitoring is concerned, the DP Act allows employers to review emails "*for the purposes of the legitimate interests pursued . . ., except where the reviewing is unwarranted in any particular case by reason of the prejudice to the rights and freedoms or legitimate interests of the individual.*" The DPA also allows the employer to review emails if the individual has freely given his explicit consent.[220]

- *The Regulation of Investigatory Powers Act 2000 (RIPA).* The RIPA requires both senders and recipients to consent to interception, unless the interception is targeted at business communications and is to prevent or detect crime or to investigate unauthorized use of the telecommunication system. Interception is not allowed if carried out wholly or in part to gain access to personal communications.
- *The Telecommunications (Lawful Business Practice) (Interception of Communications) Regulations 2000 (Regulations).* These Regulations allow employers to monitor or record employees' communications—without their consent—for the following purposes:
  - To establish the existence of facts relevant to business;
  - To ascertain compliance with regulatory or self-regulatory practices or procedures;
  - To ascertain or demonstrate standards to be achieved by employees;
  - To prevent or detect crime;
  - To investigate or detect the unauthorized use of the business system; and
  - To secure the effective system operation.

On June 14, 2005, the Information Commissioner's Office published the Employment Practices Data Protection Code (Code) in order to make the data protection principles as set forth in the

---

[220]Schedule 2 of the DPA, para 2.

Data Protection Act 1998 accessible and applicable to working environments.

Part III of the Code deals with both systematic and occasional monitoring carried out by employers.

A monitoring activity is covered by the Code when it consists of:

- Gathering information through point of sale terminals, to check the efficiency of individual supermarket check-out operators;
- Randomly opening up individual workers' emails or listening to their voice mails to look for evidence of malpractice;
- Using automated checking software to collect information about workers (i.e., to find out whether particular workers are sending or receiving inappropriate emails);
- Examining logs of Web sites visited to check that individual workers are not downloading pornography;
- Keeping recordings of telephone calls made to or from a call center either to listen to part of workers' training or simply to have a record to refer to in the event of a customer complaint about a worker;
- Systematically checking logs of telephone numbers called to detect use of premium-rate lines;
- Videoing workers outside the workplace to collect evidence that they are not in fact sick; or
- Obtaining information through credit reference agencies to check that workers are not in financial difficulties.

The Code states that the DP Act does not prevent monitoring but requires employers to make an assessment of the following factors:

- Purposes behind the monitoring arrangement and likely benefits;
- Adverse impact of the monitoring activity;
- Alternatives to the detection activity;
- Obligations arising from the monitoring activity; and
- Justifications for the monitoring activities.

If the assessment is found to be balanced in favor of the employer, then the monitoring activity can be carried out by the employer without specific concerns.

The Code sets out some core principles to be followed by employers:

- Once the person entitled to authorize the monitoring or put the monitoring system in place has been identified, the employer must ensure that the person is briefed on all responsibilities arising from the DP Act and the Code;
- If monitoring has to be used to enforce the organization's rules and standards, the employer must ensure that the rules and standards are clearly set out in a policy which also refers to the scope and extent of any associated monitoring;
- If sensitive data are collected through the monitoring activity, the employer must ensure that the data are processed in compliance with the data protection legislation;
- The employer must limit the access to personal information obtained through monitoring (i.e., by preferring security personnel to line managers) and subject those persons to security and confidentiality requirements;
- If information gathered through the monitoring activity might have an adverse impact on employees, the employer must present the employees with the information and allow them to make a representation before taking action; and
- The employer must concretely ensure the employees' right to have access to data collected through the monitoring activity.

With specific reference to electronic communications, a policy should be drafted addressing the following issues:

- The employer should clearly set out to employees the circumstances in which they may or may not use the employer's telephone systems (including mobile phones), the email system, and Internet access for private communications;
- In case of Internet access, the employer should specify clearly any restrictions on materials that can be copied or downloaded (such as pornographic material);

- The employer should make the available alternatives clear (e.g., internal postal mail rather than email);
- The employer should outline how the policy is enforced and related penalties;
- If voice mails need to be checked for business calls when employees are away, the employer must make sure the employees know this may happen and that it may be unavoidable that some personal messages are heard;
- The employer must consider the use of recorded messages informing external callers that calls may be monitored, or alternatively the employer must encourage employees to tell callers that their conversations may be monitored;
- Whenever possible, the employer should avoid opening emails, especially those clearly personal and private;
- Where practicable, the employer should ensure that those sending emails to employees (i.e., when soliciting job applications) are aware of the eventual monitoring that would be carried out;
- If it is necessary to check the email accounts of employees in their absence, the employer must make sure that they are aware that this will happen; and
- The employer should inform employees of the extent to which information about their Internet access and emails is retained in the system and for how long.

The Code also addresses some principles related to the covert monitoring to be carried out:

- Senior management should normally authorize any covert monitoring when there are grounds for suspecting criminal activity or equivalent malpractice and notifying individuals about the monitoring would prejudice its prevention or detection;
- Any covert monitoring must be strictly targeted at obtaining evidence within a set time frame and must not continue after the investigation is complete;
- Covert audio or video monitoring should not be used in areas that employees would genuinely and reasonably expect to be private;

- If a private investigator has to covertly collect information on employees, the employer should make sure that there is a contract in place that requires the private investigator to collect information in a way that satisfies the employer's obligations under the DP Act; and
- Other information collected in the course of monitoring must be disregarded or deleted unless it reveals information that no employer could reasonably be expected to ignore.

A landmark case is *Avocer Hardware plc v. Morrison*,[221] in which the complainant was a telesalesperson who had been dismissed for the content of the call made to clients. The calls, in fact, had been registered without the employee's knowledge. The Employment Tribunal did not recognize evidentiary value to the registering of the phone calls because the employee had not been informed. Nonetheless, the Employment Appeal Tribunal reversed the Employment Tribunal's decision by stating that the secret recording of the telephone calls did amount to evidence of misconduct by the employee. In this case, the Employment Appeal Tribunal sought to balance the employee's right to respect for his private life and the employer's right to a fair trial.

2. *Monitoring of Employee Telephone Calls*

The monitoring of employee telephone calls, insofar as it comprises the collection and processing of personal data belonging to an identified or identifiable person, is covered by the DP Act 1998 and the Code. The most common forms of telephone monitoring that are covered are either:

- Keeping recordings of telephone calls made to or from a call center either to listen to part of workers' training or simply to have a record to refer to in the event of a customer complaint about a worker; and
- Keeping logs of telephone numbers called by workers for checking to detect use of premium-rate lines.

[221] [2003] All ER (D) 126 (Jul).

Before conducting any form of telephone monitoring, employers must make an assessment of the following factors:

- Purposes behind the monitoring arrangement and likely benefits;
- Adverse impact of the monitoring activity;
- Alternatives to the detection activity;
- Obligations arising from the monitoring activity; and
- Justifications for the monitoring activities.

Employers should ensure that the rules and standards regarding workers' use of the telephone while at work are clearly set out in a policy which also refers to the scope and extent of any associated monitoring. In particular, employers should make sure that workers are aware of routine checking of voice mails, for example, when the worker is out of the office.

If an employer provides telephones specifically for private use, these should on no account be monitored. In the case of *Halford v. UK*[222] a police inspector was assured that her calls from a telephone provided for her private use would not be monitored. When the employer then covertly monitored her calls, the European Court of Human Rights awarded the police inspector £10,600 in damages in respect to nonpecuniary loss for the breach of her right to privacy.

3. Video Surveillance

The videoing of workers, whether in or outside the workplace, is covered by the DP Act 1998 and the Code. Video surveillance of workers in the workplace is usually focused on ensuring good performance or detecting misconduct, whereas video surveillance outside the workplace is usually to collect evidence of workers' activities that are inconsistent with their workplace behavior, most commonly that they are not in fact sick or incapable of performing certain tasks.

Again, before conducting any form of video surveillance employers must make an assessment of the following factors:

---

[222][1997] 24 EHRR 523.

- Purposes behind the monitoring arrangement and likely benefits;
- Adverse impact of the monitoring activity;
- Alternatives to the detection activity;
- Obligations arising from the monitoring activity; and
- Justifications for the monitoring activities.

Covert video surveillance, whether in or outside the workplace, should be strictly targeted at obtaining evidence within a set time frame and should not be used in areas that employees would genuinely and reasonably expect to be private. If an employer engages a private investigator to covertly collect information on workers outside the workplace, the employer should make sure that there is a contract in place that requires the private investigator to collect information in a way that satisfies the employer's obligations under the DP Act 1998.

IV. ASIA AND ASIA PACIFIC

A. Australia

1. General Requirements for Monitoring

In Australia, workplace monitoring and surveillance activities are broadly covered by the Privacy Act. According to the Guidelines on Workplace Email, Web Browsing and Privacy (The Guidelines) issued by the Office of the Privacy Commissioner, the National Privacy Principles apply to employee "emails that contain personal information other than employee records in certain circumstances" as well as logs of staff Web browsing activities.[223] The Guidelines, which are advisory only and not legally binding, recommend steps that organizations can take to ensure that their employees understand the organization's position on monitoring and surveillance.

In addition to the federal Privacy Act, there is currently only one state law in New South Wales (NSW) that regulates private

[223] *See* Guidelines on Workplace Email, Web Browsing and Privacy (30/3/2000).

sector workplace monitoring and surveillance. The Workplace Surveillance Act (WSA) entered into force in 2005.

2. *Monitoring of Employee Email*

The Guidelines recommend that employers ensure that the organization's email monitoring policies are given to and understood by employees. Those policies should:

- Be explicit about what activities are permitted and forbidden and refer to any relevant legislation;
- Specify what information is logged and who in the organization has rights to access the logs and content of employee email and browsing activities;
- Indicate, in general terms, the circumstances under which an organization will disclose the contents of emails and logs;
- Refer to the organization's computer security policy; and
- Outline in an easy-to-understand manner how the organization intends to monitor or audit staff compliance with its rules relating to acceptable usage of email and Web browsing.

In addition, policies should be reviewed on a regular basis and reissued whenever significant changes are made.

The WSA restricts and regulates the blocking by employers of emails and Internet access of employees at work. In particular, an employer may prevent delivery of an email sent to or received by, or access to a Web site by, an employee if:

- The employer has a policy on email and Internet access of which the employee has been notified to the employee in advance in such a way that it is reasonable to assume that the employee is aware of and understands the policy;
- The employer is acting in accordance with that policy; and
- In the case of an email filter, the employee is notified as soon as practicable that delivery of the email has been prevented.

The obligation to notify employees of blocked emails does not apply, however, with respect to blocking emails that are spam as defined by the federal Spam Act 2003; contain viruses that would interfere or damage the employer's computer network; or are offensive, menacing, or harassing in nature. The employer's email and Internet access policy cannot prohibit delivery of emails or access to Web sites merely because the content concerns industrial matters.[224]

3. *Video Surveillance and Other Surveillance*

Under the WSA, surveillance is defined as:

- Camera surveillance that monitors or records visual images of activities on premises or in any other place;
- Computer surveillance using software or other equipment to monitor or record the information input or output, or other use, of a computer (including, but not limited to, the sending and receipt of emails and the accessing of Internet Web sites); or
- Tracking surveillance that uses an electronic device to monitor or record geographical location or movement (such as a Global Positioning System tracking device).

The WSA requires there to be "surveillance," as that term is ordinarily understood. Computer surveillance, therefore, does not cover normal business practices such as backups of hard drives, network performance monitoring, software license monitoring, computer asset tracking, computer asset management, or the normal saving of documents because these are not normally considered to be "surveillance" activities. However, if backups, for instance, were to be used to conduct surveillance to facilitate the reading of somebody's emails, employees would need to be notified about such use. Otherwise, it would be considered to be covert surveillance.

The WSA prohibits the surveillance by employers of their employees at work (and outside the workplace where an employee

---

[224] *See* §17 of the Workplace Video Surveillance Act 1998.

is working) except where employees have been given notice or where the employer has a covert surveillance authority. Written (or emailed) notice must be given at least 14 days prior to commencing any surveillance. The notice must indicate the kind of surveillance to be carried out (camera, computer, or tracking), how the surveillance will be carried out, when the surveillance will start, whether the surveillance will be continuous or intermittent, and whether the surveillance will be for a specified limited period or ongoing. For new employees, notice must be given before they start work.

The WSA prohibits surveillance in a changing room, toilet facility, or shower or other bathing facility at a workplace.

The WSA does permit covert surveillance when approved or sanctioned by a court. The WSA regulates the carrying out of that surveillance and the storage of records resulting from the covert surveillance. In addition, the WSA restricts the use and disclosure of covert surveillance records.

The WSA prescribes additional requirements for the surveillance of employees at work. For example, surveillance of an employee must not begin without prior notice in writing to the employee. A 14-day advance (written or emailed) notice is required before conducting such surveillance and in case of a new employee, before the new employee starts to work. The notice must include the following information:

- The kind of surveillance to be carried out (camera, computer, or tracking);
- How the surveillance will be carried out;
- When the surveillance will start;
- Whether the surveillance will be continuous or intermittent; and
- Whether the surveillance will be for a specified limited period or ongoing.

Cameras used for the surveillance must be clearly visible in the place where the surveillance is taking place. Signs also must notify people that they may be under surveillance in that place and must be clearly visible at each entrance to that place. With respect to the use of tracking devices, there must be a notice clearly visible on the vehicle or other object that is being tracked, indicating that the vehicle or the object is the subject of tracking surveillance.

B. China

1. General Requirements for Monitoring

Employees have limited rights of privacy under Chinese law. Article 3 of China's Administration of Email Services Procedures protects the privacy of a citizen's email, but also provides that a person is permitted to use a computer system to send email only if authorized by the owner of the computer system. This follows the Telecommunication Regulations that provide for privacy of a telecommunication subscriber's messages, including both voice mail and email, but these protections do not extend to an employee of a subscriber. Thus, an employer is not restricted from monitoring telecommunication messages carried on the services for which it has subscribed.

The Administration of the Maintenance of Secrets in the International Networking of Computer Information Systems Provisions strengthens an employer's right to monitor email. These provisions impose affirmative obligations on a company to be responsible for all information transmitted over its computer information systems. Similarly, Article 13 of the Administration of International Linkups of Computer Information Networks Tentative Provisions requires companies and individuals to comply with People's Republic of China (PRC) laws and regulations; implement secure online systems; not engage in illegal activities; and not produce, retrieve, reproduce, or disseminate information that would hinder public security or that is obscene or pornographic. Article 1(2) of the Administrative Measures on Safety and Protection of Computer Information Networks imposes affirmative obligations on a legal entity to monitor computer/Internet activity on its equipment. China's Safe Production Law imposes an affirmative requirement that a company implement affirmative monitoring procedures for its workplace for safety reasons. There are no regulations that address privacy concerns of employees.

C. Hong Kong

The collection and use of personal data in Hong Kong is governed by the Personal Data (Privacy) Ordinance 1997 (PDPO). Any collection of personal data through monitoring of employees' email and Internet use and video surveillance is subject to the PDPO.

The Hong Kong Privacy Commissioner has issued nonbinding "Privacy Guidelines: Monitoring and Personal Data Privacy at Work" (the Employee Monitoring Guidelines), which seek to provide more detailed guidance to complement the high-level data privacy principles set out in the PDPO.[225]

1. Monitoring Guidelines

Broadly speaking, the Employee Monitoring Guidelines require the employer's legitimate business interests to be balanced against employees' personal data privacy rights. To do this, an employer should:

- Assess the risks that the employee monitoring seeks to manage and the intrusiveness of the proposed monitoring techniques; and
- Consider alternatives to employee monitoring that may be equally effective and practical in their application, yet less intrusive.

The Employee Monitoring Guidelines state that a risk should be "sufficiently realistic," but the examples provided indicate that the risk threshold is low. For example, time spent Web browsing by employees may be monitored to prevent company resources from being substantially used for private purposes that may adversely impact on productivity, or in order to avoid the risk of vicarious liability of the employer for activities such as unlicensed downloading of copyrighted materials. The contents of emails sent

---

[225] *See* "Privacy Guidelines: Monitoring and Personal Data Privacy at Work."

using company communications equipment may be monitored to ensure the integrity and security of confidential business information. The risk assessment is meant to ensure that the reasons for monitoring are well founded and that the monitoring is related to, and aligned with, the company's business needs.

Once a monitoring purpose is established, the employer should assess the likely adverse impact that it may have on employees' privacy.[226] For example, when monitoring emails, the concern is whether the message is work-related or purely private. Monitoring emails that are clearly unrelated to the employee's performance at work will likely be characterized as intrusive. As a result, the identified risk must be proportionately great (e.g., there must be a reasonable suspicion of seriously improper conduct).

As well as a risk and impact assessment, companies should adopt a transparent approach to formulating and disseminating employee monitoring policies and practices.[227] An effective way of achieving this is to implement a comprehensive written privacy policy, which should explicitly address the following:

- Business purpose(s) that employee monitoring seeks to fulfill;
- Circumstances in which monitoring may take place;
- Manner in which monitoring may be conducted;
- Kinds of personal data that may be collected by means of monitoring; and
- Purpose(s) for which the personal data collected may be used.

As a general rule, employee monitoring should be conducted openly on the basis of a clear and easily accessible employee monitoring policy or technology use policy.[228]

Under the PDPO employers must properly manage personal data collected while conducting employee monitoring. That legal obligation extends to third-party acts in which the third party acts

[226]Employee Monitoring Guidelines, §§2.1–2.3.
[227]*Id.*, §3.3.1.
[228]*Id.*, §§2.4, 3.2

as an agent on behalf of the employer.[229] Employers are also liable for all acts of employees with the responsibility of handling personal data collected in the course of employee monitoring.[230] Therefore, employers should implement security and access control measures to safeguard the personal data collected in monitoring records.

Employers also should remember that access rights under the PDPO apply to the personal data collected in the course of employee monitoring.

2. *Video Surveillance*

Under the Employee Monitoring Guidelines, covert video monitoring should be used only when it can be justified as a last resort measure that is absolutely necessary in detecting or gathering evidence of unlawful activities. Additionally, the monitoring should be appropriately limited in scope and duration. Furthermore, the purposes of monitoring, the circumstances under which monitoring will take place, and the type of personal data to be collected should be made known and communicated to the affected employees.[231]

In a case investigated by the Privacy Commissioner, pinhole cameras were found installed in the working areas and near the toilets and changing rooms of a government office. The office management explained to the Commissioner that this covert employee monitoring was for the purpose of detecting crime following a series of thefts from the office. The Commissioner concluded that the employer had contravened Data Privacy Principles 1(1), 1(2), and 5 under the PDPO because:

- Although the employer had a legitimate purpose in protecting its property from theft, the available evidence did not demonstrate the existence of sufficiently extensive risk of loss as to justify engaging in such intrusive and widespread video monitoring activities;

[229] *Id.*, §2.4.2.
[230] PDPO, §65; Employee Monitoring Guidelines, §2.4.3.
[231] Employee Monitoring Guidelines, §2.3.3.

- There was no evidence to show that due consideration had been given to the use of other less privacy-intrusive alternatives and such covert monitoring was carried out in an unreasonable and unfair manner; and
- The employer lacked an effective privacy policy covering video surveillance of employees.

D. Japan

1. General Requirements for Monitoring

Various Japanese ministries have issued guidelines on the use of personal information pursuant to the Protection of Personal Information Law (PIPL). In terms of employee monitoring and surveillance, businesses should look to the Ministry of Economy, Trade and Industry (METI) Guidelines.[232] The guidelines provide that an employer should:

- Specify the purposes of monitoring;
- Create a privacy policy that provides specific details relating to monitoring;
- Designate a person responsible for monitoring; and
- Perform audits and confirm that monitoring is being conducted appropriately.

An employer infringes privacy rights when the purpose, method, and manner of monitoring, balanced against the privacy intrusion suffered by the person being monitored, would be socially inappropriate.[233]

In general, monitoring should be balanced against the employee's expectation of privacy. Thus, notifying employees clearly and publicly in advance of the Internet and email surveillance policy is essential.

When the company implements policies that prohibit the private use of email and employees are notified about those policies,

[232] Article II 2(3)3 of the METI Guidelines. Because the guidelines apply to both monitoring and surveillance, the use of the term "monitoring" for the purposes of this section only refers to both electronic monitoring and video surveillance.

[233] Tokyo District Court (wa) 12081 of 2000.

employees' expectation of privacy is low. Thus, employee monitoring in those circumstances without a specific notice is usually acceptable, provided there is a rational reason to monitor, and the employer designates an individual responsible for monitoring. However, when a company approves or even implicitly acquiesces to the private use of emails, employees' expectations of privacy are higher. Thus, an employer would need to articulate a business need for monitoring that overcomes that higher expectation of privacy.

Although consent is not required in the two instances cited above, notice is essential. In addition, the METI Guidelines also provide that when internal regulations regarding the monitoring of employees are to be established, it is desirable to notify workers' organizations in advance, consult them as necessary, and notify the workers regarding the rules after the rules have been established.

2. *Monitoring of Computer Use*

In a 2004 case, the Tokyo District Court explained the standards that should apply to an employer's investigation of employees' computer use. The court stated:

> (1) whether or not the employers' act is an invasion of privacy rights of employees that goes against public policy depends on whether, balanced against the drawbacks suffered by the employees, the purpose or manner of the investigation goes beyond the bounds of socially accepted limits;
>
> (2) if there are acts that violate the corporate order, employers may investigate the factual relationships regarding the content, manner and degree of the violating acts, and employees must cooperate with the employer pursuant to their employment contract, but it is sufficient for such cooperation to be within the range necessary and rational in order for the employer to smoothly conduct operations.

This case involved an investigation of an employee's computer for the purpose of explaining to the supervising ministry the factual background behind a critical article written about the company by a weekly magazine. The investigation was conducted after the computer had been returned to the leasing company. The court found that the manner of the investigation was appropriate, so there was no violation of the employee's privacy rights. The court stated that "whether or not the employer's act is an invasion of privacy rights of employees that goes against public policy depends on whether, balanced against the drawbacks suffered by the employees, the purpose or manner of the investigation goes beyond the bounds of socially acceptable limits," and found no violation of the employee's privacy rights. In addition, the court found that it was within the necessary and rational range for the smooth operations of the employer's business to request the employee to appear in order to investigate the factual background behind a critical article written about the employer in a weekly magazine, and that the employee had the obligation to respond to such questioning.[234]

E. Korea

1. *Monitoring of Employee Email*

In Korea, the monitoring of work emails of employees is covered by the Act on Promotion of Information and Communications Network Utilization and Information Protection (APICNU) and the Protection of Communications Secret Law of 1993 (the Secrecy Act).[235] Under Article 48 of the APICNU, any person is prohibited from infiltrating information and communications networks without any justifiable access right or beyond the permitted access right.

Unless notice and express consent are obtained from employees, monitoring of employee emails is likely to be viewed as a violation of Article 48 of APICNU. Even if the computers are owned by the employer, without notice and consent the employer is likely to be deemed to have gone beyond the permitted access right and to be in violation of Article 48.

In addition, Article 3 of the Secrecy Act prohibits any person from censoring any mail, wiretapping any telecommunications,

---

[234]Case Number: 26741 (wa) 2003.

[235]*See* Act No. 5835, Act on Promotion of Information and Communications Network Utilization and Information Protection and Act No. 4650, the Protection of Communications Secret Law of 1993.

providing communication confirmation data, or recording or listening to conversations between others that are not made public. Emails are considered to be "telecommunications" under the Secrecy Act. Monitoring of emails under the Secrecy Act is permitted only if: (1) the sender and receiver consent; (2) monitoring is protected under the Secrecy Act (monitoring of emails of person in custody or prison; emails addressed to bankrupt person received by bankruptcy trustee, etc.); or (3) monitoring is done pursuant to the Criminal Procedure Act or Military Court Act. Therefore, unless the employees provide consent to the employer to monitor their emails, the employer will be in violation of Article 3 of the Secrecy Act. The consent of the sender of the email received by the employee or the receiver of the email sent by the employee will not likely be required, as the consent will likely be presumed in case of work emails as these emails are usually viewed as emails exchanged on behalf of the company. Penalties for violations of the Secrecy Act include imprisonment for up to 10 years.

Employers also should be aware that if reading of the emails requires the breaking of a security device (this includes something as simple as a password), this may be a violation of Article 316 of the Criminal Law.

Employers should, therefore, disclose to the employee in sufficient detail that his emails will be monitored (i.e., how the monitoring will be done, scope of monitoring, etc.) and obtain the express consent of each employee before monitoring. In Korea, an employer who fails to properly monitor employees may be deemed to commit a crime.

2. *Video Surveillance*

The Ministry of Information and Communication announced the Video Camera Privacy Guidelines on June 16, 2006. These rules are nonbinding and carry no legal penalties. Closed-circuit TV surveillance is prohibited in bathrooms, restrooms, and locker rooms. The Guidelines also prohibit the use of high-powered features such as rotation scanning, zooming, and voice recording.

F. New Zealand

1. Monitoring of Employee Email

To monitor emails in the workplace in New Zealand, employers must obtain the consent of the employees and have appropriate policies in place or a contractual provision in the employee's employment agreement that provides for such monitoring. Otherwise, any workplace monitoring must be done in accordance with the Privacy Act 1993 (the Act).

Under the Act, employers may undertake monitoring in the workplace under limited conditions. Workplace emails may be monitored for only a lawful purpose, such as to enable employer access to business information on the employee's network or investigate legitimate concerns the employer may have about possible illegal acts by the employee or activity that may be in violation of the employee's terms of employment. In addition, the information to be collected must be necessary to achieve that purpose, and unfair or unreasonably intrusive means must not be used when undertaking any such monitoring. In general, personal information must be collected from the employee unless it would "prejudice the purpose" of collecting the information.[236]

Covert monitoring, therefore, is permitted if open monitoring would prejudice the purpose for which the emails are to be monitored (i.e., to investigate potentially unlawful behavior). In such cases, employee notice or consent is not required to monitor employee emails, and the information collected must be held securely and be used only for the purposes of the investigation. Any information collected that is not relevant to the employer's investigation should be disregarded and deleted.

2. Video Surveillance

The same rules that apply to email monitoring have been applied by the Privacy Commissioner with respect to video surveillance in the workplace.

---

[236] *See* Principles 1, 2, & 4 of the Act.

G. Taiwan

1. General Requirements for Monitoring

The Republic of China Constitution protects privacy of communications of the people. Privacy is also a protected right under the Civil Code and infringement of privacy may be subject to civil liabilities. Within the legal and academic communities, the current thinking is that an employer's ability to monitor the activities and speech of its employees depends on whether or not an employee has been given a "reasonable expectation" of privacy in the activities or speech that are to be monitored.

2. Monitoring of Employee Email

In December 2003, the "reasonable expectation" test was adopted in a district court case involving the monitoring of employee emails. The district court judge explained that the employer's ability to monitor its employees' work emails depended on whether or not the employees had a reasonable expectation in terms of the privacy of their work emails. If there is no such expectation, the next issue to consider is whether or not the laws or regulations explicitly prohibit the employer from monitoring employees' emails. As to the standards for determining whether the employees have any reasonable expectation of privacy, the court stated that an employer may announce its email monitoring policy to the employees, and if the employees do not object to such a policy, the employees should be deemed as having given implied consent. The district court also concluded that there are no other laws and regulations explicitly prohibiting employers from monitoring employees' work emails.

There are, however, other laws that are relevant to this issue. The Statute Governing the Protection and Monitoring of Communications (the Statute) governs the interception and monitoring of private communications by the police and prosecution departments, but certain civil and criminal liabilities for illegal interception and monitoring apply to all persons. For an employer to be exempt from the liabilities under the Statute, the employer needs to obtain the consent of the employees, and the employer's monitoring activities cannot be for any illegal purpose.

The Criminal Code also prohibits individuals from intercepting or monitoring others' "nonpublic" speeches or activities without justification. Whether there is a reasonable justification for conducting monitoring or surveillance of employees would be determined on a case-by-case basis. Recording customer service calls, for example, may be generally justifiable for commercial reasons. In terms of monitoring employee emails, it may be justifiable to monitor the time spent on email or the number of emails sent for security or personnel management reasons, but unless there is a reasonable doubt, it would not be advisable to track the party or parties to whom the emails were sent or to read the contents of emails. It probably would not be justifiable for security or personnel management reasons to monitor employee Internet access, the time spent on the Internet, or each site entered if the employee is using the facilities provided by the employer.

Thus, if an employer is considering monitoring the activities or speech of its employees, it should: (1) provide employees notice regarding the monitoring, such as by announcing by email and circulating Work Rules revised to include a provision regarding the possibility of monitoring; and (2) obtain consent to the extent possible, such as by including such a provision in its employment contracts.

V. WHAT TO CONSIDER BEFORE MONITORING EMPLOYEES

Companies that decide to implement technologies that enable electronic monitoring of employees in the workplace should first consider the following legal and employee relations issues:

- Is the monitoring necessary? Are there preventive measures/technologies that could be used instead of monitoring? Can the same results be obtained using traditional methods of supervision?
- Have the employees received clear prior notice on the presence, use, and purpose of any monitoring technologies and on the misuse of electronic communication technologies (email, instant messaging, Internet, telephones, etc.), and is the monitoring transparent to the employees?

- Is the proposed monitoring proportionate to the concerns that it is intended to allay?
- Where applicable, have the Works Councils been informed and consulted and has an agreement been reached as required by national laws?
- Are employees entitled to have an email account for purely personal use?
- Is the use of Web-mail accounts permitted at work and does the employer recommend the use of a private Web-mail account for the purpose of using email for personal use?
- Does the company inform third parties whose emails may have been captured by the monitoring for the purpose of obtaining their consent?
- Have the employees been informed of: (1) the conditions under which private use of the Internet is permitted as well as on material that cannot be viewed or copied; (2) the systems implemented both to prevent access to certain sites and to detect misuse; (3) the extent of the monitoring activity (i.e., whether such monitoring may relate to individuals or particular sections of the company or whether the content of the sites visited is viewed or recorded by the employer in particular circumstances); (4) what use, if any, will be made of any data collected in relation to who visited what sites; and, lastly, (5) whether there has been any involvement of the employees' representatives?
- Has access to the content of employee email been arranged when the employee is absent without having given previous notice, and are the specific purposes for such access clear?
- Have the employees been informed of the backup procedures and any relevant storage periods?
- Have the employees been informed as to when email messages are definitely deleted from servers?
- Have the employees been informed of network security issues?
- Have the employees been informed of the risks involved in using Web-mail such as: (1) the risks of potentially spreading viruses; and (2) the possibility that Web-mail servers

are located in third countries where there may not be adequate protection of the personal data?

- Is video surveillance used only for monitoring production or occupational safety requirements, and are no cameras placed in locations intended for employees' private use?
- Has the company ascertained that any images collected exclusively to safeguard property or detect, prevent, and control serious offenses are not used to charge employees with minor disciplinary breaches?
- Is there a system in place whereby employees can lodge their counterclaims related to any disciplinary actions? and
- Is the company obligated to notify/register the monitoring activities with the national DPAs?

CHAPTER 4

EMPLOYEES' OFF-DUTY CONDUCT

I. Overview ... 298
II. Americas ... 299
A. United States ... 299
1. Union Membership or Affiliation ... 300
a. Off-Duty Union Activities Outside Employer's Premises ... 300
b. Off-Duty Union Activities on Employer's Premises ... 301
2. Political Activities ... 302
a. Participation in Political Campaigns ... 302
b. Freedom of Political Activities and Affiliations ... 303
3. Religious Activities ... 305
4. Fraternization/Romantic Relationships ... 305
a. Relationships Between Managers and Nonmanagers ... 306
b. Relationships Between Co-Workers ... 306
c. Relationships With Nonemployees ... 308
5. "Moonlighting" or Outside Employment ... 308
6. Off-Duty Use of Tobacco, Alcohol, or Other Legal Substances ... 309
a. Off-Duty Use of Lawful "Consumable Products" ... 309
b. Laws Protecting Off-Duty Smoking and Tobacco Use ... 310
c. Off-Duty Use of Medical Marijuana ... 310
7. Participation in Alcohol or Drug Rehabilitation Programs ... 312
8. Participation in Literacy Programs ... 312

9. Other Lawful Off-Duty Activities 313
Exhibit 4.1 U.S.: Examples of Off-Duty Conduct That May Be Legally Protected 314

III. Europe 315
A. Overview 315
B. United Kingdom 316
1. Union Membership 316
2. Political Activities 317
3. Religious Activities 319
4. Fraternization/Romantic Relationships 319
5. "Moonlighting" or Outside Employment 320

IV. Asia 320
A. China 320
1. "Moonlighting" or Outside Employment 320
2. Union Membership or Affiliation 320
B. Hong Kong 321
1. "Moonlighting" or Outside Employment 321
2. Union Membership or Affiliation 321
C. Japan 322
1. "Moonlighting" or Outside Employment 322
2. Union Membership or Affiliation 323
3. Political Activities in the Workplace 325
4. Political Activities Outside the Workplace 326

I. OVERVIEW

Privacy and employment laws intersect to protect applicants and employees against discrimination based on their off-duty conduct. Many of these laws protect off-duty conduct that tends to benefit workers or society in general, such as labor union involvement and political activities. These protections are found in the laws of the United States, United Kingdom, Japan, Hong Kong, China, and many other countries. Other laws protect off-duty conduct that is viewed as personal in nature, and not a legitimate matter for an employer to consider, such as U.S. and German laws prohibiting discrimination against employees for off-duty tobacco use.

The U.S. has a multitude of federal and state laws that prohibit employers from discriminating against applicants and employees based on assorted types of off-duty conduct. These laws counter-balance the general U.S. principle of "at-will employment," in which an employer is presumed to have the right to terminate an employee at any time, for any or no reason.[1] This chapter begins with a discussion of many, but certainly not all, of the protections for off-duty conduct that arise under U.S. law.

In comparison to the variety of laws in the U.S., the protections in the European Union (EU) and Asia may appear more limited. However, employers should keep in mind that at-will employment is a U.S. concept: employers in the EU, Japan, and a majority of other countries may dismiss an employee for only good cause. If the employer is unable to prove that the off-duty conduct was a good cause for dismissal, the employer may be liable for unjust dismissal. Consequently, U.S. protections for employees' off-duty conduct tend to be narrower than the protections in other countries, as a practical matter.

II. AMERICAS

A. United States

U.S. law does not impose blanket restrictions on an employer's ability to monitor or regulate the off-duty conduct of its employees. However, a variety of federal and state laws do protect employees against discrimination based on their off-duty activities. Many of these protections are grounded in public policy concerns, such as statutes protecting employees who engage in union or political activities. Other protections shield an employee's lawful off-duty recreational activities. At the same time, state and federal courts have sought to balance the privacy interests of employees with the legitimate interests of employers in regulating off-duty conduct affecting job performance. This section describes some of the pri-

[1]It should be noted that at-will employment in the United States is a state-law concept and is not recognized in all states. For instance, Montana is not an at-will state.

mary restrictions imposed on employer monitoring and regulation of the off-duty conduct of employees. As illustrated here, these restrictions vary substantially from state to state. Employers must be mindful of these restrictions in seeking to monitor or regulate the after-hours activities of their employees.

1. Union Membership or Affiliation

The National Labor Relations Act (NLRA) strictly prohibits employers from discriminating against any applicant or employee based on his union membership or affiliation.[2] State laws also may prohibit employers from discriminating against labor union members.[3] While a full discussion of the protections of the NLRA is beyond the scope of this book, the NLRA confers significant privacy protections with respect to employees' off-duty union activities and employer monitoring of such activities.

The following sections summarize the restrictions imposed on employer monitoring of off-duty union activities. See Chapter 3 for a more detailed discussion of limitations on employer surveillance of union activities, both during and after working hours.

a. Off-Duty Union Activities Outside Employer's Premises

As a general rule, the NLRA prohibits employers from conducting surveillance of their employees' off-duty, off-premises union activities.[4] This prohibition also applies to managers who conduct off-premises surveillance activities on their own initiative.[5] Unlawful surveillance can include monitoring of employee attendance at off-site union meetings, photographing employees engaged in union activities, and conducting audio or video sur-

---

[2] *See* 29 U.S.C. §158(a)(3). All citations herein for statutes and codes are on LexisNexis online at www.lexis.com unless otherwise indicated.

[3] *See* N.Y. LAB. LAW §201-d(2)(d) (protecting an employee's "membership in a union or any exercise of rights granted under [the NLRA or Taylor law]"). This protection has been found to extend to members of *any* union, not just members of unions subject to the NLRA or Taylor law. *See* Muhitch v. St. Gregory the Great Roman Catholic Church & Sch., 659 N.Y.S.2d 679, 680 (App. Div. 1997).

[4] *See, e.g.*, Cook Family Foods, 311 NLRB 1299, 1300–01 (1993).

[5] *See, e.g.*, BRC Injected Rubber Prods., 311 NLRB 66, 71 (1993) (manager violated NLRA by driving through parking lot of motel where he knew union meeting was being held, allegedly out of personal curiosity).

veillance of employees engaged in union activities.[6] State law may prohibit employer surveillance of employees engaged in union activities as well.[7]

b. Off-Duty Union Activities on Employer's Premises

The NLRA also restricts employer surveillance of an employee's union activities on the employer's premises outside working hours. In order to justify such surveillance, the employer generally must demonstrate that the surveillance serves a legitimate business interest, such as workplace security or quality control.[8] Additionally, the use of hidden video cameras for even routine workplace surveillance is a mandatory subject of collective bargaining in a unionized workplace.[9]

A higher standard applies to the intentional photographing or videorecording of employees engaged in peaceful union activity; these types of recordings are presumed to be unlawful unless the employer can prove a specific, legitimate justification. For example, in *Chester County Hospital*, company executives openly photographed and videotaped union members distributing union literature outside workplace entrances.[10] The company asserted that the photographs and videotapes were intended to record illegal activity by the union, such as trespassing and blocking access. The National Labor Relations Board (NLRB) disregarded the company's explanation, as the company's motivation for the surveillance was held to be unlawful.

This is not a case in which an employer, in an inconspicuous manner, simply and passively observes open union activity.

---

[6]*See generally* THE DEVELOPING LABOR LAW: THE BOARD, THE COURTS, AND THE NATIONAL LABOR RELATIONS ACT 162–66 (Patrick Hardin & John E. Higgins, Jr., eds., 4th ed. 2001).

[7]*See, e.g.*, CONN. GEN. STAT. ANN. §31-105.

[8]*See, e.g.*, NLRB v. Southern Md. Hosp. Ctr., 916 F.2d 932, 938 (4th Cir. 1990) (stating that it "is firmly established that management officials may observe public union activity, particularly where such activity occurs on company premises, without violating §8(a)(1) of the Act, unless such officials do something 'out of the ordinary'" to restrain employees from engaging in union activity).

[9]*See* Colgate-Palmolive Co., 323 NLRB 515, 515 (1997) (stating that the "use of hidden surveillance cameras in the workplace is a mandatory subject of bargaining, and [the] Union has a statutory right to bargain over the installation and continued use of these surveillance cameras").

[10]Chester County Hosp., 320 NLRB 604, 619 (1995).

Rather, the company, in a conspicuous manner, engaged in conduct that predictably tended, and was in fact designed, to intimidate its employees and thereby discourage them from receiving union literature.

As the company's motivation for its conduct was unlawful, it is immaterial, whether the union handbillers, at times, entered onto company property, temporarily blocked entrances, or otherwise engaged in unprotected conduct.

As a result, an employer's legitimate reason for photographing or videorecording union activity may be insufficient if the employer's conduct suggests that the surveillance was intended to discourage employees from engaging in union-related activities. See Chapter 3 for a more detailed discussion of restrictions on video surveillance of union activities.

2. *Political Activities*

Even though no federal law prohibits discrimination against employees based on their political beliefs or activities, a number of states provide such protection. The breadth of these protections varies by state, as illustrated by the following comparison of New York and California law.

a. *Participation in Political Campaigns*

New York law prohibits employers from taking adverse action against an employee or applicant based on involvement in political campaigns, as long as these activities occur outside working hours, outside the employer's premises, and without the use of the employer's equipment or other property.[11] Political activities are defined by the statute as running for public office; campaigning for a candidate; or participating in fund raising for a candidate, party, or advocacy group.[12] For example, a court held that an employee had stated a cause of action under this statute by alleging that she was terminated as the result of an off-duty, off-site discussion in which her political affiliations were revealed.[13]

---

[11]N.Y. LAB. LAW §201-d(2)(a).

[12]N.Y. LAB. LAW §201-d(1)(a).

[13]Cavanaugh v. Doherty, 675 N.Y.S.2d 143, 149 (App. Div. 1998).

These statutory protections apply equally to a public employee involved in a political campaign against the public official for whom he works. In *Richardson v. City of Saratoga Springs*, an employee who worked for the Commissioner of Public Works publicly supported the political campaign of the Commissioner's opponent, including wearing a campaign sticker supporting the Commissioner's opponent while at work.[14] The employee claimed that "shortly after he was directed to refrain from wearing [the] campaign sticker...the Commissioner...transferred certain of [the employee's] duties to [a] co-worker."[15] The appellate court held that the employee had established a viable legal claim that he was denied a promotion and a salary increase based on his off-duty political activities.[16]

b. Freedom of Political Activities and Affiliations

California law more broadly prohibits employers from controlling or limiting the political activities of its employees. Section 1101 of the California Labor Code prohibits employers from adopting any rule, regulation, or policy that (1) forbids or prevents employees from participating in politics or seeking public office or (2) tends to control or direct the political activities or affiliations of employees.[17] Similarly, Section 1102 states: "No employer shall coerce or influence or attempt to coerce or influence his employees through or by means of threat of discharge or loss of employment to adopt or follow or refrain from adopting or following any particular course or line of political action or political activity."[18]

---

[14]Richardson v. City of Saratoga Springs, 667 N.Y.S.2d 995, 996 (App. Div. 1998).

[15]*Id.*

[16]*Id.* at 997. It is interesting to note that the wearing of the campaign sticker was not the protected "political activity," as Section 201-d clearly requires that the political activity occur outside working hours and outside the worksite. The employee in *Richardson* wore the campaign sticker during work hours, on work premises. The court placed the infraction within the statute, stating that "the Commissioner—*knowing that* [*the employee*] *continued to express his opposing political views on his own time*... transferred certain... duties to [a] co-worker." *Id.* at 996 (emphasis added).

[17]CAL. LAB. CODE §1101.

[18]CAL. LAB. CODE §1102.

Both applicants for employment and employees are protected by these statutes.[19]

These California statutes do not define the term "political," but the California Supreme Court has described political activity as "pertaining to the exercise of the rights and privileges or the influence by which the individuals of a state seek to determine or control its public policy."[20] Protected activities include political speech[21] and participation in political organizations[22] but exclude activities that promote anarchy.[23] Although an employer cannot seek to influence or control the political activities of its employees, these statutes do not prevent the employer from sharing its own political beliefs or views with employees.[24]

---

[19]*See* Gay Law Students Ass'n v. Pacific Tel. [& Tel.] Co., 24 Cal. 3d 458, 487 & n.16 (1979).

[20]Lockheed Aircraft Corp. v. Superior Court, 28 Cal. 2d 481, 484–85 (1946) (quoting *Merriam Webster Dictionary* (2d ed.)). *See also* Mallard v. Boring, 182 Cal. App. 2d 390, 395 (1960) (stating that the term "political" includes "the espousal of a candidate or a cause, and some degree of action to promote the acceptance thereof by other persons").

[21]*See, e.g.*, Ali v. L.A. Focus Publ'n, 112 Cal. App. 4th 1477, 1487 (2003) (holding that a newspaper editor fired for publicly criticizing a public official outside that workplace had a valid claim under Section 1101 for wrongful termination); Buckley v. Valeo, 424 U.S. 1, 14 (1976) (holding that public discourse and debate on candidates are essential to the function of the government); Monitor Patriot Co. v. Roy, 401 U.S. 265, 272 (1971) (holding that the constitution protects political speech especially with "campaigns for political office").

[22]An employee's political activities, such as participation in litigation, wearing symbolic armbands, and associating with others to advance beliefs, are also protected by Sections 1101 and 1102 of the California Labor Law. *Gay Law Students*, 24 Cal. 3d at 487; Rosenfield v. Malcolm, 65 Cal. 2d 559, 561 (1967) (holding that the county could not discharge an employee who refused to resign from the Ad Hoc Committee to End Discrimination, an anti-race discrimination group).

[23]Political activity that does not "further the peaceful organization, regulation, and administration of government" is not protected by Sections 1101 and 1102 of the California Labor Law. For example, these statutes do not protect those who promote anarchy. *Lockheed*, 28 Cal. 2d at 485 (holding that an employer who created war materials at a missile plant could fire an employee "who advocates the overthrow of our government by force or whose loyalty to the United States has not been established to the satisfaction of the employer").

[24]*Id.* at 486 (allowing the management at the missile plant to express pro-government sentiment). *But see Gay Law Students*, 24 Cal. 3d at 487 (while an employer can share his own political beliefs, an employer cannot hire only individuals who share those political beliefs).

3. *Religious Activities*

Title VII of the Civil Rights Act of 1964 prohibits discrimination against employees based on their religious practices; it also requires employers to reasonably accommodate an employee's bona fide religious practices. These rights are not limited to participation in a traditionally recognized religion, but extend to any "sincere and meaningful belief that occupies in the life of its possessor a place parallel to that filled by [a traditionally recognized religion]."[25] A religious practice may be protected by Title VII even if it is not endorsed by an organized religion to which the employee belongs.[26] A number of states also protect the religious beliefs and activities of employees.[27]

An employer's obligations in responding to a request for religious accommodation are highly fact-specific. Generally speaking, if the employer is unable to grant the employee's requested accommodation, the employer must negotiate with the employee to find a reasonable compromise.[28] The employer must take steps to accommodate the employee's religious beliefs, unless it can prove that any accommodation would create undue hardship for the company or its employees.[29] Given the fact-intensive nature of this analysis, employers would be well-advised to consult counsel prior to refusing to grant an employee's request for religious accommodation.

4. *Fraternization/Romantic Relationships*

Privacy protections for U.S employees are created not only by statute, but also through case law. This section involves a topic that is currently governed by case law: the ability of employers to prohibit their employees from fraternizing with subordinates, co-workers, or nonemployees.

---

[25]United States v. Seeger, 380 U.S. 163, 176 (1965).

[26]*See* 29 C.F.R. §1605.1.

[27]*See, e.g.*, CAL. GOV'T CODE §12940 et seq.

[28]*See* Opuku-Boateng v. California, 95 F.3d 1461, 1467 (9th Cir. 1996).

[29]*Id.*

a. Relationships Between Managers and Nonmanagers

An employer generally may prohibit intimate relationships between managers and nonmanagers when there is a direct supervisory relationship. In *Crosier v. United Parcel Service, Inc.*, a manager dating a nonmanager employee was punished for violating a rule forbidding such relationships. The rule was implemented in an effort to "avoid misunderstandings, complaints of favoritism, and possible claims of sexual harassment" and "employee dissension created by romantic relationships between management and nonmanagement employees."[30] The court held that this rule served a legitimate business interest and therefore justified infringement on employee's right to privacy.[31]

b. Relationships Between Co-Workers

Certain courts have affirmed an employer's ability to terminate employees for knowingly violating a company nonfraternization policy by dating a co-worker.[32]

The enforceability of nonfraternization policies under laws protecting lawful off-duty conduct is less clear. For example, as discussed below, New York law protects employees against adverse actions based on their "legal recreational activities outside work hours, off of the employer's premises," which raises the question of whether dating may be considered a protected activity under this law.[33] New York courts have reached differing opinions about whether this statute applies to dating,[34] and the Second Circuit has

---

[30]Crosier v. United Parcel Serv., Inc., 150 Cal. App. 3d 1132, 1135, 1140 (1983).

[31]*Id.* at 1140. *See also* Shumway v. United Parcel Serv., Inc., 118 F.3d 60, 65 (2d Cir. 1997) (dismissing claims by employee terminated for dating a subordinate in violation of the employer's nonfraternization policy); Barbee v. Household Auto. Fin. Corp., 113 Cal. App. 4th 525, 531–33 (2003) (dismissing claims by an employee terminated for dating a subordinate).

[32]*See, e.g.*, Smith v. Wal-Mart Stores, 891 F.2d 1177, 1179–80 (5th Cir. 1990) (dismissing claims by an employee terminated for dating a co-worker in violation of the employer's nonfraternization policy); Watkins v. United Parcel Serv., Inc., 797 F. Supp. 1349, 1359–60 (S.D. Miss. 1992) (rejecting terminated employee's claim that employer's nonfraternization policy constituted an invasion of privacy), *aff'd mem.*, 979 F.2d 1535 (5th Cir. 1992).

[33]N.Y. LAB. LAW §201-d(2)(c).

[34]In *State v. Wal-Mart*, 621 N.Y.S.2d 158 (App. Div. 1995), the New York Appellate Division held that " 'dating' is entirely distinct from and, in fact, bears little resemblance to 'recreational activity.'" *Id.* at 159. The *Wal-Mart* court further concluded that

concluded that dating would not be considered a protected "recreational activity" under this statute.[35] As further discussed below, California law also provides that employees are protected against discrimination based on their "lawful conduct occurring during nonworking hours away from the employer's premises."[36] However, a California appellate court has held that these statutes did not prevent an employer from terminating an employee for violating the employer's nonfraternization policy.[37]

Nonfraternization policies may be subject to challenge on other grounds. In one case, for example, the District of Columbia Court of Appeals held[38] that a nonfraternization policy that prohibited employees from "fraternization" on or off duty with the client's employees or with co-employees was unenforceable because the rule failed to distinguish between union fraternizing and social fraternizing.

"the voluminous legislative history to the enactment . . . evinces an obvious intent to limit the statutory protection to certain clearly defined categories of leisure-time activities," with dating not to be included among them. *Id.* In contrast, New York district courts concluded that "the New York Court of Appeals would not construe [Section 201-d(2)(c)] so narrowly as to exclude 'cohabitation' from the class of recreational activities protected by the statute." Pasch v. Katz Media Corp., No. 94 Civ. 8554, 1995 U.S. Dist. LEXIS 11153, at *9 (S.D.N.Y. Aug. 7, 1995). *See also* Aquilone v. Republic Nat'l Bank of N.Y., No. 98 Civ. 5451, 1998 U.S. Dist. LEXIS 19531, at *17–18 (S.D.N.Y. Dec. 15, 1998) (holding that "a close personal friendship is analogous to co-habitation... [and] should be considered a protected activity for which an employer may not discriminate"). A state appellate division court even followed the determination of the Southern District, rejecting the *Wal-Mart* ruling. *See* Carey v. de Souza, 678 N.Y.S.2d 264 (App. Div. 1998) (relying on *Pasch*, and assuming without analysis that "dating is a protected recreational activity").

[35]*See* McCavitt v. Swiss Reinsurance Am. Corp., 237 F.3d 166, 168 (2d Cir. 2001) (holding that there was "no persuasive evidence... that leads us to conclude that the New York Court of Appeals would hold that romantic dating is a 'recreational activity' under [Section 201-d]"). *See also* Bilquin v. Roman Catholic Church, 729 N.Y.S.2d 519 (App. Div. 2001) (holding that cohabitation with a married co-worker does not fall under the definition of "recreational activity"); Hudson v. Goldman Sachs & Co., 725 N.Y.S.2d 318, 319 (App. Div. 2001) (holding that "romantic relationships are not protected").

[36]CAL. LAB. CODE §§96(k), 98.6.

[37]*See* Barbee v. Household Auto. Fin. Corp., 113 Cal. App. 4th 525, 531–33 (2003).

[38]Guardsmark, LLC v. NLRB, 475 F.3d 369 (D.C. Cir. 2007).

c. *Relationships With Nonemployees*

An employer also may be allowed to impose job-related restrictions on fraternization between employees and certain categories of nonemployees, although these cases have primarily arisen in the law enforcement context. For example, the Sixth Circuit held that a policy forbidding employees of the Department of Corrections from fraternizing with prisoners, parolees, probationers, or their families did not invade the employees' right of privacy in their off-duty relationships.[39] Similarly, the Eleventh Circuit dismissed the claims of a former correctional officer who was terminated for marrying an inmate.[40]

A comparable issue arose with respect to a private-sector employee in a California case.[41] In *Ortiz*, the plaintiff was employed at the Los Angeles Police Relief Association (LAPRA), a private nonprofit association, where she administered the employee benefits of current and former Los Angeles police officers.[42] She was required to leave her job after her employer discovered she planned to marry an inmate. In response to the plaintiff's claim that the employer violated her right of privacy, the employer asserted that the plaintiff's "intimate relationship with an inmate and access to confidential information about law enforcement personnel" created an actual or potential conflict of interest and could jeopardize the personal safety of LAPRA's members.[43] The court dismissed the plaintiff's claims, concluding that the employer had a "legitimate—indeed, a paramount—interest in preventing the improper disclosure of confidential information."[44]

5. *"Moonlighting" or Outside Employment*

An employer generally may prohibit its employees from engaging in outside employment that poses a conflict of interest. In *Fowler v. Varian Associates*, a California court held that an

---

[39]Akers v. McGinnis, 352 F.3d 1030, 1039–41 (6th Cir. 2003). *See also* Poirier v. Massachusetts Dep't of Corr., 532 F. Supp. 2d 275 (D. Mass. 2008).

[40]Burke-Fowler v. Orange County, 447 F.3d 1319, 1326 (11th Cir. 2006).

[41]Ortiz v. Los Angeles Police Relief Ass'n, 98 Cal. App. 4th 1288 (2002).

[42]*Id.* at 1294–95.

[43]*Id.* at 1295–96.

[44]*Id.* at 1313.

employee's pursuit of employment with a competitor while still employed with defendant constituted "good cause" for termination.[45] The court explained that "California law does not authorize an employee to transfer his loyalty to a competitor. During the term of employment, an employer is entitled to its employees' 'undivided loyalty.'"[46] The Sixth Circuit also has confirmed that an employer may legitimately forbid dual employment.[47]

6. *Off-Duty Use of Tobacco, Alcohol, or Other Legal Substances*

More than a dozen states have passed laws preserving the right of employees to engage in off-duty use of tobacco, alcohol, and other lawful substances. These laws do not interfere with an employer's ability to maintain a smoke-free workplace, but are intended to prevent employers from forbidding the use of tobacco or alcohol by employees outside work.

a. Off-Duty Use of Lawful "Consumable Products"

New York law generally prohibits an employer from taking adverse employment action based on an individual's "legal use of consumable products prior to the beginning or after the conclusion of the employee's work hours, and off of the employer's premises and without use of the employer's equipment or other property."[48] As the use of consumable products must be legal, illegal drug use is not protected by this statute, even if done outside work hours, and off work premises.[49] Minnesota law similarly prohibits an employer from taking adverse employment action against an individual because of his "use or enjoyment of lawful

---

[45]Fowler v. Varian Assocs., 196 Cal. App. 3d 34, 41 (1987).

[46]*Id.*

[47]Architectural Glass & Metal Co. v. NLRB, 107 F.3d 426, 432–33 (6th Cir. 1997).

[48]N.Y. LAB. LAW §201-d(2)(b).

[49]This section of the New York statute was apparently an expansion of language in other states that protected smokers from discrimination if they smoked off the job. New York's language was part of a national expansion that "went beyond protecting smoker's rights," and New York's statute, with its protection of political and recreational activity "took an even broader approach" than most states. *See*, Terry Morehead Dworkin, "*It's My Life—Leave Me Alone: Off the Job Employee Associational Privacy Rights*," 35 AM. BUS. L.J. 47, 51 (1997).

consumable products," although employers may restrict the use of these products during nonworking hours to the extent required by the nature of the employee's job.[50] More specifically, Missouri law protects employees who engage in lawful off-duty use of alcohol or tobacco products, unless such use interferes with an employee's performance of his job duties.[51]

b. Laws Protecting Off-Duty Smoking and Tobacco Use

In comparison, a number of states have adopted statutes prohibiting employers from requiring employees to refrain from off-duty tobacco use. Connecticut, the District of Columbia, Indiana, Louisiana, Maine, New Mexico, Oklahoma, Rhode Island, South Dakota, West Virginia, and Wyoming all prohibit employers from discriminating against employees for using tobacco products.[52] New Jersey law protects employees against discrimination on the basis of whether or not they choose to smoke or use other tobacco products.[53]

c. Off-Duty Use of Medical Marijuana

While federal law prohibits marijuana use, a number of states have passed laws permitting the use of marijuana for medical purposes.[54] This has resulted in a direct conflict between federal and state laws regarding the legality of so-called "medical marijuana"

---

[50]MINN. STAT. ANN. §181.938. *See also* MONT. CODE ANN. §39-2-903.

[51]MO. REV. STAT. §290.145.

[52]CONN. GEN. STAT. ANN. §31-40s; D.C. CODE ANN. §7-1703.03; IND. CODE ANN. §22-5-4; LA. REV. STAT. ANN. §23:966; 26 ME. REV. STAT. ANN. §597; N.M. STAT. ANN. §50-11-3; OKLA. STAT. ANN. tit. 40, §500; R.I. GEN. LAWS §23-20.10-14; S.D. CODIFIED LAWS §60-4-11; W. VA. CODE §21-3-19; WYO. STAT. ANN. §27-9-105.

[53]N.J. STAT. ANN. §34:6B-1.

[54]The following 12 states have authorized marijuana use for medical purposes: Alaska (ALASKA STAT. §11.71.090); Arizona (ARIZ. REV. STAT. ANN. §13-3412.01); California (CAL. HEALTH & SAFETY CODE §11362.5); Colorado (COLO. CONST. art. XVIII, §14); Hawaii (HAW. REV. STAT. §§329-121 to 329-128); Maine (ME. REV. STAT. ANN. tit 22, §2383-B[5]); Montana (MONT. CODE ANN. §§50-46-101 to 50-46-210); Nevada (NEV. REV. STAT. §§453A.010 to 453A.400); Oregon (OR. REV. STAT. §§475.300 to 475.346); Rhode Island (R.I. GEN. LAWS §§21-28.6-1 to 21-28.6-10); Vermont (VT. STAT. ANN. tit. 18, §§4472-4474d); Washington (WASH. REV. CODE §§69.51A.005 to 69.51A.902).

use.[55] As a result, employers may be faced with the question of whether they can refuse to employ someone who tests positive for marijuana use, if that marijuana use is permitted by state law.

The California Supreme Court addressed this issue in 2008, concluding that California law did not prohibit an employer from terminating an employee for off-duty medical marijuana use.[56] In this case, the plaintiff used marijuana at the recommendation of his physician, to alleviate pain and muscle spasms from a back injury suffered during his military service. His employment was terminated after he failed a routine pre-hire drug test, although he provided documentation of his status as a qualified medical marijuana patient under California law. The plaintiff subsequently filed a civil lawsuit, alleging that his termination violated California public policy and his right to reasonable accommodation for his back injury. The California Supreme Court rejected these claims, finding that California law does not require employers to accommodate off-duty use of marijuana, and noting that marijuana use remains illegal under federal law.[57] Following this decision, the California Legislature passed a bill that would have created employment protections for qualified medical marijuana users; this bill passed both the California Assembly and Senate but was vetoed by the Governor.[58]

---

[55]In *United States v. Oakland Cannabis Buyers' Cooperative*, 532 U.S. 483 (2001), the U.S. Supreme Court held that the federal Controlled Substances Act does not permit medical marijuana use, notwithstanding state laws to the contrary. *See also* Gonzales v. Raich, 545 U.S. 1, 26–29 (2005) (holding that provisions of the federal Controlled Substances Act (CSA) did not permit personal use or cultivation of medical marijuana under California's Compassionate Use Act, even within the state of California). As the *Raich* Court explained, "the mere fact that marijuana—like virtually every other controlled substance regulated by the [Controlled Substances Act, 21 U.S.C. §§812, 844(a),]—is used for medicinal purposes cannot possibly serve to distinguish it from the core activities regulated by the CSA." *Id.* at 28.

[56]Ross v. Ragingwire Telecomm. Inc., 174 P.3d 200 (Cal. 2008).

[57]*Id.* at 205.

[58]California Assembly Bill 2279 would have prohibited discrimination against an employee based solely on the employee's status as a qualified medical marijuana patient who uses the doctor-recommended medication outside of work. However, as the Governor explained in his veto message, "[e]mployment protection was not a goal of the initiative as passed by voters in 1996." Letter from Arnold Schwarzenegger, Governor of California, to Members of the California State Assembly (Sept. 30, 2008).

Other states have begun to consider employment protections for medical marijuana users as well. For instance, Rhode Island's Medical Marijuana Act provides that no employer may refuse to employ "or otherwise penalize a person solely for his or her status as a registered qualifying patient or a registered primary caregiver."[59] The bill was enacted over the Governor's veto in 2007, despite the U.S. Supreme Court's prior ruling that medical marijuana cultivation and use remains illegal under federal law.[60]

Given the legislative activity in this area, employers will want to consider state laws as well as federal laws in determining whether it is permissible to terminate an employee based on off-duty use of medical marijuana that is permitted by state law.

7. *Participation in Alcohol or Drug Rehabilitation Programs*

California law requires employers to "reasonably accommodate any employee who wishes to voluntarily enter and participate in an alcohol or drug rehabilitation program" as long as the accommodation does not "impose an undue hardship on the employer."[61] This "undue hardship" exception excuses an employer from accommodating an employee who is unable to do her job owing to substance abuse.[62] This exception may include poor performance, an unacceptable number of absences, or termination after unsuccessful treatment programs.[63]

8. *Participation in Literacy Programs*

Employees who seek to participate in an literacy program are also protected under California law. Under the California Labor Code, private employers with 25 or more employees must reasonably accommodate and assist any employee who reveals a problem of illiteracy and requests assistance.[64] The employer is required

---

[59]R.I. GEN. LAWS §21-28.6-4(b).

[60]*Raich*, 545 U.S. at 26–29.

[61]CAL. LAB. CODE §1025.

[62]*Id.*

[63]*See, e.g.*, Fuller v. Frank, 916 F.2d 558, 561 (9th Cir. 1990) (stating that an employer's duty to accommodate alcoholism is not unlimited); Sullivan v. Delta Air Lines, 58 Cal. App. 4th 938, 945 (1997).

[64]CAL. LAB. CODE §1041.

by statute to "make reasonable efforts to safeguard the privacy of the employee as to the fact that he or she has a problem with illiteracy."[65] In addition, the employer is prohibited from terminating an employee for disclosing his illiteracy if the employee performs his or her work satisfactorily.[66]

9. *Other Lawful Off-Duty Activities*

The laws of Colorado, Connecticut, Minnesota, New Jersey, New York, and North Dakota contain so-called "lifestyle statutes," limiting an employer's ability to regulate the lawful off-duty conduct of employees. New York law prohibits adverse employment actions based on "an individual's legal recreational activities outside work hours, off of the employer's premises and without use of the employer's equipment or other property."[67] Recreational activities are defined by the statute as "any lawful, leisure-time activity, for which the employee receives no compensation and which is generally engaged in for recreational purposes, including but not limited to sports, games, hobbies, exercise, reading and the viewing of television, movies and similar materials."[68] Colorado and North Dakota also prohibit discrimination against an employee for engaging in "lawful activity off the premises of the employer during nonworking hours," unless that conduct directly conflicts with the employer's legitimate business interests.[69]

Section 96(k) of the California Labor Code permits the California Labor Commissioner to handle claims for loss of wages

---

[65]CAL. LAB. CODE §1042.

[66]CAL. LAB. CODE §1044.

[67]N.Y. LAB. LAW §201-d(2)(c).

[68]N.Y. LAB. LAW §201-d(1)(b). The statute does not protect conduct that "creates a material conflict of interest related to the employer's trade secrets, proprietary information or other proprietary or business interest." N.Y. LAB. LAW §201-d(3)(a). In addition, an employer does not violate the statute when: (1) the employer believes that its actions are required by law; (2) the employer believes that its actions conformed to "an established substance abuse or alcohol program or workplace policy, professional contract or collective bargaining agreement"; or (3) the employee's actions "were deemed by an employer or previous employer to be illegal or to constitute habitually poor performance, incompetency or misconduct." N.Y. LAB. LAW §201-d(4). These exceptions carve out substantial areas upon which employers may make hiring and retention decisions.

[69]COLO. REV. STAT. ANN. §24-34-402.5; N.D. CENT. CODE §14-02.4-03.

resulting from "demotion, suspension, or discharge from employment for lawful conduct occurring during nonworking hours away from the employer's premises."[70] In turn, Section 98.6(a) of the California Labor Code prohibits an employer from discharging or discriminating against an employee for engaging in conduct described in Section 96(k).[71] Read together, these two statutes may suggest that employers are prohibited from discharging or discriminating against a California employee based on "lawful conduct occurring during nonworking hours away from the employer's premises." However, at least one California appellate court has held that Section 96(k) does not create a new legal protection for employees' off-duty conduct, but merely provides a new procedural remedy for claims that are already available by law.[72] Given the potential for differing interpretations of Section 96(k), however, employers should also exercise caution in taking adverse action against a California employee based on lawful off-duty conduct.

Examples of off-duty conduct that may be legally protected in the United States appear in Exhibit 4.1.

EXHIBIT 4.1
U.S.: Examples of Off-Duty Conduct That May Be Legally Protected

Union membership or affiliation—including off-duty union activities on the employer's premises
Political activities
Religious beliefs and activities
Off-duty use of tobacco, alcohol, or other legal substances
Participation in alcohol or drug rehabilitation program
Participation in illiteracy program

[70] CAL. LAB. CODE §96, subd. (k).

[71] CAL. LAB. CODE §98.6, subd. (a).

[72] *See* Barbee v. Household Auto. Fin. Corp., 113 Cal. App. 4th 525, 533–36 (2003).

III. EUROPE

A. Overview

The European Convention on Human Rights,[73] the EC Data Protection Directives,[74] and the EC Equal Treatment Directives[75] provide the legal framework in Europe that gives employees the right to a private life and protects employees against discrimination for certain off-duty activities. Furthermore, individual Member State laws may provide additional restrictions on an employer's ability to monitor or restrict employees' off-duty activities.

An employer that is monitoring the off-duty activities of employees may, in the course of monitoring, obtain personal data relating to employees. In such circumstances, the employer must comply with any applicable Member State law regarding the collection, processing, and storing of such personal data. In addition, an employer will generally require the employee's free and explicit consent to collect, store, or process sensitive personal data. What are regarded as permissible enquires regarding off-duty activities vary across the European Union. For example, in Germany an employer may not ask applicants or employees whether they smoke, as whether someone smokes or not is considered to be part of a person's private life. However, in the United Kingdom (UK),

---

[73]European Convention on Human Rights and Fundamental Freedoms 1950.

[74]The Directive 95/46/EC of the European Parliament and of the Council of October 24, 1995 on the protection of individuals with regard to the processing of personal data and on the free movement of such data; Directive 2002/58/EC of the European Parliament and of the Council of July 12, 2002 concerning the processing of personal data and the protection of privacy in the electronic communications sector (Directive on privacy and electronic communications); the Directive 2006/24/EC of the European Parliament and of the Council of March 15, 2006 on the retention of data generated or processed in connection with the provision of publicly available electronic communications services or of public communications networks; and amended Directive 2002/58/EC and Directive 97/66/EC of the European Parliament and of the Council of December 15, 1997 concerning the processing of personal data and the protection of privacy in the telecommunications sector.

[75]The Directive 2006/54/EC of the European Parliament and of the Council of July 5, 2006 on the implementation of the principle of equal opportunities and equal treatment of men and women in matters of employment and occupation and the Directive 2000/78/EC of November 27, 2000 establishing a general framework for equal treatment in employment and occupation.

if the purpose of making such an enquiry is to find out information about an employee's personal habits, for example, to accommodate smoking breaks, then it will be permissible to ask whether an employee smokes. In comparison, if the purpose is to assess the applicant's or employee's health, his status as a smoker may be regarded as health information, which would be categorized as sensitive personal data.

The employer's right to monitor or restrict employees' off-duty activities may also be governed by the contractual relationship or grounded in case law or public policy. Employers therefore should be mindful of the variety of different protections afforded to employees if they are seeking to monitor or restrict employees' off-duty activities.

B. United Kingdom

1. Union Membership

Under the Trade Union and Labour Relations (Consolidation) Act of 1992[76] (TULRCA), union members are protected against dismissal,[77] redundancy selection,[78] or being subjected to any detriment on account of their union membership or union activities at an appropriate time.[79] An appropriate time includes a time outside the employees' working hours.[80] The Employment Act 1990[81] also makes it unlawful for an employer to refuse to engage a person on the grounds of his union membership, nonmembership, or union activities.

Before the introduction of Section 174 of TULRCA,[82] a trade union was free to decide who should be or remain a member of the union. When Section 174 of TULRCA came into force, it prohibited the expulsion of union members save in very limited circumstances.[83] However, under Article 11 of the Human Rights Act of

[76]Trade Union and Labor Relations (Consolidation) Act 1992 c.52.
[77]§152 of TULRCA 1992.
[78]*Id.*
[79]§146(1) of TULRCA 1992.
[80]§146(2) of TULRCA 1992.
[81]§174(2)(a)-(d) of TULRCA 1992.
[82]Trade Union and Labor (Consolidation) Act 1992 c.52.
[83]§174(2)(a)-(d) of TULRCA 1992.

1998,[84] there is a right to freedom of assembly and of association, including the right to form and to join trade unions. In an attempt to make TULRCA comply with Article 11, the government amended Section 174 of TULRCA in 2005 to allow unions to expel members due to any activities undertaken by an individual as a member of a political party, although it remained unlawful to exclude or expel a member on the grounds of his membership in a political party. Trade unions felt that this amendment was inadequate and that TULRCA still breached their Article 11 rights. This issue was brought before the European Courts of Human Rights in the case of *Aslef v. UK*.[85] The court held that under Article 11 unions must remain free to decide, in accordance with union rules, questions concerning admission to and expulsion from the union. The decision means that unions can expel members whose opinions, which may be manifested by membership of a particular political party, are contrary to the principles of the union. The government is again amending TULRCA to delete all references to political party membership and activities. However, the prohibition on exclusion or expulsion for conduct that consists of being or ceasing to be, or having been or ceased to be, a member of another union will remain. Given that membership of a trade union is sensitive personal data, there are concerns as to how trade unions will obtain and process this information. This category of excluded conduct could also be subject to challenge on the basis that it infringes the right of freedom of assembly and association.

2. *Political Activities*

There is no specific UK law that prohibits discrimination against employees based on their political belief. There has been a debate on whether the Employment Equality (Religion or Belief) Regulations 2003,[86] which prohibit discrimination on the grounds of "religious or philosophical belief," extend to political views held

[84] 1998 c.42.

[85] Associated Soc'y of Locomotive Eng'rs & Firemen v. United Kingdom (Application No. 11002/05) [2007] IRLR 361.

[86] The Employment Equality (Religion or Belief) (Amendment) Regulations 2003 (SI 2003/2828).

by extreme political organizations such as the British National Party. However, so far case law has decided that they do not.[87]

As stated in the trade union section above, following the decision of the European Court of Human Right in *Aslef v. UK*,[88] the government is amending TULRCA to delete the prohibition on exclusion or expulsion from union membership on the grounds of membership of a political party and activities undertaken pursuant to such membership.

Practice Pointer: An employer should be cautious in dismissing an employee due to his political beliefs or action. If an employee has 12 months' continuous services with his employer, he has the right not to be unfairly dismissed. An employee's political beliefs will not normally be a fair reason to dismiss an employee unless they give rise to unacceptable conduct or behavior by the employee toward others or the employee's actions harm the reputation of the employer.

As noted above, information regarding a person's political belief is sensitive personal data and therefore an employer must ensure that it does not use collect or process such information without the employee's express consent.

---

[87]In *Baggs v. Fudge*, ET/1400114/05, April 1, 2005, the claimant argued that he had suffered discrimination on grounds of his membership in the British National Party (BNP), a right-wing political party. The employment tribunal rejected the claim and held that the BNP was "peculiar" in that it restricted its membership on racial grounds but did not require members to hold a particular religious philosophical or political belief. In the case of *Finnon v. Asda Stores Limited*, ET 2402142/05, January 4, 2006, the employment tribunal refused to strike out an application by a BNP member as having no prospect of success because the claimant had shown that he had a set of beliefs that affected his way of life and it was arguable that his ideology was capable of meeting the definition of religion or belief. The fact that a political party encapsulated this belief was not a reason to strike out the claim. However, at a full hearing the employment tribunal rejected the claim and held that the BNP did not involve a clear belief system, or a profound belief affecting a way of life or a view of the world.

[88]Associated Soc'y of Locomotive Eng'rs & Firemen v. United Kingdom (Application No. 11002/05) [2007] IRLR 361.

3. *Religious Activities*

The Employment Equality (Religion or Belief) Regulations 2003[89] implement the religious discrimination aspects of the Equal Treatment Framework Directive[90] and prohibit discrimination in the workplace by reason of any "religious belief or philosophical belief." They apply to vocational training and all aspects of employment including recruitment, terms and conditions, promotion, transfers, dismissals, and training. They cover existing and former employees and applicants.

An employee also has the right to freedom of religion and freedom to manifest religious beliefs under the Human Rights Act 1998.[91] Although only public sector employees can bring a direct claim for breach of the Human Rights Act, an employment tribunal, as a public authority body, has an obligation to consider human rights principles when deciding all claims. As a result, the common law should be compatible, and comply, with the Human Rights Act.

4. *Fraternization/Romantic Relationships*

There is no specific law in the UK on fraternization or romantic relationships in the workplace. However, a female employee who is dismissed because she has or had a relationship with a male co-worker may be able to bring a claim for sex discrimination if she is treated less favorably than a male co-worker. Employers must therefore deal with such relationships sensitively and cautiously. If an employer wants to prohibit or govern such workplace relationships it must have a clear policy on such matters and act reasonably. For example, an employer may insist that disclosures of such relationships are made and take any necessary steps where the employee has managerial responsibility for the employee with whom he or she is involved. It should be reasonable for an employer to seek to be informed of such relationships to ensure

---

[89]The Employment Equality (Religion or Belief) (Amendment) Regulations 2003 (SI 2003/2828).

[90]Directive 2000/78/EC of November 27, 2000 establishing a general framework for equal treatment in employment and occupation.

[91]1998 c.42.

that an employee is not subject to discrimination when a relationship ends.

5. "Moonlighting" or Outside Employment

There is no specific law in the UK that prohibits employees from moonlighting or taking outside employment. The right of an employee to take outside employment is generally governed by the terms of the employment contract. There is a duty of fidelity and mutual trust and confidence implied into every contract. However, taking a job outside working hours is not in itself a breach of this implied term unless the activities are likely to cause significant harm to the employer's legitimate interest. Given the limited protection provided by this implied term, an employer that wishes to restrict an employee from taking any outside employment should do so by expressly prohibiting such activities in the employment contract. In the absence of such an express term, an employee will generally be free to engage in outside employment.

IV. ASIA

A. China

1. "Moonlighting" or Outside Employment

The PRC Labor Law permits an employer to terminate an employment relationship if the employee has entered into an employment relationship with another company and in doing so has harmed the interests of the original company. This does not allow a company to prevent employees from moonlighting, but does provide a tool to terminate an employee if that moonlighting negatively affects the employee's job performance.

2. Union Membership or Affiliation

China's Labor Law provides that every employee has the right to participate in and organize trade unions in accordance with law.[92]

---

[92]PRC, Labor Law, Art. 7.

B. Hong Kong

1. "Moonlighting" or Outside Employment

While employees are subject to common law fiduciary duties and obligations to act in good faith toward their employers, these concepts are somewhat nebulous in practice and it is common practice to address moonlighting by means of express provisions in employment contracts. It should be noted that the efficacy of such provisions may be subject to common law restrictions on restraint of trade, which require the restriction to be reasonably necessary for the protection of a legitimate business interest of the employer. Accordingly, excessive scope should be avoided when drafting such restrictions.

2. Union Membership or Affiliation

Under Chapter 11 of the Employment Ordinance, every employee shall have the right to:[93]

- Be a member or an officer of a trade union;
- Take part in the activities of the trade union at any appropriate time (outside working hours, or, during working hours by arrangement and with the consent of the employer); and
- Associate with other persons for the purpose of forming or applying for the registration of a trade union.

Under the Employment Ordinance, employers are prohibited from:

- Preventing or deterring an employee from exercising his or her rights as a member or an officer of a trade union;
- Dismissing, penalizing, or discriminating against an employee for exercising the above mentioned rights; and
- Making it a condition of employment that an applicant (1) who is a member or officer of a trade union must relinquish his or her membership or office; (2) must not become a member of, or officer in, such a trade union; or (3) must

[93]Employment Ordinance (CAP. 57) §21B.

not associate with other persons for the purpose of forming or applying for the registration of a trade union.

While there is little relevant case law, it may be argued that the surveillance of an employee's union activities may have the practical effect of deterring his participation in such activities. In any event, if such monitoring involves the collection of personal data it will need to comply with the Personal Data (Privacy) Ordinance.[94] See Chapter 7 for additional details.

C. Japan

1. "Moonlighting" or Outside Employment

There is no law in Japan that prohibits employees from moonlighting. However, many businesses have corporate rules that prohibit their employees from moonlighting. In general, workers are free to use their time outside business hours in any matter they please, but the prohibition of moonlighting is permitted if it is rational. The Tokyo District Court stated that it may be rational to prohibit workers from engaging in side-businesses, because "workers must take appropriate rest outside of business hours in order to provide good faith services, and depending on the content of the side-business, such business may impair the operation and order of business of the employer."[95]

In general, the standards to determine whether a provision prohibiting moonlighting is rational are as follows:

- Whether there is a risk that the worker will be unable to provide his services by engaging in a side business, or that it will be difficult to do so (such as in the case of late-night shift work or physical labor);
- Whether the business of the side business will impair the business operations of the employer or damage the reputation and social trust of the employer (such as by working at a competitor or in the sex industry); and

---

[94]Cap. 486, Laws of Hong Kong.

[95]397 Roudou Hanrei 30 (Tokyo D. Ct., Nov. 19, 1982).

- Whether the worker will violate his fiduciary duty of loyalty or duty to give undivided attention to his work, pursuant to the employment contract.

It is necessary to keep in mind that even if the corporate rule prohibiting moonlighting is rational, not every disciplinary measure imposed for a violation of such provision by a worker may be deemed to be valid. The case law is steadfast in its general position that workers may use their time away from work as they please, and so disciplinary measures imposed for violations of the provision prohibiting moonlighting must be deemed to be rational.

If there is an agreement with the workers pursuant to Article 36.1 of the Labor Standards Law that provides for limits regarding the extension of work hours (36 Agreement),[96] employers will have an advantage. If such an agreement is in place, companies may order workers to work overtime to engage in emergency and important business, and workers must be ready to respond to such requests. Because refusing to comply with orders to work overtime is grounds for disciplinary measures, businesses may impose disciplinary measures without resorting to the provision prohibiting moonlighting.

Practice Pointer: Before imposing disciplinary measures on a worker for moonlighting, an employer should determine whether the worker is subject to the 36 Agreement, consider the nature of the side business, and check the Work Rules to confirm that a prohibition of moonlighting is in place.

2. *Union Membership or Affiliation*

Under Article 7 of the Labor Union Law,[97] the following acts by the employer are prohibited as unfair labor practices:

---

[96]Pursuant to Article 36 of the Labor Standards Law, when employers wish to have workers work in excess of statutory working hours, or to work on statutory holidays, it is necessary for labor and management to enter into a written agreement, and submit the same to the head of the relevant labor standards supervision office. This requirement is often referred to as the "36 Agreement."

[97]Labor Union Law (Law No. 174 of 1949).

- Discharge of or unfair handling of a worker because the worker is a member of a labor union, joined a labor union, tried to form a labor union, or took proper acts of a labor union;
- Making it a condition of employment for the worker not to join a labor union, or to leave a labor union. However, where a labor union represents more than a majority of the workers at a factory or workplace, the employer may make it a condition of employment for a worker to be a member of that labor union;
- Refusal to engage in negotiations with the representative of the workers without rational reason;
- Controlling the formation of or operations of a labor union, or interfering with such activities, or providing financial assistance to the operations of a labor union. (However, employers may permit workers to engage in negotiations or discussions with their employer during working hours without losing their wages, and may also contribute to a welfare fund of the labor union to prevent economic calamities and the like, and may provide a necessary minimum of office space.); and
- Discharge of or unfair handling of a worker because the worker reported to the Labor Committee that the employer violated any provision in this Article.

In a noteworthy case, a court decided against an employer that attempted to monitor the labor union activities of its employees. Central Japan Railway Company (JR Tokai) had set up a camera in February 1999 that monitored the bulletin board of its labor union, and the JR Tokai labor union asked JR Tokai to remove the camera. JR Tokai argued that it was necessary for security purposes. The labor union then made a complaint to the Osaka District Labor Committee that this was an unfair labor practice. On October 14, 2003, the Osaka District Labor Committee ordered JR Tokai to change the location of the camera.

The foregoing case involved monitoring of employees that took place before the Action Guide regarding the Protection of Personal Information of Workers (Action Guide) was issued by the Ministry of Health, Labour and Welfare (MHLW) in 2000, and before the Personal Information Protection Law of 2004 (PIPL) was enacted. Employers that are considering implementing the monitoring of their employees should now heed the Guidelines for the Protection of Personal Information in the Economic and Industrial Areas, issued by the Ministry of Economy, Trade and Industry (METI) pursuant to the PIPL. The basic requirements are to notify employees in advance regarding the purpose of monitoring, to implement corporate rules regarding monitoring and the person responsible, and to verify that the monitoring is being suitably performed. The MHLW's Employment Management Guidelines state that it is "desirable" for employers to notify the labor unions when adopting the required corporate rules for monitoring employees.

Practice Pointer: Even if the employer follows the previous guidelines regarding monitoring of employees, labor union members may still object to the monitoring of labor union activities as an unfair labor practice. Thus, in actuality, it will probably be difficult to monitor the labor union activities of employees.

3. Political Activities in the Workplace

The Supreme Court in Japan has confirmed that employers may restrict the political activities of employees in the workplace. *In the Matter of Nippon Telegraph and Telephone Public Corporation Meguro Telegraph and Telephone Agency*, the Supreme Court explained that:

> Private businesses in general are places to engage in work, not in political activities or other private activities of employees. Workers do not have a right to engage in political activity at work, since there is a risk that such activity may also cause political animosity and conflict among the workers, may impede the ability of employers to manage the workplace, and to the extent this is done during business hours, this would violate the worker's obligation to provide its services, and may prevent other workers from engaging in their duties. Even if workers engage in such activities outside business hours, such as during breaks, such activities may impede the ability of other workers freedom to use their free time as they wish, and may decrease the performance and efficiency afterwards, and there is a high risk that this will impede the maintenance of corporate order. Therefore, we find that a provision

in the work rules of a private business prohibiting workers from engaging in political activities in the workplace is rational, and should be permitted.[98]

4. Political Activities Outside the Workplace

The Supreme Court indicated that restrictions on political activities outside the workplace must be rational and permissible, as determined on a case-by-case basis. The Supreme Court of Japan stated in the case called the *Matter of the Japan National Railways Chugoku Regional Office* that:

> Disciplinary measures that employers impose on their employees are a kind of sanction in order to maintain the broader corporate order, and to make the smooth operation of business possible. By being employed, employees have the duty to maintain and secure the corporate order. Ordinarily, maintaining and securing the corporate order can be achieved by regulating the acts of the workers within the workplace, or their actions that relate to their jobs. However, there may be cases when such restrictions are not sufficient. Clearly, if there is a direct relationship with the corporate order, even acts of workers outside the workplace with no relationship to their work may be the subject of restriction. A corporation is a member of society, and damage to its social reputation may impede the smooth operation of business. If objectively speaking, the worker's actions outside the workplace may damage the social reputation of the business, there may be cases when restriction of such activity is permissible. In this matter, the employee struck a policeman on duty, and we find that such an act objectively damages the social reputation of the business.[99]

In another decision, the Supreme Court decided that a disciplinary discharge of an employee for acts outside the workplace was ineffective. This so-called "NKK Incident" involved an employee who was arrested and indicted for his political activities outside the workplace and was discharged by his employer for rea-

[98]871 Nanrei Jihou 3 (Sup. Ct., Dec. 13, 1977), regarding restricting the political activities of workers in the workplace. Note that in Japan, Supreme Court cases do not necessarily have the same effect over the lower courts as in the United States. Cases rarely reach the courts in Japan, and when they do, judges often look to influential academics to decide their cases, not just to other cases.

[99]733 Hanrei Jihou 18 (Sup. Ct., Feb. 28, 1974).

son of severe damage to its social reputation. The Supreme Court stated that:

> In order to determine that the dishonorable actions of an employee have damaged the reputation of the business, it is not necessarily required that there be specific incidents of interruption of business or disadvantages suffered in business transactions. However, the act must be objectively determined to be considerably detrimental to the social reputation of the company, looking comprehensively at factors such as the nature of the act, circumstances of the act, the type, manner and scale of the company's business, the status of the company in the business world, the company's policies, the position and duties of the employee at the company, and other relevant matters.[100]

The Supreme Court then found that the act of the employee could not be objectively determined to be damaging to the reputation of NKK, and declared the disciplinary discharge of the employee ineffective.

Practice Pointer: Note also that the Action Guide prohibits the collection of personal information about workers regarding their "philosophy, faith or religious beliefs."[101] Employers should not inquire into the political activities of the worker outside the workplace, as doing so may result in the breach of this prohibition.

---

[100] Supreme Court, 3/15/74, Second Petty Bench.

[101] Action Guide, §2.2(3).

CHAPTER 5

CONFIDENTIALITY OF HEALTH INFORMATION

I. Overview ... 333
II. Americas ... 334
  A. United States ... 334
    1. Health Insurance Portability and Accountability Act of 1996 ... 334
      a. Business Associates ... 334
      b. Covered Entities ... 335
        i. Health Care Providers ... 335
        ii. Health Plans ... 335
        iii. Group Health Plans ... 336
      c. Health Care ... 336
      d. Health Care Operations ... 337
      e. Health Information ... 337
      f. Individually Identifiable Health Information ... 338
      g. Payment ... 338
      h. Protected Health Information ... 339
      i. Treatment ... 339
      j. Summary of the Privacy Rules ... 339
      k. Compliance Issues for Employers ... 340
        i. Initial Compliance Issues ... 340
          (a) Distinction Between Health Plan and Employer/Sponsor ... 340
          (b) Identification and Classification of Health Plans ... 341
          (c) Scope of Compliance Responsibilities ... 341
        ii. Common Operational Issues Involving Health Information ... 343
          (a) Benefit Plan Administration ... 343

(b) Information Sharing 344
(c) Participant Advocacy 344
iii. Specific Health Plan Compliance Requirements 345
iv. Administrative Safeguards.................. 346
(a) Appointment of a Privacy Official and Contact Person....................... 346
(b) Privacy Training for Plan's Workforce.................................... 347
(c) Implementation of Procedural Safeguards.................................... 347
(d) "Minimum Necessary" Policies.... 348
(e) Complaint Procedures.................. 349
(f) Sanctions for Members of the Workforce Who Violate HIPAA Privacy Rules................................ 349
(g) Duty to Mitigate Harmful Effects of Improper Uses or Disclosures... 350
(h) Prohibitions on Retaliation and Waiver 350
(i) Policies, Procedures, and Documentation 350
(j) Notice of Privacy Practices 351
v. Plan Amendment Requirements 353
vi. Individual Rights 355
vii. Business Associate Issues................... 355
(a) Business Associate Agreements.... 356
(b) Violation of Business Associate Agreements 357
viii. Implementation Deadlines.................. 358
ix. De-Identification of Health Information 358
x. Health Information Relating to Deceased Individuals.......................... 359
xi. Disclosures to Family Members and Friends 359
xii. Disclosures Relating to Minors 360
xiii. Other Disclosures Required or Permitted by the Privacy Rules........... 360
(a) Response to a Complaint.............. 360
(b) Reporting of Crimes..................... 361

xiv. Consents to Disclosure 361
xv. Authorizations 361
(a) Psychotherapy Notes.................... 363
(b) Marketing 363
xvi. Impact of State Medical Privacy Laws.. 364
l. Individual Privacy Rights 364
i. Right of Access 365
ii. Right to Request Amendment/ Correction 367
iii. Right to Accounting of Nonroutine Disclosures... 369
(a) Notice of Privacy Practices 370
(b) Voluntary Restrictions on Disclosure of Health Information.................................. 371
(c) Confidential Communications 371
(d) Complaints to HHS 371
m. Enforcement 372
i. Responsibility for Enforcement.......... 372
ii. Compliance Investigations by HHS..... 372
iii. Sanctions.. 373
iv. Private Enforcement Rights 374
v. HHS Approach to Enforcement.......... 375
n. HIPAA Security Rules................................ 375
i. Employer Compliance Issues 378
ii. Individual Rights Relating to the Security Rules.................................... 378
2. Other U.S. Federal Rules Relating to Confidentiality of Health Information 378
a. Americans With Disabilities Act 379
3. State Rules in the United States Relating to Confidentiality of Medical Information............. 379
a. California.. 379
i. Summary of Key Statutory Provisions 380
ii. Employer Compliance Responsibilities.................................. 381
(a) Adoption of Procedural Safeguards 381
(b) Prohibition on Discrimination....... 381

(c) Disclosure of Medical Information 382
(d) Authorized Disclosures 383
(e) Receipt of Medical Information 384
(f) Effects on Vendor Relationships 385
(g) Document Destruction Requirements 386
(h) Health Care Providers Acting as Employers 386
(i) Improper Use or Disclosure of Medical Information 387
(j) Disclosure of Genetic Data 387
(k) HIV/AIDS Status 388
(l) Prohibition on Waivers 388
(m) Right of Access 388
(n) Enforcement of Rights 389
iii. Additional California Medical Privacy Laws 390
b. New York 390
i. Access to Patient Information 391
(a) Confidentiality of Records Received Under Section 18 391
(b) Violations of Section 18 392
ii. On-Site Medical Facilities and Patient Health Records 392
(a) Conflicts Between Medical Ethics and Employer Instructions 393
(b) Employee Access to Information 394
iii. Privacy Rights of Government Employees 394
iv. New York Workers' Compensation Law 395
v. Laws Regarding Confidentiality of HIV/AIDS Information 396
(a) Confidentiality Required 396
(b) Enforcement Provisions 396
III. Europe 397
A. France 397
1. Subject Access Requests by Individual Employees 398
2. Applicable Fee and Consultation Terms 399

3. Denial of Subject Access Requests 399
B. Germany 400
C. United Kingdom 401
IV. Asia and Asia Pacific 404
A. Australia 404
1. NSW Health Records and Information Privacy Act 2002 404
2. ACT Health Records (Privacy and Access) Act 1997 406
3. Victoria Health Records Act 2001 406
B. China 407
C. Hong Kong 407
1. Employment Candidates 408
2. Existing Employees 408
D. Japan 410
1. Mental Health Information 412
2. Additional Guidance 413
E. New Zealand 413

I. OVERVIEW

While most countries seek to protect the confidentiality of employees' health information, this principle is addressed in very different ways. The United States tends to focus on entities that generally control and have access to health information, placing the greatest obligations on health care providers, health plans, and health care clearinghouses. In contrast, European Union (EU) Member States, such as France, Germany, and the United Kingdom (UK), seek to apply uniform protections for health information, regardless of whether this information is held by medical providers, employers, or others. Moreover, most countries with privacy laws cover health information with specific legislation, as the U.S. does, or else have omnibus laws that provide greater protection for health information. Thus health and medical information tends to be among the most protected information globally.

This chapter describes the general legal protections for employee health information in the United States and representative countries in Europe and Asia. In turn, the next chapter

(Chapter 6) describes legal and procedural requirements an employer must follow in collecting health information from applicants and employees through medical examinations and drug testing.

II. AMERICAS

A. United States

In the United States, the key protections for health information have evolved from the Health Insurance Portability and Accountability Act of 1996 (HIPAA).[1] HIPAA (or the Privacy Rules) applies to health care providers, health plans, and health care clearinghouses; as a result, it does not necessarily apply to employers. However, employers may be subject to state medical confidentiality laws, even if they are not subject to HIPAA. This section begins with a detailed discussion of HIPAA, followed by examples of state medical confidentiality laws.

1. Health Insurance Portability and Accountability Act of 1996

HIPAA is a rather technical statute and in order to understand the interactions of the various provisions and the implications for employers, it is important that some basic terms are defined.

a. Business Associates

A business associate is any entity or person that performs certain services on behalf of, or provides certain services to, a covered entity that involves the use or disclosure of individually identifiable health information.[2] Members of a covered entity's workforce are not its business associates.[3] In addition, neither an

---

[1]Pub. L. No. 104-191, 110 Stat. 1936 (1996). HIPAA and its related regulations (including both proposed and final regulations) are available online at http://www.hhs.gov/ocr/hipaa/.

[2]45 C.F.R. §160.103; 65 Fed. Reg. 82,475–82,476 (Dec. 28, 2000).

[3]45 C.F.R. §160.103; 65 Fed. Reg. 82,475 (Dec. 28, 2000). A covered entity's workforce includes its employees, volunteers, trainees, and other persons who perform work under its direct control, whether or not they are paid by the covered entity. 45 C.F.R. §160.103; 65 Fed. Reg. at 82,480 (Dec. 28, 2000). For purposes of this defini-

employer nor a health insurance issuer acting as such are business associates of a health plan sponsored by the employer.[4] Professional service providers such as attorneys, accountants, actuaries, and consultants may be business associates.[5]

b. Covered Entities

The Privacy Rules are directly applicable only to health care providers, health plans, and health care clearinghouses. These three entities are referred to as covered entities.[6] Many people believe that the obligations under HIPAA "stick" to the data, that is, just because an employer receives health information from an employee, the employer is covered by HIPAA. That understanding is incorrect. Only entities that are regulated by the Department of Health and Human Services (HHS) such as hospitals and health plans are directly covered by HIPAA.

i. Health Care Providers

A health care provider is an entity that provides health care services or which furnishes, bills, or is paid for the provision of such services in the ordinary course of its business.[7] Health care providers include physicians, dentists, clinics, hospitals, skilled nursing facilities, home health agencies, and many other health care professionals. Thus, employers that provide on-site health care or a clinic for employees may be considered a health care provider under HIPAA.

ii. Health Plans

A health plan is any individual or group plan that provides, or pays the cost of, medical care.[8] It includes, among other things, group health plans, health insurance issuers, health maintenance

---

tion, individuals who perform services in connection with a group health plan maintained by their employer will be regarded as members of the plan's workforce.

[4]65 Fed. Reg. at 82,508 (Dec. 28, 2000).

[5]*Id.*; 65 Fed. Reg. 82,475 (Dec. 28, 2000).

[6]45 C.F.R. §160.103.

[7]45 C.F.R. §160.103; 42 U.S.C. §1320d(3); 65 Fed. Reg. at 82,477–82,478 (Dec. 28, 2000). This definition encompasses both "providers of services" (as defined in 42 U.S.C. §1395x(u)) as well as "providers of medical or health services" (as defined in 42 U.S.C. §1395x(s)).

[8]45 C.F.R. §160.103.

organizations (HMOs), issuers of long-term care policies, and multiple-employer welfare benefit plans.[9]

iii. Group Health Plans

A group health plan is any "employee welfare benefit plan" as defined under Employee Retirement Income Security Act (ERISA)[10] that provides medical care to employees and their dependents directly or through insurance, reimbursement, or otherwise.[11] This term includes both fully insured and self-insured plans. Plans that have fewer than 50 participants and that are self-administered are not included in this definition.[12] A plan or arrangement providing certain excepted benefits is not included within this definition.[13]

c. Health Care

The Privacy Rules adopt a very broad definition of health care. Health care includes preventive, diagnostic, therapeutic, rehabilitative, maintenance, and counseling care, services, or supplies relating to an individual's physical or mental condition or functional status or that affects the structure or function of the body.[14]

---

[9]*Id.* The Privacy Rules also include as health plans the Medicare and Medicaid programs, issuers of long-term care policies, multiple-employer welfare benefit arrangements, and a variety of other government-sponsored programs providing health care.

[10]An "employee welfare benefit plan" is any

> plan, fund, or program... established or maintained by an employer or by an employee organization, or by both... for the purpose of providing for its participants or their beneficiaries, through the purchase of insurance or otherwise, (A) medical, surgical, or hospital care or benefits, or benefits in the event of sickness, accident, disability, death or unemployment, or vacation benefits, apprenticeship or other training programs, or day care centers, scholarship funds, or prepaid legal services, or (B) any benefit described in section 302(c) of the Labor Management Relations Act of 1947 (other than pensions on retirement or death, and insurance to provide such pensions).

29 U.S.C. §1002(1).

[11]45 C.F.R. §160.103.

[12]45 C.F.R. §160.103; 65 Fed. Reg. at 82,478 (Dec. 28, 2000).

[13]*Id.* (citing 42 U.S.C. §300gg-91(c)(1)); 65 Fed. Reg. at 82,479 (Dec. 28, 2000). Excepted benefits include group term life insurance, disability income benefits, automobile liability insurance, and workers' compensation benefits. 42 U.S.C. §300gg-91(c)(1).

[14]45 C.F.R. §160.103; 65 Fed. Reg. at 82,477 (Dec. 28, 2000).

In addition, health care includes the sale or dispensation of a drug, device, piece of equipment, or other item by prescription.[15]

d. Health Care Operations

The term "health care operations" refers to the administrative functions of covered entities and includes quality assessment and improvement, evaluation of health care professionals, underwriting, premium rating, and other activities relating to the creation, renewal, or replacement of health insurance contracts or health benefits, arranging and conducting medical review, legal and auditing services, business planning and management, management activities, customer service, and resolution of internal grievances.[16]

e. Health Information

Health information is any information in any form that is created or received by a covered entity or an employer, life insurer, public health authority, school, or university that relates to the past, present, or future physical or mental health or condition of an individual, the provision of health care to the individual, or the past, present, or future payment for health care services for the individual.[17]

---

[15] *Id.*

[16] 45 C.F.R. §164.501; 65 Fed. Reg. at 82,489–82,491 (Dec. 28, 2000). With respect to group health plans, the term "health care operations" includes many activities that are commonly referred to as "plan administration functions," including claims processing and payment and auditing. However, health care operations do not include activities involving the amendment, modification, or termination of a group health plan. 65 Fed. Reg at. 82,508 (Dec. 28, 2000). Under ERISA, these are the sorts of activities that are commonly referred to as "settlor functions." *See, e.g.*, DOL Adv. Op. 2001-01A; Lockheed Corp. v. Spink, 517 U.S. 882, 890 (1996).

[17] 45 C.F.R. §160.103. Section 105(a) of the Genetic Information Nondiscrimination Act of 2008, Pub. L. No. 110-233, 122 Stat. 890 (GINA), amends the Public Health Service Act (PHSA) by adding Section 1180, effective as of May 21, 2008, regulating the use and disclosure of "genetic information" relating to individual's participating in group health plans and covered by group health insurance policies and Medicare supplemental policies. GINA incorporates amendments to both ERISA and Internal Revenue Code (in addition to the PHSA), applying a number of substantial limitations on the use of genetic information by group health plans and health insurance carriers. Supplementing these statutory requirements, GINA directs the Secretary of HHS to amend the Privacy Rules to explicitly bring "genetic information" within the definition of "health information." For this purpose, "genetic information" generally includes

f. Individually Identifiable Health Information

Individually identifiable health information is any health information that identifies the individual to whom it relates or with respect to which there is a reasonable basis to believe that the information could be used to identify the individual to whom it relates.[18]

g. Payment

Payment functions include, among other things, activities undertaken by health plans to obtain premiums or to pay for the costs of medical care incurred by covered employees and their dependents.[19] More specifically, payment functions can include determinations of eligibility or coverage, coordination of benefits and subrogation, risk adjusting, billing, claims management, collection activities, securing reinsurance, medical necessity reviews, precertification, utilization reviews, and credit reporting.[20]

---

information about an individual's "genetic tests," the genetic tests of the individual's "family members," and any evidence of the manifestation of any disease or disorder in the individual's "family members." 42 U.S.C. §300gg-91(16). A "genetic test" includes any "analysis of human DNA, RNA, chromosomes, proteins, or metabolites, that detects genotypes, mutations, or chromosomal changes" or any "analysis of proteins or metabolites that is directly related to a manifested disease, disorder, or pathological condition that could reasonably be detected by a health care professional with appropriate training and expertise in the field of medicine involved." 42 U.S.C. §300gg-91(17). An individual's "family members" include any dependents or other individuals who are related in the first, second, third, or fourth degree. 42 U.S.C. §300gg-91(15). GINA imposes specific limitations on the use and disclosure of genetic information by group health plans and health insurance carriers; these limitations are more extensive than those applicable to health information generally. Section 105(a) of GINA directs HHS to issue the revised regulations within 60 days of GINA's initial effective date (i.e., May 21, 2009); the revised regulations will be effective upon their issuance. Note that the statutory limitations on the use of genetic information by group health plans and health insurance carriers are independent of the regulatory limitations and may become effective after the regulatory limitations depending on the circumstances. *See* GINA 101(f)(2), 102(d) & 103(f) (for group health plans and health insurance carrier, the ERISA, Internal Revenue Code, and PHSA amendments are effective as of the first plan year commencing after May 21, 2009). See note 40 below for further discussion of the regulatory limitations mandated by GINA.

[18] 45 C.F.R. §160.503; 65 Fed. Reg. at 82,493 (Dec. 28, 2000).

[19] 45 C.F.R. §164.501; 65 Fed. Reg. 82,495–82,496 (Dec. 28, 2000).

[20] *Id.*

h. Protected Health Information

Protected health information (PHI) is any individually identifiable health information that is transmitted in electronic form or maintained or transmitted in any other form or medium.[21] Notably, employment records held by an employer are excluded from this definition even if such records contain health information that might otherwise be subject to the Privacy Rules.[22]

i. Treatment

Treatment means the provision, coordination, or management of health care and related services by one or more health care providers.[23] Treatment functions can include interactions between health care providers and their business associates.[24]

j. Summary of the Privacy Rules

The Privacy Rules prohibit covered entities from using or disclosing any PHI except as authorized by the person to whom the information relates or as is otherwise permitted or required by applicable law. The Privacy Rules also indicate that, in general, only the minimum amount of PHI necessary to accomplish the intended purpose may be provided by a covered entity to a non-covered entity (such as an employer or business associate).

As discussed in more detail below, covered entities are permitted to use and disclose PHI to perform treatment and payment functions as well as health care operations. In addition, PHI can be freely disclosed to the individual to whom it relates. Protected health information also may be used or disclosed in accordance with an authorization from the individual. PHI must be disclosed to the individual pursuant to the rights of access and accounting and to HHS for investigative purposes.

---

[21]45 C.F.R. §160.503; 65 Fed. Reg. 82,496–82,497 (Dec. 28, 2000). In the preamble to the initial final Privacy Rules, HHS indicates that its intention is to regulate the use and disclosure of individually identifiable health information by covered entities. As a result, there is little, if any, practical distinction between individually identifiable health information and protected health information, as defined by the Privacy Rules. 65 Fed. Reg. at. 82,496 (Dec. 28, 2000).

[22]45 C.F.R. §164.501; 67 Fed. Reg. 53,182, 53,192–53,193 (Aug. 14, 2002).

[23]45 C.F.R. §164.501; 65 Fed. Reg. at 82,497 (Dec. 28, 2000).

[24]*Id.*

Any entities that are business associates of a covered entity (such as claims administrators, payroll providers, consultants, etc.) also may be indirectly subject to the privacy regulation to the extent they use or receive PHI from a covered entity. The Privacy Rules regulate business associates indirectly by limiting a covered entity's ability to disclose PHI to them absent contractual guarantees that the PHI will be used in only a permissible manner. A business associate is permitted to use or access PHI only when its agreement with the covered entity expressly limits its use and disclosure of any PHI it creates, receives, or maintains.

k. Compliance Issues for Employers

i. Initial Compliance Issues

(a) Distinction Between Health Plan and Employer/Sponsor

The Privacy Rules do not regulate employers acting as employers or in their capacity as the sponsor of health plans.[25] Nevertheless, because most health plans do not have a formal workforce (relying instead on their sponsor's personnel), employers often have de facto responsibility for taking action to bring their health plans into compliance with the Privacy Rules.

In determining the scope of an employer's compliance obligations, it is important to bear in mind the artificial distinction created by the Privacy Rules between the employer and its health plan. Although most health plans are technically distinct from their sponsoring employers, they rarely have a separate existence.[26] In other words, most health plans do not have their own employees, offices, or computer systems; the employer's personnel are usually responsible for administering or overseeing the administration of their health plan. As a result, many of the requirements imposed

---

[25] 65 Fed. Reg. at 82,507–82,508 (Dec. 28, 2000).
[26] *Id.*

by the Privacy Rules on the use and disclosure of PHI by health plans are conceptually troublesome in actual application.[27]

(b) Identification and Classification of Health Plans

Health plans can be configured in many ways. An employer may maintain an "umbrella" health plan that provides a comprehensive array of welfare benefits (e.g., medical, dental, vision) or might provide each benefit through a separate plan. Although these distinctions are important for purposes of ERISA, the Privacy Rules apply to each component benefit within a health plan. For instance, if an employer self-insures its medical benefits but provides dental benefits through an insurance contract, even though this arrangement might be regarded as a single plan for purposes of ERISA, the Privacy Rules arguably apply to each component benefit separately.[28] In other words, for purposes of the Privacy Rules, the self-insured medical component and the fully insured dental component are regarded as separate plans (although they might form an organized health care arrangement).

(c) Scope of Compliance Responsibilities

The two key determinants to an employer's compliance responsibilities relative to its health plan are: (1) the type of plan at issue (fully insured or self-funded)[29] and (2) the degree of

---

[27]For example, before a group health plan can permit its sponsor to receive any PHI generated or maintained by the plan, the plan document must be amended to include certain limitations relating to the sponsor's use of that PHI. 45 C.F.R. §164.504(f)(1)(i). The plan sponsor is required to certify in writing to the plan that these amendments have been adopted. 45 C.F.R. §164.504(f)(2)(ii). In most instances, this requirement will be satisfied by the plan sponsor's certification to itself (acting on behalf of the plan as its administrator) that it has adopted the required amendments.

[28]*See* 65 Fed. Reg. at 82,548 (Dec. 28, 2000) (discussing distribution of notice of privacy practices in the context of an umbrella welfare benefits plan).

[29]A "fully insured" health plan is a plan that provides benefits solely through an insurance or HMO contract. 45 C.F.R. §164.530(k)(1)(i). A "self-funded" health plan is a plan under which the benefits are paid out of the plan sponsor's general assets. 65 Fed. Reg. at 82,507 (Dec. 28, 2000). In some instances, a health plan may have dual characteristics (e.g., a minimum premium arrangement). As a general rule of thumb, under a fully insured health plan, an insurance company or HMO is at risk for claims in excess of premiums paid. Under a self-funded plan, the sponsoring employer is typically at risk for all claims; the fact that the employer may have procured stop-loss

involvement the employer desires in the administration of the plan. In the case of a fully insured health plan, the Privacy Rules differentiate between the group health plan and the underlying insurance or HMO contract through which benefits are funded.[30] In most instances, the administration of fully insured health plans is performed by a health insurer, itself a "health plan" under the Privacy Rules, and the sponsoring employer has no formal role other than to periodically provide enrollment and disenrollment information and to remit the appropriate premiums. In this configuration, the sponsoring employer (or its broker) often receives claims reports from the health insurance issuer for use in tracking claims experience under the plan and for establishing future premiums.[31] Because of the minimal involvement an employer has in this sort of health plan, the Privacy Rules excuse the employer from many compliance responsibilities.[32]

In contrast, for the typical self-funded health plan, the sponsoring employer usually has a much greater degree of involvement in the ongoing administration of the plan. In this configuration, the health plan might be funded by the sponsoring employer on a pay-as-you-go basis from its general assets or might be funded by contributions to a tax-exempt trust. The sponsoring employer

---

insurance coverage for particularly large claims does not change the self-funded character of the plan.

[30]*See* 45 C.F.R. §164.520(a)(2)(iii), 45 C.F.R. §164.530(k)(1).

[31]Cognizant of their responsibilities as covered entities under the Privacy Rules, many of the health insurers and HMOs now limit the amount of information they provide to employers and redact claims reports to eliminate information that could be used to identify participants. A sponsor of a fully insured health plan can amend the plan to permit access to more detailed information (including PHI) for plan administration functions pursuant to Section 164.504(f)(2) of the Privacy Rules.

[32]As discussed in more detail below, for fully insured plans where the sponsoring employer does not actively involve itself in plan administration, the Privacy Rules impose two negative requirements: to avoid intimidating or retaliating against covered individuals for exercising their privacy rights and to avoid requiring covered individuals to waive their privacy rights. In particular, such an employer is obligated to refrain from intimidating, threatening, coercing, discriminating against, or taking other retaliatory action against individuals for: exercising their privacy rights; filing a complaint; participating in an investigation; or opposing any improper practice under the Privacy Rules. In addition, the sponsoring employer cannot require individuals to waive their rights under the Privacy Rules as a condition of treatment, payment, enrollment, or eligibility to participate in its health plan.

might process claims internally or could instead outsource claims processing to a third-party administrator (TPA).[33] Appeals that arise under a self-funded plan may be resolved by an internal committee or by a TPA, although in virtually every instance, the sponsoring employer will retain ultimate authority to approve or deny a claim under the plan. Thus, self-funded health plans almost inevitably have a greater degree of employer involvement than do fully insured health plans, and, as a result, the compliance responsibilities associated with self-funded health plans are also more extensive.

ii. Common Operational Issues Involving Health Information

(a) Benefit Plan Administration

It is important to maintain the distinction between employer and health plan because health information received by an employer acting as employer is not subject to the Privacy Rules, but health information received by an employer acting as plan administrator is likely to be subject to the Privacy Rules.[34] PHI can be generated in many ways during the course of administering a health plan, whether the plan is self-administered or administered by a TPA. In particular, PHI can be found in such things as explanation of benefits forms; invoices or statements from health care providers; notes or oral statements relating to a participant's claim or treatment; medical records, files, and reports; and detailed claims experience reports provided by brokers or health insurance issuers. Although it may be possible for an employer to have access to some or all of this information, that ability cannot be taken for granted under the Privacy Rules.

However, there are many common records relating to employees that may contain health information, much of which will relate

---

[33]Many health insurers also have the capability to serve as claims administrators to self-funded health plans. When they act in this capacity, these entities are regarded as business associates rather than as covered entities. 65 Fed. Reg. at 82,476 (Dec. 28, 2000).

[34]*See* 65 Fed. Reg. at 82,507–82,508 (Dec. 28, 2000).

to excepted benefits or will constitute "employment records."[35] As a result, the Privacy Rules will not limit an employer's ability to access such information.

(b) Information Sharing

The Privacy Rules are designed to encourage the exchange of PHI between covered entities and their business associates for the purpose of better serving covered individuals. Thus, when appropriate, an individual's PHI can be readily shared (subject to the minimum necessary standard discussed below) between a health care provider and a health plan or between the members of an organized health care arrangement.[36] The Privacy Rules generally permit the ready use and disclosure of PHI in the ordinary course of plan administration only when the entities that are exchanging that information are all obligated to follow the Privacy Rules.

(c) Participant Advocacy

Employers are often asked to intercede on behalf of participants in their health plans to secure additional information regarding claims that are denied by a health insurer, HMO, or TPA. The Privacy Rules indicate clearly that a plan sponsor is free to assist participants in its health plan with claims issues without becoming subject to the full range of compliance responsibilities.[37] Even in this context, however, the plan sponsor generally may not receive PHI from the health plan, except as permitted under the Privacy Rules. In the absence of a participant authorization, unless the

---

[35]45 C.F.R. §164.501; 67 Fed. Reg. at 53,192 (Aug. 14, 2002). Among the common types of information that fall into these categories are employment records relating to the Family Medical Leave Act or other medical leaves of absence; alcohol and drug-free workplace laws; fitness-for-duty reports; reports relating to the Americans With Disabilities Act; information relating to short- and long-term disability claims, group life insurance, accidental death and dismemberment insurance, and business travel accident insurance; and information relating to workers' compensation coverage and claims.

[36]An organized health care arrangement (OCHA) is an organized health care system in which more than one covered entity participates and that holds itself out to the public as participating in a joint arrangement. 45 C.F.R. §164.501; 65 Fed. Reg. at 82,494–82,495 (Dec. 28, 2000). A group health plan and a health insurance issuer or HMO can form an OCHA with respect to the covered individuals, as can multiple health plans maintained by a single employer. *Id.*

[37]65 Fed. Reg. at 82,648 (Dec. 28, 2000).

health plan is amended to include disclosures of PHI relating to claims assistance as a "plan administration function" (and the other requirements discussed below are satisfied), the plan sponsor will not be able to receive PHI from a health plan (or its business associates) or a health insurer or HMO.

iii. Specific Health Plan Compliance Requirements[38]

For health plans,[39] there are three primary categories of compliance responsibilities: (1) implementation of appropriate administrative safeguards; (2) adoption of policies and procedures to safeguard and allow for the free exercise of the individual rights conferred by the Privacy Rules; and (3) adoption of certain plan amendments and implementation of a "firewall" to safeguard PHI held by the plan.

The Privacy Rules permit health plans to use or disclose a participant's PHI without authorization for performing treatment and payment functions and health care operations.[40] The use or

---

[38]As an initial observation, the adoption of the Privacy Rules (and related regulations) has spawned a cottage industry of consultants and other professionals who seek to provide guidance to employers and health plans (among other entities). As HHS itself has noted, much of this purported guidance is inaccurate, incomplete, or misleading. *See* HHS Comments on HIPAA Privacy Marketing available online at http://www.hhs.gov/ocr/hipaa/misleadingmarketing.html. Despite the best intentions of HHS, there are many ambiguities in the Privacy Rules, but there is currently no well-developed body of administrative guidance. Faced with this situation, many covered entities and third-party vendors have adopted overly conservative compliance positions or have misinterpreted or misapplied the Privacy Rules. Employers should carefully review their compliance efforts to ensure that they are not undertaking unnecessary action or otherwise "overcomplying" with the Privacy Rules and should cast a skeptical eye toward compliance activities taken by the individuals and entities that provide services to them and their health plans.

[39]Throughout this discussion, references to "health plans" are intended to include only group health plans, except as otherwise indicated. As health plans, health insurers and HMOs are also subject to the Privacy Rules, although plan sponsors will obviously have little involvement in the compliance efforts of such entities.

[40]45 C.F.R. §164.502(a)(1)(ii). As discussed in note 17, as directed by Section 105(a) of GINA, the Privacy Rules are to be amended by HHS to clarify the circumstances in which genetic information about health plan participants and their family members may be used or disclosed by a group health plan, a health insurance carrier, or their respective workforce members and business associates While GINA does permit the use of genetic information in connection with "payment" functions, it is clear that a group health plan or health insurance carrier may request only the minimum amount of genetic information necessary to complete the payment function at issue. ERISA 702(c)(3)(B); I.R.C. §9802(c)(3)(B); 42 U.S.C. §300gg-1(c)(3)(B). Further, GINA cat-

disclosure of PHI for any other purpose is generally prohibited unless authorized by the participant at issue. However, as discussed below, the Privacy Rules do permit the use and disclosure of PHI to an employer to facilitate "plan administration functions."[41]

iv. Administrative Safeguards

Under the Privacy Rules, health plans[42] are required to implement a variety of so-called administrative safeguards to protect the confidentiality of health information and to prevent its misuse or improper disclosure. The majority of these requirements can be addressed through the adoption of appropriate privacy policies and procedures.

(a) Appointment of a Privacy Official and Contact Person

Health plans must designate a privacy officer who is responsible for the development and implementation of appropriate privacy policies and procedures, including (1) developing and maintaining a notice describing the anticipated uses and disclosures of PHI under each plan, each participant's rights under the Privacy Rules, and the self-funded plans' legal duties with respect to the use and disclosure of PHI; and (2) developing training schedules and programs so that all workforce members receive the necessary training to permit them to carry out their designated functions in connection with these plans.[43] The role of privacy officer may be an additional responsibility given to an existing employee or a newly created position.

---

egorically precludes the use or disclosure of genetic information by group health plans or health insurance carriers for "underwriting purposes." ERISA 702(c)(4); I.R.C. §9802(c)(4); 42 U.S.C. §300gg-1(c)(4); GINA 105(a). "Underwriting purposes" includes (1) rules governing eligibility (including enrollment and continued eligibility) for benefits or coverage; (2) determination of premium or contribution amounts; (3) application of any pre-existing condition limitations; or (4) any other activities to the creation, renewal, or replacement of health insurance benefits. 42 U.S.C. §300g-91(19).

[41]45 C.F.R. §164.504(f)(3).

[42]Fully insured health plans are not subject to the foregoing administrative requirements if they do not create or receive PHI other than summary health information and enrollment and disenrollment information. 45 C.F.R. §164.530(k).

[43]45 C.F.R. §164.530(a)(1)(i); 65 Fed. Reg. at 82,561 (Dec. 28, 2000).

Health plans must also designate a contact person (who may or may not be the same as the privacy officer) or office for receiving complaints and for providing additional information about matters that are covered in the notice of privacy practices.[44]

Both of these appointments must be documented by the health plan.[45]

(b) Privacy Training for Plan's Workforce

Health plans must provide training to all members of their workforce regarding their privacy policies and procedures, as necessary and appropriate for the members of the workforce to carry out their assigned functions.[46] For this purpose, a health plan's "workforce" includes both employees of the plan as well as employees of the sponsoring employer's workforce who perform services in connection with the plan.[47] All training must be documented.[48] To comply with the training mandate, the health plan must:

- Provide the training to each member of its workforce by the applicable compliance date;
- Provide the training to each new member of its workforce within a reasonable time after joining the workforce; and
- Retrain each member of its workforce as material changes in privacy procedures or policies occur and document the training.[49]

(c) Implementation of Procedural Safeguards

Health plans are required to implement appropriate administrative, technical, and physical safeguards to protect the PHI they maintain.[50] These safeguards must reasonably safeguard PHI from

---

[44] *Id.*

[45] 45 C.F.R. §164.530(a)(2).

[46] 45 C.F.R. §164.530(b)(1); 65 Fed. Reg. at 82,561 (Dec. 28, 2000).

[47] 45 C.F.R. §164.503; 65 Fed. Reg. at 82,480 (Dec. 28, 2000).

[48] 45 C.F.R. §164.530(b)(2)(ii).

[49] 45 C.F.R. §§164.530(b)(2)(i)(A)–(C).

[50] 45 C.F.R. §164.530(c)(1); 65 Fed. Reg. at 82,561–82,562 (Dec. 28, 2000). The Privacy Rules do not mandate that particular safeguards be implemented in light of the differing needs of health plans and other covered entities of various sizes. 65 Fed. Reg. at 82,562 (Dec. 28, 2000). Note that the Security Rules (as discussed below in

intentional or unintentional misuse or disclosure.[51] In addition, health plans must take reasonable steps to limit uses or disclosures of PHI that are incidental to permitted uses and disclosures.[52]

(d) "Minimum Necessary" Policies

In connection with their use and disclosure of PHI, health plans are required to adopt a "minimum necessary" policy.[53] Under this requirement, even uses and disclosures that are permitted by the Privacy Rules must be limited to the minimum amount of PHI that is reasonably necessary to accomplish the intended purpose.[54] The Privacy Rules do permit some degree of flexibility in this regard such that covered entities can adopt policies and procedures that are tailored to their own individual circumstances.[55] Incidental disclosures of PHI in a manner not in conformance with the Privacy Rules are permitted so long as the covered entity has adopted a minimum necessary policy and implemented appropriate administrative safeguards to avoid such disclosures.[56]

There are a number of exceptions to the minimum necessary standard. They include disclosures to health care providers for treatment purposes; disclosures to the covered individual; disclosures required or permitted by the Privacy Rules; disclosures made pursuant to an authorization; and various disclosures required by law.[57]

To comply with the minimum necessary standard, covered entities must identify the persons or classes of persons who require access to PHI to perform their job functions and impose appropriate limitations on their right of access.[58]

---

more detail) supplement this requirement imposed by the Privacy Rules. *See* Health Insurance Reform: Security Standards, 68 Fed. Reg. 8,334 (Feb. 20, 2003) *codified* at 45 C.F.R. pts. 160, 162, & 164.

[51] 45 C.F.R. §164.530(c)(2)(i).

[52] 45 C.F.R. §164.530(c)(2)(ii).

[53] 45 C.F.R. §164.514(d)(1); 65 Fed. Reg. at 82,543–82,545 (Dec. 28, 2000).

[54] 45 C.F.R. §164.514(d)(3)(ii). Note that the use or disclosure of genetic information by group health plans and health insurance carriers is subject to a statutory "minimum necessary" requirement under ERISA, the Internal Revenue Code, and the PHSA. ERISA 702(c)(3)(B); I.R.C. §9802(c)(3)(B); 42 U.S.C. §300gg-1(c)(3)(B).

[55] 67 Fed. Reg. at 53,195 (Aug. 14, 2002).

[56] 45 C.F.R. §164.502(a)(1)(iii). *See* 67 Fed. Reg. at 53,194 (Aug. 14, 2002).

[57] 45 C.F.R. §§164.502(b)(2)(i)–(vi).

[58] 45 C.F.R. §§164.514(d)(2)(i)(A)–(B).

For any types of routine or recurring disclosures of PHI, a covered entity must adopt appropriate policies and procedures to ensure that only the minimum amount of PHI necessary to accomplish the purpose of the disclosure is released or requested.[59] For all other disclosures of PHI, covered entities must develop guidelines to limit the amount of PHI that is released or requested and individually review requests for disclosures using those guidelines.[60]

In narrow circumstances, disclosures are deemed to satisfy the minimum necessary standard.[61] Health plans and other covered entities are obligated to limit their requests for PHI to the minimum amount necessary.[62]

(e) Complaint Procedures

Health plans must adopt a procedure for allowing covered individuals to make complaints regarding its policies and procedures and must maintain a record of any such complaints and their dispositions.[63]

(f) Sanctions for Members of the Workforce Who Violate HIPAA Privacy Rules

Health plans are required to design a system of written disciplinary policies and appropriate sanctions for workforce members who violate the Privacy Rules.[64]

---

[59] 45 C.F.R. §164.514(d)(3)(i); 65 Fed. Reg. at 82,544–82,545 (Dec. 28, 2000).

[60] 45 C.F.R. §164.514(d)(3)(ii); 65 Fed. Reg. at 82,545 (Dec. 28, 2000).

[61] 45 C.F.R. §164.514(d)(3)(iii); 65 Fed. Reg. at 82,545 (Dec. 28, 2000). Among other things, disclosures requested by another covered entity and disclosures requested by a professional member of the workforce or a business associate are deemed to satisfy the minimum necessary standard. 45 C.F.R. §§164.514(d)(3)(iii)(B) & (C).

[62] 45 C.F.R. §164.514(d)(4); 65 Fed. Reg. at 82,545 (Dec. 28, 2000).

[63] 45 C.F.R. §164.530(d)(1); 65 Fed. Reg. at 85,562 (Dec. 28, 2000).

[64] 45 C.F.R. §164.530(e)(1); 65 Fed. Reg. at 85,562 (Dec. 28, 2000). Violation of a covered entity's privacy policies and procedures by a member of the workforce can be a basis for terminating the member's employment. *See, e.g.*, Verinder v. Rite Aid Corp., No. 3:06cv0024, 2007 U.S. Dist. LEXIS 90931, *87–88 (W.D. Va. Dec. 11, 2007) (discussing impact of potential violation of HIPAA disclosure policies on employer's decision to terminate an employee).

(g) Duty to Mitigate Harmful Effects of Improper Uses or Disclosures

A health plan must mitigate, to the extent practicable, any harmful effect of which it is aware resulting from an improper use or disclosure of PHI by a member of its workforce, its sponsoring employer, or a business associate.[65]

(h) Prohibitions on Retaliation and Waiver

Health plans may not intimidate or retaliate against covered individuals for making complaints (internally or to HHS), testifying, participating, or assisting in certain proceedings or good-faith opposition to any act or practice that violates the Privacy Rules (providing the opposition does not involve an impermissible disclosure of PHI).[66] In addition, health plans may not require covered individuals to waive their privacy rights as a condition of treatment, payment, enrollment, or eligibility.[67]

(i) Policies, Procedures, and Documentation

Health plans are obligated to adopt policies and procedures to comply with the requirements imposed by the Privacy Rules.[68] These policies and procedures must be reasonably designed and can be tailored to address the particular activities undertaken by the plan (and its business associates) that involve the use or disclosure of PHI.[69] Health plans must promptly document and implement changes to their policies and procedures as necessary or appropriate to comply with changes in the law, standards, requirements, and implementation specifications (including changes and modifications in the Privacy Rules).[70] Other changes may be made at any

---

[65] 45 C.F.R. §164.530(f); 65 Fed. Reg. at 85,562–85,563 (Dec. 28, 2000). This duty encompasses both violations of the Privacy Rules as well as violations of the policies and procedures adopted by the health plan. 65 Fed. Reg. at 85,563 (Dec. 28, 2000).

[66] 45 C.F.R. §164.530(g); 65 Fed. Reg. at 85,563 (Dec. 28, 2000). Note that although this prohibition applies only to health plans and other covered entities by its terms, because of the close relationship between most health plan sponsors and their plans, it would be inadvisable for an employer to attempt to retaliate against an individual who makes a complaint.

[67] 45 C.F.R. §164.530(h); 65 Fed. Reg. at 85,563 (Dec. 28, 2000).

[68] 45 C.F.R. §164.530(i)(1); 65 Fed. Reg. at 85,563 (Dec. 28, 2000).

[69] *Id.*

[70] 45 C.F.R. §§164.530(i)(2)–(3); 65 Fed. Reg. at 85,563 (Dec. 28, 2000).

time but must be documented.[71] However, changes that affect the content of the privacy notice must be reflected in a revised notice and generally may not be retroactive.[72]

The documentation of any policies and procedures, actions, activities, and designations may be maintained in either written or electronic form for at least six years following their adoption.[73]

(j) Notice of Privacy Practices

In general, individuals have a right to receive a notice of privacy practices from each covered entity that maintains their PHI.[74] Participants in health plans are entitled to receive a privacy notice from either the plan itself or the health insurance issuer, depending on the plan's funding mechanism.[75] Self-funded health plans must provide their own privacy notices, but fully insured health plans are excepted in most instances.[76] However, fully insured health plans that create or receive PHI must maintain a privacy notice and provide copies upon request.[77] A health plan may not use or disclose PHI in a manner that is inconsistent with its notice of privacy practices.

The Privacy Rules require that privacy notices contain a variety of provisions. In particular, a notice must be written in plain language and describe the uses and disclosures of PHI that the plan may make; indicate whether the plan will disclose PHI to its sponsor; and describe participant's rights of access, amendment, and accounting and rights to request confidential communications and restrictions on the use and disclosure of PHI.[78] Privacy notices can be distributed electronically, but participants must have the

---

[71] 45 C.F.R. §164.530(i)(5).

[72] The ability of a health plan to change its policies and procedures is limited unless it documents its reservation of amendment rights in its notice of privacy practices. 45 C.F.R. §164.530(i)(4)(ii).

[73] 45 C.F.R. §164.530(j); 65 Fed. Reg. at 85,563 (Dec. 28, 2000).

[74] 45 C.F.R. §164.520(a)(1); 65 Fed. Reg. at 85,547 (Dec. 28, 2000).

[75] 45 C.F.R. §164.520(a)(2)(i); 65 Fed. Reg. at 85,547–85,548 (Dec. 28, 2000).

[76] 45 C.F.R. §164.520(a)(2)(i)(A) (self-funded health plans); 45 C.F.R. §164.520(a)(2)(iii) (fully insured health plans). *See* 65 Fed. Reg. at 85,547–85,548 (Dec. 28, 2000).

[77] 45 C.F.R. §164.520(a)(2)(ii); 65 Fed. Reg. at 85,548 (Dec. 28, 2000).

[78] 45 C.F.R. §164.520(b)(1); 65 Fed. Reg. at 85,548–85,550 (Dec. 28, 2000).

right to request paper copies.[79] The notice must also describe the plan's responsibilities under the Privacy Rules.[80] In order to be permitted to modify the privacy practices described in the notice on other than a prospective basis, the covered entity must expressly reserve its amendment rights.[81] The notice must explain the plan's complaint procedure and identify the privacy official and contact person.[82] The notice must also indicate its effective date.[83]

The notice must be promptly revised and distributed whenever a material change to its substance is made.[84] In general, no such change can be implemented prior to the effective date set forth in the revised notice.[85]

Health plans must provide the notice by their initial compliance date and thereafter to new enrollees.[86] Revised notices must be distributed within 60 days after a material change is made.[87] At least once every three years, the plan must notify participants of their right to request a copy of the notice.[88] If a health plan has more than one notice, it can comply with a request for the notice by providing the notice that is applicable to the requesting individual.[89] Although the Privacy Rules specify that notices are to be written in plain language,[90] it is often difficult to satisfy this requirement while still addressing each of the mandatory provisions. To minimize the risk of confusion associated with lengthy notices, HHS has indicated that "layered" notices are permissible.[91] Under this

---

[79] 45 C.F.R. §164.520(c)(3)(ii); 65 Fed. Reg. at 85,551 (Dec. 28, 2000).

[80] 45 C.F.R. §164.520(b)(1)(v); 65 Fed. Reg. at 85,550 (Dec. 28, 2000).

[81] 45 C.F.R. §164.520(b)(2); 65 Fed. Reg. at 85,550–85,551 (Dec. 28, 2000).

[82] 45 C.F.R. §§164.520(b)(1)(vi)–(vii); 65 Fed. Reg. at 85,550 (Dec. 28, 2000).

[83] 45 C.F.R. §164.520(b)(1)(vii); 65 Fed. Reg. at 85,550 (Dec. 28, 2000).

[84] 45 C.F.R. §164.520(b)(3); 65 Fed. Reg. at 85,550 (Dec. 28, 2000).

[85] *Id.*

[86] 45 C.F.R. §§164.520(c)(1)(i)(A)–(B); 65 Fed. Reg. 85,551 (Dec. 28, 2000). The notice need be distributed only to the covered employee. 45 C.F.R. §164.520(c)(1)(iii); 65 Fed. Reg. at 85,551 (Dec. 28, 2000) ("if a named insured and one or more dependents are covered by the same policy, the health plan can satisfy the distribution requirement with respect to the dependents by sending a single copy of the notice to the named insured").

[87] 45 C.F.R. §164.520(c)(1)(i)(C); 65 Fed. Reg. at 85,551 (Dec. 28, 2000).

[88] 45 C.F.R. §164.520(c)(1)(ii); 65 Fed. Reg. at 85,551 (Dec. 28, 2000).

[89] 45 C.F.R. §164.520(c)(1)(iv); 65 Fed. Reg. at 85,551 (Dec. 28, 2000).

[90] 45 C.F.R. §164.520(b)(1).

[91] 67 Fed. Reg. at 53,242–53,243 (Aug. 14, 2002).

approach, a health plan would distribute an abbreviated notice in lieu of a more comprehensive notice; the comprehensive notice would be made available to participants upon request.

If a health plan maintains a Web site, the notice must also be posted there.[92] The notice can be provided electronically if the individual at issue agrees to receive it in this manner.[93]

v. Plan Amendment Requirements

In order for a health plan to disclose PHI to its sponsoring employer or to permit such disclosure by a health insurance issuer or an HMO, the plan must ensure that the plan documents restrict the plan sponsor's use and disclosure of the PHI in a manner consistent with the Privacy Rules.[94] Health plans (including health insurers and HMOs) may disclose summary health information to their sponsoring employers for the purposes of obtaining premium bids for replacement coverage and for plan design (i.e., amending, modifying, or terminating the plan).[95] In addition, a health plan may disclose enrollment and disenrollment information to its sponsor.[96]

If an employer requires greater access to PHI generated by its health plan (including a health insurer or HMO), it must adopt appropriate amendments to the plan document.[97] Note that even

---

[92]45 C.F.R. §164.520(c)(3)(i); 65 Fed. Reg. at 85,551 (Dec. 28, 2000).

[93]45 C.F.R. §164.520(c)(3)(ii); 65 Fed. Reg. at 85,551 (Dec. 28, 2000). Note that these electronic distribution provisions are somewhat more restrictive than those permitted by the Department of Labor and Internal Revenue Service. *See* I.R.S. Notice 99-1; 1999-2 I.R.B. 8; 65 Fed. Reg. 6001, 6004 (Feb. 8, 2000); 29 C.F.R. §2520.104b-1.

[94]45 C.F.R. §164.504(f)(1)(i); 65 Fed. Reg. at 82,508 (Dec. 28, 2000).

[95]45 C.F.R. §164.504(f)(1)(ii); 65 Fed. Reg. at 82,508–82,509 (Dec. 28, 2000). Summary health information is individually identifiable health information that summarizes claims history, claims expenses, or the types of claims experienced by a participant in a group health plan and that has been redacted to remove 19 specific identifiers. 45 C.F.R. §164.504(a). The 19 identifiers that must be removed from individually identifiable health information to create summary health information are set forth in 45 C.F.R. Section 164514(b)(2)(i) and include identifiers such as names, addresses, birth dates, and identification and account numbers. As distinguished from de-identified health information, summary health information may include five-digit Zip codes. Id.

[96]45 C.F.R. §164.504(f)(1)(iii); 67 Fed. Reg. at 53,207–53,208 (Aug. 14, 2002). Absent this exception, a health plan could not readily disclose participation data to its sponsoring employer because it would constitute PHI.

[97]45 C.F.R. §164.504(f)(2); 65 Fed. Reg. at 82,508 (Dec. 28, 2000).

with such amendments, any PHI received from a health plan (including a health insurer or HMO) by its sponsoring employer can be used only to perform plan administration functions.[98] In addition, if PHI is to be disclosed to the sponsor, the plan's notice of privacy practices must advise participants of this fact.[99] No PHI can be disclosed to a plan sponsor for employment-related purposes or in connection with any other employee benefit plan maintained by the sponsor.[100]

The health plan documents must be amended to: (1) establish the permitted and required uses of PHI by the sponsor and (2) mandate that PHI can be disclosed to the plan sponsor only after the plan receives a written certification from the sponsor that the plan documents contain the requisite provisions.[101] In addition, the plan sponsor must implement a "firewall" between plan operations and other noncovered functions to ensure that any PHI it receives from the health plan (or a related health insurer or HMO) is handled in a manner consistent with the Privacy Rules and the plan documents.[102] In this regard, the plan documents must describe which employees or classes of employees will have access to PHI and must limit access by all other employees.[103] In addition, the plan document must incorporate appropriate procedures to ensure that any instances of noncompliance are promptly remedied.[104]

Before disclosing (or permitting a health insurer, HMO, or business associate to disclose) PHI to its sponsor, a health plan

---

[98] 45 C.F.R. §164.504(f)(3)(i); 65 Fed. Reg. at 82,508 (Dec. 28, 2000). Plan administration functions include administrative functions performed by a sponsoring employer on behalf of its health plan but excludes administrative functions relating to any other benefit or benefit plan of the employer. 45 C.F.R. §164.504(a); 65 Fed. Reg. at 82,508 (Dec. 28, 2000).

[99] 45 C.F.R. §164.520(a)(2)(ii); 65 Fed. Reg. at 82,548 (Dec. 28, 2000).

[100] 45 C.F.R. §164.504(f)(3)(iv); 65 Fed. Reg. at 82,508 (Dec. 28, 2000).

[101] 45 C.F.R. §§164.504(f)(2)(ii)(A)–(J); 65 Fed. at Reg. 82,508 (Dec. 28, 2000).

[102] 45 C.F.R. §164.504(f)(2)(iii); 65 Fed. Reg. at 82,508 (Dec. 28, 2000).

[103] 45 C.F.R. §164.504(f)(2)(iii)(B). Any employee who receives PHI relating to payment functions or health care operations for the plan in the ordinary course of plan administration must be included within the firewall. 65 Fed. Reg. at 82,508 (Dec. 28, 2000).

[104] 45 C.F.R. §164.504(f)(2)(iii)(C); 65 Fed. Reg. at 82,508 (Dec. 28, 2000).

must first receive written certification from the sponsor that the foregoing amendments have been adopted.[105]

vi. Individual Rights

As discussed in more detail below, the Privacy Rules mandate that individuals have access to their PHI held by health plans and other covered entities to inspect and copy it, and to amend or correct inaccuracies.[106] In addition, individuals have a right to a periodic accounting of nonroutine disclosures of PHI[107] and are entitled to receive a notice describing the privacy procedures and policies adopted by the plan.[108] These rights are applicable only with respect to PHI held in designated record sets.[109] If a health plan (or its business associates) maintains PHI in a designated record set, the plan will be responsible for implementing appropriate procedures to enable participants to exercise these rights.[110]

vii. Business Associate Issues

Many employers retain third-party vendors to assist in the operation of their health plans.[111] For purposes of the Privacy Rules, all of these entities are potentially "business associates" of the health plans for which they perform services if they create or maintain PHI on their behalf.

---

[105] 45 C.F.R. §164.504(f)(2)(ii); 65 Fed. Reg. at 82,508 (Dec. 28, 2000). The written certificate of amendment is intended to ease the compliance burden placed on health plans, health insurers, and HMOs by providing reasonable assurances that the plan sponsor will not misuse the PHI that it receives. 65 Fed. Reg. at 82,508 (Dec. 28, 2000).

[106] 45 C.F.R. §164.524 (access), 45 C.F.R. §164.526 (amendment), 45 C.F.R. §164.528 (accounting); 65 Fed. Reg. at 82,554–82,559 (Dec. 28, 2000).

[107] 45 C.F.R. §164.528 (accounting); 65 Fed. Reg. at 82,559–82,561 (Dec. 28, 2000).

[108] 45 C.F.R. §164.520(a)(2); 65 Fed. Reg. at 82,547 (Dec. 28, 2000).

[109] 45 C.F.R. §164.524(a) (access), 45 C.F.R. §164.526(a) (amendment), 45 C.F.R. §164.528(a) (accounting). A designated record set is a collection of records maintained by a covered entity that contains, among other things, data relating to enrollment, payment, and claims adjudication for a health plan or that is used, in whole or in part, by a covered entity to make individual decisions. 45 C.F.R. §164.501; 65 Fed. Reg. at 82,489 (Dec. 28, 2000).

[110] 45 C.F.R. §164.503(i)(1); 65 Fed. Reg. at 82,563 (Dec. 28, 2000).

[111] For health plans, typical third-party vendors include insurance brokers or agents, third-party claims administrators, accountants, attorneys, actuaries, and consultants.

(a) Business Associate Agreements

A health plan may disclose PHI to a business associate and can allow a business associate to create or receive PHI on its behalf only if it receives satisfactory assurances from the business associate that the information will be handled in conformance with the Privacy Rules.[112] Disclosures by health plans to health care providers are not subject to this requirement.[113] In addition, no agreement is necessary to permit group health plans or health insurance issuers to disclose PHI to the sponsor of the plan, provided the sponsor has implemented the required provisions of the Privacy Rules.[114] Violation of this requirement will violate the Privacy Rules.[115] Compliance with these requirements must be documented in a written agreement with the applicable business associates.[116]

Business associate agreements must establish the permitted or required uses of PHI in connection with the provision of specified services.[117] The agreement cannot authorize the business associate to use or disclose PHI in a manner that is inconsistent with the Privacy Rules but may permit the use or disclosure of PHI to facilitate the business associate's management and to perform data aggregation services with the PHI.[118] The Privacy Rules mandate that business associate agreements contain a variety of substantive guarantees to protect the confidentiality of any PHI the business associate handles. In particular, business associate agreements must:

---

[112]45 C.F.R. §164.502(e)(1)(i); 65 Fed. Reg. at 82,499 (Dec. 28, 2000). This is the same concept applicable to the use and disclosure of PHI by the sponsors of health plans.

[113]45 C.F.R. §164.502(e)(1)(ii)(A).

[114]45 C.F.R. §164.502(e)(1)(ii)(B).

[115]45 C.F.R. §164.502(e)(1)(iii).

[116]45 C.F.R. §164.502(e)(1)(2).

[117]45 C.F.R. §164.504(e)(2)(i); 65 Fed. Reg. at 82,504 (Dec. 28, 2000). If a covered entity and its business associate are both governmental entities, a written memorandum of understanding can be substituted for a formal business associate agreement. 45 C.F.R. §164.502(e)(1)(ii)(C); 65 Fed. Reg. at 82,504 (Dec. 28, 2000).

[118]45 C.F.R. §§164.504(e)(2)(i)(A)–(B); 65 Fed. Reg. at 82,505 (Dec. 28, 2000). Data aggregation refers to the aggregation of PHI from two or more covered entities by a common business associate for the purpose of analyzing the health care operations of the covered entities. 45 C.F.R. §164.501; 65 Fed. Reg. at 82,489 (Dec. 28, 2000).

- Establish the permitted uses and disclosures of PHI;
- Prohibit the use or disclosure of PHI in a manner contrary to the Privacy Rules;
- Mandate the implementation of safeguards to prevent the improper use or disclosure of PHI;
- Mandate the reporting of any instances of improper uses or disclosures of PHI;
- Impose similar restrictions on any subcontractors;
- Require that PHI be made available in compliance with the rights of access, amendment, and accounting;
- Require access to books and records for HHS auditing purposes;
- Require the return or destruction of PHI upon the termination of the relationship; and
- Authorize the termination of the agreement if the business associate violates a material term.[119]

(b) Violation of Business Associate Agreements

Health plans (and their proxies, plan sponsors) must monitor business associate compliance with the terms of their agreements and the Privacy Rules. If a plan sponsor becomes aware of a pattern of noncompliance by a business associate, it is required to take reasonable steps to cure the noncompliance.[120] It is important to note that a health plan cannot be held directly responsible for a business associate's conduct, although neither can plan sponsors avoid this requirement by intentionally ignoring violations.[121] If a health plan cannot successfully cure the noncompliance, it must terminate the agreement or, if termination is not feasible, report the noncompliance to HHS.[122] Depending on the relationships between the health plan and the business associate at issue, termination of an agreement may not be feasible (or, indeed, may be

---

[119]45 C.F.R. §§164.504(e)(2)(ii)(A)–(I); 65 Fed. Reg. at 82,503–82,504 (Dec. 28, 2000).

[120]45 C.F.R. §164.504(e)(1)(ii); 65 Fed. Reg. at 82,505 (Dec. 28, 2000).

[121]65 Fed. Reg. at 82,505 (Dec. 28, 2000) (". . .a covered entity is nonetheless expected to investigate when they [sic] receive complaints or other information that contain substantial and credible evidence of violations by a business associate, and it must act upon any knowledge of such violation that it possesses").

[122]45 C.F.R. §164.504(e)(1)(ii); 65 Fed. Reg. at 82,505 (Dec. 28, 2000).

impossible). In such circumstances, reporting the noncompliance to HHS may be the only available alternative.

viii. Implementation Deadlines

Under the Privacy Rules, large health plans were given until April 14, 2003, to incorporate the required business associate provisions in their contracts; small plans had an additional year to comply.[123] However, a transition period applied to written contracts in place on October 15, 2002, that had not been renewed or modified prior to April 14, 2003.[124] For these contracts, the compliance deadline became the earlier of the date on which the contract was amended or renewed or April 14, 2004.[125] Contracts that were entered into after October 15, 2002, were not eligible for this extension.[126] Further, if no written contract is in place between a business associate and a covered entity, the extension is not available.[127] Even where the extension applies, health plans are required to comply with the access, accounting, amendment, and mitigation requirements and the compliance review provisions relating to HHS.[128]

ix. De-Identification of Health Information

The Privacy Rules exclude from the definition of individually identifiable health information, health information that does not identify the individual to whom it relates and with respect to which there is no reasonable basis for believing the individual could be identified.[129] In order for health information to satisfy these criteria, the Privacy Rules require either that, under generally accepted statistical principles and methods, a qualified person determines that the risk of identification associated with the information (and any other reasonably available information) at issue

---

[123] 45 C.F.R. §164.532; 65 Fed. Reg. at 82,565 (Dec. 28, 2000).

[124] 45 C.F.R. §164.532(e); 67 Fed. Reg. at 53,250 (Aug. 14, 2002).

[125] 45 C.F.R. §164.532(e)(2); 67 Fed. Reg. at 53,250 (Aug. 14, 2002).

[126] 67 Fed. Reg. at 53,250 (Aug. 14, 2002).

[127] *Id.*

[128] 45 C.F.R. §164.532(e)(3); 67 Fed. Reg. at 53,250 (Aug. 14, 2002).

[129] 45 C.F.R. §164.514(a); 65 Fed. Reg. at 82,542–82,543 (Dec. 28, 2000); 67 Fed. Reg. at 53,232–53,233 (Aug. 14, 2002). As distinguished from summary health information, de-identified health information can generally include the initial three digits of Zip codes. 45 C.F.R. §164.514(b)(2)(i)(B).

is very small or that 19 specified identifiers are removed from the information to be disclosed.[130] After PHI has been de-identified, it may be freely used by a health plan, employer, or other persons or entities.

Covered entities can develop re-identification codes as long as such codes are not derived from or related to information about the individual at issue and are safeguarded.[131]

x. Health Information Relating to Deceased Individuals

The Privacy Rules protect the use and disclosure of PHI relating to deceased individuals.[132] If an individual has authority to act on behalf of a deceased individual or his estate under applicable state law, a covered entity must treat that individual as a personal representative.[133]

xi. Disclosures to Family Members and Friends

If an individual is present or available prior to a disclosure and permits the disclosure or does not express an objection to it, a health plan may disclose relevant PHI to an individual's family members or other relatives, close personal friends, or any other persons designated by the individual.[134] In addition, a health plan may use or disclose PHI to notify a family member, personal representative, or other person responsible for the care of the individual or of

---

[130] 45 C.F.R. §164.514(b)(2)(i); 65 Fed. Reg. at 82,543 (Dec. 28, 2000).

[131] 45 C.F.R. §164.514(c); 65 Fed. Reg. at 82,543 (Dec. 28, 2000).

[132] 45 C.F.R. §164.502(f); 65 Fed. Reg. at 82,499–82,500 (Dec. 28, 2000).

[133] 45 C.F.R. §164.502(g)(1); 65 Fed. Reg. at 82,500–82,501 (Dec. 28, 2000). This requirement is also applicable to individuals who have authority to act on behalf of adults and emancipated minors. 45 C.F.R. §164.502(g)(2); 65 Fed. Reg. at 82,500 (Dec. 28, 2000). In addition, parents and other individuals who act in loco parentis relative to an unemancipated minor must generally be allowed to act on behalf of their child or ward under the Privacy Rules. 45 C.F.R. §164.502(g)(3)(i); 65 Fed. Reg. at 82,500 (Dec. 28, 2000). If an unemancipated minor is capable of consenting to receive health care services without approval by a parent or guardian under applicable state law or the parent or guardian has consented to a confidentiality agreement between the minor and the provider, the covered entity need not treat the parent or guardian as the personal representative of the minor. 45 C.F.R. §164.502(g)(3)(ii); 65 Fed. Reg. at 82,500 (Dec. 28, 2000).

[134] 45 C.F.R. §§164.510(b)(1)(i), 164.510(b)(2); 65 Fed. Reg. at 82,522–82,523 (Dec. 28, 2000).

the individual's whereabouts, general condition, or death, subject to certain procedural limitations.[135] If the individual is not present or does not have an opportunity to object because of incapacity or exigent circumstances, the health plan may use its professional judgment to determine whether the disclosure is in the individual's best interests and, if so, may disclose PHI that is directly relevant to the recipient's relationship with the individual.[136]

xii. Disclosures Relating to Minors

A health plan can disclose PHI relating to an unemancipated minor to his parent or legal guardian as permitted or required by applicable state law.[137] If a parent or legal guardian is not acting as the personal representative of a child and there is no state law prohibiting disclosure, a health plan may (but is not required to) disclose the minor's PHI; the decision to make such a disclosure must be made by a licensed health care professional and must be consistent with state law.[138]

xiii. Other Disclosures Required or Permitted by the Privacy Rules

There also are a number of circumstances when a covered entity can disclose PHI without authorization and without allowing the individual to object.[139]

(a) Response to a Complaint

A health plan will not violate the Privacy Rules if a member of its workforce discloses PHI in a good-faith complaint regarding the use or disclosure of PHI by the plan.[140] Any such disclosures can be made only to a health oversight agency, public health authority, or an attorney retained by the individual at issue.[141]

---

[135] 45 C.F.R. §164.510(b)(1)(ii); 65 Fed. Reg. at 82,522–82,523 (Dec. 28, 2000).
[136] 45 C.F.R. §164.510(a)(3); 65 Fed. Reg. at 82,522 (Dec. 28, 2000).
[137] 45 C.F.R. §164.502(g)(3)(ii); 65 Fed. Reg. at 82,500 (Dec. 28, 2000).
[138] 45 C.F.R. §164.502(g)(3)(ii)(C); 65 Fed. Reg. at 82,500 (Dec. 28, 2000).
[139] 45 C.F.R. §164.512(b)(3)(ii); 65 Fed. Reg. at 82,524–82,542 (Dec. 28, 2000).
[140] 45 C.F.R. §164.502(j); 65 Fed. Reg. at 82,501–82,502 (Dec. 28, 2000).
[141] *Id.*

(b) Reporting of Crimes

A member of a health plan's workforce may disclose certain PHI to law enforcement officials if he was the victim of a criminal act and the information relates to the suspected perpetrator.[142]

xiv. Consents to Disclosure

Health plans may, but are not required to, obtain individual consent to use or disclose PHI in connection with treatment and payment functions and health care operations.[143]

xv. Authorizations

Health plans can use and disclose PHI to perform treatment and payment functions and health care operations. However, except for certain other disclosures mandated by law, health plans cannot use or disclose PHI for any other purposes without first securing authorization from the individual to whom the PHI relates.[144]

In order for an authorization to be valid under the Privacy Rules, it must contain certain substantive provisions and must not contain any additional provisions that are inconsistent with the Privacy Rules.[145] Authorizations must be written in plain language.[146] At a minimum, valid authorizations must: (1) describe the health information to be used or disclosed; (2) identify the persons or class of persons who are authorized to make the requested use or disclosure; (3) identify the intended recipient of the information;

---

[142]45 C.F.R. §164.502(j)(2); 65 Fed. Reg. at 82,502 (Dec. 28, 2000).

[143]45 C.F.R. §164.506; 65 Fed. Reg. at 82,509–82,513 (Dec. 28, 2000).

[144]45 C.F.R. §§164.502(a)(iv), 164.508(a); 65 Fed. Reg. at 82,498–82,499 (Dec. 28, 2000). A health plan or other covered entity may not use or disclose PHI for marketing purposes without first securing authorizations from the individuals to whom the marketing will be directed. 45 C.F.R. §164.508(a)(3); 67 Fed. Reg. at 53,186 (Aug. 14, 2002). Marketing refers to communications about a product or service that is intended to encourage the recipients to purchase or use the product or service. 45 C.F.R. §164.501; 65 Fed. Reg. at 82,493–82,494 (Dec. 28, 2000). It also includes any arrangements between a covered entity and another entity involving the disclosure of PHI for direct or indirect remuneration to facilitate the other entity's use of such information to communicate about its own products or services. *Id.* Marketing does not include communications made by a covered entity to describe benefits it provides, for treatment purposes, or to direct or recommend alternate treatments, providers, etc., to the individual. 45 C.F.R. §164.501; 67 Fed. Reg. at 53,186 (Aug. 14, 2002).

[145]45 C.F.R. §164.508(b)(1); 65 Fed. Reg. at 82,515 (Dec. 28, 2000).

[146]45 C.F.R. §164.508(b)(3); 67 Fed. Reg at. 53,222 (Aug. 14, 2002).

(4) describe the intended uses or disclosures;[147] (5) specify its expiration date (or an expiration event); and (6) be executed and dated by the individual (or the individual's personal representative).[148] In addition, a valid authorization must inform the individual that: (1) the authorization can be revoked and describe the process for making and any limitations on revocations;[149] (2) treatment, payment, enrollment, and eligibility decisions cannot be preconditioned on the provision of an authorization;[150] and (3) any information disclosed pursuant to the authorization may be re-disclosed by the recipient and is no longer protected by the Privacy Rules.[151]

An authorization is invalid and cannot be relied upon after its stated expiration date.[152] In addition, if the authorization form omits any required information; is revoked; contains any material false information; appears in an impermissible compound authorization; or is required as a precondition for treatment, payment, enrollment, or eligibility, it will be invalid.[153]

Compound authorizations are generally permitted unless treatment, payment, enrollment, or eligibility is contingent on the execution of the authorization.[154] Multiple authorizations relating to psychotherapy notes can be combined but not with authorizations relating to other types of PHI.[155]

The Privacy Rules generally prohibit covered entities from conditioning treatment, payment, enrollment, or eligibility on the execution of an authorization.[156] However, a health plan may condition enrollment or eligibility on the provision of an authoriza-

---

[147] A statement that a use or disclosure is made "at the request of the individual" is sufficient when the individual initiates the request. 45 C.F.R. §164.508(c)(1)(iv).

[148] 45 C.F.R. §164.508(c)(1); 65 Fed. Reg. at 82,517–18 (Dec. 28, 2000).

[149] 45 C.F.R. §164.508(c)(2)(i); 67 Fed. Reg. at 53,221 (Aug. 14, 2002).

[150] 45 C.F.R. §164.508(c)(2)(ii); 67 Fed. Reg. at 53,221 (Aug. 14, 2002). The authorization must also indicate any consequences of a failure to provide an authorization. 45 C.F.R. §164.508(c)(2)(ii)(B).

[151] 45 C.F.R. §164.508(c)(2)(iii); 67 Fed. Reg. at 53,221 (Aug. 14, 2002).

[152] 45 C.F.R. §164.508(b)(2); 67 Fed. Reg. at 53,221 (Aug. 14, 2002).

[153] 45 C.F.R. §164.508(b)(2); 67 Fed. Reg. at 53,220–21 (Aug. 14, 2002).

[154] 45 C.F.R. §164.508(b)(3); 67 Fed. Reg. at. 53,221 (Aug. 14, 2002).

[155] 45 C.F.R. §164.508(b)(3)(ii); 67 Fed. Reg. at 53,221 (Aug. 14, 2002).

[156] 45 C.F.R. § 164.508(b)(4); 67 Fed. Reg. at 53,221 (Aug. 14, 2002).

tion if the request is based on the plan's need for information for underwriting or risk rating purposes and does not relate to psychotherapy notes.[157] In addition, a covered entity may condition the provision of health care services that are intended for disclosure to a third party on the execution of an authorization.[158]

Authorizations can be revoked at any time by providing a written notice to the relevant covered entity.[159] However, such a revocation will be effective only to the extent the health plan has not taken action in reliance on the authorization.[160]

Health plans must document and retain all authorizations for at least six years following their receipt.[161]

(a) Psychotherapy Notes

The Privacy Rules require authorizations for most uses of psychotherapy notes including treatment and payment functions and health care operations.[162]

(b) Marketing

In order to use or disclose PHI for marketing purposes, a health plan must first secure an authorization from the relevant individuals unless the communication at issue is made in person with a member of the plan's workforce (or a business associate) or is a promotional gift of nominal value provided by the plan (or a

---

[157] 45 C.F.R. §164.508(b)(4)(ii); 65 Fed. Reg. at 82,516–17 (Dec. 28, 2000); 67 Fed. Reg. at 53,221 (Aug. 14, 2002).

[158] 45 C.F.R. §164.508(b)(4)(iii); 65 Fed. Reg. at 82,516–17 (Dec. 28, 2000). This exception is of particular use in the context of pre-employment physical examinations and drug testing. For example, suppose an employer requires a physical examination and/or drug test as a condition of employment and retains a health care professional to perform the examination or testing. If the prospective employee refuses to authorize the release of the results of the examination or testing, the health care professional can refuse to perform the examination or testing.

[159] 45 C.F.R. §164.508(b)(5); 65 Fed. Reg. at 82,517 (Dec. 28, 2000).

[160] 45 C.F.R. §164.508(b)(5)(i); 65 Fed. Reg. at 82,517 (Dec. 28, 2000).

[161] 45 C.F.R. §164.508(b)(6); 65 Fed. Reg. at 82,517 (Dec. 28, 2000).

[162] 45 C.F.R. §164.508(a)(2); 65 Fed. Reg. at 82,514–15 (Dec. 28, 2000).

business associate).[163] If the covered entity is to receive any direct or indirect compensation for providing the PHI, the authorization must so indicate.

xvi. Impact of State Medical Privacy Laws

The Privacy Rules are intended to provide minimum standards of conduct for covered entities. To the extent state law provides less stringent protection for PHI, the Privacy Rules will supersede them. HHS has authority to modify this general rule upon application by a covered entity.[164] State laws that provide more stringent protection for PHI or other health information continue to be effective and supplement the Privacy Rules as applicable.[165]

l. Individual Privacy Rights[166]

Individuals covered by health plans have three primary rights under the Privacy Rules as well as a number of ancillary rights:

---

[163]45 C.F.R. §164.508(a)(3); 67 Fed. Reg. at 53,220 (Aug. 14, 2002). In most instances, this requirement will affect health care providers to a greater extent than health plans. However, when a health plan's business associates propose to use PHI for marketing purposes (most likely as a source for a mailing list), this requirement will be critical to avoid a violation of the Privacy Rules. Note that the largest penalties that can be imposed on improper uses and disclosures of PHI are tied to marketing functions. Also note that any penalties would not be imposed on the business associate but on the health plan itself.

[164]45 C.F.R. §160.203(a).

[165]It is unclear how the preemption principles incorporated into the Privacy Rules will interact with Section 514 of ERISA, which broadly preempts any state laws that "relate to" employee benefit plans. 29 U.S.C. §1104 (ERISA preempts state laws that "relate to" employee benefit plans). Although states generally do not attempt to directly regulate employee benefit plans, they often enact legislation that indirectly affects such plans. For example, in California, the CMIA does not apply to employee benefit plans, although it does regulate HMOs and health insurers. For fully insured group health plans, this is tantamount to regulating the plans themselves. ERISA permits this sort of indirect regulation because it does not preempt state laws that regulate the business of insurance. However, a further qualification on this exception is that self-funded health plans are not deemed to be in the business of insurance. As a result, state laws that may otherwise indirectly affect fully insured health plans will not apply to self-funded health plans. This means that self-funded health plans are subject to the requirements imposed by the Privacy Rules but not to more stringent state laws, and fully insured health plans are indirectly subject to more stringent state laws.

[166]In addition to the Privacy Rules themselves (and accompanying regulatory preambles), HHS provides individual interpretive guidance in the form of frequently asked questions. The OCR will also respond to individual questions and complaints.

right of access; right to request amendment or correction; and right to accounting of nonroutine disclosures.

i. Right of Access

Under the Privacy Rules, individuals are entitled to have access to any of their PHI that is maintained by a health plan in a designated record set.[167] A designated record set may include such information as enrollment, payment, claims adjudication, and case management records.[168] However, individuals are not generally entitled to access PHI comprising psychotherapy notes or materials compiled in anticipation of or for use in civil or criminal litigation or administrative proceedings.[169]

In some circumstances, an individual's right of access can be limited by a health plan (or other covered entity). In particular, a request for access can be denied if it seeks PHI that is not otherwise subject to disclosure; information protected by the Federal Privacy Act;[170] or PHI obtained from an entity other than a health care provider under a promise of confidentiality, among other things.[171] If a request for access is denied on any of these grounds, the requesting individual has no right to a review of the denial.[172]

A request for access to PHI also may be denied if a licensed health care professional retained by a health plan determines that the release of the requested information is reasonably likely to endanger the life or physical safety of the requesting individual or another person;[173] or the PHI refers to another person and the licensed health care professional determines that its release would

---

Depending on the configuration of the health plan at issue, it may be necessary to exercise individual access, amendment, and/or accounting through the plan's business associates, health insurers, or HMOs. The notice of privacy practices distributed by the health plan and any related health insurers or HMOs should provide additional information regarding the exercise of these rights.

[167]45 C.F.R. §164.524(a); 65 Fed. Reg. at 82,554 (Dec. 28, 2000).

[168]45 C.F.R. §164.501; 65 Fed. Reg. at 82,489 (Dec. 28, 2000). Not all PHI maintained by or on behalf of a health plan is considered to be part of a designated record set. As a result, individuals do not have a right to access all PHI maintained by a health plan that relates to them.

[169]45 C.F.R. §§164.524(a)(1)(i)–(iii); 65 Fed. Reg. at 82,554 (Dec. 28, 2000).

[170]5 U.S.C. §552a.

[171]45 C.F.R. §164.524(a)(2); 65 Fed. Reg. at 82,554–56 (Dec. 28, 2000).

[172]*Id.*

[173]45 C.F.R. §164.524(a)(3)(i); 65 Fed. Reg. at 82,555–56 (Dec. 28, 2000).

be reasonably likely to result in harm to that person.[174] If a request for access is denied on either of these grounds, the requesting individual has a right to seek review of the denial.[175]

A health plan must either approve or deny a request for access within 30 days of receipt.[176] If a request relates to PHI that is not stored or accessible electronically, this deadline is extended to 60 days.[177] If necessary, the health plan can extend the deadline for responding by up to 30 days if it provides a written statement explaining the reasons for the delay and providing the date when a response will be forthcoming; only one such extension is permitted per request.[178]

If a request for access is approved, the individual must be allowed to inspect the requested PHI and to request copies.[179] The health plan must provide the requested information in the form requested if the information is readily accessible in that form; all other materials must be provided in hard copy or another form as agreed by the parties.[180] The health plan may provide a summary of the requested information in lieu of the actual documents if the requesting individual agrees in advance.[181] The health plan must allow the requested access in a timely manner and may discuss the scope, format, and other issues relating to the request with the requesting individual as necessary to facilitate the timely provision of the requested information.[182] If a health plan does not maintain the requested information itself but knows where it can

---

[174] 45 C.F.R. §164.524(a)(3)(ii); 65 Fed. Reg. at 82,555–56 (Dec. 28, 2000). In addition, if a request for access is made by an individual's personal representative and a licensed health care professional determines that releasing the requested information would be likely to endanger the individual to whom it relates, the health plan may deny the request, subject to the personal representative's right of review. 45 C.F.R. §164.524(a)(3)(iii); 65 Fed. Reg. at 82,556 (Dec. 28, 2000).

[175] 45 C.F.R. §164.524(a)(4); 65 Fed. Reg. at 82,556 (Dec. 28, 2000). The review of a denial of access must be performed by a health care professional designated by the covered entity who did not participate in the initial review and denial process. A denial of access must be provided in writing within the requisite time period.

[176] 45 C.F.R. §164.524(b)(2)(i); 65 Fed. Reg. at 82,556 (Dec. 28, 2000).

[177] 45 C.F.R. §164.524(b)(2)(ii); 65 Fed. Reg. at 82,556 (Dec. 28, 2000).

[178] 45 C.F.R. §164.524(b)(2)(iii); 65 Fed. Reg. at 82,556 (Dec. 28, 2000).

[179] 45 C.F.R. §164.524(c)(1); 65 Fed. Reg. at 82,556–57 (Dec. 28, 2000).

[180] 45 C.F.R. §164.524(c)(2)(i); 65 Fed. Reg. at 82,556–57 (Dec. 28, 2000).

[181] 45 C.F.R. §164.524(c)(2)(ii); 65 Fed. Reg. at 82,556–57 (Dec. 28, 2000).

[182] 45 C.F.R. §164.524(c)(3); 65 Fed. Reg. at 82,557 (Dec. 28, 2000).

be found, the plan must inform the requesting individual.[183] The health plan can charge a reasonable fee for copying the requested information.[184]

If a request for access is denied, the health plan must permit access to any PHI for which no grounds for denial exist.[185] In addition, the health plan must provide a written notice of denial explaining in plain language the basis for the denial, an explanation of the requesting individual's review rights (if any), and a description of the plan's complaint process (including contact information).[186]

A health plan must document and retain the designated record sets that are subject to individual access and the individuals responsible for responding to requests for access.[187]

ii. Right to Request Amendment/Correction

Individuals have the right to request that erroneous or incomplete PHI held by a health plan in a designated record set be corrected or amended.[188] In general, a health plan may deny a request for amendment if it did not create the PHI at issue, if the PHI is not part of a designated record set, if the PHI is not available for inspection or access under the Privacy Rules, or if the PHI is accurate and complete.[189]

Upon receiving a request for amendment, a health plan must respond within 60 days.[190] If necessary, the health plan can extend the deadline for responding by up to 30 days if it provides a written statement explaining the reasons for the delay and providing the date when a response will be forthcoming; only one such extension is permitted per request.[191]

---

[183]45 C.F.R. §164.524(d)(3); 65 Fed. Reg. at 82,557 (Dec. 28, 2000).

[184]45 C.F.R.§164.524(c)(4); 65 Fed. Reg. at 82,557 (Dec. 28, 2000). In the preamble to the initial final Privacy Rules, HHS encouraged health plans and other covered entities to limit their duplication fees. 65 Fed. Reg at 82,557 (Dec. 28, 2000).

[185]45 C.F.R. §164.524(d)(1); 65 Fed. Reg. at 82,557 (Dec. 28, 2000).

[186]45 C.F.R. §§164.524(d)(2)(i)–(iii); 65 Fed. Reg. at 82,557 (Dec. 28, 2000).

[187]45 C.F.R. §164.524(e); 65 Fed. Reg. at 82,558 (Dec. 28, 2000).

[188]45 C.F.R. §164.526(a)(1); 65 Fed. Reg. at 82,558 (Dec. 28, 2000).

[189]45 C.F.R. §§164.526(a)(2)(i)–(iv); 65 Fed. Reg. at 82,558 (Dec. 28, 2000).

[190]*Id.*

[191]45 C.F.R. §164.526(b)(2); 65 Fed. Reg. at 82,558 (Dec. 28, 2000).

If the request is denied, the plan must provide a written notice of denial to the requesting individual.[192] If a health plan accepts a proposed amendment, it must incorporate the amendment into the designated record set at issue.[193] In addition, the plan must inform the requesting individual that the amendment has been so incorporated and obtain his agreement as to the persons to be notified about the amendment.[194] The plan must make reasonable efforts to inform individuals who have previously received the PHI at issue and others who have access to the PHI and who may have relied upon it to their detriment.[195]

If a request of an amendment is denied, the plan must provide a written notice of denial explaining the basis for the denial, informing the requesting individual of his right to submit a written statement of disagreement, and describing the plan's complaint process (including contact information).[196] A plan must permit an individual to submit a written statement of disagreement, although it may place reasonable limits on the length of any such statements.[197] In addition, the plan may prepare a written rebuttal statement in response to the statement of disagreement; any such rebuttal must be provided to the requesting individual.[198] The plan must maintain records of the request for amendment, any accepted amendments, any notices of disagreement, and any rebuttal statements.[199]

If a statement of disagreement is submitted, the plan must include the appended material with any subsequent disclosures to which the disagreement relates.[200] If no such statement is submitted, the plan must include either the request for amendment

---

[192]45 C.F.R. §164.526(a)(2)(i)(B); 65 Fed. Reg. at 82,558 (Dec. 28, 2000).

[193]45 C.F.R. §164.526(c)(1); 65 Fed. Reg. at 82,558 (Dec. 28, 2000). The plan must also ensure that its business associates update their designated record sets, if applicable. 45 C.F.R. §164.526(c)(3)(ii); 65 Fed. Reg. at 82,559 (Dec. 28, 2000).

[194]45 C.F.R. §164.526(c)(2); 65 Fed. Reg. at 82,559 (Dec. 28, 2000).

[195]45 C.F.R. §164.526(c)(3); 65 Fed. Reg. at 82,559 (Dec. 28, 2000). This requirement also includes business associates who maintain the applicable PHI in a designated record set. 45 C.F.R. §164.526(c)(3)(ii).

[196]45 C.F.R. §§164.526(d)(1)(i)–(iv); 65 Fed. Reg. at 82,559 (Dec. 28, 2000).

[197]45 C.F.R. §164.526(d)(2); 65 Fed. Reg. at 82,559 (Dec. 28, 2000).

[198]45 C.F.R. §164.526(d)(3); 65 Fed. Reg. at 82,559 (Dec. 28, 2000).

[199]45 C.F.R. §164.526(d)(4); 65 Fed. Reg. at 82,559 (Dec. 28, 2000).

[200]45 C.F.R. §164.526(d)(5)(i); 65 Fed. Reg. at 82,559 (Dec. 28, 2000).

and related denial or a summary of the same in all subsequent disclosures but only if the individual so requests.[201] If any such subsequent disclosure is made in a standard transaction such that the appended materials cannot be included, the plan must provide those materials separately.[202]

If a health plan is informed of an amendment accepted by another covered entity relating to PHI the plan holds, it must incorporate the amendment into its designated record set as applicable.[203]

A health plan must document and retain the designated record sets that are subject to individual amendment and that document the individuals responsible for responding to requests for amendments.[204]

iii. Right to Accounting of Nonroutine Disclosures

Individuals have a right to receive an accounting of nonroutine disclosures of their PHI made by a covered entity in the six years (or a specified shorter period) preceding the date on which the request is made.[205] For purposes of the Privacy Rules, routine disclosures of PHI include those made: (1) for treatment and payment functions; (2) for health care operations; (3) to the individual to whom the PHI relates; (4) incident to a use or disclosure otherwise permitted or required by the Privacy Rules; (5) pursuant to an authorization; or (6) for incidents that occurred prior to the applicable compliance date for the health plan.[206] The Privacy Rules do not require health plans to include routine disclosures in statements of accounting.

The statement of accounting must include all relevant nonroutine disclosures of PHI (including those made by business associates) and must indicate the dates of the disclosures, the name and address of the recipient, a brief description of the PHI, and a brief statement of the purpose of the disclosure (or a copy of

---

[201] 45 C.F.R. §164.526(d)(5)(ii); 65 Fed. Reg. at 82,559 (Dec. 28, 2000).
[202] 45 C.F.R. §164.526(d)(5)(iii); 65 Fed. Reg. at 82,559 (Dec. 28, 2000).
[203] 45 C.F.R. §164.526(e); 65 Fed. Reg. at 82,559 (Dec. 28, 2000).
[204] 45 C.F.R. §164.526(f); 65 Fed. Reg. at 82,559 (Dec. 28, 2000).
[205] 45 C.F.R. §164.528(a)(1); 65 Fed. Reg. at 82,560 (Dec. 28, 2000).
[206] *See* 45 C.F.R. §§164.528(a)(1)(i)–(ix); 65 Fed. Reg. at 82,560 (Dec. 28, 2000).

the request).[207] Multiple disclosures during the period at issue may include the frequency and periodicity or number of disclosures in addition to the foregoing information.[208]

A health plan must respond to a request for accounting within 60 days of receiving that request.[209] If necessary, the health plan can extend the deadline for responding by up to 30 days if the health plan provides a written statement explaining the reasons for the delay and providing the date when a response will be forthcoming; only one such extension is permitted per request.[210]

Health plans must provide the first accounting statement in any 12-month period free of charge.[211] However, they may impose a reasonable fee for subsequent requests during the same 12-month period, provided they notify the requesting individual and allow for the request to be withdrawn.[212]

A health plan must document and retain the PHI that is subject to accounting requests and must identify the members of its workforce responsible for responding to requests for accountings.[213]

(a) Notice of Privacy Practices

Individuals who are covered by a health plan are entitled to receive a copy of the plan's notice of privacy practices upon their initial enrollment in the plan.[214] In addition, as material changes are made to the health plan's privacy policies and procedures, the Privacy Rules require the plan to update its notice of privacy practices and make the updated notice available to participating individuals.[215]

---

[207] 45 C.F.R. §164.528(b)(2); 65 Fed. Reg. at 82,560 (Dec. 28, 2000).

[208] 45 C.F.R. §164.528(b)(3); 65 Fed. Reg. at 82,560 (Dec. 28, 2000).

[209] 45 C.F.R. §164.528(c)(1); 65 Fed. Reg. at 82,560–61 (Dec. 28, 2000).

[210] 45 C.F.R. §164.528(c)(1)(ii); 65 Fed. Reg. at 82,560–61 (Dec. 28, 2000).

[211] 45 C.F.R. §164.528(c)(2); 65 Fed. Reg. at 82,561 (Dec. 28, 2000).

[212] *Id.*

[213] 45 C.F.R. §164.528(d); 65 Fed. Reg. at 82,561 (Dec. 28, 2000).

[214] 45 C.F.R. §164.520(a)(1); 65 Fed. Reg. at 82,547 (Dec. 28, 2000). Depending on the configuration of the health plan at issue, an individual might receive a notice of privacy practices from a health insurer or HMO or from the plan itself (either automatically or upon request).

[215] 45 C.F.R. §164.520(b)(3); 65 Fed. Reg. at 82,550–51 (Dec. 28, 2000).

(b) Voluntary Restrictions on Disclosure of Health Information

Individuals have the right to request that uses and disclosures of their PHI be limited to a greater extent than required by the Privacy Rules.[216] Health plans are not required to agree to such requests, but if the plans do, they must abide by the agreed-upon restrictions absent exigent circumstances.[217] Any such restriction may be terminated by agreement with the requesting individual or unilaterally by the health plan, but only with respect to PHI created or received after the notice of termination.[218] Health plans must document any such restrictions to which they agree.[219]

(c) Confidential Communications

Individuals have the right to request that communications regarding PHI be made by alternative means or in alternative locations.[220] Although health care providers are required to accommodate all reasonable requests for confidential communications, health plans are not.[221] Instead, health plans are not required to accommodate such requests unless the requesting individual clearly indicates that the disclosure of the information at issue could endanger his safety.[222]

Health plans can require that all requests for confidential communications be made in writing and can condition the approval of such requests on the requesting individual's provision of information regarding how payment issues will be addressed and alternate contact information will be specified.[223]

(d) Complaints to HHS

Any person who believes a health plan (or other covered entity) or one of its business associates is not in compliance with

---

[216] 45 C.F.R. §164.522(a)(1)(i); 65 Fed. Reg. at 82,552 (Dec. 28, 2000).

[217] 45 C.F.R. §§164.522(a)(1)(ii)–(iii); 65 Fed. Reg. at 82,552 (Dec. 28, 2000).

[218] 45 C.F.R. §164.522(a)(2); 65 Fed. Reg. at 82,553 (Dec. 28, 2000).

[219] 45 C.F.R. §164.522(a)(3); 65 Fed. Reg. at 82,553 (Dec. 28, 2000).

[220] 45 C.F.R. §164.522(b)(1); 65 Fed. Reg. at 82,553–54 (Dec. 28, 2000).

[221] 45 C.F.R. §164.522(b)(1)(i); 65 Fed. Reg. at 82,553 (Dec. 28, 2000).

[222] 45 C.F.R. §§164.522(b)(1)(ii), 164.522(b)(2)(iv); 65 Fed. Reg. at 82,553 (Dec. 28, 2000).

[223] 45 C.F.R. §§164.522(b)(2)(i)–(ii); 65 Fed. Reg. at 82,553–54 (Dec. 28, 2000).

the Privacy Rules can file a complaint with the Secretary of HHS.[224] Such complaints must be in writing (in paper or electronic form), provide the name of the covered entity, describe the acts or omissions that are alleged to violate the Privacy Rules, and be filed within 180 days of the complainant's becoming aware of the alleged violation.[225]

m. Enforcement

i. Responsibility for Enforcement

Enforcement authority for the Privacy Rules has been delegated to the Office of Civil Rights (OCR) at HHS.[226] Under the Privacy Rules, enforcement activities may include: (1) working with covered entities to secure voluntary compliance through the provision of technical assistance and other means; (2) responding to questions regarding the Privacy Rules and providing interpretations and guidance; (3) investigating complaints and conducting compliance reviews; and (4) where voluntary compliance cannot be achieved, seeking civil monetary penalties and making referrals for criminal prosecution.[227] The Department of Justice is responsible for enforcing HIPAA's criminal sanctions.

ii. Compliance Investigations by HHS

HHS may perform periodic reviews to measure compliance with the Privacy Rules.[228] The Privacy Rules indicate that HHS will, to the extent possible, take a cooperative approach to enforcement and will provide technical assistance to facilitate compliance.

---

[224] 45 C.F.R. §160.306(a); 65 Fed. Reg. at 82,487 (Dec. 28, 2000).

[225] 45 C.F.R. §160.306(b); 65 Fed. Reg. at 82,487 (Dec. 28, 2000).

[226] 65 Fed. Reg. at 82,472 (Dec. 28, 2000). The OCR is responsible for enforcing the Security Rules as well. HHS has promulgated interim final regulations relating to the enforcement of the Privacy Rules, and the Security Rules. HIPAA Administrative Simplification: Enforcement, 71 Fed. Reg. 8390 (Feb. 16, 2006) *codified* at 45 C.F.R. pts. 160 & 164 (Enforcement Rules). The Centers for Medicare and Medicaid Services are responsible for enforcing the Transaction Rules. *See* HHS News Release (Oct. 15, 2002).

[227] 45 C.F.R. §160.304 (Dec. 28, 2000); 65 Fed. Reg. at 82,472 (Dec. 28, 2000).

[228] 45 C.F.R. §160.308; 65 Fed. Reg. at 82,487 (Dec. 28, 2000).

Covered entities must be able to provide compliance reports on request to the HHS and must cooperate with complaint investigations and compliance reviews.[229] In addition, covered entities must permit access to facilities, books, records, and other data during normal business hours.[230] If another entity holds information sought by HHS and will not produce it, the covered entity must so certify to HHS.[231]

If, following a complaint investigation, HHS determines that a violation has occurred, it will advise the covered entity and attempt to resolve the violation by informal means if possible.[232] Failing this, HHS can issue a written notice of noncompliance to the covered entity and pursue civil or criminal penalties as provided by HIPAA and the Privacy Rules. If HHS determines that no violation occurred, it will notify the covered entity of that fact.[233]

iii. Sanctions

HIPAA provides for the imposition of both civil and criminal penalties for violations of its requirements.[234] In particular, HIPAA authorizes HHS to assess penalties for violations of the Privacy Rules.[235]

HHS may assess civil money penalties of up to $100 per violation to an annual maximum of $25,000 for multiple violations of a single provision of the Privacy Rules.[236] In addition, any person who knowingly obtains or discloses PHI in violation of HIPAA is subject to a fine of $50,000 and up to one year of imprisonment.[237] These criminal penalties are subject to increase if the misconduct involved false pretenses.[238] Procuring PHI with the intent to sell, transfer, or use it for commercial advantage, personal gain,

---

[229] 45 C.F.R. §§160.310(a) & (b); 65 Fed. Reg. at 82,487 (Dec. 28, 2000).

[230] 45 C.F.R. §160.310(c); 65 Fed. Reg. at 82,487 (Dec. 28, 2000).

[231] 45 C.F.R. §160.310(c)(2); 65 Fed. Reg. at 82,487 (Dec. 28, 2000).

[232] 45 C.F.R. §160.312(a)(1); 65 Fed. Reg. at 82,487 (Dec. 28, 2000).

[233] 45 C.F.R. § 160.312(a)(2); 65 Fed. Reg. at 82,487 (Dec. 28, 2000); 68 Fed. Reg. at 18,897 (Apr. 17, 2003).

[234] 42 U.S.C. §1320d-5.

[235] *Id.*

[236] 42 U.S.C. §1320d-5(a)(1).

[237] 42 U.S.C. §1320d-6(b)(1).

[238] 42 U.S.C. §1320d-6(b)(2).

or malicious harm is subject to a $250,000 penalty and up to ten years of imprisonment.[239]

iv. Private Enforcement Rights

Neither HIPAA nor the Privacy Rules provide for a private right of action. As a result, individuals cannot directly enforce their rights under the Privacy Rules. Instead, individuals may avail themselves of the complaint procedures each covered entity must adopt or may file complaints with the OCR.[240]

In addition, in some instances, individuals may have direct enforcement rights under either ERISA or state law independent of any rights they might have under HIPAA or the Privacy Rules. If a health plan has been amended to incorporate provisions addressing the Privacy Rules, the sponsoring employer is obligated to follow the terms of the plan.[241] Adherence to this requirement can be enforced by plan participants or beneficiaries or by the Department of Labor.[242] As a practical matter, this enforcement option is likely to be viable primarily in the context of self-funded health plans; most fully insured health plans will not incorporate HIPAA amendments.[243]

State contract and tort laws may also provide viable individual enforcement alternatives. That is, the privacy standards set forth in the Privacy Rules may be viewed by state courts as de facto minimum standards of conduct under state law such that violations may subject covered entities or other persons or entities to civil or criminal liability. Further, misuses of health information

---

[239] 42 U.S.C.§1320d-6(b)(3).

[240] 45 C.F.R. § 160.306.

[241] Under ERISA, the fiduciaries of employee benefit plans are required to act in accordance with the governing plan documents. 29 U.S.C. §1104(a)(1)(D). Thus, if an employer amends its health plan as provided under Section 164.504(f)(2) of the Privacy Rules and then fails to adhere to the terms of the plan as amended, it will have arguably breached this duty and may be subject to liability under ERISA.

[242] *See* 29 U.S.C. §1132(a) (describing the circumstances in which plan participants and the Department of Labor can bring civil actions under ERISA).

[243] Note, however, that state insurance law may provide some recourse against a health insurer that mishandles health information. *See, e.g.*, CAL. INS. CODE §791.20 (private right of action against insurance entities that improperly disclose medical information).

can be subject to stricter state privacy law requirements, many of which do provide for private enforcement.[244]

v. HHS Approach to Enforcement

HHS has indicated that its initial approach to enforcement under the Privacy Rules will be cooperative. The enforcement process will be complaint-driven. HHS will attempt to encourage voluntary compliance through informal means rather than through enforcement action and will provide technical assistance to covered entities.[245]

In furtherance of its enforcement responsibilities, HHS will have the ability to issue investigational subpoenas and to make investigational inquiries.[246] If attempts to secure voluntary compliance are unsuccessful, HHS may issue a notice of proposed determination specifying the basis for a proposed penalty assessment and its amount.[247] The respondent may either pay the assessment or request a hearing before an administrative law judge.[248] Penalties assessed under the Privacy Rules may be collected by HHS in the federal courts.[249] All enforcement actions under the Privacy Rules are subject to a six-year statute of limitations.[250]

n. HIPAA Security Rules

In addition to the Privacy Rules, covered entities are required to take action to protect the confidentiality and integrity of the PHI they transmit and maintain in electronic form (Security Rules).[251] The Security Rules became effective in April 2005 for most covered entities.[252]

---

[244]*See, e.g.*, Confidentiality of Medical Information Act, CAL. CIV. CODE §§56–56.37.

[245]68 Fed. Reg. 18,895, 18,897 (Apr. 17, 2003).

[246]45 C.F.R. §160.504; 68 Fed. Reg. at 18,902 (Apr. 17, 2003).

[247]45 C.F.R. §160.514; 68 Fed. Reg. at 18,902–03 (Apr. 17, 2003).

[248]*See* 45 C.F.R. §160.516; 68 Fed. Reg. at 18,903 (Apr. 17, 2003).

[249]45 C.F.R. §160.518(b); 68 Fed. Reg. at 18,903 (Apr. 17, 2003).

[250]45 C.F.R. §160.522; 68 Fed. Reg. at 18,903 (Apr. 17, 2003).

[251]Health Insurance Reform: Security Standards, 68 Fed. Reg. at 8334 (Feb. 20, 2003) (to be codified at 45 C.F.R. pts. 160, 162, and 164). The Security Rules do not affect PHI that is not maintained in electronic form. 45 C.F.R. §164.104(a).

[252]45 C.F.R. §164.318(a)(1). The compliance date for small health plans is April 20, 2006. 45 C.F.R. §164.318(a)(2).

The Security Rules impose several general requirements on covered entities. In particular, covered entities must: ensure the confidentiality, integrity, and availability of all PHI they create, receive, maintain, or transmit electronically; protect against reasonably foreseeable threats to the security of this information; protect against reasonably foreseeable misuse or improper disclosures of this information; and ensure that their workforces comply with the Security Rules.[253] The Security Rules make clear, however, that covered entities have a significant amount of flexibility and discretion to take appropriate action to comply with these requirements.[254]

To address the requirements imposed by the Security Rule, covered entities must adopt policies and procedures to prevent, detect, contain, and correct security violations involving PHI.[255] In addition, covered entities must implement safeguards to limit physical access to computer systems on which PHI is stored.[256] Finally, covered entities must implement technical safeguards to ensure the integrity of its computer systems.[257] The Security Rules also mandate that covered entities adopt policies and procedures to comply with the foregoing requirements.[258]

To ensure that business associates also comply with the Security Rules, covered entities must incorporate specific provi-

---

[253]45 C.F.R. §§164.306(a)(1)–(4).

[254]45 C.F.R. §164.306(b).

[255]45 C.F.R. §164.308(a)(1)(i). This process should include a thorough risk analysis, implementation of risk management and sanctions policies, and periodic review of system activity. 45 C.F.R. §§164.308(a)(1)(ii)(A)–(D). In addition, covered entities must appoint a security official to develop and implement their security policies and procedures. 45 C.F.R. §164.308(a)(2). Members of a covered entity's workforce must be subject to a security clearance and authorization process to ensure that their level of access to PHI is appropriate. 45 C.F.R. §164.308(3).

[256]45 C.F.R. §164.310. Under this requirement, covered entities must take action to limit physical access to computer systems on which PHI is stored. 45 C.F.R. §164.310(a)(1). Among the required actions are the development of a disaster recovery and facility security plan; implementation of access control, role-based validation, and physical controls over computer workstations and maintenance performed on them; and adoption of data storage and destruction policies. *Id.*

[257]45 C.F.R. §164.312. Technical safeguards include such things as access control and identification procedures, audit controls, data authentication procedures, data encryption, and transmission security. *Id.*

[258]45 C.F.R. §164.316(a).

sions into existing business associate agreements.[259] Specifically, agreements must: (1) obligate business associates to implement administrative, physical, and technical safeguards to protect the PHI they create or maintain for a covered entity;[260] (2) ensure that their agents and subcontractors comply with the Security Rules;[261] and report any instances of noncompliance of which they become aware.[262]

The Security Rules also mandate specific procedures for use by group health plans in connection with the electronic transmission of PHI to the sponsoring employer.[263] A group health plan must ensure that its plan documents have been amended to obligate its sponsoring employer to reasonably and appropriately safeguard the PHI that is created, received, maintained, or transmitted by or to the employer on behalf of the plan.[264] To comply with this requirement, the sponsoring employer must amend the group health plan document to implement administrative, physical, and technical safeguards to: (1) protect the confidentiality, integrity, and availability of PHI it creates, receives, maintains, or transmits on behalf of the plan; (2) ensure that its firewall is supported by reasonable and effective security measures;[265] (3) ensure that its agents and subcontractors comply with the Security Rules;[266] and (4) report any security breaches to the plan.[267]

---

[259] 45 C.F.R. §164.314(a)(1)(i). In addition to these specific security requirements, business associate agreements remain subject to the requirements imposed by the Privacy Rules generally. For example, if a covered entity becomes aware of a pattern of activity by a business associate that violates the Security Rules, it must take reasonable steps to cure the violation or terminate the agreement if cure is not possible. 45 C.F.R. §§164.314(a)(1)(ii); 164.314(a)(2)(i)(D).

[260] 45 C.F.R. §164.314(a)(2)(i)(A).

[261] 45 C.F.R. §164.314(a)(2)(i)(B).

[262] 45 C.F.R. §164.314(a)(2)(i)(C).

[263] 45 C.F.R. §164.314(b)(1). These requirements are not applicable with respect to the electronic transmission of summary health information pursuant to 45 C.F.R. Section 164.504(f)(1)(ii) or enrollment and disenrollment information pursuant to 45 C.F.R. Section 164.504(f)(1)(iii).

[264] 45 C.F.R. §164.314(b)(1).

[265] 45 C.F.R. §164.314(b)(2)(ii).

[266] 45 C.F.R. §164.314(b)(2)(iii).

[267] 45 C.F.R. §164.314(b)(2)(iv).

i. Employer Compliance Issues

As is the case with the Privacy Rules, the extent to which employer-sponsored health plans will be required to take action under the Security Rules depends upon the scope of the plans' use and maintenance of PHI. For fully insured health plans that do not share PHI with their sponsors, compliance with the Security Rule will be limited to ensuring that the applicable business associate agreements are amended to incorporate the required provisions. For fully insured plans that do share PHI with their sponsors and for virtually all self-funded plans,[268] the Security Rules will require the sponsoring employers to take action on behalf of their plans to implement appropriate administrative, physical, and technical safeguards, and amend plan documents and business associate agreements.

ii. Individual Rights Relating to the Security Rules

The Security Rules neither alter the individual rights conferred by the Privacy Rules nor provide additional enforcement options. Individuals affected by breaches of security relating to PHI that is maintained in electronic forms by covered entities may submit a complaint to the OCR.[269]

2. *Other U.S. Federal Rules Relating to Confidentiality of Health Information*

Although employers may not provide medical benefits to employees and may not administer a health plan, employers often have access to a great deal of health information relating to employees. Employers receive information directly from employees, when assisting employees in obtaining benefits, and sometimes in the course of litigation.

---

[268] A self-funded health plan that fully outsources its administration to business associates and avoids creating or maintaining any PHI would presumably not be subject to compliance responsibilities under Security Rules.

[269] 45 C.F.R. §160.300.

a. Americans With Disabilities Act

The employer's use of the results of health information should be limited. The Americans With Disabilities Act (ADA) provides that the medical information or history of a job applicant must be "collected and maintained on separate forms and in separate files and [be] treated as a confidential medical record."[270] Moreover, the ADA allows three types of individuals to have access to the confidential medical information. First, supervisors and managers may be informed about an employee's work-related restrictions and the necessary accommodations that the employee may need. Second, first aid and safety personnel can be informed if necessary. Finally, government officials investigating ADA compliance may be informed as well.[271]

Under the ADA, personnel and employment records must be retained for a period of one year from the later of (1) the date the record is created or (2) the date the personnel action involved is taken.[272] These records include requests for reasonable accommodation, applications, compensation records, and records related to hiring, promotion, demotion, transfer, layoff, or termination. Longer retention periods may be imposed by state law.[273]

3. State Rules in the United States Relating to Confidentiality of Medical Information

a. California

In 1981, California enacted the Confidentiality of Medical Information Act (CMIA) to protect the confidentiality of individually identifiable medical information[274] created and disclosed

---

[270]42 U.S.C. §12112(d)(3)(B).

[271]*Id.*

[272]29 C.F.R. §1602.14.

[273]*See, e.g.*, CAL. CODE REGS. tit. 2, §7287.0(c); CAL. GOV'T CODE §12946 (requiring personnel records to be retained for two years from the later of the date the record is created or the date the personnel action is taken).

[274]For purposes of the CMIA, "medical information" is

> any individually identifiable information, in electronic or physical form, in possession of or derived from a provider of health care, health care service plan, pharmaceutical company, or contractor regarding a patient's medical history, mental or physical condition, or treatment. 'Individually identifiable' means that

by health care providers.[275] The CMIA also imposes a variety of restrictions on the use of such information by employers doing business in California.[276]

i. Summary of Key Statutory Provisions

The CMIA's primary provisions are designed to limit the use and disclosure of medical information by health care providers and employers except in certain specific circumstances or as otherwise authorized by the individual to whom the information relates. In addition, the CMIA mandates that all entities that maintain medical information provide access to the individuals to whom that

---

> the medical information includes or contains any element of personal identifying information sufficient to allow identification of the individual, such as the patient's name, address, electronic mail address, telephone number, or social security number, or other information that, alone or in combination with other publicly available information, reveals the individual's identity.

CAL. CIV. CODE §56.05(f).

[275] 1981 Cal. Stat. 782, *codified as amended* at CAL. CIV. CODE §§56B56.36. *See, e.g.*, Loder v. City of Glendale, 927 P.2d 1200, 1207 (Cal. 1997) (discussing the legislative intent behind the CMIA). California originally enacted medical privacy legislation in 1979, but that act was repealed and replaced by the CMIA. *See* Heller v. Norcal Mut. Ins. Co., 32 Cal. Rptr. 2d 200, 203–04 (Cal. 1994); California Consumer Health Care Council v. Kaiser Found. Health Plan, Inc., 47 Cal. Rptr. 3d 593, 596–600 (Ct. App. 2006) (citing Pettus v. Cole, 57 Cal. Rptr. 2d 46 (Ct. App. 1996), and *Heller* in analyzing the CMIA).

For purposes of the CMIA, a "provider of health care" is

> any person licensed or certified pursuant to Division 2 (commencing with Section 500) of the Business and Professions Code; any person licensed pursuant to the Osteopathic Initiative Act or the Chiropractic Initiative Act; any person certified pursuant to Division 2.5 (commencing with Section 1797) of the Health and Safety Code; any clinic, health dispensary, or health facility licensed pursuant to Division 2 (commencing with Section 1200) of the Health and Safety Code.

CAL. CIV. CODE §56.05(j).

[276] Chapter 2 of the CMIA imposes substantial limits on the disclosure of medical information by health care providers, health care service plans, and contractors. *See* CAL. CIV. CODE §§56.10–.17. Although employers are not directly regulated by these provisions, their ability to secure medical information relating to employees from health care providers, health care service plans, and contractors will be restricted by these provisions. "Health care service plans" are any entities that are regulated under the Knox-Keene Health Care Service Plan Act of 1975. CAL. HEALTH & SAFETY CODE §§1340–1399.904 (e.g., HMOs). "Contractors" include, among other things, medical groups, pharmaceutical benefit managers, and other medical service organizations that are neither health care providers nor health care service plans. CAL. CIV. CODE §56.05(c). The term does not include issuers of health or other forms of insurance. *Id.*; *see also* CAL. INS. CODE §791.02(k) (defining "insurance institution").

information relates upon their request. Finally, the CMIA provides for both a private right of action and governmental enforcement for violations of its restrictions on the use and disclosure of medical information.

ii. Employer Compliance Responsibilities

The CMIA imposes broad requirements on the use and maintenance of medical information by employers. These requirements are discussed in more detail below.

(a) Adoption of Procedural Safeguards

An employer that receives medical information relating to its employees is obligated to adopt procedures to safeguard that information from unauthorized use or disclosure.[277]

(b) Prohibition on Discrimination

Employers may not discriminate against employees who refuse to authorize the use or disclosure of their medical information, although they may take appropriate action to address the absence of such information.[278] However, it is permissible to condition an initial employment decision on an individual's authorization of the release of the results of a medical examination or drug test to the employer.[279] As long as the examination or testing at issue is otherwise permissible, the CMIA does not prohibit

---

[277]CAL. CIV. CODE §56.20(a). Among the recommended procedures suggested by the CMIA are training for employees who handle medical information and implementation of technical and other security mechanisms to restrict access to such information. *Id.* In the absence of more detailed guidance, an employer may be able to rely upon the administrative policies and procedures its health plan adopts in connection with the HIPAA privacy regulations, 45 C.F.R. Parts 160 and 164, to comply with the requirement.

[278]Employers are permitted to refuse to hire or to terminate employees who refuse to authorize the use or disclosure of their medical information. *See* Loder v. City of Glendale, 927 P.2d 1200, 1209 (Cal. 1997). This ability is consistent with the limitations imposed on mandatory authorizations under the HIPAA privacy regulations. *See* Standards for Privacy of Individually Identifiable Health Information, 65 Fed. Reg. at 82,592 (Dec. 28, 2000); 67 Fed. Reg. at 53,193 (Aug. 14, 2002). Neither the CMIA nor the HIPAA privacy regulations preclude employers from requiring authorizations as a condition of employment.

[279]*Loder*, 927 P.2d at 1209.

disqualification of an applicant who refuses to authorize release of examination or test results.[280]

(c) Disclosure of Medical Information

Employers are generally prohibited from allowing their employees or agents to use or disclose medical information in their possession without first securing an authorization from the affected employee.[281] However, in some circumstances, employers are permitted to disclose medical information without employee authorization.[282] In particular, the CMIA permits employers to disclose medical information without authorization: (1) if required by judicial or administrative process or otherwise by applicable law;[283] (2) if the information to be disclosed is relevant in a lawsuit, arbitration, grievance, or other challenge to which the employer and employee are parties and in which the employee has placed his medical history, mental or physical condition, or treatment at issue;[284] (3) in the course of administering employee benefit plans (including health plans, short- and long-term disability plans, workers' compensation programs, and eligibility determinations

---

[280] *Id.* at 1208.

[281] A health care provider retained by an employer for the purpose of examining an employee and reporting on his or her medical condition remains subject to the limitations imposed by Chapter 2 of the CMIA and cannot disclose any medical information to the employer regarding the employee without authorization or as otherwise provided by the CMIA. Pettus v. Cole, 57 Cal. Rptr. 2d 46, 66 (Ct. App. 1996). In such circumstances, a health care provider may release information describing an employee's functional limitations to only the employer qua employer, although full disclosure could be made to the employer in its capacity as sponsor or administrator of a benefit plan. *Id.* at 67–69. As is the case under the HIPAA privacy regulations, identifying the capacity in which an employer is acting relative to a benefit plan is often quite difficult.

[282] CAL. CIV. CODE §§56.20(c)(1)–(4).

[283] CAL. CIV. CODE §56.20(c)(1).

[284] CAL. CIV. CODE §56.20(c)(2). A request for disability leave does not constitute a "proceeding" for purposes of Section 56.20(c)(2). *Pettus*, 57 Cal. Rptr. 2d at 67–68. An employer can disclose a former employee's medical file to its counsel in connection with defending against an employment action brought by the former employee. Doe v. City of Chula Vista, 196 F.R.D. 562, 571 (S.D. Cal. 1999). *But see* Fitzgerald v. United States Dist. Ct. for the N. Dist. of Cal., 216 F.R.D. 632, 638 (N.D. Cal. 2003) (implicitly rejecting *Doe* to adopt a narrow view of waiver of privacy rights under California law).

relating to medical leaves of absence);[285] or (4) if provided to a health care provider to facilitate an employee's treatment.[286]

As interpreted by the California courts, the CMIA precludes employer access to detailed family or medical histories of their employees without first securing consent to the contemplated disclosure.[287]

If an employer agrees with one or more of its employees to preserve the confidentiality of medical information to a greater extent than required by the CMIA, the employer is obligated to comply with that agreement and to seek authorization before using or disclosing such information in a manner inconsistent with the agreement.[288]

(d) Authorized Disclosures

The CMIA contains detailed requirements specifying the format and content of employee authorizations.[289] In particular, an authorization is valid only if it:

- Appears in a typeface no smaller than eight point or is handwritten;
- Is clearly separated from other material printed on the same page;
- Is executed by a signature used only for purposes of the authorization;
- Is signed and dated by the employee, the employee's legal representative, or the personal representative of a deceased employee;
- States the limitations on the use or disclosure it contemplates;
- Identifies the person authorized to make the disclosure and the intended recipient of the disclosure;
- Specifies the date on which the authorization will expire; and

---

[285] CAL. CIV. CODE §56.20(c)(3).
[286] CAL. CIV. CODE §56.20(c)(4).
[287] *Pettus*, 57 Cal. Rptr. 2d at 73–74.
[288] CAL. CIV. CODE §56.20(d).
[289] CAL. CIV. CODE §56.21.

- Advises the employee of his of her right to receive a copy of the authorization.[290]

Authorizations can be canceled or modified at any time, but any such cancellation or modification is effective only after the employer receives actual written notice.[291]

An employer that discloses medical information pursuant to an authorization is required to inform the recipient of any limitations or restrictions on further use or disclosure that are imposed by the authorization.[292] If an employer complies with this requirement in good faith, it will not be liable for subsequent misuse of the information by the recipient.[293] Recipients of medical information pursuant to an authorization are generally prohibited from making further disclosures absent a new authorization or legal requirement mandating such disclosures.[294]

(e) Receipt of Medical Information

The CMIA provisions restricting the disclosure of medical information by health care providers indirectly affect both employers and employees. The CMIA broadly prohibits health care providers from disclosing medical information about their patients without prior authorization, although it does permit disclosures compelled by court or administrative orders, subpoenas, search warrants, and other official directives.[295] In addition, the CMIA exempts a variety of uses and disclosures of medical information from its prohibitions.[296]

A number of common situations involving the use or disclosure of medical information are specifically permitted by the

---

[290] An employee is entitled to receive a copy of any authorizations he or she executes. CAL. CIV. CODE §56.22.

[291] CAL. CIV. CODE §56.24.

[292] CAL. CIV. CODE §56.23.

[293] *Id.*

[294] CAL. CIV. CODE §56.245.

[295] CAL. CIV. CODE §§56.10(b)(1)–(9).

[296] CAL. CIV. CODE §56.30. Of particular interest to employers are the exceptions for disclosures relating to investigations of workplace injuries and alcohol and drug abuse. *See* CAL. CIV. CODE §§56.30(h)–(i).

CMIA. A health care provider may disclose medical information to other providers for diagnosis or treatment purposes.[297] In addition, a provider may disclose medical information to an insurer, employer, HMO, employee benefit plan, governmental authority, or any other person or entity responsible for paying for health care rendered to an individual to the extent necessary to determine the appropriate payment amount and to facilitate payment of that amount.[298] Health care providers are also permitted to disclose medical information to other providers to assist in the collection of payments for health care.[299] This information may also be disclosed to any persons or entities that assist in the billing, claims management, data processing, or administration of any of the foregoing entities.[300]

A health care provider that creates employment-related medical information at the prior specific written request and expense of the employer may disclose such information to the extent it is relevant in a lawsuit or other proceeding in which the patient has placed his medical history, physical or mental condition, or treatment at issue, or which describes the patient's functional limitations relating to the patient's fitness for duty.[301] Unless the provider is notified in advance that disclosure of the information is prohibited, it may disclose the information to a sponsor, insurer, or administrator of an insured or self-insured plan or policy under which the individual is seeking coverage.[302]

(f) Effects on Vendor Relationships

In addition to regulating the use and disclosure of medical information by employers, the CMIA also limits the use of medical

[297]CAL. CIV. CODE §56.10(c)(1).

[298]CAL. CIV. CODE §56.10(c)(2). As a practical matter, this provision exempts most of the uses of medical information that employers are likely to require relative to their employee benefit plans.

[299]CAL. CIV. CODE §56.10(c)(2).

[300]CAL. CIV. CODE §56.10(c)(3).

[301]CAL. CIV. CODE §56.10(c)(8). *See* Pettus v. Cole, 57 Cal. Rptr. 2d 46, 67–69 (Ct. App. 1996).

[302]CAL. CIV. CODE §56.10(c)(9).

information by TPAs.[303] In particular, TPAs are generally prohibited from knowingly using, disclosing, or permitting their employees to use or disclose medical information received in the course of performing services for employers and other entities except for legitimate purposes.[304] This requirement effectively precludes the circumvention of the CMIA's restrictions through the use of TPAs to accomplish what employers otherwise could not.

(g) Document Destruction Requirements

Health care providers, HMOs, pharmaceutical companies, and contractors[305] are obligated to dispose of medical information regarding their patients in a manner that preserves the confidentiality of that information.[306] Employers and TPAs are not subject to this requirement.

(h) Health Care Providers Acting as Employers

The CMIA sets forth a number of exceptions for health care providers acting in their capacity as employers. Such an employer is not deemed to violate the CMIA because it discloses medical information pursuant to Section 56.10.[307] In addition, such an employer will not violate the CMIA if an employee or agent who provides health care discloses medical information pursuant to Section 56.10.[308] Finally, a health care provider's disclosure of

---

[303]CAL. CIV. CODE §56.26. Chapter 5 of the CMIA (relating to disclosures of medical information by TPAs) does not apply to employers or health care providers acting as such. CAL. CIV. CODE §56.26(c). In addition, it does not apply to entities that are subject to the Insurance Information Privacy Act. CAL. INS. CODE §§791–791.27.

[304]CAL. CIV. CODE §56.26(a). Authorizations relating to medical information disclosed by TPAs must be in the same format and contain the same substantive provisions as employer authorizations. CAL. CIV. CODE §56.26(b).

[305]A "contractor" includes medical groups, medical service organizations, pharmaceutical benefits managers, and independent practice associates that are not otherwise regarded as health care providers or health care service plans. CAL. CIV. CODE §56.05(c).

[306]CAL. CIV. CODE §56.101.

[307]CAL. CIV. CODE §56.25(a).

[308]CAL. CIV. CODE §56.25(b).

medical information regarding its employees as provided under Section 56.20 will not violate the CMIA.[309]

(i) *Improper Use or Disclosure of Medical Information*

If a health care provider, health care service plan, contractor, employer, or TPA uses or discloses medical information in a manner that is inconsistent with the CMIA or an authorization provided thereunder, both civil and criminal liabilities can be imposed.[310]

(j) *Disclosure of Genetic Data*

The results of genetic testing contained in an individual's medical records maintained by an HMO may not be disclosed without specific authorization; a separate authorization is required for each disclosure.[311] Negligent violations of this prohibition are subject to a $1,000 fine per violation.[312] Willful violations are subject to penalties of up to $5,000 per violation.[313] Any negligent or willful disclosure that results in economic, bodily, or emotional

---

[309]Information held by a provider relating to its employees is not considered to be "medical information" unless such information would be deemed to be such if it was received by an employer that is not a health care provider. CAL. CIV. CODE §56.25(c).

[310]Rights of enforcement under the CMIA apply not just to the entities it expressly covers but also extend to any persons or entities that misuse medical information. An employer may be liable for the improper use of medical information about its employees if it receives such information from a health care provider in violation of the CMIA. Pettus v. Cole, 57 Cal. Rptr. 2d 46, 79–80 (Ct. App. 1996). Employers that maintain on-site health clinics should be particularly attuned to this issue and should ensure that adequate separation is maintained between employment functions and the operations of the clinic.

However, if a disclosure of medical information by a provider falls within one of the exceptions set forth in Sections 56.10 or 56.16 of the CMIA, an employer's use of that information for employment or other purposes will not violate the CMIA. Shaddox v. Bertani, 110 Cal. App. 4th 1406, 1417–18 (2003); Garrett v. Young, 1 Cal. Rptr. 3d 134, 142 (Ct. App. 2003).

[311]CAL. CIV. CODE §56.17; CAL. INS. CODE §§742.407. Section 10123.35 of the Insurance Code purports to impose a similar requirement on self-funded welfare benefit plans. ERISA almost certainly preempts this requirement to the extent it relates to employee welfare benefit plans themselves, regardless of their funding mechanism. CAL. INS. CODE §10123.35.

[312]CAL. CIV. CODE §56.17(b); CAL. INS. CODE §742.407(b).

[313]CAL. CIV. CODE §56.17(c); CAL. INS. CODE §742.407(c).

harm is a misdemeanor punishable by a fine of up to $10,000 per violation.[314]

(k) HIV/AIDS Status

The CMIA does not prevent the use or disclosure of medical information regarding an individual's human immunodeficiency virus/acquired immune deficiency syndrome (HIV/AIDS) status without prior authorization unless the individual is an injured worker claiming to have been exposed to HIV in the course of his employment.[315]

(l) Prohibition on Waivers

Except to the extent a purported waiver of rights under the CMIA conforms to the content requirements for authorizations, it will be void and unenforceable.[316] In addition, no health care provider, HMO, or contractor may require an individual, as a condition of receiving services, to authorize, waive, or consent to the disclosure of medical information that may not otherwise be disclosed without authorization.[317] An HMO or health or disability carrier can require medical information as part of the medical underwriting process, however.[318]

(m) Right of Access

Generally, any entity (including a health care provider or employer) that compiles or maintains medical information is obligated to provide, upon request and at no charge, a copy of any medical summary, profile, or medical information it maintains about the requesting individual.[319] No such request is deemed to be an authorization to disclose the information to any other party.[320] However, records that are subject to inspection under the Patient

---

[314] CAL. CIV. CODE §56.17(d); CAL. INS. CODE §742.407(d).

[315] CAL. CIV. CODE §56.31.

[316] CAL. CIV. CODE §56.37(b).

[317] CAL. CIV. CODE §56.37(a).

[318] *Id.*

[319] CAL. CIV. CODE §56.07. In addition, with respect to medical information maintained by health care providers, individuals have rights of access under the Patient Access to Medical Records Act. CAL. HEALTH & SAFETY CODE §§123100–123149.5 (1995).

[320] CAL. CIV. CODE §56.07(b).

Access to Medical Records Act are not subject to this requirement.[321] Neither are records maintained by HMOs or health and disability insurers.[322]

(n) Enforcement of Rights

The CMIA provides for both a private right of action as well as criminal penalties for violations of its requirements. A violation of the CMIA that results in economic loss or personal injury to an individual is a misdemeanor.[323] In addition, an individual who sustains an economic loss or personal injury resulting from a unauthorized disclosure of his medical information can recover compensatory damages of up to $3,000, up to $1,000 in attorneys' fees, and the costs of litigation.[324]

In addition, an affected individual may bring an action against any person or entity that negligently discloses the individual's medical information to recover the greater of $1,000 in nominal damages or actual damages.[325] A person or entity that negligently discloses such information also is subject to an administrative penalty of up to $2,500 per violation regardless of the amount of damage sustained by the affected individual.[326]

Any person or entity that knowingly obtains, discloses, or uses medical information in a manner contrary to the CMIA is subject to an administrative penalty of up to $25,000 per violation.[327] Furthermore, any person or entity that obtains or uses medical information in violation of the CMIA for financial gain is subject to administrative penalties of up to $250,000 per violation and disgorgement of any proceeds obtained.[328] Any person or entity who is not permitted to receive medical information under the CMIA and who knowingly and willfully obtains such information without prior authorization is liable for a civil penalty of

---

[321] CAL. CIV. CODE §56.07(c).

[322] *Id.*

[323] CAL. CIV. CODE §56.36(a).

[324] CAL. CIV. CODE §56.35.

[325] CAL. CIV. CODE §56.36(b).

[326] CAL. CIV. CODE §56.36(c)(1).

[327] CAL. CIV. CODE §56.36(c)(2). Enhanced penalty provisions were incorporated into the CMIA in 1999. Act of September 28, 1999, ch. 526, 1999, Cal. Stat. §8.

[328] CAL. CIV. CODE §56.36(c)(3)(A).

up to $250,000.[329] The foregoing penalties can be assessed and sought by the Attorney General, any district attorney, and other specified public counsel.[330]

In addition to the penalties contemplated by the CMIA, the California Constitution also guarantees the individual right to privacy and can support a cause of action against persons or entities that violate that right.[331]

iii. Additional California Medical Privacy Laws

In addition to the CMIA, California has enacted numerous other health care privacy laws. These laws do not directly impact the employer-employee relationship but do confer rights on individuals to access medical information in the hands of health care providers and other entities and also place limits on the ability of providers, insurers, health care service plans, and state governmental entities to collect, use, or disclose personal information (including medical information) about individuals. In addition, California has enacted more specific privacy laws relating to various medical conditions and treatments including birth defects,[332] cancer,[333] HIV/AIDS status,[334] mental health,[335] and substance abuse,[336] among others. Attempts to obtain medical information for unlawful purposes are also subject to separate criminal penalties.[337]

b. New York

New York State does not have a statutory provision that specifically governs the confidentiality of medical records in the workplace. Generally speaking, employers are subject to privacy laws,[338] and there exist statutory provisions dealing specifically

---

[329]CAL. CIV. CODE §56.36(c)(5). "Knowing" and "willful" have the meanings ascribed under the California Penal Code. CAL. PENAL CODE §7.

[330]CAL. CIV. CODE §56.36(e)(1).

[331]CAL. CONST. art. I, §1. *See, e.g.,* Pettus v. Cole, 57 Cal. Rptr. 2d 46, 70–71 (Ct. App. 1996); Hill v. NCAA, 865 P.2d 633, 641 (Cal. 1994).

[332]CAL. HEALTH & SAFETY CODE §§103825–103850.

[333]CAL. HEALTH & SAFETY CODE §§103875–103885.

[334]CAL. HEALTH & SAFETY CODE §§120975–121020.

[335]CAL. WELF. & INST. CODE §§5328, 5540.

[336]CAL. HEALTH & SAFETY CODE §11977.

[337]CAL. PENAL CODE §530.5(a).

[338]*See, e.g.*, N.Y. PUB. HEALTH LAW §18.

with public sector employees[339] and certain types of records.[340] Violations of confidentiality requirements may expose an employer to statutory penalties,[341] and an employee may have a statutory cause of action against a medical practitioner who improperly discloses confidential information to an employer.[342]

i. Access to Patient Information

The statutory provision most generally applicable to employee medical records is found in Public Health Law Section 18 governing Access to Patient Information.[343] This provision restricts a health care provider's release of medical records to a third party—such as an employer—and restricts the third party's conduct once it possesses such records. Access to an individual's medical records is subject to the notification and consent of the individual[344] and subject to the physician's denial of access after considering, among other factors, any potential harm that could be caused by the release of sensitive information.[345]

(a) Confidentiality of Records Received Under Section 18

An entity that receives confidential medical information under this statute will in turn be subject to the statute's requirements and must keep the information confidential.[346] Accordingly, if an employer receives employee medical information from a

---

[339] *See, e.g.*, N.Y. GEN. MUN. LAW §207-c.

[340] *See, e.g.*, N.Y. WORK. COMP. LAW §110(1) (confidentiality of records related to workers' compensation claims); N.Y. PUB. HEALTH LAW §2782 (confidentiality of HIV-related information).

[341] *See, e.g.*, N.Y. PUB. HEALTH LAW §§12, 12-b (establishing penalties for violations of, inter alia, §18), 2783(2) (providing for penalties of up to $5,000 for violations of §2782).

[342] N.Y. PUB. HEALTH LAW §§12, 12-b, 2783(2).

[343] N.Y. PUB. HEALTH LAW §18.

[344] N.Y. PUB. HEALTH LAW §18(3)(c).

[345] N.Y. PUB. HEALTH LAW §18(3)(d) (in determining whether to deny access to some or all requested information, "the provider may consider...the extent to which the information contains sensitive materials disclosed to the practitioner...which would be injurious to the subject's relationships with other persons...").

[346] The statute provides that "[i]nformation...disclosed [pursuant hereto] should be kept confidential by the party receiving such information and the limitations on such disclosure in this section shall apply to such party." N.Y. PUB. HEALTH LAW §18(6).

medical practitioner, the employer may not release the information to another party without notifying the employee[347] and must maintain a copy of the employee's written authorization or a record of the party to whom the records were disclosed.[348]

(b) Violations of Section 18

A violation of this provision exposes the medical practitioner or employer to civil penalties of up to $2,000 per violation[349] or, for a willful violation, imprisonment of up to one year and a fine of up to $2,000.[350] The Public Health Law provides a private right of action for employees whose rights under the statute are violated.[351]

At least one New York state court has held an employer liable for violation of this provision upon releasing employee records to a third party.[352]

ii. On-Site Medical Facilities and Patient Health Records

New York state law concerning doctor-patient privilege applies to employers most directly when the employer sponsors an on-site medical facility. Pursuant to the law, "[n]o person charged with the custody and care of the health records of employees treated at an on-site employer sponsored occupational health service facility shall release or disclose any employee-patient record to an employer, except on the express authorization of the employee-patient, or as otherwise authorized by law."[353] As one federal district court held, an employee's allegations that his

---

[347] N.Y. PUB. HEALTH LAW §18(3)(c).

[348] N.Y. PUB. HEALTH LAW §18(6).

[349] N.Y. PUB. HEALTH LAW §12(1).

[350] N.Y. PUB. HEALTH LAW §12-b(2).

[351] N.Y. PUB. HEALTH LAW §13 (providing that "[t]he performance of any duty or the doing of any act enjoined, prescribed or required by this chapter, may be enforced by a proceeding pursuant to article seventy-eight of the civil practice law and rules at the instance . . . of any citizen of full age resident of the municipality where the duty should be performed or the act was done").

[352] Rockland County Patrolmen's Benevolent Ass'n v. Collins, 638 N.Y.S.2d 747 (App. Div. 1996) (finding that employer violated Section 18(6) in releasing employment records to the New York State Retirement System without the employee's authorization).

[353] N.Y. LAB. LAW §201-e.

employer "disclosed intimate details about [his] medical condition to third parties" formed the basis of a cause of action for violation of the New York Public Health Laws.[354]

(a) Conflicts Between Medical Ethics and Employer Instructions

The New York Court of Appeals recently held that when there is a conflict between standards of medical ethics and the employer's directions to an on-site physician in its employ, the employer's orders may trump other considerations.[355] In that case, Dr. Sheila Horn alleged that she had been fired when she refused directions by her employer, the *New York Times*, to provide *Times* personnel with confidential employee medical records, and to misinform employees whether their injuries were eligible for workers' compensation claims.[356] The court held that Dr. Horn's allegation could not overcome the common-law presumption of employment at will because her position required her to "apply[ ] her professional expertise in furtherance of her corporate responsibilities as a part of corporate management."[357]

Horn follows previous New York decisions holding that employees do not have a reasonable expectation of confidentiality when receiving medical attention from an on-site medical facility.[358] In *International Paper*, the court held that records of medical conditions reported by employees to a nurses' station maintained by an industrial paper company were not subject to physician-patient privilege but rather were business records properly discoverable in a toxic tort action against the employer.[359] The court in *General Electric* followed *International Paper* to hold that the doctor-patient privilege did not restrict disclosure of similar documents in a lawsuit when the company had previously used those records in 10 scientific studies and did not "produce any

[354]Carevo v. Nielsen Media Research, No. 01 Civ. 9609 2003 U.S. Dist. LEXIS 941, at *22 (S.D.N.Y. Jan. 22, 2003).

[355]Horn v. New York Times, 100 N.Y.2d 85 (N.Y. 2003).

[356]*Id.*

[357]*Id.*

[358]*See, e.g.*, Smith v. International Paper Co., 531 N.Y.S.2d 58 (App. Div. 1988); New York v. General Elec. Co., 607 N.Y.S.2d 181 (App. Div. 1994).

[359]*International Paper*, 531 N.Y.S.2d at 59.

evidence in the record to suggest that its employees expected this information to remain confidential."[360]

(b) Employee Access to Information

Although employees do not have a reasonable expectation of privacy with respect to information obtained from a medical examination at an employer's on-site facility, employees are nevertheless entitled to information obtained via such an examination. If an employer undertakes an examination of a current or future employee (i.e., a pre-employment examination) wherein the employer discovers a dangerous disease or health condition, it may have a duty to inform the employee of that disease or condition.[361] Workers' compensation laws do not provide the sole remedy for an employee whose employer has negligently failed to inform him of the result of certain medical testing performed by doctors in the defendant's employ.[362] Rather, such a claim may be brought under an ordinary theory of negligence.[363]

iii. Privacy Rights of Government Employees

A fair amount of litigation has concerned confidentiality of medical records under General Municipal Law Section 207-c, which generally provides for wages and medical expenses to be paid to police officers injured in the line of duty.[364] Section 207-c provides such benefits subject to a mandatory medical examination and a determination that the officer is permanently disabled and may be retired.[365] In a challenge to a municipal law requiring police officers applying for benefits under Section 207-c to waive confidentiality of medical records, the New York Court of Appeals held that an employee can voluntarily waive confidentiality of medical records regarding an on-the-job injury absent collective bargaining, although waiver of unrelated medical records must

---

[360] *General Elec.*, 607 N.Y.S.2d at 183.

[361] Wojcik v. Aluminum Co. of Am., 183 N.Y.S.2d 351 (1959).

[362] *Id.*; *see also* New York Workers' Compensation Law, N.Y. LAB. LAW §5.03[2][d].

[363] McKinney v. Bellevue Hosp., 183 A.D.2d 563 (1992). *See generally* 52 N.Y. JUR. *Employment Relations* §198 (2006).

[364] N.Y. GEN. MUN. LAW §207-c(1).

[365] N.Y. GEN. MUN. LAW §207-c(2).

be the subject of collective bargaining.[366] The Appellate Division held that an employee, by applying for benefits under Section 207-c, "affirmatively placed his medical condition in issue and effectively waived the physician-patient privilege."[367] Another appellate court found that release of municipal employees' medical records pursuant to applications for disability benefits under a program established by the collective bargaining agreement was subject to collective bargaining and accordingly, the union's "sole remedy lies in the grievance and arbitration procedure under the collective bargaining agreement."[368]

iv. New York Workers' Compensation Law

Although employers are required to maintain records of workplace injuries and illnesses,[369] an employer has a legal obligation to maintain the confidentiality of those files.[370] New York workers' compensation law requires that "[a]n employer, or a third party designated by the employer, shall record any injury or illness incurred by one of its employees in the course of employment" using forms prescribed by the workers' compensation board.[371] Whether or not a claim is filed with the board with the respect to the injury, it is unlawful for the employer to disclose individually identifiable information regarding the injury, illness, or potential claim to any person or entity not legally entitled to obtain such information.[372] Entities legally authorized to receive such information include only those affiliated with the workers' compensation board, the employee who is the subject of the information, court officers, insurers, and health benefit plans.[373]

---

[366] Schenectady Police Benevolent Ass'n v. New York State Public Employment Relations Bd., 85 N.Y.2d 480 (N.Y. 1995).

[367] Burns v. New York State & Local Police & Fire Ret. Sys., 685 N.Y.S.2d 322, 323 (App. Div. 1999).

[368] Suffolk County Ass'n of Mun. Employees v. County of Suffolk, 629 N.Y.S.2d 792, 794 (App. Div. 1995).

[369] N.Y. WORKERS' COMP. LAW §110.

[370] N.Y. WORKERS' COMP. LAW §110-a(4).

[371] N.Y. WORKERS' COMP. LAW §110(1).

[372] N.Y. WORKERS' COMP. LAW §110-a(4).

[373] N.Y. WORKERS' COMP. LAW §110-a(2).

v. Laws Regarding Confidentiality of HIV/AIDS Information

In 1988, the New York State legislature enacted Public Health Law Article 27-F, which established the confidentiality rights of HIV-positive individuals.[374] Under this law, an individual's HIV-related information may be released only to persons and entities specifically permitted by statute,[375] and in accordance with prescribed procedures.[376] These provisions provide an employee with a cause of action if his medical practitioner discloses his HIV status to his employer without his consent.[377]

(a) Confidentiality Required

If an employee's HIV status is properly disclosed to an employer, the statute requires the employer to maintain the confidentiality of that information.[378] Similar to the general medical record confidentiality requirements,[379] the confidentiality obligations of the statute attach to a third party to whom the information is disclosed under the statute.

(b) Enforcement Provisions

New York courts have held that an employee has a private right of action under Public Health Law Article 27-F against his physician for unlawful disclosure of his HIV status to his employer.[380] In *Doe v. Roe*, a physician was directed to release the plaintiff's medical records in conjunction with his workers' compensation claim.[381] The medical information the physician submitted to the attorney for the plaintiff's employer included not only the conditions related to the condition for which he claimed eligibility for workers' compensation but also the undisputedly unrelated fact that he was HIV positive.[382] The court held that whether the phy-

[374] N.Y. PUB. HEALTH LAW §§2780 et seq.
[375] N.Y. PUB. HEALTH LAW §2782(1).
[376] N.Y. PUB. HEALTH LAW §2782(4).
[377] *See, e.g.,* Doe v. Roe, 190 A.D.2d 463, 469–70 (1993).
[378] N.Y. PUB. HEALTH LAW §2782(3).
[379] N.Y. PUB. HEALTH LAW §18(6); see also text accompanying note 12.
[380] *Doe*, 190 A.D.2d at 469–70.
[381] *Id.* at 469.
[382] *Id.*

sician's unlawful disclosure of plaintiff's HIV status was a proximate cause of plaintiff's injuries was a question of fact properly determined by a jury, and not a matter of law to be determined by the court.[383] Although the employee's HIV status may be disclosed to an insurer,[384] the court found that an employer was not an "insurance institution" within the meaning of the statute.[385]

III. EUROPE

Employers who collect, use, or share health information in the EU must comply with the local laws applicable in the relevant Member State. Unlike U.S. law, Member State law, in most cases, does not generally establish specific requirements for health information. Rather, health information is protected as other "sensitive data"[386] and there are specific consent requirements, enhanced security obligations, as well as registration and prior authorization provisions that are explained in more detail in Chapter 6.

A. France

Article 8 of the 1978 French Data Protection Act of 1978[387] provides that the collection and processing of personal data relating to health is prohibited unless such processing is necessary for the purposes of preventive medicine, medical diagnosis, provision of healthcare or treatment, or for the management of healthcare services. The Act also provides that such processing is to be carried out by a member of a medical profession, or by any other person who, due to his functions, is bound by a duty of confidentiality

---

[383] Doe v. Roe, 239 A.D.2d 878 (1997).

[384] N.Y. PUB. HEALTH LAW §2782(1)(j). The information may be released to an insurer only if, inter alia, accompanied by a valid authorization signed by the protected individual or another statutorily authorized person. *Id.*

[385] *Doe*, 190 A.D.2d at 472.

[386] Article 8 of the Directive defines sensitive data to include personal data revealing racial or ethnic origin, political opinions, religious or philosophical beliefs, trade union membership, and health issues.

[387] Article 8 of the French Data Protection Act of 1978.

provided for in Article 226-13 of the French Criminal Code.[388] Processing necessary for medical research also is allowed under certain circumstances defined by law.

In France, health professionals are responsible for health data confidentiality and cannot communicate individual health information to employers.

Additionally, employers cannot refuse to hire, dismiss, or take any adverse action against an employee based on his sickness or health condition. Noncompliance with this principle amounts to discrimination, which is punishable by three years' imprisonment and a 45,000€ fine[389] (or 225,000€ fine if the discrimination is committed by a company).

Medical tests are allowed by French Labor Law in limited cases[390] before hiring to determine if the potential employee is fit for work, after suspending an employment contract due to a health issue, and periodically in the normal course of employment. However, medical tests are to be performed by work doctors, and thus employees do not have access to any health data. Medical records established by work doctors cannot be communicated to employers.[391] In summary, employers in France cannot use, collect, or share health data. Employers must comply with the confidentiality of health data.

1. Subject Access Requests by Individual Employees

Any applicant, current employee, or former employee may ask an employer[392] whether personal information relating to the employee is held by an employer. If personal information is held about an employee, the individual may request:

---

[388] Article 226-13 of French Criminal Code.

[389] Articles 225-1, 225-2 and 225-4 of French Criminal Code and article 131-8 of French Criminal Code.

[390] Articles R.241-48 to R.241-51 of French Labor Code.

[391] Article R.241-56 of French Labor Code.

[392] Article 39 of the French Data Protection Act No. 78-17 of January 6, 1978 on Data Processing Files and Individual Liberties provides for an entire section on access rights to data subjects.

- A description of the type of data held, the purposes for which this information is being processed, and the recipients or types of recipients to whom such data may be disclosed;
- Information relating to the transfers of personal data outside the EU, if applicable;
- A copy in an accessible form of the personal data relating to an employee as well as any available information on the origin of the data. Codes, logograms, and abbreviations contained in this communication must be explained; and
- Information enabling this individual to know and to object to the methodology of the automatic processing; here a decision is taken based on automatic processing and producing legal effects in relation to the data subject.

The right to access personal data under the 1978 French Data Protection Act covers data directly disclosed by the employees, potentially collected from third parties, or originally collected from recruitment methods.

The right to access personal data also covers data concerning performance at work, ranking, professional scoring or valuation, as well as data concerning whistleblowing, which must comply with the required confidentiality about the identity of the whistleblower.

2. *Applicable Fee and Consultation Terms*

Access to the requested personal data must be provided free of charge and without undue delay (usually within two months after the request is made). The employer may, however, charge for the actual cost of making copies.

When the consultation takes place on the premises, protection of third parties' personal data must be guaranteed.

3. *Denial of Subject Access Requests*

Access may be denied only when:

- The employer can prove that the request is "abusive," "repetitive," or "systematic" (the burden of proof will here lie on the data controller who has received the request);

- The French Data Protection Authority (CNIL) determines that personal information is stored in a form that poses no risk of violating the individual's privacy and for a period that does not exceed that required for statistical or research purposes; or
- The disclosure of the data would infringe the employer's or a third-party copyright.

The CNIL recommends that the information requested by the employee be given to the employee in a written format, irrespective of the type of information requested.[393]

B. Germany

In Germany, no statute specifically governs data relating to medical examinations. Rather, the collection, processing, and use of medical examination information are addressed through a plethora of different laws and regulations.

Generally, an employer is obliged under data protection and labor laws to treat health information relating to its employees with particular care. Any health and related information is considered "particularly sensitive personal data" requiring the employer to obtain the explicit consent of employees, or to comply with one of the conditions in Section 28 of the Federal Data Protection Act when collecting, storing, or processing such data. Guidance by the data protection authorities suggests that obtaining the individual's consent is not on its own sufficient to ensure compliance with the Data Protection Act.[394] Rather, any collection, processing, and use must be required for performing the labor relationship. The employer is obligated to ensure that the health information is relevant, accurate, up to date, and secure; that is, any such data must be protected through particular technical and organizational measures such as encryption or locked filing cabinets. Health-related data should be kept separate from other data, if feasible.

---

[393]This requirement is provided in the CNIL decision: Deliberation n02/017 du 21 mars 2002 portant adoption d'une recommendation relative a la collecte et au traitement d'inforactions nominatives lors d'operations de recrutement.

[394]Unabhangiges Landeszentrum fur Datenschutz Schleswig-Holstein: Gesundheitsdatem im Arbeitsverhaltnis.

Doctors are generally subject to confidentiality obligations, and breach of the same is penalized through criminal sanctions. These confidentiality obligations also exist towards employers (e.g., sickness leave certificates should contain only the fact that the employee is not capable of working, and the duration, but not the reason, for his absence).

Practice Pointers: A contractual provision in an employment contract that releases a doctor from his confidentiality obligations is unlikely to be construed as valid consent. In comparison, a contractual provision that states that the employee agrees to undergo a medical examination and to permit the disclosure of any subsequent report to the employer is useful for those circumstances.

C. United Kingdom

In the United Kingdom (UK), an employer must treat health information relating to its employees with care and respect. As such, information will amount to "sensitive personal data" requiring the employer to obtain the explicit consent of employees or comply with one of the conditions in schedule 3 of the Data Protection Act (DP Act) when collecting, storing, or processing health information. The Code[395] also recommends core principles for the employer to abide by and suggests that obtaining the individual's consent is not on its own sufficient to ensure compliance with the DP Act. The employer is still obligated to ensure that the health information obtained through medical examination is relevant, accurate, up to date, and secure. The DP Act gives an individual the right to access health records[396] held by the employer or medical practitioner by making a data subject access request to the data controller. The data controller can refuse to disclose such data if the disclosure is likely to cause serious harm to the physical or mental well-being of the individual. If an individual feels that the information contained in his health records is incorrect,

---

[395]The Information Commissioner's "Employment Practices Code, Part 4."

[396]Under the DP Act, "Health Records" is defined as "a record consisting of information about the physical or mental health or condition of an identifiable individual made by or on behalf of a health professional in connection with the care of that individual."

he should approach the medical practitioner and discuss amending the record. The individual can also file a complaint with the Information Commissioner for a review of the record to determine whether the information should be rectified, blocked, or erased. Guidance[397] suggests that an opinion or judgment recorded by a health professional, whether accurate or not, should not be amended as it may be relevant in understanding the clinical decision that was made and the level of care that was provided. In such cases, good practice suggests that a statement could be included from the individual to record that he disagrees with the opinion or judgment.

In addition to the DP Act, the Access to Medical Reports Act 1998 (AMRA) provides individuals with a right of access to medical reports[398] provided by his medical practitioner[399] to his employer or insurance companies. The scope of AMRA is quite broad and covers employees. However, the position with regard to those who work on a self-employed basis is less clear. Commentary suggests that the general interpretation of AMRA is that it was not intended to cover those in self-employment; however, there has been no case law on this point.

An employer is permitted to apply for a medical report that is covered by AMRA only if the employer notifies the employee that the employer needs to obtain a medical report, obtains the employee's explicit consent, and informs the employee of his rights under AMRA. Under AMRA an individual has the right to: (1) withhold his consent; (2) consent to the application for the report and agree

---

[397]Department of Health Guidance for Access to Health Records Request under the DPA Act 1998.

[398]Under Section 2(l) of the Access to Medical Reports Act 1998, a "medical report" is defined as a report "relating to the physical or mental health of [an] individual prepared by a medical practitioner who is or has been responsible for the clinical care of the individual."

[399]Under Section 2(l) of the Access to Medical Reports Act 1998, a "medical practitioner" for the purposes of the Access to Medical Reports Act 1998 has to be registered under the Medical Act 1983 and responsible for the individual's care, which includes "examination, investigation, or diagnosis for the purposes of, or in connection with, any form of medical treatment." One-off medical reports prepared by company doctors, occupational health consultants, or independent specialist therefore may not be covered.

that it can be sent directly to the employer;[400] or (3) consent to the application but indicate that he wishes to see the report before it is supplied to the employer. When an employee has agreed to send the report directly to the employer, he has a limited opportunity in which to request access to the report. If the report has not yet been provided to the employer, the medical practitioner must allow 21 days for the employee to see the report before it is sent to the employer.[401] Irrespective of whether the report has been sent to the employer, an individual is entitled to a copy of the report from the medical practitioner anytime up to six months after it was supplied to the employer.[402]

Practice Pointers: A contractual provision in an employment contract is unlikely to be construed as consent for the purposes of AMRA because the AMRA relates to consent being given for a particular report to be obtained. It is recommended that where AMRA applies, the employer provide the employee with a written consent from to sign setting out the employee's rights under AMRA. However, a contractual provision that states that the employee agrees to undergo a medical examination, and for any subsequent report to be disclosed to the employer, is useful for those circumstances in which AMRA does not apply to such a report prepared by a company doctor or occupational health consultant. It should be noted that the British Medical Association has issued guidelines that state that when AMRA does not apply; it is considered best practice for employers to provide the employee with a copy of any medical report so that the parties can openly assess and discuss the content and recommendations.

---

[400] Under Section 4(1)(a) of the Access to Medical Reports Act 1998, the employer must inform the medical practitioner that the individual wishes to see the report. The employer must also inform the individual at the same time the application for a report is made as the individual has 21 days to request a copy of the report from the medical practitioner. If the individual fails to make the request within 21 days, the medical practitioner is entitled to assume that he or she no longer wishes to see the report and that he or she has given his or her consent for the report to be supplied to the employer.

[401] Sections 4(2) and (3) of the Access to Medical Reports Act 1998.

[402] Section 6(2) of the Access to Medical Reports Act 1998.

IV. ASIA AND ASIA PACIFIC

A. Australia

As discussed in Chapter 1, the Privacy Act regulates the collection and use of personal health information. Health information about an individual may be collected only in certain circumstances, including where the individual has consented or collection is authorized by law. Health information about an employee, however, is covered by the Employee Records Exemption and, therefore, may be collected and used by an organization without consent. Health information of all other workers such as independent contractors or temporary agents of an organization or prospective employees is not covered by this exemption, and therefore, consent is required to collect such information. In addition, organizations must comply with the other requirements of the Act as described in Chapter 1 with respect to the collection and use of personal information of all other workers.

In addition to the federal privacy law, there are state and territory laws in the Australian Capital Territory (ACT), New South Wales (NSW), and Victoria that regulate the handling of personal health information in the private sector. Organizations that operate in those states and territories must also comply with these laws.

1. NSW Health Records and Information Privacy Act 2002

The NSW Health Records and Information Privacy Act 2002 (HRIP Act) applies to health service providers of any size and organizations that handle health information[403] and have annual

[403]Under the NSW Health Records and Information Privacy Act, health information includes personal information that is information or an opinion about the physical or mental health or a disability of an individual. It also includes personal information that is information or an opinion about:

- A health service provided, or to be provided, to an individual;
- An individual's express wishes about the future provision of health services to him or her;
- Other personal information collected in connection with the donation of human tissue; and
- Genetic information that is or could be predictive of the health of an individual or the individual's relatives or descendants.

revenues in excess of A$3 million. The 15 Health Privacy Principles (HPPs) contained in the HRIP Act describe what public and private sector organizations must do when they collect, hold, use, and disclose health information.

Unless an exemption applies, covered entities are required to:

- Collect health information for a lawful purpose;
- Ensure the information is relevant, accurate, up to date, and not excessive;
- Collect directly from the individual unless it is unreasonable or impracticable to do so;
- Provide notice about what health information they hold about the individual, the purposes for which the information is being collected and used, to whom it might be disclosed, and what rights the individual has to access it;
- Provide individuals with access to and the ability to correct the information and advise them of the consequences of not providing the information;
- Protect the health information from unauthorized access, use, and disclosure;
- Store the health information securely and dispose of it in an appropriate manner when it is no longer required;
- Use and disclose the health information for the purpose for which it was collected, or a directly related purpose that the individual would expect unless consent is obtained (or an exemption applies); and
- Transfer information outside NSW only if the recipient of the information is subject to a law, binding scheme, or contract that provides substantially similar protection or the individual consents to the transfer.

As with the Privacy Act, health information of employees is covered by an Employee Records Exemption in the HRIP Act. The definition of an Employee Record is taken directly from the federal Privacy Act.

The exemptions in the HPPs are more fully defined in four legally binding statutory guidelines.[404] These guidelines describe how the exemption applies and what organizations need to do in order to comply with the exemptions. Organizations seeking to rely on an exemption in the HPPs to collect, use, or disclose health information must also comply with the statutory guidelines (if any) accompanying that exemption. The statutory guidelines are as important as the exemptions. An exemption cannot be relied upon unless the organization is in compliance with the applicable guidelines. A failure to comply with the guidelines constitutes a breach of the Act.

2. ACT Health Records (Privacy and Access) Act 1997

The Health Records (Privacy and Access) Act 1997 covers health records held in the public sector in the ACT and applies to acts or practices in the private sector. The Health Records Act contains 14 privacy principles based on the federal privacy law but modified to suit the requirements of the health care sector. The Act does not, however, contain an equivalent Employee Records Exemption. Employers, therefore, are not permitted to collect health information unless the employee consents or the collection is authorized by law. To the extent that it contains personal health information, the Act gives people access to their health records and any other record. The ACT Community and Health Services Complaints Commissioner handles health record privacy complaints.

3. Victoria Health Records Act 2001

Victoria's Health Records Act 2001 regulates the handling of all health information held by the private health sector. The Act contains 11 Health Privacy Principles adapted from the NPPs. Like the ACT law, the Victoria Act does not have an Employee Records Exemption. Employers, therefore, are not permitted to

---

[404]*See* "Statutory guidelines on the management of health services," "Statutory guidelines on training," "Statutory guidelines on research" and "Statutory guidelines on notifying a person when you have collected health information about them from someone else."

collect health information unless the employee consents or the collection is authorized by law. The Act also gives employees and other individuals a legally enforceable right of access to health information.

B. China

It is standard practice for employers in China to require prospective employees to undergo a physical examination and provide the results of that examination to the employee. However, under the Employment Promotion Law, an employer cannot refuse to hire someone on the basis that the person is carrier of an infectious disease.[405]

An employee's medical information is considered personal information that an employer cannot publicly disclose. Various court cases in recent years have been successfully brought by employees who have had their private medical information disclosed by their employers.

Practice Pointer. In order to limit potential liability, access to employee health information should be limited to the extent possible, and measures should be taken so that employers handle only the information necessary.

C. Hong Kong

In Hong Kong, the collection and use of personal data relating to employee health (Health Data) is governed by the Personal Data Privacy Ordinance (PDPO).[406] The Hong Kong Privacy Commissioner has issued a Code of Practice on Human Resource Management (the HR Code), which seeks to provide more detailed guidance to complement the high-level data privacy principles set out in the PDPO.

It should be noted that the provisions of the HR Code are not legally binding. A breach of the HR Code by a data user, however, will give rise to a presumption against the data user in any legal proceedings under the PDPO.

---

[405]Employment Promotion Law, Art. 30.

[406]Laws of Hong Kong, Cap. 486.

Under the PDPO and the HR Code, the collection of personal data relating to the health of potential employees or employees is restricted as follows:

1. Employment Candidates

The collection of Health Data with respect to potential employees must be limited to that required to confirm the suitability of the candidate for the inherent requirements of the position in question. Health Data should be collected only for such purposes after the employer has made an offer of employment to the selected candidate conditional upon the fulfillment of the basic requirements (e.g., by means of a medical examination).

On or before the collection of any Health Data, the employer must give the employee notice relating to the collection and use of the health information. Specifically, the employer should notify the candidate of: (1) the purpose for which the data are to be used; (2) the classes of persons to whom the data may be transferred; (3) whether it is obligatory or voluntary to supply the data; and (4) the candidate's right to request access and corrections to Health Data held. This is typically effected by means of a Personal Information Collection Statement (PICS).

Health Data relating to unsuccessful candidates should not be retained for longer than two years unless the candidate has given consent, or there is another good reason for retaining the information (i.e., potential legal proceedings).

2. Existing Employees

The collection of Health Data regarding employees must be for a purpose that is either:[407]

- Directly related to an assessment of the suitability of the employee's continuance in employment (e.g., where the nature of a post requires a certain level of health); or
- Directly related to the employer's administration of medical or other benefits or compensation provided to the employee.

---

[407] HR Code, §3.2.4.

In each case, the Health Data should be collected by fair means, limited to what is required for the purpose, and must not be excessive for that purpose. For example, an employer should seek only the minimum information about an employee's sick leave application that is required to verify or calculate the entitlement to sick leave and other related benefits but not the details of the treatment prescribed for the medical condition afflicting the employee.[408]

On or before the collection of any Health Data, the employer should notify the employee of: (1) the purpose for which the data are to be used; (2) the classes of persons to whom the data may be transferred; (3) whether it is obligatory or voluntary to supply the data; and (4) the data subject's right to request access and corrections to Health Data held. This is typically effected by means of a PICS statement incorporated in the employee's terms of employment. In addition, the employer must ensure that it has a policy covering medical checking, prior notice of which has been brought to the attention of the employee concerned.[409]

The HR Code requires employers to take all practicable steps to ensure that Health Data are kept secure, having regard to the generally sensitive nature of such data.

Practice Pointer. As a matter of good practice, Health Data should be accessible only to authorized staff using appropriate procedures. Measures suggested in the HR Code include the use of secure terminals, access protocols, audit trail software, logging, and compliance checks. Where Health Data are stored in hard copy form, they should be held in a secure area accessible only to authorized personnel on a "need-to-know" basis.[410]

Both candidates and existing employees have the right to request access to the Health Data collected.[411] More detailed information on access rights is contained in Chapter 7. Health Data will be exempt from those access right provisions if their application would be likely to cause serious (and, implicitly, lasting)

---

[408] HR Code, §3.2.1.
[409] HR Code, §3.2.5.
[410] HR Code, §3.2.6.
[411] Data Protection Principles (DPP), Schedule 1 of PDPO, §6.

harm to the physical or mental health of the employee or any other individual.[412]

D. Japan

In carrying out their obligations to provide such health examinations and take measures to maintain the health of their employees (see Chapter 6), employers must heed the general obligations regarding the use and handling of personal information under the Protection of Personal Information Act (PIPL), the Ministry of Health, Labour and Welfare's (MHLW) Guidelines for the Appropriate Handling of Personal Information in Employment Management (MHLW Guidelines), and the Commentary to the Guidelines (Commentary), which are described in Chapter 1 of this book. In addition, there are also special limitations to the collection, use, and handling of employee health information, which are described below.

The MHLW's Matters to Consider when Handling Health Information in Employment Management (the Health Information Guidelines) issued pursuant to the PIPL provides that when it is necessary to collect health information from medical institutions or health insurance associations and the like, it is desirable for businesses to obtain the consent of the worker after providing notice regarding the purpose of collection, and if necessary, to obtain such information from the worker directly.[413]

In terms of the handling of health information, the Health Information Guidelines provide that in terms of raw data from health examinations (i.e., actual test results or doctors notes), such information should be handled only by specialists, such as industrial physicians (occupational health business-related worker), who have specialized medical knowledge for diseases.[414] Raw data should not be provided to nonspecialists such as the employee's supervisor or human resource personnel.[415]

---

[412]PDPO, §59

[413]Health Information Guidelines, §3.1.

[414]Health Information Guidelines, §3.2.

[415]Commentary to the Guidelines, Reference III, "Points regarding Matters to Consider in Handling Health Information of Personal Information Related to Employment Management."

Practice Pointer. Thus, although the employer will have access to raw data, they should not be disseminated.

Even if it is necessary to use health examination results to take employment measures (such as recommending taking time off), the Commentary to the Health Information Guidelines provides that it is unnecessary for nonspecialists such as the employee's supervisor or human resource personnel to have raw data, and only a doctor's findings should be provided to such personnel.[416]

Practice Pointer. Access to employee health information should be limited to the extent possible, and measures should be taken so that employers handle only essential information that has gone through necessary processing by specialists.

To ensure that health information is properly handled, the Health Information Guidelines and Commentary provide that it is desirable that: (1) businesses develop internal company rules for handling such information, after discussions with the labor unions as necessary; (2) these rules be made known to employees and those handling such information; and (3) such rules be followed in the handling of such information.[417]

In terms of safeguard measures for health information, the Health Information Guidelines provide that the health information of workers should be handled in accordance with the safeguard measures provided in the Guidelines for the Proper Handling of Personal Information at Medical and Nursing Related Businesses and Guidelines for the Proper Handling of Personal Information at Health Insurance Associations, Etc.[418] The security provisions in these guidelines are more stringent than the MHLW Guidelines and Ministry of Economy, Trade and Industry (METI) Guidelines, and include specific additional security requirements such as taking measures to prevent degradation of media on which the information will be stored for long periods, and before disposing or deleting personal information, ensuring that personal information will be made irretrievable.

---

[416] *Id.*

[417] Health Information Guidelines, §§3.4(1), 3.4(2).

[418] Health Information Guidelines, §3.4(5).

1. Mental Health Information

Section 7 of the Guidelines regarding the Maintenance and Promotion of the Mental Health of Workers (Mental Health Guidelines), issued by MHLW in March 2006 pursuant to the Occupational Safety Law, provides additional guidance on the handling of mental health information. The Mental Health Guidelines provide that it is desirable to obtain the consent of the worker when obtaining such information from the doctor or the worker's family, and that consent of the worker is also generally necessary when such personal health information is to be provided to a third party such as a medical institution, unless it is necessary to protect the worker's life or health in an emergency or other important situations.[419] Workplaces that have industrial physicians on staff should consult such doctors to make determinations as to what information is required and how it is to be handled.[420]

Industrial physicians that acquire personal information, including physical and mental health information, through consultations with the workers, should provide as little as possible to the employer to achieve the required purpose.[421] In addition, before providing such information, industrial physicians must appropriately process the information by summarizing, sorting, and interpreting the information so that the necessary information will be accurately communicated and appropriate workplace measures can be implemented to protect the worker's health and privacy.[422]

The Mental Health Guidelines also provide that it is desirable for the diagnosis and raw data from test results to be handled by the industrial physicians or other health staff, and it is particularly important to handle information regarding diagnoses that indicate mental disorders very carefully.[423] Like the Health Information Guidelines, the Mental Health Guidelines state that there should be internal company rules that provide for the appropriate and confidential handling of mental health information.[424]

---

[419] Mental Health Guidelines, §7(1).

[420] *Id.*

[421] Mental Health Guidelines, §7(2).

[422] *Id.*

[423] *Id.*

[424] Mental Health Guidelines, §7(3).

2. *Additional Guidance*

Employers also should heed the Action Guide regarding the Protection of Personal Information of Workers (Action Guide) issued by the MHLW in 2000. Although it does not have the force of law, it is generally regarded by businesses as agency rules that should be followed.

The Action Guide states that health information may be collected if the collection is pursuant to law, if there are confidentiality obligations imposed on workers handling health information, and if it is pursuant to achieving one of the following purposes: (1) necessity for a certain type of work (such as to confirm the vision of a driver at a transportation company); (2) to implement measures for occupational health and safety or protection of mothers (measures taken pursuant to law); or (3) when it is clear that the collection will be for the benefit of the worker, and it is recognized that there is a justifiable reason for the collection of such health information (e.g., if a worker requests to take a leave of absence or change in position due to health reasons, and the business requests a medical certificate).

E. New Zealand

Employers in New Zealand who collect, use, or share health information of their employees must comply with the requirements of the Privacy Act 1993 (the Act), discussed in Chapter 1. The Act applies to all personal information that is collected, used, and disclosed; it does not distinguish between sensitive and non-sensitive information and, therefore, does not extend any special protections to sensitive information such as health information. Employers that operate in the health sector (and their employees), however, are subject to special rules on the collection, use, and disclosure of health information. In 1994, the Privacy Commissioner issued a legally binding Health Information Privacy Code (the Code)[425] that contains industry-specific information privacy

[425]*See* Health Information Privacy Code 1994, available online at www.privacy.org.nz/filestore/docfiles/38197000.pdf.

principles; the Code substitutes for the information privacy principles in the Act.

The Code sets out 12 rules that apply to health information about an identifiable individual, including information about a person's health or disabilities, a person's medical history, any health or disability services provided to someone, or information about patients that is collected while providing health and disability services to them. The rules largely mirror the principles contained in the Act. In addition, the Code requires health organizations to establish a complaints process. In particular, a health organization must:

- Designate a person or persons to handle complaints;
- Acknowledge complaints in writing within five days of receipt of the complaint;
- Inform the complainant of relevant internal and external complaint procedures;
- Document the complaint and the actions of the organization regarding the complaint;
- Decide within 10 working days of acknowledging the complaint whether or not it accepts that the complaint is justified or whether it needs more time to investigate the complaint and if so, how much more time is required (if more than 20 working days are required, then it must notify the complainant of that determination and its reasons for that determination); and
- Inform the individual as soon as possible once a determination is made of the reasons for the decision, any actions the organization proposes to take, any appeal procedure the organization has in place, and any right to complain to the Privacy Commissioner.[426]

---

[426] *See* Health Information Privacy Code, Part III, clause 7.

CHAPTER 6

MEDICAL EXAMINATIONS AND DRUG TESTING OF APPLICANTS AND EMPLOYEES

I. Overview 417
II. Americas 418
A. United States 418
1. Medical Examinations 418
Exhibit 6.1 U.S.: Timing of Inquiries Under the ADA 419
a. What Is a Medical Examination? 420
i. Psychological Examinations 420
ii.. Personality Assessments 421
iii. Physical Agility Tests 422
b. Medical Examinations of Job Applicants 423
i. Prior to Job Offer 423
ii. After Conditional Job Offer, Prior to Employment 423
(a) Standards for Conditional Job Offer 424
(b) Scope of Medical Examinations Pursuant to a Conditional Job Offer 425
c. Medical Examinations of Employees 426
i. EEOC Standards 426
ii. Standards Defined by Courts 426
iii. Fitness for Duty Evaluations 427
d. Standing to Bring Claim for Unlawful Medical Examinations Under the ADA 429
2. Other Inquiries Related to Physical or Mental Condition 429
a. Examples of Permissible Job-Related Inquiries 429
b. Examples of Impermissible Disability-Related Inquiries 430

c. Inquiries Following Voluntary Disclosure of Disability 431
3. Drug Testing 432
a. Inquiries About Current Illegal Drug Use 432
b. Inquiries About Past Drug or Alcohol Use 433
c. State Laws Regulating Drug Testing 434
i. California 434
ii. Connecticut 435
iii. Iowa 435
iv. Minnesota and Maine 436
v. Oklahoma 436
vi. Vermont 436
4. Additional Limitations on Physical or Mental Testing of Applicants 436
Exhibit 6.2 U.S.: Examples of Other Legally Restricted Inquiries 437
a. Genetic Information Nondiscrimination Act of 2008 437
i. Restrictions on Collecting Genetic Information 438
ii. Protection Against Discrimination Based on Genetic Information 440
iii. Confidentiality of Genetic Information 441
b. State Laws Restricting Genetic Testing 444
c. HIV/AIDS Testing 445
d. Lie Detector and Polygraph Examinations 445
i. Employee Polygraph Protection Act 446
ii. State Restrictions on Lie Detector and Polygraph Tests 447
B. Brazil 449
1. Medical Examinations 449
2. Drug Testing 449
C. Canada 450
1. Medical Examinations 450
2. Drug Testing 450
D. Mexico 450
1. Medical Examinations 450
2. Drug Testing 450
III. Europe 451
A. Belgium 451

1. Medical Examinations 451
2. Drug Testing 451
B. France 452
C. Germany 454
D. Italy 456
1. Medical Examinations 456
2. Drug Testing 456
E. United Kingdom 457
IV. Asia 460
A. China 460
B. Hong Kong 461
1. Medical Examinations 461
2. Drug and Genetic Testing 462
C. Japan 462
1. Health Examinations 462
2. Generally Prohibited Tests 464
D. Korea 465
1. Medical Examinations 465
2. Drug Testing 465

I. OVERVIEW

Medical examinations and drug testing allow an employer to detect impairments that may interfere with an individual's job performance. At the same time, medical examinations and drug testing pose the risk of screening out qualified individuals for improper reasons, ranging from stereotypical assumptions about individuals with disabilities to inaccurate drug testing results. Countries attempt to mitigate these risks by regulating when and how medical examinations and drug testing may be conducted—and even whether such examinations or testing may be conducted at all—or may be used to make an employment decision.

The U.S. regulates privacy on a sectoral basis and health information is one of the key areas of concern and thus regulations relating to health information are abundant. Similarly in the European Union (EU) health information is considered sensitive information and thus is subject to heightened regulation. Thus medical examinations are heavily regulated in nearly every country that has privacy regulation.

Genetic testing has become a growing area of regulation due to the rapid advances in genetic research. The United States is one of a number of countries that strictly limit genetic testing by employers, and other countries (such as Germany) are actively working on similar legislation. These laws respond to concerns that genetic testing may result in widespread and systematic discrimination, such as employers refusing to hire individuals with apparent genetic predispositions to serious medical conditions. These laws also are intended to promote and foster genetic research, by allaying such fears.

This chapter describes procedures that must be followed in requiring medical examinations or drug testing of applicants and employees, as well as legal risk factors that may influence an employer's decisions about medical screening.

II. AMERICAS

A. United States

1. Medical Examinations

The federal Americans with Disabilities Act (ADA) prohibits employers from discriminating against qualified individuals on the basis of physical or mental disability[1] and regulates an employer's ability to ask job applicants or employees to undergo "medical examinations" to assess physical or mental health. These limitations are discussed below and summarized in Exhibit 6.1. The ADA is supplemented by state laws that further restrict health-related inquiries of employees or applicants.

---

[1]For purposes of the ADA, a "disability" is defined as: (1) a physical or mental impairment that substantially limits one or more major life functions; (2) a history of such an impairment; or (3) being regarded as having such an impairment. 42 U.S.C. §12102(2). The ADA Amendments Act of 2008 clarifies that "major life activities" include performing manual tasks, seeing, hearing, eating, sleeping, walking, standing, lifting, bending, speaking, breathing, learning, reading, concentrating, thinking, communicating, and working. *Id.* "Major life activities" also include the operation of a major bodily function, such as functions of the immune system; normal cell growth; and digestive, bowel, bladder, neurological, brain, respiratory, circulatory, endocrine, and reproductive functions. *Id.*

EXHIBIT 6.1
U.S.: Timing of Inquiries Under the ADA

Timing of Inquiries Under the ADA			
Inquiry	Prior to Job Offer	After Conditional Offer, Prior to Employment	Post-Hire
Asking whether individual can perform job functions, with or without reasonable accommodation	Permissible	Permissible	Permissible
Medical/Psychological Examination or Inquiry	Not permitted	Permissible after bona fide job offer, if requirement is applied consistently to post-offer candidates	Permissible only if job-related and consistent with business necessity (e.g., employer has objective evidence that employee cannot safely perform job functions)
Physical Agility Tests	Permissible if test cannot be used to screen out candidates with disabilities	Permissible if test cannot be used to screen out candidates with disabilities. If test could be used for this purpose, employer must demonstrate that test is job-related and consistent with business necessity	Permissible if test cannot be used to screen out candidates with disabilities. If test could be used for this purpose, employer must demonstrate that test is job-related and consistent with business necessity
Personality Assessments	Permissible if test cannot be used to screen out candidates with disabilities	Permissible if test cannot be used to screen out candidates with disabilities. If test could be used for this purpose, employer must demonstrate that test is job-related and consistent with business necessity	Permissible if test cannot be used to screen out candidates with disabilities. If test could be used for this purpose, employer must demonstrate that test is job-related and consistent with business necessity

a. What Is a Medical Examination?

The Equal Employment Opportunity Commission (EEOC) defines a "medical examination" as a procedure or test that "seeks information about an individual's physical or mental impairments or health."[2] Additionally, the EEOC has identified a number of factors that indicate whether a procedure constitutes a medical examination under the ADA, including: (1) who conducts the procedure/test; (2) who interprets the result; (3) the procedure's ability to reveal impairment of physical or mental health; (4) the invasiveness of the procedure; (5) what characteristics are measured by the procedure; (6) the setting in which the procedure is conducted; and (7) the type of equipment used.[3]

i. Psychological Examinations

The EEOC has taken the position that psychological examinations are medical examinations if "they provide evidence that would lead to identifying a mental disorder or impairment (for example, those listed in the American Psychiatric Association's most recent Diagnostic and Statistical Manual of Mental Disorders (DSM))."[4]

As an illustration, a Florida district court held that a clinical evaluation arranged by a potential employer was an unlawful pre-employment medical examination. The evaluation was conducted

---

[2]EEOC Compliance Manual, ADA Enforcement Guidance: Preemployment Disability-Related Questions and Medical Examinations, No. 915.002 (Oct. 10, 1995), ¶6903, at 5376 (CCH 2006). While the EEOC guidelines are not binding on the courts, many courts give the guidelines substantial deference. *See, e.g.*, Karraker Rent-A-Center, Inc., 411 F.3d 831, 835 & n.2 (7th Cir. 2005) (citing Meritor Sav. Bank v. Vinson, 477 U.S. 57, 65 (1986)); Grenier v. Cyanamid Plastics, Inc., 70 F.3d 667, 672 (1st Cir. 1995). *See also* St. Clair v. City of Plano, No. 3:06-cv-1485, 2007 U.S. Dist. LEXIS 32583 (N.D. Tex. 2007) (denying the defendant's summary judgment motion on determining that employers who make improper medical inquires during the pre-offer stage of hiring violate the ADA and are subject to the same claims and damages available to any ADA plaintiff; noting that the employer's pre-offer procedures required the applicant to take a polygraph examination and to answer a "health condition questionnaire" for a polygraph examination, asking questions such as "Have you ever been treated for serious sickness, illness, or disease in your lifetime?" and "Did you ever have a back, neck, spinal column or head injury?" and "Do you understand that you may be asked to verify the truthfulness of health questionnaire with the polygraph?").

[3]*Id.*

[4]EEOC Compliance Manual, No. 915.002 (Oct. 10, 1995), ¶6903, at 5377.

by a licensed psychologist, involved analysis of the applicant's medical history, and applied psychological tests.[5] The court held that this type of assessment elicited information that could be used to identify mental disorders and, therefore, constituted an impermissible pre-offer medical examination.[6]

ii. Personality Assessments

Some employers view personality tests as a means of assessing a candidate's suitability for a particular job. To the extent that it is based on a mental health diagnostic assessment, however, the personality test may be considered an impermissible medical inquiry. For example, in *Karraker v. Rent-A-Center, Inc.*, the Seventh Circuit held that an employer's use of the Minnesota Multiphasic Personality Inventory (MMPI) as a personality test constituted a medical examination under the ADA.[7] The Seventh Circuit rejected the employer's argument that it used the MMPI only as a personality test, not for the purpose of identifying disabilities.[8] The court held that the test was an impermissible medical examination under the ADA because the MMPI was likely to screen out applicants with protected mental disabilities.[9]

Personality tests that inquire about personal matters unrelated to the job also may violate an applicant's privacy rights under state law. In *Soroka v. Dayton Hudson Corp.*, a California court invalidated an employer's use of a personality test based on the MMPI and the California Psychological Inventory to evaluate candidates for security officer positions at retail stores.[10] The personality test included questions related to the applicant's religious faith and sexual orientation, and the answers were assessed by a psychology firm that made hiring recommendations based on the applicant's ratings in the areas of emotional stability, interpersonal style, addiction potential, dependability and reliability, and socialization. The court explained that inquiries about the private life of

---

[5]Barnes v. Cochran, 944 F. Supp. 897, 904-05 (S.D. Fla. 1996), *aff'd mem.*, Barnes v. Broward County Sheriff's, 130 F.3d 443 (11th Cir. 1997).

[6]*Id.*

[7]Karraker v. Rent-A-Center, Inc., 411 F.3d 831, 835-37 (7th Cir. 2005).

[8]*Id.*

[9]*Id.* at 837.

[10]Soroka v. Dayton Hudson Corp., 18 Cal. App. 4th 1200 (1991).

an applicant or employee must be justified by a compelling interest and serve a job-related purpose.[11] As applied to the personality test used in *Soroka*, the court recognized that the employer "unquestionably has an interest in employing emotionally stable persons" to be security officers. However, the court concluded that the employer failed to establish a compelling interest to inquire about religious beliefs or sexual orientation, and also failed to demonstrate how these inquiries had any bearing on the emotional stability or suitability of candidates for security officer positions.[12] The court therefore determined that the personality test constituted an invasion of privacy under California law. It should be noted that not all states recognize a common-law right of privacy, however. See Chapter 3, Section II.A.

Practice Pointer. Because many personality tests are based on psychological assessment tools such as the MMPI, employers should inquire about the origin of any personality test prior to using it. Personality tests that are based on psychological diagnostic tests should be used only in compliance with the ADA and state law. Employers also should ensure that the personality test does not contain intrusive questions about topics such as religion, sexual orientation, or past drug or alcohol addiction.

iii. Physical Agility Tests

Under the federal regulations to the ADA, "[p]hysical agility tests are not medical examinations and so may be given at any time in the application or employment process."[13] It must be noted, however, that such examinations cannot be used to screen out indi-

---

[11] *Id.* at 1214.

[12] *Id.* Additionally, the court held that these inquiries violated the California Fair Employment and Housing Act, which prohibits nonjob-related inquiries that express "direct[ly] or indirectly, any limitation, specification, or discrimination" related to religion, sexual orientation, or other protected classifications. *Soroka*, 18 Cal. App. 4th at 1215 (citing CAL. GOV'T CODE §12940(d)). In order to justify such inquiries, the employer must demonstrate that the inquiry is sufficiently related to an essential function of the position to warrant the inquiry's use. *Id.* (citing CAL. CODE REGS. tit. 2 §7287.3(b)(1)).

[13] 29 C.F.R. pt 1630, App., §1630.14(a). It should be noted that the Code of Federal Regulations Appendix describes the views of the EEOC and is not binding on the courts. *See* Sullivan v. River Valley Sch. Dist., 197 F.3d 804, 811–12 (6th Cir. 1999).

viduals with disabilities unless the employer can show that the test is job-related and consistent with business necessity.[14]

b. Medical Examinations of Job Applicants

As a general rule, an employer may not ask a job applicant to undergo any type of medical examination prior to receiving a bona fide offer of employment. However, the employer may condition the offer of employment on the applicant's successful completion of a job-related medical examination. This examination would be conducted after the candidate receives a job offer but before he starts employment.

i. Prior to Job Offer

The ADA generally prohibits an employer from conducting a medical examination or making other disability-related inquiries prior to a job offer. Specifically, the ADA states that "a covered entity shall not conduct a medical examination or make inquiries of a job applicant as to whether such applicant is an individual with a disability or as to the nature or severity of such disability."[15] Therefore, the key considerations for an employer when making pre-offer inquiries concern: (1) whether the inquiries equate to a "medical examination"; and (2) whether the inquiries may be viewed as seeking information about disabilities.

ii. After Conditional Job Offer, Prior to Employment

Once the employer makes a conditional offer of employment to the applicant, the ADA permits legitimate job-related medical examinations and disability-related inquiries. The deferral of these medical-related inquiries serves three purposes. First, it limits the risk of disability-based discrimination in the hiring process, because the employer would have made the job offer without the results of these medical inquiries. Second, it forces an employer to show that the reason for rescission of an offer is job-related, or a business necessity. Third, it requires an employer to make an effort to reasonably accommodate an applicant's disability.[16]

---

[14] *Id.*

[15] 42 U.S.C. §12112(d)(2)(A).

[16] Barnes v. Cochran, 944 F. Supp. 897, 905 (S.D. Fla. 1996).

(a) Standards for Conditional Job Offer

In order to seek a medical examination, the employer must first provide a bona fide offer of employment. The EEOC takes the position that an employment offer is not "real" unless the "employer has evaluated all relevant non-medical information which it reasonably could have obtained and analyzed prior to giving the offer."[17] Therefore, to be a "real" offer, an employer should make the offer contingent on no additional screening other than the medical examination.

Conditioning the job offer on requirements beyond the medical examination may cause the offer not to qualify as bona fide for purposes of the ADA. In *Buchanan v. City of San Antonio*, the Fifth Circuit held that the employer's job offer was not "real" because "the offer was not conditioned solely on a medical examination, but was instead conditioned on successful completion of 'the entire screening process.'"[18] The plaintiff in *Buchanan* had applied for a job at the San Antonio Police Department and was given a conditional offer of employment. This offer, however, required "'physical and psychological examinations, a polygraph examination, a physical fitness test, an assessment board, and an extensive background investigation.'"[19] The court held that these conditions of employment prevented the offer from being considered "real."[20]

It is advisable for an employer to complete all nonmedical screening processes before making the conditional offer of employment under the ADA. As an illustration, in *O'Neal v. City of New Albany*, the Seventh Circuit found that a job offer was bona fide when the employer had completed all screening measures except for the medical examination.[21] Unlike *Buchanan*, the employer in *O'Neal* had administered all the nonmedical screening tests before distributing the offer. The court noted that the employer

---

[17]EEOC Compliance Manual, No. 915.002 (Oct. 10, 1995), ¶6903, at 5378.

[18]Buchanan v. City of San Antonio, 85 F.3d 196, 199 (5th Cir. 1996).

[19]*Id.*

[20]*See also* Leonel v. American Airlines, Inc., 400 F.3d 702, 709 (9th Cir. 2005); Downs v. Massachusetts Bay Transp. Auth., 13 F. Supp. 2d 130, 137–38 (D. Mass. 1998) (holding that a conditional offer was not "real" because it was contingent on multiple steps other than a medical examination).

[21]O'Neal v. City of New Albany, 293 F.3d 998, 1008-09 (7th Cir. 2002).

"probably could not have required O'Neal to take [the remaining tests] until after [it] gave him the conditional offer."[22] Therefore, the court affirmed the trial court's summary judgment in favor of the employer on the ADA claim.[23]

(b) Scope of Medical Examinations Pursuant to a Conditional Job Offer

If a "real" offer is given to an applicant, the ADA provides that pre-hire medical examinations are "not required to be job-related and consistent with business necessity."[24] Under the ADA, an employer is permitted to conduct a pre-hire medical examination of the applicant as long as three conditions are met. First, all entering employees must be subject to the examination.[25] Second, information obtained from examinations must be kept in separate forms and in separate files. Third, the information must be used only in accordance with the other sections of the ADA.[26]

In contrast, state laws may impose much greater restrictions than the ADA. Unlike the ADA, California law *does* require all medical examinations to be "job-related and consistent with business necessity."[27]

Under either federal or state law, an employer cannot use post-offer examinations to avoid hiring candidates with disabilities unless the individual would be unable to perform the essential functions of the job even with reasonable accommodation.[28]

---

[22] *Id.* at 1009.

[23] *Id.* at 1010.

[24] 29 C.F.R. §1630.14(b). *See, e.g.*, Norman-Bloodsaw v. Lawrence Berkeley Lab., 135 F.3d 1260, 1273–74 (9th Cir. 1998) (affirming summary judgment for employer on ADA claim since there was no requirement that post-offer testing be job-related or consistent with business necessity).

[25] *See* Farmiloe v. Ford Motor Co., 277 F. Supp. 2d 778, 794 (N.D. Ohio 2002) (rejecting summary judgment based partly on the lack of evidence that the test administered was given to all post-offer applicants).

[26] 42 U.S.C. §12112(d)(3).

[27] CAL. GOV'T CODE §12940(e)(3).

[28] 29 C.F.R. §1630.14(b)(3). *See* Fuzy v. S&B Eng'rs & Constructors, Ltd., 332 F.3d 301, 303 (5th Cir. 2003) (holding that failure to fulfill 100-pound lifting requirement in post-offer test was sufficient to rescind offer); Flores v. American Airlines, Inc., 184 F. Supp. 2d 1287, 1293–94 (S.D. Fla. 2002) (holding that an applicant was not a "qualified individual with a disability" because a post-offer screening showed that he could not perform an essential function of the job).

c. *Medical Examinations of Employees*

Once the candidate has begun employment, any medical examinations and disability-related inquiries must be job-related and consistent with business necessity.

i. *EEOC Standards*

The EEOC considers an inquiry "'job-related and consistent with business necessity' when an employer 'has a reasonable belief, based on *objective* evidence, that: (1) an employee's ability to perform essential job functions will be impaired by a medical condition; or (2) an employee will pose a *direct threat* due to a medical condition.'"[29] The reasonable belief can be based on reliable third-party information. When determining reliability, the EEOC considers these five factors: "(1) the relationship of the person providing the information...; (2) the seriousness of the medical condition at issue; (3) the possible motivation of the person providing the information; (4) how the person learned the information...; and (5) other evidence that the employer has that bears on the reliability of the information provided." [30]

ii. *Standards Defined by Courts*

In *Conroy v. New York State Department of Correctional Services*, the Second Circuit held that, in order to prove "business necessity," an employer must show that (1) the "'business necessity' is vital to the business," and (2) the "examination or inquiry genuinely serves the asserted business necessity."[31]

---

[29] EEOC Compliance Manual, Enforcement Guidance: Disability-Related Inquiries and Medical Examinations of Employees Under the Americans with Disabilities Act (ADA), No. 915.002 (July 27, 2000), ¶6910, at 5485 (CCH 2006) (emphasis added) (citation omitted).

[30] *Id.* at 5487.

[31] Conroy v. New York State Dep't of Corr. Servs., 333 F.3d 88, 97–98 (2d Cir. 2003). *See also* Gajda v. Manhattan & Bronx Surface Transit Operating Auth., 396 F.3d 187, 188–89 (2d Cir. 2005) (following the reasoning of *Conroy*); Transportation Workers Union of Am. v. New York City Transit Auth., 341 F. Supp. 2d 432, 446–47 (S.D.N.Y. 2004); EEOC v. Murray, Inc., 175 F. Supp. 2d 1053, 1064 (M.D. Tenn. 2001) (stating that tests revealing specific medical conditions are allowed only if such tests "always cause specific physical or mental limitations that prevent the individuals" from doing their jobs). *See also* Mickens v. Polk County Sch. Bd., 430 F. Supp. 2d 1265, 1278 (M.D. Fla. 2006) (citing *Conroy* and, referring to the jury instructions,

Moreover, in *Sullivan v. River Valley School District*, the Sixth Circuit held that "there must be significant evidence that could cause a *reasonable* person to inquire as to whether an employee is still capable of performing his job. . . . [T]here must be [a] genuine reason to doubt whether [the] employee can 'perform job-related functions.'"[32] Therefore, the employer is allowed to require medical examinations of an employee only if its belief in the "job-relatedness" and "business necessity" is reasonable.

iii. Fitness for Duty Evaluations

In certain circumstances, employers may be allowed to require medical examinations of employees in order to reassess their ability to perform the functions of the job. This situation often arises in the context of employees returning from leave due to injury or disability, for example. Such examinations are commonly called "fitness for duty" examinations.

A fitness for duty evaluation may be warranted if the employee's physical or mental condition calls into doubt his ability to continue performing the job. For example, in *Yin v. California*, the Ninth Circuit held that an employer's request for an employee to submit to a medical examination was job-related and consistent with business necessity.[33] The plaintiff had a history of absenteeism and the state requested a "fitness for duty" medical examination, which she refused.[34] The Ninth Circuit explained that even if the goal of the examination was to determine the nature or severity

---

stating that "[i]n demonstrating that a requested medical or psychological examination is job-related and consistent with a reasonable business necessity, the employer has the burden to show that the examination is more than merely convenient or beneficial to the conduct of the business of the employer. The particular necessities of a business, of course, vary from workplace to workplace, and [the jury] may consider the particular requirements of each workplace, including the need for safety and security. Also, the employer must show that the particular request for an examination is not materially broader or more intrusive than reasonably necessary." *Id.* at 1279.).

[32]Sullivan v. River Valley Sch. Dist., 197 F.3d 804, 811 (6th Cir. 1999) (citing 42 U.S.C. §12112(d)(4)(B)) (emphasis added). *See also* Denman v. Davey Tree Expert Co., 266 Fed. Appx. 377, 380 (6th Cir. 2007) (citing *Sullivan* and stating, *id.*, that "any examination ordered by the employer must be restricted to discovering whether the employee can continue to fulfill the essential functions of the job . . . a job function is essential if its removal would fundamentally alter the position.").

[33]Yin v. California, 95 F.3d 864, 868 (9th Cir. 1996).

[34]*Id.* at 867.

of the employee's disability, the examination was not a violation of the ADA because it was job-related.[35] The plaintiff's absenteeism was hurting her work and, as a result, the court found that the requirement of a medical examination was sufficiently related to the job.[36]

Further, in *Riechmann v. Cutler-Hammer, Inc.*, the district court distinguished between "job-related" and "business necessity" with respect to fitness for duty examinations.[37] In *Riechmann*, the court found that the employer legitimately required an independent medical examination following the employee's return, but that the employer asked impermissibly broad questions about the employee's lawful use of prescription drugs. The court noted that "[r]equiring employees to disclose all legal, prescription medications used improperly solicits information about employees' disabilities in violation of the ADA."[38] Moreover, the court held that when an employer informs a physician of specific questions to ask

---

[35] *Id.* at 868.

[36] *Id. See also* Porter v. U.S. Alumoweld Co., 125 F.3d 243, 249 (4th Cir. 1997) (holding that an employer's request for a "fitness for duty" examination following employee's surgery and leave was job-related and consistent with business necessity); *Sullivan*, 197 F.3d at 811–12 (holding that an employer's requirement of a mental examination based on employee's bizarre behavior was a permissible fitness for duty examination); Dyrek v. Garvey, 334 F.3d 590, 599 (7th Cir. 2003) (holding that termination was justified based on the employee's refusal to provide medical documentation showing his ability to safely perform the job); Rodriguez v. Loctite Puerto Rico, Inc., 967 F. Supp. 653, 660–62 (D.P.R. 1997) (holding that it was job-related and consistent with business necessity to require an independent medical examination of an employee requesting two months of leave); Miller v. Champaign Cmty. Unit Sch. Dist., 983 F. Supp. 1201, 1206–07 (C.D. Ill. 1997) (holding that requiring a psychiatric evaluation of a school employee displaying erratic behavior was job related and consistent with business necessity); Mickens v. Polk County Sch. Bd., 430 F. Supp. 2d 1265, 1279–80 (M.D. Fla.) (holding that a psychiatric evaluation requirement for a school employee was job related and consistent with business necessity as a matter of law), *aff'd*, No. 05-16579, 2006 U.S. App. LEXIS 23546 (11th Cir. Sept. 14, 2006); McDonald v. Potter, No. 1:06-cv-1, 2007 U.S. Dist. LEXIS 57983 (holding that the employer had a legitimate, nondiscriminatory reason for a fitness for duty examination when the plaintiff had admitted sensitivity to fragrances and had requested for a fragrance ban in the company, "even if the examination might disclose whether the employee is disabled or the extent of any disability" because the health problems significantly affected the employee's performance of essential job functions. *Id.* at *138).

[37] Riechmann v. Cutler-Hammer, Inc., 95 F. Supp. 2d 1171, 1186–87 (D. Kan. 2000).

[38] *Id.* at 1186.

in a medical examination, the employer must bear the responsibility of posing such questions.[39]

d. Standing to Bring Claim for Unlawful Medical Examinations Under the ADA

The Eighth and Tenth Circuits have concluded that an employee does not need to be disabled in order to bring a claim for illegal medical examinations or disability-related inquiries under the ADA.[40] In this respect, the ADA appears to confer privacy rights on applicants and employees, regardless of whether they have a disability covered by the ADA.

2. *Other Inquiries Related to Physical or Mental Condition*

Apart from medical examinations, the ADA also limits an employer's ability to ask applicants or employees about their physical or mental condition. A useful principle is that an employer may ask about the *ability* of an applicant or employee to perform the essential functions of the job, but should avoid inquiring about *disabilities* generally.

a. Examples of Permissible Job-Related Inquiries

Some inquiries are expressly allowed in order to determine an applicant's ability to perform "job-related" functions. First, an employer may "describe or demonstrate the job function and inquire whether or not the applicant can perform that function with or without reasonable accommodation."[41] If the applicant responds that he can perform such function, the employer is then permitted to ask him to describe or demonstrate, with or without reasonable accommodation, how he will perform the function.[42] "Employers may ask about an applicant's ability to perform *both* essential *and* marginal job functions," although an employer cannot refuse

---

[39] *Id.*

[40] 42 U.S.C. §12112(d)(4)(A). *See* Cossette v. Minnesota Power & Light, 188 F.3d 964, 969 (8th Cir. 1999) ("whether or not [the employee] is disabled, the ADA protects her from unauthorized disclosures of medical information by her employer"); Griffin v. Steeltek, Inc., 160 F.3d 591, 595 (10th Cir. 1998) (holding that an employee did not need to be disabled to bring a claim under the ADA for unlawful medical inquiries).

[41] 29 C.F.R. pt. 1630, App., §1630.14(a).

[42] *Id.*

to hire an applicant based on inability to perform marginal job functions.[43]

For example, in *EEOC v. Texas Bus Lines*, the court held that pre-offer inquiries related to "physical defect" were permissible when hiring for a bus driver position.[44] In its application, Texas Bus Lines requested that applicants disclose "'any physical defects such as eyesight, hearing, limb impairment, diabetes, back or heart trouble, high blood pressure, fits, convulsions, fainting, etc.,' all of which are expressly addressed by the DOT regulations."[45] The court held that such "physical defect" inquiry was reasonably related to the job as a bus driver and that the "physical defects" as stated by the DOT were job-related and consistent with business necessity.[46]

b. *Examples of Impermissible Disability-Related Inquiries*

Even if questioning by a potential employer would not equate to a "medical examination" under the ADA, an employer must still be mindful that its questions should not be too closely related to disability. If the questions are too closely related, they will likely violate the ADA. The EEOC takes the position that a question is too closely related to disability if it is "likely to elicit information about a disability."[47] The EEOC, however, notes that "if there are many possible answers to a question and only one of those possible answers would contain disability-related information, that question is not 'disability-related.'"[48]

---

[43] *Id.*

[44] EEOC v. Texas Bus Lines, 923 F. Supp. 965, 981 (S.D. Tex. 1996). *See also* Adeyemi v. District of Columbia, No. 04-1684, 2007 U.S. Dist. LEXIS 24179 (D.D.C. 2007) (holding that it was reasonable for an employer to explore whether and how effectively the hearing-impaired plaintiff would function in various employer offices where no one else used sign language).

[45] *Id.*

[46] *Id.*

[47] EEOC Compliance Manual, ADA Enforcement Guidance: Preemployment Disability-Related Questions and Medical Examinations, No. 915.002 (Oct. 10, 1995), ¶6903, at 5372 (CCH 2006).

[48] *Id.* Note that too broad a question such as "Can you stand?" may not be sufficiently tailored to an applicant's specific ability to perform essential job functions and may be impermissible. EEOC Compliance Manual, No. 915.002 (Oct. 10, 1995) ¶6903, at 5373.

In *Downs v. Massachusetts Bay Transportation Authority*, the district court followed the EEOC's approach, stating that an employer may not ask an applicant about previous work-related injuries or workers' compensation claims.[49] *Downs* involved an employee who, in response to a pre-employment inquiry, falsely denied having ever received workers' compensation benefits or suffered joint pain. The employer discovered the false statements and terminated him. The employee claimed that the inquiry violated the ADA, and therefore, termination based on his false statements was unlawful.[50] Although the court dismissed the claim based on the running of the statute of limitations, it proceeded to explain that the inquiry was impermissible prior to a "real" offer because the inquiry was disability-related.[51]

The types of pre-offer inquiries approved by the EEOC include questions regarding: (1) reasonable accommodation for the hiring process only; (2) ability to meet attendance requirements; (3) certifications or licenses; (4) arrests or convictions; and (5) current illegal drug use.[52]

c. *Inquiries Following Voluntary Disclosure of Disability*

When it has direct knowledge of an applicant's disability, an employer may address the applicant's need for accommodation. This situation is handled similarly to the case of an employee returning from disability leave. For example, when a former employee reapplies for a job, the employer is not required to disregard a known disability that may affect the former employee's ability to perform the job. In *Grenier v. Cyanamid Plastics*, the plaintiff was placed on medical leave owing to psychological problems, and subsequently was terminated after exhausting his available medical leave time.[53] He later reapplied for a position with the same employer, which requested notice from his physician that he was "'prepared to return to work without restrictions or identifying

---

[49]Downs v. Massachusetts Bay Transp. Auth., 13 F. Supp. 2d 130, 138 (D. Mass. 1998).

[50]*Id.* at 137.

[51]*Id.* at 138.

[52]EEOC Compliance Manual, No. 915.002 (Oct. 10, 1995), ¶6903, at 5372–76.

[53]Grenier v. Cyanamid Plastics, Inc., 70 F.3d 667, 669–70 (1st Cir. 1995).

those reasonable accommodations that may be necessary.'"[54] The court held that: (1) the inquiry into Grenier's ability to function effectively in the workplace and get along with his co-workers was not a prohibited inquiry under the ADA; and (2) "the ADA does not preclude an employer from asking an applicant with a known disability who seeks a reasonable accommodation to specify the type of accommodation."[55] The court noted that "[t]he central purpose of the prohibition on pre-offer inquiries generally is to ensure that an applicant's hidden disability remains hidden."[56] Therefore, when the disability is already known, the court found no reason to limit the pre-offer determination of what reasonable accommodation would be necessary.[57]

3. *Drug Testing*

The ADA neither endorses nor prohibits drug testing of applicants or employees. Indeed, the ADA explicitly states that it should not "be construed to encourage, prohibit, or authorize the conducting of drug testing for the illegal use of drugs by job applicants or employees or making employment decisions based on such tests."[58] Irrespective of this neutral policy, an employer still must ensure that its drug testing does not reveal information about *legal* drug use, such as use of prescription drugs. Such information could reveal the disability of an applicant or employee in violation of the ADA.

Although the ADA does not expressly regulate drug testing of applicants or employees, many states do regulate this practice, as discussed below.

a. Inquiries About Current Illegal Drug Use

The ADA explicitly states that "a test to determine the illegal use of drugs shall not be considered a medical examination."[59]

---

[54] *Id.* at 670.

[55] *Id.* at 677.

[56] *Id.*

[57] *See also* Harris v. Harris & Hart, Inc., 206 F.3d 838, 845 (9th Cir. 2000) (holding that an employer's "request for a medical release as a prerequisite to re-hiring plaintiff, a former employee with a known disability, did not run afoul of the ADA").

[58] 42 U.S.C. §12114(d)(2).

[59] 42 U.S.C. §12114(d)(1).

Therefore, the ADA does not restrict testing for *current* use of illegal drugs. An employer must, however, ensure that any testing for illegal drugs is narrowly tailored to only reveal use of *illegal* drugs.

Although the ADA prohibits drug testing relating to legal drug use, a positive test for illegal drugs may allow some leeway for an employer to ask about legal drug use. The EEOC states that following a positive test, the following types of questions are permissible: "What medications have you taken that might have resulted in this positive test result? Are you taking this medication under a lawful prescription?"[60]

b. Inquiries About Past Drug or Alcohol Use

Past illegal drug addiction is considered a disability under the ADA. Consequently, inquiries relating to past drug use are limited in the pre-offer setting. Questions that relate merely to past use, but not addiction, are allowed under the ADA. If, however, the drug-related questions are likely to elicit information regarding addiction, then they are not allowed before an employment offer is made.[61] For example, the EEOC maintains that the following types of questions about drug use are improper because they are too likely to convey information regarding a disability: "How often did you use illegal drugs in the past? Have you ever been treated for drug abuse?"[62]

The EEOC has taken the position that limited inquiries about alcohol consumption are allowable before a conditional offer is given. Such questions, however, cannot be used to elicit information about a disability (i.e., alcoholism). The EEOC, therefore, asserts that an employer should not question an applicant about *how much* alcohol he drinks because such questioning may lead to information regarding alcoholism.[63]

---

[60]EEOC Compliance Manual, No. 915.002 (Oct. 10, 1995), ¶6903, at 5375.
[61]*Id.*
[62]*Id.*
[63]EEOC Compliance Manual, No. 915.002 (Oct. 10, 1995), ¶6903, at 5376.

c. *State Laws Regulating Drug Testing*

Although the ADA does not cover drug testing, many states have adopted laws that regulate drug testing of employees or applicants. States with drug-testing laws that apply to private-sector employers include Alaska, Arizona, Arkansas, Connecticut, Florida, Georgia, Hawaii, Idaho, Iowa, Louisiana, Maine, Maryland, Minnesota, Mississippi, Montana, Nebraska, North Carolina, Rhode Island, Tennessee, Texas, Utah, and Vermont.[64] The requirements and limitations imposed by these state laws vary considerably.

i. *California*

California courts have held that drug testing implicates the privacy rights of employees under the California Constitution and state common-law principles.[65] The California Supreme Court also has indicated that current employees have greater privacy rights against routine or suspicionless drug testing than job applicants.[66] Although *Loder* involved testing of public-sector employees, California courts have confirmed that the same constitutional protections apply to private-sector employees.[67]

Practice Pointer: Although there are few clear-cut rules about employee drug testing under common law or other state privacy rights, there is one key point to keep in mind: the absence of a state drug testing statute does not mean that the state freely

---

[64]*See* ALASKA STAT. §§23.10.600–.699; ARIZ. REV. STAT. ANN. §§23-493.01–.11; ARK. CODE ANN. §11-14-104; CONN. GEN. STAT. ANN. §§31-51(t)–(aa); FLA. STAT. ANN. §440.101; GA. CODE ANN. §§34-9-410 to 34-9-421; HAW. REV. STAT. ANN. §§329-1 to 329-128; IDAHO CODE ANN. §§72-1701 to 72-1717; IOWA CODE ANN. §730.5; LA. REV. STAT. ANN. §§49:1011–1012; ME. REV. STAT. ANN. tit. 26, §§681–690; MD. CODE ANN., HEALTH-GEN. §17-214; MINN. STAT. ANN. §§181.950–.957; MISS. CODE ANN. §§71-7-1 to 71-7-33; MONT. CODE ANN. §§39-2-205 to 39-2-211; NEB. REV. STAT. ANN. §§48-1901 to 48-1910; N.C. GEN. STAT. ANN. §§95-230 to 95-235; R.I. GEN. LAWS §28-6.5-1 to 28-6.5-3; TENN. CODE ANN. §§50.9-107 to 50.9-114; TEX. LAB. CODE ANN. §21.120; UTAH CODE ANN. §§34-38-1 to 34-38-15; VT. STAT. ANN. tit. 21, §§511–520.

[65]*See* Loder v. City of Glendale, 14 Cal. 4th 846, 896 (Cal. 1997) (stating that an employee drug testing program "unquestionably implicates privacy interests protected by the [California] Constitution").

[66]*Id.* at 897–98.

[67]*See, e.g.*, Wilkinson v. Times Mirror Corp., 215 Cal. App. 3d 1034, 1040–44 (1989).

allows drug testing by employers. To the contrary, the restrictions imposed by California courts are more extensive than the express drug testing statutes of many other states. Any drug testing program should be structured to comply with the statutory and judicial standards of each state covered by the program.

ii. Connecticut

Connecticut law requires the employer to inform a job applicant in writing at the time of the application that a drug test will be required.[68] Connecticut law also limits the circumstances in which an employer may require periodic or random drug testing of current employees.[69]

iii. Iowa

Iowa law strikes a middle course by permitting drug testing of current employees, as long as the testing is conducted under a written policy that is given to every employee.[70]

If an employer fails to comply with state drug testing laws, the employer may be prohibited from taking adverse action based on the test results. For example, in *McVey v. National Organization Service*, an employer conducted random drug testing and terminated an employee who tested positive for marijuana use.[71] The employee filed a lawsuit demanding reinstatement, claiming that the employer had failed to provide a written copy of its drug testing policy, as required by state law.[72] The Iowa Supreme Court allowed the employee to proceed with her case, confirming that "a discharge from employment may be based on an employee drug-testing program only if that program is being carried out in compliance with the governing statutory law."[73]

---

[68]CONN. GEN. STAT. ANN. §31-51v.

[69]CONN. GEN. STAT. ANN. §31-51x.

[70]IOWA CODE ANN. §730.5(9)(a)(1).

[71]McVey v. National Org. Serv., Inc., 719 N.W.2d 801, 802 (Iowa 2006).

[72]*Id.*

[73]*Id.* at 803.

iv. Minnesota and Maine

Minnesota and Maine laws provide that an employer cannot ask an applicant to submit to a drug test until after receiving a job offer.[74]

v. Oklahoma

Oklahoma law provides that employers may not require an applicant or employee to undergo drug or alcohol testing unless the employer has first adopted a written, detailed policy setting forth the specifics of the testing program; the employees who are subject to testing; and the circumstances under which testing may be requested or required.[75] The policy must explain the testing methods and collection procedures, the consequences of refusing to undergo testing, and the potential adverse consequences of a positive result.

vi. Vermont

Vermont law goes a step further, by prohibiting random or companywide drug tests of current employees, except when required by federal law.[76]

4. Additional Limitations on Physical or Mental Testing of Applicants

Federal and state laws also restrict certain types of testing procedures based on public policy concerns, such as genetic testing, human immunodeficiency virus/acquired immune deficiency syndrome (HIV/AIDS) testing, and lie detector examinations. Exhibit 6.2 provides examples of these legally restricted inquiries.

---

[74]MINN. STAT. ANN. §181.951(2); ME. REV. STAT. ANN. tit. 26, §684(1)(A).

[75]State Standards for Workplace Drug and Alcohol Testing Act, OKLA. STAT. tit. 40, §§551–65.

[76]VT. STAT. ANN. tit. 21, §513(b).

EXHIBIT 6.2
U.S.: Examples of Other Legally Restricted Inquiries

Drug testing;

Past addiction to illegal drugs;

Alcoholism;

Past work-related injuries or workers' compensation claims;

Genetic testing;

HIV/AIDS testing; and

Lie detector and polygraph examinations.

a. Genetic Information Nondiscrimination Act of 2008

As of November 2009, the federal Genetic Information Nondiscrimination Act of 2008 (GINA)[77] will place strict limitations on genetic testing and collection of "genetic information" by employers. GINA will also impose similar limitations on group health plans and insurers, as described in Chapter 5, Section II.A.1.e.

"Genetic information" is defined as information about: (1) an individual's genetic tests;[78] (2) genetic tests of the individual's family members; and (3) the "manifestation of a disease or disorder" in the individual's family members.[79]

---

[77]Genetic Information Nondiscrimination Act of 2008, H.R. 493, 110th Congress (2008) (GINA).

[78]Under GINA, a "genetic test" includes any analysis of human DNA, RNA, chromosomes, proteins, or metabolites that detects genotypes, mutations, or chromosomal changes. Tests that do not detect abnormalities and those that are directly related to manifested disease or disorder or pathological conditions that could reasonably be detected by a health care professional with appropriate training and expertise are not encompassed within this definition. GINA §§101(7), 102(d)(4)(17), 103(d)(8), 104(3)(C), 201(7).

[79]Under GINA, "family members" include a dependent and "any other individual who is a first-degree, second-degree, third-degree, or fourth-degree relative of such individual or such individual's dependent." GINA, §§101(d)(5)(B), 102(a)(4)(15)(B), 103(d)(6)(B), 104(b)(3)(A), 201(3)(b). The legislative history explains that GINA "applies to spouses and adopted children of an individual because of the potential discrimination an employee...could face because of an employer's or other entities' concern over potential medical or other costs and their effect on insurance rates." H.R. Rep. No. 110-28, pt. 1 (Mar. 5, 2007). Accordingly, GINA appears to prohibit discrimination based on the family medical history of an individual's dependent, even if the individual does not share the same family medical history.

GINA imposes three categories of restrictions on employers: (1) it restricts an employer's acquisition of genetic information; (2) it prohibits employers from discriminating on the basis of genetic information; and (3) and it requires employers to take specific measures to maintain the confidentiality of genetic information.

i. Restrictions on Collecting Genetic Information

GINA generally prohibits an employer from requesting, requiring, or purchasing genetic information related to an employee or his family members,[80] subject to the following limited exceptions (or "safe harbors"):

- *Inadvertent Requests of Genetic Information.*[81] This exception applies when an employer "inadvertently requests or requires family medical history of the employee or family member of the employee." The legislative history explains that this exception was intended to address the "so-called 'water cooler problem,'" in which an employer may unintentionally elicit information about family health or medical history through "casual conversations" in the workplace.[82]
- *Employee Wellness Programs.*[83] This exception is intended to preserve employer-sponsored wellness programs by allowing the employer's receipt of genetic information when:
  - the employer offers health or genetic services, including as part of a wellness program;
  - the individual provides prior, knowing, voluntary, and written authorization;
  - only the individual receiving genetic services and the licensed health care service provider receives individually identified results of such services; and

[80]GINA §202(b).

[81]GINA §§202(b)(1), 203(b)(1), 204(b)(1), 205(b)(1).

[82]H.R. Rep. No. 110-28, pt. 1 (Mar. 5, 2007).

[83]GINA §§202(b)(2), 203(b)(2), 204(b)(2), 205(b)(2).

- the employer receives information about such services only in aggregate terms that do not disclose the identity of specific employees.

- *Requests for Family Medical Leave.*[84] This exception allows an employer to request family medical history to comply with the certification provisions of the Family and Medical Leave Act or similar state family or medical leave laws.
- *Purchase of Commercially and Publicly Available Documents.*[85] This exception applies when an employer purchases documents that are commercially and publicly available, such as newspapers or magazines, which include family medical history. For example, the legislative history indicates that this exception should apply when an employer purchases a local newspaper containing the obituary of an employee's parent who died of breast cancer.[86] This exception does not apply to the purchase of medical databases or court records.[87]
- *Genetic Monitoring of Biological Effects of Workplace Toxins.*[88] This exception allows an employer to conduct genetic monitoring[89] of the biological effects of toxic substances in the workplace, but only if:
  - the employer provides written notice of the genetic monitoring to the employee;
  - the employee provides prior, knowing, voluntary, and written authorization or genetic monitoring is required by law;
  - the employee is informed of the individual genetic monitoring results;

---

[84]GINA §§202(b)(3), 203(b)(3), 204(b)(3), 205(b)(3).

[85]GINA §§202(b)(4), 203(b)(4), 204(b)(4), 205(b)(4).

[86]H.R. Rep. No. 110-28, pt. 1 (Mar. 5, 2007).

[87]GINA §§202(b)(4), 203(b)(4), 204(b)(4), 205(b)(4).

[88]GINA §§202(b)(5), 203(b)(5), 204(b)(5), 205(b)(5).

[89]"Genetic monitoring" refers to "the periodic examination of employees to evaluate acquired modifications to their genetic material, such as chromosomal damage or evidence of increased occurrence of mutations, that may have developed in the course of employment due to exposure to toxic substances in the workplace, in order to identify, evaluate, and respond to the effects of or control adverse environmental exposures in the workplace." GINA §201(5).

- the monitoring is in compliance with federal or state genetic monitoring regulations, such as regulations issued under the Occupational Safety and Health Act, the Federal Mine Safety and Health Act, or the Atomic Energy Act; and
- the employer, excluding any licensed health care professional or board certified genetic counselor involved in the genetic monitoring program, receives the monitoring results only in aggregate terms that do not disclose the identity of specific individuals.

• *Law Enforcement Purposes.*[90] This narrow exception applies when an employer conducts DNA analysis for law enforcement purposes as a forensic laboratory. Such an employer may require its employees to provide genetic information, but only to the extent that this information is used for analysis of DNA identification markers for quality control, to detect sample contamination.

Even if it can establish a lawful basis to collect genetic information, an employer may still be liable for using this information for discriminatory purposes or in violation of GINA's confidentiality requirements, as discussed below.

ii. Protection Against Discrimination Based on Genetic Information

GINA adds "genetic information" as a protected characteristic under Title VII of the Civil Rights Act of 1964, which prohibits discrimination based on race, color, religion, sex, national origin, or other specified characteristics.[91] Consequently, employers are prohibited from discriminating against an applicant or employee based on genetic information.[92] GINA also prohibits an employer from retaliating against an individual for filing a claim of genetic information discrimination.[93]

---

[90]GINA §§202(b)(5), 203(b)(5), 204(b)(5), 205(b)(5).

[91]Civil Rights Act of 1964 §703(a); 42 U.S.C. §2000e-2.

[92]GINA §§202(a)(2), 203(a)(2), 204(a)(2), 205(a)(2).

[93]GINA §207(f).

iii. Confidentiality of Genetic Information

Even if it is allowed to possess genetic information under one of the safe harbors described above, GINA requires the genetic information to be maintained as a confidential medical record under the ADA. See Chapter 5, Section II.A.2.a., for additional information about these confidentiality requirements under the ADA.

GINA further limits the disclosure of genetic information, providing that it can be disclosed only as follows:

- to the individual to whom the information relates at that individual's written request;
- to an occupational or other health researcher if research is in compliance with the regulations and protections of 45 C.F.R. 46, which addresses the protections for human research subjects;
- in response to a court order;[94]
- to government officials investing in compliance with this title;
- to the extent disclosure is made with employee's compliance with Section 103 of the Family and Medical Leave Act or similar state family and medical leave laws; and
- to federal, state, or local public health agency only with regard to the manifestation of a contagious disease in a family member that presents an imminent hazard of death or life-threatening illness and the employee whose family member(s) are the subject of the disclosure is notified.

Practice Pointer. Due to the rising costs of health care coverage, many employers are considering or implementing employee wellness programs, offering such features as blood pressure tests, weight control programs, cholesterol screens, smoking cessation programs, and cancer detection tests. These programs are intended to improve employee health, emphasize preventative care, and

---

[94]Genetic information disclosed pursuant to a court order may include only the genetic information expressly authorized by the order and if the court order was secured without the individual's knowledge, the employer, employment agency, labor organization, or training program receiving the court order must inform the individual of the order and any information disclosed pursuant to the order.

help manage the expense of providing health insurance. Employers offering such programs should look to the ADA, GINA, and state laws for guidance on relevant privacy restrictions:[95]

- *Medical Examinations and Inquiries.* While it limits an employer's ability to request medical examinations of employees, the ADA provides an exemption for voluntary medical examinations, such as voluntary employee wellness programs.[96] According to the EEOC, a "voluntary" wellness program neither requires employee participation nor penalizes those who do not participate.[97] Employers are advised to communicate these principles clearly to employees by developing a written policy and using consent forms that reflect the voluntary nature of the program. Under this exemption, any personal medical information obtained through the examination process must be stored separately and treated as a confidential medical record.[98] A number of states have adopted laws that further restrict medical

---

[95]Employers covered under HIPAA, such as health care providers, will need to evaluate their obligations under HIPAA as well. See Chapter 5 for information on HIPAA compliance issues.

[96]42 U.S.C. §12112(d)(4)(B) ("A covered entity may conduct voluntary medical examinations, including voluntary medical histories, which are part of an employee health program available to employees at that work site.") The EEOC interprets an "employee health plan" to include voluntary wellness programs, which need not be part of a formal health plan. *See* Enforcement Guidance: Disability-Related Inquiries and Medical Examinations of Employees Under the Americans with Disabilities Act (ADA), Question 22.

[97]*Id.*

[98]42 U.S.C. §12112(d)(3)(B)–(C). In general, access to information obtained through an employee wellness program regarding the medical condition or history of any employee must be maintained in confidence, except that: (1) supervisors and managers may be informed regarding necessary restrictions on the work or duties of the employee and necessary accommodations; (2) first aid and safety personnel may be informed, when appropriate, if the disability might require emergency treatment; and (3) government officials investigating compliance with this chapter shall be provided relevant information on request. *Id.* An employer may consider retaining a third-party health care provider to collect and analyze the personal medical informaiton, to limit internal access to such information. As noted below, the employer should ensure its contract with the third party contains appropriate privacy and data security provisions.

examinations and inquiries. For information on employee medical examinations generally, see Section II.A.

- *Genetic Information and Testing.* GINA, which generally prohibits an employer from collecting "genetic information" about employees, also offers a narrow exception for wellness programs. Significantly, GINA defines "genetic information" to include information about the "manifestation of a disease or disorder" in the employee's family members or dependents, as well as genetic test results.[99] As a result, GINA is not limited to genetic testing services, but also may affect employee wellness programs that solicit information about family medical history. GINA permits the collection of genetic information in a wellness program, but does not allow the employer to have access to that information in individually identifiable form. Instead, GINA provides that access to this individual genetic information must be limited to the employee and the licensed health care professional involved in the wellness program; the employer may receive data only in aggregate form.[100] Effectively, this may require the employer to use a third-party vendor to provide employee wellness program services that involve collection of genetic information, rather than providing such services in-house. GINA further requires the employer to obtain the employee's voluntary and written authorization to participate in the employee wellness program.[101] Many states also have passed laws restricting genetic testing by employers. Section II.A.4.b. provides more detailed information about these requirements.
- *Avoiding Discrimination Claims.* Even if it has complied with laws such as the ADA and GINA in collecting health-related information, an employer may be subject to discrimination claims for misusing this information. Employers should take measures to prevent adverse action from being taken against employees based on information obtained through employee wellness programs. Employers

[99]GINA §201(4). See Section II.A.4.a.i. of this chapter.

[100]GINA §202(b)(2)(C), (D).

[101]GINA §202(b)(2)(B).

also may wish to consider using a third party to administer the employee wellness program, to limit its access to legally protected health information that could give rise to a discrimination claim.

- *Effect of State Laws.* State laws also may limit the collection, use, and disclosure of health-related information about employees. For example, California's Confidentiality of Medical Information Act generally prevents health care providers from disclosing individual medical records absent the patient's written authorization.[102] California law also requires California residents to be notified in the event of a security breach affecting computerized data containing their medical information, which further underscores the importance of maintaining adequate data security practices.[103] If the employer uses a third party to provide employee wellness program services, the employer also should ensure that its contract with the third party contains privacy, confidentiality, and data security provisions that are appropriate given the nature of the information being collected.

b. State Laws Restricting Genetic Testing

California, Connecticut, Massachusetts, Minnesota, and Oregon are among the many states that restrict genetic testing of job applicants or employees.[104] GINA does not preempt or limit more protective state and federal employment laws.[105] Thus, employers interested in conducting genetic testing must carefully consider both GINA and any applicable state restrictions.

Practice Pointer: An employer contemplating any type of genetic testing or screening should consult legal counsel concerning the applicable limitations under these laws, as well as laws

[102] CAL. CIV. CODE §56.10(a).

[103] CAL. CIV. CODE §1798.29.

[104] *See* CAL. GOV'T CODE §12940(o); CONN. GEN. STAT. ANN. §46a-60(a)(11); MASS. GEN. LAWS ANN. ch. 151B, §4; MINN. STAT. ANN. §181.974; OR. REV. STAT. ANN. §659A.300(1).

[105] GINA, §209(a)(1).

prohibiting discrimination based on medical condition or genetic characteristics.

c. *HIV/AIDS Testing*

In addition to protections available under the ADA, California and Vermont prohibit employers from asking an applicant or employee to be tested for HIV or AIDS as a condition of employment.[106] Washington law also prohibits employers from discriminating against applicants or employees based on the results of a test for HIV or hepatitis C, unless the absence of these conditions is a bona fide occupational requirement of the job at issue.[107]

New York law prohibits an employer from performing HIV testing without an employee's written and informed consent or from conditioning employment on the test.[108] Such informed consent must be memorialized in a written statement by the individual and is subject to certain other requirements.[109] In addition, a private right of action exists for violations of the statute.[110]

d. *Lie Detector and Polygraph Examinations*

Just as employers may seek psychological examinations of applicants, employers may wish to conduct polygraph or lie detector examinations of employees suspected of misconduct. However, the use of lie detector or polygraph examinations by private-sector employers is strictly limited by federal and state law. Even in circumstances in which a lie detector test is legally permissible, employers are prohibited from taking adverse action based solely on the test results. The notice and procedural requirements imposed by these laws may substantially lessen the perceived value of the lie detector test as well. As explained below, these

---

[106]*See* CAL. HEALTH & SAFETY CODE §§120980, 120990, 121115, 121025; VT. STAT. ANN. tit. 21, §495.

[107]*See* WASH. REV. CODE ANN. §49.60.172.

[108]N.Y. PUB. HEALTH LAW §2781.

[109]N.Y. PUB. HEALTH LAW §2781(2). The requirements include that the consent be signed by the subject and include an explanation of the test, procedure followed, and the confidentiality protections for HIV-related information afforded by the law.

[110]Claimant v. State, 566 N.Y.S.2d 987, 989 (Ct. Cl. 1991) (an allegation that an employer has, without authorization, disclosed any information obtained via such an examination forms the basis for a cause of action against the employer). Doe v. Roe, 599 N.Y.S.2d 350, 352–53 (App. Div. 1993).

restrictions cannot be avoided by seeking the voluntary consent of the applicant or employee to submit to the lie detector test. Such a request may itself violate the laws regulating lie detector and polygraph examinations in the employment context.

i. Employee Polygraph Protection Act

The federal Employee Polygraph Protection Act (EPPA) generally prohibits any employer engaged in or affecting interstate commerce to ask any applicant or employee to submit to a lie detector test.[111] The EPPA covers private-sector employers but excludes governmental employers.[112] The term "lie detector" is broadly defined to include "a polygraph, deceptograph, voice stress analyzer, psychological stress evaluator, or any similar device (whether mechanical or electrical) that is used . . . for the purpose of rendering a diagnostic opinion regarding the honesty or dishonesty of an individual."[113]

The EPPA provides a limited exception allowing private-sector employers to request (but not require) an employee to submit to a polygraph test in connection with an ongoing investigation involving theft, embezzlement, misappropriation, or other economic loss or harm to the employer.[114] Even in these circumstances, an employee can be asked to submit to a polygraph examination only if he had access to the stolen or misused property and the employer has a reasonable suspicion[115] that he was involved in the incident or activity under investigation.[116] The employer also must give the employee a written statement stating "with particularity the specific incident or activity being investigated," identifying the "specific economic loss or injury" to the employer, stating that the employee had access to the property that is the subject of the investigation, and explaining the basis of the employer's reasonable suspicion that the employee was involved in the incident or activ-

---

[111] 29 U.S.C. §2002.

[112] 29 U.S.C. §2006(a).

[113] 29 U.S.C. §2001(3).

[114] 29 U.S.C. §2006(d).

[115] The EPPA regulations explain that the fact that an employee had access or opportunity to commit the offense does not, in itself, qualify as "reasonable suspicion." 29 C.F.R. §801.12(f)(1).

[116] 29 C.F.R. §2006(d)(2)–(3).

ity under investigation.[117] This statement must be signed on behalf of the company and given to the employee prior to the lie detector test.[118] The employee is entitled to refuse to participate in the lie detector test, and the employer cannot take any adverse action against the employee based on this refusal.[119] If the employee does consent to participate in the lie detector test, the EPPA imposes detailed rules about how the testing must be conducted.

The EPPA is not limited to polygraph examinations conducted in person by a polygraph examiner but may include analysis of a recording of an employee's voice. In *Veazey v. Communications & Cable of Chicago*, an employer suspected an employee of leaving a threatening anonymous voice mail message. The employer required the employee to provide a "voice exemplar," in which he would be tape-recorded reading a transcript of the threatening message.[120] When the employee refused to read the message into a tape recorder, the employer terminated his employment.[121] The terminated employee alleged that the employer's demand for a "voice exemplar" violated the EPPA because it could be used to perform a voice stress analysis to assess his honesty. The Seventh Circuit concluded that a tape recorder, when used in conjunction with a voice stress analyzer or similar device, could fall within the definition of "lie detector" under the EPPA.[122] This case illustrates that an employer cannot avoid the restrictions of the EPPA by performing the analysis on a recording of the employee's voice, rather than during an in-person examination.

ii. State Restrictions on Lie Detector and Polygraph Tests

Many states also prohibit employers from asking an applicant or employee to submit to a lie detector or polygraph test. These states include Alaska, California, Connecticut, Delaware, Hawaii,

---

[117]29 C.F.R. §2006(d)(4); 29 C.F.R. §801.12.

[118]The employer is also required to keep a copy of the signed written statement for three years. 29 U.S.C. §2006(d)(4)(C).

[119]29 U.S.C. §2007(a)(1); 29 C.F.R. §801.20.

[120]Veazey v. Communications & Cable of Chi., Inc., 194 F.3d 850, 853 (7th Cir. 1999).

[121]*Id.*

[122]*Id.* at 859.

Idaho, Illinois, Iowa, Maine, Maryland, Massachusetts, Michigan, Minnesota, Montana, Nebraska, Nevada, New Jersey, New York, Oregon, Pennsylvania, Rhode Island, Texas, Vermont, Virginia, Washington, West Virginia, and Wisconsin, as well as the District of Columbia.[123]

Practice Pointer. Certain states prohibit employers from asking an applicant or employee to submit to a lie detector test in any circumstances. Therefore, an employer should check the applicable laws before making such a request. Even if the lie detector test is legally permissible, the employer should evaluate the practical effect of any notice requirements. Statutes such as the EPAA effectively prevent "fishing expeditions" by employers, and require employers to provide an official written statement of their reasons for suspecting the individual being asked to submit to the test. If this written statement provides insufficient detail, the employee may allege that the employer lacked "reasonable suspicion" to request the examination, or improperly withheld information that was required to be disclosed in the notice. If the written statement overstates or exaggerates the grounds for the employer's "reasonable suspicion," the employee may allege that the employer made intentional misrepresentations to induce the employee to submit to the request for a lie detector test. In either case, the employee may seek to use the employer's official written statement as evidence in legal proceedings against the employer, such as a claim of wrongful termination. For all of these reasons, an employer should exercise caution in preparing the written statement required by EPPA.

---

[123]*See* ALASKA STAT. §23.10.037; CAL. LAB. CODE §432.2; CONN. GEN. STAT. ANN. §31-51g; DEL. CODE ANN. tit. 19, §704; D.C. CODE ANN. §32-902; HAW. REV. STAT. ANN. §378-26.5; IDAHO CODE ANN. §44-903; 225 ILL. COMP. STAT. ANN. 430/14.1; IOWA CODE ANN. §730.4(2); ME. REV. STAT. ANN. tit. 32, §7166; MD. CODE ANN., LAB. & EMPL. §3-702(c); MASS. GEN. LAWS ANN. ch. 149, §19B; MICH. COMP. LAWS ANN. §37.202; MINN. STAT. ANN. §181.75; MONT. CODE ANN. §39-2-304; NEB. REV. STAT. ANN. §81-1932; NEV. REV. STAT. ANN. §613.480; N.J. STAT. ANN. §2C:40A-1; N.Y. LAB. LAW §735; OR. REV. STAT. ANN. §659.840(1); 18 PA. CONS. STAT. ANN. §7321; R.I. GEN. LAWS §28-6.1-1; TEX. GOV'T CODE ANN. §§441.0074–.00741; VT. STAT. ANN. tit. 21, §494a; VA. CODE §40.1-51.4:3; WASH. REV. CODE ANN. §49.44.120; W. VA. CODE §21-5-5b; WIS. STAT. ANN. §111.31(4). (All citations to statutes and codes are cited to LexisNexis online at www.lexis.com unless otherwise indicated.)

B. Brazil

1. Medical Examinations

Brazilian employers may request medical examinations as a condition of employment. In fact, certain pre-employment screening procedures are required by statute. Employees of Brazil must maintain a Program of Health Control and Occupational Health (PCMSO), which aims to identify and prevent work-related harm to employee health.[124] Under PCMSO, employees must submit to very general health examinations both before and during their employment to ascertain their fitness to perform required job functions.

Consent of the applicant is necessary to conduct pre-employment medical screenings. An offer letter that states that medical exams are a necessary condition of employment, signed by the employee, may be interpreted as the applicant's consent to be examined. A candidate may be denied employment based on his refusal to undergo pre-employment medical testing.

Denial of employment based on medical exam results would be justified only if the results revealed that a candidate's working capacity, safety, or reliability would be materially impaired by his medical condition. Otherwise, the employer may face liability for discrimination.

An employer's failure to preserve the confidentiality of employee medical records may be deemed to violate the individual right of intimacy guaranteed by the Brazilian Constitution.[125]

2. Drug Testing

An employer's failure to preserve the confidentiality of employee drug test results may violate the individual right of intimacy guaranteed by the Brazilian Constitution.[126]

---

[124]Labor Standards Act, Art. 39, ¶(1).

[125]Brazilian Federal Constitution, Article 5, subsection X.

[126]*Id.*

C. Canada

1. Medical Examinations

As a general matter, medical exams cannot be a prerequisite for employment in Canada.

2. Drug Testing

Canadian employers may condition employment on the satisfactory completion of a drug test only in limited circumstances involving safety-sensitive positions or interstate truck-driving work. Outside of these exceptions, employment may not be denied based on an applicant's refusal to submit to a drug test.

D. Mexico

1. Medical Examinations

Under Mexican law, employers may condition employment upon the satisfactory completion of a medical examination. However, such a request must precede any offer of employment. A pre-employment medical exam requires the consent of the applicant. Any proof of consent must contain specific language indicating that the candidate agrees to submit to medical testing. A candidate's refusal to consent to a medical examination provides grounds to deny employment. The results of employee medical examinations must be treated as strictly confidential and retained by the employer for a period of at least five years.

2. Drug Testing

Employment offers may be made contingent upon negative drug test results. As with medical examinations, any request for a drug screen must be made prior to extending an offer of employment. An employer may elect not to hire a candidate if he refuses to consent to a drug test. Records of employee drug screens are highly confidential and must be retained by the employer for at least five years.

III. EUROPE

A. Belgium

1. Medical Examinations

Belgian law prescribes pre-employment medical examinations where an employee's duties would involve high-risk activities, the performance of safety functions, functions requiring high vigilance, or direct contact with food. Legal authorities differ as to whether employers are barred from requiring medical examinations for other categories of employees. Examinations detecting genetic conditions or HIV/AIDS, however, are strictly prohibited in nearly all cases. Employers must send a confidential notice via registered mail to any applicant for whom testing is sought at least ten days prior to the scheduled examination. The letter must detail all examinations and health information sought, as well as explain the employer's reason for requesting the examinations.

Employment-related medical examinations in Belgium are conducted by a prevention advisor, a physician specializing in industrial medicine. After the examination, the prevention advisor confirms to the employer whether, based on the results, the candidate is suited for the position in question. The examination results of candidates who are not hired must be destroyed within a reasonable period of time. Employers may refuse to hire an applicant who will not consent to a statutory-required medical examination.

2. Drug Testing

In the four categories of safety-related employment listed above, pre-employment drug tests may be conducted at the recommendation of the prevention advisor. For other categories of employees, drug tests are permissible insofar as the health and safety of affected parties require them. As with medical examinations, an employee must receive a confidential notice via registered mail at least ten days prior to a scheduled drug test. Based on the exam results, the prevention advisor confirms to the employer whether the applicant is suited for employment. If a candidate is not hired, the employer must destroy his drug test results within a reasonable period time. When a prevention advisor finds drug testing to be necessary, an employee who refuses to submit to a drug screen may be denied employment.

B. France

French law rarely allows genetic testing for purposes other than medical or scientific research or for identification purposes in judiciary cases.[127] The French Criminal Code article 226-25[128] provides for an offense of unlawful genetic testing punishable by one year's imprisonment and a 15,000€ fine for a first-time offender or a 75,000€ fine if the offense is committed by a company.[129]

The French Labor Code[130] also more specifically prohibits taking into account genetic markers to recruit, dismiss, or take any decision concerning an employee. This offense is punishable by three years' imprisonment and a 45,000€ fine for a first-time offender or a 225,000€ if the offense is committed by a company.[131]

The French Data Protection Act and further guidance by the French Data Protection Authority (CNIL) have permitted, in specific and limited cases, the collection of biometric data. The French Data Protection Act allows the collection of biometric data only with express consent from the individual and prior authorization granted by the CNIL.[132] The use of such biometric information is strictly limited and the CNIL has been extremely vigilant in limiting the scope of the collection of biometric data.

The CNIL distinguishes between two kinds of biometrics: "trace-leaving biometrics" (e.g., fingerprint) "trace-free biometrics" (e.g., hand geometry, hand veins, voice). The CNIL considers that trace-free biometrical data can be stored in a centralized

---

[127] French Civil Code (Code Civil) Arts. 16-10 & 16-11.

[128] Article 226-25 of French Criminal Code.

[129] Article 131-8 of French Criminal Code.

[130] Article L.122-45 of French Labor Code (new article L. 1132-1).

[131] Articles 225-1, 225-2 & 225-4 of French Criminal Code.

[132] Art. 25 §I.8.

database because there are no particular risks with respect to fundamental rights and freedoms.[133]

Conversely, the centralization of trace-leaving biometrical data could potentially be used for other means than the original collection purpose and cannot protect employees against such misuse. In addition, employees have no control over this process and database. According to the CNIL, only specific security requirements could justify storing personal data in a database. This is why the CNIL denied a hospital the right to control the employees' working time by fingerprint recognition.[134]

However, the CNIL allows the storing of trace-leaving biometrical data on personal chips carried by the employees themselves.[135] In a previous decision, the CNIL allowed employers to collect fingerprints mainly in order to control access on the condition that personal data were uniquely stored on a personal device, such as a swipe card, and not on a centralized database.[136]

In addition, employers will need to put into place specific data storage systems for their employees' biometric data, ensuring privacy and security of the data.

Employers have to seek the CNIL's authorization to use biometric data. There are two different declarations—normal or simplified—depending on the kind of biometrics used and the purpose pursued. Companies also will have to show the CNIL that the system complies with these principles and that no other use of the data, other than for the original purpose of the collection, is possible.

In any case, any biometrical process must be appropriate, proportionate, and justified in comparison with the original purpose of the collection.[137]

---

[133]CNIL decision n°2007-248 of September 13, 2007 (concerning voice), and CNIL decisions n°2007-335 to n°2007-339 of November 8, 2007 (concerning hand veins).

[134]CNIL decisions n°04-017 and n°04-018 on April 8, 2004.

[135]CNIL decision n°2005-01 of January 13, 2005.

[136]*Id.*

[137]Tribunal de Grande Instance of Paris decision on April 19, 2005, n° 05-382, Comité d'entreprise d'Effia Services et a. c/ Sté Effia Services.

Moreover, the CNIL recommends the use of swipe cards only to control authorizations and not to check employees' entries and exits.

French law prohibits the collection of personal health information by an employer when the specific job does not justify the collection of such data.[138] Further, according to Article L.120-2 of French Labor Code, systematic and general screening of alcohol or drugs by employers is prohibited because it amounts to a violation of rights and individual freedoms.

Thus the issue of medical testing and drug or alcohol screening is two-fold with respect to both the protection of personal data and the preservation of rights and individual freedoms.

An employer therefore is prohibited from asking an applicant to be tested for HIV or AIDS unless the job justifies such testing (e.g., if a job were to require an employee to be entirely fit for a mission in the army). In the same way, an internal rule can provide for drug or alcohol screening only if this rule is neither general nor systematic. Indeed, the French Supreme Court has considered that internal rules concerning alcohol screening are lawful only if they allow the employee to contest the finding and if the employee's intoxication could endanger persons or property, given the nature of this employee's work.[139] Employees must be informed about drug or alcohol screening before it happens.

C. Germany

Drug and genetic testing will result in the collection of medical information that is considered "sensitive data." Under the Federal Data Protection Act[140] sensitive data may be collected only with the individual's specific written consent, and the individual must be notified of the information obtained, the purposes for which the information is used, and all possible recipients.[141] In addition, if the applicant or employee refuses to consent to a drug

---

[138]CNIL decision 02-017 of 21 March 2002 regarding the collection of employee's personal information.

[139]Cour de Cassation, Chambre Sociale, May 22, 2002, n°99-45.878; Cour de Cassation, Chambre Sociale, February 24, 2004, n°01-47.000.

[140]Bundesdatenschutzgesetz (BDSG), as amended on May 18, 2001.

[141]Federal Data Protection Act (*Bundesdatenschutzgesetz*).

or genetic test, there must be no negative consequences resulting from his failure to consent. Also, upon request from the individual, the results of the test must be deleted.

In relation to drug testing, case law and commentary permit drug testing where a potential addiction could have a severe impact on the prospective or actual employees' ability to perform professional duties (e.g., in case of a severe alcohol addiction).[142] However, explicit consent is required, and applicants and employees are not under an obligation to accept drug testing. In this respect, the Supreme Labor Court has expressly stated, in their ruling on the complaint of a security guard who refused testing,[143] that employees may refuse routine drug testing.

As regards HIV or AIDS testing, employers are generally prohibited from carrying out such tests unless a positive result would be directly relevant for the employment relationship. Guidance suggests that AIDS tests are permissible and may be used for making employment decisions if it affects the applicant's ability to perform his duties, or if there is a general risk of infecting co-workers, customers, or patients (e.g., for personnel at food manufacturers or staff in the health sector such as doctors or nurses).[144]

There is no statute specifically governing genetic tests yet. Commentary suggests that genetic tests generally do infringe privacy rights of applicants and employees.[145] Data protection authorities have issued guidance that prohibits genetic tests even with prior approval from the candidate. The logic behind this is that applicants and employees cannot freely refuse such a test because they may not be offered or retained in the job if they did. Therefore, such consent would be invalid.[146] The German government, which has been working on this issue for years without much success, has now just recently published a paper outlining the basic

---

[142]BAG, ZTR 2000, 132; Gola/Wronka, Handbuch zum Arbeitnehmerschutz, Rdn. 255, 256.

[143]BAG, DB 1999, 2369.

[144]Richardi NZA 1988, 75.

[145]Gola/Wronka, Handbuch zum Arbeitnehmerschutz, Rdn. 245.

[146]13 Tätigkeitsbericht des Landesbeauftragten für den Datenschutz Rheinland-Pfalz; LT-Drs. 12/800, Berliner Datenschutzbeauftragter, Jahresbericht 1989, S. 10; Entschliessung der Konferenz der datenschutzbeauftragten des Bundes und der Länder vom 26.10.2001, DuD 200, S. 150.

elements of a Genetic Testing Act that will contain serious restrictions on the possibilities of genetic testing in order to protect individuals' rights. Generally, individuals shall be able to freely decide whether and how their genetic health information is collected and used, mainly to avoid any discrimination based on genetic issues. Employers shall be allowed to demand genetic tests only in strictly drafted exceptional cases, for example, to assess physical ability to perform the work or if health issues may constitute physical dangers to others. When the Genetic Test Act will become statutory reality is, however, still unclear.

D. Italy

1. Medical Examinations

Generally, it is unlawful for employers to make satisfactory completion of a medical examination a condition of employment in Italy, except for general assessments of a candidate's fitness for a particular job, regulated and performed by the National Health Service. Employers must request these assessments before an employment offer is made. A candidate must provide separate consent, including a handwritten signature, to undergo pre-employment medical testing. An employer may decline to hire a candidate who refuses to submit to a National Health Service exam when one is required. Access to records of employee medical examinations must be limited to interested parties.[147] There is no legal requirement to retain these records.

2. Drug Testing

Relevant legislation restricts pre-employment drug screening to positions for which drug use would pose some risk to the security, safety, and health of third parties. Drug testing requests must be extended before an employment offer is made and require a separate consent, including the handwritten signature of the appli-

[147]In Italy, sensitive information such as employee health data is subject to the Authorisation no. 1/2005 Concerning Processing of Sensitive Data in the Employment Context (Autorizzazione n. 1/2005 al trattamento dei dati sensibili nei rapporti di lavoro – 21 dicembre 2005).

cant. An employer may decline to hire a candidate who refuses to submit to drug screening if the nature of the vacant position warrants a drug test. Access to records of employee drug screens must be limited to interested parties. There is no legal requirement to retain these records.

E. United Kingdom

Drug and genetic testing will involve the collection of medical information that is considered "sensitive data." Sensitive data are afforded particular protection under the Data Protection Act 1998 (DPA).[148] The Information Commissioner (the United Kingdom's data protection authority) has published two documents that give employers helpful guidance on how to comply with the DPA when conducting background checks: the Employment Practices Code (Code) and the Employment Practices Code Supplementary Guidance (Supplementary Guidance), including drug and genetic testing.

The Code advises employers undertaking medical testing generally to be satisfied that the testing is a necessary and justified measure to determine whether the (prospective) employee is fit or likely to remain fit to carry out the job in question, to meet any legal requirements for testing, or to determine the terms on which a (prospective) employee is eligible to join a pension or insurance scheme.

The Supplementary Guidance notes that medical examination and testing are intrusive and should be used only to obtain information when necessary. Employers should not subject all applicants for a job or even all those short-listed to examination or testing. Ideally only when there is an intention to appoint, subject to satisfactory examination or test results, should such examination or testing be undertaken. It is, however, recognized that practical considerations may dictate that medical examination or testing are undertaken in parallel with other pre-employment checks.

To ensure that employers are in compliance with the DPA when undertaking any medical testing, the Code advises them to:

---

[148] Data Protection Act 1998 c29.

- Record the business purpose for which examination or testing is to be introduced and the sensitive data condition that can be satisfied;
- Consider less intrusive ways of meeting the objectives, for example, using a health questionnaire as an alternative to a medical examination or as a means to select those required to undergo a full examination; and
- Make it clear early on in the recruitment process that individuals may be subjected to medical examination or testing once there is a likelihood that they will be appointed.

Regarding drug testing, the Code is clear that very few employers will be justified in testing to detect illegal use on safety grounds. Testing to detect illegal use may, in exceptional cases, be justified where illegal use would:

- Breach the (prospective) employee's contract of employment, conditions of employment, or disciplinary rules; or
- Cause serious damage to the employer's business (e.g., by substantially undermining public confidence in the integrity of a law enforcement agency).

If an employer does undertake drug testing, it should:

- Use the least intrusive form of testing practicable to deliver the benefits to the business that the testing is intended to bring;
- Tell (prospective) employees what drugs they are being tested for;
- Base any testing on reliable scientific evidence of the effect of particular substances on employees;
- Limit testing to those substances and the extent of exposure that will have a significant bearing on the purpose(s) for which the testing is conducted;
- Make sure information gathered through testing is designed to ensure safety at work rather than reveal the illegal use of substances in a (prospective) employee's private life;

- Ensure that (prospective) employees are fully aware that drug testing is taking place, and of the possible consequences of being tested;
- Ensure that information is obtained only through drug testing that is of sufficient technical quality to support any decisions or opinions that are derived from it, subject to rigorous integrity and quality control procedures and conducted under the direction of, and positive test results interpreted by, a person who is suitably qualified and competent in the field of drug testing;
- Ensure that (prospective) employees have access to a duplicate of any sample taken to enable them to have it independently analyzed as a check on the accuracy of the employer's results; and
- Not assume that the tests are infallible and be prepared to deal properly with disputes arising from their use.

The Supplementary Guidance notes that genetic testing has the potential to provide employers with information predictive of the likely future general health of (prospective) employees or with information about their genetic susceptibility to occupational diseases. Genetic testing is, though, still under development and in most cases has an uncertain predictive value. It is rarely, if ever, used in the employment context. The Human Genetics Commission advises that employers should not demand that an individual take a genetic test as a condition of employment. A genetic test should therefore be introduced only after very careful consideration, if at all.[149] At the present time, very few genetic tests are available that give information to either an employer or a (prospective) employee that could validly be used in the context of decisions concerning employment. This situation may change in the future, but an employer will still have to demonstrate a genetic test's relevance to health protection of (prospective) employees, reliability and reproducibility, and level of predictive value.

---

[149] Human Genetics Comm'n Info. Sheet on Genetics and Employment.

In such a sensitive area, it is obviously extremely important that procedures for genetic testing are as reliable as possible, as provision of incorrect information to an employer or a (prospective) employee could have far-reaching consequences. All stages of a scientifically satisfactory testing procedure should have built-in negative and positive controls to ensure the reliability of the test result. Good laboratory practice should be observed at all times, including detailed documentation of procedures and results. Even when testing procedures are optimized, false negatives and false positives will emerge and validation procedures for the tests may be required.

The Code recommends employers not to insist that a (prospective) employee disclose the results of a previous genetic test. Genetic testing should be used only to obtain information where it is clear that a (prospective) employee with a particular, detectable genetic condition is likely to pose a serious safety risk to others or where it is known that a specific working environment or practice might pose specific risks to (prospective) employees with particular genetic variations.

Practice Pointer: An employer contemplating any type of genetic testing or screening should consult legal counsel concerning the applicable limitations under these laws, as well as laws prohibiting discrimination based on medical condition or genetic characteristics.

IV. ASIA

A. China

In China, it is a standard condition of employment that employees undergo an annual health examination, paid for by the employer, and to have the employee return those results to the employer.

Although an employer can require an employee to undergo an annual health examination as a condition of employment, an employer cannot independently obtain an employee's health information. The *Law on Practicing Doctors*[150] requires that doctors

[150] Law on Practicing Doctors of the People's Republic of China (1998).

not reveal to third parties health information obtained when treating a patient. Doctors who violate the law face criminal penalties. The government also has promulgated regulations directing that personal information of patients with HIV/AIDS be kept secret and that the legal rights and interests of those people and their relatives should not be infringed. All units and individuals in charge of diagnosis, treatment, and management work are instructed not to publish any personal information about HIV/AIDS patients.[151]

B. Hong Kong

1. Medical Examinations

The collection and use in Hong Kong of personal data relating to employee health (Health Data) is governed by the Personal Data (Privacy) Ordinance (PDPO).[152] The Hong Kong Privacy Commissioner has issued a Code of Practice on Human Resource Management (the HR Code), which seeks to provide more detailed guidance to complement the high-level data privacy principles set out in the PDPO.

The PDPO and the HR Code restrict the circumstances in which medical examinations can be required and the scope of the data that can be collected by the employer.

In relation to employment candidates, a prospective employer may require a pre-employment medical examination if:

- The examination directly relates to the inherent requirements of the job; and
- The employment is conditional upon the fulfillment of the medical examination.[153]

The employer should seek only the minimum information about the candidate's health condition that supports the medical practioner's opinion that he is fit for employment. Details of the candidate's medical history and treatment might be relevant in

---

[151] Regulation on the Prevention and Treatment of HIV/AIDS (2006).
[152] Laws of Hong Kong, Cap. 486.
[153] HR Code, §2.9.1.

conducting the medical check but these details should generally not be collected by the employer.

In relation to existing employees, as with the collection of any health data, medical examinations must be for a purpose that is either:[154]

- Directly related to an assessment of the suitability of the employee's continuance in employment (e.g., where the nature of a post requires a certain level of health); or
- Directly related to the employer's administration of medical or other benefits or compensation provided to the employee.

The health data collected from the medical examination must be limited to what is required for the purpose and must not be excessive.[155]

Restrictions upon the collection, use, and management of health data are discussed in more detail in Chapter 5.

2. *Drug and Genetic Testing*

Hong Kong has not implemented any legislation or codes that specifically address drug or genetic testing of employees or potential employees.

Data relating to such testing will constitute personal data and as such the collection and use of the same will be subject to the PDPO and the HR Code in the same way as any other form of medical examination (see above).

Restrictions upon the collection, use, and management of Health Data are discussed in more detail in Chapter 5.

C. Japan

1. *Health Examinations*

Under the Japanese Occupational Health and Safety Law (Occupational Safety Law), employers in Japan are required to

---

[154] HR Code, §3.2.4.
[155] HR Code, §3.2.1.

ensure that their employees are provided with health examinations conducted by doctors and dentists, to record the results of such health examinations, and to inquire with the doctors and dentists as to the necessary measures to maintain the health of the workers.[156] There are other obligations to promote the health of workers that are codified in the ministry guidelines and ministry orders issued under the Occupational Safety Law, such as the Guidelines for the Maintenance and Promotion of Mental Health of Workers (Mental Health Guidelines) and the General Strategies to Prevent Health Issues Caused by Overworking.

Under the Occupational Safety Law and the regulations promulgated thereunder, employers are required to provide employees with medical examination at the inception of employment.[157] If an employee can provide the employer with medical examination reports less than three months old, the employee may be exempted from certain or all of the examination requirements.[158] Also, employers are required to provide employees with an annual medical examination in order to maintain employees' health.[159] The regulations enumerate the types of examinations required. The results of such examinations are given to both the employees and the employers. Employers are obligated to keep the medical examination reports for five years.[160]

The Ministry of Health, Labour and Welfare's (MHLW) Matters to Consider when Handling Health Information in Employment Management (the Health Information Guidelines) issued pursuant to the Personal Information Protection Law (PIPL) provides that when it is necessary to collect health information from medical institutions or health insurance associations and the like (such as the results of the health examinations explained above), it is desirable for businesses to obtain the consent of the worker after

---

[156] Occupational Safety Law, Art. 66.

[157] *Id.*; Occupational Health and Safety Regulations, Art. 43.

[158] *Id.*

[159] Occupational Safety Law, Art. 66; Occupational Health and Safety Regulations, Art. 44.

[160] Occupational Safety Law, Art. 66; Occupational Health and Safety Regulations, Art. 51.

providing notice regarding the purpose of collection, and if necessary, to obtain such information from the worker directly.[161]

Employers also should heed the MHLW's Action Guide regarding to the Protection of Personal Information of Workers (Action Guide), which does not have the force of law, but is generally regarded by businesses as agency rules that should be followed. The Action Guide states that health information may be collected if it is pursuant to law, if there are confidentiality obligations imposed on workers handling health information, and if pursuant to achieving one of the following purposes: (1) to satisfy the necessity for a certain type of work (such as to confirm the vision of a driver at a transportation company); (2) to implement measures for occupational health and safety or protection of mothers (measures taken pursuant to law); or (3) when it is clear that collecting the health information will be for the benefit of the worker, and it is recognized that there is a justifiable reason for the collection of such health information (e.g., if a worker requests to take a leave of absence or change in position due to health reasons, and the business requests a medical certificate).

2. *Generally Prohibited Tests*

HIV testing and genetic testing are prohibited under the Action Guide.[162] In terms of HIV testing, the Guidelines Regarding AIDS Issues in the Workplace[163] also prohibit such testing. The Health Information Guidelines also provide that employers should not obtain information regarding (1) infectious diseases that are unlikely to infect others in the office, such as HIV and hepatitis B; or (2) genetic information, such as abnormal color sensation, unless there is a particular need in business operations.[164]

In terms of drug and alcohol testing, the general rule clarified in the Action Guide is that unless there is a special need in connection with a job (if there is a rational need to conduct such tests where the job has a direct impact on the safety of other people),

---

[161] Health Information Guidelines, §3.1.

[162] Action Guide, Art. 2.6(1).

[163] Labor Standards Agency Issuance No. 75; Employment Security Office Issuance No. 97 (February 20, 1995).

[164] Health Information Guidelines, §3.4 (4).

and clear consent has been obtained from the worker, such testing must not be conducted.[165]

Practice Pointer. Japanese law obligates employers to conduct frequent medical examinations of its workers, but prohibits tests regarding certain protected health conditions likely to lead to unfair discrimination, such as HIV, hepatitis B, and genetic testing.

D. Korea

1. Medical Examinations

Under Korean law, an employer may condition job offers upon the satisfactory completion of a medical examination. However, an employer cannot require an applicant to undergo a pre-hire medical examination that would reveal whether the individual has a disability. Such examinations may take place only after the candidate has been hired, although the employer may request one either before or after an offer is extended. The candidate must provide consent to undergo the medical examination, such as by signing an offer letter that identifies the examination as a condition of employment. Under the Labor Standards Act, an employer must retain medical examination records for a minimum of three years.

2. Drug Testing

Korean employers may require satisfactory completion of a drug test as a condition of employment. Such a request may be extended before or after a job offer is made. An applicant must consent to testing; an offer letter signed by the applicant stating that a drug test is a condition of hire would satisfy the consent requirement. The Labor Standards Act requires that employers keep drug test results for at least three years.

---

[165] Action Guide, Art. 2.6(3).

CHAPTER 7

PERSONNEL RECORDS

I. Overview ... 468
II. Americas ... 468
A. United States ... 468
1. Employee Rights to Personnel Records ... 468
a. Definition of "Personnel Records" ... 469
2. Occupational Health and Safety Records ... 471
3. Employee's Addition of Explanatory Statement ... 472
4 Laws Requiring Employee's Consent for Disclosure to Third Parties ... 472
5. Laws Requiring Notice to Employee of Subpoena for Personnel Records ... 473
6. Potential Consequences of Improper Disclosure of Employee Information ... 474
7. Restrictions on Use and Printing of Social Security Numbers ... 474
8. Security Breach Notification Issues Related to Personnel Data ... 474
9. Confidentiality of Medical Information ... 475
10. Defamation and Other Legal Claims ... 475
III. Europe ... 478
A. European Union ... 478
B. France ... 480
1. Subject Access Requests by Individual Employees ... 480
2. Applicable Fee ... 481
3. Denial of Subject Access Requests ... 481
C. Germany ... 482
1. Subject Access Requests by Individual Employees ... 482
2. Applicable Fee ... 483
3. Denial of Subject Access Requests ... 483
D. United Kingdom ... 483

1. Subject Access Requests by Individual Employees 483
2. Applicable Fee 485
3. Denial of Subject Access Requests 486
IV. Asia 489
A. China 489
B. Hong Kong 489
1. Access Requests 490
2. Relevant Process Exemption 491
3. Personal References Exemption 492
4. General Exemptions 492
5. Costs and Fees 493
C. Japan 493
1. Access Requests 494
2. Requests for Correction 495
3. Requests to Cease Use 496
4. Disclosure of Personal Records to Third Parties 497

I. OVERVIEW

Personnel records are subject to very different requirements from jurisdiction to jurisdiction. While the European Union (EU) and Japan give employees broad access rights to their personnel records, and the U.S. and Hong Kong provide limited access rights, China currently provides no access rights. Certain countries, particularly Japan, also strictly limit the employer's ability to disclose personnel records to affiliates or third parties. This chapter describes many of the key obligations and considerations when handling personnel records of employees in the U.S., EU (especially France, Germany, and the United Kingdom (UK), Hong Kong, Japan, and China.

II. AMERICAS

A. United States

1. Employee Rights to Personnel Records

Many states entitle an employee to review his personnel records upon reasonable request. These states include Alaska,

California, Connecticut, Delaware, Illinois, Iowa, Maine, Massachusetts, Michigan, Minnesota, Nevada, New Hampshire, Oregon, Pennsylvania, Rhode Island, Washington, and Wisconsin.[1] Some of these states also allow the employee to obtain a copy of his personnel records.[2] These statutes generally cover only current employees, although some expressly cover former employees as well.[3] Additionally, public-sector employees may be subject to different personnel file access rights than employees covered by the general laws discussed here.

Not all states give employees the right to review their personnel records, however. In New York, employees generally do not have the right to access or inspect their personnel files. Public employees, however, may access their personnel files under New York's Personal Privacy Protection Law and the Freedom of Information Law (FOIL).[4] Similarly, public-sector employees of other states also may be subject to different personnel file access rights than those in the general laws.

a. *Definition of "Personnel Records"*

There is no uniform definition of "personnel records" under these laws. Some states limit the employee's access right to records that have been used or may be used to make employment-related decisions. For example, Connecticut describes "personnel

---

[1] *See, e.g.*, ALASKA STAT. §23.10.430; CAL. LAB. CODE §1198.5; CONN. GEN. STAT. ANN. §31-128b; DEL. CODE ANN. tit. 19, §732; 820 ILL. COMP. STAT. ANN. 40/2; IOWA CODE ANN. 91B.1; ME. REV. STAT. ANN. tit. 26, §631; MASS. GEN. LAWS ANN. ch. 149, §52C; MICH. COMP. LAWS §423.503; MINN. STAT. ANN. §181.961; NEV. REV. STAT. ANN. §613.075(1)(a); N.H. REV. STAT. ANN. §275:56(I); OR. REV. STAT. §652.750; 43 PA. CONS. STAT. ANN. §1322; R.I. GEN. LAWS §28-6.4-1; WASH. REV. CODE ANN. §49.12.250; WIS. STAT. ANN. §103.13(2).

[2] *See, e.g.*, ALASKA STAT. §23.10.430; CONN. GEN. STAT. ANN. §31-128g; 820 ILL. COMP. STAT. ANN. 40/3; IOWA CODE ANN. §91B.1; ME. REV. STAT. ANN. tit. 26, §631; MASS. GEN. LAWS ANN. ch. 149, §52C; MICH. COMP. LAWS §423.504; MINN. STAT. ANN. §181.961, subd. (2)(b); NEV. REV. STAT. ANN. §613.075(1)(b); N.H. REV. STAT. ANN. §275:56(I). In comparison, California law entitles an applicant or employee to receive only copies of documents that he or she has signed. CAL. LAB. CODE §432.

[3] *See, e.g.*, ALASKA STAT. §23.10.430; CONN. GEN. STAT. ANN. §31-128a; ME. REV. STAT. ANN. tit. 26, §631; MASS. GEN. LAWS ANN. ch. 149, §52C; MICH. COMP. LAWS §423.501. All citations herein for statutes and codes are to LexisNexis, available online at www.lexis.com unless otherwise indicated.

[4] N.Y. PUB. OFF. LAW §§91–99 & 84–90.

records" as any documents used by the employer "to determine such employee's eligibility for employment, promotion, additional compensation, transfer, termination, disciplinary or other adverse personnel action including employee evaluations or reports relating to such employee's character, credit and work habits."[5] In comparison, certain other states do not expressly limit personnel records to those used to make employment decisions. The access right under California law, for instance, applies to personnel records maintained by the employer "related to the employee's performance or to any grievance concerning the employee."[6]

These access rights typically exclude letters of reference and records of criminal investigations.[7] These exceptions vary by state and should be considered in responding to an employee's request to review his personnel records.

Practice Pointer: Despite the differences in state law and the fact that in many instances there is no statutory right, the common practice in the U.S. is to provide an employee with access to his "official" personnel file upon reasonable request. Employee access rights are not necessarily limited to the "official" personnel file maintained by the employer, but may include documents kept in other locations. Employers should assess whether they operate in a jurisdiction that entitles employees to access their personnel records. If so, employers should consider the scope of "personnel records" covered by the applicable access rights, in order to ensure that all these records are maintained in a centralized location. This will facilitate the employer's response to an employee's request to review his personnel records.

---

[5] CONN. GEN. STAT. ANN. §31-128a.

[6] CAL. LAB. CODE §1198.5, subd. (a). However, employees do not have a right to review "personnel records" that are protected by the attorney-client privilege. *See, e.g.*, Wellpoint Health Networks, Inc. v. Superior Court, 59 Cal. App. 4th 110, 124–125 (1997), in which the court stated: "[W]hile the statute [CAL. LAB. CODE §1198.5] mandates unconstrained employee access to personnel files, it does not express a legislative intention to overthrow the traditional protections afforded attorney-client communications and work product documents. . . . We refuse to read into the Labor Code an implied exception to the attorney-client privilege or work product doctrine."

[7] *See, e.g.*, CAL. LAB. CODE §1198.5, subd. (c)(3); CONN. GEN. STAT. ANN. §31-128a; DEL. CODE ANN. tit. 19, §731(3); 820 ILL. COMP. STAT. ANN. 40/10; MICH. COMP. LAWS §423.501(2)(c); MINN. STAT. ANN. §181.960, subd. (4); 43 PA. CONS. STAT. ANN. §1321.

2. *Occupational Health and Safety Records*

The federal Occupational Health and Safety Act (OSHA) entitles present and former employees and their designated representatives[8] to access employee exposure and medical records pertaining to their workplace exposure to toxic substances or harmful physical agents.[9] Employers that obtain or create such records are required to keep them for a period of 30 years after the employment relationship ends, in order to ensure ongoing access to this information.[10]

A current or former employee, or his designated representative, is entitled to review exposure records and medical records regarding the employee's exposure to toxic substances or harmful physical agents in the workplace.[11] When a present or former employee (or his designated representative) requests access to such records, the employer must provide a response within 15 working days. If the employer cannot reasonably provide access to the records within that 15-day period, the employer must inform the requesting party of the reason for the delay and the earliest date on which the records can be made available for review.[12] The employee (or his designated representative) is entitled to obtain a copy of the exposure or medical records upon request.[13] Similar access rights are provided under state occupational health and safety laws.[14]

---

[8]A "designated representative" is any individual or organization authorized in writing by the employee to access his or her records under OSHA. A recognized or certified collective bargaining agent is automatically treated as a designated representative for purposes of access to employee exposure records, but requires written authorization to access employee medical records. 29 C.F.R. §1910.1020(c)(3).

[9]29 C.F.R. §1910.1020(b).

[10]29 C.F.R. §1910.1020(d).

[11]29 C.F.R. §1910.1020(b)(1).

[12]29 C.F.R. §1910.1020(e)(1).

[13]29 C.F.R. §1910.1020(e)(1)(iii).

[14]*See, e.g.*, CAL. CODE REGS. tit. 8, §3204.

3. *Employee's Addition of Explanatory Statement*

Although employees are not legally entitled to modify information contained in their personnel files,[15] a few states allow employees to submit a written statement in response to any disputed information in the personnel file. States providing this right include Connecticut, Delaware, Illinois, Massachusetts, Michigan, Minnesota, Nevada, New Hampshire, and Wisconsin.[16] This written statement must be maintained as part of the employee's permanent personnel file as long as the disputed information is kept in the file.[17]

4. *Laws Requiring Employee's Consent for Disclosure to Third Parties*

Connecticut law generally requires an employee's consent to the disclosure of personally identifiable information contained in his personnel file or medical records to third parties, although this rule is subject to a number of exceptions.[18] Consent is not required when the disclosed information is limited to verifying dates of employment, job title or position, or wages.[19] Additionally, consent is not required to disclose such records: (1) to a vendor that maintains employment records or performs other employment-related services for the employer; (2) to comply with a legal process, such as a subpoena or court order, or a government investigation; (3) to a law enforcement agency, with respect to providing the employee's home address and dates of attendance at work; (4) in response to an apparent medical emergency or to inform the employee's doc-

---

[15]Employees represented by a labor union may file a grievance to expunge disputed information from their personnel files. *See, e.g.*, Trus Joist MacMillan, 341 NLRB 369, 373–74 (2004) (ordering any reference to unlawful disciplinary actions or discharges removed from employee personnel files).

[16]*See* CONN. GEN. STAT. ANN. §31-128e; DEL. CODE ANN. tit. 19, §734; 820 ILL. COMP. STAT. ANN. 40/6; MASS. GEN. LAWS ANN. ch. 149, §52C; MICH. COMP. LAWS §423.505; MINN. STAT. ANN. §181.962. *Cf.* NEV. REV. STAT. ANN. §613.75(1)(a)(2); N.H. REV. STAT. ANN. §275:56(II); WIS. STAT. ANN. §103.13(4).

[17]*See* CONN. GEN. STAT. ANN. §31-128e; DEL. CODE ANN. tit. 19, §734; 820 ILL. COMP. STAT. ANN. 40/6; MASS. GEN. LAWS ANN. ch. 149, §52C; MICH. COMP. LAWS §423.505; MINN. STAT. ANN. §181.962. *Cf.* NEV. REV. STAT. ANN. §613.75(1)(a)(2); N.H. REV. STAT. ANN. §275:56(II); WIS. STAT. ANN. §103.13(4).

[18]CONN. GEN. STAT. ANN. §31.128f.

[19]*Id.*

tor of a medical condition of which the employee may be unaware; (5) to comply with applicable legal requirements; or (6) in accordance with the terms of a collective bargaining agreement.[20]

Illinois and Michigan laws do not require the employee's consent to disclose the personnel file to a third party but require the employer to remove any disciplinary records that are more than four years old prior to releasing the file, except when the disclosure is ordered to a party in a legal action or arbitration.[21] Additionally, Michigan and Illinois laws provide that an employer or former employer shall not disclose disciplinary records to a third party without prior written notice to the employee.[22]

5. *Laws Requiring Notice to Employee of Subpoena for Personnel Records*

State laws also may create special protections for employees whose personnel files are sought for litigation purposes. For example, California law requires the party issuing the subpoena to notify the employee whose records are sought by the subpoena.[23] If the employee is not a party to the lawsuit, the employee can block production of the records by serving a written objection. In contrast, if the employee is a party to the lawsuit, the employee would need to file a motion to quash or modify the subpoena.[24]

Practice Pointer: These laws place the burden on the party issuing the subpoena, rather than the employer, to notify the employee of the subpoena. When receiving a subpoena for personnel records, however, the employer still must review all the documentation carefully and comply with the applicable timing requirements.

---

[20] *Id.*

[21] 820 Ill. Comp. Stat. Ann. 40/8; Mich. Comp. Laws §423.507.

[22] 820 Ill. Comp. Stat. Ann. 40/7(1); Mich. Comp. Laws §423.506(1).

[23] Cal. Civ. Proc. Code §1985.6.

[24] Cal. Civ. Proc. Code §1985.6. *See also* Vt. Stat. Ann. tit. 12, §1691a (requiring an employee to be given notice and an opportunity to object to the production of his or her personnel records in response to a subpoena).

6. *Potential Consequences of Improper Disclosure of Employee Information*

Personnel records routinely contain personal information that, if improperly disclosed, could expose an employee to the risk of identity theft. These records also may contain legally protected medical information, as well as other sensitive information about employees. The improper disclosure of personnel information, whether intentional or accidental, may have a variety of legal consequences for the employer such as the need to comply with the breach notification laws. See Chapter 9 on breach notification, Chapter 8 on violations of state Social Security Number laws, or Chapter 5 on violations of laws restricting the disclosure of health information.

7. *Restrictions on Use and Printing of Social Security Numbers*

An employer should avoid using an employee's Social Security Number (SSN) as his identification number for employment purposes. Many states have adopted laws prohibiting the public posting or display of an individual's SSN.[25] See Chapter 8 for more information. Based on these laws, an employer should not, for example, print an employee's SSN on an identification badge or on a mailing label.

8. *Security Breach Notification Issues Related to Personnel Data*

Although employers may continue to use employees' SSNs for certain internal purposes, employers should limit the internal use and distribution of SSNs. Nearly all states have adopted data security breach notification laws, which require an employer to notify any individual whose "personal information" is reasonably believed to have been compromised by a data security

[25] *See* CAL. CIV. CODE §1798.85; MICH. COMP. LAWS §45.83; MINN. STAT. ANN. §325E.59.

breach.[26] If it experiences a data security breach that affects the "personal information" of individuals located in any of these states, a company must notify the individuals of the breach.[27] See Chapter 9 for more information.

9. *Confidentiality of Medical Information*

An employer that receives medical information must establish appropriate procedures to protect that information from unauthorized use or disclosure. See Chapter 5 for a detailed discussion of privacy and data security requirements related to employee medical information.

10. *Defamation and Other Legal Claims*

Employers must be cautious in responding to reference checks about present or former employees because of the risk of defamation or other legal claims. For example, it is a misdemeanor under California law for an employer to make "misrepresentations" to try to prevent a former employee from obtaining other employment.[28] This statute does not prohibit an employer from giving "upon special request" a "truthful statement concerning the reason" for the employee's departure.[29] Moreover, California law gives employers a qualified immunity in responding to a reference check.[30] In order for this qualified immunity to apply, the employer's reference must be based on credible evidence, made without malice, and given upon the specific request of a prospective employer (or someone reasonably believed to be a prospective employer).[31] If it fails to meet the standards for this qualified immunity, an employer should

---

[26] A security "breach" is typically defined as the unauthorized access or disclosure of data containing "personal information." *See, e.g.*, CAL. CIV. CODE §1798.82. Thus, these statutes are not limited to external "hacking" activities, but also cover data theft by employees and the loss or theft of equipment or media containing data (e.g., stolen laptops).

[27] The employer's notice obligation is not limited to the laws of the state in which the employer is located, but includes the laws of the states in which the affected individuals are located.

[28] CAL. LAB. CODE §1050.

[29] CAL. LAB. CODE §1053.

[30] CAL. CIV. CODE §47, subd. (c).

[31] *Id.*

be prepared to prove the truthfulness of any statement made about the former employee.[32]

Similarly, New York courts recognize the existence of a qualified privilege in giving employment references for the purpose of allowing employers "to give a prospective employer honest information as to the character of a former employee."[33] Still, defamation claims may be possible in New York under certain circumstances.[34]

Defamation claims are not limited to information disclosed by the employer, but may be based on an individual's "compelled self-publication" of negative information that would otherwise be disclosed by his prior employer. This type of claim may arise if an employer maintains defamatory information about a former employee, and the former employee knows the information would be disclosed in response to a reference check. The theory is that the former employee is compelled to tell prospective employers this defamatory information, because the prospective employer would otherwise obtain this information directly from the prior employer and assume that the individual was trying to conceal it.[35] Under this theory, the employer would be liable for defamation by maintaining defamatory information about the former employee, compelling the former employee to disclose it to prospective employers. Significantly, this claim will fail if the disclosure was not truly compelled. For example, if the applicant knows that the prior employer has a strict policy of confirming only dates of employment in response to reference checks, the applicant was not compelled to disclose the information and this claim should fail.[36] This provides another incentive for employers to maintain

---

[32]*See, e.g.*, Conkle v. Jeong, 853 F. Supp. 1160, 1168–69 (N.D. Cal. 1994) (applying California law and granting summary judgment for employer because the statements he made about a former employee in response to reference checks were truthful).

[33]De Sapio v. Kohlmeyer, 52 A.D.2d 780 (1976).

[34]*See, e.g.*, Konowitz v. Archway Sch. Inc., 65 A.D.2d 752 (1978) (denying summary judgment where the discrepancy between the reason for discharge given by employer to the employee and to a third party was found sufficient to raise a triable question of fact on the issue of malice).

[35]*See, e.g.*, McKinney v. County of Santa Clara, 110 Cal. App. 3d 787, 796–98 (1980).

[36]*See* Davis v. Consolidated Freightways, 29 Cal. App. 4th 354, 448–49 (1994).

a policy of confirming only dates of employment and job title in response to reference checks.

On the other side of the spectrum, an employer may be liable for providing a deceptively favorable reference, if that reference conceals that the employee presents a substantial and foreseeable risk of physical injury to third parties. For example, in *Randi W. v. Muroc Joint Unified School District*, a student who was sexually molested by a school vice principal sued the school districts that formerly employed that vice principal, based on their role in helping him obtain a job at her school. The school district officers had provided glowing letters of recommendation for the vice principal as part of his departure, despite their alleged knowledge of complaints of the vice principal's sexual misconduct toward students. The California court acknowledged that former employers are not required to provide negative information to prospective employers. However, the court concluded that a former employer may be held liable for recommending a former employee without reservation or qualification, if that recommendation amounts to an affirmative representation that presents a substantial and foreseeable risk of physical injury to third parties.[37]

Practice Pointer. Given the risks associated with providing references, it is common for employers to adopt a policy of confirming only job title and dates of employment in response to requests for references. (Employers often choose to confirm final salary as well, usually with the former employee's authorization.) This type of policy must be applied uniformly in order to serve its intended purpose. If an employer provides favorable references for good former employees, but declines to provide any reference for lackluster former employees, the refusal to provide a reference will cease to be a matter of policy and may instead indicate a negative assessment of that individual.

After confirming job title and dates of employment, a skilled recruiter may ask other questions to try to ascertain if the employee left in good standing. For example, a recruiter may ask if the former employee would be eligible for rehire by that company. Although these questions may seem harmless, employers should

---

[37]Randi W. v. Muroc Joint Unified Sch. Dist., 929 P.2d 582, 591 (Cal. 1997).

avoid deviating from their standard policy or practice concerning responses to reference checks. It is a good practice to require all reference check requests to be directed to the human resources department or to a manager experienced with reference check issues.

III. EUROPE

A. European Union

One of the keystones of the Directive 95/46/EC of the European Parliament and of the Council of October 24, 1995 on the protection of individuals with regard to the processing of personal information and on the free movement of such data (Directive)[38] is the right of individuals to access their personal information. Each Member State is required to implement a law that guarantees every individual the right to obtain information relating to his personal information from the person or entity controlling that personal information.[39] Although the Directive is not binding on any organization and does not confer rights on individuals, the Directive is a convenient way to discuss the common elements across the EU Member States. The Directive provides that an individual may request the following without constraint at reasonable intervals and without excessive delay or expense:

- Confirmation as to whether or not personal information relating to him is being processed and the purposes for which such information is being processed, the categories of personal information collected and used, and the recipients or categories of recipients to whom the personal information is disclosed;
- Communication to him in an intelligible form of the personal information undergoing processing and of any available information as to the source of the personal information; and

---

[38]Published in the Official Journal on November 23, 1995, L 281/31.
[39]Art. 12 of the Directive.

- Knowledge of the logic involved in any automatic processing of data concerning him, at least in the case of the automated decisions referred to in Article 15(1) of the Directive.

However, the right of access is not absolute. The right of access to personal information may be restricted where necessary to safeguard national security, defense, or public security; for the prevention, investigation, detection, and prosecution of criminal offenses or breaches of ethics for regulated professions; for an important economic or financial interest of a Member State or of the EU, including monetary, budgetary, and taxation matters; for a monitoring, inspection, or regulatory function connected, even occasionally, with the exercise of official authority in cases of public security; for an important economic or financial interest of a Member State; or for the protection of the individual or of the rights and freedoms of others.[40]

On June 27, 2007, the Article 29 Working Party issued WP136[41] on the concept of personal data. WP136 seeks to give a common understanding of the concept, as well as explain the situations in which national data protection legislation should be applied and the way it should be applied in different situations. It contains many useful examples for those who are required to determine whether certain categories of information constitute personal data. The Article 29 Working Party has agreed to "adopt a broad notion of personal data." However, as they themselves accept that the notion is not unlimited, some uncertainties remain as to how each of the data protection regulators in each Member State will interpret the concept.

Practice Pointer. A subject access request will generally allow employees to see the following types of documents in their personnel files:

- Performance reviews and appraisals;
- Warnings or minutes of disciplinary interviews;

---

[40] Art. 13 of the Directive (Exemptions and Restrictions).

[41] *See* Article 29 Working Party WP136, Opinion 4/2007 on the concept of persona data, adopted on 20th June 2007.

- Information generated by computer systems involved in automated decision making (e.g., in respect to performance and conduct);
- Sickness absence records;
- Training records;
- Pay statements; and
- Other documents of which employees are the subject, including expressions of opinion or intention (e.g., about performance and promotion).

It is important to make managers and others aware of the extent and nature of the information to which an individual could gain access. This awareness should encourage managers to record only what is truly relevant and useful and thus make subject access requests much less burdensome and more relevant for all concerned.

The difference among the rights of access in a few Member States illustrates the variations in the local implementation of the Directive. The following sections highlight the requirements in France, Germany, and the United Kingdom.

B. France

1. Subject Access Requests by Individual Employees

Any applicant, current employee, or former employee may ask his employer[42] whether personal information relating to him is held by the employer, and if personal information is held about him, the individual may request:

- A description of the type of data held, the purposes for which this information is being processed, the names of the recipients or the types of recipients to whom such data may be disclosed, and an explanation of whether that data can be transferred outside the EU;
- A copy of the personal information and any information available to the employer as to the source of the data; and

---

[42] Article 39 of the French Data Protection Act No. 78-17 of January 6, 1978 on Data Processing, Data Files and Individual Liberties provides for an entire section on access rights to data subjects.

- Information about the process that is likely to constitute the sole basis for any decision significantly affecting the individual, and the logic involved in that decision-making process, if the data are processed by automatic means for the purpose of evaluating matters relating to the employee (such as his performance at work, creditworthiness, reliability, or conduct).

2. *Applicable Fee*

Access must be provided without undue delay and free of charge. The employer may, however, charge for the actual cost of making copies.

3. *Denial of Subject Access Requests*

Access may be denied only where:

- The employer can prove that the request is "abusive," "repetitive," or "systematic" (the burden of proof will here lie on the data controller who has received the requests);
- The French Data Protection Authority (CNIL) determines that personal information is stored in a form that poses no risk of violating the individual's privacy and for a period that does not exceed that required for statistical or research purposes; or
- The disclosure of the data would infringe the employer's or a third-party copyright.

The CNIL recommends that the information requested by the employee be given to him in a written format, irrespective of type of information requested.[43]

---

[43]This requirement is provided in the French Data Protection Authority's (CNIL) recommendation: Délibération n°02/017 du 21 mars 2002 portant adoption d'une recommendation relative à la collecte et au traitement d'informations nominatives lors d'opérations de recrutement.

C. Germany

1. Subject Access Requests by Individual Employees

Any applicant, current employee, or former employee may request the following information with respect to data relating to him:

- The data held about him, including the source(s) of the data;
- The recipients or categories of recipients to whom personal data are disclosed; and
- The purposes for which personal data are collected, processed, or used.[44]

No particular form of request is required. The individual seeking the information should specify the type of data about which information is to be provided.

In addition, anyone may request information on:

- The full legal name, address, and legal officers of the employer entity controlling the data;
- The purposes for which personal data are collected, processed, or used;
- The types of personal data retained;
- The types of individuals to whom the data relate;
- The recipients or categories of recipients to whom personal data are disclosed;
- Data retention periods;
- Transfers to non-EU countries; and
- The technical and organizational security measures.[45]

The above information should be held on record by the data protection officer (Verfahrensverzeichnis); a template document is available on the data protection authority's Web site at http://www.lfd.nrw.de/fachbereich/fach_0_komplett.html.

---

[44]Federal Data Protection Act (BDSG) §34, Works Council Act (BetrVG) §83.
[45]BDSG §§4g(2)2, 4e.

2. *Applicable Fee*

Any request must be answered in writing (even when denied), unless a vital interest of the individual concerned requires choosing another form. Information must be provided free of charge.[46]

3. *Denial of Subject Access Requests*

The employer is exempt from providing access where:

- The data are retained for the sole purpose of complying with statutory or contractual retention obligations or security requirements;
- The data must be kept confidential due to legal requirements or privacy interests of third parties;
- The data are derived from public source only; or
- No overriding interest of the individual in obtaining the information exists, to the extent to which access would be likely to prejudice the conduct of the employer's business.[47]

Employers are not required to provide the reason for the denial of an access request if provision of the reasons would jeopardize the purpose for which the access request is being denied. In such a case the employer should inform the employee that he or she may appeal to the Federal Commissioner for Data Protection.

D. United Kingdom

1. *Subject Access Requests by Individual Employees*

Employees have the right to request access to their personal information held by their employer (a "subject access request").[48] Subject access requests may be made with respect to computer files, email correspondence, and manual files (if the data are

---

[46]BDSG §34(5).
[47]BDSG §34, BetrVG §83.
[48]Data Protection Act 1998 (DPA) §7, 1998 c29.

recorded as part of a relevant filing system or with the intention that they should form part of a relevant filing system.)[49]

There is some guidance from the courts on what is meant by "personal information" and "relevant filing system" in the context of a subject access request.[50] Personal information does not extend to all information that mentions a specific individual. Rather, in order to constitute personal information, data must fall in a "continuum of relevance or proximity to the data subject as distinct, say, from transactions or matters in which he may have been involved to a greater or lesser degree." Employers should consider two questions when determining whether information is personal information:

- Is the information biographical in a significant sense?
- Does the information have the individual as its focus?

A "relevant filing system" can be described as follows:

- The files are structured or referenced in such a way that they clearly indicate at the outset of the search whether specific information capable of amounting to "personal information" is held within the system and, if so, in which file or files it is held; and
- The system has, as part of its own structure or referencing mechanism, a sufficiently sophisticated and detailed means of readily indicating whether and where in an individual file or files specific criteria or information about the data subject can easily be located.

Manual files will come within this definition if they are structured in a way that is comparable to a computerized file, so that not just the files themselves but also the relevant personal

[49]"Relevant filing system" means any set of information relating to individuals to the extent that, although the information is not to be processed by means of equipment operating automatically in response to instructions given for that purpose, the set is structured, either by reference to individuals or by reference to criteria relating to individuals, in such a way that specific information relating to a particular individual is readily accessible (DPA §1(1)).

[50]Durant v. Financial Servs. Auth. [2003] EWCA Civ 1746.

information within those files can be identified and isolated without the data controller actually having to search through them. Accordingly, and rather perversely, the better organized a manual filing system is, the more likely it is that the employer will have to comply with subject access requests.

To ensure that subject access requests are handled appropriately, the Information Commissioner (the United Kingdom's data protection authority) has published a guidance document, the Employment Practices Code (Code). The Code advises employers to:

- Assess what personal information about workers exists and who is responsible for it;
- Ensure that the information is accessible;
- Establish who in the organization is responsible for responding to subject access requests;
- Ensure that all workers who are likely to receive subject access requests can recognize them and know who deals with them;
- Have a checklist in place listing all places where personal information might be held that should be checked in response to such a request;
- Use the checklist to gather all personal information in time to enable a response within 40 days at the latest;
- Brief anyone responsible for responding to a subject access request on how to check the identity of the person making it; and
- Inform managers and other relevant people in the organization of the nature of information that will be released to individuals who make subject access requests.

2. *Applicable Fee*

A fee of up to £10[51] per access request may be charged by the employer. The Data Protection Act 1998 (DPA) lays down strict rules as to how subject access requests should be made and

---

[51] As of May 3, 2009.

dealt with. A valid subject request must be in writing[52] and must identify the data to which the person seeks access. An employer does not have to comply with an employee's request for access if the employee has not supplied such information as the employer may reasonably require to locate the information requested.[53] For example, an employer could ask an employee to define his request by date range, author, recipient, or subject matter.

3. *Denial of Subject Access Requests*

An employer may refuse to comply with a subject access request if the same employee has previously made a similar or identical request and a reasonable time interval has not yet elapsed between compliance with the previous request and the making of the current request.[54] A "reasonable time interval" is not defined in the DPA, so it is unclear how much time should have elapsed before the employer can rely on this provision.

Some limited exemptions apply to the duty to comply with a subject access request and include circumstances in which the personal information held relates to:

- Management forecasting or planning, if its disclosure would be likely to prejudice the employer's conduct of their business (e.g., plans to make employees redundant);[55]
- Negotiations with employees, again if its disclosure would be likely to prejudice the negotiations (e.g., the employer's "bottom line" in pay negotiations);[56]
- Information that, if disclosed, might affect the price of a company's shares or other financial instrument (the "corporate finance" exemption);[57]
- Information to which claim to legal professional privilege could be maintained;[58]

---

[52]DPA §7(2)(a).
[53]DPA §7(3).
[54]DPA §8(3).
[55]DPA §8(3), ¶5 of Schedule 7.
[56]DPA §8(3), ¶7 of Schedule 7.
[57]DPA §8(3), ¶6 of Schedule 7.
[58]DPA §8(3), ¶9 of Schedule 7.

- References,[59] although this exemption does not apply to references held by the recipient employer—accordingly, references contained in employees' or job applicants' files are subject to disclosure; and
- Data about another person (see further below).

A partial exemption also exists when the provision of a permanent copy of the information requested would require disproportionate effort.[60] The DPA does not define "disproportionate effort." According to the Employment Practices Code Supplementary Guidance (Supplementary Guidance), matters to be taken into account include the cost, the length of time responding to the request would take, the difficulty of providing the information, and the size of the organization to which the request has been made. These factors have to be balanced against the impact on the individual of not providing a copy. The Supplementary Guidance advises that, given the significance of employment records, an employer should rely on the disproportionate effort exemption only in exceptional circumstances.

The Code gives some guidance on how to respond when the information covered by a subject access request could include information that identifies another person (e.g., a work colleague). Responding fully to a subject access request could lead to the third party's rights under the DPA being violated. In many cases simply removing the third party's name from the information before it is released may solve the problem. The employer therefore has to strike a balance between the right of the employee to access the information and the right of the third party to privacy. The Code advises an employer to follow a clear decision-making process before releasing any such information to ensure that it gets the balance right. The Supplementary Guidance suggests that the following factors should be taken into account:

- Whether the information can easily be edited to remove the part that reveals the identity of a third party without

[59] DPA §8(3), ¶1 of Schedule 7.

[60] DPA §8(2).

significantly changing the information's likely value to the employee;

- Whether releasing the information would breach a duty of confidence owed by the employer to the third party;
- Whether a third party has expressly refused consent to the release of the information and the reasons given, if any;
- What the third party was told when the information was supplied about its possible release or, if told nothing, what the third party's reasonable expectations would be;
- The impact the information has had or might have in the future on actions or decisions affecting the employee;
- The nature of the information, in particular whether its release could be damaging to the third party or whether it would reveal sensitive data about the third party;
- The extent to which the employee is likely to be aware already of the information;
- Whether the information includes facts of which the employee ought to be made aware because he might dispute them;
- Whether the information identifies the third party in a business or personal capacity; and
- The fact that if the information is released in error, the error cannot subsequently be corrected, but if information is withheld in error, that error can subsequently be corrected by its later release.

Practice Pointer. When an employer receives a subject access request, the employer should:

- If necessary, verify the identity of the person requesting access to the data to ensure that personal information is disclosed only to the person who is its subject;
- Inform the person making the application whether a fee is payable; and
- Having checked identity (if necessary) and received a fee (if required), provide the person requesting access with copies of the relevant information, subject to the exemp-

tions referred to above, in an intelligible permanent form promptly and at least within 40 calendar days.[61]

IV. ASIA

A. China

China has a government-administered system of personnel records. These records are maintained by government departments charged with handling such information.[62] Foreign-invested enterprises are prohibited from viewing these official personnel records. When a foreign-invested enterprise hires Chinese nationals, it is required to engage a domestic organization authorized by the Chinese government to handle personnel records to maintain the personnel records of its Chinese employees.[63]

A company can maintain its own personnel records; there is no statutory restriction on the collection of personal data relating to employees in China. A company is required to maintain the confidentiality of that information, and is not permitted to publicly disclose that information without the consent of the employee.

Employees have no right to view their official personnel records, nor an employer-maintained personnel record.

B. Hong Kong

The collection, use, and access to personal data relating to employees in Hong Kong is governed by the Personal Data (Privacy) Ordinance (PDPO).[64] The Hong Kong Privacy Commissioner has issued a Code of Practice on Human Resource Management

[61] Information Commissioner's Office, Employment Practices Code Supplementary Guidance, 2005, §2.8.

[62] Law of the People's Republic of China Governing Personnel Files, Law of the People's Republic of China for Maintenance of Confidentiality, and Regulations for the Administration of Personnel Files of Enterprise Employees.

[63] Regulations for the Administration of Personnel Files of Enterprise Employees.

[64] Cap. 486, Laws of Hong Kong.

(the HR Code), which seeks to provide more detailed guidance to complement the high-level data privacy principles set out in the PDPO.

It should be noted that the provisions of the HR Code are not legally binding. A breach of the HR Code by a data user, however, will give rise to a presumption against the data user in any legal proceedings under the PDPO.

1. Access Requests

Under the PDPO, an individual, which includes a job applicant, current employee, or a former employee, or an authorized person or attorney acting on behalf of such individual, has the right to request access to that person's personal data held by the employer.[65]

In order to be effective, data access requests must be made in the form issued by the Privacy Commissioner (the Prescribed Form).[66]

Unless one of the exemptions described below applies, the employer is required to provide a copy of the relevant personal data no later than 40 days after receiving the data request.[67] Any time extension needed by the employer must be communicated in writing to the requester, with reasons, before the expiration of the period and the employer must provide the data as soon as practicable thereafter.

Personal data subject to employee access include (without limitation) the following:

1. For employment candidates:
    a. Job application form;
    b. Written assessment of the candidate in a selection interview;
    c. Assessment report of any tests (e.g., psychological tests) that the candidate is required to take; and

---

[65]PDPO, §18(1).

[66]PDPO, §§20(3) & 67. The Prescribed Form can be found at the Privacy Commissioner's Web site, www.pcpd.org.hk.

[67]PDPO, §19(1) of the Ordinance.

   d. Personal references obtained from the candidate's current or former employers or other sources.
2. For existing employees:
   a. Remuneration and benefits records;
   b. Job postings, transfer, and training records;
   c. Performance reviews and appraisals;
   d. Warnings or minutes of disciplinary interviews;
   e. Sickness absence records, medical checks, and other medical claims;
   f. Staff planning exercises involving employees; and
   g. Promotion records.

An employer responding to a data access request must not disclose to the requesting party any data identifying any other individual unless the other individual consents.[68] However, the employer cannot simply refuse to provide a copy of a relevant document on the ground that it contains personal data of a third party. Rather, the employer must either: (1) obtain consent from the third party to make the disclosure or (2) edit out the personal data relating to the third party before releasing a copy to the requesting party.

2. Relevant Process Exemption

An employer may decline to comply with a data access request in respect to data that are the subject of a Relevant Process until the Relevant Process is completed.[69] The PDPO defines a "Relevant Process" as:

- A recruitment process, promotion process, contract tendering process, academic or other award process, and disciplinary proceedings
- For which a right of appeal exists (whether statutory, contractual, or otherwise) in relation to the determination made on the completion of the process.

[68]PDPO, §§20(1)(b) & 20(2).
[69]PDPO, §55.

In order for the employer to rely on this exemption, both of these conditions must be fulfilled. Note, however, that the availability of appeal governs only whether the Relevant Process qualifies for the exemption from compliance with granting of the data access and does not mean that the appeal period is part of the Relevant Process period.[70]

As a matter of good practice, employers should have a written policy that documents the procedures and personal data collected for the purpose of conducting each Relevant Process applicable to the business. This policy should stipulate a right of appeal against the decision of such Relevant Process and any conditions pertaining to that right.[71]

3. *Personal References Exemption*

An employer should decline to comply with a data access request made by a job applicant in respect to personal references given by a third party unless: (1) the third party has given the employer consent to such disclosure or (2) the applicant has been informed in writing that he has been accepted or rejected for the position.[72]

4. *General Exemptions*

Other general grounds for declining data access requests include:

- The request is not in writing in Chinese or English in the Prescribed Form;
- The employer is not provided with sufficient information to locate the requested data;
- The request follows two or more similar requests made by the employee or a relevant person on his or her behalf and it is unreasonable for the employer to comply;

---

[70] HR Code, §§2.11.2.2 & 3.8.2.

[71] HR Code, §§2.11.2.2 & 3.8.2.

[72] PDPO, §56.

- Another data user controls the use of the personal data concerned in such a way that prohibits the employer receiving the data access request from complying with it; or
- Other statutory grounds (e.g., detection of crime).

If the employer declines to comply with a data access request for any reason, it must inform the requestor in writing with the reasons of the refusal within 40 days of receiving the request. If it refuses to comply with a data access request because another data user controls the use of the personal data concerned in such a way that prohibits it from complying with the request, it is required, in the notice to the data subject, to provide the name and address of the other data user concerned.[73]

The employer as a data user is required to keep and maintain a log book of any refusals to comply with data access requests and the reasons therefore. The log book must be kept in Chinese or English. The particulars in the log book must be kept for a minimum period of four years.[74]

5. *Costs and Fees*

The employer may charge a fee for complying with a data access request, but the fee must not be excessive.[75] Although the PDPO does not prescribe a particular fee, the Privacy Commissioner's view is that the employer should not charge more than the direct cost of complying with the request.

C. Japan

In responding to requests by employees to disclose, correct, supplement, delete, or suspend use of "Held Personal Data,"[76]

---

[73]PDPO, §21(1).

[74]PDPO, §27.

[75]PDPO, §28; Data Protection Principles (DPP), Schedule 1 of PDPO, §6.

[76]"Held Personal Data" is defined as Personal Information (information that relates to a living individual, which can be used to identify specific individuals by name, date of birth, or other description (including information that can be easily compared with other information to identify a specific individual)) that comprises a Personal Information Database (a collection of information that contains personal information which is systematically structured so to enable the searching of specific personal in-

employers must heed the requirements of the Protection of Personal Information Law (PIPL), Ministry of Health, Labour and Welfare's (MHLW) Guidelines for the Appropriate Handling of Personal Information in Employment Management (MHLW Guidelines), and the Commentary to the Guidelines (Commentary). Note that the PIPL does not distinguish between employee data and customer data, so that the obligations of responding to access requests are basically the same, whether they are made by employees or customers. Therefore, applicable industry-specific guidelines, such as the Ministry of Economy, Trade and Industry (METI) Guidelines, must also be heeded. In terms of the handling of health information of employees, see Chapter 5, Section IV.D.

In addition, the Action Guide regarding the Protection of Personal Information of Workers (Action Guide) issued by the MHLW should be heeded. As explained previously, the Action Guide does not have the force of law, but is generally regarded by businesses as agency rules that should be followed.

1. Access Requests

Under Article 25 of the PIPL, an employer that has been requested by an employee to disclose Held Personal Data regarding the employee must respond to such disclosure without delay in writing.[77]

However, disclosures do not have to be made in the following cases: (1) if it is likely that there will be harm to life, person, property, or other rights and interests of the individual or third party;[78] (2) if it is likely that the proper functioning of business operations of the enterprise handling personal information would be markedly impaired; or (3) in the event that disclosure would constitute

---

formation) for which an enterprise handling personal information holds the full authority to disclose, make corrections, additions, or deletions to the content thereof, cease to use, erase, and suspend the provision thereof to third parties, on the request of the principal or its agents, and will not be erased within six months.

[77]Method prescribed as per Article 6 of the Enforcement Order for the Law Concerning the Protection of Personal Information (Cabinet Order No. 507 of 2003) (Cabinet Order).

[78]METI Guidelines Section 2-2-5-2 provides that an example of this would be when a hospital is asked to disclose the name of the disease, where there is a risk that to do so would result in the deterioration of the patient's medical and physical condition.

a violation of other laws and ordinances. The example given in the METI Guidelines regarding what it means for business operations to be "markedly impaired" is where the same individual repeatedly requests disclosure of the same content requiring a complicated process, and requests by others cannot be processed due to such requests.[79]

The Action Guide also sheds some light on what situations would constitute matters likely to markedly impair proper business operations. The Action Guide provides that if the access request concerns the test results or evaluations of the employees, and if it is likely that proper functioning of business operations would be impaired, then the employer does not have to disclose all or a part of the personal information.[80]

In addition, the METI Guidelines and MHLW Guidelines provide that employers should establish guidelines concerning when access requests by employees may be denied as likely to markedly impair proper business operations, upon prior mutual consultation with labor unions (the term includes any representative of a majority of the workers), and should ensure that these guidelines are made known to the employees.[81] Note that the foregoing is considered desirable, but not mandatory.

When it provides notice to the requesting employee that the employer does not plan on making all or a part of the requested disclosure, the employer must strive to provide the employee with an explanation of the reason.[82]

2. *Requests for Correction*

Pursuant to the PIPL, when an employer has been requested by an employee to correct the contents of Held Personal Data regarding the employee, the employer must promptly conduct an investigation regarding the matter if the alleged inaccuracy would

---

[79]§2-2-5-2 of the METI Guidelines.

[80]Art. 3.1(2) of the Action Guide.

[81]§2-2-5-2 of the METI Guidelines; §3.6 of the MHLW Guidelines (commentary).

[82]Art. 28 of the PIPL.

affect the purpose of use.[83] The employer is not required to make the requested correction if the investigation determines that there was no inaccuracy, or if the inaccuracy would not affect the purpose of use for such data. The example provided by the METI Guidelines of when it is not necessary for the employer to carry out the requested correction is when the request is regarding information related to the employee's evaluation and not a fact subject to a correction.[84]

The employer must notify the employee without delay in the event that a decision has been made not to perform the requested correction, or, if performed, of the content of the correction.[85] The employer must strive to provide the employee with an explanation for the decision taken.[86]

3. Requests to Cease Use

When an employer is requested by an employee to cease use of or to delete his Held Personal Data because the Held Personal Data is being used for purposes other than the specified purpose of use in violation of Article 16 of the PIPL, or because the Held Personal Data was acquired by the employer using improper methods in violation of Article 17 of the PIPL, the employer must, in principle, take the requested action with respect to such Held Personal Data without delay, to the extent necessary to rectify the violation, if it is determined that there are grounds for this request. The PIPL also provides that if excessive expense would be required or if there is extreme difficulty involved in suspending the use of or deleting that Held Personal Data, the employer may choose to take substitute measures that would protect the rights and interests of the employee.[87] For example, in a case in which the employee requests the deletion of all Held Personal Data, if it is possible to correct the procedural violations by ceasing use, then by taking

---

[83] Art. 26 of the PIPL.
[84] §2-2-5-3 of the METI Guidelines.
[85] *Id.*
[86] Art. 28 of the PIPL.
[87] Art. 27 of the PIPL.

such measure the obligation will be fulfilled. So it is not always necessary to take the requested measures.[88]

Employers must provide notice of the suspension of use or deletion without delay, and, if it does not plan on making all or a part of the requested disclosure, the employer must strive to provide the employee with an explanation of the reason.[89]

4. *Disclosure of Personal Records to Third Parties*

The PIPL generally requires an employer to obtain the consent of the employee before disclosing the employee's personal data to third parties.[90] Note that, under the PIPL, "third parties" may include affiliates, subsidiaries, and other group companies, and consent would need to be obtained unless the business complied with the requirements of the "joint use" exception, or other applicable exception.

The other exceptions under the PIPL include the following:

- *Transfer pursuant to opt-out notice.* If transfer of personal data to third parties has been specified as a purpose of use, then such transfer can be made without the opt-in consent of the employee, provided that a valid opt-out notice has been provided in advance. The opt-out notice must specify the items of personal information to be transferred, means and methods of transfer of the personal data, and the cessation of the transfer of personal data upon request. METI's examples of businesses that might use this exception are residential map makers and businesses that prepare and sell name lists to direct mailing operations.
- *Transfer to delegatees (service providers).* A delegatee is not considered a "third party" under the PIPL. Therefore, if personal data of employees are provided to service providers of the employer within the scope necessary to achieve the purposes of use of such personal data, no consent needs to be obtained from the employees. Note that under Article

[88]§2-2-5-4 of the METI Guidelines.
[89]Art. 28 of the PIPL.
[90]Art. 23 of the PIPL.

22 of the PIPL, the employer is obligated to supervise the delegatees.

- *Merger and acquisition (M&A) exception.* In cases in which there is a transfer of personal data to a successor due to a merger, company spin off, or transfer of business, the PIPL deems that the successor is not a "third party" and therefore consent of the individuals is not needed. However, businesses must take care to note that this exception does not apply to the due diligence process preceding the transfer, even with a nondisclosure agreement in place. Businesses that want to share employee information for due diligence purposes in the M&A context must take care to either make the personal data anonymous or obtain consent (both of which may be costly and impractical solutions).
- *Transfer pursuant to joint use notice.* In the event personal data is used jointly with other parties, consent need not be obtained from the individual if the individual is notified in advance of: (1) the joint use; (2) the items of personal data to be used jointly; (3) the scope of person or persons engaged in the joint use; (4) the purpose of use of the personal data; and (5) the name or title of the person or entity responsible for the management of the jointly used personal data.
- *Other general exceptions.* Other exceptions from the requirement to obtain the employee's consent to the transfer of personal data are: (1) if pursuant to law or ordinance;[91] (2) if necessary for the protection of life, person, or property, when it is difficult to obtain consent; (3) if necessary in order to improve public hygiene or promote the health of children, when it is difficult to obtain consent; or (4) in the event cooperation is required for a national agency, a local public entity, or a person delegated thereby to carry out official work prescribed by law or ordinance, when it is likely that the carrying out of that operation could be hindered through obtaining the principal's consent.

---

[91]The Ministries have provided guidance that "law or ordinance" applies only to Japanese laws and ordinances. *See, e.g.*, Responses to Comments to the Draft FSA Guidelines, Q&A.

In cases in which references are sought by a third party regarding an employee, it is unlikely that any of the exceptions above would apply, and consent should be obtained from such employee. The METI Guidelines provide the following examples of cases where consent would be deemed to have been obtained:[92]

- Verbal or written confirmation from the consenting party (including records created in an electronic format, magnetic format, or other format that cannot be recognized by human senses);
- Receipt of a consent form or other document signed by the party or affixed with the name and seal impression thereof;
- Receipt of mail from the party stating consent;
- Placement of check in a consent verification box;
- Click of a button on a Web site, which signifies consent; and
- Consent by voice input; touching a touch panel; or input by button, switch, or the like.

The METI Guidelines provide that when employee personal data, such as personnel ratings, are provided to third parties pursuant to consent (and not pursuant to any of the exceptions such as joint use, opt out, etc.), such as when an employee is seconded to a subsidiary or if a worker is dispatched, employers should "pay attention to" the following matters (language suggests that these are not mandatory):

- The party being provided data has established that the personal data learned with regard to the employee in the handling of the corresponding personal data must not be divulged or misused;
- The third party has confirmed that it will not leak or divulge the personal data or use data for another purpose;
- The prior written approval of the business is to be obtained when engaging in a subsequent provision of the personal data;

[92] §2-1-10 of the METI Guidelines.

- The copying and duplication of personal data (excluding that required for backup purposes under security control) are prohibited for the party being provided the data;
- The party being provided the data will clarify the retention term; and
- The personal data will be returned, destroyed, deleted, or handled by the combination thereof, after achieving the purpose of use, and the party that was provided the data will provide confirmation of the same.

CHAPTER 8

USE OF GOVERNMENT IDENTIFIERS AND SOCIAL SECURITY NUMBERS

I. Overview 502
II. Americas 503
A. United States 503
Exhibit 8.1 U.S.: Summary of State Social Security Number Disclosure Laws 504
1. Application to Employers 503
2. Types of Information Covered 506
3. Prohibited Activities 507
a. Method of Mailing Documents Containing SSNs 508
b. Electronic or Facsimile Transmission of SSNs 508
c. Sale of SSNs 508
d. Use of SSNs as Account Numbers 509
e. Collection of SSNs 509
f. Disclosure of Employee's Personal Identifying Information 509
4. Exceptions 510
a. Court Filings 510
b. Verifications and Investigations 511
c. Maintenance and Reporting of Employment Records 512
d. Other Exemptions 512
5. Privacy Policy Requirements 513
a. SSN Policy Laws Requiring Internal Policies 513
i. Michigan 513
ii. New Mexico 514
iii. New York 514
b. SSN Policy Laws Requiring External Policies 515

i. Connecticut ... 515
ii. Texas ... 515
6. Additional Requirements ... 516
7. Enforcement and Administration ... 517
8. Compliance Issues for Employers ... 519
B. Brazil ... 522
C. Canada ... 522
D. Mexico ... 523
III. Europe ... 523
A. Belgium ... 523
B. Germany ... 523
C. Italy ... 523
D. United Kingdom ... 524
IV. Asia and Asia Pacific ... 524
A. Australia ... 524
B. Hong Kong ... 525
1. Employment Candidates ... 526
2. Existing Employees ... 527
C. Japan ... 528
D. Korea ... 529
E. New Zealand ... 529

I. OVERVIEW

Many employers rely on government identifiers and Social Security Numbers (SSNs) to identify and track employees for a variety of purposes, ranging from tax reporting to benefit plan enrollment to employee ID numbers. Due to the increasing incidence of identity theft, many employees have become more concerned about the use of their Government Identifiers and SSNs as passwords or employer identifiers and laws in several countries limit the use of government ID numbers. In contrast to the U.S., many countries use government ID numbers for identification on a regular basis but not for financial purposes and, thus, the concerns relating to financial fraud connected to the use of government identifiers is of less significance outside of the U.S.

II. AMERICAS

A. United States

There currently is no federal legislation regulating the collection and use of SSNs by private sector businesses, but it is possible that federal legislation will be introduced and enacted in the future. Furthermore, state legislatures are actively pursuing legislation in this area. To date, 31 states and Puerto Rico have adopted laws restricting or prohibiting the collection, use, or disclosure of SSNs, which generally apply to all commercial entities (SSN Protection Laws).[1] The SSN Protection Laws vary widely, and this chapter provides an overview of these laws to illustrate the differences among them. In addition, a summary of these laws appears in Exhibit 8.1.

This chapter is intended to provide an overview of the SSN Protection Laws, rather than an exhaustive account of their requirements. It is important to review the text of each applicable SSN Protection Law to gain a comprehensive understanding. In addition, other state laws also may regulate the collection, use, or disclosure of SSN data; for example, this chapter does not address state laws that regulate the collection, use, or disclosure of SSN data by insurance entities, given the specialized nature of those laws.

1. Application to Employers

Most SSN Protection Laws are drafted to apply to any person or entity doing business in a particular state, and to regulate

---

[1]States that have enacted legislation regulating the use of SSNs, include, Alaska, Arizona, Arkansas, California, Colorado, Connecticut, Georgia, Hawaii, Idaho, Illinois, Kansas, Maine, Maryland, Michigan, Minnesota, Missouri, Nebraska, New Jersey, New Mexico, New York, North Carolina, Oklahoma, Oregon, Pennsylvania, Puerto Rico, Rhode Island, South Carolina, Tennessee, Texas, Utah, Vermont, and Virginia. These state statutes have varying effective dates. The current Texas law governing the disclosure of SSNs shall be repealed as of April 1, 2009, and revised provisions shall become effective as of that date. *See* TEX. BUS. & COM. CODE §35.581; 2005 Tex. Gen. Laws 198.

EXHIBIT 8.1
U.S.: Summary of State Social Security Number Disclosure Laws

This chart identifies which states have SSN Protection Laws as well as the key requirements under those laws, but does not address other state laws relating to insurance.

STATE	SSN Disclosure Law	Specifically Addresses Truncated SSNs	Generally Prohibits Publicly Posting or Displaying SSNs to the General Public[1]	Limits Mailing of Documents that Include SSNs	Limits Printing of SSNs for Specific Purposes	SSN Policy Law
Alabama	No					
Alaska[2]	Yes	No	Yes	Yes	No	
Arizona	Yes	Yes[3]	Yes	Yes	Yes	
Arkansas	Yes	No	Yes	Yes	Yes	
California	Yes	No	Yes	Yes	Yes	
Colorado	Yes	No	Yes	Yes	Yes	
Connecticut	Yes	No	Yes	No	Yes	Yes
Delaware	No					
D.C.	No					
Florida	No					
Georgia	Yes	No	Yes	Yes	No	
Hawaii	Yes	No	Yes	Yes	Yes	
Idaho	Yes	No	Yes	No	No	
Illinois	Yes	No	Yes	Yes	Yes	
Indiana	No					
Iowa	No					
Kansas	Yes	No	No	Yes	No	
Kentucky	No					
Louisiana	No					
Maine	Yes	No	No	No	Yes	
Maryland	Yes	No	Yes	Yes	Yes	
Massachusetts	No					No[4]
Michigan	Yes	Yes	Yes	Yes	Yes	Yes
Minnesota	Yes	No	Yes	Yes	Yes	
Mississippi	No					
Missouri	Yes	No	Yes	No	No	
Montana	No					

STATE	SSN Disclosure Law	Specifically Addresses Truncated SSNs	Generally Prohibits Publicly Posting or Displaying SSNs to the General Public[1]	Limits Mailing of Documents that Include SSNs	Limits Printing of SSNs for Specific Purposes	SSN Policy Law
Nebraska	No	Yes	Yes	No	No	
Nevada	No					
New Hampshire	No					
New Jersey	Yes	Yes	Yes	Yes	Yes	
New Mexico	Yes	No	Yes	Yes	Yes	Yes
New York	Yes	Yes	Yes	Yes	Yes	Yes
North Carolina	Yes	No	Yes	Yes	Yes	
North Dakota	No					
Ohio	No					
Oklahoma	Yes	No	Yes	Yes	Yes	
Oregon	Yes	Yes[5]	Yes	Yes	Yes	
Pennsylvania	Yes	No	Yes	Yes	Yes	
Puerto Rico	Yes	No	Yes	No	Yes	
South Carolina[6]	Yes	Yes	Yes	Yes	Yes	
South Dakota	No					
Tennessee	Yes	No	Yes	Yes	No	
Texas	Yes	No	Yes	Yes	Yes	Yes
Utah	Yes	No	Yes[7]	No	No	
Vermont	Yes	No	Yes	Yes	Yes	
Virginia	Yes	No	Yes	Yes	Yes	
Washington	No					
West Virginia	No					
Wisconsin	No					
Wyoming	No					

[1]The California SSN disclosure law defines "public post" or "public display" as intentionally communicating or otherwise making available, in any manner, an individual's SSN. CAL. CIV. CODE §1798.84(a)(1). Several state SSN disclosure laws include similar language.

[2]Effective July 1, 2009.

[3]Effective January 1, 2009.

[4]Massachusetts does not have a regulation specifically for SSNs but does require an organization to adopt a policy to ensure that SSNs are properly safeguarded.

[5]The Oregon law refers to redacted SSNs.

[6]Effective December 31, 2008.

[7]Prohibits the displaying of SSNs in a manner or location likely to be open to public view.

the handling of any SSNs by that person or entity.[2] Thus, they tend to apply indirectly to employers: an employer doing business in that state would need to comply with its SSN Protection Law in handling any SSNs, whether of employees, customers, or other individuals. In comparison, some SSN Protection Laws expressly apply to employers, such as those in Nebraska,[3] New York,[4] and Oklahoma,[5] as well as Puerto Rico. [6]

Some SSN Protection Laws provide exemptions for certain entities. For example, the Colorado and Pennsylvania laws exempt entities covered by the federal Health Insurance Portability and Accountability Act of 1996 (HIPAA).[7] The Pennsylvania and South Carolina laws exempt a financial institution covered by the Gramm-Leach-Bliley Act (GLBA).[8] The Pennsylvania law also exempts a "licensee" regulated under Pennsylvania law or any entity subject to the Fair Credit Reporting Act (FCRA).[9]

In addition to its SSN Protection Law, New York also has recently enacted legislation that specifically prohibits employers from communicating an employee's "personally-identifying information," including SSNs, to the general public (the N.Y. Employee PII Law).[10]

2. *Types of Information Covered*

The SSN Protection Laws typically do not define the term "Social Security Number" and thus do not specifically address whether the law applies to the use of the entire SSN, or to truncated or redacted numbers. Some states laws, however, include specific language regarding truncated or redacted numbers, even though those laws do not define a "Social Security Number." For

---

[2]*See, e.g.*, N.Y. GEN. BUS. LAW §399-dd(2); N.C. GEN. STAT. §75-62(a); TEX. BUS. & COM. CODE §35.581(a).

[3]NEB. REV. STAT. §48-237(2).

[4]N.Y. LAB. LAW §203-d.

[5]OKLA. STAT. tit. 40, §173.1(A)(1).

[6]20 P.R. LAWS ANN. §621a(a).

[7]COLO. REV. STAT. §6-1-715(4)(b); 74 PA. STAT. ANN. §204.

[8]74 PA. STAT. ANN. §204; S.B. 453, 117th S.C. Gen. Assem., 2d Sess. (S.C. 2008) (to be codified at S.C. CODE ANN. §37-20-180(A) (effective Dec. 31, 2008)).

[9]74 PA. STAT. ANN. §204.

[10]N.Y. LAB. LAW §203-d (effective Jan. 3,2009).

example, the SSN Protection Laws of Hawaii[11] and New Mexico[12] specify that the prohibitions apply to the use of the "entire" SSN, while the Arizona,[13] Michigan,[14] Nebraska,[15] New Jersey,[16] North Carolina,[17] South Carolina[18] and Vermont[19] laws specifically apply to the use of truncated or redacted numbers.

In this regard, the New York SSN Protection Law appears to be the most stringent. The New York law applies to a "Social Security Account Number" (SSAN), which is defined as "includ[ing] the number issued by the federal Social Security Administration and any number derived from such number. Such term shall not include any number that has been encrypted."[20]

3. *Prohibited Activities*

The SSN Protection Laws generally prohibit using SSNs in a manner that provides access to a SSN by the general public. For example, the California law prohibits any person or entity from:

- publicly displaying an individual's SSN;
- printing an individual's SSN on any card used to access products or services provided by the person;
- encoding or embedding an SSN in or on a card or document;
- requiring an individual to transmit his SSN via the Internet unless the connection is secure or the SSN is encrypted;
- requiring an individual to use his SSN to access an Internet Web site unless an additional password or personal identification number (PIN) is also required; or
- printing an individual's SSN on any materials mailed to him absent a federal or state law requirement that the SSN

---

[11] HAW. REV. STAT. ANN. §487J-2(a).
[12] N.M. STAT. ANN. §57-12B-4(A).
[13] ARIZ. REV. STAT. §1373.02.
[14] MICH. COMP. LAWS §445.83.
[15] NEB. REV. STAT. §48-237(2)(a).
[16] N.J. REV. STAT. §56:8-164(a)(1).
[17] N.C. GEN. STAT. §75-62(b)(7).
[18] S.B. 453, 117th S.C. Gen. Assem., 2d Sess. (S.C. 2008).
[19] VT. STAT. ANN. tit. 9, §2440(c)(7).
[20] N.Y. GEN. BUS. LAW §399-dd(1).

be included, except for applications or forms sent by mail as part of an application or enrollment process.[21]

Many other state laws contain similar prohibitions.[22] The SSN Protection Laws also impose a variety of other restrictions, as presented in the following sections.

a. Method of Mailing Documents Containing SSNs

Even when an entity is permitted to mail an individual's SSN, the SSN should not be visible from the outside of the mailing. Specifically, the SSN should not be printed, in whole or in part, on a postcard or other mailer not requiring an envelope, and it should not be visible on the envelope or without the envelope having been opened.[23]

b. Electronic or Facsimile Transmission of SSNs

Unlike the California SSN Protection Law, which does not specifically reference the transmission of SSNs via electronic mail or facsimile, the Maryland law[24] specifically prohibits the inclusion of an individual's SSN on any material that is electronically transmitted or transmitted by facsimile to the individual.

c. Sale of SSNs

Some state laws, such as those in Minnesota,[25] North Carolina,[26] and Vermont,[27] specifically prohibit a person or entity from selling an individual's SSN to a third party. Some state laws, such

[21] CAL. CIV. CODE §§1798.85(a)(1)–(5), 1798.85(f).

[22] *See, e.g.*, 815 ILL. COMP. STAT. §505/2RR(a), (f); N.J. STAT. ANN. §56:8-164(a); TEX. BUS. & COM. CODE §35.58(a). The Minnesota law, however, specifically provides that if any entity receives a number from a third party in connection with a transaction involving or otherwise relating to an individual, the receiving entity is under no obligation to inquire or otherwise determine whether the number is or includes the individual's SSN, and may print the number on materials mailed to the individual, unless the receiving entity has actual knowledge that the number is or includes the individual's SSN. MINN. STAT. §325E.59 Subd. 1(a)(5).

[23] *See, e.g.*, CAL. CIV. CODE §1798.85(a)(5); COLO. REV. STAT. §6-1-715(1)(e); 815 ILL. COMP. STAT. §505/2RR(a)(5).

[24] MD. CODE ANN. COM. LAW §3402(a)(6).

[25] MINN. STAT. §325E.59 Subd. 1(a)(7).

[26] N.C. GEN. STAT. §75-62(a)(6).

[27] VT. STAT. ANN. tit. 9, §2440(a)(6).

as Minnesota[28] and New York,[29] require entities to restrict access to SSNs to employees who have a legitimate purpose and need to access SSNs to perform their job duties.

d. Use of SSNs as Account Numbers

The Michigan law prohibits the use of an individual's entire SSN as the individual's primary account number,[30] and the Minnesota law prohibits assigning or using a number as the primary account identifier that is identical to or incorporates the individual's complete SSN, except in conjunction with an employee or member retirement or benefit plan or human resources or payroll administration.[31]

e. Collection of SSNs

The Alaska law, which goes into effect July 1, 2009, may be the most stringent in this regard. The Alaska law prohibits any person from requesting and collecting SSNs unless the person falls within a specifically enumerated exception.[32] Similarly, the Alaska law prohibits sale, lease, loan, trade, renting, or other disclosure of an individual's SSN to a third party unless such disclosure is specifically permitted under the law, and the Alaska law permits disclosure to employees, agents, and independent contractors only for specific purposes, such as for a legitimate purpose established and directed by the person disclosing the SSN.[33]

f. Disclosure of Employee's Personal Identifying Information

In addition to its SSN Protection Law, New York has a new law protecting the personal identifying information of employees, including SSNs (the New York Employee PII Law). The New York Employee PII Law prohibits employers from communicating an employee's personal identifying information to the general

---

[28]MINN. STAT. §325E.59 Subd. 1(b).
[29]N.Y. GEN. BUS. LAW §399-dd(4).
[30]MICH. COMP. LAWS §445.83(b).
[31]MINN. STAT. §325E.59 Subd. 1(a)(6).
[32]ALASKA STAT. §45.48.10.
[33]ALASKA STAT. §§45.48.20–.30, 45.48.50.

public.[34] "Personal identifying information" is defined as an employee's SSN, home address, or telephone number, personal email address, Internet identification name or password, parent's maiden name, or driver's license number.[35] This law provides for civil penalties of up to $500 for any "knowing violation." As discussed in Section 5, below, an employer must establish internal policies and procedures to prevent such disclosures, to avoid an automatic presumption that any violation was "knowing."

Practice Pointer. As a practical matter, employers should use an employee identification number that is not derived from the employee's SSN. This will minimize an employer's risk of violating SSN Protection Laws, as well as reduce access to employees' SSNs. Because SSNs are vulnerable to identity theft, state breach notification laws generally require a company to notify individuals of a security breach that may have compromised their SSNs or other specified personal information. These laws are discussed in detail in Chapter 9. Employers can help reduce the risk of a security incident requiring notice under these laws by restricting their collection and use of SSNs and other protected types of data.[36]

4. *Exceptions*

A majority of the SSN Protection Laws include some exceptions for the use of SSNs.

a. *Court Filings*

For example, the California law provides an exception for documents that are required to be open to the public pursuant to other specified provisions of California law or records that are required by statute, case law, or California Rule of Court, to be made available to the public by certain entities under the California Constitution.[37] Moreover, the California SSN disclosure law does not prevent the collection, use, or release of SSNs as required

---

[34]N.Y. LAB. LAW §203-d(1)(d).

[35]*Id.*

[36]Note, however, that the North Dakota security breach notification law requires notification of a breach when the breach involves any identification number assigned by an employer. N.D. CENT. CODE §51-30-01(2)(a)(7).

[37]CAL. CIV. CODE §1798.85(c).

by state or federal law or the use of SSNs for internal verification or administrative purposes.[38]

Other states are limiting the filing of documents containing SSNs, however. Effective January 3, 2009, the New York SSN Protection Law will prohibit filing documents that contain SSAN of any other person for public inspection, unless such other person is a dependent child, has consented to such filing, or if such filing is required by federal or state law or regulation or by court rule.[39]

b. Verifications and Investigations

The Michigan law does not apply to the use of the SSN as the primary account number or the printing of the SSN on any information mailed to a person, as long as the use or printing is for an administrative purpose in the ordinary course of business to:

- Verify an individual's identity, identify an individual, or accomplish a similar administrative purpose related to a current or proposed account, transaction, product, service, or employment;
- Investigate an individual's claim, credit, criminal, or driving history;
- Detect, prevent, or deter identity theft or other crime;
- Lawfully pursue or enforce a person's legal rights;
- Lawfully investigate, collect, or enforce a child or spousal support obligation or tax liability; or
- Provide or administer employee or health insurance or membership benefits, claims, or retirement programs or to administer the ownership of shares of stock or other investments.[40]

Under the New York SSN Protection Law, the prohibitions do not prevent the collection, use, or release of a SSAN as required

---

[38]CAL. CIV. CODE §1798.85(b).

[39]N.Y. GEN. BUS. LAW §399-dd(7).

[40]MICH. COMP. LAWS §445.83(3)(a). Moreover, the Michigan law permits the use of an SSN as a primary account number if the use began before the effective date of the law and the use is ongoing, continuous, and in the ordinary course of business; however, if the use is stopped for any reason, this exemption no longer applies. *Id.*, §445.83(3)(b).

by state or federal law or the use of the number for internal verification, fraud investigation, or administrative purposes, or for any business function specifically authorized by certain provisions of the GLBA.[41]

c. Maintenance and Reporting of Employment Records

The South Carolina law specifically permits the submission and use of an SSN or other personally identifying information as part of the maintenance and reporting of employment records, employment verification, or in the course of the administration or provision of employee benefits programs, claims, and procedures related to employment, including termination, retirement, injuries suffered during the course of employment, and other such claims, benefits, and procedures.[42]

d. Other Exemptions

Other state laws include a more expanded list of exceptions to the prohibitions against the use of an SSN. For example, the Hawaii, North Carolina, and Vermont SSN Protection Laws permit:

- use of an SSN in an application or in documents related to an enrollment process, or to establish, amend, or terminate an account, or to confirm the accuracy of the SSN for the purpose of obtaining a credit report pursuant to the FCRA;[43]
- the collection, use, or release of an SSN for internal verification or administrative purposes; the opening of an account or the provision of or payment for a product or service authorized by an individual;
- the collection, use, or release of an SSN related to prevention and investigation of fraud, background checks, social, or scientific research, collection of debt, obtaining a credit

[41]N.Y. GEN. BUS. LAW §399-dd(3).

[42]S.B. 453, 117th S.C. Gen. Assem., 2d Sess. (S.C. 2008).

[43]HAW. REV. STAT. ANN. §487J-2(b)(1); N.C. GEN. STAT. §75.62(a); VT. STAT. ANN. tit. 9, §2440(c)(1). However, a SSN that is permitted to be mailed under this exception may not be printed, in whole or in part, on a postcard or other mailer not requiring an envelope, or visible on the envelope or without the envelope having been opened. *Id.*

report from or furnishing data to a consumer reporting agency pursuant to the FCRA, or other permissible purpose enumerated under the GLBA, or locating an individual who is missing; or

- business activities pursuant to a court order, warrant, subpoena, or when otherwise required by law; a business providing the SSN to a federal, state, or local government entity, including a law enforcement agency, court, or their agents or assigns; or disclosure of an SSN that has been redacted.[44]

5. *Privacy Policy Requirements*

While SSN Protection Laws prohibit improper disclosures of SSNs, a more recent legislative trend requires businesses to take affirmative measures to prevent such disclosures. This trend is most clearly demonstrated in the state laws requiring an entity that collects or uses SSNs to have a privacy policy regarding the protection of SSNs (SSN Policy Laws). Some of these laws require only internal policies and procedures, while others require publicly facing policy statements.

a. *SSN Policy Laws Requiring Internal Policies*

i. *Michigan*

Michigan's SSN Policy Law requires a person who obtains one or more SSNs in the ordinary course of business to create a privacy policy that must, at a minimum: (1) ensure, to the extent practicable, the confidentiality of the SSN; (2) prohibit unlawful disclosure of SSNs; (3) limit access to information that contains an SSN; (4) describe the proper disposal of documents containing an SSN; and (5) establish penalties for the violation of the privacy policy.[45] The privacy policy must be published in an employee handbook, procedures manual, or other similar document.[46]

---

[44]HAW. REV. STAT. ANN. §§487J-2(b)(2)–(10); N.C. GEN. STAT. §75-62(b); VT. STAT. ANN. tit. 9, §§2440(c)(2)–(7).

[45]The privacy policy requirements do not apply to persons who obtain an individual's SSN in the ordinary course of business and in compliance with the FCRA or subtitle A of Title V of the GLBA. MICH. COMP. LAWS §445.84(3).

[46]*Id.*, §445.84.

ii. New Mexico and Texas

The New Mexico SSN Policy Law requires a company acquiring or using SSNs to adopt internal policies that limit access to the SSNs to those employees authorized to have access to that information to perform their duties and hold employees responsible if the SSNs are released to unauthorized persons.[47] The Texas law prohibits an entity from requiring an individual to disclose the individual's SSN to obtain goods or services from or to enter into a transaction with the entity, unless the entity adopts a privacy policy, makes the privacy policy available to the individual, and maintains under the privacy policy the confidentiality and security of an SSN disclosed to the entity.[48]

iii. New York

The New York SSN Policy Law requires any person who is in possession of the SSN of any individual, to the extent that such SSN is maintained for the conduct of business or trade, to take reasonable measures to ensure that no officer or employee has access to the SSN for any purpose other than for a legitimate or necessary purpose related to the conduct of such business or trade and to provide safeguards necessary or appropriate to preclude unauthorized access to the SSN and to protect the confidentiality of the SSN.[49] In addition, the New York SSN disclosure law provides a safe harbor if a person can show, by a preponderance of the evidence, that any violation of the New York SSN disclosure law was not intentional and resulted from a bona fide error made notwithstanding the maintenance of procedures reasonably adopted to avoid such error.[50]

Additionally, New York's SSN Employee PII Law indirectly penalizes an employer that fails to maintain internal policies and procedures to avoid improper disclosures of employees' SSNs and other personal identifying information. The law further provides

[47]N.M. STAT. ANN. §57-12B-3(D).

[48]TEX. BUS. & COM. CODE §35.581. The Texas law provides for exceptions to this requirement of providing a privacy policy for certain entities, including an entity required to maintain and disseminate a privacy policy number under the GLBA. *See id.*

[49]N.Y. GEN. BUS. LAW §399-dd(4).

[50]*Id.*, §399-dd(6).

that it will be presumptive evidence that a violation was knowing if the employer has not put in place any policies or procedures to safeguard against such violation, including procedures to notify relevant employees of these provisions.[51]

b. SSN Policy Laws Requiring External Policies

i. Connecticut

Connecticut has recently enacted a broad privacy policy requirement that would apply to any person who collects SSNs in the course of business.[52] The policy must be published or publicly displayed, and must protect the confidentiality of SSNs, prohibit unlawful disclosure of SSNs, and limit access to SSNs.[53] "Publicly displayed" includes posting on an Internet Web site.[54]

ii. Texas

The Texas law prohibits any person from requiring an individual to disclose his SSN in order to obtain goods or services from, or enter into a business transaction with, the person unless the person:

- adopts a privacy policy;
- makes the privacy policy available to the individual; and
- maintains the confidentiality and security of the SSN under its privacy policy.[55]

A covered person's privacy policy must describe:

- how personal information is collected;
- how and when personal information is used;
- how the personal information is protected;

---

[51]N.Y. LAB. LAW §203-d(3).

[52]H.B. 5658, Gen. Assem. Sess. 2008, §1(b) (Conn. 2008) (effective Oct. 1, 2008). Because the Connecticut law is not limited to entities collecting SSNs from Connecticut residents, this provision may apply broadly.

[53]*Id.*

[54]*Id.*

[55]TEX. BUS. & COM. CODE §35.581(a).

- who has access to the personal information; and
- the method of disposal of the personal information.[56]

However, the privacy policy requirements under the Texas law do not apply to:

- a person who is required to maintain and disseminate a privacy policy under the GLBA, the HIPAA, or the Family Educational Rights and Privacy Act;
- a covered entity under specific Texas insurance regulations;
- specific government bodies; and
- a person with respect to a loan transaction if the person is not engaged in the business of making loans. [57]

Practice Pointer. Employers should establish privacy policies addressing the collection and use of SSNs, including limiting access to SSNs to employees who need to have such access for the conduct of legitimate business, as well as addressing the disposal of materials containing SSNs. In addition, employers should develop policies to maintain, update, and administer their privacy policies.

6. *Additional Requirements*

In addition to the various prohibitions on the use of SSNs and exceptions to the prohibitions, a number of the laws include additional requirements. For example, the Puerto Rico SSN Protection Law required covered employers to certify to the Puerto Rico Department of Labor and Human Resources their compliance with the law by March 2008. If the covered employer cannot provide such a certification, the employers were required to file with the Puerto Rico Department of Labor and Human Resources a working plan for implementing compliance measures by October 2008.[58] As another example, the North Carolina SSN

[56] *Id.*, §35.581(b). The Texas statute does not define the term "personal information."

[57] *Id.*, §35.581.

[58] *See* 29 P.R. LAWS. ANN. §62a(d).

Protection Law requires a business covered by the state SSN disclosure law to make reasonable efforts to cooperate, through systems testing and other means, to ensure that the requirements are implemented.[59]

7. *Enforcement and Administration*

As with the provisions regarding the use of SSNs, the state laws differ widely with respect to enforcement and administration. While some state laws have no express penalties for the violation of the restrictions imposed by these provisions and no state agency is charged with responsibility for issuing regulations,[60] others, such as the Michigan law,[61] provide for criminal and civil penalties for the violation of such laws.

Although the California law does not expressly address enforcement of the state's SSN disclosure law, the California Attorney General may have enforcement authority under the general unfair commercial practices provisions of the California Business and Professions Code.[62] In addition, the California Office of Privacy Protection has published recommended practices for complying with the law.[63] The California Office of Privacy Protection also may undertake some amount of administrative investigation and informal enforcement.

In contrast, the Michigan law provides that a person who knowingly violates the provisions prohibiting the use of SSNs is guilty of a misdemeanor punishable by imprisonment for not more than 93 days or a fine of not more than $1,000, or both.[64] In addition, an individual may bring a civil action against a person who uses a SSN in violation of the prohibitions and may recover actual

---

[59] N.C. GEN. STAT. §65-62(c).

[60] *See, e.g.*, CAL. CIV. CODE §§1798.85–.89; N.M. STAT. ANN. §§57-12B-3, 57-12B-4.

[61] MICH. COMP. LAWS §445.86.

[62] *See* CAL. BUS. & PROF. CODE §17200. Other state laws, which do not include specific enforcement provisions, may similarly be enforced by those states' Attorneys General under the unfair trade practices laws of those states.

[63] Recommended Practices on Protecting the Confidentiality of Social Security Numbers, Office of Privacy Protection (Apr. 2008).

[64] MICH. COMP. LAWS §445.86.

damages, or, in the event of a knowing violation, the greater of actual damages or $1,000 and reasonable attorney's fees.[65] There is no private right of action, however, for conduct by an employee or agent of the person in violation of a privacy policy created pursuant to the requirements of the Michigan statute or in compliance with the FCRA, or subtitle A of title V of the GLBA, if the person has taken reasonable measures to enforce its policy and to correct and prevent the reoccurrence of any known violations.[66]

The New York SSN Protection Law provides the New York Attorney General with enforcement authority, and the Attorney General may seek an injunction against any violation of the statute.[67] In addition, a court may impose a civil penalty[68] if there is a violation of the prohibitions imposed by the statute.[69] However, no person shall be deemed to have violated the provisions of the New York statute if the person can show, by a preponderance of the evidence, that the violation was not intentional and resulted from a bona fide error made notwithstanding the maintenance of procedures reasonably adopted to avoid such error.[70] The New York Employee PII Law provides for civil penalty of up to $500 on any employer for any knowing violation of the law. As explained above, an employer's failure to implement policies or procedures to safeguard against such a violation will be treated as a "knowing" violation.[71] A number of other state laws also provide for Attorney General enforcement.[72]

---

[65] *Id.*

[66] *Id.*

[67] N.Y. GEN. BUS. LAW §399-dd(6).

[68] The penalty can be up to and including $1,000 for a single violation and up to and including $100,000 for multiple violations resulting from a single act or incident. Any subsequent violation is punishable by a civil penalty of not more than $5,000 for a single violation and not more than $250,000 for multiple violation resulting from a single act or incident. *Id.*

[69] *Id.*

[70] *Id.*

[71] N.Y. LAB. LAW §203-d(3).

[72] *See, e.g.*, HAW. REV. STAT. ANN. §487J-3 (providing that a business that violates any provision of the Hawaii SSN disclosure law shall be subject to penalties of not more than $2,500 for each violation and the Hawaii Attorney General or the Executive Director of the Office of Consumer Protection may bring an action, and the business also shall be liable for any actual damages to any injured party); VT. STAT. ANN. tit. 9, §2440(g) (providing that with respect to any entity other than an entity licensed by

Under the North Carolina SSN Protection Law, a violation of this law is treated as a violation of the provisions regarding unfair competition and unfair or deceptive trade practices.[73] As such, a private right of action may exist in addition to the North Carolina Attorney General's authority to enforce the provisions regarding the protection of SSNs. Similarly, a number of other states also deem a violation of the SSN disclosure law as a violation of the state's consumer protection laws.[74]

8. *Compliance Issues for Employers*

Although the state SSN disclosure laws generally limit the use of SSNs, these laws do not preclude employers from requiring applicants or employees to provide their SSN information to meet the employer's legal obligations or for internal verification purposes. Indeed, employers generally must collect an employee's SSN in completing routine new-hire documentation, such as a Form I-9 to verify eligibility to work in the United States and a Form W-4 for tax withholdings.[75]

Courts have confirmed that employers may legitimately require an individual to provide his SSN as a condition of employment, at least for purposes of complying with these legal requirements. For example, in *Sutton v. Providence St. Joseph Medical Center*, an applicant brought a claim of religious discrimination under Title VII of the Civil Rights Act of 1964 when he was denied employment for refusing to provide his SSN on pre-employment

---

or registered with the Department of Banking, Insurance, Securities and Health Care Administration, the Attorney General and State's Attorney shall have sole and full authority to investigate potential violations; enforce, prosecute, obtain, and impose remedies for a violation; and to adopt rules with respect to the state SSN disclosure laws; the Department of Banking, Insurance, Securities and Health Care Administration shall have full authority to investigate potential violations and to prosecute, obtain, and impose remedies for any violation with respect to an entity licensed by or registered with the department).

[73]N.C. Gen. Stat. §75-1.1.

[74]*See, e.g.*, 815 Ill. Comp. Stat. §505/2RR(g); Va. Code Ann. §59.1-444.

[75]*See* Sutton v. Providence St. Joseph Med. Ctr., 192 F.3d 826, 830 (9th Cir. 1999) ("Specifically, the Immigration and Naturalization Services (INS), 8 C.F.R. §274a.2(a) & (b)(1)(i), 8 C.F.R. §274a.10(b)(2); Immigration Form I-9; and the Internal Revenue Code (IRC), 26 U.S.C. §6109(a)(3) & (d), require employers to provide the social security numbers of their employees.").

forms.[76] (According to the court, the applicant believed that the SSN was "the 'Mark of the Beast' prophesied in the Book of Revelations.")[77] Although there was no dispute about the sincerity of the applicant's religious beliefs, the Ninth Circuit held that the employer was not required to accommodate the applicant's religious belief because it directly conflicted with the employer's own legal obligations to collect the SSN.[78] Other courts have reached similar conclusions.[79]

In addition, SSNs are in widespread use in the course of administering group health plans. Applications for health and other insurance, enrollment and claims forms, billing statements, and other materials almost invariably include SSNs as a primary identifier. Moreover, health care providers frequently rely on SSNs as identifiers for patients to link health plans, hospitals, pharmacists, and other providers for treatment and payment purposes. Employers and health insurers use SSNs for tracking and processing claims under health plans and for reporting to state and federal welfare programs such as Medi-Cal or Medicare. Similarly, employee benefit plans governed by the Employee Retirement Income Security Act of 1974 (ERISA) rely on the use of SSNs even though such uses are not excepted from coverage under a majority of the state SSN disclosure laws.[80] In addition, neither the employers that sponsor such plans nor any third-party vendors that may provide services to them are exempted from coverage.

However, the state SSN disclosure laws pose significant compliance issues for all of these common practices. To comply with the requirements of the state SSN disclosure laws, employers may be required to implement many changes to their current operations. These changes may include:

---

[76] *Id.* at 826.

[77] *Id.* at 830.

[78] *Id.*

[79] *See, e.g.*, Seaworth v. Pearson, 203 F.3d 1056 (8th Cir. 2000); Baltgalvis v. Newport News Shipbuilding, Inc., 132 F. Supp. 2d 414 (E.D. Va.), *aff'd*, 15 Fed. Appx. 172, 2001 U.S. App. LEXIS 18349 (4th Cir. 2001) (unpublished decision).

[80] Note, however, that ERISA may preempt the application of the state SSN disclosure laws to employee welfare benefit plans. *See* ERISA §514, 29 U.S.C. §1114 (state laws that "relate to" ERISA-governed employee benefit plans are preempted).

- creation of alternate identification numbers for employees and their dependents;
- reprogramming of computer systems to replace references to SSNs with alternative identifiers;[81]
- removal of SSNs from identification cards;
- removal of SSNs from correspondence, claims forms and statements, and other materials provided by health plans and health insurers; and
- removal of SSNs from benefit statements and similar materials provided in connection with retirement and welfare benefit plans.

In addition, covered entities may wish to evaluate their use of SSNs to ensure that continuing uses are consistent with the requirements imposed by the various state SSN disclosure laws.

The California Office of Privacy Protection has published recommended practices for complying with the law.[82] In particular, the California Office of Privacy Protection recommends that entities: reduce their efforts to collect SSNs; provide information to individuals when SSNs are collected explaining the purpose, the intended use, whether the SSN must be provided, and the consequences of failing to provide the SSN; eliminate the public display of SSNs; control access to SSNs; protect SSNs with appropriate security measures; and implement accountability procedures to monitor the handling of SSNs.[83] As a result, many employers and insurers have taken steps to reduce their reliance on SSNs, particularly where external communications are involved.

---

[81]To ensure that Internet-based benefits and payroll administrative services provided by third-party vendors are provided in compliance with these provisions, employers should consult with their vendors and require assurances that any continuing uses of SSNs are consistent with the requirements. In addition, employers may wish to encourage their vendors to consider using alternative identifiers in lieu of SSNs even when these provisions would not otherwise require them to do so.

[82]Recommended Practices for Protecting the Confidentiality of Social Security Numbers, Office of Privacy Protection (April 2008).

[83]*Id.*

Employers should consider whether to conform their systems to the various state SSN laws or maintain separate systems for tracking and identifying employees.[84]

B. Brazil

Under Brazilian law, employers may collect national identification numbers and use them as employee identification numbers, as long as their use is for internal purposes only. Improper disclosure of such information, however, may violate the employee's constitutional right to privacy.[85] In addition to national identification numbers, Brazil requires all employees to obtain a Work and Social Security Card (CTPS), which provides cardholders with a separate work-related personal identification number.

C. Canada

Canadian Employers must verify new hires' social insurance numbers (SIN) within their first three days of work. Canadian law does not restrict use of the SIN as an employee identification number. While employers are not bound by any specific data security requirements, they are expected to take appropriate safeguards of employee SIN numbers. An employer must retain insurance records, which contain the SINs of individual employees, for at least six years.

---

[84]HIPAA mandates that the U.S. Department of Health and Human Services (HHS) develop a uniform national identifier for use in the health care system. 42 U.S.C. §1320d-2(b). Final regulations relating to employers and health care providers have been issued pursuant to this directive; national standards for employee and health plan identification have not yet been promulgated. *See* Health Insurance Reform: National Standard Employer Identifier, 67 Fed. Reg. 38,009 (May 31, 2002) (codified at 45 C.F.R. pt. 162); National Standard Health Care Provider Identifier, 69 Fed. Reg. 3434 (proposed Jan. 23, 2004) (codified at 45 C.F.R. pt. 162). In light of these forthcoming national standards for employee and health plan identifiers, employers may wish to consider delaying extensive efforts to devise alternative employee identifiers to replace SSNs pending further official guidance.

[85]Brazilian Federal Constitution, Article 5, subsection X.

D. Mexico

Employers in Mexico may collect the national identification numbers of their employees and use them as employee identification numbers, although such personal information is considered confidential and should be used for internal purposes only.

III. EUROPE

A. Belgium

In Belgium, an employer may collect national identification numbers from employees and prospective employees for use as employee identification numbers. Generally speaking, such personal data may not be retained longer than is necessary for the purposes for which they were originally gathered.

B. Germany

The collection, processing, or use of data relating to passports, identity cards, social security numbers, or other identifiers is not subject to any specific requirements in Germany, but rather is governed by the general data protection regime established by the German Federal Data Protection Act. As such, identifiers must not be collected, used, or processed, unless there is statutory permission or an individual's consent that permits such collection, processing, or use. Additionally, the processing must be limited appropriately (e.g., even if there is a statute requiring the identification of an individual through passport details, this does not necessarily permit the collection of the data by making a copy of the passport).

C. Italy

Italy does not have national identification numbers but does have numbers that are derived from a formula aggregating various personal pieces of information. Accordingly, these are not widely relied upon by employers as definitive proof of a person's identity, or as an employee identifier.

D. United Kingdom

National Insurance is a government insurance system that provides certain state benefits and a state retirement pension to employees. These benefits are funded through payroll deductions and employer contributions, which are credited to the employee's National Insurance Number (NIN). The NIN is a unique government identification number that remains unchanged throughout the person's life. The employer may use the NIN solely for the purpose of processing the deduction of income tax payments and National Insurance Contributions. Individuals are advised to keep their NIN confidential and disclose it to their employer for only this purpose. Therefore, an employer should not use the NIN or any portion of the NIN as an employee identification number. An employer should disclose an employee's NIN only to a person or company responsible for processing the company payroll, to the UK tax authority, Her Majesty's Revenue and Customs, to the Department for Public Works and Pensions, or to the Social Security Agency in Northern Ireland.

As an employer collects not only an employee's NIN but also other employee data from which the employee can be identified, the NIN will be considered personal data for the purposes of the Data Protection Act 1998, and the employer should collect, store, and process NINs in accordance with the provisions of that Act.

IV. ASIA AND ASIA PACIFIC

A. Australia

The collection and use of government identity numbers is governed by the Privacy Act 1988 (Cth) (the Privacy Act). In particular, National Privacy Principle (NPP) 7 prohibits an organization from using government identifiers or identity numbers as its own identity number. In addition, the organization is prohibited from using or disclosing a government identifier unless the use or disclosure is necessary for the organization to fulfill its obligations to the government, or is permitted under one of the exceptions listed in the Privacy Act. Such exceptions include, for example, situations in which disclosure is necessary to prevent a serious and imminent threat to an individual's life or public health or public safety or when the organization suspects an illegal act has occurred.

According to an information fact sheet on the use of government identifiers used by the health sector issued by the Privacy Commissioner,[86] private sector health organizations should collect government identifiers only for the purpose of providing care and treatment to a client that is authorized by, and will be financed by, a specific government agency, for example, collecting the Medicare number for treatments under the Medicare Benefits Scheme, or the Department of Veterans Affairs (DVA) Card number for treatment under DVA entitlements. These identifiers then should be used or disclosed only to fulfill reporting obligations to the government agency that assigned the identifier and not for any other purpose (including research purposes), unless specifically authorized by the government.

B. Hong Kong

The collection and use of data relating to Hong Kong Identity Cards (HKID Cards) and the unique serial number embossed thereon are governed by the Personal Data (Privacy) Ordinance (PDPO).[87] The Hong Kong Privacy Commissioner has issued a Code of Practice on the Identity Card number and other Personal Identifiers (the ID Code), which seeks to provide detailed guidance to complement the high level data privacy principles set out in the PDPO.

It should be noted that the provisions of the ID Code are not legally binding. A breach of the ID Code by a data user, however, will give rise to a presumption against the data user in any legal proceedings under the PDPO.

---

[86]*See* "Information Sheet 15—2002: National Privacy Principle 7—Identifiers in the Health Sector."

[87]Cap. 486, Laws of Hong Kong.

1. Employment Candidates

In order to prevent the employment of any person not lawfully employable in Hong Kong, there is a statutory requirement under Section 17J of the Immigration Ordinance[88] requiring the employer to inspect the HKID Card or passport/travel documents ("other immigration document") of a prospective employee before employment commences.

Notwithstanding this inspection obligation, the ID Code states that the prospective employer should not collect a copy of the HKID Card unless the applicant has accepted the offer of employment[89] (see below).

The prospective employer may collect the HKID Card number of a job applicant provided that there is no less privacy-intrusive and practicable alternative and it is necessary for:

- The correct identification of the applicant;
- The correct attribution of records the employer holds relating to the applicants; or
- Checking whether the applicant has applied for a position with it before, or is a former employee (in circumstances where a large number of applicants or former employees may be involved).

On or before the collection of the HKID Card number, the employer should notify the applicant of:

- The purpose for which the HKID Card number will be used;
- The classes of persons to whom the HKID Card number may be transferred;
- Whether it is obligatory or voluntary to supply the HKID Card number; and
- The applicant's right to request access and corrections to personal data held; this is typically effected by means of a Personal Information Collection Statement (PICS) statement.[90]

---

[88]Cap. 115, Laws of Hong Kong.

[89]ID Code §3.3.2.

[90]*See* ¶1.06[2][a].

The HKID Card numbers of unsuccessful candidates should not be retained for longer than two years unless the candidate has given consent, or a subsisting reason (e.g., potential legal proceedings) exists.

2. *Existing Employees*

Section 17K of the Immigration Ordinance requires the employer to keep at the place of employment of each of its employees a record of:

- The full name of the employee as shown in his HKID Card (or other immigration document); and
- The type of HKID Card or other immigration document held by the employee, and the unique number set out therein.

HKID Card numbers collected from employees may be used only for the purposes set out in the ID Code.[91] These purposes include compliance with statutory obligations; use for linking, retrieving, or otherwise processing records held by it relating to the employee; and any other purpose for which the employee has given prescribed consent.

The employer may collect a copy of the employee's HKID Card provided that the employer notifies the employee of: (1) the purpose for which the copy will be used; (2) the classes of persons to whom the copy may be transferred; (3) whether it is obligatory or voluntary to supply the copy; and (4) the applicant's right to request access and corrections to the copy. This is typically effected by means of a PICS statement incorporated in the employee's terms of employment.[92] The ID Code further provides that, at the time of making such a copy, the employer must check the copy against the original and mark it with the word "COPY" (or its equivalent in Chinese), across the entire image of the HKID Card in the presence of the employee in question.[93]

The employer must:

---

[91] ID Code §§2.3 & 2.6.

[92] *See* ¶1.06[2][a].

[93] ID Code §3.9.

- Take all reasonably practicable steps to ensure that the HKID Card number and the name of the holder are not displayed together publicly or made visible or otherwise accessible together to any person other than a person who needs to carry out activities related to permitted uses of the identity card number;[94] and
- Ensure that HKID Card copies are treated as confidential and kept under secure conditions with access restricted to individuals carrying out activities related to permitted uses.[95]

When employees or former employees are issued with identification documents relating to their employment (e.g., site security cards or employee club cards), such identification documents should not bear the HKID Card number of the employee in a legible form (or an altered form from which it is reasonably practicable to deduce the HKID Card number). Note, however, that the inclusion of the employee's HKID Card number in nondirectly legible form (e.g., as a bar code or upon a magnetic strip) is not prohibited.[96]

C. Japan

Japan residents are issued 11-digit identification numbers under Japan's Basic Resident Registry Law (the Law). Article 30, item 43 of the Law restricts the use of this government-issued identification number by anyone other than the individual resident, national and local governments, and certain entities specifically designated by the Law. Accordingly, private sector employers in Japan should not collect these government-issued identification numbers from applicants or employees, or request to inspect government-issued identification cards containing these numbers.

---

[94]ID Code §2.7.
[95]ID Code §3.9.
[96]ID Code §2.8.

D. Korea

Korean employers are permitted to use an individual's resident registration number as his employee identification number; however, the Resident Registration Act requires employers to keep the number confidential and protect it from misuse.

E. New Zealand

The Privacy Act 1993 restricts the use of unique identifiers—such as Inland Revenue Department numbers, bank customer numbers, driver's license numbers, and passport numbers. Under the Privacy Act, such identifiers must not be assigned to individuals unless this is necessary for the organization to carry out its functions efficiently. The identifiers must be truly unique to each individual (except in some tax-related circumstances), and the identity of individuals must be clearly established. No one is required to disclose his unique identifier unless it is for, or related to, one of the purposes for which the identifier was assigned.

Practice Pointer. Given the number of countries that have limitations on the use of a government identifier, employers should consider assigning numbers other than government-issued identification numbers as employee IDs and begin to modify internal systems to allow for an alternative to a government-issued identifier as the internal ID.

CHAPTER 9

SECURITY BREACH NOTIFICATION REQUIREMENTS

I. Overview ... 532
II. Americas ... 533
 A. United States ... 533
  Exhibit 9.1 U.S.: Summary of State Security Breach Notification Laws ... 534
  1. State Notification Laws ... 536
  2. Scope and Coverage ... 539
   a. Information Brokers and Other Species of Covered Entities ... 540
   b. Paper Records ... 542
  3. Covered Information ... 542
   a. Exceptions for Publicly Available Information ... 546
  4. Notification Triggers ... 547
   a. Unauthorized Acquisition ... 547
   b. Risk-Based Triggers for Notification ... 548
   c. Employee Exception to Notification Obligation ... 553
  5. Timing Requirements ... 555
   a. Generally ... 555
   b. Delay for Law Enforcement Investigation ... 557
  6. Notice to Specified State Authorities ... 559
  7. Notification Methods ... 559
   a. Thresholds for Providing Substitute Notice ... 562
   b. Methods of Providing Substitute Notice ... 565
  8. Notice Contents ... 568
   a. Coordination With Consumer Reporting Agencies ... 570

9. Safe Harbors 572
a. Other Exemptions 575
B. Canada 578
1. Personal Information Covered 579
2. Risk Assessment 579
3. Timing and Content of the Notice 580
4. Prevention of Future Breaches 581
5. Ontario Personal Health Information Privacy Act, 2004 (PHIPA) 582
III. Europe 583
A. European Union 583
B. Norway 584
C. United Kingdom 585
IV. Middle East 587
A. United Arab Emirates 587
V. Asia Pacific 588
A. Australia 588
1. Personal Information Covered 588
2. Risk Assessment 589
3. Timing and Content of the Notice 589
B. Japan 590
C. New Zealand 592
1. Personal Information Covered 592
2. Risk Assessment 592
3. Timing and Content of the Notice 593

I. OVERVIEW

Information is the lifeblood of a company and, fundamentally, a company must appropriately protect data containing personal information in order to serve its customers and manage its employees. The United States, Canada, and other countries have developed laws that expressly impose what a company's business environment implicitly mandates, namely, an obligation to develop an information security program that is reasonably designed to protect personal information from unauthorized or unlawful use or disclosure.

Apart from, but not unrelated to, the general obligation to protect data containing personal information, a company must grapple with the consequences of a potential breach of its data security controls. An essential element of each company's overall information security program is designing a process to investigate possible security breach incidents, secure information systems if a breach occurs, and take appropriate steps to respond to the breach. Moreover, developing an effective response program in advance of a security breach incident and updating the program, if necessary, after experiencing a breach, strengthens a company's ability to fulfill the notification duties under laws that arise in the event of a breach. This chapter addresses the main features of security breach notification laws that bear on a company's actions in response to suspected security breach incidents.

II. AMERICAS

A. United States

More than 40 states in the United States have enacted laws imposing notification obligations on companies that discover, or are themselves notified about, a breach of security of their information systems. In general, these laws impose two types of requirements: first, to notify individuals about a breach affecting their personal information; and second, to notify the entities that own or license the data containing the personal information. If a company both owns or licenses data and maintains other data for another entity, the company may need to satisfy both types of notification requirements.

In general, state security breach notification laws are understood to be modeled on the California breach notification law, which went into effect on July 1, 2003 (California Law).[1] Although these state laws vary in many important respects, including the potential penalties and enforcement measures, they share a common policy objective, perhaps best stated by the California Office of Information Security and Privacy Protection: "The purpose of notifying individuals of such incidents is to enable them to take actions to protect themselves against, or mitigate the damage from, identity theft or other possible harm."[2]

---

[1]CAL. CIV. CODE §1798.82.

[2]Recommended Practices of Notice of Security Breach Involving Personal Information, California Office of Information Security & Privacy Protection, May 2008, p. 12.

This section addresses the key requirements of these state notification laws, including certain obligations to notify specified state authorities about a breach of security. These key requirements are also summarized in Exhibit 9.1. Because the steps necessary

EXHIBIT 9.1
U.S.: Summary of State Security Breach Notification Laws

State	Security Breach Notification Law	Applies Only to Computerized Data[a]	Specific Risk-Based Trigger[b]	Notice to Regulators	Notice to Consumer Reporting Agencies	Notice Content Requirements
Alabama	No					
Alaska	Yes	No	Yes	Yes	Yes	No
Arizona	Yes	Yes	Yes	No	No	No
Arkansas	Yes	Yes	Yes	No	No	No
California[c]	Yes	Yes	No	No	No	No
Colorado	Yes	Yes	Yes	No	Yes	No
Connecticut	Yes	Yes	Yes	No	No	No
Delaware	Yes	Yes	Yes	No	No	No
D.C.	Yes	No	No	No	Yes	No
Florida	Yes	Yes	Yes	No	Yes	No
Georgia[d]	Yes	Yes	No	No	Yes	No
Hawaii	Yes	No	Yes	Yes	Yes	Yes
Idaho	Yes	Yes	Yes	No	No	No
Illinois	Yes	Yes	No	No	No	No
Indiana	Yes	No	Yes	No	Yes	No
Iowa	Yes	Yes	No	No	Yes	No
Kansas	Yes	Yes	Yes	No	Yes	No
Kentucky	No					
Louisiana	Yes	Yes	Yes	Yes[e]	No	No
Maine	Yes	Yes	Yes	Yes	Yes	No
Maryland	Yes	Yes	Yes	Yes	Yes	Yes
Massachusetts	Yes	No	Yes	Yes	Yes	Yes
Michigan	Yes	Yes	Yes	No	Yes	Yes
Minnesota	Yes	Yes	No	No	Yes	No
Mississippi	No					
Missouri	No					
Montana	Yes	Yes	Yes	No	Yes	No
Nebraska	Yes	Yes	Yes	No	No	No
Nevada	Yes	Yes	No	No	Yes	No
New Hampshire	Yes	Yes	Yes	Yes	Yes	Yes

State	Security Breach Notification Law	Applies Only to Computerized Data[a]	Specific Risk-Based Trigger[b]	Notice to Regulators	Notice to Consumer Reporting Agencies	Notice Content Requirements
New Jersey	Yes	Yes	Yes	Yes	Yes	No
New Mexico	No					
New York[f]	Yes	Yes	No	Yes[g]	Yes	Yes
North Carolina	Yes	No	Yes	Yes	Yes	Yes
North Dakota	Yes	Yes	No	No	No	No
Ohio	Yes	Yes	Yes	No	Yes	No
Oklahoma	Yes	Yes	Yes	No	No	No
Oregon	Yes	Yes	Yes	No	Yes	Yes
Pennsylvania	Yes	Yes	Yes	No	Yes	No
Puerto Rico	Yes	Yes	No	Yes	No	No
Rhode Island	Yes	Yes	Yes	No	No	No
South Carolina	Yes	Yes	Yes	Yes	Yes	No
South Dakota	No					
Tennessee	Yes	Yes	No	No	Yes	No
Texas	Yes	Yes	No	No	Yes	No
Utah	Yes	Yes	Yes	No	No	No
Vermont	Yes	Yes	Yes	Yes[h]	Yes	Yes
Virginia	Yes	Yes	Yes	Yes	Yes	Yes
Washington	Yes	Yes	Yes	No	No	No
West Virginia	Yes	Yes	Yes	No	Yes	Yes
Wisconsin	Yes	No	Yes	No	Yes	Yes
Wyoming	Yes	Yes	Yes	No	No	Yes

[a]Certain state notification laws, such as the Connecticut, District of Columbia, and New Jersey laws, also apply to electronic files or media, or a device or equipment.

[b]As applicable to persons or entities that own data containing personal information.

[c]Office of Privacy Protection: Recommended Practices on Notice of Security Breach Involving Personal Information, updated February 2007, is available online at www.privacy.ca.gov/recommendations/secbreach.pdf.

[d]Applies only to certain entities defined as "information brokers."

[e]Pursuant to the final rule adopted by the Louisiana Attorney General. 33 La. Reg. 466.

[f]Additional information, including the reporting form, is available online at www.cscic.state.ny.us/ security/securitybreach/index.htm.

[g]The Reporting Form is available online at www.cscic.state.ny.us/security/securitybreach/ReportForm.pdf.

[h]Regulator must be notified if notice is *not* provided to individuals because misuse of information is not reasonably possible.

to comply with state law requirements to notify the data owner or licensee about a breach of security are relatively straightforward and common for all of these state laws, this section focuses on the various requirements to notify individuals. Taking the California Law as the basis for analysis and for comparison, this section analyzes the central aspects of these state security breach notification laws, namely the:

- Scope and coverage of the laws;
- Covered information;
- Triggers for notification;
- Timing requirements;
- Notification methods;
- Notice contents;
- Responsibilities to coordinate with consumer reporting agencies (CRAs); and
- Safe harbors for compliance and limited exemptions.

1. State Notification Laws

The California Law generally requires any person or business that conducts business in California, and that owns or licenses *computerized data* that includes "personal information," to notify the individuals about whom that information relates about any breach of the security of the system in which "unencrypted personal information was, or is reasonably believed to have been, acquired by an unauthorized person."[3]

As originally enacted, the California Law defined *personal information* as an individual's name combined with specified "data elements," when either the name or a data element is unencrypted.[4] Data elements include:

- Social Security number (SSN);
- driver's license or California identification card number; or

[3]CAL. CIV. CODE §1798.82.
[4]CAL. CIV. CODE §1798.82(e).

- account, credit card, or debit card number in combination with any required security code or password that would permit access to an individual's financial account.

Most states have enacted notification laws that cover computerized data containing information similar to the personal information covered by the California Law. In addition, many of these state laws follow the California Law by providing an exception for certain types of information "available to the general public";[5] however, the Alaska, Arkansas, and Rhode Island notification laws, for example, do not contain an exception for publicly available information. In addition, a few state laws apply to a breach of security affecting *paper records* containing personal information. As a result, companies that endeavor to respond to a breach of security on a nationwide basis should not assume that notification is not required if the affected data contains information that is a matter of public record or had been stored in paper records.

The California Law requires a company to notify potentially affected individuals in the "most expedient time possible and without unreasonable delay" after the company discovers, or is itself notified of, the breach of security.[6] The statute provides three methods for notice: written notice, electronic notice, or "substitute notice," which specifically provides for certain methods of generally publicizing the notice.[7] The California Law also provides that notification may be delayed if law enforcement determines that notification will impede a criminal investigation.[8]

---

[5]*See, e.g.*, MINN. STAT. §325E.61, subd. 1(f).

[6]CAL. CIV. CODE §1798.82(a).

[7]CAL. CIV. CODE §1798.82(g).

[8]CAL. CIV. CODE §1798.82(c).

More than 40 states, including Alaska,[9] Arizona,[10] Arkansas,[11] Colorado,[12] Connecticut,[13] Delaware,[14] Florida,[15] Georgia,[16] Hawaii,[17] Idaho,[18] Illinois,[19] Indiana,[20] Iowa,[21] Kansas,[22] Louisiana,[23] Maine,[24] Maryland,[25] Massachusetts,[26] Michigan,[27] Minnesota,[28] Montana,[29] Nebraska,[30] Nevada,[31] New Hampshire,[32] New Jersey,[33] New York,[34] North Carolina,[35] North Dakota,[36] Ohio,[37] Oklahoma,[38] Oregon,[39] Pennsylvania,[40] Rhode Island,[41] South

---

[9]H.B. 65, 25th Legis., 1st Sess. (Alaska 2008) (to be codified at ALASKA STAT. §§45.48.010–45.48.090).

[10]ARIZ. REV. STAT. §44-7501.

[11]ARK. CODE ANN. §4-110-101 et seq.

[12]COLO. REV. STAT. §6-1-716.

[13]CONN. GEN. STAT. §36a-701b.

[14]DEL. CODE ANN. tit. 6, §12B-101 et seq.

[15]FLA. STAT. ANN. §817.5681.

[16]GA. CODE ANN. §10-1-910 et seq.

[17]HAW. REV. STAT. ANN. §§487N-1 to 487N-4.

[18]IDAHO CODE ANN. §§28-51-104, 28-51-107.

[19]815 ILL. COMP. STAT. 530/1 et seq.

[20]IND. CODE §24-4.9-1-1 et seq.

[21]S.B. 2308, 82nd Gen. Assem., 2d Sess. (Iowa. 2008) (to be codified at IOWA CODE §715C.1–.2).

[22]KAN. STAT. ANN. §§50-7a01 to 50-7a04.

[23]LA. REV. STAT. ANN. §51:3071 et seq.

[24]ME. REV. STAT. ANN. tit. 10, §1346 to 1350-A.

[25]MD. CODE ANN., COM. LAW §§14-3501 to 14-3508.

[26]MASS. GEN. LAWS ch. 93H, §§1–6.

[27]MICH. COMP. LAWS §§445.63, 445.72.

[28]MINN. STAT. §325E.61.

[29]MONT. CODE ANN. §§30-14-1701 et seq.

[30]NEB. REV. STAT. ANN. §§87-801 to 87-807.

[31]NEV. REV. STAT. ANN. §§603A.010 et seq.

[32]N.H. REV. STAT. ANN. §§359-C:19 to 359-C:21.

[33]N.J. STAT. §56:8-163.

[34]N.Y. STATE TECH. LAW §208; NY GEN. BUS. LAW §899-aa.

[35]N.C. GEN. STAT. §75-65.

[36]N.D. CENT. CODE §51-30-01 to 51-30-07.

[37]OHIO REV. CODE ANN. §1349.19.

[38]H.B. 2245, 51st Leg., 2d Sess. (Okla. 2008) (to be codified at OKLA. STAT. tit. 24, §§161–166).

[39]OR. REV. STAT. §§646A.602, 646A.604.

[40]73 PA. CONS. STAT. §2301 et seq.

[41]R.I. GEN. LAWS §§11-49.2-1 to 11-49.2-6.

Carolina,[42] Tennessee,[43] Texas,[44] Utah,[45] Vermont,[46] Virginia,[47] Washington,[48] West Virginia,[49] Wisconsin,[50] and Wyoming,[51] as well as the District of Columbia[52] and Puerto Rico,[53] have enacted similar laws that, in general, require companies to notify consumers of a breach of security in which certain personal information relating to those consumers was or is reasonably believed to have been acquired[54] by an unauthorized person in a manner that compromises the security, confidentiality, or integrity of the personal information.

2. *Scope and Coverage*

The California Law imposes two types of notification obligations in the event of a "breach of security" affecting *computerized data*, depending on whether a person or business "owns or licenses" or "maintains" the data. Specifically, the California Law provides that a person or business that

- "conducts business in California, and that owns or licenses computerized data that includes personal information" notify individual residents about whom the information relates upon discovery or notification of the breach;[55] or

---

[42]S.B. 453, 117th Gen. Assem., 2d Reg. Sess. (S.C. 2008) (to be codified at S.C. ANN. §39-1-90).

[43]TENN. CODE ANN. §47-18-2107.

[44]TEX. BUS. & COM. CODE ANN. §§48.101 – 48.103.

[45]UTAH CODE ANN. §§13-44-102, 13-44-202, 13-44-301.

[46]VT. STAT. ANN. tit. 9, §2435.

[47]VA. CODE ANN. §182.186.6.

[48]WASH. REV. CODE §19.255.010.

[49]W. VA. CODE ANN. §§46A-2A-101 to 46A-2A-105.

[50]WIS. STAT. §895.507.

[51]WYO. STAT. ANN. §§40-12-501 to 40-12-509.

[52]D.C. CODE §§28-3851 to 28-3853.

[53]10 P.R. LAWS ANN. §§4051–4055.

[54]Connecticut's notification law defines a security breach as unauthorized access to, or acquisition of, computerized data containing personal information, CONN. GEN. STAT. §36a-701b, and the New Jersey notification law defines a breach as unauthorized access to such data. N.J. STAT. §56:8-163.

[55]CAL. CIV. CODE §1798.82(a).

- "maintains computerized data that includes personal information that they *do not* own" notify the owner or licensee of the information about the breach.[56]

Many states have enacted security breach notice laws that follow the language of the California Law,[57] but there are several notable variations. For example, the New Jersey law applies to entities that *compile or maintain* such data;[58] the Wisconsin Law applies to entities that *maintain or license* such covered data;[59] and the Florida Law requires only that an entity maintain such data.[60]

a. Information Brokers and Other Species of Covered Entities

Whereas the California Law, as well as the notification laws enacted by most other states, applies to a "person or business," several states specifically define the entity that is subject to notification duties. The Georgia and Maine notification laws apply to a specifically defined "information broker"[61] that does business in the state, although the Maine law has been amended also to apply to other types of companies.[62] An "information broker" under the Georgia and Maine laws is generally defined as a person or entity who "for monetary fees or dues, engages in whole or in part

---

[56] CAL. CIV. CODE §1798.82(b) (emphasis added).

[57] COLO. REV. STAT. §6-1-716(2)(a)–(b); DEL. CODE ANN. tit. 6, §102(a)–(b); IDAHO CODE ANN. §28-51-105(1)–(2); LA. REV. STAT. ANN. §51:3074(A)–(B); MINN. STAT. ANN. §325E.61(1)(a)–(b); MONT. CODE ANN. §30-14-1704(1)–(2); NEB. REV. STAT. ANN. §87-803; N.H. REV. STAT. ANN. §359-C:20(I)(a)–(b); N.Y. STATE TECH. LAW §208(2)–(3); N.C. GEN. STAT. §75-65(a)–(b); N.D. CENT. CODE §51-30-02–03; OHIO REV. CODE ANN. §§1349.19(B)(1), 1349.19(C); UTAH CODE ANN. §§13-44-202(1)(A), 13-44-202(3)(A); WASH. REV. CODE §19.255.010(1)–(2).

[58] N.J. STAT. ANN. §56:8-163(a)–(b).

[59] WIS. STAT. §§895.507(2)(a), 895.507(2)(bm).

[60] FLA. STAT. §817.5681(1)(a).

[61] The Georgia law and the Maine law define an "information broker" as "any person or entity who, for monetary fees or dues, engages in whole or in part in the business of collecting, assembling, evaluating, compiling, reporting, transmitting, transferring, or communicating information concerning individuals for the primary purpose of furnishing personal information to nonaffiliated third parties.... [It] does not include any governmental agency whose records are maintained primarily for traffic safety, law enforcement, or licensing purposes." GA. CODE ANN. §10-1-911(2); ME. REV. STAT. ANN. tit. 10, §1347(3).

[62] ME. REV. STAT. ANN. tit. 10, §1348(1)–(2).

in the business of collecting, assembling, evaluating compiling, reporting, transmitting, transferring, or communicating information concerning individuals *for the primary purpose of furnishing personal information to nonaffiliated third parties.*"[63] Thus, if a company does not have as its primary purpose an objective of collecting, assembling, transmitting, or otherwise communicating information to "nonaffiliated third parties," the company should not be subject to the Georgia and Maine notification laws.

By contrast, other states have developed particular terms for companies that are subject to notification duties, but these definitions are broad and likely would cover any type of company that owns, licenses, or maintains personal information, regardless of the extent to which the company handles the information. For example, the Illinois and Nevada laws apply only to "data collectors,"[64] and the Vermont law applies to yet a different definition of "data collector."[65] The Indiana law defines a covered entity as a "data base owner" conducting business in the state,[66] and the Tennessee law applies to an "information holder."[67]

[63]*See, e.g.*, GA. CODE ANN. §10-1-912(a) (emphasis added); ME. REV. STAT. ANN. tit. 10, §1347(3) (emphasis added).

[64]The Illinois law, like the Nevada law, defines "data collector[s]" as including, but not limited to, government agencies, public and private universities, privately and publicly held corporations, financial institutions, retail operators, and any other entity that, for any purpose, handles, collects, disseminates, or otherwise deals with nonpublic personal information. 815 ILL. COMP. STAT. ANN. §§530/5 & 530/10(a)–(b); NEV. REV. STAT. §603A.030.

[65]The Vermont law mirrors the Illinois and Nevada laws in its definition of data collectors. The Vermont law includes, but does not limit, the term to the state, state agencies, political subdivisions of the state, public and private universities, privately and publicly held corporations, limited liability companies, financial institutions, retail operators, and any other entity that, for any purpose, whether by automated collection or otherwise, handles, collects, disseminates, or otherwise deals with nonpublic personal information. VT. STAT. ANN. tit. 9, §2430(3). *See also* VT. STAT. ANN. tit. 9, §2435(b)(1)–(2).

[66]Indiana law defines a "data base owner" as a person that owns or licenses computerized data that includes personal information. IND. CODE §24-4.9-2-3(6); *see also id.* §§24-4.9-3-1, 24-4.9-3-2.

[67]The Tennessee law defines "information holder" as any person or business that conducts business in the state, or any agency of the state or any of its political subdivisions, that owns or licenses computerized data that includes personal information. TENN. CODE ANN. §47-18-2107(a)(2); *see also id.* §47-18-2107(b)–(c).

b. Paper Records

The overwhelming majority of state notification laws apply only to computerized data that include personal information. But a few state laws—namely, the Alaska, Hawaii, Indiana, Massachusetts, North Carolina, and Wisconsin laws—stand as important exceptions, and special care must be taken to investigate potential security breach incidents that involve paper records. The Hawaii and North Carolina laws expressly apply to personal information "in any form," including information stored in paper records. Even though the Wisconsin law is silent as to whether personal information must be in a particular medium, that state's law should not be misinterpreted as applying only to computerized data.[68] The Indiana notification law applies to computerized data that includes personal information and that has been "transferred to another medium, including paper, microfilm, or a similar medium, even if the transferred data are no longer in a computerized format."[69] And the District of Columbia notification law is triggered by the unauthorized acquisition of any equipment or device storing data that compromises the security, confidentiality, or integrity of "personal information" subject to the law.

Practice Pointer: In the event of an apparent breach of a company's information security controls, one of the first issues to address is the form of the records. If the incident appears to be confined to paper records, the company can focus its compliance efforts with respect to possible notification obligations under state laws to those that cover such paper records; state laws requiring notice for a breach of security limited to "computerized data" should not be implicated by the incident.

3. Covered Information

The California Law, as amended, defines "personal information" as an individual's first name or initial and last name in combination with one or more "data elements," if either the name or the data elements are not encrypted. These data elements are:

---

[68]WIS. STAT. ANN. §895.507(2)(a)–(b).
[69]IND. CODE §24-4.9-2-2(a).

- SSN;
- Driver's license number or state identification card number;
- Account, credit card, or debit card number, in combination with any required security code, access code, or password that would permit access to an individual's financial account;
- Medical information;
- Health insurance information.

Many states' notification laws define "personal information" in similar terms, except that they usually omit the data elements of "medical information" and "health insurance information."[70] However, several laws provide that only the data element need not be encrypted, redacted, or secured by another method rendering the element unreadable or unusable, for the data to be considered "personal information."[71]

One notable difference between the data elements covered under the California Law and the notification laws of other states involves the coverage of an account number, by itself, rather than in combination with a security code or password that would permit access to an individual's financial account. For example, the Alaska notification law covers an account number as a data element if an account number can be misused without a personal iden-

---

[70] CONN. GEN. STAT. §36a-701b(a); DEL. CODE ANN. tit. 6, §101(4)(a)–(c); IDAHO CODE ANN. §28-51-104(5)(a)–(c); S.B. 2308, 82nd Gen. Assem., Second Sess. (Iowa 2008) (to be codified at IOWA CODE §715C.1(11)(d)) (covering unique electronic identification or routing code, in combination with a security code, that would permit access to an individual's financial account); LA. REV. STAT. ANN. §51:3073(4)(a)(i)–(iii); MINN. STAT. ANN. §325E.61(1)(e)(1)–(3); MONT. CODE ANN. §30-14-1704(4)(b)(i)(A)–(C); NEV. REV. STAT. §603A.040; N.H. REV. STAT. ANN. §359-C:19(IV)(a)(1)–(3); N.J. STAT. ANN. §56:8-161; R.I. GEN. LAWS §11-49.2-5(c)(1)–(3); TENN. CODE ANN. §47-18-2107(a)(3)(A)(i)–(iii); TEX. BUS. & COM. CODE ANN. §48.002(2)(A)(i)–(iii); VA. CODE ANN. §182.186.6(A); W. VA. CODE ANN. §46A-2A-101(6). Even though the Texas notification law uses the term "sensitive personal information," the definition is substantively similar to the definition of personal information under the California Law as originally enacted.

[71] *See, e.g.*, ARIZ. REV. STAT. §§44-7501(L)(7)(A)(i)–(iii); COLO. REV. STAT. §6-1-716(1)(d)(I)(A)–(C); OHIO REV. CODE ANN. §1349.19(A)(7)(a)(i)–(iii); 73 PA. STAT. ANN. §2302.

tification number (PIN).[72] The Kansas notification law provides that a financial account, credit card, or debit card number, *alone or* in combination with any required security code, access code, or password that would permit access to a consumer's financial account counts as a data element.[73] The District of Columbia and Illinois statutes include as a data element an account, credit card, or debit card number, by itself, *or* an account or credit card number in combination with any required security code, access code, or password that would permit access to an individual's financial account.[74] Similarly, the Hawaii notification law provides that an account number, credit card or debit card number, access code, *or* password that would permit access to an individual's financial account is a covered data element.[75] Correspondingly, several states include as a data element account passwords; PINs; account, credit card, or debit card numbers, if circumstances exist wherein such a number could be used without additional identifying information; access codes or passwords; or other access codes.[76]

Several state notification laws expand the scope of personal information, as originally enacted in the California Law, to include different types of data elements. For example, the Arkansas law includes medical information as an additional data element,[77] and the Wisconsin law includes unique biometric data as a data element.[78] In addition to those covered under the California Law, the North Carolina law includes several other data elements: a passport number, account number, digital signature, biometric data, and fingerprints.[79] The North Dakota law includes among the covered data elements an individual's date of birth, the maiden name of the individual's mother, an identification number assigned to the individual by the individual's employer, and the individual's

[72]H.B. 65, 25th Leg., First Sess. (Alaska 2008) (to be codified at ALASKA STAT. §45.48.090(7)(B)(iii)).

[73]*See, e.g.,* KAN. STAT. ANN. §50-7a01(g)(3).

[74]D.C. CODE §28-3851(3); 815 ILL. COMP. STAT. ANN. §530/5.

[75]HAW. REV. STAT. §487N-1.

[76]ME. REV. STAT. ANN. tit. 10, §1347(6)(A)–(E); VT. STAT. ANN. tit. 9 §2430(5)(A)(I)–(IV); WASH. REV. CODE §19.255.010(5)(a)–(c).

[77]ARK. CODE ANN §4-110-103(7)(A)–(D).

[78]WIS. STAT. §895.507(1)(b)(1)–(5).

[79]N.C. GEN. STAT. §75-61(10); *see also* N.C. GEN. STAT. §14-113.20(b).

digitized or other electronic signature.[80] The Maryland law defines personal information to include an "individual taxpayer identification number,"[81] and the Wyoming law includes a "tribal identification card."[82]

The Georgia notification law, which, as discussed above, applies only to an "information broker," defines personal information, in relevant part, to include any of the prescribed data elements when not in combination with the individual's first name or first initial and last name, if the information compromised would be sufficient to perform or attempt to perform identity theft against the person whose information was compromised.[83]

The New York notification law applies to a breach of security involving the unauthorized acquisition of "private information," which consists of "personal information," in combination with an individual's SSN, driver's license number, or state identification card number, or a credit or debit card account number along with any required security code or password that would permit access to an individual's financial account. Under the New York law, "personal information" is defined as "any information concerning a natural person which, because of name, number, personal mark, or other identifier, can be used to identify such natural person."[84] For example, an individual's date of birth may be viewed as a "number" or "other identifier" within the meaning of the definition of "personal information" under the New York law.

In contrast to the structure of the definition of personal information under the California Law, the Indiana notification law defines "personal information" as (1) an SSN that is not encrypted or redacted; *or* (2) an individual's first and last names, or first initial and last name and one or more of the following unencrypted and unredacted data elements: (a) a driver's license number; (b) a state identification card number; (c) a credit card number; or (d) a financial account number or debit card number in combination with a security code, password, or access code that would permit

---

[80]N.D. CENT. CODE §51-30-01(2)(a)(1)–(8).
[81]MD. CODE ANN., COM. LAW §14-3501(D)(1)(iv).
[82]WYO. STAT. ANN. §40-12-1501(a)(vii)(D).
[83]GA. CODE ANN. §10-1-911(5)(A)–(E).
[84]N.Y. GEN. BUS. §899-aa(1)(a)–(b).

access to the person's account.[85] The Utah law does not include a driver's license or state identification card among the covered data elements.[86]

a. Exceptions for Publicly Available Information

The California Law provides that personal information does not include publicly available information that is lawfully made available to the general public from federal, state, or local government records.[87] Many states use substantively similar language in their notification laws.[88] Several state notification laws provide an exception for publicly available information that is lawfully made available to the general public "in widely distributed media."[89] However, the North Carolina law provides an exception only for publicly available directories containing information an individual has voluntarily consented to have publicly disseminated or listed, including name, address, and telephone number.[90] In comparison, the Nevada law makes a general exception for *all* publicly available information that is lawfully made available to the general public.[91]

---

[85] IND. CODE §24-4.9-2-10(1)–(2).

[86] UTAH CODE ANN. §13-44-102(3)(A)(i)–(iii).

[87] CAL. CIV. CODE §1798.82(f).

[88] ARIZ. REV. STAT. §44-7501(L)(7)(b); DEL. CODE ANN. tit. 6, §101(4); HAW. REV. STAT. §487N-1; 815 ILL. COMP. STAT. ANN. §530/5; IND. CODE §24-4.9-2-10; S.B. 2308, 82nd Gen. Assem., Second Sess. (Iowa 2008) (to be codified at IOWA CODE §715C.1(11)); KAN. STAT. ANN. §50-7a01(g)(3); LA. REV. STAT. ANN. §51:3073(4)(b); MINN. STAT. ANN. §325E.61(1)(f); MONT. CODE ANN. §30-14-1704(4)(b)(ii); NEB. REV. STAT. ANN. §87-802(5); N.H. REV. STAT. ANN. §359-C:19(IV)(b); N.Y. STATE TECH. LAW §208(1)(a); N.D. CENT. CODE §51-30-01(d)(b); OR. REV. STAT. §646A.602(11)(C); 73 PA. STAT. ANN. §2302; TENN. CODE ANN. §47-18-2107(a)(3)(B); TEX. BUS. & COM. CODE ANN. §48.002(2)(B); VT. STAT. ANN. tit. 9, §2430(5)(B); WASH. REV. CODE §19.255.010(6).

[89] COLO. REV. STAT. §6-1-716(1)(d)(II); CONN. GEN. STAT. §36a-701b(a); FLA. STAT. §817.5681(5); GA. CODE ANN. §10-1-911(5); IDAHO CODE ANN. §28-51-104(5); ME. REV. STAT. ANN. tit. 10, §1347(6); N.J. STAT. ANN. §56:8-161; OHIO REV. CODE ANN. §1349.19(A)(7)(b)(i)–(iv); H.B. 2245, 51st Leg., Second Sess. (Okla. 2008) (to be codified at OKLA. STAT. tit. 24, §162(6)); S.B. 453, 117th Gen. Assem., 2d Reg. Sess. (S.C. 2008) (to be codified at S.C. ANN. §39-1-90(D)(3)); UTAH CODE ANN. §13-44-102(3)(B); VA. CODE ANN. §182.186.6(A); W. VA. CODE ANN. §46A-2A-101(6); WIS. STAT. §895.507(1)(c)(1)–(2); WYO. STAT. ANN. §40-12-1501(b).

[90] N.C. GEN. STAT. §75-61(10); *see also* MD. CODE ANN., COMM LAW §14-3501(D)(2).

[91] NEV. REV. STAT. §603A.040.

As noted earlier, the Alaska, Arkansas and Rhode Island laws do not provide any exceptions for publicly available information.

4. *Notification Triggers*

a. *Unauthorized Acquisition*

The California Law provides that covered entities must disclose a breach of the security of the system following discovery or notification of the breach to any resident of California whose unencrypted personal information was, or is reasonably believed to have been, *acquired* by an unauthorized person.[92] Further, the California Law defines a "breach of the security of the system" as the "unauthorized acquisition of computerized data that compromises the security, confidentiality, or integrity of personal information maintained by the person or business."[93] Under the California Law, a company should evaluate whether the breach has *compromised*, or is reasonably likely to *compromise*, the security, confidentiality, or integrity of the information, and, if so, notify potentially affected individuals accordingly. Many other state laws prescribe a standard for notifying individuals that is substantially similar to the standard under the California Law.[94] For example, the Louisiana law contains language similar to the California Law regarding a company's duty to notify a resident following the discovery of a breach of security,[95] but defines a "[b]reach of the security of the system" as "the compromise of the security, confidentiality, or integrity of computerized data that results in, or there is a reasonable basis to conclude has resulted in, the unauthorized acquisition of and access to personal information maintained by the [company]."[96] By contrast, the North Dakota

---

[92]CAL. CIV. CODE §1798.82(a) (emphasis added).

[93]CAL. CIV. CODE §1798.82(d).

[94]ARK. CODE ANN. §4-110-105(a)(1); COLO. REV. STAT. §6-1-716(1)(a)); DEL. CODE ANN. tit. 6, §101(a); D.C. CODE §28-3852; GA. CODE ANN. §10-1-912(a); 815 ILL. COMP. STAT. ANN. §530/10(a); S.B. 2308, 82nd Gen. Assem., Second Sess. (Iowa 2008) (to be codified at IOWA CODE §715C.1(1)); ME. REV. STAT. ANN. tit. 10, §1348(1); MINN. STAT. ANN. §325E.61(1)(a); NEB. REV. STAT. ANN. §87-803; N.H. REV. STAT. ANN. §359-C:19(V); N.Y. STATE TECH. LAW §208(2); TEX. BUS. & COM. CODE ANN. §48.103(b); WASH. REV. CODE §19.255.010(1).

[95]LA. REV. STAT. ANN. §51:3074(A).

[96]LA. REV. STAT. ANN. §51:3073(2).

notification law defines a breach of security, in relevant part, as the unauthorized acquisition of computerized data when access to personal information has not been secured by encryption or by any other method or technology that renders the electronic files, media, or databases unreadable or unusable.[97]

b. Risk-Based Triggers for Notification

Several state notification laws describe a breach of security as the "unauthorized acquisition" of covered information, but impose notification obligations based upon a determination that the acquisition creates, relative to the California Law, a heightened risk of harm to an individual, such as a risk of identity theft or other fraud that could be committed against the individual. For example, the Florida law includes a notification trigger that is similar to the standard under the California Law[98] but, in the definition of a breach of security, provides that the acquisition must be *unlawful* or unauthorized and must *materially compromise* the security, confidentiality, or integrity of the information.[99]

The North Carolina and Ohio laws specifically provide that notification is triggered if the breach creates a *material risk of harm* to a consumer.[100] The North Carolina Law defines "security breach" as the unauthorized access to and acquisition of unencrypted or unredacted records or data containing personal information where illegal use of the personal information has occurred,

[97]N.D. CENT. CODE §51-30-01(1).

[98]FLA. STAT. §817.5681(1)(a).

[99]FLA. STAT. §817.5681(4) (emphasis added). The notification standards under the Montana and Oregon laws similarly provide that a breach consists of the unauthorized acquisition of covered information that materially compromises the security, confidentiality, or integrity of the information, and the acquisition must cause, or be reasonably believed to cause, loss or injury to a resident. MONT. CODE ANN. §30-14-1704(4)(a); OR. REV. STAT. §§646A.602(1)(a), 646A.604(7). Under the Oregon law, a company must maintain a written record of its determination that no reasonable likeliness of harm to consumers has or will occur as a result of the breach. Similarly, the Tennessee law provides that the acquisition must materially compromise the security, confidentiality, or integrity of personal information and that the data must be unencrypted. TENN. CODE ANN. §47-18-2107(a)(1). The Nevada law provides for substantially the same trigger but differs from the California Law's definition of a breach by providing that the acquisition must materially compromise the security, confidentiality, or integrity of personal information. NEV. REV. STAT. §603A.020.

[100]N.C. GEN. STAT. §75-65(a); OHIO REV. CODE ANN. §1349.19(B)(1).

or is reasonably likely to occur, and that creates a material risk of harm to a person. It also includes any incident of unauthorized access to and acquisition of encrypted records or data containing personal information along with the confidential process or key.[101] The Ohio law provides that unauthorized access to and acquisition of data that causes, reasonably is believed to have caused, or reasonably is believed will cause a material risk of identity theft or other fraud to the person or property of a state resident constitutes a security breach.[102]

The Pennsylvania notification law defines a breach of security, in relevant part, as the acquisition of personal information that materially compromises the security, confidentiality, or integrity of the information. Additionally, under the Pennsylvania law, the acquisition must cause, or be reasonably believed to cause, loss or injury to a state resident to constitute a breach.[103]

The Massachusetts law requires notice to individuals of unauthorized acquisition or use of unencrypted data that is capable of compromising the security, confidentiality, or integrity of personal information and that "creates a substantial risk of identity theft or fraud against a resident."[104]

The Wisconsin notification law imposes a general duty on a company whose "principal place of business is located in this state or . . . that maintains or licenses personal information in this state" to notify an individual if the company "knows that personal information in the [company's] possession has been acquired by a person whom the [company] has not authorized to do so."[105] Nevertheless, notification is not required under the Wisconsin law if the unauthorized acquisition of personal information does not create a material risk of identity theft or fraud to the subject of the information.[106]

Several states provide that when a covered entity becomes aware of an incident of unauthorized *acquisition and access* to unencrypted or unredacted computerized data that includes an

---

[101] N.C. GEN. STAT. §75-61(14).
[102] OHIO REV. CODE ANN. §1349.19(A)(1)(a).
[103] 73 PA. STAT. ANN. §2302.
[104] MASS. GEN. LAWS ch. 93H, §1(a).
[105] WIS. STAT. §895.507(2)(a).
[106] *Id.*

individual's personal information, the entity shall conduct a reasonable investigation to promptly determine if there has been a breach of the security system. If the investigation results in a determination that there has been a breach in the security system, the entity is obligated to notify the individuals potentially affected.[107] For example, the Arizona law defines a breach of security as the unauthorized acquisition of and access to unencrypted or unredacted computerized data that materially compromises the security or confidentiality of personal information maintained by a person as part of a database of personal information regarding multiple individuals; additionally, the acquisition and access must cause or be reasonably likely to cause substantial economic loss to an individual.[108] The Hawaii notification law defines "security breach" as the unauthorized access to and acquisition of unencrypted or unredacted records or data containing personal information where illegal use of the personal information has occurred, or is reasonably likely to occur, and that creates a risk of harm to a person.[109] The South Carolina notification law provides a similar risk-based standard for notification obligations.[110]

If a company in Vermont determines that "misuse" of the personal information that is subject to the breach "is not reasonably possible," notice to individuals is not required. However, the company must notify the appropriate Vermont regulator of its determination. The Alaska law provides a similar risk-based standard that alleviates the duty to notify potentially affected individuals, yet requires written notice to the Alaska Attorney General. Moreover, a company that notifies the Alaska Attorney General must document its determination and maintain the documentation for five years.[111]

---

[107] ARIZ. REV. STAT. §44-7501(A); HAW. REV. STAT. §487N-2 (a); 73 PA. STAT. ANN. §2303(a).

[108] ARIZ. REV. STAT. §44-7501(L)(1). The Michigan notification law imposes a similar standard for notification to individuals. MICH. COMP. LAWS §445.72.

[109] The Hawaii law also includes any incident of unauthorized access to and acquisition of encrypted records or data containing personal information along with the confidential process or key. HAW. REV. STAT. §487N-1.

[110] S.B. 453, 117th Gen. Assem., 2d Reg. Sess. (S.C. 2008) (to be codified at S.C. CODE ANN. §39-1-90(D)(1)).

[111] H.B. 65, 25th Leg., First Sess. (Alaska 2008) (to be codified at ALASKA STAT. §45.48.010(c)).

The Vermont notification law differs from Arizona, Hawaii, and Pennsylvania laws in the applicable trigger, providing that either acquisition of *or* access to the data triggers notification,[112] and defines a breach of security in terms that are substantially similar to those in the California Law: defining it as the unauthorized acquisition of computerized data that compromises the security, confidentiality, or integrity of personal information maintained by the person or business.[113]

The Connecticut and New Jersey laws provide that a covered entity shall disclose any breach of security following the discovery of the breach to any resident whose personal information was, or is reasonably believed to have been, *accessed* by an unauthorized person through a breach of security.[114] Despite the potentially lower threshold of "access to," as opposed to "acquisition of," data, the Connecticut law provides that a breach of security must "materially compromise[] the security or confidentiality of personal information maintained by a person as part of a database of personal information regarding multiple individuals"[115] in order to warrant notification to potentially affected individuals. The New Jersey law defines a breach of security as unauthorized access to electronic files, media, or data containing personal information that compromises the security, confidentiality, or integrity of personal information when access to the personal information has not been secured by encryption or by any other method or technology rendering it unreadable or unusable.[116] Similarly, the Puerto Rico notification law is triggered by access to personal information by unauthorized persons or entities, including access through the removal of databases or recording media.[117]

Several states provide that a covered entity shall, when it becomes aware of a breach of the security of the system, conduct a prompt investigation in good faith to determine the likelihood that personal information has been or will be misused. Notice shall be made unless the investigation determines that no misuse of

[112] VT. STAT. ANN. tit. 9 §2435(B)(1).
[113] VT. STAT. ANN. tit. 9 §2430(8)(A).
[114] CONN. GEN. STAT. §36a-701b(b); N.J. STAT. ANN. §56:8-163(a).
[115] CONN. GEN. STAT. §36a-701b(a).
[116] N.J. STAT. ANN. §56:8-161.
[117] 10 P.R. LAWS ANN. §4051.

information has occurred and no such misuse is reasonably likely to occur. The Maryland and Maine laws impose notification duties based on this standard.[118]

The Colorado, Delaware, and Nebraska laws define a breach of security in terms that are substantially similar to those of the California Law—the unauthorized acquisition of computerized data that compromises the security, confidentiality, or integrity of personal information maintained by the person or business—but add that the acquired data must be unencrypted.[119] The Idaho law provides that the acquisition must be *unlawful* or unauthorized and must *materially compromise* the security, confidentiality, or integrity of the information.[120]

The Kansas, Oklahoma, Virginia and West Virginia laws define "breach of security" as the unauthorized acquisition of and access to unencrypted or unredacted computerized data that materially compromises the security or confidentiality of personal information maintained by a person as part of a database of personal information regarding multiple individuals. Additionally, these laws provide that the entity must reasonably believe the acquisition and access has caused or will cause identity theft to any consumer.[121] The Wyoming law similarly defines a "breach of security," and further establishes a standard for notifying individuals based on whether the entity's investigation of the incident, which is mandated by the Wyoming law, determines that misuse

---

[118]COLO. REV. STAT. §6-1-716(2)(a); DEL. CODE ANN. tit. 6, §102(a); IDAHO CODE ANN. §28-51-105(1); KAN. STAT. ANN. §50-7a02(a); NEB. REV. STAT. ANN. §87-803(1); N.H. REV. STAT. ANN. §359-C:20(I)(a); MD. CODE ANN., COM. LAW §14-3504(B); ME. REV. STAT. ANN. tit. 10, §1348(1)(A).

[119]COLO. REV. STAT. §6-1-716(1)(a); DEL. CODE ANN. tit. 6, §101(a); NEB. REV. STAT. ANN. §87-801(a).

[120]IDAHO CODE ANN. §28-51-104(2).

[121]KAN. STAT. ANN. 50-7a01(h); H.B. 2245, 51st Leg., Second Sess. (Okla. 2008) (to be codified at OKLA STAT. tit. 24, §§162(1), 161(3)); VA. CODE ANN. §182.186.6(A); W. VA. CODE ANN. §46A-2A-101(1). The Oregon law similarly defines a "breach of security" (OR. REV. STAT. §646A.602(1)(a)) and requires notification when a company determines that the breach has resulted or will result in a reasonable likelihood of harm. In addition, under the Oregon law, the company must maintain a written record of such determination for five years. OR. REV. STAT. §646A.604(7).

of personal identifying information has occurred or is reasonably likely to occur.[122]

The Indiana and Utah laws specifically provide that if the entity knows, or should have known, that the unauthorized acquisition constituting the breach has resulted in or could result in identity deception, identity theft, or fraud affecting the resident, notification must be made.[123] Additionally, both state laws define a breach of the security of the system, in terms substantively similar to the California Law, as the unauthorized acquisition of computerized data that compromises the security, confidentiality, or integrity of personal information maintained by the person or business.[124]

The Rhode Island law defines a breach of security, in terms substantively similar to the California Law, as the unauthorized acquisition of computerized data that compromises the security, confidentiality, or integrity of personal information maintained by the person or business, with the added provision that the data be unencrypted.[125] In addition, the Rhode Island law provides that notification is required if there is a *significant risk of identity theft.*[126]

c. *Employee Exception to Notification Obligation*

The California Law provides an exception to the definition of breach of security, in the case of good-faith acquisition of personal information by an employee or agent of the person or business for the purposes of the person or business. Acquisition under these circumstances, even if otherwise "unauthorized," is not a breach of the security of the system, provided that the personal information is not used or subject to further unauthorized disclosure.[127] As a result, a company would have no duty to notify individuals about those types of incidents that occur for the purposes of the company's business, when the information acquired will not be further

---

[122] WYO. STAT. ANN. §40-12-502(a).

[123] IND. CODE §24-4.9-3-1(A)(1)–(2); UTAH CODE ANN. §13-44-202(1)(a).

[124] IND. CODE §24-4.9-2(2)-2(a); UTAH CODE ANN. §13-44-102(1)(9).

[125] R.I. GEN. LAWS §11-49.2-5(b).

[126] R.I. GEN. LAWS §11-49.2-3(a).

[127] CAL. CIV. CODE §1798.82(d).

disclosed. The majority of state security breach notification laws have similar language.[128] However, neither the Connecticut nor the Puerto Rico laws provide such an exception for good-faith acquisition by an employee or agent.[129]

The Arizona law contains a similar exception that applies to incidents involving employees or agents, and further specifies that no breach of security occurs as long as there is no further willful unauthorized disclosure.[130]

Several state notification laws provide that the information must have been acquired by the employee or agent for the lawful[131] or *legitimate* purposes of the person or business.[132] The Florida law states that, for this exception to apply, the information must not be used for a purpose unrelated to the business.[133] Alternatively, some states' laws provide that the information must not be used for a purpose other than a *lawful* purpose of the business for the exception to apply.[134]

Several laws limit this exception to circumstances in which it can be determined that the information was not used for an unlawful purpose.[135] The Indiana law states that the information must

---

[128]H.B. 65, 25th Legis., First Sess. (Alaska 2008) (to be codified at ALASKA STAT. §45.48.050); COLO. REV. STAT. §6-1-716(1)(a); DEL. CODE ANN. tit. 6, §101(1); D.C. CODE §28-3851(1); GA. CODE ANN. §10-1-911(1); IDAHO CODE ANN. §28-51-104(2); S.B. 2308, 82nd Gen. Assem., Second Sess. (Iowa 2008) (to be codified at IOWA CODE §715C.1(1)); KAN. STAT. ANN. §50-7a01(h); LA. REV. STAT. ANN. §51:3073(2); MD. CODE ANN., COM. LAW §14-3504(A)(2); MASS. GEN. LAWS ANN. ch. 93H, §1(a); MICH. COMP. LAWS §445.63(b); ME. REV. STAT. ANN. tit. 10, §1347(1); MINN. STAT. ANN. §325E.61(1)(d); MONT. CODE ANN. §30-14-1704(4)(a); NEB. REV. STAT. ANN. §87-802(1); N.H. REV. STAT. ANN. §359-C:19(V); N.Y. STATE TECH. LAW §208(1)(b); N.D. CENT. CODE §51-30-01(1); H.B. 2245, 51st Leg., Second Sess. (Okla. 2008) (to be codified at OKLA. STAT. tit. 24, §162(1)); R.I. GEN. LAWS §11-49.2-5(b); TENN. CODE ANN. §47-18-2107(a)(1); TEX. BUS. & COM. CODE ANN. §48.103(a); VA. CODE ANN. §182.186.6(A); W. VA. CODE ANN. §46A-2A-101(1); WASH. REV. CODE §19.255.010(4); WYO. STAT. ANN. §40-12-501(a)(i).

[129]CONN. GEN. STAT. §36a-701b; 10 P.R. LAWS ANN. §4051(c).

[130]ARIZ. REV. STAT. §44-7501(L)(1).

[131]IND. CODE §24-4.9-2-2(b)(1).

[132]ARK. CODE ANN. §4-110-103(1)(B); SB 583 §2(1)(b) (Or. 2007).

[133]FLA. STAT. §817.5681(4).

[134]HAW. REV. STAT. §487N-1; 815 ILL. COMP. STAT. ANN. §530/5; NEV. REV. STAT. §603A.020; N.J. STAT. ANN. §56:8-161; N.C. GEN. STAT. §75-61(14); VT. STAT. ANN. tit. 9, §2430(8)(B).

[135]OHIO REV. CODE ANN. §1349.19(A)(1)(b)(i); 73 PA. STAT. ANN. §2302; UTAH CODE ANN. §13-44-102(1)(b).

have been obtained for the lawful purposes of the person or business,[136] while the Wisconsin law provides only that, for the exception to apply, the personal information must have been acquired in good faith by an employee or agent of the entity, and the information may be used only for a lawful purpose of the entity.[137]

5. *Timing Requirements*

a. Generally

The California Law provides that, after discovering or being notified of a breach of security, a company must disclose the breach to potentially affected individuals "in the most expedient time possible and without unreasonable delay, consistent with the legitimate needs of law enforcement or any measures necessary to determine the scope of the breach and restore the reasonable integrity of the data system."[138] Many states have adopted substantially the same language.[139] The Arkansas law provides that notice must be made in the most expedient time *and manner* possible.[140] However, the Illinois law does not provide a delay for law enforcement investigation.[141]

Several states expressly allow time for a company to determine the nature and scope of the breach, to identify individuals

---

[136] IND. CODE §24-4.9-2-2(b)(1).

[137] WIS. STAT. §895.507(2)(cm)(2).

[138] CAL. CIV. CODE §1798.82(a).

[139] H.B. 65, 25th Leg., First Sess. (Alaska 2008) (to be codified at ALASKA STAT. §45.48.010(b)); COLO. REV. STAT. §6-1-716(2)(a); DEL. CODE ANN. tit. 6, §102(a); D.C. CODE §28-3852(a); GA. CODE ANN. §10-1-92(a); IND. CODE §24-4.9-3-3(a); KAN. STAT. ANN. §50-7a02(1); LA. REV. STAT. ANN. §51:3074(C); ME. REV. STAT. ANN. tit. 10, §1348(1); MICH. COMP. LAWS §445.72(4)(a); MONT. CODE ANN. §30-14-1704(1); NEB. REV. STAT. ANN. §87-803; NEV. REV. STAT. §603A.220(1); N.J. STAT. ANN. §56:8-163(a); N.Y. STATE TECH. LAW §208(2); N.D. CENT. CODE §51-30-02; 10 P.R. LAWS ANN. §4052; 73 PA. STAT. ANN. §2303(a); R.I. GEN. LAWS §11-49.2-3(a); S.B. 453, 117th Gen. Assem., 2nd Reg. Sess. (S.C. 2008) (to be codified at S.C. CODE ANN. §39-1-90(A)); TENN. CODE ANN. §47-18-2107(b); TEX. BUS. & COM. CODE ANN. §48.103(b); UTAH CODE ANN. §13-44-202(2); VA. CODE ANN. §182.186.6(B); WASH. REV. CODE §19.255.010(1). VT. STAT. ANN. tit. 9 §2435(b)(1); W. VA. CODE ANN. §46A-2A-102(a); WYO. STAT. ANN. §40-12-502(a).

[140] ARK. CODE ANN. §4-110-105(a)(2).

[141] 815 ILL. COMP. STAT. ANN. §530/10(a).

affected, or to restore the reasonable integrity of the data system.[142] However, the Massachusetts law is silent with respect to these aspects of investigating the scope of the incident and timing of the notice.[143]

The Hawaii, North Carolina, and Oregon laws also provide that the general duty to expeditiously notify individuals is to be balanced against the work necessary for a company to determine sufficient contact information.[144] Similarly, the Ohio law also provides time to determine which residents' personal information was accessed and acquired.[145] The New Hampshire law provides only that notification should be made as soon as possible, consistent with the legitimate needs of law enforcement.[146]

The Florida notification law provides that, in general, notice shall be made without unreasonable delay, consistent with the legitimate needs of law enforcement, or subject to any measures necessary to determine the presence, nature, and scope of the breach and restore the reasonable integrity of the system. Yet the Florida law also imposes a timetable: notification must be made not later than 45 days following the determination of the breach, unless otherwise delayed due to a request from law enforcement.[147] Similarly, the Wisconsin law provides that notification shall be made within a reasonable time, not to exceed 45 days after the entity learns of the acquisition of personal information. A determination as to reasonableness shall include consideration of the number of notices that an entity must provide and the methods of communication available to the entity.[148]

---

[142]ARIZ. REV. STAT. §44-7501(A); CONN. GEN. STAT. §36a-701b(b); IDAHO CODE ANN. §28-51-105(1); S.B. 2308, 82nd Gen. Assem., Second Sess. (Iowa 2008) (to be codified at IOWA CODE §715C.2(1)); MD. CODE ANN., COM. LAW §14-3504(D); MINN. STAT. ANN. §325E.61(1)(a).

[143]MASS. GEN. LAWS ch. 93H, §3(a)-(b).

[144]HAW. REV. STAT. §487N-2 (a); N.C. GEN. STAT. §75-65(a); OR. REV. STAT. §646A.604(1).

[145]OHIO REV. CODE ANN. §1349.19(B)(2).

[146]N.H. REV. STAT. ANN. §359-C:20(I)(a).

[147]FLA. STAT. §817.5681(1)(a).

[148]WIS. STAT. §895.507(3)(a).

b. Delay for Law Enforcement Investigation

The California Law provides that notification may be delayed if a law enforcement agency determines that the notification will impede a criminal investigation. Notice shall be provided after the law enforcement agency determines that notification will no longer compromise the investigation.[149] Many states have adopted substantially similar language.[150] In addition, several state laws also provide for a delay if notification may jeopardize national security.[151]

Some state laws require that a request for delay by a law enforcement agency must be made in writing, or the business may document the request contemporaneously in writing, including the name of the law enforcement officer making the request and the officer's law enforcement agency engaged in the investigation.[152] The Pennsylvania law further provides that the law enforcement agency must advise the entity in writing, specifically referencing the state law, that the notification will impede the investigation.[153] The Minnesota law requires the law enforcement agency to affirmatively determine that notification will impede a criminal inves-

---

[149]CAL. CIV. CODE §1798.82(c).

[150]H.B. 65, 25th Leg., First Sess. (Alaska 2008) (to be codified at ALASKA STAT. §45.48.020); ARIZ. REV. STAT. §44-7501(C); ARK. CODE ANN. §4-110-105(c)(1)–(2); COLO. REV. STAT. §6-1-716(2)(c); CONN. GEN. STAT. §36a-701b(d); D.C. CODE §28-3852(d); DEL. CODE ANN. tit. 6, §102(c); FLA. STAT. §817.5681(3); GA. CODE ANN. §10-1-912(c); IDAHO CODE ANN. §28-51-105(3); S.B. 2308, 82nd Gen. Assem., Second Sess. (Iowa 2008) (to be codified at IOWA CODE §715C.2(3)); KAN. STAT. ANN. §50-7a02(c); LA. REV. STAT. ANN. §51:3074(D); MD. CODE ANN., COM. LAW §14-3504(D); ME. REV. STAT. ANN. tit. 10, §1348(3); MICH. COMP. LAWS §445.72(4)(b); MONT. CODE ANN. §30-14-1704(3); NEB. REV. STAT. ANN. §87-803(3); NEV. REV. STAT. §603A.220(3); N.Y. STATE TECH. LAW §208(4); N.D. CENT. CODE §51-30-04; S.B. 453, 117th Gen. Assem., 2d Reg. Sess. (Okla. 2008); 10 P.R. LAWS ANN. §4052; R.I. GEN. LAWS §11-49.2-3(c); S.B. 453, 117th Gen. Assem., 2d Reg. Sess. (S.C.) (to be codified at S.C. CODE ANN. §39-1-90(C)); TENN. CODE ANN. §47-18-2107(d); TEX. BUS. & COM. CODE ANN. §48.103(d); UTAH CODE ANN. §13-44-202(4)(a)–(b); WASH. REV. CODE §19.255.010(3).

[151]N.H. REV. STAT. ANN. §359-C:20(II); OHIO REV. CODE ANN. §1349.19(D); H.B. 2245, 51st Leg. 2d Sess. (Okla. 2008) (to be codified at OKLA. STAT. tit. 24, §163(3)(D)); VA. CODE ANN. §182.186.6(B); W. VA. CODE ANN. §46A-2A-102(e).

[152]HAW. REV. STAT. §487N-2 (c); N.C. GEN. STAT. §75-65(c); OR. REV. STAT. §646A.604.

[153]73 PA. STAT. ANN. §2304.

tigation,[154] and the Wyoming law provides that delay is warranted if a law enforcement agency determines in writing that notification may *seriously* impede a criminal investigation.[155] The New Jersey notification law allows the company to delay if the notice will impede a criminal *or civil* investigation.[156] The Massachusetts law requires the law enforcement agency to notify the state's Attorney General, *in writing*, rather than the entity itself, of the determination regarding the delay.[157] As noted above, the Illinois law does not provide a delay for law enforcement investigation.

The Indiana law provides a delay in response to a request from the attorney general or a law enforcement agency to delay disclosure because disclosure will impede a criminal or civil investigation or jeopardize national security. Notification will be made as soon as possible after the attorney general or a law enforcement agency notifies the person that notice will no longer impede the investigation or jeopardize national security.[158]

The Vermont law provides that notification will be delayed if it will impede a law enforcement investigation or a national or homeland security investigation or jeopardize public safety or national or homeland security interests. Such request must be made in writing, or the business may document the request contemporaneously in writing, including the name of the law enforcement officer making the request and the officer's law enforcement agency engaged in the investigation. Notification will be made once the law enforcement agency no longer believes that notification will be an impediment.[159] The Wisconsin law uses substantively similar language but does not specifically require that the request be in writing.[160]

---

[154] MINN. STAT. ANN. §325E.61(1)(c).
[155] WYO. STAT. ANN. §40-12-502(b).
[156] N.J. STAT. ANN. §56:8-163(c)(2).
[157] MASS. GEN. LAWS ch. 93H, §3(b).
[158] IND. CODE §§24-4.9-3-3(a)(3), 24-4.9-3-3(b)(2).
[159] VT. STAT. ANN. tit. 9 §2435(b)(3).
[160] WIS. STAT. §895.507(5).

6. *Notice to Specified State Authorities*

Even though the California Law does not require notification to a state regulator, a number of states, including Alaska, Hawaii, Louisiana, Maine, Maryland, Massachusetts, New Hampshire, New Jersey, New York, North Carolina, South Carolina, Vermont and Virginia, as well as Puerto Rico, require notification of specified state authorities about the breach of security. Under the Louisiana notification law, for example, a regulation adopted by that state's Attorney General's office requires an entity to provide a written notice detailing the breach of security, including the names of affected Louisiana citizens, to the Consumer Protection Section of the Attorney General's office within 10 days of distributing notices to Louisiana citizens.[161] The New Jersey law requires a company to notify that state's Division of State Policy *prior to* notifying a customer who resides in New Jersey.[162] And, in general, the Alaska and Vermont laws require notice to state authorities when a security breach occurs but, because the breach does *not* pose a risk of identity theft, notice to individuals is not required.[163]

7. *Notification Methods*

The California Law provides that notice to individuals may be provided by one of the following methods: [164]

> (1) written notice;
>
> (2) electronic notice, if the notice provided is consistent with the provisions regarding electronic records and signatures set forth in the Electronic Signatures in Global and National Commerce Act (E-SIGN Act) (15 USC §7001); or
>
> (3) substitute notice.

Most state security breach notification laws contain similar provisions regarding the methods of notifying individuals about a

---

[161] 33 La. Reg. 466.

[162] N.J. STAT. §56:8–163c(1).

[163] H.B. 65, 25th Legis., First Sess. (Alaska 2008) (to be codified at ALASKA STAT. §45.48.010(c)); VT. STAT. ANN. tit. 9, §2435(d)(1).

[164] CAL. CIV. CODE §1798.82(g)(1)–(3).

breach.[165] The Florida law specifies that electronic notice may be provided if it is consistent with the provision regarding electronic records and signatures set forth in the E-SIGN Act *or* if the person or business providing the notice has a valid email address for the subject person and the subject person has agreed to accept communications electronically.[166]

In addition to the methods prescribed by the California Law, several state notification laws also allow telephonic notice.[167] Some state notification laws contain language similar to that of the California Law and include a provision for telephonic notice, but require that telephonic notice be used only if contact is made directly with the affected persons. However, a few states impose certain restrictions on the use of telephonic notice. For example, the Pennsylvania law allows telephonic notice only if the customer can be reasonably expected to receive it and the notice is (1) given in a clear and conspicuous manner; (2) describes the incident in general terms; and (3) verifies personal information but does not require the customer to provide personal information. Additionally, the customer must be provided with a telephone number to call or an Internet Web site to visit for further information or assistance. Similarly, the Vermont law provides that telephonic notice may not be made through a prerecorded message.

Several state notification laws also impose certain conditions on the use of electronic notice that vary from, or are in addition to, the general requirement under the California Law to con-

---

[165] ARK. CODE ANN. §4-110-105(e)(1)–(3); D.C. CODE §28-3851(2); GA. CODE ANN. §10-1-911(3)(a)–(c); 815 ILL. COMP. STAT. ANN. §530/10(c)(1)–(3); KAN. STAT. ANN. §50-9a01(c)(1)–(3); LA. REV. STAT. ANN. §51:3074(E)(1)–(3); ME. REV. STAT. ANN. tit. 10, §1347(4)(A)–(C); MASS. GEN. LAWS ch. 93H, §1(a); MICH. COMP. LAWS §445.72(5); MINN. STAT. ANN. §325E.61(1)(g)(1)–(3); NEV. REV. STAT. §603A.220(4)(a)–(c); N.J. STAT. ANN. §56:8-163(d)(1)–(3); N.D. CENT. CODE §51-30-05(1)–(3); 10 P.R. LAWS ANN. §4053; R.I. GEN. LAWS §11-49.2-5(d)(1)–(3); TENN. CODE ANN. §47-18-2107(e)(1)–(3); TEX. BUS. & COM. CODE ANN. §48.103(e)(1)–(3); WASH. REV. CODE §19.255.010(7)(a)–(c).

[166] FLA. STAT. §817.5681(6)(a)–(c).

[167] CONN. GEN. STAT. §36a-701b(e)(1)–(4); DEL. CODE ANN. tit. 6, §101(3)(a)–(d); IDAHO CODE ANN. §28-51-104(4)(a)–(d); MD. CODE ANN., COM. LAW §14-3504(E); MONT. CODE ANN. §30-14-1704(5)(a)(i)–(iv); NEB. REV. STAT. ANN. §87-802(4)(a)–(d); H.B. 2245, 51st Leg., Second Sess. (Okla. 2008) (to be codified at OKLA. STAT. tit. 24, §162(7)); OR. REV. STAT. §646A.604(4); VA. CODE ANN. §182.186.6(A); W. VA. CODE ANN. §46A-2A-101(7).

form with the E-SIGN Act. For example, the Pennsylvania Law allows electronic notification only if a prior business relationship exists.[168] Likewise, the Vermont law allows electronic notice only if the data collector does not have a mailing address or telephone number for the individual, and provides that the electronic notice may not request, or contain a hypertext link to a request, that the consumer provide personal information. The law requires that the electronic notice conspicuously warn consumers not to provide personal information in response to electronic communications regarding security breaches.[169]

The New York law allows electronic notice only if the person entitled to notification has expressly consented to receiving such a notice in electronic form and a log of each such notification is kept by the entity that notifies affected persons in such form; provided further, however, that in no case shall any person or business require a person to consent to accepting such notices in electronic form as a condition of establishing any business relationship or engaging in any transaction. Additionally, the New York law permits telephonic notification only if a log of each such notification is kept by the entity which notifies affected persons.[170] The New Hampshire law also provides that telephonic notice may be made only if a log of each such notification is kept by the person or business which notifies affected persons.[171]

For electronic mail notice, these states require only that a business or government agency have a valid electronic mail address and that the individual has agreed to receive communications electronically, if the notice is consistent with the provisions regarding electronic records and signatures set forth in the E-SIGN Act.[172] The Maryland notification law permits an entity to notify individuals through electronic mail if the individuals have expressly consented to receive electronic notice or if the entity itself conducts its business "primarily through Internet account transactions or by the Internet."[173]

---

[168] 73 PA. STAT. ANN. §2302.
[169] VT. STAT. ANN. tit. 9 §2435(b)(5)(A)–(B).
[170] N.Y. STATE TECH. LAW §208(5)(a)–(d); N.Y. GEN. BUS. LAW §899-aa(5)(b)-(c).
[171] N.H. REV. STAT. ANN. §359-C:20(III)(a)–(d).
[172] HAW. REV. STAT. §487N-2(e)(1)–(4); N.C. GEN. STAT. §75-65(e)(1)-(4).
[173] MD. CODE ANN., COM. LAW §14-3504(E)(2).

The Indiana law is substantively similar to the California law, but allows telephonic notice *or* notice by facsimile.[174]

Some states allow written notice and substitute notice, as well as telephonic notice, but specify that electronic notice may be used only if the person's primary means of communication with the individual is by electronic means *or* if the notice is consistent with the provisions regarding electronic records and signatures set forth in the E-SIGN Act.[175]

The Utah law allows: written notification by first-class mail; electronic notice, to be used if the person's primary means of communication with the resident is electronic or if the notice is consistent with the provisions regarding electronic records and signatures set forth in the E-SIGN Act; telephonic notice, including the use of automatic dialing technology not prohibited by other law; or by publishing notice of the breach of system security in a newspaper of general circulation.[176]

The Wisconsin Law requires only that notice be made "by mail or by a method the entity has previously employed to communicate with the subject of the personal information. If an entity, through reasonable diligence, cannot determine the mailing address of the subject of the personal information, and if the entity has not previously communicated with the subject of the personal information, the entity shall provide notice by a method reasonably calculated to provide actual notice to the subject of the personal information."[177]

a. Thresholds for Providing Substitute Notice

The California Law provides for substitute notice if the person or business demonstrates that the cost of providing notice would exceed $250,000 or that the affected class of subject persons to be notified exceeds 500,000, or the person or business does not

---

[174]IND. CODE §24-4.9-3(4)(A)(1)–24-4.9-3(4)(A)(4).

[175]H.B. 65, 25th Leg.. First Sess. (Alaska 2008) (to be codified at ALASKA STAT. §45.48.030); ARIZ. REV. STAT. §44-7501(D)(1)–(4); COLO. REV. STAT. §6-1-716(1)(c)(I)–(IV); OHIO REV. CODE ANN. §1349.19(E)(1)–(4); S.B. 453, 117th Gen. Assem., 2nd Reg. Sess. (S.C. 2008) (to be codified at S.C. ANN. §39-1-090(E)(4)).

[176]UTAH CODE ANN. §13-44-202(5)(a)(i)–(iv).

[177]WIS. STAT. §895.507(3)(b).

have sufficient contact information.[178] The majority of states have adopted this language.[179]

However, the Indiana law does not contain a provision allowing a company to provide "substitute notice" in the event that the company lacks sufficient contact information about the potentially affected residents. As a result, unless the breach of security affects more than 500,000 Indiana residents or the cost of disclosure exceeds $250,000, the Indiana law requires a company to directly notify each of the individuals who is potentially affected by the breach. Accordingly, the law appears to require the company to obtain contact information for the individuals in the event the company does not already have the information.[180]

The Kansas and Vermont laws describe the affected class of individuals to be notified as *consumers* (rather than "subject persons"), whereas other state laws such as the laws of Colorado and Delaware use the term "residents." The use of the term "residents" suggests that a company should first determine the number of individuals potentially affected by the security breach on a state-by-state basis to assess whether the applicable threshold has been met. There is a possibility that a state notification law that provides for substitute notice in the event that the affected class of "subject *persons* to be notified" exceeds a certain threshold could be interpreted as relating to the total number of individuals potentially affected by the breach of security. However, the better view is that the threshold necessary to warrant substitute notice is determined only on the basis of affected state residents, consistent with the scope of the state's police powers to require notification to its residents. In addition, substitute notice provisions contained in

---

[178] CAL. CIV. CODE §1798.82(g)(3).

[179] ARK. CODE ANN. §4-110-105(e)(3)(A)(i)–(iii); CONN. GEN. STAT. §36a-701b(e)(4); FLA. STAT. §817.5681(6)(c); GA. CODE ANN. §10-1-911(3)(c); 815 ILL. COMP. STAT. ANN. §530/10(c)(3); LA. REV. STAT. ANN. §51:3074(E)(3); MASS. GEN. LAWS ch. 93H, §1(a); MICH. COMP. LAWS §445.72(5)(d); MINN. STAT. ANN. §325E.61(1)(g)(3); MONT. CODE ANN. §30-14-1704(5)(a)(iv)(A)–(C); NEV. REV. STAT. §603A.220(4)(c); N.J. STAT. ANN. §56:8-163(d)(3); N.Y. STATE TECH. LAW §208(5)(d); N.D. CENT. CODE §51-30-05(3); S.B. 453, 117th Gen. Assem., 2d Reg. Sess. (S.C. 2008) (to be codified at S.C. ANN. §39-1-90(E)(4)); TENN. CODE ANN. §47-18-2107(e)(3); TEX. BUS. & COM. CODE ANN. §48.103(f); WASH. REV. CODE §19.255.010(7)(c).

[180] IND. CODE ANN. §24-4.9-3-4(a); H.B. 2245, 51st Leg., Second Sess. (Okla. 2008) (to be codified at OKLA. STAT. tit. 24, §162(7)(d)).

most state laws are predicated on notice "required by" those laws and, therefore, fundamentally apply only to state residents.

Several states have adopted language regarding substitute notice that is substantively similar to the California Law, but have established different thresholds for the costs of notification or the population of individuals who are potentially affected by the breach. For example, the Alaska law requires costs to exceed $150,000 or more than 300,000 affected residents;[181] the Arizona, Oklahoma, Virginia, and West Virginia laws require costs in excess of $50,000 or more than 100,000 in the affected class;[182] the Colorado law requires costs in excess of $250,000 or more than 250,000 affected residents;[183] the Delaware and Nebraska laws require costs in excess of $75,000 and more than 100,000 affected residents;[184] the Hawaii law requires costs in excess of $100,000 or more than 200,000 in the affected class;[185] the Idaho law requires costs in excess of $25,000 and more than 50,000 affected residents;[186] the Indiana and Ohio laws require costs in excess of $250,000 and more than 500,000 affected residents;[187] the Iowa law requires costs in excess of $250,000 or more than 300,000 persons in the affected class of consumers;[188] the Kansas law requires costs in excess of $100,000 and an affected class of consumers of more than 5,000;[189] the Maine and New Hampshire laws require costs in excess of $5,000 or more than 1,000 in the affected class;[190] the Maryland law requires costs to exceed $100,000 or the affected class of consumers to be more than

---

[181] H.B. 65, 25th Legis., First Sess. (Alaska 2008) (to be codified at ALASKA STAT. §45.48.030(3)).

[182] ARIZ. REV. STAT. §44-7501(D)(4); H.B. 2245, 51st Leg., Second Sess. (Okla. 2008) (to be codified at OKLA. STAT. tit. 24, §162(7)(d)); VA. CODE ANN. §182.186.6(A); W. VA. CODE ANN. §46A-2A-101(7)(D).

[183] COLO. REV. STAT. §6-1-716(1)(c)(IV).

[184] DEL. CODE ANN. tit. 6, §101(3)(d); NEB. REV. STAT. ANN. §87-802(4)(d).

[185] HAW. REV. STAT. §487N-2 (e)(4).

[186] IDAHO CODE ANN. §28-51-104(4)(d).

[187] IND. CODE §24-4.9-3-4(b); OHIO REV. CODE ANN. §1349.19(E)(4).

[188] S.B. 2308, 82nd Gen. Assem., Second Sess. (Iowa 2008) (to be codified at IOWA CODE §715C.2(4)(c)).

[189] KAN. STAT. ANN. §50-7a01(c)(3).

[190] ME. REV. STAT. ANN. tit. 10, §1347(4)(c); N.H. REV. STAT. ANN. §359-C:20(III)(d).

$175,000;[191] the Oregon law requires costs in excess of $250,000 and an affected class of 350,000 consumers;[192] the Pennsylvania law requires costs in excess of $100,000 or more than 175,000 in the affected class;[193] the Puerto Rico law requires costs to be "expressly onerous" due to various factors or more than $100,000; the Rhode Island law requires costs in excess of $25,000 or more than 500,000 in the affected class;[194] and the Vermont law requires costs in excess of $5,000 and an affected class of 5,000 consumers to be notified by written or telephonic consent.[195]

The Hawaii and North Carolina laws are substantively similar to the California Law and also specify that if the person or business has sufficient contact information for some affected individuals but not others, substitute notice may be made only to those affected individuals without sufficient contact information.[196]

The substitute notice provisions of the Nebraska and Ohio laws, which are generally substantively similar to the substitute notice provision of the California Law, also contain separate substitute notice provisions that apply to a company that has ten employees or fewer and demonstrates that the cost of providing notice will exceed $10,000.[197]

b. Methods of Providing Substitute Notice

The California Law provides that substitute notice shall consist of the following:

- Email notice when the person or business has an email address for the subject persons;
- Conspicuous posting of the notice on the Web site page of the person or business, if the person or business maintains one; and
- Notification to major statewide media.[198]

---

[191] MD. CODE ANN., COM. LAW §14-3504(E)(4).
[192] OR. REV. STAT. §646A.604(4)(d).
[193] 73 PA. STAT. ANN. §2302.
[194] R.I. GEN. LAWS §11-49.2-5(d)(3).
[195] VT. STAT. ANN. tit. 9 §2435(b)(5)(B).
[196] HAW. REV. STAT. §487N-2(e)(4); N.C. GEN. STAT. §75-65(e)(4).
[197] NEB. REV. STAT. ANN. §87-802(4)(e); OHIO REV. CODE ANN. §1349.19(E)(5).
[198] CAL. CIV. CODE §1798.82(g)(3)(A)–(C).

Most state notification laws have adopted substantively similar provisions for the methods of substitute notice.[199] The California Law, among other similar state laws, requires "substitute notice" to be provided, in part, through a "[c]onspicuous posting of the notice on the [company's] Web site page."[200] However, these state laws do not articulate standards for a conspicuous notice on a Web site and are silent on whether the entire notice must itself be posted on the Web site, instead of providing a link to the notice on the Web site. In addition, the guidance published by the California Office of Privacy Protection does not address these issues regarding the particular methods of substitute notice.

If applicable to a particular security breach incident, substitute notice is required through one or more methods, and (with rare exceptions) posting the notice on a Web site is not the sole method of notification. For example, the California Law, as noted above, also requires a company to provide notification to major statewide media. In light of the structure of the substitute notice provisions, a strong argument can be made that posting a bulletin that includes a link to the complete notice should be sufficient to satisfy the "conspicuously posting" requirement. However, a company should take steps to confirm that the bulletin is "conspicuous." For example, a company should review the size and location of a notice posted on the Web site to confirm that the notice is not

---

[199]H.B. 65, 25th Leg., First Sess. (Alaska 2008) (to be codified at ALASKA STAT. §45.48.030); ARIZ. REV. STAT. §44-7501(D)(4)(A)–(C); ARK. CODE ANN. §4-110-105(e)(3)(B)(i)–(iii); COLO. REV. STAT. §6-1-716(1)(c)(IV)(A)–(C); CONN. GEN. STAT. §36a-701b(e)(4)(A)–(C); DEL. CODE ANN. tit. 6, §101(3)(d)(1)–(3); D.C. CODE §28-3851(2)(C); FLA. STAT. §817.5681(6)(c)(1)–(3); GA. CODE ANN. §10-1-911(c)(i)–(iii); HAW. REV. STAT. §487N-2(e)(4)(A)–(C); IDAHO CODE ANN. §28-51-104(d)(i)–(iii); 815 ILL. COMP. STAT. ANN. §530/10(c)(3)(i)–(iii); KAN. STAT. ANN. §50-7a01(e)(1); LA. REV. STAT. ANN. §51:3074(E)(3)(a)–(c); ME. REV. STAT. ANN. tit. 10, §1347(4)(C)(1)–(3); MD. CODE ANN., COM. LAW §14-3504(E)(4); MASS. GEN. LAWS ch. 93H, §1(a); MICH. COMP. LAWS §445.72(5)(d); MINN. STAT. ANN. §325E.61(1)(g)(3)(i)–(iii); MONT. CODE ANN. §30-14-1704(5)(b)(i)–(iii); NEB. REV. STAT. ANN. §87-802(4)(d); NEV. REV. STAT. §603A.220(4)(c)(1)–(3); N.H. REV. STAT. ANN. §359-C:20(III)(d)(1)–(3); N.J. STAT. ANN. §56:8-163(d)(3)(a)–(c); N.Y. STATE TECH. LAW §208(5)(d)(1)–(3); N.C. GEN. STAT. §75-65(e)(4)(a)–(c); N.D. CENT. CODE §51-30-05(3)(a)–(c); 73 PA. STAT. ANN. §2302; R.I. GEN. LAWS §11-49.2-5(d)(3)(A)–(C); TENN. CODE ANN. §47-18-2107(e)(3)(A)–(C); TEX. BUS. & COM. CODE ANN. §48.103(f)(1)–(3); WASH. REV. CODE §19.255.010(7)(c)(i)–(iii); W. VA. CODE ANN. §46A-2A-101(7)(D).

[200]CAL. CIV. CODE §1798.82(g)(3)(B).

obscure or otherwise could be viewed as indistinguishable from the existing contents on the company's Web site; if so, the company should revise the notice to make it more prominent—in larger font sizes, with different colors, and set off through the use of graphic devices—than other information displayed on the Web site.

In contrast to the substitute notice provisions under most state laws, the Ohio law generally provides that notification through major media outlets is permissible only to the extent that the cumulative total of the readership, viewing audience, or listening audience of all the outlets so notified equals or exceeds 75 percent of the population of the state.[201] As a result, a company seeking to avail itself of substitute notice on a nationwide basis should take steps to confirm that its "notification to major media outlets" satisfies either (or all) of the thresholds under the Ohio law.

Under the Ohio law, a small company that meets these standards may provide substitute notice by paid advertisement in a local newspaper that is distributed in the geographic area in which the company is located, subject to certain requirements regarding the size of the advertisement and frequency of publication. (As noted above, the Ohio law contains a separate substitute notification provision that applies to a business entity with ten or fewer employees if the cost of providing notice to individual residents exceeds $10,000.[202]) In addition, the company must conspicuously post the notice on its Web site, if it has one, and provide "notification to major media outlets in the geographical area in which the . . . entity is located."[203] The Nebraska law contains a similar provision for substitute notice applicable to small businesses, and permits the substitute notification to be provided by all the methods described in the Ohio law, as well as by electronic mail.[204]

The Indiana, Vermont, and Wyoming laws allow substitute notice only by conspicuous posting of the notice on the Web site of the person or business, if the person or business maintains one, or notification to major news media in the geographic area where

---

[201] OHIO REV. CODE ANN. §1349.19(E)(4)(a)–(c).
[202] OHIO REV. CODE ANN. §1349.19(E)(5).
[203] OHIO REV. CODE ANN. §1349.19(E)(5)(a)–(c).
[204] NEB. REV. STAT. ANN. §87-802(4)(e)(i)–(iv).

residents affected by the breach reside.[205] The Oregon law provides that substitute notice consists of both conspicuous posting of the notice or a link to the notice on the company's home page and notification to major television and newspaper media.[206] Similarly, the Puerto Rico notification law provides for substitute notice to be made by conspicuously posting a notice on the entity's Web site, if the entity maintains a site, and notification to the media, subject to particular requirements.[207]

The Wisconsin law does not have a specific substitute notice provision, but provides that if an entity cannot with reasonable diligence determine the mailing address of the subject of the personal information, and if the entity has not previously communicated with the subject of the personal information, the entity shall provide notice by a method reasonably calculated to provide actual notice to the subject of the personal information."[208]

Utah does not have a substitute notice provision.

8. *Notice Contents*

The California Law currently does not provide specific requirements for the contents of a notice, and the large majority of state security breach notification laws also do not have such provisions.[209] Nevertheless, several state laws impose content requirements for notices provided to individuals. As a result, a company that provides notices to individuals must take steps to confirm that the contents of its notice conforms to the requirements of the applicable state law.

The Hawaii, North Carolina and Virginia laws provide that the notice shall be clear and conspicuous and shall include (1) a description of the incident in general terms; (2) the type of per-

---

[205] IND. CODE §24-4.9-3-4(b)(1)–(2); VT. STAT. ANN. tit. 9, §2435(b)(5)(B)(i)–(ii); WYO. STAT. ANN. §40-12-502(c)(iv).

[206] OR. REV. STAT. §646A.604(4)(d).

[207] 10 P.R. LAWS ANN. §4053(2)(a).

[208] WIS. STAT. §895.507(3)(b).

[209] Arizona, Arkansas, Colorado, Connecticut, Delaware, Florida, Georgia, Idaho, Illinois, Indiana, Kansas, Louisiana, Maine, Minnesota, Montana, Nebraska, Nevada, New Jersey, North Dakota, Ohio, Pennsylvania, Rhode Island, Tennessee, Texas, Utah, and Washington.

sonal information that was subject to the unauthorized access and acquisition; (3) the general acts of the business to protect the personal information from further unauthorized access; (4) a telephone number that the person may call for further information and assistance (if one exists); and (5) advice that directs the person to remain vigilant by reviewing account statements and monitoring free credit reports.[210] The Vermont law requires each of these five items of information and further requires the entity to provide a *toll-free* telephone number.[211]

The Maryland notification law requires a notice to include: (1) the categories of information that were, or are, reasonably believed to have been acquired; (2) contact information for the entity making the notification, including its address and telephone number, as well as a toll-free number if one is maintained; (3) toll-free telephone numbers for the major CRAs; and (4) the toll-free telephone numbers, addresses, and Web sites for the Federal Trade Commission (FTC) and Maryland Office of Attorney General, as well as a statement that an individual can obtain information from these sources about steps to avoid identity theft.[212]

The Massachusetts law requires notice to a resident to include "the consumer's right to obtain a police report, how a consumer requests a security freeze and the necessary information to be provided when requesting the security freeze, and any fees to be paid to any of the consumer reporting agencies," but must *not* include "the nature of the breach or... the number of residents of [Massachusetts] affected by the breach."[213]

The New Hampshire law provides that notice shall include, at a minimum, (1) a description of the incident in general terms; (2) the approximate date of breach; (3) the type of personal information obtained as a result of the security breach; (4) and the telephonic contact information of the person subject to the law.[214] The Oregon law requires a notice to include all of the items of information prescribed by the New Hampshire law, as summarized above,

---

[210] HAW. REV. STAT. §§487N-2(d)(1)–(5); N.C. GEN. STAT. §75-65(d)(1)–(5); VA. CODE ANN. §182.86.6(A).

[211] VT. STAT. ANN. tit. 9 §§2435(b)(4)(A)–(E).

[212] MD. CODE ANN., COM. LAW §14-3504(G).

[213] MASS. GEN. LAWS ch. 93H, §3(b).

[214] N.H. REV. STAT. ANN. §359-C:20(IV)(a)–(d).

plus contact information for the major CRAs and advice for the consumer to report suspected identity theft to law enforcement, including the FTC.[215]

The New York notification law requires a notice to include contact information for the entity and a "description of the categories of information that were, or are reasonably believed to have been, acquired by a person without valid authorization, including specification of which of the elements of personal information and private information were, or are reasonably believed to have been, so acquired."[216]

The Wisconsin law provides that the notice must indicate that the entity knows of the unauthorized acquisition of personal information pertaining to the resident of the state.[217] In addition, the law contains a separate provision that allows an individual who has received such notice to request, in writing, the information that was acquired.[218] In anticipation of such requests by individuals, a company should consider identifying in the notice itself the personal information that was, or is reasonably believed to have been, acquired.

The West Virginia law requires the notice to include a description of the categories reasonably believed to have been accessed or acquired, including SSNs, driver's license numbers or state identification numbers and financial data; a telephone number or Web site address for an individual to learn about the types of information the entity maintained and whether information about that individual was maintained; and toll-free telephone numbers and addresses for the major CRAs and information about how to place a fraud alert or security freeze on the individual's file.[219]

a. Coordination With Consumer Reporting Agencies

The California law does not require a company to coordinate with CRAs regarding the notices it provides to consumers about a breach of security. Many other state notification laws are similarly

---

[215] SB 583 §3(5) (Or. 2007).
[216] N.Y. STATE TECH. LAW §208(6); N.Y. GEN. BUS. LAW §899-aa(7).
[217] WIS. STAT. §895.507(2)(a).
[218] WIS. STAT. §895.507(3)(c).
[219] W. VA. CODE §46A-2A-102(d).

silent on this issue. However, several state laws require a company to notify, or coordinate with, the nationwide CRAs about the timing and distribution of notices provided to individuals.

The Colorado law, for example, provides that if an individual or commercial entity is required to notify more than 1,000 residents of a breach of security, the individual or commercial entity shall also notify, without unreasonable delay, all nationwide CRAs of the anticipated date of the notification and the approximate number of residents who are to be notified.[220] The Georgia and Ohio laws similarly require that the notification to the CRAs contain information on the timing, distribution, and content of the notification to residents.[221] The Maine law provides for notification to CRAs based on the number of *persons* (rather than residents) to be notified, and also requires that the date of the breach be included in the notice to the CRAs.[222] The New York law requires a company to notify the CRAs about the distribution and content of the notice if more than 5,000 residents would be notified of the breach.[223]

Several state notification laws provide that if a person discovers circumstances requiring notification of more than 1,000 persons at a single time, he shall also notify, without unreasonable delay, all nationwide CRAs of the *timing, distribution, and content* of the notices.[224] The Hawaii law provides that the notification must be made in writing;[225] the Nevada law provides that the notification to the CRAs must describe the timing and content of

---

[220]COLO. REV. STAT. §6-1-716(2)(d).

[221]GA. CODE ANN. §10-1-912(d); OHIO REV. CODE ANN. §1349.19(G).

[222]ME. REV. STAT. ANN. tit. 10, §1348(4).

[223]N.Y. STATE TECH. LAW §208(7)(b); N.Y. GEN. BUS. LAW §899-aa(8)(b).

[224]H.B. 65, 25th Leg., First Sess. (Alaska 2008) (to be codified at ALASKA STAT. §45.48.040); D.C. CODE §28-3852(c) (however, under the D.C. law, this requirement does not apply to certain financial institutions that comply with rules issued by the federal bank regulatory agencies); FLA. STAT. §817.5681(12); KAN. STAT. ANN. 50-7a02(f); MD. CODE ANN., COM. LAW §14-3506(A); MICH. COMP. LAWS §445.72(8) (however, under the Michigan law, this requirement does not apply to a financial institution); N.J. STAT. ANN. §56:8-163(f); N.C. GEN. STAT. §75-65(f); OR. REV. STAT. §646A.604(6); 73 PA. STAT. ANN. §2305; TENN. CODE ANN. §47-18-2107(g); VT. STAT. ANN. tit. 9 §2435(c); VA. CODE ANN. §182.186.6(E); W. VA. CODE ANN. §46A-2A-102(f); WIS. STAT. §895.507(2)(br).

[225]HAW. REV. STAT. §487N-2(f).

the notices sent to individuals;[226] the New Hampshire law provides that the notification must describe the timing, number of persons to be notified, and content;[227] and the Indiana law provides that, in the event a database owner is required to notify more than 1,000 consumers, the database owner must disclose to each CRA information necessary to assist the CRA in preventing fraud, including personal information of a resident affected by the breach of security.[228]

The Texas law sets the threshold number of persons to be notified at 10,000 in order to require notice to the nationwide CRAs.[229] The Minnesota law provides the lowest threshold for notifying the nationwide CRAs: if a company discovers circumstances requiring notification of more than 500 persons at one time, the company shall also notify, within 48 hours, all nationwide CRAs about the timing, distribution, and content of the notices.[230]

The Montana law does not contain a particular threshold of the individuals to be notified. Instead, the Montana notification provides that if a business notifies any individual about a security breach and if the notice suggests, indicates, or implies to an individual that the individual may obtain a copy of the file on the individual from a CRA, the business shall coordinate with the CRA as to the timing, content, and distribution of the notice to the individual. In addition, the coordination with the CRA may not unreasonably delay the notice to the potentially affected individuals.[231]

9. *Safe Harbors*

The California Law provides a limited type of safe harbor from the notification methods if a company maintains its own notification procedures as part of an information security policy for treatment of personal information that is otherwise consistent with the timing requirements of the law.[232] Other state laws

---

[226] NEV. REV. STAT. §603A.220(6).
[227] N.H. REV. STAT. ANN. §359-C:20(VI)(a).
[228] IND. CODE §24-4.9-3-1(b).
[229] TEX. BUS. & COM. CODE ANN. §48.103(h).
[230] MINN. STAT. ANN. §325E.61(2).
[231] MONT. CODE ANN. §30-14-1704(7).
[232] CAL. CIV. CODE §1798.82(h).

contain more expansive forms of safe harbors for companies that maintain their own information security programs, which include procedures for notification in response to a breach of security.

In connection with the requirements prescribing the methods of "notice," the California law provides:

> Notwithstanding subdivision (g), a person or business that maintains its own notification procedures as part of an information policy for the treatment of personal information and is otherwise in compliance with the timing requirements of this part, shall be deemed to be in compliance with the notification requirements of this section if the person or business notifies subject persons in accordance with its policies in the event of a breach of security of the system.[233]

In light of the language at the outset of subsection (h)—"[n]otwithstanding subdivision (g)"—this provision of the California Law likely affords an alternative basis for complying with the notification methods prescribed in subsection (g), rather than for complying generally with the requirements of the law. As a result, a company should not, for example, assume that the standards under its own response program for determining whether a breach of security has occurred should apply; rather, consistent with the language of subsection (h), a company should assess an incident in light of the statutory definition of a "breach of security of the system," and comply with other applicable provisions of the California Law.

Many state notification laws contain substantively similar provisions that allow companies to avail themselves of their own notification methods.[234] Additionally, several state laws require that the company's procedures be in compliance with all requirements of the state notification law, not just the timing requirements.[235]

---

[233] *Id.*

[234] ARK. CODE ANN. §4-110-105(f); GA. CODE ANN. §10-1-911(3); 815 ILL. COMP. STAT. ANN. §530/10(d); KAN. STAT. ANN. §50-7a02(d); LA. REV. STAT. ANN. §51:3074(F); MINN. STAT. ANN. §325E.61(1)(h); NEV. REV. STAT. §603A.220(5)(a); N.D. CENT. CODE §51-30-06; H.B. 2245, 51st Leg., Second Sess. (Okla. 2008) (to be codified at OKLA. STAT. tit. 24, §164(A)); TENN. CODE ANN. §47-18-2107(f); VA. CODE ANN. §182.186.6(F); WASH. REV. CODE §19.255.010(8); W. VA. CODE ANN. §46A-2A-103(a).

[235] *See, e.g.*, ARIZ. REV. STAT. §44-7501(E); 73 PA. STAT. ANN. §2307(a).

The Montana law provides that as long as the company does not unreasonably delay notice, as opposed to maintaining procedures to comply with the timing requirements, the company shall be deemed in compliance with the notification requirements.[236]

Several state laws describe the scope of the safe harbor in terms of notifying "affected state residents" as opposed to "subject persons."[237]

In addition to the safe harbor for notification methods, several states allow a company that maintains security breach procedures pursuant to the rules, regulations, procedures, or guidelines established by a primary or functional regulator to be deemed to be in compliance with the security breach notification requirements of the state law, provided that the company notifies subject persons in accordance with the policies of the rules, regulations, procedures, or guidelines established by the primary or functional regulator in the event of a breach of security of the system.[238] This provision is designed to facilitate compliance by an entity that is functionally regulated under the Gramm-Leach-Bliley Act (GLBA) and subject to certain privacy and security requirements under state or federal regulations. A few state laws provide a safe harbor only for a person engaged in trade or commerce that is subject to federal laws and that maintains procedures for security breach notification pursuant to the laws, rules, regulations, guidance, or guidelines issued by a state or federal regulator.[239] The Maine law allows a person who complies with the security breach notification requirements of rules, regulations, procedures, or guidelines established pursu-

---

[236] MONT. CODE ANN. §30-14-1704(6).

[237] COLO. REV. STAT. §6-1-716 (3)(a); DEL. CODE ANN. tit. 6, §103(a); IDAHO CODE ANN. §28-51-106(1); NEB. REV. STAT. ANN. §87-804(1); UTAH CODE ANN. §13-44-202(5)(b).

[238] ARIZ. REV. STAT. §44-7501(F); COLO. REV. STAT. §6-1-716(3)(b); CONN. GEN. STAT. §36a-701b(f); DEL. CODE ANN. tit. 6, §103(b); FLA. STAT. §817.5681(9)(a)–(b); IDAHO CODE ANN. §28-51-106(2); KAN. STAT. ANN. §50-7a02(e); NEB. REV. STAT. ANN. §87-804(2); H.B. 2245, 51st Leg., Second Sess. (Okla. 2008) (to be codified at OKLA. STAT. tit. 24, §164(B)); 73 PA. STAT. ANN. §2307(b)(2); R.I. GEN. LAWS §11-49.7-7; S.B. 453, 117th Gen. Assem., 2d Reg. Sess. (S.C. 2008) (to be codified at S.C. ANN. §39-1-90(J)) (limited to a financial institution subject to and in compliance with the GLBA); UTAH CODE ANN. §13-44-202(5)(c); VA. CODE ANN. 182.186.6(H); W. VA. CODE ANN. §46a-2A-103(c).

[239] N.H. REV. STAT. ANN. §359-C:20(V); OHIO REV. CODE ANN. §1349.19(F)(1).

ant to federal or state law to be considered in compliance with the state's security breach notification law, as long as such law, rules, regulations, or guidelines provided are at least as protective as the state notification law.[240]

The Massachusetts law contains a similar safe harbor, and further requires the company to also provide notice to Massachusetts authorities; the notice must include any steps the company has taken or plans to take pursuant to the applicable law.[241]

The Indiana law provides that a database owner that maintains its own disclosure procedures as part of an information privacy policy or a security policy is not required to make a separate disclosure under that state's notification law if the database owner's information privacy policy or security policy is at least as stringent as the disclosure requirements provided in the state law.[242]

The Oregon law contains exemptions for a company that (1) complies with notification requirements that provide "greater protection for personal information" established by its primary or functional regulator or (2) complies with "a state or federal law that provides greater protection to personal information and at least as thorough disclosure requirements."[243]

Several state notification laws are silent with respect to a safe harbor provision for notification methods, although these laws provide other types of safe harbors, as discussed below. However, the New York notification law does not provide any safe harbor that would allow alternative methods of compliance with the requirements of that state's law.

a. Other Exemptions

Many state notification laws, including the California Law, do not provide outright exemptions from the requirements for notifying individuals or data owners or licensees in the event of a breach of security.[244] A few state notification laws provide exemptions

---

[240]ME. REV. STAT. ANN. tit. 10, §1349(4).

[241]MASS. GEN. LAWS ch. 93H, §5.

[242]IND. CODE §24-4.9-3-4(c).

[243]OR. REV. STAT. §646A.604(8)(a).

[244]These states include Colorado, Connecticut, Delaware, Florida, Georgia, Idaho, Illinois, Kansas, Maine, Montana, Nebraska, New Jersey, New York, Texas, and Washington.

for a "financial institution" that is subject to regulation under the GLBA.[245] However, several state notification laws contain a more limited provision that allows a financial institution to be deemed in compliance with the state law if the institution is subject to and in compliance with the federal Interagency Guidance on Response Programs for Unauthorized Access to Consumer Information and Customer Notice, adopted under the GLBA rules (GLBA Guidance),[246] by the Board of Governors of the Federal Reserve System, the Federal Deposit Insurance Corporation, the Office of the Comptroller of the Currency, and the Office of Thrift Supervision (collectively, the Banking Agencies), or are subject to certain requirements applicable to federal credit unions under 12 C.F.R. part 748.[247] Some states limit an exemption only to entities that are subject to the jurisdiction of the Banking Agencies and, thus, must comply with the GLBA Guidance.[248]

In addition, several state laws provide that a health plan or health care provider that is subject to and in compliance with the standards for privacy of individually identifiable health information and the security standards for the protection of electronic health information under the Health Insurance Portability and Accountability Act of 1996 (HIPAA) is exempt from the notification requirements.[249]

The Indiana law also exempts a database owner that maintains its own disclosure procedures as part of an information privacy, security policy, or compliance plan under the USA PATRIOT Act, Executive Order 13224, the Federal Driver's Privacy Protection Act, the federal Fair Credit Reporting Act, or the GLBA, if the

---

[245] S.B. 2308, 82d Gen. Assem., Second Sess. (Iowa 2008) (to be codified at IOWA CODE §715C.2(7)(c)); MINN. STAT. §325E.61 subd. 4; OR. REV. STAT. §646A.604(8); S.B. 453, 117th Gen. Assem., 2d Reg. Sess. (S.C. 2008) (to be codified at S.C. ANN. §39-1-90(I)).

[246] 70 Fed. Reg. 15,736 (Mar. 29, 2005).

[247] D.C. CODE §28-3852(c); HAW. REV. STAT. §487N-2(g)(1); LA. REV. STAT. ANN. §51:3076; N.C. GEN. STAT. §75-65(h); OHIO REV. CODE ANN. §1349.19(F)(2); VT. STAT. ANN. tit. 9, §2435(f)(1)–(2).

[248] IND. CODE §24-4.9-3-4(e); MD. CODE ANN., COM. LAWS §14-3507(c); MICH. COMP. LAWS §445.72(9); N.D. CENT. CODE §51-30-06; 73 PA. STAT. ANN. §2307(b)(1); R.I. GEN. LAWS §11-49.7-7; WYO. STAT. ANN. §40-12-502(c).

[249] ARIZ. REV. STAT. §44-7501(J)(2); HAW. REV. STAT. §487N-2(g)(2); MINN. STAT. ANN. §325E.61(4); R.I. GEN. LAWS §11-49.7-7.

database owner's information privacy, security policy, or compliance plan requires that Indiana residents be notified of a breach of the security of a system without unreasonable delay.[250]

However, the New Hampshire law exempts financial institutions only from the requirement under the state's law to notify CRAs.[251]

The Arkansas, Iowa, and Oregon laws generally exempt a person or business that is regulated by a state or federal law that provides greater protection to personal information and at least as thorough disclosure requirements for breaches of the security of personal information than that provided by that state's law.[252]

The Wisconsin notification law exempts any entity that is subject to the privacy and security requirements of 15 U.S.C. §§6801–6827, or a person that has a contractual obligation to such an entity, if the entity or person has in effect a policy concerning breaches of information security. In addition, the Wisconsin law broadly exempts a "covered entity" under HIPAA, as described in 45 C.F.R. §164.104(a), if the covered entity complies with the security and privacy standards of 45 C.F.R. part 164.[253]

Practice Pointer: Fundamentally, each company needs to develop a response plan that is designed to operate as an extension of its overall information security program. The response plan must involve key personnel from the departments or divisions of the company that are responsible for maintaining data systems and communicating with customers, as well as appropriate members from the company's human resources and legal departments. In any particular incident, there are three basic steps that every company could take as part of its response:

1. Assess the media and the categories of information potentially affected—namely, assess whether computerized data or paper records are affected, and which items

---

[250] IND. CODE §24-4.9-3-4(d)(1)–(6).

[251] N.H. REV. STAT. ANN. §359-C:20(VI)(b).

[252] ARK. CODE ANN. §4-110-106(a)(1); S.B. 2308, 82nd Gen. Assem. (Iowa 2008) (to be codified at IOWA CODE §715C(7)(c)); OR. REV. STAT. §646A.604(8).

[253] WIS. STAT. §895.507(3m).

of information are involved—to determine whether the personal information is subject to state notification laws;
2. Establish and document the facts and circumstances of the incident, and keep records of the investigation up to date; and
3. Identify the number of individuals potentially affected and where they reside so that the company can be sure to satisfy various statutory requirements that depend, in part, on the number of affected individuals.

Beyond these core elements of a response program, the specific circumstances of an incident will dictate the steps to be taken to determine whether to notify individuals or, if the company does not own or license the data, notify the data owner or licensee. Only after investigating an incident and assessing the crucial factors involved in light of the various duties under state notification laws will a company be able to determine (1) whether a "breach of security," within the meaning of these state laws, has occurred; (2) the individuals, and possibly regulators, who must be notified; and (3) the appropriate methods and content of the notices that will be required.

B. Canada

At present, there is only one law in Canada at the provincial level, Ontario's Personal Health Information Privacy Act, 2004 (PHIPA), that expressly requires organizations that handle personal information to notify those individuals who are affected by a data breach. Efforts are currently underway, however, to introduce legislation that would impose federal security breach notification requirements. In May 2007, a Parliamentary committee, tasked with conducting the first mandated five-year review of the Personal Information Protection and Electronic Documents Act (PIPEDA), issued a report[254] recommending amendments to

---

[254] *See* Recommendations 23, 24, and 25, Statutory Review of the Personal Information Protection and Electronic Documents Act (PIPEDA), Fourth Report of the Standing Committee on Access to Information, Privacy, and Ethics, May 2007, 39th Parliament, 1st Session.

PIPEDA in a number of areas including security breach notification. In the fall of 2007, the government launched a public consultation on breach notification and is now drafting a proposed model that will be used as the basis for legislative amendments for data breach notification under PIPEDA. As an interim measure, the Office of the Privacy Commissioner (OPC) issued voluntary data breach notification guidelines in August 2007.[255] Overviews of the OPC guidelines and PHIPA's breach notification requirements are provided below.

1. Personal Information Covered

Organizations are advised to look at the data elements that have been inappropriately disclosed; the sensitivity of the information; the context of the personal information involved; whether the data are adequately encrypted, anonymized, or not otherwise easily accessible; and how the information could be used. The OPC guidelines note that a combination of personal information is typically more sensitive than a single piece of personal information and that combinations of certain types of specific personal information along with name, address, and date of birth pose a higher risk due to the potential for identity theft.

2. Risk Assessment

Organizations will need to assess the potential harm to individuals, organizations, and the public that may result from the breach and/or notification. For individuals, possible harms include: security risks; identity theft; financial loss; loss of business or employment opportunities; or humiliation and damage to reputation or relationships. Possible harm to organizations might include: loss of trust, loss of assets, financial exposure, or legal proceedings such as class action lawsuits. The harm to the public that could result from breach notifications includes risks to public health and/or public safety.

Each incident, therefore, must be considered on a case-by-case basis to determine whether security breach notification is required. Organizations also are encouraged to inform the

---

[255]*See* "Key Steps for Organizations in Responding to Privacy Breaches."

appropriate privacy commissioner(s) of material security breaches so they are aware of the breach. The key consideration in deciding whether to notify affected individuals should be whether notification is necessary to avoid or mitigate harm to that individual if his personal information has been inappropriately accessed, collected, used, or disclosed. Organizations should also take into account the ability of the individual to take specific steps to mitigate any such harm. Other factors are to be evaluated when assessing whether to report a breach to the OPC (see below).

3. *Timing and Content of the Notice*

The OPC guidelines recommend that affected individuals be notified "as soon as reasonably possible following assessment and evaluation of the breach," unless a delay is warranted to ensure that the investigation is not compromised. The preferred method of notification is direct—by phone, letter, email, or in person. The Privacy Commissioner believes that indirect notification—Web site information, posted notices, or mass media—should generally occur only when direct notification could cause further harm, is prohibitive in cost, or when the contact information for affected individuals is unknown. Using multiple methods of notification may, in certain cases, be appropriate. Organizations should also consider whether the method or level of detail in the notification might increase the risk of harm (e.g., by alerting a laptop thief of the value of the information contained therein).

In addition, it should be the organization that has a direct relationship with the customer, client, or employee that notifies the affected individuals. Typically this would also include notification of breaches that occur at a third-party service provider that has been contracted to maintain or process personal information. However, there may be circumstances in which notification by a third party is more appropriate (e.g., in case of a breach relating to credit card information at a retail merchant, whereby the credit card issuer may need to provide notice since the merchant may not have the necessary contact information).

Lastly, the OPC guidelines encourage organizations to report data breaches to the appropriate Privacy Commissioner(s). Before doing so, an organization should consider: (1) any applicable legislation that may require notification; (2) whether the personal information is subject to privacy legislation; (3) the type of personal information affected, including whether the disclosed information could be used to commit identity theft, as well as whether there is a reasonable risk of harm from the disclosure, including non-monetary losses; (4) the number of people affected by the breach; (5) whether the individuals affected have been notified; and (6) if there is a reasonable expectation that the OPC may receive complaints or inquiries about the breach.

In addition to the Privacy Commissioner(s), others should be informed of the breach: the police, if theft or other crime is suspected; insurers or others, if required by contractual obligations; professional or other regulatory bodies, if professional or regulatory standards require notification to these bodies; credit card companies, financial institutions, or credit reporting agencies, if their assistance is necessary to contact individuals or to assist in mitigating harm; and other internal or external parties not already notified (e.g., third-party contractors or other parties who may be impacted; internal business units not previously advised of the privacy breach, such as government relations, communications and media relations, senior management, etc.; or union or other employee bargaining units).

Organizations should consider the potential impact that the breach and notification may have on third parties and should take action accordingly (e.g., third parties may be affected if individuals cancel their credit cards or if financial institutions issue new cards).

4. *Prevention of Future Breaches*

Organizations are also encouraged to consider developing a plan to prevent future breaches, depending on whether the breach that occurred was systemic or an isolated incident. The plan may include: audits of both physical and technical security practices; reviews of internal policies and procedures (e.g., security policies, record retention, and collection policies); reviews of employee training practices; and reviews of the practices and procedures of service providers and business partners.

5. *Ontario Personal Health Information Privacy Act, 2004*

The Ontario Personal Health Information Privacy Act, 2004 (PHIPA) applies to organizations and individuals involved in the delivery of health care services and establishes rules regarding the collection, use, and disclosure of personal health information. In particular, covered organizations are required to take reasonable steps to ensure that personal health information in their custody or control is protected against theft, loss, and unauthorized use or disclosure. In the event of a data breach, such organizations are required to notify the individual at the first reasonable opportunity if personal health information about the individual is lost, stolen, or accessed by unauthorized persons.

The manner in which notification must be carried out is not specified in the Act; however, the Information and Privacy Commissioner of Ontario (IPC) has issued breach notification guidelines for the health sector.[256] These guidelines encourage covered organizations to report breaches to the IPC so the IPC can help the organization fulfill its obligations under the Act and take remedial steps necessary to prevent future breaches. They recommend that organizations develop a "privacy breach protocol" to ensure that appropriate staff (and where appropriate, senior management) are notified immediately of the breach. Once the organization has identified the scope of the potential breach and taken steps to contain it, it must then identify those individuals whose privacy was breached and notify them of the breach.

Because there are numerous factors that need to be considered when deciding on the best form of notification, such as the sensitivity of the information, organizations are encouraged to contact the IPC to discuss the most appropriate form of notification. In their notices to individuals, organizations are expected to provide details of the extent of the breach and the specifics of the personal health information involved. In particular, affected individuals should be advised of the steps that have been or will be taken to address the breach, and when financial information

---

[256]*See* "What To Do When Faced With A Privacy Breach: Guidelines for the Health Sector," issued by the Information and Privacy Commission/Ontario, Dec. 1, 2006.

or information from government-issued documents is involved, urged to contact their bank, credit card company, and appropriate government departments to advise them of the breach and monitor their accounts and transaction statements for any suspicious activities.

III. EUROPE

A. European Union

The need for security breach notification obligations has been debated for some time, particularly in the context of the review of the European Union (EU) telecommunications regulatory framework. In fact, the European Commission proposed introducing mandatory breach notification requirements for any "provider of publicly available electronic communications services"[257] through amendments to the Electronic Communications Directive 2002/58.[258]

An "electronic communications service" is defined as a "service normally provided for remuneration which consists wholly or mainly in the conveyance of signals on electronic communications networks, including telecommunications services and transmission services in networks used for broadcasting, but excluding services providing, or exercising editorial control over, content transmitted using electronic communications networks and services." The Electronic Communications Directive gives no further guidance on how to interpret the terms "publicly" or "normally provided for remuneration."

Therefore, while the Electronic Communications Directive is aimed at telecommunications operators and Internet service pro-

---

[257]Proposal for a Directive of the European Parliament and of the Council amending Directive 2002/22/EC on universal service and users' rights relating to electronic communications networks, Directive 2002/58/EC concerning the processing of personal data and the protection of privacy in the electronic communications sector and Regulation (EC) No. 2006/2004 on consumer protection cooperation (COM (2007) 698 final).

[258]Directive 2002/58/EC of the European Parliament and of the Council of July 12, 2002 concerning the processing of personal data and the protection of privacy in the electronic communications sector (O.J. L 201/37).

viders, the broad wording could be used by national regulators and law enforcement agencies to regulate employers providing employees with email, internet cafes or hotels allowing guests to use communications devices, or even universities facilitating the use of the internet.

As the proposal was made in the context of the review of the EU telecommunications framework, and possible amendment to the Electronic Communications Directive 2002/58,[259] it is unlikely that the end result will impose obligations on organizations other than communication services providers. That said, there is growing interest in steering the debate towards a broader notification regimen. Consequently, debate on breach notification is likely to continue even after the final amendments to the Electronic Communications Directive are finally approved and may lead to proposals for enactment of a wider data breach law at the EU level.

In addition, recent highly publicized security breaches in the United Kingdom (UK) and elsewhere in Europe have resulted in some Member States, including Germany, Ireland, the Netherlands, and the UK considering the possible adoption of national statutes that would require breach notification.

B. Norway

At present, Norway, which is not a member of the EU, is the only European country that imposes any breach notification obligations. Under the Norwegian Data Protection Regulations implementing the Data Protection Law,[260] the Norwegian Data Protection Authority (Datatilsynet) must be made aware of any unauthorized disclosure of personal data that requires confidential treatment. For example, breaches involving sensitive data such as health information or financial data require notification. There is no obligation, however, to notify the data subject (the individual) whose personal data have been wrongfully disclosed to third parties or when the disclosure involves data that are not subject to confidential treatment (e.g., nonsensitive data). Nonetheless, the Data Protection Authority may require organizations to notify individu-

---

[259] *Id.*

[260] *See* Section 2-6 of the Regulations on the processing of personal data (Personal Data Regulations), Nov. 4, 2005.

als if it deems notification to be necessary in light of the nature and quantity of personal data that were wrongfully disclosed.

The regulations do not specify the timing required for notification; however, the Data Protection Authority has unofficially said that it would expect any such notification to be made within one week of the breach occurring. In addition, the causes of the breach and the measures taken to correct the breach need to be documented by the data controller or data processor.

C. United Kingdom

In April 2008, the Information Commissioner's Office (ICO) released guidance on data security breach management.[261] The paper suggests that the adoption of a security breach response plan could be viewed as one of the appropriate security measures organizations are obligated to adopt under the Directive and national implementation legislation.

According to the guidance paper, a response plan should include four distinct elements:

1. *Containment and recovery.* Following a data breach, in addition to the initial response to investigate and contain the breach, a more thorough recovery plan is necessary in order to limit damages. In particular, the plan should consider who should take the lead in the investigation, who should be notified, whether there is anything the organization could do to recover the losses and limit damages, and whether it is appropriate to inform the police.
2. *Assessment of the risk.* The risk assessment for determining the necessary steps should focus on the analysis of the types of data involved and their sensitivity; whether data have been lost or stolen; whether the data were protected, including by encryption; how many individuals' data are affected by the breach; who the individuals whose data have been breached are; what harm can come to those individuals; and whether there are wider consequences to consider.

---

[261] ICO Guidance on data security breach management.

3. *Notification of breach.* The ICO stresses that notification is not an end in itself. The preferred approach seems to be to "encourage" organizations to notify the ICO and, according to the Notification of Data Security Breaches paper,[262] there is a "presumption" that all "serious breaches" will be reported to the ICO, providing details on:

   - the types of data and number of records;
   - the circumstances of the loss, release, or corruption;
   - the action taken to mitigate effect on individuals involved, including whether they have been informed, and details on how the breach is being investigated;
   - whether any other regulatory body has been informed and its response;
   - the security measures in place, such as encryption, and any remedial action taken to prevent future occurrence; and
   - any information about whether the media are aware of the breach.

   The ICO would then decide, together with the organization, whether notification to affected individuals is required, depending on the nature and seriousness of the breach (e.g., where a high volume of personal data is concerned, or where there is a high risk of individuals suffering some harm, or where particularly sensitive data were lost, released, or unlawfully corrupted). The ICO may also decide that no further action is required, or decide on specific other actions to prevent harm, including formal enforcement action where the organization declines to take any recommended action, or where the ICO has other reasons to doubt future compliance or where there is a need to provide reassurance to the public. The ICO may also "recommend" that the organization make a breach public "where it is clearly in the interests of the individuals concerned or there is a strong public interest argument to do so."

[262] *See* Notification of Data Security Breaches to the ICO.

4. *Evaluation of response.* In determining an effective response, an organization should consider whether sensitive data are involved and whether these data have been shared with or disclosed to others. The organization should establish a group of technical and nontechnical staff to discuss "what if" scenarios.

In summary, while the ICO suggests that a response plan including notification may be legally required for an organization to meet its obligation to maintain appropriate security measures, the ultimate determination is for the organization to make. As a result, organizations are in a legal limbo as to how to react to breaches and whether to notify or not; and if they do, they may possibly face scrutiny from the Information Commissioner and the public.

IV. MIDDLE EAST

A. United Arab Emirates

In 2006, the Dubai International Financial Center Authority (DIFC) amended its privacy law to include, among other things, limited breach notification obligations. The law, DIFC Law No. 1 of 2007, however, applies only to data controllers within the DIFC, a 110-acre free zone area of Dubai, focusing on banking services, capital, asset management, fund registration, insurance and re-insurance, Islamic finance, business processing operations, and professional service providers. Dubai is one of seven Emirates that make up the United Arab Emirates (UAE).

Under the DIFC law,[263] organizations must notify the Commissioner of Data Protection as soon as reasonably practicable about any unauthorized intrusion into any database containing personal information. The law does not distinguish among data elements and there is no obligation to notify the affected individuals.

---

[263]Dubai International Financial Centre Law 1/2007

V. ASIA PACIFIC

A. Australia

Like Canada and New Zealand, Australia is undertaking a comprehensive review of its national privacy law, the Privacy Act 1988, to determine if amendments are required in such areas as security breach notification. In August 2008, the Australian Law Reform Commission, tasked with reviewing and recommending changes to the Privacy Act, issued its formal recommendations[264] and specifically recommended that breach notification be required by law. Immediately following the issuance of the Law Commission's recommendations, the Office of the Privacy Commissioner issued voluntary guidance[265] to assist government agencies, businesses, and nonprofit organizations in responding to data breaches as well as to lay out an approach that could serve as the basis for the government's response to the Law Commission's recommendations. The guidance is based on and virtually identical to the voluntary guidance issued by the Office of the Privacy Commissioner of Canada. See Section II.B.

1. Personal Information Covered

Organizations are advised to consider the type of personal information involved in the breach and whether it creates a greater risk of harm, be it physical, financial, or psychological. Health information; government-issued identifiers such as Medicare, driver's license, health care; and financial account numbers, such as credit or debit card numbers, are cited as examples of the type of information that poses a greater risk of harm to the individual than their name and address.

Another aspect to be considered is who is affected by the breach because certain people in particular may be at risk of harm. While a breach involving the name and address typically might not be considered to be high risk, it may in fact be high risk

---

[264]*See* "For Your Information: Australian Privacy Law and Practice," ALRC Report 108, Australian Law Reform Commission, Aug. 11, 2008..

[265]*See* "Guide to Handling Personal Information Security Breaches," Office of the Privacy Commissioner, Aug. 2008.

if it involves, for example, disclosure of names and addresses of women from a domestic violence shelter.

2. *Risk Assessment*

If a breach creates a real risk of serious harm to the individual, those affected should be notified. Organizations should also consider whether the individual is able to avoid or mitigate possible harm if notified of a breach. Even if the individual would not be able to take steps to rectify the situation, disclosure of very sensitive information or information that is likely to cause humiliation or embarrassment for the individual may still warrant notification. Organizations will also want to consider whether there are legal and contractual obligations to and the consequences of such information.

3. *Timing and Content of the Notice*

Accordance to the guidance, notification of affected individuals should occur as soon as reasonably possible. The preferred method is direct notification either by telephone, letter, email, or in person to the affected individuals. The notice should "stand alone" and not be bundled with other material unrelated to the breach. Multiple methods of notification may be appropriate in certain cases. Indirect notification, such as via a Web site or posted notices, should be used only when direct notification could cause further harm, the cost of such notification is prohibitive, or the organization does not have contact information for the affected individuals. When a breach involves multiple organizations, the organization that has the direct relationship with the individual should be responsible for the notification.

The contents of the notice will vary depending on the breach but, in general, the organization should provide information about the incident in general terms, a description of the information involved in the breach, an account of what the organization has done to control the situation or reduce the harm, and proposed future steps that are planned. In addition, the organization should indicate what it will do to assist the affected individuals, what steps the individuals can take to further protect themselves, and whether other parties such as the Office of the Privacy Commissioner, law enforcement, insurers, financial institutions, and/or regulatory bodies have been notified.

B. Japan

Japan also has a breach notification law. Japan's Protection of Personal Information Law (PIPL)[266] went into effect as to the private sector on April 1, 2005.[267] The PIPL itself does not provide for an explicit obligation to provide breach notification, but the ministry guidelines that implement the PIPL provide for breach notification as a desirable measure to take to comply with the mandatory obligation to take "necessary and appropriate security control measures to prevent the leakage, loss or damage of personal data." Thus, most organizations in Japan understand this as an affirmative obligation to provide notice following a security breach involving personal information.

Under the Ministry of Economy, Trade and Industry Guidelines (METI Guidelines) as amended in March 2007, organizations "must" take measures to deal with incidents or breaches, and when there has been a breach of personal information, it is "desirable" for them to (1) investigate the facts surrounding the breach and cause of breach; (2) identify the extent of the security breach; (3) deliberate and implement measures to prevent further security incidents; (4) provide notice to individuals who may be affected by the security breach; (5) provide notice to METI or any other relevant ministry; and (6) publicly announce the facts surrounding the breach and measures taken to prevent further incidents.[268] Although the language suggests that the obligation for breach notification is not mandatory, in practice, businesses have been treating the obligation to provide notice both to individuals and to METI as mandatory.

Unlike the prior version of the METI Guidelines, the METI Guidelines as revised in March 2007 incorporate the concept of risk of harm and provide for exceptions to breach notification to

---

[266]Personal Information Protection Law (Law No. 57 of 2003).

[267]*Id.*, Art. 36.

[268]METI Guidelines (revised March 2007), §2-2-3-2, Organizational Security Measures. Examples of desirable measures to carry out "responses to accidents and violations."

individuals—more in line with the breach notification laws in the United States. The revised METI Guidelines provide that if the rights of the individual have not been infringed, and there is very little possibility of infringement of rights of the individual in the future, there is no need to notify the individual about such a breach. For example, if the lost or disclosed personal information (1) was promptly retrieved after the breach without any third party accessing the data; (2) was protected by a high level of encryption; or (3) was in a form in which no one other than the business could have derived meaning, then no notice would be required. A similar standard is in place for when public announcements regarding the security breach may be required.

Standards of notification to ministries, however, have not been similarly modified in the revised METI Guidelines, except that organizations may choose to report nonserious breaches (breaches that do not involve sensitive information such as religion, race, ethnicity, domicile, medical information, criminal history, union membership, political organization membership, or credit information or credit card numbers) to Approved Personal Information Protection Organizations (APIPOs) instead of the relevant ministry unless the organization is a repeat offender. Even security breaches that will not require that notice be provided to individuals should be reported to the relevant ministry or an APIPO.

It is important to note that other ministry guidelines to which organizations may be subject may not incorporate the concept of harm, and will not have an exception for notice to individuals even if there is very little risk of harm, such as when the information has been encrypted. For example, organizations subject to the jurisdiction of the Financial Services Agency (FSA) and its guidelines must provide notice regarding the relevant facts of the breach to affected individuals "promptly," and to the applicable minister(s) immediately, and a public announcement must be promptly made regarding the relevant facts of the breach and measures taken to prevent further incidents.[269]

---

[269]*See* "Key Steps for Agencies in Responding to Privacy Breaches and Privacy Breach Checklist," Office of the New Zealand Privacy Commissioner, Mar. 5, 2008.

C. New Zealand

Like Australia and Canada, New Zealand is undertaking a comprehensive review of its national privacy law, the Privacy Act 1993, to determine if amendments are required in such areas as breach notification. As an interim step, the New Zealand Privacy Commissioner, who has expressed support for a change in law to require organizations to notify affected individuals, issued voluntary breach notification guidelines in March 2008.[270] The voluntary guidelines are comprised of a privacy breach checklist and a document outlining key steps for organizations to take in response to data breach incidents. The New Zealand guidance documents are based on and virtually identical to the voluntary guidance issued by the Office of the Privacy Commissioner of Canada. See Section II.B.

1. Personal Information Covered

There is no clear-cut guidance on the type of information covered but an assessment along the same lines as those set out by the Canadian Privacy Commissioner is recommended. In general, the more sensitive the information, the higher the risk of harm to individuals and the greater the need for notification. Some personal information, such as health information; government-issued identification, such as driver's license numbers; and financial account details, such as credit or debit card numbers, is more sensitive than others. Again, as for the Canadian model, a combination of personal information is typically more sensitive than a single piece of personal information.

2. Risk Assessment

If an individual's identity, dignity, physical safety, reputation, or financial security has been put at risk by an unauthorized or improper release of personal information, it may be advisable to inform the affected individuals. This may enable the affected individuals to take steps to protect themselves from any harmful effects. Also the same factors listed in the Canadian guide-

[270] *See id.*

lines should be considered when deciding whether or not to report a breach to the New Zealand Privacy Commissioner or to other officials.

3. Timing and Content of the Notice

Similar to the Canadian breach notification obligation, notification to individuals affected should occur as soon as reasonably possible following assessment and evaluation of the breach. The New Zealand Privacy Commissioner explained that the approach to notification would vary depending on the type and scale of the breach. With regard to how notification should be made, direct notification, by telephone, email, or post is usually the most appropriate means of communication. However, when the organization does not hold contact details for affected individuals, public notification (e.g., Web site information, posted notices, media) might be appropriate. Organizations should also consider what information should be included in the notification. Notification should therefore include (1) information about the incident and its timing in general terms, (2) a description of the personal information involved in the breach, (3) a general account of what the organization has done to control or reduce the harm, (4) what the organization will do to assist the affected individuals, and (5) whether the organization has notified the office of the Privacy Commissioner

CHAPTER 10

DATA SECURITY: MAINTAINING AN INFORMATION SECURITY PROGRAM

I. Introduction 595
II. Overview of Data Security Laws and Regulations 598
III. Creating an Information Security Program 600
Exhibit 10.1 Selected Domestic and International Data Security Requirements 601
A. Personal Information 600
B. Written Security Program 603
C. Risk Assessment 605
D. Security Program Coordinator 608
E. Employee Training and Awareness 609
F. Access Controls 612
G. Physical Access Controls 614
H. Technical Security Controls 615
I. Data Destruction/Retention Limits 618
J. Documentation of Security Breach Responses 620
K. Oversight of Service Providers 621
L. Internal Audits/Reviews 623

I. INTRODUCTION

Traditionally, many data security laws focused on protecting specific types of information or information relating to specific types of individuals, such as the Gramm-Leach-Bliley Act (GLBA) protections for information relating to customers of financial institutions. Today, however, data security laws tend to focus on personal information generally, without regard to the categories of individuals to whom such information may relate (e.g., requirements relating to any Social Security Number (SSN) maintained by a company, as opposed to SSNs relating to customers). Accordingly, a company may be required to protect all personal information, including personal information that relates to prospective, existing, and past customers, employees, vendors, and other individuals. Nonetheless, many companies still tend to focus their information security efforts on maintaining the security of information relating to customers. All companies, however, maintain sensitive personal information relating to their employees, such as national identification numbers that are collected for tax reporting purposes and financial account information that is used for payroll direct deposit purposes. As a result, companies must ensure that they protect sensitive personal information relating to their employees, not only because it is a best practice and will help maintain employee trust, but also because it is often required by applicable law.

Over the past few years, the issue of data security has received heightened legislative scrutiny, both internationally and within the United States. The principal focus of this scrutiny has been the extent to which companies maintain the security of sensitive personal information relating to individuals. Initially, data security laws tended to focus on how to respond to an information security incident, which is the topic of Chapter 9. More recently, however, the growing trend in data security laws is to prescribe substantive requirements for how companies should protect information. That is, data security laws now tend to be more prophylactic in nature and designed to prevent, as opposed to respond to, information security incidents. As a result, the varied data security laws have begun to regulate how and when organizations must safeguard personal information to avoid its unintended access or disclosure. As will become evident in this chapter, the data security obligations have a great deal in common, and seem to be coalescing around a common set of practices for protecting personal information that requires input from the human resources group and the technology services organization within a company.

Not long ago, a company's human resources department would handle all matters related to the company's employees, while the company's information technology (IT) department would handle its IT issues, with little overlap or interaction between the departments. Today, however, a number of factors compel a different approach, including the growing risk of information security incidents and a common understanding that many of these incidents are rooted in a company's internal processes. A company must take precautions against both inadvertent and intentional breaches and/or disclosures of the company's data by its own employees and also by contractors and vendors. At the same time, a company must train and empower its employees to protect the information that provides the company's livelihood. Only by capitalizing on its investment in its employees, as well as in appropriate technological solutions, can a company successfully protect its data against the growing array of internal and external threats to the security and confidentiality of that data. A company should foster a culture of information security as a core value. This is most readily accomplished when the entire company (e.g., the human resources, IT, physical security and legal departments, and the business owners) all work in concert to address information security.

A company must appreciate that sound information security practices are essential for conducting its business. As more countries and more states within the United States impose information security requirements, more and more companies will need to adopt information security programs and practices in order to comply with those obligations. As a result, this chapter describes the key elements of an information security program that a company may need to develop in order to comply with the growing array of laws that impose requirements with respect to the company's information security practices.

In connection with describing the key elements of an information security program, this chapter provides an overview and sampling of data security laws throughout the world. With respect to the United States, this chapter focuses on detailed information security regulations issued by the Massachusetts Office of Consumer Affairs and Business Regulations (hereinafter, Massachusetts Program Rule).[1] The Massachusetts Program Rule, which will become effective on January 1, 2010, is not only the most recent data security regulation in the United States, but it is also the most comprehensive effort in the United States to regulate the information security practices of companies. In addition, this chapter describes important international data security requirements

---

[1]201 MASS. CODE REGS. §§17.03–17.05.

by highlighting obligations in Argentina, Italy, Japan, Norway, Poland, and Spain. As a result, this chapter should assist a company in its efforts to strengthen its information security program by highlighting key steps that the company can take to protect data and, in the process, comply with some of the more restrictive data security laws.[2]

II. OVERVIEW OF DATA SECURITY LAWS AND REGULATIONS

Within the United States, various laws and regulations require that employers protect personal information relating to their employees. Some of these laws are targeted specifically at employee information. For example, New York law prohibits an employer from communicating an employee's "personal identifying information" to the general public. The New York law further provides that it is presumptive evidence of a "knowing violation" of the law, which may result in a civil penalty, "if the employer has not put in place any policies or procedures to safeguard against such violation."[3] In addition, as discussed in Chapter 8, a number of state laws impose data security requirements on employers with respect to employee SSNs.

The vast majority of data security laws that require employers to protect employee information, however, are focused more generally on personal information that relates to any individual, not simply employees. For example, California and Texas have enacted laws that require companies that own or license personal information about residents in those states, including employees, to implement reasonable security procedures to protect that information from unauthorized use or disclosure.[4] Apart from state

---

[2]For clarity, this chapter does not attempt to provide an overview of all international laws on data security, or an overview of any particular international law on data security. Rather, this chapter notes certain obligations required by some of the more restrictive international data security laws—those of Argentina, Italy, Japan, Norway, Poland and Spain—as guidelines for a company's international data security practices.

[3]N.Y. LAB. LAW §230-d.

[4]CAL. CIV. CODE §1798.81.5; TEX. BUS. & COM. CODE §48.102.

laws that impose general mandates to protect personal information, some companies may be subject to laws or rules that require the implementation of a comprehensive information security program. For example, the Massachusetts Program Rule requires "[e]very person that owns, licenses, stores or maintains personal information about [Massachusetts] resident [to] develop, implement, maintain and monitor a comprehensive, written information security program applicable to any records containing such personal information."[5]

In addition, the Federal Trade Commission (FTC) has adopted rules under the GLBA[6] (the Safeguards Rule) that require a financial institution to implement a written, comprehensive information security program that, in general, is designed to protect customer information against anticipated threats or hazards to the security of the information, as well as to guard against unauthorized access to, or use of, the information that could result in substantial harm or inconvenience to any customer. At first blush, it appears that the Safeguards Rule does not apply to most companies because the Rule applies only to financial institutions subject to the FTC's jurisdiction and only with respect to financial information relating to their customers. Nonetheless, the Safeguards Rule is important for all companies. The FTC, and even state attorneys general, frequently use the Safeguards Rule as a general benchmark or standard when bringing data security enforcement actions against companies and have taken the position informally that the Safeguards Rule is a "best practice" that should be adopted by all companies.

If a company also operates outside of the United States, it is likely subject to additional data security obligations with respect to personal information relating to its employees. Many foreign

---

[5]201 MASS. CODE REGS. §17.03(1).

[6]16 C.F.R. pt. 314. The FTC and the federal banking agencies have adopted substantially similar regulations under the GLBA, which apply to the financial institutions subject to their jurisdiction. *See, e.g.*, 12 C.F.R. pt. 364, app. B (FDIC). For the sake of clarity, this chapter focuses on the FTC's Safeguards Rule. However, companies that act as service providers to financial institutions should be mindful of the information security requirements that apply to their financial institution customers and, indirectly, to their service providers. Accordingly, a company acting as a service provider should be prepared to enter into an agreement with a financial institution that, in relevant part, requires the company to use appropriate security controls to protect the institution's customer information.

laws, including laws in Argentina, Italy, Japan, Norway, Poland, and Spain, require companies to implement written information security programs to protect the security and confidentiality of personal information, including personal information relating to employees.

III. CREATING AN INFORMATION SECURITY PROGRAM

As described above, many laws, both foreign and domestic, require a company to implement a written information security program to protect personal information, including personal information relating to employees. In developing an information security program, it is important for a company not to focus solely on the technological aspects of data protection, such as firewalls and encryption. While technology often forms the cornerstone of an information security program, many companies tend to neglect a critical component of any effective information security program, namely, their employees. A company's investment in firewalls, encryption, password protection, and other security measures can be completely undermined, even accidentally, by a single employee. At the same time, employees can be one of the company's strongest lines of defense against internal and external information security threats.

In order to comply with the myriad data security laws that are coming into force, companies need to create information security programs and practices that protect the company's information from inadvertent as well as intentional misconduct. This task may seem daunting. Many of the key obligations in data security laws and regulations around the world, however, are in fact similar. Exhibit 10.1 provides a brief overview of some of the common obligations.

A. Personal Information

Before discussing the steps that a company should take to develop a robust information security program, it is important to discuss in greater detail the types of information covered by data security laws and regulations. While some data security laws apply

EXHIBIT 10.1
Selected Domestic and International Data Security Requirements

Security Requirement	Safeguards Rule	Massachusetts	Spain	Poland	Japan[1]
Written Security Program	Yes	Yes	Yes	Yes	Yes [METI & MHLW]
Security Program Coordinator	Yes	Yes	Yes	Yes	Yes [MHLW] Desirable [METI]
Risk Assessment	Yes	Yes	N/A	N/A	Yes [METI]
Document Security Breach Responses	N/A	Yes	Yes	N/A	Desirable [METI]
Oversight of Service Providers	Yes	Yes	Yes	Yes	Yes [METI & MHLW]
Employee Training	N/A	Yes	N/A	N/A	Yes [METI & MHLW]
Authentication	N/A	Yes	Yes	Yes	Yes [METI] Desirable [MHLW]
Access Controls	N/A	Yes	Yes	Yes	Yes [METI & MHLW]
Password Requirements	N/A	Yes	Yes	Yes	Desirable [METI & MHLW]
Unauthorized Use	N/A	Yes	Yes	Yes	Desirable [METI]
Malware Controls	N/A	Yes	N/A	Yes	Yes [METI]
Encryption of Data Communicated via Public Network	N/A	Yes	Yes	Yes	Desirable [METI]
Physical Access Controls	N/A	Yes	Yes	Yes	Yes [METI]
Controls on Portable Devices	N/A	Yes	Yes	Yes	N/A
Data Destruction/ Retention Limits	Yes	Yes	Yes	Yes	Desirable [METI]
Internal Audits/ Reviews	N/A	Yes	Yes	N/A	Desirable [METI]
Back-ups	N/A	N/A	Yes	Yes	Desirable [METI]

[1]Guidelines issued by the Ministry of Economy, Trade and Industry (METI) and by the Ministry of Health, Labor, and Welfare (MHLW). The guidelines use the term "desirable" to refer to actions that are not required, but that, if not followed, require the company to articulate the alternative method used.

broadly to all personally identifiable information, many of these laws apply only to narrower categories of personal information.

For example, the Massachusetts Program Rule applies only to a narrow subset of personal information. Specifically, the Massachusetts Program Rule applies only to an individual's

> first name and last name or first initial and last name in combination with any one or more of the following data elements that relate to such [individual]: (a) Social Security number; (b) driver's license number or state-issued identification card number; or (c) financial account number, or credit or debit card number, with or without any required security code, access code, personal identification number or password, that would permit access to a resident's financial account.[7]

On the other hand, many foreign data security laws tend to apply quite broadly to any form or type of personal information. For example, Spain's data security law applies with respect to any "personal data," which is defined as "any information concerning identified or identifiable natural persons."[8]

Notwithstanding the differing scope of the personal information that is covered under data security laws, a company may elect to apply its information security program broadly to most types of personal information that it maintains. The growing trend in data security regulation is clearly moving toward more detailed and proscriptive requirements for information security programs that protect personal information generally. For a company that operates in multiple jurisdictions, developing a robust information security program that applies broadly to various types of personal information may reduce future compliance costs when new jurisdictions adopt comprehensive data security regulations. Moreover, it may simply be more efficient and less costly for a company to apply its information security program to personal information beyond that which is required, as opposed to attempting to apply

---

[7]201 MASS. CODE REGS. §17.02. Under the Massachusetts Program Rule, the term "personal information" does "not include information that is lawfully obtained from publicly available information, or from federal, state or local government records lawfully made available to the general public." *Id.*

[8]Spanish Organic Law 15/1999 of 13 December on the Protection of Personal Data, Article 3(a).

various procedures to some types of personal information and not others.

B. Written Security Program

As discussed above, any company with personal information relating to individuals, including employees, should develop a comprehensive information security program that covers risks arising from both technical failures and human foibles. For companies operating solely or primarily in the United States, the requirements of the Massachusetts Program Rule provide a particularly useful roadmap for developing comprehensive information security programs. For example, the Massachusetts Program Rule requires companies to implement, maintain, and update from time to time a comprehensive, written information security program that is appropriate to the size, complexity, nature, and scope of the activities of the particular entity.[9] Although the data security laws in Argentina, Italy, Japan, Norway, Poland, and Spain impose similar requirements, companies that operate outside the U.S. may need to modify their policies to satisfy specific jurisdictional requirements.[10] For example, in Poland, a company must maintain a data security policy and instructions on computer system management. The policy should be prepared in Polish, as it must be provided to employees and, in case of inspection, to the data protection authority.[11] Under Argentinean law, a company must implement a written information security program that specifies the security measures and procedures that must be followed for

---

[9]201 MASS. CODE REGS. §17.03(1).

[10]Argentinean Regulation 11/2006, Security Measures for the Processing and Maintenance of Personal Data Contained in Files, Records, Databanks, and Databases, Annex 1, Basic Level, paras. 1–10 (Argentinean Regulation); Italian Personal Data Protection Code, Section 34(1)(g) (Italian Code); Japanese Guidelines Targeting Economic and Industrial Sectors with Regard to the Law Concerning the Protection of Personal Information, Ministry of Economy, Trade and Industry, §11.2(3)(2) (METI Guidelines); Norwegian Regulations on the Processing of Personal Data, §§2-3, 2-7, 2-14, 2-16 (Norwegian Regulations); Polish Regulation on Personal Data Processing Documentation, §§4, 5, 7 (Polish Regulation); Spanish Royal Decree 1720/2007 of 21 December, Regulation Implementing the Organic Law on the Protection of Personal Data 15/1999, Art. 88 (Spanish Royal Decree).

[11]Polish Regulation, §4.

information systems that contain personal information, and must update and revise its program when any changes are made to the underlying information systems.[12] Spanish law requires a company to develop an internal security document, which must be binding on employees who access the information systems.[13]

The steps described below should assist any company in developing a comprehensive, written information security program that strikes a workable balance between a company's security needs and its operational requirements. Information security policies are of little use if the policies would prevent employees from having access to the information that they need to perform their jobs. As a result, the policies, as well as the particular technological controls, must be tailored to the company's individual needs and practices.[14]

To begin, a company should ensure that the relevant policies and procedures that make up its information security program are memorialized in writing. This written information security program should describe, among other things, the company's data classification system; mandatory and recommended uses of access controls; and limitations on the access, use, and disclosure of personal information. The program also may address related issues, such as a requirement for each employee to sign a confidentiality agreement and required elements for agreements with vendors relating to information safeguards and nondisclosure. In addition, the program should identify the process owner and encourage employees to direct questions or concerns to the process owner or her delegate. Companies also may consider providing a means for employees to report concerns or assure employees that the company will not permit any reprisal against an employee for raising a good-faith concern about information security practices.

Moreover, a company should take steps to ensure its written program is followed in actual practice. An information security program should be a living, breathing document that is modified to reflect changes in technology, changes in business operations, and new threats to a company's information. As described in more

---

[12]Argentinean Regulation, Annex 1, Basic Level, paras. 1–10.

[13]Spanish Royal Decree, Art. 88.

[14]*See* 16 CFR §314.3(a).

detail below, a company should regularly monitor its written program to ensure that its risk-based controls continue to be reasonably designed to prevent unauthorized access to, or unauthorized use of, personal information. A company should periodically and regularly revisit its existing security procedures and controls and upgrade its procedures and security controls as appropriate.

C. Risk Assessment

The foundation for any information security program is a risk assessment. A company's information security program should take into account the reasonably foreseeable threats or hazards to its data in light of the nature and scope of the company's business and the sensitivity of the personal information contained in the data. In addition, the company must periodically modify its program, as appropriate, to address the changing nature of these threats and hazards.

Moreover, many jurisdictions now require that a company perform a risk assessment. For example, the Massachusetts Program Rule requires that a company identify and assess reasonably foreseeable internal and external risks to the security, confidentiality, and integrity of its electronic, paper, and other records that contain personal information.[15] Moreover, after completing this risk assessment, a company must evaluate and improve, where necessary, its safeguards in order to limit any identified risks.[16] In sum, a company's risk assessment should highlight for the company where the greatest threats to its information lie and allow the company to implement security controls to limit those risks.

Similarly, a number of foreign jurisdictions impose specific requirements for risk assessments that companies must perform. For example, Italy requires companies that process sensitive data to include in their security policy documents an analysis of risks applying to data and measures to be taken to ensure data integrity, availability, and protection.[17] Under Norwegian law, a company must establish criteria for acceptable risks associated with the

---

[15] 201 MASS. CODE REGS. §17.03(3)(2).

[16] *Id.*

[17] Italian Code, Annex B, paras. 19.3–19.4.

processing of personal information and carry out a risk assessment to determine the probability and consequences of information security incidents, followed by a comparison of the risk assessment to the established criteria for acceptable risk.[18]

A company's risk assessment need not take into account every conceivable threat or hazard, only those that are reasonably foreseeable. To begin, a company should consider each aspect of its systems used to process, store, and transmit electronic and paper records containing personal information, including employee information. A company also must take care to assess the systems used by its service providers to perform these functions on the company's behalf. To initiate its risk assessment, a company could consider posing various questions, such as:

- *who* has access to each of its systems used to process, store, and transmit personal information (e.g., employees, contractors, customers);
- *where* are the company's systems located (e.g., at retail locations, the company's domestic and foreign offices);
- *what* types of environmental hazards pose threats to those systems and how frequently do these hazards occur (e.g., fire, flood, or earthquake); and
- *what* types of existing safeguards has the company implemented to protect personal information (e.g., employee training, encryption, an information classification scheme).

In addition, this assessment should be based on the sensitivity of the data stored in the company's information systems. For example, the company should assess the nature or severity of the threat or hazard depending on whether the data contain personal information about individuals, including employees.

As part of its risk assessment, a company should assess the various forms in which data are maintained. It is not uncommon for information security policies to contain state-of-the-art protections for computerized data, while neglecting to address the creation or handling of paper copies of the same data. In addition, employees may transport data in other forms, such as files saved

[18]Norwegian Regulations, §§2–4.

on the hard drives of their laptop computers or spreadsheets stored in their personal data assistants (PDAs). A company may find that its employees are storing and transporting data in new ways that have not been considered or approved by management. Unless these practices are identified and evaluated, there inevitably will be gaps in the coverage of the information security program. Accordingly, a company should review its information systems and paper records, including electronic databases, computing systems, and storage media, to identify where personal information is commonly maintained or processed. In fact, the Massachusetts Program Rule requires such an identification of personal information.[19] This identification should assist a company in determining where its information security program should be applied.

After assessing the forms in which its data are maintained, the company should begin evaluating the level of confidentiality protection that should apply to each type of data. This classification process requires balancing the company's aim of keeping all of its data confidential against its real-world operational needs. It does little good to classify all employee data as uniformly confidential if, in practice, the same confidentiality safeguards will not be followed. In fact, automatically classifying all data as confidential may be counterproductive because, for example, it may increase the difficulty of enforcing trade secret or confidentiality protections. In the event that a company does not comply with its own information security policy, an argument could be made that the company's noncompliance is evidence that the company does not actually treat the data as secret or confidential. Consequently, a company needs to approach its confidentiality classifications in a realistic manner and avoid setting standards that the company itself cannot meet.

Moreover, a company should review its information collection procedures to assess whether personal information is collected only as reasonably necessary to accomplish the legitimate purposes for which it is collected. As discussed below, limiting the collection of personal information and, further, limiting access to the information to those persons (employees or service providers)

---

[19]201 MASS. CODE REGS. §17.03(3)(8).

who are reasonably required to know such information to carry out the company's legitimate purposes are essential elements of the company's program to protect personal information. In addition, a company should limit the amount of time the personal information is retained to periods that are anticipated as reasonably necessary for accomplishing the company's legitimate purposes. These steps are in fact required by the Massachusetts Program Rule.[20]

D. Security Program Coordinator

Establishing a comprehensive information security program is not a one-time project. Instead, a company must continually administer its program and, in light of the changing nature of the reasonably foreseeable threats and hazards to its data and information systems, periodically evaluate and update its program to control these threats and hazards. As a result, a company generally should identify a particular individual or group as the "owner" of this ongoing process. The process owner should be responsible for ensuring that each category of data is appropriately classified and protected. Additionally, the process owner should take more long-term responsibility for proposing modifications to the information security program based on the company's evolving business needs and practices.

Many jurisdictions actually require a company to designate a process owner to oversee its information security program. For example, the Massachusetts Program Rule requires that a company "designat[]e one or more employees to maintain the [company's] comprehensive information security program."[21] In addition, a number of foreign jurisdictions, including Japan, Poland, and Spain, have a similar requirement.[22] Under Japanese law, a company must appoint a process owner who has the required knowledge

---

[20] *Id.* §17.03(3)(7).

[21] *Id.* §17.03(1). *See also* 16 C.F.R. §314.4(a) (FTC Safeguards Rule).

[22] Japanese Guidelines Relating to Measures to be Taken by Businesses in Order to Ensure the Proper Handling of Personal Information Relating to Employment Management, Ministry of Health, Labor and Welfare, §III.4 (MHLW Guidelines); Polish Act of 29 August 1997 on the Protection of Personal Data, Art. 36.3 (Polish Act); Spanish Royal Decree, Arts. 95, 109.

and experience to be responsible for the protection of employment data.[23]

E. Employee Training and Awareness

In order to effectuate a company's information security program, the company's employees must be aware of, and familiar with, their underlying obligations to safeguard personal information. To begin, companies should consider creating a contractual obligation for their employees to maintain the confidentiality of their data. In some countries, such as Japan, a contract with employees relating to the protection of personal information is part of the specific security requirements.[24] In Norway, a company's staff must be subject to a duty of confidentiality concerning personal data where confidentiality is necessary; the duty of confidentiality must also apply to other data of significance.[25] This contractual protection can be created by requiring each employee to sign a confidentiality agreement (also known as a nondisclosure agreement). The confidentiality agreement can include a broad definition of information that is considered confidential and should provide specific examples of confidential data (such as formulas, inventions, and customer lists). Additionally, the company can bolster the confidentiality agreement by requiring new employees to sign new-hire certificates and requiring departing employees to sign termination certificates confirming their obligations to maintain the company's data in confidence.[26] The confidentiality obligations contained under these agreements create legal protections for the company's data, even if it does not qualify for trade secret protection. Regardless of the particular legal status of the data, maintaining appropriate levels of confidentiality is integral

---

[23]Japanese MHLW Guidelines, §III.4.

[24]Japanese METI Guidelines, §II.2(3)(2).

[25]Norwegian Regulations, §2-9.

[26]Many jurisdictions require that a business take steps to limit the access terminated employees have to personal information. For example, the Massachusetts Program Rule requires that a company prevent terminated employees from access to records containing personal information by immediately terminating both their physical and their electronic access to such information. 201 MASS. CODE REGS. §17.03(3)(5).

for preserving any type of legal protection against disclosure of the data.

The ultimate purpose of the information security program is to improve and standardize security practices throughout the company. This will happen only if employees know about and understand the particular policies that apply to the company's data and information systems. Generally, a company cannot sufficiently implement its program merely by distributing certain policies to its employees. Instead, a company should consider a variety of methods to educate its employees and other workers (including temporary and contract employees) about the security controls relevant to the data and information systems with which they work. One of the best ways to reinforce the elements of a company's program is to provide employees with training that covers both the basic and more advanced aspects of the relevant information security controls. For instance, employees should be periodically reminded of the importance of everyday precautions, such as deleting or shredding confidential information once it is no longer needed, password-protecting confidential files, and exercising caution in using the public Internet outside the company's firewall.

Moreover, many jurisdictions require that a company regularly train its employees about relevant information security procedures. For example, the Massachusetts Program Rule requires a company to train its employees, including temporary and contract employees, regarding the company's information security program, including the proper use of the company's computer security system and the importance of personal information security.[27] Various foreign jurisdictions, including Italy and Japan, impose similar requirements.[28] For example, under Japanese law, a company must provide education and training to those responsible for employee personal data management, as well as those who handle employee personal data.[29] In Italy, a company must schedule training sessions for individuals on data management, liability in data

---

[27] 201 MASS. CODE REGS. §§17.03(3)(2), 17.04(8).
[28] Italian Code, Annex B, para. 19.6; Japanese MHLW Guidelines, §III.3(5).
[29] Japanese MHLW Guidelines, §III.3(5).

processing, and continuous updating. A description of this training session must be included in the security policy document.[30]

Beyond the basics, employees should be trained about how to handle a worst-case scenario, such as an incident involving a potential breach of security or an environmental hazard that threatens part of the company's information systems. All employees should know who to call if an information security incident is suspected, and employees with IT responsibilities also should be trained in taking actions to stop or minimize unauthorized access upon learning of a breach. In jurisdictions requiring notice of a security breach, management should be prepared to contact knowledgeable attorneys to discuss the company's legal obligations and whether to involve law enforcement to respond to the incident. An information security incident requires a rapid response, and by the time such a breach occurs, it might be too late for this type of planning. Moreover, as discussed below, many jurisdictions require that a company document its response to information security incidents.

In addition, in order to lend credibility to its information security policies and procedures, a company should establish measures to enforce compliance with these policies and procedures. For example, a company should impose disciplinary measures for personnel and vendors that commit violations of the company's program. In addition, this may be required under applicable law. The Massachusetts Program Rule, for instance, requires a company to impose disciplinary measures on its employees for violations of the company's information security program.[31]

The importance of informing and training employees about information security practices cannot be overstated. Without employees actively involved in fulfilling the company's information security program, the policies themselves will be of limited value, if any. Moreover, in order to comply with its varied legal obligations, a company must have well-educated and well-trained employees who are prepared to implement and maintain all aspects of the company's information security program. While employee training need not be conducted on a rigid time frame, a company

---

[30]Italian Code, Annex B, para. 19.6.

[31]201 MASS. CODE. REGS. §17.03(3)(4).

should ensure that all relevant employees are in fact periodically trained. Moreover, a company should have flexibility in terms of how it provides such training (e.g., posting training modules on the company's internal Web site and conducting formal training sessions alike should suffice, depending on the particular subject matter).

F. Access Controls

One of the most fundamental principles of information security is limiting internal and external access to sensitive information. While many companies take appropriate steps to limit external access to information, such as by protecting information systems with firewalls and limiting the third parties with whom they share personal information, companies frequently fail to limit internal access to information. Simply stated, a company should permit employees to have access to personal information, including employee information, only if those employees need that information to perform their job duties.

Many jurisdictions expressly require companies to establish both external and internal access controls. As an example, the Massachusetts Program Rule requires that a company limit access to personal information to those individuals who are reasonably required to know such information in order to accomplish the legitimate purpose for which the information was collected.[32] Similarly, the Massachusetts Program Rule requires that a company restrict electronic access to records and files containing personal information to those individuals who need such information to perform their job duties.[33] The laws of many foreign jurisdictions, including those of Argentina, Italy, Japan, Norway, Poland, and Spain, also require companies to establish access controls.[34] In Poland, for example, a company must apply access control

---

[32]201 MASS. CODE REGS. §17.03(3)(7).

[33]*Id.*

[34]Argentinean Regulation, Annex 1, Medium Level, paras. 3–5.2; Italian Code, Annex B, paras. 1–11; Japanese METI Guidelines, §II.2(3)(2); Norwegian Regulations, §§2-10 to 2-12; Polish Regulation Appendix, Section II; Spanish Royal Decree, Article 83.

mechanisms in computer systems that are used to process personal data; in Spain, a company must adopt adequate measures to limit employee access to personal data.[35]

Aside from minimizing the risk of an information security incident, assigning different levels of confidentiality is essential in preserving the company's trade secret or other applicable legal rights. Trade secret protection requires that a company prove that: (1) certain data are economically valuable because such data are not known to others; and (2) the company has taken reasonable measures to protect the secrecy of such data. The greater the number of employees with access to the alleged trade secret data, the greater the difficulty of proving that the company has taken reasonable measures to maintain its secrecy. In other words, a company should maintain policies that, in general, support an inverse relationship between the value of certain data and the number of employees with access to that data. Otherwise, the company may not be able to proffer sufficient evidence that would authorize a court to recognize the data as a trade secret, and thus deprive the company of remedies available under the Uniform Trade Secrets Act or similar laws prohibiting the misappropriation of trade secrets. Nonetheless, a company should take measures to create and preserve legal protections for its confidential data, even if the data may not qualify as the company's trade secret.

In classifying the level of confidentiality that should apply to each category of data, companies generally will find that different data fields or data sets within a single database require different levels of confidentiality and thus different levels of access. For instance, employee compensation is generally treated as confidential, but government identification numbers should be subject to an even greater degree of confidentiality because of the risk of identity theft. Thus, managers may be granted access to compensation data from the company's payroll database, while not being allowed access to the SSNs contained in the same database. In fact, countries such as Argentina and Italy actually require different levels of security and access control for different types of

[35]Polish Regulation Appendix, Section II; Spanish Royal Decree, Article 83.

data.[36] In other words, simply because various types of data are stored or processed in the same systems does not mean that all such data should be accorded identical treatment under the company's information security program.

Additionally, a company must not overlook the access controls necessary to guard against the risk of unauthorized access by former employees or vendors. A company should establish procedures and security controls designed to prevent terminated employees (or vendors whose service contracts have ended) from accessing records or computer systems used to store or transmit personal information. This includes developing procedures to deactivate an employee's user name and password for the company's computer system immediately when the employee is terminated, which, as described below, is required by the Massachusetts Program Rule.

G. Physical Access Controls

Companies frequently make the mistake of focusing solely on electronic access controls. While a company that predominately maintains and processes personal information in electronic form may reasonably determine that its most significant threat involves electronic access, all companies should implement controls to limit physical access to personal information as well. Simply stated, a company must develop policies and procedures to limit access to physical records containing personal information to those individuals who need such access to perform their job duties. In fact, the Massachusetts Program Rule requires that a company establish reasonable restrictions upon physical access to personal information.[37] The Massachusetts Program Rule further requires that a company implement a written procedure that sets forth the manner in which physical access to personal information is restricted, including the storage of personal information in locked facilities, storage areas, or containers.[38] Similarly, under Spanish law, only

---

[36] Argentina requires a detailed access registry to be made available for databases that contain sensitive personal data. *See* Argentinean Regulation, Annex 1, Critical Level, para. 2. Italy requires access to archives containing sensitive or judicial data to be controlled. *See* Italian Code, Annex B, paras. 19–24.

[37] 201 MASS. CODE REGS. §17.03(3)(9).

[38] *Id.*

personnel authorized in the written security document may have access to the physical equipment that supports the information systems.[39]

Personal information, including employee information, should not be left in areas in which unauthorized individuals may access such information. Instead, personal information in paper form should be locked in filing cabinets, drawers, or other secure areas. Moreover, a company should implement physical controls over areas of its premises that frequently contain personal information or where personal information is processed. For example, a company should implement card key access to rooms or areas that contain personal information, such as rooms that house servers.

H. Technical Security Controls

Technical security measures often form some of the most fundamental elements of an information security program. The growing trend in data security legislation is for jurisdictions to impose express and detailed requirements for technical controls that companies must adopt. For example, the Massachusetts Program Rule requires a company to adopt security controls that are specifically tailored to its computer systems, including its wireless systems, such as detailed requirements for the authentication of users of a company's computer systems.[40] The Massachusetts Program Rule also includes various requirements for firewalls, malware, and virus protection.[41] Moreover, the Massachusetts Program Rule requires that a company monitor its computer systems for unauthorized use of or access to personal information.[42] These technical security controls will play an important role in assuring that only authorized individuals have access to personal information. A number of foreign jurisdictions have similar provisions. The laws of Spain and Italy also contain authentication requirements.[43] In addition, in Poland, Norway, and Argentina, companies must take measures to secure their computer systems

[39]Spanish Royal Decree, Art. 99.
[40]201 MASS. CODE REGS. §17.04(1).
[41]*Id.* §§17.04(6)–(7).
[42]*Id.* §17.04(4).
[43]Spanish Royal Decree, Art. 93; Italian Code, Annex B, paras. 1-11.

against malicious software.[44] Norway, Spain, and Poland all have laws that require steps to limit the unauthorized use of or access to personal information.[45]

In implementing technical security controls, a company should ensure that it does not overlook systems or devices used to store or transport personal information, including employee information. As discussed above, a company should develop appropriate controls to protect information stored both in electronic and paper form. In addition, a company should consider the various devices used to process, store, and transmit the company's data. For example, PDAs are increasingly used to store information, and, among other risks, PDAs are easy to misplace or lose, owing to their small size and portable nature. At a minimum, companies should place password protections on laptops, PDAs, and other devices containing confidential information.

Companies that allow employees to store confidential data on their personal or noncompany-managed devices, such as personal laptops, home computers, or PDAs, should reconsider this practice. Not only does a company face obstacles to ensure that personally owned (or noncompany-managed) devices are equipped with appropriate access controls, but a company can rarely ensure that all company data will be permanently deleted from the device when the employment relationship ends. In addition, in those instances in which the company needs access to documents stored on a computer (such as in response to a document request or subpoena), if the company does not own or control the computer or device, gaining access can be tricky. Ideally, the company should have ready access to all laptops, PDAs, and other devices used to store confidential company data. Passwords also should be used to protect individual files or documents containing highly confidential information. An organization should consider adopting a policy that any documents that contain highly sensitive information should be password-protected.

---

[44]Polish Regulation, §5; Norwegian Regulations, §2-13; Argentinean Regulation, Annex 1, Basic Level, para. 9.

[45]Norwegian Regulations, §§2-11, 2-14; Spanish Royal Decree, Art. 98; Polish Act, Arts. 36–39.

Encryption deserves special discussion because of the security breach notification laws enacted in numerous states in the United States and other jurisdictions (see Chapter 9). In general, these laws require any person or business conducting business in the relevant state to provide notice in the event of a security breach of computerized data containing unencrypted "personal information" relating to that state's residents. Under these laws, "personal information" is generally defined as an individual's name in combination with one or more specified data elements, such as an SSN, if either the name or the data element is unencrypted. If the company's controls are breached and personal information is acquired by an unauthorized person, including by an employee under certain circumstances, the company must notify each of the individuals potentially affected by the breach. The costs of notifying individuals, particularly the company's customers, about a security breach are not solely monetary but can include reputation and relationship damage as well. As a consequence, companies should reevaluate whether it is truly necessary to maintain SSNs or other sensitive data elements that may trigger a notice obligation. These security breach notification laws also provide a significant incentive for companies to encrypt the personal information that they do maintain, thus limiting or avoiding entirely notification obligations under these laws.

Notwithstanding these security breach notification laws, a likely growing trend in data security legislation is to prescribe explicit encryption requirements. For example, the Massachusetts Program Rule prescribes several standards for the encryption of personal information that is stored and transmitted. More specifically, the Massachusetts Program Rule requires the following types of encryption: (1) encryption of all personal information that is stored on laptops and other portable devices; and (2) encryption of all records and files containing personal information that is transmitted by the company and will travel across public networks or that will be transmitted wirelessly.[46] In addition, Nevada has enacted a law that specifically prohibits a business in that state from "transfer[ring] any personal information of a customer

---

[46] *See, e.g.*, 201 MASS. CODE REGS. §§17.04(3), 17.04(5).

through an electronic transmission other than a facsimile to a person outside of the secure system of the business unless the business uses encryption to ensure the security of the electronic transmission."[47] Similarly, the laws of Argentina, Poland, and Spain contain requirements that certain personal data on portable devices be encrypted.[48] In Argentina, sensitive personal data that are transmitted through communications networks must be encrypted or otherwise protected.[49] In Poland, the law requires implementation of physical and logical security measures if at least one of the computer system devices used to process personal data is connected to the public network.[50] In Spain, personal data that contain sensitive information must be encrypted or otherwise protected when transmitted via electronic communications, or public or wireless networks.[51]

I. Data Destruction/Retention Limits

A company can often limit its risk of harmful information security incidents simply by not retaining personal information, including employee information, beyond the time period for which the company actually needs such information to conduct its business. If a company fails to dispose of personal information after it no longer needs such information, the damage of an information security event can often be magnified quite significantly. For example, if a company collects government identification numbers from its employees for tax reporting purposes only, the company should not maintain numbers relating to past employees beyond the time period for which it will actually need them, for example, to respond to tax audit.

Many jurisdictions now impose express requirements that companies limit how long they retain personal information. For example, the Massachusetts Program Rule requires that a company limit the amount of time personal information is retained to

---

[47] NEV. REV. STAT. ANN. §597.970(1).

[48] Argentinean Regulation 11/2006; Polish Regulation Appendix, §§V, IX; Spanish Royal Decree, Art. 101.

[49] Argentinean Regulation, Annex 1, Critical Level, para. 4.

[50] Polish Regulation Appendix, §XII.

[51] Spanish Royal Decree, Art. 104.

that which is reasonably necessary to accomplish the purpose for which the information was collected.[52] The laws of the European Union (EU) Member States and many other countries have similar requirements.[53]

Companies also must take appropriate measures to protect data from unauthorized access during the disposal process. In fact, along with security breach notification, the disposal of information was part of the initial focus of data security legislation. Now, many jurisdictions impose disposal requirements. For example, under Connecticut law, a company must "destroy, erase or make unreadable" any data, computer files, and documents containing any information "capable of being associated with a particular individual" prior to its disposal.[54] Moreover, the FTC has issued a rule regarding the disposal of information in the context of the Fair Credit Reporting Act, the federal statute regulating the use of consumer report information. Specifically, the FTC's rule provides that any person in possession of a consumer report or information derived from a consumer report "must properly dispose of such information by taking reasonable measures to protect against unauthorized access to or use of the information in connection with its disposal."[55] While this rule expressly only applies with respect to consumer report and related information, the FTC has taken the position in the context of enforcement actions relating to unfair and deceptive acts and practices that all sensitive personal information, not just consumer report information, should be disposed of in accordance with this standard.

Similarly, many foreign jurisdictions with data security laws, including Argentina, Italy, Japan, Norway, Poland, and Spain, impose some form of disposal requirement.[56] For example, under Argentinean law, a company must destroy personal data once it

---

[52]201 Mass. Code Regs. §17.03(3)(7).

[53]*See, e.g.*, Norwegian Act of 14 April 2000 No. 31 Relating to the Processing of Personal Data, §28 (Norwegian Law); Polish Act, Art. 26.1.4.

[54]Conn. Pub. Act No. 08-167, §§1(a), 1(c).

[55]16 C.F.R. §682.3(a).

[56]Argentinean Personal Data Protection Act, Act 25,326, §4.7 (Argentinean Act); Italian Code, Annex B, para. 22; Japanese METI Guidelines, §II.2(3)(2); Norwegian Regulations, §2-11; Polish Regulation Appendix, §VI; Spanish Royal Decree, Arts. 92, 112.

ceases to be necessary or relevant to the purposes for which it was collected.[57] Similarly, under Spanish law, whenever a company intends to discard a document or medium containing personal information, the company must destroy or delete the document or medium by adopting measures to avoid access to the information contained therein or its subsequent recovery.[58]

J. Documentation of Security Breach Responses

As discussed in the Chapter 9, a company's comprehensive information security program should include a plan that is designed to facilitate its ability to respond in a timely manner to an information security incident. The response plan needs to involve key personnel from multiple departments within the company who are responsible for maintaining data systems and communicating with customers, as well as appropriate members from the company's human resources and legal departments.

In any particular incident, there are three basic steps that every company should take as part of its response:

1. Assess the media and the categories of information potentially affected—namely, assess whether computerized data or paper records are affected and which items of information are involved—to determine whether the affected personal information is subject to notification laws;
2. Establish and document the facts and circumstances of the incident, and keep records of the investigation up to date; and
3. Determine the number of individuals potentially affected and where they reside so that the company can be sure to satisfy various statutory requirements that depend, in part, on the number of affected individuals.

Beyond these core elements of a response program, the specific circumstances of an incident will dictate the steps to be taken to determine whether to notify individuals or, if the company does

---

[57] Argentinean Act, §4.7.

[58] Spanish Royal Decree, Article 92.

not own or license the data, notify the data owner or licensee. Only after investigating an incident and assessing the crucial factors under notification laws will a company be able to determine: (1) whether a "breach of security," within the meaning of these laws, has occurred; (2) the individuals, and possibly regulators, who must be notified; and (3) the appropriate methods and content of the notification.

In addition, a company should document the responsive actions taken in connection with any incident involving a security breach so that the company can make appropriate changes in its business practices, if any, relating to the protection of personal information. This step is actually required under the Massachusetts Program Rule.[59] The law of Spain requires similar documentation.[60] In Japan, it is "desirable" for companies to: (1) establish a system for reporting incidents and contacting representatives or the like when personal data has been divulged or other accidents have occurred or there is high probability that they will occur; (2) establish a system for providing information to principals who may be impacted and for providing reports to the Minister and authorized personal information protection groups; (3) make public announcements of factual relationships and measures to prevent reoccurrence following accidents and violations; (4) investigate the facts; (5) identify the scope of impact; (6) examine the causes; and (7) examine and implement measures to prevent any recurrence.[61]

K. Oversight of Service Providers

Companies that provide personal information, including employee information, to vendors or other third parties should implement appropriate policies that require these service providers to protect the information, such as by adhering to nondisclosure agreements. In Japan, companies are required to have contractors sign a nondisclosure agreement.[62] At a minimum, a

---

[59] 201 MASS. CODE REGS. §17.03(3)(12).

[60] Spanish Royal Decree, Art. 90.

[61] Japanese METI Guidelines, §II.2(3)(2). The Guidelines use the term "desirable" to refer to actions that are not required, but that, if not followed, require the company to articulate the alternative method used.

[62] Japanese METI Guidelines, §II.2(3)(2).

nondisclosure agreement should prohibit a vendor from disclosing the company's data without written permission, or from using the data for any purpose other than performing the terms of the contract. Typically, companies require their vendors to represent that the vendors (as well as their subcontractors) will implement appropriate technological and procedural safeguards to protect the company's data and that these safeguards will be at least equal to the safeguards that the company uses to protect its own data. Some companies also require vendors to represent that each of their employees has signed a confidentiality agreement that would cover the company's data.

Additionally, a company may negotiate an indemnification provision that requires its vendor to reimburse the company for any losses or expenditures that result from a breach of security affecting the company's data maintained by the vendor. This type of indemnification provision is likely to become more common owing to the potential expense of notifying individuals of a security breach under the various notification laws.

Many jurisdictions have imposed express requirements establishing how a company must oversee its service providers that have access to personal information. For example, under the Massachusetts Program Rule, a company must take reasonable steps to verify that its service providers with access to personal information have the capacity to protect such information in the manner required by the Rule.[63] Moreover, the Rule requires that a company also take reasonable steps to ensure that a service provider is actually applying security measures that are at least as strong as those required by the Rule.[64] Various other countries impose similar requirements. In Norway, companies must make certain that service providers ensure data security and document the data system and security measures.[65] Under Spanish law, a company must ensure that its service providers comply with the data protection regulations.[66] In Japan, a company must engage in necessary and appropriate supervision of service providers to ensure compliance

[63]201 MASS. CODE REGS. §17.03(3)(7).

[64]*Id.*

[65]Norwegian Law, §13.

[66]Spanish Royal Decree, Art. 20.

with required security control measures.[67] Italy requires service providers to give a company contractual guarantees about data security and compliance with the Code.[68] In Argentina, when personal data processing services are provided by service providers, the data cannot be used by the service providers for any purpose other than that appearing in the contract, nor can it be communicated to other parties, even for storage purposes.[69]

L. Internal Audits/Reviews

An integral part of maintaining an effective information security program is ensuring that the program continues to operate in the manner in which it was designed. As a result, a company should regularly monitor its written program to ensure that its risk-based controls continue to be reasonably designed to prevent unauthorized access to, or unauthorized use of, personal information, including when the company experiences a material change in its business operations or when the nature of its needs for personal information change. Even if a company does not experience a material change in its operations, the company should periodically and regularly revisit its existing security procedures and controls. In fact, this is required in many jurisdictions. For example, under the Massachusetts Program Rule, a company must regularly monitor its information security program to ensure that it is operating in a manner that is designed to prevent unauthorized access to, or use of, personal information and upgrade its information safeguards as necessary to limit these risks.[70] In addition, under the Rule, a company must review the scope of its security measures at least annually or whenever there is a material change in the company's business practices that may implicate the security or integrity of personal information.[71]

Italy, Japan, Norway, and Spain, require companies to update their written information security programs on a regular or annual

[67] Japanese METI Guidelines §II.2(3)(4).

[68] Italian Code, §29.

[69] Argentinean Act, §25.1.

[70] 201 MASS. CODE REGS. §17.03(10).

[71] *Id.* §17.03(3)(11). *See also* 16 C.F.R. §314.3(e) (FTC Safeguards Rule).

basis.[72] For example, under Italian law, companies that process sensitive data must draft a security policy document each year that analyzes the risk to the company's personal information and that describes the company's measures to ensure data integrity, availability, and protection. In addition, the authorization profiles of persons in charge of processing must be verified on at least an annual basis.[73] Moreover, under Norwegian law, a company must carry out regular security audits that are documented and that include an assessment of the company's security measures.[74] In Spain, data files must be audited at least every two years to verify compliance with the Royal Decree.[75] Finally, in Japan, it is "desirable" to designate a person responsible for audits and establish a system for implementing audits.

---

[72]Italian Code, Annex B, paras. 19.3–19.4; Japanese METI Guidelines, §II.2(3)(2); Norwegian Regulations, Section 2-5; Spanish Royal Decree, Art. 88.

[73]Italian Code, Annex B, paras. 19.3–19.4, 14.

[74]Norwegian Regulations, Section 2-5.

[75]Spanish Royal Decree, Art. 110.

APPENDIX A

ABOUT MORRISON & FOERSTER'S PRIVACY LIBRARY

Morrison & Foerster's Privacy Library is a free online resource, providing links to privacy laws, regulations, reports, multilateral agreements, and government authorities for more than 90 countries around the world, including the United States. The Privacy Library can be accessed though Morrison & Foerster's Web site at www.mofo.com or through its own URL at www.mofoprivacy.com. No registration is necessary.

The Privacy Library is the most comprehensive collection of privacy laws and regulations ever assembled, the result of years of research and experience working with clients around the world.

The Global Privacy and Data Security practice group at Morrison & Foerster recognized that simply finding copies of the relevant regulations could be challenging. The practice group's members used their extensive experience advising clients on privacy strategies to identify the relevant source materials and compile them into a user-friendly collection that provides an easy way to find text of the key laws and regulations—the first step in any compliance strategy.

Materials in the collection are located via three tabs: "United States"; "Other Countries"; and "Multilateral Organizations."

- Under the "United States" tab, the materials are grouped under "States and Territories" or "Federal" with a separate section devoted to "Key Court Cases" including enforcement actions and decrees.

  Example: To review California's breach notification law, select the "United States" tab and click on "California." Doing this directs you to a page containing links to a variety of California privacy laws, listed in alphabetical order by topic. Scroll down this page to "Security Breach Notice," where there is a link to the California breach notification law.

- Where possible, for each country included in the "Other Countries" tab, the library includes a link to the Web site of the national data protection authority in that country, as well as to privacy laws and regulations. English translations of documents are provided where available.

  Example: To review a copy of Germany's Federal Data Protection Act, select the "Other Countries" tab and click on "Germany." This will take you to a page containing links to key German privacy laws and regulations, including a link to an English translation of the Federal Data Protection Law.
- The "Multilateral Organizations" tab brings together resources from agencies such as the Asia-Pacific Economic Cooperation, Council of Europe, European Union, Organization for Economic Cooperation and Development, and United Nations.

The Privacy Library also links to client alerts and articles on key privacy topics that Morrison & Foerster posts on a regular basis.

Appendix B

EU STANDARD CLAUSES FOR CROSS-BORDER TRANSFERS OF PERSONAL INFORMATION

As discussed in Section III.D of Chapter 1, the EU Directive[1] restricts transfers of personal information from the European Union (EU) to any non-EU country, unless that country is deemed to provide "adequate" data protection or the parties have implemented "adequate safeguards" to protect the transferred or shared data. For transfers to U.S.-based employers, the options include the U.S.-EU Safe Harbor Framework, consent from the individuals, Binding Corporate Rules, or the standard contractual clauses approved by the European Commission.

The Safe Harbor Framework negotiated between the EU and the U.S. Department of Commerce applies only to transfers from the EU to the U.S., and does not apply to transfers to other non-EU countries. If an employer in the EU needs to share EU data with entities in multiple countries outside the EU, the Safe Harbor may provide only a partial solution.

In such situations, employers instead may choose to use standard contractual clauses approved by the European Commission as a method of ensuring "adequate" safeguards for the transfer of personal data to non-EU countries (Standard Clauses).[2] Thus, the

---

[1]Directive 95/46/EC of the European Parliament and of the Council of 24 October 1995 on the protection of individuals with regard to the processing of personal information and on the free movement of such data (Directive).

[2]A significant advantage of the Standard Clauses is that they do not require approval by the local EU data protection authorities, provided that these Clauses are used without modification. If the parties modify the Standard Clauses, or draft their own contractual provisions for data transfers, these "ad hoc" contracts generally require the review and approval of each applicable data protection authority. Since the approval process for ad hoc contracts can be quite time-consuming, it is common to use the Standard Clauses without modification.

Standard Clauses are a valuable option for U.S. employers with multinational operations.

To date, the European Commission has approved three sets of Standard Clauses, which are discussed further below. Two sets of Standard Clauses may be used for transfers between data controllers, while the third set of Standard Clauses applies to transfers between a data controller and a data processor.[3] All three sets are currently valid.[4]

A. Commission decision of 15 June 2001 on standard contractual clauses for the transfer of personal data to third countries, under Directive 95/46/EC (2001/497/EC) (the "2001 Clauses")

The European Commission's first set of Standard Clauses apply to personal data transfers from a data exporter controller located within the EU to a data controller located outside of the EU. See Exhibit App 2.1 below.

B. Commission decision of 27 December 2001 on standard contractual clauses for the transfer of personal data to third countries, under Directive 95/46/EC (2002/16/EC) (the "Controller-to-Processor Clauses")

In December 2001, the European Commission approved a second set of Standard Clauses to provide for adequate protection of personal data that is transferred from a controller located within the EU to a data processor located outside of the EU. Pursuant to these Clauses, the data importer agrees, among other things, to process data only on the data exporter's behalf, in compliance with the Clauses and the exporter's instructions. See Exhibit App 2.2 below.

---

[3]The issue of whether the recipient is a data controller or a data processor is a fact-intensive issue that should be assessed by legal counsel, to ensure the parties select an appropriate set of Standard Clauses.

[4]Electronic copies of these Standard Clauses may be found at www.mofoprivacy.com, by clicking the "Other Countries" tab, selecting "European Union," and locating the "Model Contracts" category.

C. Commission decision of 27 December 2004 on amending Decision 2001/497/EC as regards the introduction of an alternative set of standard contractual clauses for the transfer of personal data to third countries (2004/915/EC) (the "2004 Clauses")

The most recent set of Standard Contractual Clauses was approved by the European Commission in 2004, as an alternative for controller-to-controller contracts. See Exhibit App 2.3 below. Some of the differences between the 2001 Clauses and the 2004 Clauses are highlighted below.

Liability: While the 2001 Clauses provide for joint and several liability (Clause 6), the 2004 Clauses (Clause III) require each party to be liable for the damages it causes. To compensate for lack of joint and several liability, however, the 2004 Clauses (Clause I(b)) contain a due diligence clause that requires the exporter to guarantee that it "used reasonable efforts to determine that the importer is able to satisfy the requirements established by [the 2004 Clauses]." This provision, therefore, could create liability for the data exporter for damages caused by the importer where the exporter was found to be in breach of its due diligence obligations.

Audits: The 2001 Clauses (Clause 5(d)) mandate that the importer submit the data processing facilities, upon the exporter's request, for an audit executed by either the exporter or any independent third party. The exporter may select the members of the independent inspection body, *where applicable in agreement with the supervisory authority.* In comparison, the 2004 Clauses also afford the choice of the auditors to the exporter and require the *necessary consent or approval* from the EU regulator, but they allow the audit to be done by the exporter or an independent third party. In addition, the 2004 Clauses require reasonable notice and allow the audit only during regular business hours.

Jurisdiction: The 2001 Clauses (Clauses 8 and 5c) require the importer to cooperate with the competent supervisory authorities and abide by their advice, while the 2004 Clauses (Clause V) only require the parties to warrant that they will cooperate with the supervisory authority. The 2001 Clauses (Clause 7) require the data importer to agree to accept the decision of the data subject to refer the matter to arbitration or mediation or the relevant court. Under the 2004 Clauses (Clause V), the parties also agree to respond to any nonbinding mediation procedure initiated by the data subject, but need only consider participating in arbitration and other data protection dispute resolution mechanisms. The data importer, however, must agree to abide by the decision of a competent court, which is final.

Another and perhaps more significant difference between the 2001 Clauses and the 2004 Clauses is that the data protection authorities have greatly increased enforcement powers under the 2004 Clauses and can more easily prohibit or suspend data transfers. In particular, transfers based on the 2004 Clauses may be prohibited where the data exporter refuses to take appropriate steps to enforce contractual obligations against the data importer or the latter refuses to cooperate in good faith with the competent (EU) authorities (Recital 7).

Third-Party Beneficiary Rights: The 2001 Clauses (Clause 3) create third-party beneficiary rights in data subjects, allowing them to enforce certain provisions of the agreement, presumably against both parties. The 2004 Clauses, in contrast, permit the data subject to take enforcement actions against the importer but *only if the exporter does not take an enforcement action against the importer within a reasonable time.* The 2004 Clauses indicate that, under normal circumstances, the exporter must take action and resolve any complaint within one month.

Technical and Organizational Measures: With respect to technical and organizational measures, the 2001 Clauses require that these measures be implemented prior to the transfer and that the measures correspond to Member State law applicable to contractual clauses. The 2004 Clauses (Clause II(a)) state that the importer *will have in place measures* to protect the data against accidental loss, alteration, disclosure, etc. No reference to Member State legislation is made.

Exhibit App B.1. "2001 Clauses"

4.7.2001 EN Official Journal of the European Communities L 181/19

II

(Acts whose publication is not obligatory)

COMMISSION

COMMISSION DECISION

of 15 June 2001

on standard contractual clauses for the transfer of personal data to third countries, under Directive 95/46/EC

(notified under document number C(2001) 1539)

(Text with EEA relevance)

(2001/497/EC)

THE COMMISSION OF THE EUROPEAN COMMUNITIES,

Having regard to the Treaty establishing the European Community,

Having regard to Directive 95/46/EC of the European Parliament and of the Council of 24 October 1995 on the protection of individuals with regard to the processing of personal data and on the free movement of such data (1), and in particular Article 26(4) thereof,

Whereas:

(1) Pursuant to Directive 95/46/EC, Member States are required to provide that a transfer of personal data to a third country may only take place if the third country in question ensures an adequate level of data protection and the Member States' laws, which comply with the other provisions of the Directive, are respected prior to the transfer.

(2) However, Article 26(2) of Directive 95/46/EC provides that Member States may authorise, subject to certain safeguards, a transfer or a set of transfers of personal data to third countries which do not ensure an adequate level of protection. Such safeguards may in particular result from appropriate contractual clauses.

(3) Pursuant to Directive 95/46/EC, the level of data protection should be assessed in the light of all the circumstances surrounding the data transfer operation or set of data transfer operations. The Working Party on Protection of Individuals with regard to the processing of personal data established under that Directive (2) has issued guidelines to aid with the assessment (3).

(1) OJ L 281, 23.11.1995, p. 31.
(2) The Internet address of the Working Party is:
http://www.europa.eu.intlcomm/internal_market/en/medial/dataprot/wpdocs/index.htm.
(3) WP 4 (5020/97) 'First orientations on transfers of personal data to third countries working document — possible ways forward in assessing adequacy', a discussion document adopted by the Working Party on 26 June 1997.
WP 7 (5057/97) 'Judging industry self regulation: when does it make a meaningful contribution to the level of data protection in a third country?', working document: adopted by the Working Party on 14 January 1998.
WP 9 (3005/98) 'Preliminary views on the use of contractual provisions in the context of transfers of personal data to third countries', working document: adopted by the Working Party on 22 April 1998.
WP 12: 'Transfers of personal data to third countries: applying Articles 25 and 26 of the EU data protection directive', working document adopted by the Working Party on 24 July 1998, available, in the web-working document site 'europa.eu.int/comm/internal_markt/en/media.dataprot/wpdocs/wp12/en' hosted by the European Commission.

(4) Article 26(2) of Directive 95/46/EC, which provides flexibility for an organisation wishing to transfer data to third countries, and Article 26(4), which provides for standard contractual clauses, are essential for maintaining the necessary flow of personal data between the Community and third countries without unnecessary burdens for economic operators. Those Articles are particularly important in view of the fact that the Commission is unlikely to adopt adequacy findings under Article 25(6) for more than a limited number of countries in the short or even medium term.

(5) The standard contractual clauses are only one of several possibilities under Directive 95/46/EC, together with Article 25 and Article 26(1) and (2), for lawfully transferring personal data to a third country. It will be easier for organisations to transfer personal data to third countries by incorporating the standard contractual clauses in a contract. The standard contractual clauses relate only to data protection. The data exporter and the data importer are free to include any other clauses on business related issues, such as clauses on mutual assistance in cases of disputes with a data subject or a supervisory authority, which they consider as being pertinent for the contract as long as they do not contradict the standard contractual clauses.

(6) This Decision should be without prejudice to national authorisations Member States may grant in accordance with national provisions implementing Article 26(2) of Directive 95/46/EC. The circumstances of specific transfers may require that data controllers provide different safeguards within the meaning of Article 26(2). In any case, this Decision only has the effect of requiring the Member States not to refuse to recognise as providing adequate safeguards the contractual clauses described in it and does not therefore have any effect on other contractual clauses.

(7) The scope of this Decision is limited to establishing that the clauses in the Annex may be used by a controller established in the Community in order to adduce sufficient safeguards within the meaning of Article 26(2) of Directive 95/46/EC. The transfer of personal data to third countries is a processing operation in a Member State, the lawfulness of which is subject to national law. The data protection supervisory authorities of the Member States, in the exercise of their functions and powers under Article 28 of Directive 95/46/EC, should remain competent to assess whether the data exporter has complied with national legislation implementing the provisions of Directive 95/46/EC and, in particular, any specific rules as regards the obligation of providing information under that Directive.

(8) This Decision does not cover the transfer of personal data by controllers established in the Community to recipients established outside the territory of the Community who act only as processors. Those transfers do not require the same safeguards because the processor acts exclusively on behalf of the controller. The Commission intends to address that type of transfer in a subsequent decision.

(9) It is appropriate to lay down the minimum information that the parties must specify in the contract dealing with the transfer. Member States should retain the power to particularise the information the parties are required to provide. The operation of this Decision should be reviewed in the light of experience.

(10) The Commission will also consider in the future whether standard contractual clauses submitted by business organisations or other interested parties offer adequate safeguards in accordance with Directive 95/46/EC.

(11) While the parties should be free to agree on the substantive data protection rules to be complied with by the data importer, there are certain data protection principles which should apply in any event.

(12) Data should be processed and subsequently used or further communicated only for specified purposes and should not be kept longer than necessary.

(13) In accordance with Article 12 of Directive 95/46/EC, the data subject should have the right of access to all data relating to him and as appropriate to rectification, erasure or blocking of certain data.

(14) Further transfers of personal data to another controller established in a third country should be permitted only subject to certain conditions, in particular to ensure that data subjects are given proper information and have the opportunity to object, or in certain cases to withold their consent.

(15) In addition to assessing whether transfers to third countries are in accordance with national law, supervisory authorities should play a key role in this contractual mechanism in ensuring that personal data are adequately protected after the transfer. In specific circumstances, the supervisory authorities of the Member States should retain the power to prohibit or suspend a data transfer or a set of transfers based on the standard contractual clauses in those exceptional cases where it is established that a transfer on contractual basis is likely to have a substantial adverse effect on the guarantees providing adequate protection to the data subject.

(16) The standard contractual clauses should be enforceable not only by the organisations which are parties to the contract, but also by the data subjects, in particular, where the data subjects suffer damage as a consequence of a breach of the contract.

(17) The governing law of the contract should be the law of the Member State in which the data exporter is established, enabling a third-party beneficiary to enforce a contract. Data subjects should be allowed to be represented by associations or other bodies if they so wish and if authorised by national law.

(18) To reduce practical difficulties which data subjects could experience when trying to enforce their rights under the standard contractual clauses, the data exporter and the data importer should be jointly and severally liable for damages resulting from any violation of those provisions which are covered by the third-party beneficiary clause.

(19) The Data Subject is entitled to take action and receive compensation from the Data Exporter, the Data Importer or from both for any damage resulting from any act incompatible with the obligations contained in the standard contractual clauses. Both parties may be exempted from that liability if they prove that neither of them was responsible.

(20) Joint and several liability does not extend to those provisions not covered by the third-party beneficiary clause and does not need to leave one party paying for the damage resulting from the unlawful processing of the other party. Although mutual indemnification between the parties is not a requirement for the adequacy of the protection for the data subjects and may therefore be deleted, it is included in the standard contractual clauses for the sake of clarification and to avoid the need for the parties to negotiate indemnification clauses individually.

(21) In the event of a dispute between the parties and the data subject which is not amicably resolved and where the data subject invokes the third-party beneficiary clause, the parties agree to provide the data subject with the choice between mediation, arbitration or litigation. The extent to which the data subject will have an effective choice will depend on the availability of reliable and recognised systems of mediation and arbitration. Mediation by the supervisory authorities of a Member State should be an option where they provide such a service.

(22) The Working Party on the protection of individuals with regard to the processing of personal data established under Article 29 of Directive 95/46/EC has delivered an opinion on the level of protection provided under the standard contractual clauses annexed to this Decision, which has been taken into account in the preparation of this Decision (1).

(23) The measures provided for in this Decision are in accordance with the opinion of the Committee established under Article 31 of Directive 95/46/EC,

(1) Opinion No 1/2001 adopted by the Working Party on 26 January 2001 (DG MARKT 5102/00 WP 38), available in the website 'Europa' hosted by the European Commission.

HAS ADOPTED THIS DECISION:

Article 1

The standard contractual clauses set out in the Annex are considered as offering adequate safeguards with respect to the protection of the privacy and fundamental rights and freedoms of individuals and as regards the exercise of the corresponding rights as required by Article 26(2) of Directive 9/46/EC.

Article 2

This Decision concerns only the adequacy of protection provided by the standard contractual clauses for the transfer of personal data set out in the Annex. It does not affect the application of other national provisions implementing Directive 95/46/EC that pertain to the processing of personal data within the Member States.

This Decision shall not apply to the transfer of personal data by controllers established in the Community to recipients established outside the territory of the Community who act only as processors.

Article 3

For the purposes of this Decision:

(a) the definitions in Directive 95/46/EC shall apply;

(b) 'special categories of data' means the data referred to in Article 8 of that Directive;

(c) 'supervisory authority' means the authority referred to in Article 28 of that Directive;

(d) 'data exporter' means the controller who transfers the personal data;

(e) 'data importer' means the controller who agrees to receive from the data exporter personal data for further processing in accordance with the terms of this Decision.

Article 4

1. Without prejudice to their powers to take action to ensure compliance with national provisions adopted pursuant to chapters II, III, V and VI of Directive 95/46/EC, the competent authorities in the Member States may exercise their existing powers to prohibit or suspend data flows to third countries in order to protect individuals with regard to the processing of their personal data in cases where:

(a) it is established that the law to which the data importer is subject imposes upon him requirements to derogate from the relevant data protection rules which go beyond the restrictions necessary in a democratic society as provided for in Article 13 of Directive 95/46/EC where those requirements are likely to have a substantial adverse effect on the guarantees provided by the standard contractual clauses; or

(b) a competent authority has established that the data importer has not respected the contractual clauses; or

(c) there is a substantial likelihood that the standard contractual clauses in the Annex are not being or will not be complied with and the continuation of transfer would create an imminent risk of grave harm to the data subjects.

2. The prohibition or suspension pursuant to paragraph 1 shall be lifted as soon as the reasons for the prohibition or suspension no longer exist.

3. When Member States adopt measures pursuant to paragraphs 1 and 2, they shall without delay inform the Commission which will forward the information to the other Member States.

Article 5

The Commission shall evaluate the operation of this Decision on the basis of available information three years after its notification to the Member States. It shall submit a report on the endings to the Committee established under Article 31 of Directive 95/46/EC. It shall include any evidence that could affect the evaluation concerning the adequacy of the standard contractual clauses in the Annex and any evidence that this Decision is being applied in a discriminatory way.

Article 6

This Decision shall apply from 3 September 2001.

Article 7

This Decision is addressed to the Member States.

Done at Brussels, 15 June 2001.

For the Commission

Frederik BOLKESTEIN

Member of the Commission

L 181/24 EN Official Journal of the European Communities 4.7.2001

ANNEX

STANDARD CONTRACTUAL CLAUSES

for the purposes of Article 26(2) of Directive 95/46/EC for the transfer of personal data to third countries which do not ensure an adequate level of protection

Name of the data exporting organisation: ....

....

Address: ....

Tel. .... **fax** .... **e-mail:** ....

Other information needed to identify the organisation: ....

('the data **exporter**')

and

Name of the data importing organisation: ....

....

Address: ....

tel. .... **fax** .... **e-mail:** ....

Other information needed to identify the organisation: ....

('the data **importer**')

HAVE AGREED on the following contractual clauses ('the Clauses') in order to adduce adequate safeguards with respect to the protection of privacy and fundamental rights and freedoms of individuals for the transfer by the data exporter to the data importer of the personal data specified in Appendix 1:

Clause 1

Definitions

For the purposes of the Clauses:

a) '**personal data**', '**special categories of data**', '**process/processing**', '**controller**', '**processor**', '**data subject**' and '**supervisory authority**' shall have the same meaning as in Directive 95/46/EC of the European Parliament and of the Council of 24 October 1995 on the protection of individuals with regard to the processing of personal data and on the free movement of such data ('hereinafter the Directive');

b) the '**data exporter**' shall mean the controller who transfers the personal data;

c) the '**data importer**' shall mean the controller who agrees to receive from the data exporter personal data for further processing in accordance with the terms of these clauses and who is not subject to a third country's system ensuring adequate protection.

Clause 2

Details of the transfer

The details of the transfer, and in particular the categories of personal data and the purposes for which they are transferred, are specified in Appendix 1 which forms an integral part of the Clauses.

Clause 3

Third-party beneficiary clause

The data subjects can enforce this Clause, Clause 4(b), (c) and (d), Clause 5(a), (b), (c) and (e), Clause 6(1) and (2), and Clauses 7, 9 and 11 as third-party beneficaries. The parties do not object to the data subjects being represented by an association or other bodies if they so wish and if permitted by national law.

Clause 4

Obligations of the data exporter

The data exporter agrees and warrants:

(a) that the processing, including the transfer itself, of the personal data by him has been and, up to the moment of the transfer, will continue to be carried out in accordance with the relevant provisions of the Member State in which the data exporter is established (and where applicable has been notified to the relevant authorities of that State) and does not violate the relevant provisions of that State;

(b) that if the transfer involves special categories of data the data subject has been informed or will be informed before the transfer that this data could be transmitted to a third country not providing adequate protection;

(c) to make available to the data subjects upon request a copy of the Clauses; and

(d) to respond in a reasonable time and to the extent reasonably possible to enquries from the supervisory authority on the processing of the relevant personal data by the data importer and to any enquiries from the data subject concerning the processing of this personal data by the data importer.

Clause 5

Obligations of the data importer

The data importer agrees and warrants:

(a) that he has no reason to believe that the legislation applicable to him prevents him from fulfilling his obligations under the contract and that in the event of a change in that legislation which is likely to have a substantial adverse effect on the guarantees provided by the Clauses, he will notify the change to the data exporter and to the supervisory authority where the data exporter is established, in which case the data exporter is entitled to suspend the transfer of data and/or terminate the contract;

(b) to process the personal data in accordance with the mandatory data protection principles set out in Appendix 2;

or, if explicitly agreed by the parties by ticking below and subject to compliance with the mandatory data protection principles set out in Appendix 3, to process in all other respects the data in accordance with:

— the relevant provisions of national law (attached to these Clauses) protecting the fundamental rights and freedoms of natural persons, and in particular their right to privacy with respect to the processing of personal data applicable to a data controller in the country in which the data exporter is established, or

— the relevant provisions of any Commission Decision under Article 25(6) of Directive 95/46/EC finding that a third country provides adequate protection in certain sectors of activity only, if the data importer is based in that third country and is not covered by those provisions, in so far as those provisions are of a nature which makes them applicable in the sector of the transfer;

(c) to deal promptly and properly with all reasonable inquiries from the data exporter or the data subject relating to his processing of the personal data subject to the transfer and to cooperate with the competent supervisory authority in the course of all its inquries and abide by the advice of the supervisory authority with regard to the processing of the data transferred;

(d) at the request of the data exporter to submit its data processing facilities for audit which shall be carried out by the data exporter or an inspection body composed of independent members and in possession of the required professional qualifications, selected by the data exporter, where applicable, in agreement with the supervisory authority;

(e) to make available to the data subject upon request a copy of the Clauses and indicate the office which handles complaints.

Clause 6

Liability

1. The parties agree that a data subject who has suffered damage as a result of any violation of the provisions referred to in Clause 3 is entitled to receive compensation from the parties for the damage suffered. The parties agree that they may be exempted from this liability only if they prove that neither of them is responsible for the violation of those provisions.

2. The data exporter and the data importer agree that they will be jointly and severally liable for damage to the data subject resulting from any violation referred to in paragraph 1. In the event of such a violation, the data exporter or the data importer or both.

3. The parties agree that if one party is held liable for a violation referred to in paragraph 1 by the other party, the latter will, to the extent to which it is liable, indemnify the first party for any cost, charge, damages, expenses or loss it has incurred. (*).

Clause 7

Mediation and jurisdiction

1. The parties agree that if there is a dispute between a data subject and either party which is not amicably resolved and the data subject invokes the third-party beneficiary provision in clause 3, they accept the decision of the data subject:

(a) to refer the dispute to mediation by an independent person or, where applicable, by the supervisory authority;

(b) to refer the dispute to the courts in the Member State in which the data exporter is established.

2. The parties agree that by agreement between a data subject and the relevant party a dispute can be referred to an arbitration body, if that party is established in a country which has ratified the New York convention on enforcement of arbitration awards.

3. The parties agree that paragraphs 1 and 2 apply without prejudice to the data subject's substantitve or procedural rights to seek remedies in accordance with other provisions of national or international law.

Clause 8

Cooperation with supervisory authorities

The parties agree to deposit a copy of this contract with the supervisory authority if it so requests or if such deposit is required under national law.

Clause 9

Termination of the Clauses

The parties agree that the termination of the Clauses at any time, in any circumstances and for whatever reason does not exempt them from the obligations and/or conditions under the Clauses as regards the processing of the data transferred.

Clause 10

Governing Law

The Clauses shall be governed by the law of the Member State in which the Data Exporter is established, namely ....

....

Clause 11

Variation of the contract

The parties undertake not to vary or modify the terms of the clauses.

On behalf of the data exporter:

Name (written out in full): ....

Position: ....

Address: ....

(*) Paragraph 3 is optional.

Other information necessary in order for the contract to be binding (if any): ....

....

....
(signature)

(stamp of organisation)

On behalf of the data importer:

Name (written out in full): ....

Position: ....

Address: ....

Other information necessary in order for the contract to be binding (if any): ....

....

....

....
(signature)

(stamp of organisation)

Appendix 1

to the standard contractual clauses

This Appendix forms part of the Clauses and must be completed and signed by the parties.

(The Member States may complete or specify, according to their national procedures, any additional necessary information to be contained in this Appendix.)

Data exporter

The data exporter is (please specify briefly your activities relevant to the transfer):

....

....

....

Data importer

The data importer is (please specify briefly your activities relevant to the transfer):

....

....

....

Data subjects

The personal data transferred concern the following categories of data subjects (please specify):

....

....

....

Purposes of the transfer

The transfer is necessary for the following purposes (please specify):

....

....

....

Categories of data

The personal data transferred fall within the following categories of data (please specify):

....

....

....

Sensitive data (if appropriate)

The personal data transferred fall within the following categories of sensitive data (please specify):

....

....

....

Recipients

The personal data transferred may be disclosed only to the following recipients or categories of recipients (please specify):

....

....

....

Storage limit

The personal data transferred may be stored for no more than (please indicate): .... (months/years)

Data exporter	Data importer
Name:	Name: ....
.... (Authorised signature)	.... (Authorised signature)

L 181/30 EN Official Journal of the European Communities 4.7.2001

Appendix 2

to the standard contractual clauses

Mandatory data protection principles referred to in the first paragraph of Clause 5(b)

These data protection principles should be read and interpreted in the light of the provisions (principles and relevant exceptions) of Directive 95/46/EC.

They shall apply subject to the mandatory requirements of the national legislation applicable to the data importer which do not go beyond what is necessary in a democratic society on the basis of one of the interests listed in Article 13(1) of Directive 95/46/EC, that is, if they constitute a necessary measure to safeguard national security, defence, public security, the prevention, investigation, detection and prosecution of criminal offences or of breaches of ethics for the regulated professions, an important economic or financial interest of the State or the protection of the data subject or the rights and freedoms of others.

1. *Purpose limitation*: data must be processed and subsequently used or further communicated only for the specific purposes in Appendix I to the Clauses. Data must not be kept longer than necessary for the purposes for which they are transferred.

2. *Data quality and proportionality*: data must be accurate and, where necessary, kept up to date. The data must be adequate, relevant and not excessive in relation to the purposes for which they are transferred and further processed.

3. *Transparency*: data subjects must be provided with information as to the purposes of the processing and the identity of the data controller in the third country, and other information insofar as this is necessary to ensure fair processing, unless such information has already been given by the data exporter.

4. *Security and confidentiality*: technical and organisational security measures must be taken by the data controller that are appropriate to the risks, such as unauthorised access, presented by the processing. Any person acting under the authority of the data controller, including a processor, must not process the data except on instructions from the controller.

5. *Rights of access, rectification, erasure and blocking of data*: as provided for in Article 12 of Directive 95/46/EC, the data subject must have a right of access to all data relating to him that are processed and, as appropriate, the right to the rectification, erasure or blocking of data the processing of which does not comply with the principles set out in this Appendix, in particular because the data are incomplete or inaccurate. He should also be able to object to the processing of the data relating to him on compelling legitimate grounds relating to his particular situation.

6. *Restrictions on onwards transfers*: further transfers of personal data from the data importer to another controller established in a third country not providing adequate protection or not covered by a decision adopted by the Commission pursuant to Article 25(6) of Directive 95/46/EC (onward transfer) may take place only if either:

   (a) data subjects have, in the case of special categories of data, given their unambiguous consent to the onward transfer or, in other cases, have been given the opportunity to object.

   The minimum information to be provided to data subjects must contain in a language understandable to them:

   — the purposes of the onward transfer,

   — the identification of the data exporter established in the Community,

   — the categories of further recipients of the data and the countries of destination, and

   — an explanation that, after the onward transfer, the data may be processed by a controller established in a country where there is not an adequate level of protection of the privacy of individuals; or

   (b) the data exporter and the data importer agree to the adherence to the Clauses of another controller which thereby becomes a party to the Clauses and assumes the same obligations as the data importer.

7. *Special categories of data*: where data revealing racial or ehtnic origin, political opinions, religious or philosophical beliefs or trade union memberships and data concerning health or sex life and data relating to offences, criminal convictions or security measures are processed, additional safeguards should be in place within the meaning of Directive 95/46/EC, in particular, appropriate security measures such as strong encryption for transmission or such as keeping a record of access to sensitive data.

8. *Direct marketing*: where data are processed for the purposes of direct marketing, effective procedures should exist allowing the data subject at any time to 'opt-out' from having his data used for such purposes.

9. *Automated individual decisions*: data subjects are entitled not to be subject to a decision which is based soley on automated processing of data, unless other measures are taken to safeguard the individual's legitimate interests as provided for in Article 15(2) of Directive 95/46/EC. Where the purpose of the transfer is the taking of an automated decision as referred to in Article 15 of Directive 95/46/EC, which produces legal effects concerning the individual or significantly affects him and which is based solely on automated processing of data intended to evaluate certain personal aspects relating to him, such as his performance at work, creditworthiness, reliability, conduct, etc., the individual should have the right to know the reasoning for this decision.

Appendix 3

to the standard contractual clauses

Mandatory data protection principles referred to in the second paragraph of Clause 5(b)

1. *Purpose limitation*: data must be processed and subsequently used or further communicated only for the specific purposes in Appendix I to the Clauses. Data must not be kept longer than necessary for the purposes for which they are transferred.

2. *Rights of access, rectification, erasure and blocking of data*: as provided for in Article 12 of Directive 95/46/EC, the data subject must have a right of access to all data relating to him that are processed and, as appropriate, the right to the rectification, erasure or blocking of data the processing of which does not comply with the principles set out in this Appendix, in particular because the data is incomplete or inaccurate. He should also be able to object to the processing of the data relating to him on compelling legitimate grounds relating to his particular situation.

3. *Restrictions on onward transfers*: further transfers of personal data from the data importer to another controller established in a third country not providing adequate protection or not covered by a decision adopted by the Commission pursuant to Article 25(6) of Directive 95/46/EC (onward transfer) may take place only if either:

   (a) data subjects have, in the case of special categories of data, given their unambiguous consent to the onward transfer, or, in other cases, have been given the opportunity to object.

   The minimum information to be provided to data subjects must contain in a language understandable to them:

   — the purposes of the onward transfer,

   — the identification of the data exporter established in the Community,

   — the categories of further recipients of the data and the countries of destination, and

   — an explanation that, after the onward transfer, the data may be processed by a controller established in a country where there is not an adequate level of protection of the privacy of indidividuals; or

   (b) the data exporter and the data importer agree to the adherence to the Clauses of another controller which thereby becomes a party to the Clauses and assumes the same obligations as the data importer.

Exhibit App. B.2. "Controller-to-Processor Clauses"

L 6/52 EN Official Journal of the European Communities 10.1.2002

II

(Acts whose publication is not obligatory)

COMMISSION

COMMISSION DECISION

of 27 December 2001

on standard contractual clauses for the transfer of personal data to processors established in third countries, under Directive 95/46/EC

(notified under document number C(2001) 4540)

(Text with EEA relevance)

(2002/16/EC)

THE COMMISSION OF THE EUROPEAN COMMUNITIES,

Having regard to the Treaty establishing the European Community,

Having regard to Directive 95/46/EC of the European Parliament and of the Council of 24 October 1995 on the protection of individuals with regard to the processing of personal data and on the free movement of such data ([1]), and in particular Article 26(4) thereof,

Whereas:

(1) Pursuant to Directive 95/46/EC Member States are required to provide that a transfer of personal data to a third country may only take place if the third country in question ensures an adequate level of data protection and the Member States' laws, which comply with the other provisions of the Directive, are respected prior to the transfer.

(2) However, Article 26(2) of Directive 95/46/EC provides that Member States may authorise, subject to certain safeguards, a transfer or a set of transfers of personal data to third countries which do not ensure an adequate level of protection. Such safeguards may in particular result from appropriate contractual clauses.

(3) Pursuant to Directive 95/46/EC the level of data protection should be assessed in the light of all the circumstances surrounding the data transfer operation or set of data transfer operations. The Working Party on the Protection of Individuals with regard to the Processing of Personal Data established under that Directive ([2]) has issued guidelines to aid with the assessment ([3]).

([1]) OJ L 281, 23.11.1995, p. 31.

([2]) The web address of the Working Party is:
http://europa.eu.int/comm/internal_market/en/dataprot/wpdocs/index.htm.

([3]) **WP 4 (5020/97)**: 'First orientations on Transfers of Personal Data to Third Countries — Possible Ways Forward in Assessing Adequacy', a discussion document adopted by the Working Party on 26 June 1997.
WP 7 (5057/97): Working document: 'Judging industry self-regulation: when does it make a meaningful contribution to the level of data protection in a third country?', adopted by the Working Party on 14 January 1998.
WP 9 (5005/98): Working Document: 'Preliminary views on the use of contractual provisions in the context of transfers of personal data to third countries', adopted by the Working Party on 22 April 1998.
WP 12: Transfers of personal data to third countries: Applying Articles 25 and 26 of the EU data protection directive, adopted by the Working Party on 24 July 1998, available on the website
'http://europa.eu.int/comm/internal_market/en/dataprot/wpdocs/wp12en.htm' hosted by the European Commission.

(4) The standard contractual clauses relate only to data protection. The data exporter and the data importer are free to include any other clauses on business related issues which they consider as being pertinent for the contract as long as they do not contradict the standard contractual clauses.

(5) This Decision should be without prejudice to national authorisations Member States may grant in accordance with national provisions implementing Article 26(2) of Directive 95/46/EC. This Decision only has the effect of requiring the Member States not to refuse to recognise as providing adequate safeguards the contractual clauses set out in it and does not therefore have any effect on other contractual clauses.

(6) The scope of this Decision is limited to establishing that the clauses which it sets out may be used by a data controller established in the Community in order to adduce adequate safeguards within the meaning of Article 26(2) of Directive 95/46/EC for the transfer of personal data to a processor established in a third country.

(7) This Decision should implement the obligation provided for in Article 17(3) of Directive 95/46/EC and does not prejudice the content of the contracts or legal acts established pursuant to that provision. However, some of the standard contractual clauses, in particular as regards the data exporter's obligations, should be included in order to increase clarity as to the provisions which may be contained in a contract between a controller and a processor.

(8) Supervisory authorities of the Member States play a key role in this contractual mechanism in ensuring that personal data are adequately protected after the transfer. In exceptional cases where data exporters refuse or are unable to instruct the data importer properly, with an imminent risk of grave harm to the data subjects, the standard contractual clauses should allow the supervisory authorities to audit data importers and, where appropriate, take decisions which are binding on data importers. The supervisory authorities should have the power to prohibit or suspend a data transfer or a set of transfers based on the standard contractual clauses in those exceptional cases where it is established that a transfer on contractual basis is likely to have a substantial adverse effect on the warranties and obligations providing adequate protection for the data subject.

(9) The Commission may also consider in the future whether standard contractual clauses for the transfer of personal data to data processors established in third countries not offering an adequate level of data protection, submitted by business organisations or other interested parties, offer adequate safeguards in accordance with Article 26(2) of Directive 95/46/EC.

(10) A disclosure of personal data to a data processor established outside the Community is an international transfer protected under Chapter IV of Directive 95/46/EC. Consequently, this Decision does not cover the transfer of personal data by controllers established in the Community to controllers established outside the Community who fall within the scope of Commission Decision 2001/497/EC of 15 June 2001 on standard contractual clauses for the transfer of personal data to third countries, under Directive 95/46/EC ([1]).

(11) The standard contractual clauses should provide for the technical and organisational security measures ensuring a level of security appropriate to the risks represented by the processing and the nature of the data to be protected that a data processor established in a third country not providing adequate protection must apply. Parties should make provision in the contract for those technical and organisational measures which, having regard to applicable data protection law, the state of the art and the cost of their implementation, are necessary in order to protect personal data against accidental or unlawful destruction or accidental loss, alteration, unauthorised disclosure or access or any other unlawful forms of processing.

(12) In order to facilitate data flows from the Community, it is desirable that processors providing data processing services to several data controllers in the Community be allowed to apply the same technical and organisational security measures irrespective of the Member State from which the data transfer originates, in particular in those cases where the data importer receives data for further processing from different establishments of the data exporter in the Community, in which case the law of the designated Member State of establishment should apply.

([1]) OJ L 181, 4.7.2001, p. 19.

(13) It is appropriate to lay down the minimum information that the parties must specify in the contract dealing with the transfer. Member States should retain the power to particularise the information the parties are required to provide. The operation of this Decision should be reviewed in the light of experience.

(14) The data importer should process the transferred personal data only on behalf of the data exporter and in accordance with his instructions and the obligations contained in the clauses. In particular the data importer should not disclose the personal data to a third party unless in accordance with certain conditions. The data exporter should instruct the data importer throughout the duration of the data processing Services to process the data in accordance with his instructions, the applicable data protection laws and the obligations contained in the clauses. The transfer of personal data to processors established outside the Community does not prejudice the fact that the processing activities should be governed in any case by the applicable data protection law.

(15) The standard contractual clauses should be enforceable not only by the organisations which are parties to the contract, but also by the data subjects, in particular where the data subjects suffer damage as a consequence of a breach of the contract.

(16) The data subject should be entitled to take action and, where appropriate, receive compensation from the data exporter who is the data controller of the personal data transferred. Exceptionally, the data subject should also be entitled to take action, and, where appropriate, receive compensation from the data importer in those cases, arising out of a breach by the data importer of any of his obligations referred to in the second paragraph of clause 3, where the data exporter has factually disappeared or has ceased to exist in law or has become insolvent.

(17) In the event of a dispute between a data subject, who invokes the third-party beneficiary clause and the data importer, which is not amicably resolved, the data importer should agree to provide the data subject with the choice between mediation, arbitration or litigation. The extent to which the data subject will have an effective choice should depend on the availability of reliable and recognised systems of mediation and arbitration. Mediation by the data protection supervisory authorities of the Member State in which the data exporter is established should be an option where they provide such a service.

(18) The contract should be governed by the law of the Member State in which the data exporter is established enabling a third-party beneficiary to enforce a contract. Data subjects should be allowed to be represented by associations or other bodies if they so wish and if authorised by national law.

(19) The Working Party on the Protection of Individuals with regard to the processing of Personal Data established under Article 29 of Directive 95/46/EC has delivered an opinion on the level of protection provided under the standard contractual clauses annexed to this Decision, which has been taken into account in the preparation of this Decision (1).

(20) The measures provided for in this Decision are in accordance with the opinion of the Committee established under Article 31 of Directive 95/46/EC,

HAS ADOPTED THIS DECISION:

Article 1

The standard contractual clauses set out in the Annex are considered as offering adequate safeguards with respect to the protection of the privacy and fundamental rights and freedoms of individuals and as regards the exercise of the corresponding rights as required by Article 26(2) of Directive 95/46/EC.

(1) Opinion No 7/2001 adopted by the Working Party on 13 September 2001 (DG MARKT....), available on the website 'Europa' hosted by the European Commission.

Article 2

This Decision concerns only the adequacy of protection provided by the standard contractual clauses set out in the Annex for the transfer of personal data to processors. It does not affect the application of other national provisions implementing Directive 95/46/EC that pertain to the processing of personal data within the Member States.

This Decision shall apply to the transfer of personal data by controllers established in the Community to recipients established outside the territory of the Community who act only as processors.

Article 3

For the purposes of this Decision:

(a) the definitions in Directive 95/46/EC shall apply;

(b) 'special categories of data' means the data referred to in Article 8 of that Directive;

(c) 'supervisory authority' means the authority referred to in Article 28 of that Directive;

(d) 'data exporter' means the controller who transfers the personal data;

(e) 'data importer' means the processor established in a third country who agrees to receive from the data exporter personal data intended for processing on the data exporter's behalf after the transfer in accordance with his instructions and the terms of this Decision and who is not subject to a third country's system ensuring adequate protection;

(f) 'applicable data protection law' means the legislation protecting the fundamental rights and freedoms of natural persons and, in particular, their right to privacy with respect to the processing of personal data applicable to a data controller in the Member State in which the data exporter is established;

(g) 'technical and organisational security measures' means those measures aimed at protecting personal data against accidental or unlawful destruction or accidental loss, alteration, unauthorised disclosure or access, in particular where the processing involves the transmission of data over a network, and against all other unlawful forms of processing.

Article 4

1. Without prejudice to their powers to take action to ensure compliance with national provisions adopted pursuant to Chapters II, III, V and VI of Directive 95/46/EC, the competent authorities in the Member States may exercise their existing powers to prohibit or suspend data flows to third countries in order to protect individuals with regard to the processing of their personal data in cases where:

(a) it is established that the law to which the data importer is subject imposes upon him requirements to derogate from the applicable data protection law which go beyond the restrictions necessary in a democratic society as provided for in Article 13 of Directive 95/46/EC where those requirements are likely to have a substantial adverse effect on the guarantees provided by the applicable data protection law and the standard contractual clauses; or

(b) a competent authority has established that the data importer has not respected the contractual clauses in the Annex; or

(c) there is a substantial likelihood that the standard contractual clauses in the Annex are not being or will not be complied with and the continuing transfer would create an imminent risk of grave harm to the data subjects.

2. The prohibition or suspension pursuant to paragraph 1 shall be lifted as soon as the reasons for the suspension or prohibition no longer exist.

3. When Member States adopt measures pursuant to paragraphs 1 and 2, they shall, without delay, inform the Commission which will forward the information to the other Member States.

Article 5

The Commission shall evaluate the operation of this Decision on the basis of available information three years after its notification to the Member States. It shall submit a report on the findings to the Committee established under Article 31 of Directive 95/46/EC. It shall include any evidence that could affect the evaluation concerning the adequacy of the standard contractual clauses in the Annex and any evidence that this Decision is being applied in a discriminatory way.

Article 6

This Decision shall apply from 3 April 2002.

Article 7

This Decision is addressed to the Member States.

Done at Brussels, 27 December 2001.

For the Commission
Frederik BOLKESTEIN
Member of the Commission

ANNEX

Standard Contractual Clauses (processors)

For the purposes of Article 26(2) of Directive 95/46/EC for the transfer of personal data to processors established in third countries which do not ensure an adequate level of data protection

Name of the data exporting organisation: ....

address ....

....

tel.: ....; fax: .... ; e-mail: ....

Other information needed to identify the organisation

....
(the data **exporter**)

and

Name of the data importing organisation: ....

address ....

....

tel.: ....; fax: .... ; e-mail: ....

Other information needed to identify the organisation:

....
(the data **importer**)

HAVE AGREED on the following Contractual Clauses (the Clauses) in order to adduce adequate safeguards with respect to the protection of privacy and fundamental rights and freedoms of individuals for the transfer by the data exporter to the data importer of the personal data specified in Appendix 1.

Clause 1

Definitions

For the purposes of the Clauses:

(a) 'personal data', 'special categories of data', 'process/processing', 'controller', 'processor', 'data subject' and 'supervisory authority' shall have the same meaning as in Directive 95/46/EC of the European Parliament and of the Council of 24 October 1995 on the protection of individuals with regard to the processing of personal data and on the free movement of such data (the Directive) [1];

(b) 'the data exporter' shall mean the controller who transfers the personal data;

(c) 'the data importer' shall mean the processor who agrees to receive from the data exporter personal data intended for processing on his behalf after the transfer in accordance with his instructions and the terms of these Clauses and who is not subject to a third country's system ensuring to adequate protection;

(d) 'the applicable data protection law' shall mean the legislation protecting the fundamental rights and freedoms of natural persons and, in particular, their right to privacy with respect to the processing of personal data applicable to a data controller in the Member State in which the data exporter is established;

(e) 'technical and organisational security measures' shall mean those measures aimed at protecting personal data against accidental or unlawful destruction or accidental loss, alteration, unauthorised disclosure or access, in particular where the processing involves the transmission of data over a network, and against all other unlawful forms of processing.

Clause 2

Details of the transfer

The details of the transfer and in particular the special categories of personal data where applicable are specified in Appendix 1 which forms an integral part of the Clauses.

(1) Parties may reproduce definitions and meanings contained in Directive 95/46/EC within this Clause if they considered it better for the contract to stand alone.

L 6/58 EN Official Journal of the European Communities 10.1.2002

Clause 3

Third-party beneficiary clause

The data subject can enforce against the data exporter this Clause, Clause 4(b) to (h), Clause 5(a) to (e), and (g), Clause 6(1) and (2), Clause 7, Clause 8(2), and Clauses 9, 10 and 11, as third-party beneficiaries.

The data subject can enforce against the data importer this Clause, Clause 5(a) to (e) and (g), Clause 6(1) and (2), Clause 7, Clause 8(2), and Clauses 9, 10 and 11, in cases where the data exporter has factually disappeared or has ceased to exist in law.

The parties do not object to a data subject being represented by an association or other body if the data subject so expressly wishes and if permitted by national law.

Clause 4

Obligations of the data exporter

The data exporter agrees and warrants:

(a) that the processing, including the transfer itself, of the personal data has been and will continue to be carried out in accordance with the relevant provisions of the applicable data protection law (and, where applicable, has been notified to the relevant authorities of the Member State where the data exporter is established) and does not violate the relevant provisions of that State;

(b) that he has instructed and throughout the duration of the personal data processing services will instruct the data importer to process the personal data transferred only on the data exporter's behalf and in accordance with the applicable data protection law and these clauses;

(c) that the data importer shall provide sufficient guarantees in respect of the technical and organisational security measures specified in Appendix 2 to this contract;

(d) that after assessment of the requirements of the applicable data protection law, the security measures are appropriate to protect personal data against accidental or unlawful destruction or accidental loss, alteration, unauthorised disclosure or access, in particular where the processing involves the transmission of data over a network, and against all other unlawful forms of processing, and that these measures ensure a level of security appropriate to the risks presented by the processing and the nature of the data to be protected having regard to the state of the art and the cost of their implementation;

(e) that he will ensure compliance with the security measures;

(f) that, if the transfer involves special categories of data, the data subject has been informed or will be informed before, or as soon as possible after, the transfer that his data could be transmitted to a third country not providing adequate protection;

(g) that he agrees to forward the notification received from the data importer pursuant to Clause 5(b) to the data protection supervisory authority if he decides to continue the transfer or to lift his suspension;

(h) to make available to the data subjects upon request a copy of the Clauses set out in this Annex, with the exception of Appendix 2 which shall be replaced by a summary description of the security measures.

Clause 5

Obligations of the data importer [1]

The data importer agrees and warrants:

(a) to process the personal data only on behalf of the data exporter and in compliance with his instructions and the clauses; if he cannot provide such compliance for whatever reasons, he agrees to inform promptly the data exporter of his inability to comply, in which case the data exporter is entitled to suspend the transfer of data and/or terminate the contract;

(b) that he has no reason to believe that the legislation applicable to him prevents him from fulfilling the instructions received from the data exporter and his obligations under the contract and that in the event of a change in this legislation which is likely to have a substantial adverse effect on the warranties and obligations provided by the Clauses, he will promptly notify the change to the data exporter as soon as he is aware, in which case the data exporter is entitled to suspend the transfer of data and/or terminate the contract;

(c) that he has implemented the technical and organisational security measures specified in Appendix 2 before processing the personal data transferred;

(1) Mandatory requirements of the national legislation applicable to the data importer which do not go beyond what is necessary in a democratic society on the basis of one of the interests listed in Article 13(1) of Directive 95/46/EC, that is, if they constitute a necessary measure to safeguard national security defence, public security, the prevention, investigation, detection and prosecution of criminal offences or of breaches of ethics for the regulated professions, an important economic or financial interest of the State or the protection of the data subject or the rights and freedoms of others, are not in contradiction with the standard contractual clauses. Some examples of such mandatory requirements which do not go beyond what is necessary in a democratic society are, *inter alia*, internationally recognised sanctions, tax-reporting requirements or anti-money-laundering reporting requirements.

(d) that he shall promptly notify the data exporter about:

(i) any legally binding request for disclosure of the personal data by a law enforcement authority unless otherwise prohibited, such as a prohibition under criminal law to preserve the confidentiality of a law enforcement investigation;

(ii) any accidental or unauthorised access; and

(iii) any request received directly from the data subjects without responding to that request, unless he has been otherwise authorised to do so;

(e) to deal promptly and properly with all inquiries from the data exporter relating to his processing of the personal data subject to the transfer and to abide by the advice of the supervisory authority with regard to the processing of the data transferred;

(f) at the request of the data exporter to submit his data processing facilities for audit of the processing activities covered by the clauses which shall be carried out by the data exporter or an inspection body composed of independent members and in possession of the required professional qualifications bound by a duty of confidentiality, selected by the data exporter, where applicable, in agreement with the supervisory authority;

(g) to make available to the data subject upon request a copy of the Clauses set out in this Annex, with the exception of Appendix 2 which shall be replaced by a summary description of the security measures in those cases where the data subject is unable to obtain a copy from the data exporter.

Clause 6

Liability

1. The parties agree that a data subject, who has suffered damage as a result of any violation of the provisions referred to in Clause 3 is entitled to receive compensation from the data exporter for the damage suffered.

2. If a data subject is not able to bring the action referred to in paragraph 1 arising out of a breach by the data importer of any of his obligations referred to in Clause 3 against the data exporter because the data exporter has disappeared factually or has ceased to exist in law or became insolvent, the data importer agrees that the data subject may issue a claim against the data importer as if he were the data exporter.

3. The parties agree that if one party is held liable for a violation of the clauses committed by the other party, the latter will, to the extent to which it is liable, indemnify the first party for any cost, charge, damages, expenses or loss it has incurred.

Indemnifaction is contingent upon:

(a) the data exporter promptly notifying the data importer of a claim; and

(b) the data importer being given the possibility to cooperate with the data exporter in the defence and settlement of the claim [1].

Clause 7

Mediation and jurisdiction

1. The data importer agrees that if the data subject invokes against him third-party beneficiary rights and/or claims compensation for damages under the clauses, the data importer will accept the decision of the data subject:

(a) to refer the dispute to mediation, by an independent person or, where applicable, by the supervisory authority;

(b) to refer the dispute to the courts in the Member State in which the data exporter is established.

2. The data importer agrees that, by agreement with the data subject, the resolution of a specific dispute can be referred to an arbitration body if the data importer is established in a country which has ratified the New York Convention on enforcement of arbitration awards.

3. The parties agree that the choice made by the data subject will not prejudice his substantive or procedural rights to seek remedies in accordance with other provisions of national or international law.

Clause 8

Cooperation with supervisory authorities

1. The data exporter agrees to deposit a copy of this contract with the supervisory authority if it so requests or if such deposit is required under the applicable data protection law.

2. The parties agree that the supervisory authority has the right to conduct an audit of the data importer which has the same scope and is subject to the same conditions as would apply to an audit of the data exporter under the applicable data protection law.

[1] Paragraph 3 is optional.

L 6/60 EN Official Journal of the European Communities 10.1.2002

Clause 9

Governing Law

The Clauses shall be governed by the law of the Member State in which the data exporter is established, namely ....

Clause 10

Variation of the contract

The parties undertake not to vary or modify the terms of the Clauses.

Clause 11

Obligation after the termination of personal data processing services

1. The parties agree that on the termination of the provision of data processing services, the data importer shall, at the choice of the data exporter, return al the personal data transferred and the copies thereof to the data exporter or shall destroy all the personal data and certify to the data exporter that he has done so, unless legislation imposed upon the data importer prevents him from returning or destroying all or part of the personal data transferred. In that case, the data importer warrants that he will guarantee the confidentiality of the personal data transferred and will not actively process the personal data transferred anymore.

2. The data importer warrants that upon request of the data exporter and/or of the supervisory authority, he will submit his data processing facilities for an audit of the measures referred to in paragraph 1.

On behalf of the data exporter:

Name (written out in full): ....

Position: ....

Address: ....

Other information necessary in order for the contract to be binding (if any): ....

Signature ....

(stamp of organisation)

On behalf of the data importer:

Name (written out in full): ....

Position: ....

Address: ....

Other information necessary in order for the contract to be binding (if any): ....

Signature ....

(stamp of organisation)

10.1.2002 EN Official Journal of the European Communities L 6/61

Appendix 1

to the Standard Contractual Clauses

This Appendix forms part of the Clauses and must be completed and signed by the parties

(*) The Member States may complete or specify, according to their national procedures, any additional necessary information to be contained in this Appendix)

Data exporter

The data exporter is (please specify briefly your activities relevant to the transfer):

....

....

....

Data importer

The data importer is (please specify briefly activities relevant to the transfer):

....

....

....

Data subjects

The personal data transferred concern the following categories of data subjects (please specify):

....

....

....

Categories of data

The personal data transferred concern the following categories of data (please specify):

....

....

....

Special categories of data (if appropriate)

The personal data transferred concern the following special categories of data (please specifiy):

....

....

....

Processing operations

The personal data transferred will be subject to the following basic processing activities (please specify):

....

....

....

DATA EXPORTER DATA IMPORTER

Name: ....

Authorised signature

....

L 6/62 EN Official Journal of the European Communities 10.1.2002

Appendix 2

to the Standard Contractual Clauses

This Appendix forms part of the Clauses and must be completed and signed by the parties

Description of the technical and organisational security measures implemented by the data importer in accordance with Clauses 4(d) and 5(c) (or document/legislation attached):

....

....

....

....

Exhibit App B.3. "2004 Clauses"

L 385/74 EN Official Journal of the European Union 29.12.2004

COMMISSION DECISION

of 27 December 2004

amending Decision 2001/497/EC as regards the introduction of an alternative set of standard contractual clauses for the transfer of personal data to third countries

(notified under document number C(2004) 5271)

(Text with EEA relevance)

(2004/915/EC)

THE COMMISSION OF THE EUROPEAN COMMUNITIES,

Having regard to the Treaty establishing the European Community,

Having regard to Directive 95/46/EC of the European Parliament and of the Council of 24 October 1995 on the protection of individuals with regard to the processing of personal data and on the free movement of such data [1], and in particular Article 26(4) thereof,

Whereas:

(1) In order to facilitate data flows from the Community, it is desirable for data controllers to be able to perform data transfers globally under a single set of data protection rules. In the absence of global data protection standards, standard contractual clauses provide an important tool allowing the transfer of personal data from all Member States under a common set of rules. Commission Decision 2001/497/EC of 15 June 2001 on standard contractual clauses for the transfer of personal data to third countries under Directive 95/46/EC [2] therefore lays down a model set of standard contractual clauses which ensures adequate safeguards for the transfer of data to third countries.

(2) Much experience has been gained since the adoption of that Decision. In addition, a coalition of business associations [3] has submitted a set of alternative standard contractual clauses designed to provide a level of data protection equivalent to that provided for by the set of standard contractual clauses laid down in Decision 2001/497/EC while making use of different mechanisms.

(3) Since the use of standard contractual clauses for international data transfers is voluntary as standard contractual clauses are only one of several possibilities under Directive 95/46/EC, for lawfully transferring personal data to a third country, data exporters in the Community and data importers in third countries should be free to choose any of the sets of standard contractual clauses, or to choose some other legal basis for data transfer. As each set as a whole forms a model, data exporters should not, however, be allowed to amend these sets or totally or partially merge them in any manner.

(4) The standard contract clauses submitted by the business associations aim at increasing the use of contractual clauses among operators by mechanisms such as more flexible auditing requirements and more detailed rules on the right of access.

(5) Moreover, as an alternative to the system of joint and several liability provided for in Decision 2001/497/EC, the set now submitted contains a liability regime based on due diligence obligations where the data exporter and the data importer would be liable vis-à-vis the data subjects for their respective breach of their contractual obligations; the data exporter is also liable for not using reasonable efforts to determine that the data importer is able to satisfy its legal obligations under the clauses (*culpa in eligendo*) and the data subject can take action against the data exporter in this respect. The enforcement of clause I(b) of the new set of standard contractual clauses is of particular importance in this regard, in particular in connection with the possibility for the data exporter to carry out audits on the data importers' premises or to request evidence of sufficient financial resources to fulfil its responsibilities.

[1] OJ L 281, 23.11.95, p. 31. Directive as amended by Regulation (EC) No 1883/2003 (OJ L 284, 31.10.2003, p. 1).

[2] OJ L 181, 4.7.2001, p. 19.

[3] The International Chamber of Commerce (ICC), Japan Business Council in Europe (JBCE), European Information and Communications Technology Association (EICTA), EU Committee of the American Chamber of Commerce in Belgium (Amcham), Confederation of British Industry (CBI), International Communication Round Table (ICRT) and the Federation of European Direct Marketing Associations (FEDMA).

29.12.2004 EN Official Journal of the European Union L 385/75

(6) As regards the exercise of third party beneficiary rights by the data subjects, greater involvement of the data exporter in the resolution of data subjects' complaints is provided for, with the data exporter being obliged to make contact with the data importer and, if necessary, enforce the contract within the normal period of one month. If the data exporter refused to enforce the contract and the breach by the data importer still continues, the data subject may then enforce the clauses against the data importer and eventually sue him in a Member State. This acceptance of jurisdiction and the agreement to comply with a decision of a competent court or data protection authority does not prejudice any procedural rights of data importers established in third countries, such as rights of appeal.

(7) In order, however, to prevent abuses with this additional flexibility, it is appropriate to provide that data protection authorities can more easily prohibit or suspend data transfers based on the new set of standard contractual clauses in those cases where the data exporter refuses to take appropriate steps to enforce contractual obligations against the data importer or the latter refuses to cooperate in good faith with competent supervisory data protection authorities.

(8) The use of standard contractual clauses will be made without prejudice to the application of national provisions adopted pursuant to Directive 95/46/EC or to Directive 2002//58/EC of the European Parliament and of the Council concerning the processing of personal data and the protection of privacy in the electronic communications sector (Directive on privacy and electronic communications) [1], in particular as far as the sending of commercial communications for the purposes of direct marketing is concerned.

(9) On that basis, the safeguards contained in the submitted standard contractual clauses can be considered as adequate within the meaning of Article 26(2) of Directive 95/46/EC.

(10) The Working Party on the Protection of Individuals with regard to the Processing of Personal Data established under Article 29 of Directive 95/46/EC has delivered an opinion [2] on the level of protection provided under the submitted standard contractual clauses which has been taken into account.

(11) In order to assess the operation of the amendments to Decision 2001/497/EC, it is appropriate that the Commission evaluates them three years after their notification to the Member States

(12) Decision 2001/497/EC should be amended accordingly.

(13) The measures provided for in this Decision are in accordance with the opinion of the Committee established under Article 31 of Directive 95/46/EC,

HAS ADOPTED THIS DECISION:

Article 1

Decision 2001/497/EC is amended as follows:

1. In Article 1 the following paragraph is added:

'Data controllers may choose either of the sets I or II in the Annex. However, they may not amend the clauses nor combine individual clauses or the sets.'

2. In Article 4 paragraphs 2 and 3 are replaced by the following:

'2. For the purposes of paragraph 1, where the data controller adduces adequate safeguards on the basis of the standard contractual clauses contained in set II in the Annex, the competent data protection authorities are entitled to exercise their existing powers to prohibit or suspend data flows in either of the following cases:

(a) refusal of the data importer to cooperate in good faith with the data protection authorities, or to comply with their clear obligations under the contract;

(b) refusal of the data exporter to take appropriate steps to enforce the contract against the data importer within the normal period of one month after notice by the competent data protection authority to the data exporter.

(1) OJ L 201, 31.7.2002, p. 37.
(2) Opinion No 8/2003, available at: http://europa.eu.int/comm/privacy

For the purposes of the first subparagraph, refusal in bad faith or refusal to enforce the contract by the data importer shall not include cases in which cooperation or enforcement would conflict with mandatory requirements of the national legislation applicable to the data importer which do not go beyond what is necessary in a democratic society on the basis of one of the interests listed in Article 13(1) of Directive 95/46/EC, in particular sanctions as laid down in international and/or national instruments, tax-reporting requirements or anti-money-laundering reporting requirements.

For the purposes of point (a) of the first subparagraph co-operation may include, in particular, the submission of the data importer's data processing facilities for audit or the obligation to abide by the advice of the data protection supervisory authority in the Community.

3. The prohibition or suspension pursuant to paragraphs 1 and 2 shall be lifted as soon as the reasons for the prohibition or suspension no longer exist.

4. When Member States adopt measures pursuant to paragraphs 1, 2 and 3, they shall without delay inform the Commission which will forward the information to the other Member States.'.

3. In Article 5 the first sentence is replaced by the following:

'The Commission shall evaluate the operation of this Decision on the basis of available information three years after its notification and the notification of any amendment thereto to the Member States.'.

4. The Annex is amended as follows:

1. After the title the term 'SET I' is inserted.

2. The text set out in the Annex to this Decision is added.

Article 2

This Decision shall apply from 1 April 2005.

Article 3

This Decision is addressed to the Member States.

Done at Brussels, 27 December 2004.

For the Commission
Charlie McCREEVY
Member of the Commission

29.12.2004 EN Official Journal of the European Union L 385/77

ANNEX

'SET II

Standard contractual clauses for the transfer of personal data from the Community to third countries (controller to controller transfers)

Data transfer agreement

between

______________________________ (name)

______________________________ (address and country of establishment)

hereinafter "data exporter")

and

______________________________ (name)

______________________________ (address and country of establishment)

hereinafter "data importer"

each a "party"; together "the parties".

Definitions

For the purposes of the clauses:

(a) "personal data", "special categories of data/sensitive data", "process/processing", "controller", "processor", "data subject" and "supervisory authority/authority" shall have the same meaning as in Directive 95/46/EC of 24 October 1995 (whereby "the authority" shall mean the competent data protection authority in the territory in which the data exporter is established);

(b) "the data exporter" shall mean the controller who transfers the personal data;

(c) "the data importer" shall mean the controller who agrees to receive from the data exporter personal data for further processing in accordance with the terms of these clauses and who is not subject to a third country's system ensuring adequate protection;

(d) "clauses" shall mean these contractual clauses, which are a free-standing document that does not incorporate commercial business terms established by the parties under separate commercial arrangements.

The details of the transfer (as well as the personal data covered) are specified in Annex B, which forms an integral part of the clauses.

I. **Obligations of the data exporter**

The data exporter warrants and undertakes that:

(a) The personal data have been collected, processed and transferred in accordance with the laws applicable to the data exporter.

(b) It has used reasonable efforts to determine that the data importer is able to satisfy its legal obligations under these clauses.

(c) It will provide the data importer, when so requested, with copies of relevant data protection laws or references to them (where relevant, and not including legal advice) of the country in which the data exporter is established.

(d) It will respond to enquiries from data subjects and the authority concerning processing of the personal data by the data importer, unless the parties have agreed that the data importer will so respond, in which case the data exporter will still respond to the extent reasonably possible and with the information reasonably available to it if the data importer is unwilling or unable to respond. Responses will be made within a reasonable time.

(e) It will make available, upon request, a copy of the clauses to data subjects who are third party beneficiaries under clause III, unless the clauses contain confidential information, in which case it may remove such information. Where information is removed, the data exporter shall inform data subjects in writing of the reason for removal and of their right to draw the removal to the attention of the authority. However, the data exporter shall abide by a decision of the authority regarding access to the full text of the clauses by data subjects, as long as data subjects have agreed to respect the confidentiality of the confidential information removed. The data exporter shall also provide a copy of the clauses to the authority where required.

II. **Obligations of the data importer**

The data importer warrants and undertakes that:

(a) It will have in place appropriate technical and organisational measures to protect the personal data against accidental or unlawful destruction or accidental loss, alteration, unauthorised disclosure or access, and which provide a level of security appropriate to the risk represented by the processing and the nature of the data to be protected.

(b) It will have in place procedures so that any third party it authorises to have access to the personal data, including processors, will respect and maintain the confidentiality and security of the personal data. Any person acting under the authority of the data importer, including a data processor, shall be obligated to process the personal data only on instructions from the data importer. This provision does not apply to persons authorised or required by law or regulation to have access to the personal data.

(c) It has no reason to believe, at the time of entering into these clauses, in the existence of any local laws that would have a substantial adverse effect on the guarantees provided for under these clauses, and it will inform the data exporter (which will pass such notification on to the authority where required) if it becomes aware of any such laws.

(d) It will process the personal data for purposes described in Annex B, and has the legal authority to give the warranties and fulfil the undertakings set out in these clauses.

(e) It will identify to the data exporter a contact point within its organisation authorised to respond to enquiries concerning processing of the personal data, and will cooperate in good faith with the data exporter, the data subject and the authority concerning all such enquiries within a reasonable time. In case of legal dissolution of the data exporter, or if the parties have so agreed, the data importer will assume responsibility for compliance with the provisions of clause I(e).

(f) At the request of the data exporter, it will provide the data exporter with evidence of financial resources sufficient to fulfil its responsibilities under clause III (which may include insurance coverage).

(g) Upon reasonable request of the data exporter, it will submit its data processing facilities, data files and documentation needed for processing to reviewing, auditing and/or certifying by the data exporter (or any independent or impartial inspection agents or auditors, selected by the data exporter and not reasonably objected to by the data importer) to ascertain compliance with the warranties and undertakings in these clauses, with reasonable notice and during regular business hours. The request will be subject to any necessary consent or approval from a regulatory or supervisory authority within the country of the data importer, which consent or approval the data importer will attempt to obtain in a timely fashion.

(h) It will process the personal data, at its option, in accordance with:

(i) the data protection laws of the country in which the data exporter is established, or

(ii) the relevant provisions [1] of any Commission decision pursuant to Article 25(6) of Directive 95/46/EC, where the data importer complies with the relevant provisions of such an authorisation or decision and is based in a country to which such an authorisation or decision pertains, but is not covered by such authorisation or decision for the purposes of the transfer(s) of the personal data [2], or

(iii) the data processing principles set forth in Annex A.

Data importer to indicate which option it selects: ______________________

Initials of data importer: ______________________;

(i) It will not disclose or transfer the personal data to a third party data controller located outside the European Economic Area (EEA) unless it notifies the data exporter about the transfer and

(i) the third party data controller processes the personal data in accordance with a Commission decision finding that a third country provides adequate protection, or

(ii) the third party data controller becomes a signatory to these clauses or another data transfer agreement approved by a competent authority in the EU, or

(iii) data subjects have been given the opportunity to object, after having been informed of the purposes of the transfer, the categories of recipients and the fact that the countries to which data is exported may have different data protection standards, or

(iv) with regard to onward transfers of sensitive data, data subjects have given their unambiguous consent to the onward transfer

III. **Liability and third party rights**

(a) Each party shall be liable to the other parties for damages it causes by any breach of these clauses. Liability as between the parties is limited to actual damage suffered. Punitive damages (i.e. damages intended to punish a party for its outrageous conduct) are specifically excluded. Each party shall be liable to data subjects for damages it causes by any breach of third party rights under these clauses. This does not affect the liability of the data exporter under its data protection law.

(b) The parties agree that a data subject shall have the right to enforce as a third party beneficiary this clause and clauses I(b), I(d), I(e), II(a), II(c), II(d), II(e), II(h), II(i), III(a), V, VI(d) and VII against the data importer or the data exporter, for their respective breach of their contractual obligations, with regard to his personal data, and accept jurisdiction for this purpose in the data exporter's country of establishment. In cases involving allegations of breach by the data importer, the data subject must first request the data exporter to take appropriate action to enforce his rights against the data importer; if the data exporter does not take such action within a reasonable period (which under normal circumstances would be one month), the data subject may then enforce his rights against the data importer directly. A data subject is entitled to proceed directly against a data exporter that has failed to use reasonable efforts to determine that the data importer is able to satisfy its legal obligations under these clauses (the data exporter shall have the burden to prove that it took reasonable efforts).

(1) "Relevant provisions" means those provisions of any authorisation or decision except for the enforcement provisions of any authorisation or decision (which shall be governed by these clauses).

(2) However, the provisions of Annex A.5 concerning rights of access, rectification, deletion and objection must be applied when this option is chosen and take precedence over any comparable provisions of the Commission Decision selected.

IV. **Law applicable to the clauses**

These clauses shall be governed by the law of the country in which the data exporter is established, with the exception of the laws and regulations relating to processing of the personal data by the data importer under clause II(h), which shall apply only if so selected by the data importer under that clause.

V. **Resolution of disputes with data subjects or the authority**

(a) In the event of a dispute or claim brought by a data subject or the authority concerning the processing of the personal data against either or both of the parties, the parties will inform each other about any such disputes or claims, and will cooperate with a view to settling them amicably in a timely fashion.

(b) The parties agree to respond to any generally available non-binding mediation procedure initiated by a data subject or by the authority. If they do participate in the proceedings, the parties may elect to do so remotely (such as by telephone or other electronic means). The parties also agree to consider participating in any other arbitration, mediation or other dispute resolution proceedings developed for data protection disputes.

(c) Each party shall abide by a decision of a competent court of the data exporter's country of establishment or of the authority which is final and against which no further appeal is possible.

VI. **Termination**

(a) In the event that the data importer is in breach of its obligations under these clauses, then the data exporter may temporarily suspend the transfer of personal data to the data importer until the breach is repaired or the contract is terminated.

(b) In the event that:

(i) the transfer of personal data to the data importer has been temporarily suspended by the data exporter for longer than one month pursuant to paragraph (a);

(ii) compliance by the data importer with these clauses would put it in breach of its legal or regulatory obligations in the country of import;

(iii) the data importer is in substantial or persistent breach of any warranties or undertakings given by it under these clauses;

(iv) a final decision against which no further appeal is possible of a competent court of the data exporter's country of establishment or of the authority rules that there has been a breach of the clauses by the data importer or the data exporter; or

(v) a petition is presented for the administration or winding up of the data importer, whether in its personal or business capacity, which petition is not dismissed within the applicable period for such dismissal under applicable law; a winding up order is made; a receiver is appointed over any of its assets; a trustee in bankruptcy is appointed, if the data importer is an individual; a company voluntary arrangement is commenced by it; or any equivalent event in any jurisdiction occurs

then the data exporter, without prejudice to any other rights which it may have against the data importer, shall be entitled to terminate these clauses, in which case the authority shall be informed where required. In cases covered by (i), (ii), or (iv) above the data importer may also terminate these clauses.

(c) Either party may terminate these clauses if (i) any Commission positive adequacy decision under Article 25(6) of Directive 95/46/EC (or any superseding text) is issued in relation to the country (or a sector thereof) to which the data is transferred and processed by the data importer, or (ii) Directive 95/46/EC (or any superseding text) becomes directly applicable in such country.

(d) The parties agree that the termination of these clauses at any time, in any circumstances and for whatever reason (except for termination under clause VI(c)) does not exempt them from the obligations and/or conditions under the clauses as regards the processing of the personal data transferred.

VII. **Variation of these clauses**

The parties may not modify these clauses except to update any information in Annex B, in which case they will inform the authority where required. This does not preclude the parties from adding additional commercial clauses where required.

VIII. **Description of the Transfer**

The details of the transfer and of the personal data are specified in Annex B. The parties agree that Annex B may contain confidential business information which they will not disclose to third parties, except as required by law or in response to a competent regulatory or government agency, or as required under clause I(e). The parties may execute additional annexes to cover additional transfers, which will be submitted to the authority where required. Annex B may, in the alternative, be drafted to cover multiple transfers.

Dated: ______________________

______________________	______________________
FOR DATA IMPORTER	FOR DATA EXPORTER
....	....
....	....
....	....

ANNEX A

DATA PROCESSING PRINCIPLES

1. Purpose limitation: Personal data may be processed and subsequently used or further communicated only for purposes described in Annex B or subsequently authorised by the data subject.

2. Data quality and proportionality: Personal data must be accurate and, where necessary, kept up to date. The personal data must be adequate, relevant and not excessive in relation to the purposes for which they are transferred and further processed.

3. Transparency: Data subjects must be provided with information necessary to ensure fair processing (such as information about the purposes of processing and about the transfer), unless such information has already been given by the data exporter.

4. Security and confidentiality: Technical and organisational security measures must be taken by the data controller that are appropriate to the risks, such as against accidental or unlawful destruction or accidental loss, alteration, unauthorised disclosure or access, presented by the processing. Any person acting under the authority of the data controller, including a processor, must not process the data except on instructions from the data controller.

5. Rights of access, rectification, deletion and objection: As provided in Article 12 of Directive 95/46/EC, data subjects must, whether directly or via a third party, be provided with the personal information about them that an organisation holds, except for requests which are manifestly abusive, based on unreasonable intervals or their number or repetitive or systematic nature, or for which access need not be granted under the law of the country of the data exporter. Provided that the authority has given its prior approval, access need also not be granted when doing so would be likely to seriously harm the interests of the data importer or other organisations dealing with the data importer and such interests are not overridden by the interests for fundamental rights and freedoms of the data subject. The sources of the personal data need not be identified when this is not possible by reasonable efforts, or where the rights of persons other than the individual would be violated. Data subjects must be able to have the personal information about them rectified, amended, or deleted where it is inaccurate or processed against these principles. If there are compelling grounds to doubt the legitimacy of the request, the organisation may require further justifications before proceeding to rectification, amendment or deletion. Notification of any rectification, amendment or deletion to third parties to whom the data have been disclosed need not be made when this involves a disproportionate effort. A data subject must also be able to object to the processing of the personal data relating to him if there are compelling legitimate grounds relating to his particular situation. The burden of proof for any refusal rests on the data importer, and the data subject may always challenge a refusal before the authority.

6. Sensitive data: The data importer shall take such additional measures (e.g. relating to security) as are necessary to protect such sensitive data in accordance with its obligations under clause II.

7. Data used for marketing purposes: Where data are processed for the purposes of direct marketing, effective procedures should exist allowing the data subject at any time to "opt-out" from having his data used for such purposes.

8. Automated decisions: For purposes hereof "automated decision" shall mean a decision by the data exporter or the data importer which produces legal effects concerning a data subject or significantly affects a data subject and which is based solely on automated processing of personal data intended to evaluate certain personal aspects relating to him, such as his performance at work, creditworthiness, reliability, conduct, etc. The data importer shall not make any automated decisions concerning data subjects, except when:

   (a) (i) such decisions are made by the data importer in entering into or performing a contract with the data subject, and

   (ii) (the data subject is given an opportunity to discuss the results of a relevant automated decision with a representative of the parties making such decision or otherwise to make representations to that parties.

   or

   (b) where otherwise provided by the law of the data exporter.

29.12.2004 EN Official Journal of the European Union L 385/83

ANNEX B

DESCRIPTION OF THE TRANSFER

(To be completed by the parties)

Data subjects

The personal data transferred concern the following categories of data subjects:

....

....

....

....

Purposes of the transfer(s)

The transfer is made for the following purposes:

....

....

....

....

Categories of data

The personal data transferred concern the following categories of data:

....

....

....

....

Recipients

The personal data transferred may be disclosed only to the following recipients or categories of recipients:

....

....

....

Sensitive data (if appropriate)

The personal data transferred concern the following categories of sensitive data:

....

....

....

....

Data protection registration information of data exporter (where applicable)

....

....

Additional useful information (storage limits and other relevant information)

....

....

Contact points for data protection enquiries

Data importer	**Data exporter**
....	....
....	....
....	....

ILLUSTRATIVE COMMERCIAL CLAUSES (OPTIONAL)

Indemnification between the data exporter and data importer:

"The parties will indemnify each other and hold each other harmless from any cost, charge, damages, expense or loss which they cause each other as a result of their breach of any of the provisions of these clauses. Indemnification hereunder is contingent upon (a) the party(ies) to be indemnified (the "indemnified party(ies)") promptly notifying the other party(ies) (the "indemnifying party(ies)") of a claim, (b) the indemnifying party(ies) having sole control of the defence and settlement of any such claim, and (c) the indemnified party(ies) providing reasonable cooperation and assistance to the indemnifying party(ies) in defence of such claim.".

Dispute resolution between the data exporter and data importer (the parties may of course substitute any other alternative dispute resolution or jurisdictional clause):

"In the event of a dispute between the data importer and the data exporter concerning any alleged breach of any provision of these clauses, such dispute shall be finally settled under the rules of arbitration of the International Chamber of Commerce by one or more arbitrators appointed in accordance with the said rules. The place of arbitration shall be [ ]. The number of arbitrators shall be [ ]."

Allocation of costs:

"Each party shall perform its obligations under these clauses at its own cost."

Extra termination clause:

"In the event of termination of these clauses, the data importer must return all personal data and all copies of the personal data subject to these clauses to the data exporter forthwith or, at the data exporter's choice, will destroy all copies of the same and certify to the data exporter that it has done so, unless the data importer is prevented by its national law or local regulator from destroying or returning all or part of such data, in which event the data will be kept confidential and will not be actively processed for any purpose. The data importer agrees that, if so requested by the data exporter, it will allow the data exporter, or an inspection agent selected by the data exporter and not reasonably objected to by the data importer, access to its establishment to verify that this has been done, with reasonable notice and during business hours." '.

INDEX

*References are to chapter and section numbers (e.g., **4:** IV.C.2 refers to sections IV.C.2 of Chapter 4) and to exhibits (Exh.). Alphabetization is word-by-word (e.g., "Data security" precedes "Database").*

A

Access codes as personal information, ***9:*** II.A.3
Access controls to information, ***10:*** III.F, III.G
Access to personnel records. *See* Personnel records
Account numbers
as personal information, ***9:*** II.A.3
SSNs as, ***8:*** II.A.3.d
Accuracy of data, ***1:*** IV.B.4, IV.E.5, IV.F.6
Action Guide Regarding the Protection of Personal Information of Workers (Japan)
applicants, background checks on, ***2:*** IV.C.1
health information, collection of, ***2:*** IV.C.1.e, ***5:*** IV.D.2, ***6:*** IV.C.1
HIV testing of employees, ***6:*** IV.C.2
personal information, rules for handling, ***2:*** IV.C.1.d
political activities, employer prohibitions against, ***4:*** IV.C.4
religious information, collection of, ***4:*** IV.C.4
union activities, employer monitoring of, ***4:*** IV.C.2
workplace surveillance, ***4:*** IV.C.2
ADA. *See* Americans With Disabilities Act
Administrative measures. *See* China
AIDS. *See* HIV/AIDS testing of employees and job applicants
Alaska
SSNs, restrictions on collection and use of, ***8:*** II.A.3.e
Alcohol
California alcohol rehabilitation programs, employee participation in, ***4:*** II.A.7
off-duty use by employees, ***4:*** II.A.6.a
past illegal drug or alcohol use, inquiries about, ***6:*** II.A.3.b
Alcohol testing
Japan, ***6:*** IV.C.2
Americans With Disabilities Act (ADA)
conditional job offers, medical examinations, ***6:*** II.A.1.b.ii
drug testing of employees and job applicants, ***6:*** II.A.3
generally, ***1:*** I.B.1.b.ii
health information, use of by employers, ***5:*** II.A.2.a
inquiries by employer
drug or alcohol use, ***6:*** II.A.3.a, II.A.3.b
permissible, ***6:*** II.A.2.a
timing of, ***Exh.*** 6.1
voluntary disclosure of disabilities, following, ***6:*** II.A.2.c
medical examinations of employees and applicants, ***6:*** II.A
after conditional job offer, ***6:*** II.A.1.b.ii
physical agility tests, ***6:*** II.A.1.a.iii
prior to job offer, ***6:*** II.A.1.b.i
unlawful medical examination, ***6:*** II.A.1.d
Applicants for jobs
conditional job offers, medical examinations, ***6:*** II.A.1.b.ii
drug testing, ***6:*** II.A.3. *See also* Drug testing of applicants and employees

Applicants for jobs—*cont'd*
genetic information
collection of, nondiscrimination, ***6:*** II.A.4.a
testing, state laws, ***6:*** II.A.4.b
HIV/AIDS testing, ***6:*** II.A.4.c. *See also* HIV/AIDS testing of employees and job applicants
Hong Kong
drug testing, ***6:*** IV.B.2
genetic testing, ***6:*** IV.B.2
medical examinations, ***6:*** IV.B.1
Japan, background checks, ***2:*** IV.C.1
lie detector examinations, ***6:*** II.A.4.d
EPPA provisions, ***6:*** II.A.4.d.i
medical examinations, ***Ch.*** 6, ***6:*** II.A.1.b. *See also* Medical examinations of applicants and employees
after conditional offer, ***6:*** II.A.1.b.ii
prior to offer, ***6:*** II.A.1.b.i
personality assessments, ***6:*** II.A.1.a.ii
physical agility tests, ***6:*** II.A.1.a.iii
polygraph examinations, ***6:*** II.A.4.d
psychological examinations, ***6:*** II.A.1.a.i
Argentina
access and correction, ***1:*** V.A.3
consent, ***1:*** V.A.2
cross-border transfers, ***1:*** V.A.6
data security, generally, ***1:*** V.A
database registration, ***1:*** V.A.3
dispute resolution, ***1:*** V.A.2
notice, ***1:*** V.A.1
onward transfer agreements, ***1:*** V.A.7
security and data retention, ***1:*** V.A.4
use limitations, ***1:*** V.A.2
Arrests and background checks, *2:* II.A.8.a
Audits of information security programs, *10:* III.L
Australia
Australian Capital Territory (ACT) Health Records (Privacy and Access) Act (1997), ***5:*** IV.A.2
data security, ***1:*** IV.
Employee Records Exemption, ***1:*** IV.A.2, IV.A.3
health information, ***1:*** IV.A.5
onward transfer agreements, ***1:*** IV.A.3
overview, ***1:*** IV.A.1
penalties, ***1:*** IV.A.4
workplace monitoring and surveillance, ***1:*** IV.A.6
email, monitoring of by employers, ***3:*** IV.A.2
government identity numbers, use of, ***8:*** IV.A
health information, confidentiality of
Employee Records Exemption, ***5:*** IV.A
health service providers, use of information by (NSW), ***5:*** IV.A.1
private sector, health records held by (Victoria), ***5:*** IV.A.3
public sector, health records held by (ACT), ***5:*** IV.A.2
Health Records (Privacy and Access) Act (1997) (ACT), ***5:*** IV.A.2
National Privacy Principals, ***1:*** IV.A.3
New South Wales (NSW) Health Records and Information Privacy Act (2002), ***5:*** IV.A.1
Privacy Act. *See* Privacy Act (Australia, 1988)
security breach notifications, ***9:*** V.A
contents of notice, ***9:*** V.A.3
personal information covered, ***9:*** V.A.1
risk assessments, ***9:*** V.A.2
timing of, ***9:*** V.A.3
Spam Act (2003), ***3:*** IV.A.2
Victoria Health Records Act (2001), ***5:*** IV.A.3
video surveillance by employers, ***3:*** IV.A.3
Workplace Email, Web Browsing and Privacy Guidelines, ***3:*** IV.A.1, IV.A.2
workplace monitoring, general requirements for, ***3:*** IV.A.1
Workplace Surveillance Act (New South Wales), ***3:*** IV.A.1–IV.A.3
Australian Capital Territory (ACT) Health Records (Privacy and Access) Act (1997), *5:* IV.A.2

B

Background checks and investigations, ***Ch.*** 2
access and correction rights, ***2:*** II.A.4
adverse actions, notice requirements, ***2:*** II.A.2.b, II.A.2.b.ii
arrests, ***2:*** II.A.8.a
Bankruptcy Act, ***2:*** II.A.8.d
Belgium, ***2:*** III.A.1
Brazil, ***2:*** II.B.1
California, ***2:*** II.A.8.c
Canada, ***2:*** II.C.1
China, ***2:*** IV.A.1, IV.A.2
consumer reports
consumer reporting agencies, defined, ***2:*** II.A.1.a
defined, ***2:*** II.A.1.b
notice and consent requirements, ***2:*** II.A.2.a, II.A.2.a.i, II.A.2.a.ii
content limitations, ***2:*** II.A.3
criminal investigations, ***3:*** II.A.9
direct inquiries, limitations on, ***2:*** II.A.8
disposal of background information, ***2:*** II.A.9, II.A.10
employer liability, ***2:*** II.A.5, II.A.8.b.iii
by employers, ***2:*** II.A.7
European Union, ***2:*** III
FCRA. *See* Fair Credit Reporting Act
fingerprinting, ***2:*** II.A.8.c
France. *See* France
Germany. *See* Germany
Hong Kong. *See* Hong Kong
Italy, ***2:*** III.D.1
Japan. *See* Japan
Korea, ***2:*** IV.D.1
Mexico, ***2:*** II.D.1
New York, ***2:*** II.A.8.b, II.A.8.b.i, II.A.8.c
OFAC-designated nationals, ***2:*** II.A.9
overview, ***2:*** I
pre-adverse action notice requirements, ***2:*** II.A.2.b.i
prior convictions, ***2:*** II.A.8.b, II.A.8.b.i, II.A.8.b.ii
sample process
European Union, ***Exh.*** 2.5
United States, ***Exh.*** 2.4
sealed or expunged convictions, ***2:*** II.A.8.a
specially designated nationals, ***2:*** II.A.9
state laws, ***2:*** II.A.2.a.ii, II.A.5, II.A.6, II.A.8.a, II.A.12
Texas, ***2:*** II.A.12
United Kingdom. *See* United Kingdom
United States, ***2:*** II.A, II.A.9
by vendors, ***2:*** II.A.1, II.A.6

Bankruptcy Act (U.S.), ***2:*** II.A.3, II.A.8.d

Basic Act (Germany), ***2:*** III.C.1

Basic Resident Registry Law (Japan), ***8:*** IV.C

Belgium
background checks, ***2:*** III.A.1
drug testing, ***6:*** III.A.2
employment verification requests, ***2:*** III.A.2
medical examinations, ***6:*** III.A.1
national identification numbers, use of, ***8:*** III.A

Biometric data, collection of (France), ***6:*** III.B

Brazil
background checks, ***2:*** II.B.1
drug testing, ***6:*** II.B.2
employment verification requests, ***2:*** II.B.2
medical examinations of applicants and employees, ***6:*** II.B.1
national identification numbers, use of, ***8:*** II.B

Breach of security. *See* Security breaches

British Columbia
personal information protections, ***1:*** V.B.3

Business associates
agreements with, ***5:*** II.A.1.k.vii.a, II.A.1.k.vii.b
defined, ***5:*** II.A.1.a

C

California
background checks and investigations
fingerprinting, ***2:*** II.A.8.c
by vendors, ***2:*** II.A.6.a

California—*cont'd*
CMIA. *See* Confidentiality of Medical Information Act (California)
Consumer Credit Reporting Agencies Act, ***1:*** I.C.2.c, ***2:*** II.A.6.a
drug testing of employees and job applicants, ***6:*** II.A.3.c.i
Financial Information Privacy Act, ***1:*** I.C.2.a
health information, confidentiality of, ***5:*** II.A.3.a
HIV status, confidentiality of, ***1:*** I.C.2.b
Invasion of Privacy Act, ***3:*** II.A.13
Investigative Consumer Reporting Agencies Act, ***1:*** I.C.2.c, ***2:*** II.A.2.a.ii, II.A.6.a
monitoring and surveillance by employers
amplifying or recording devices used, ***3:*** II.A.13
of email, ***3:*** II.A.6.b
invasion of privacy claims, ***3:*** II.A.15.a
location-based restrictions on, ***3:*** II.A.12
of telephone calls, ***3:*** II.A.4
undercover investigators, ***3:*** II.A.14
off-duty conduct of employees
alcohol rehabilitation programs, employee participation in, ***4:*** II.A.7
illiteracy programs, employee participation in, ***4:*** II.A.8
political activities and affiliations, ***4:*** II.A.2.b
personal information, ***9:*** II.A.1, II.A.3, II.A.3.a
security breach notification laws
authorities, notice to, ***9:*** II.A.6
consumer reporting agencies, coordination with, ***9:*** II.A.8.a
covered information, ***9:*** II.A.3
exemptions, ***9:*** II.A.9.a
generally, ***9:*** II.A.1
information brokers, ***9:*** II.A.2.a
law enforcement investigations, delays for, ***9:*** II.A.5.b
notice contents, ***9:*** II.A.8
notification, risk-based triggers for, ***9:*** II.A.4.b
notification methods, ***9:*** II.A.7
paper records, ***9:*** II.A.2.b
safe harbors, ***9:*** II.A.9
scope and coverage, ***9:*** II.A.2
substitute notice, ***9:*** II.A.7.a
timing requirements, ***9:*** II.A.5
unauthorized acquisition, ***9:*** II.A.4.a
Security Safeguard Act, ***1:*** I.C.3.a
SSNs, use of
court filings, privacy exceptions, ***8:*** II.A.4.a
employer compliance issues, ***8:*** II.A.8
prohibited activities, ***8:*** II.A.3
Canada
background checks, ***2:*** II.C.1
data security, ***1:*** V.B.2.j
access, ***1:*** V.B.2.g
audits, ***1:*** V.B.2.f
complaint handling, ***1:*** V.B.2.i
consent, ***1:*** V.B.2.b
cross-border transfers, ***1:*** V.B.2.h
data processing contracts, ***1:*** V.B.2.d
database registration, ***1:*** V.B.2.c
federal statutes, ***1:*** V.B.1
notice, ***1:*** V.B.2.a
Personal Health Information Protection Act (Ontario), ***1:*** V.B.3
Personal Information Protection Act (British Columbia), ***1:*** V.B.3
PIPEDA. *See* Personal Information Protection and Electronic Documents Act (Canada)
policies and practices, implementation of, ***1:*** V.B.2.f
privacy officers, designation of, ***1:*** V.B.2.e
Protection of Personal Information in the Private Sector Act (Quebec), ***1:*** V.B.3
provincial privacy laws, ***1:*** V.B.3
retention of data, ***1:*** V.B.2.k
drug testing, ***6:*** II.C.2
employment verification requests, ***2:*** II.C.2
medical examinations, ***6:*** II.C.1
security breach notification, ***9:*** II.B

authorities, notice to, **9:** II.B.3
contents of notice, **9:** II.B.3
methods of, **9:** II.B.3
personal information covered, **9:** II.B.1
PHIPA requirements, **9:** II.B.5
prevention of future breaches, **9:** II.B.4
risk assessments, **9:** II.B.2
timing, **9:** II.B.3
social insurance numbers (SINs), **8:** II.C

Central Registry Act (Germany), *2:* III.C.1

CFAA (Computer Fraud and Abuse Act, U.S.), *1:* I.B.2.a

Character questions in background checks
France, **2:** III.B.7.e
Germany, **2:** III.C.7.e
United Kingdom, **2:** III.E.7.e

Children's Online Privacy Protection Act of 1998 (COPPA, U.S.), *1:* I.B.1.d

Chile
collection, use, and disclosure, limitations on, **1:** V.C.4
consent, **1:** V.C.3
cross-border limitations, **1:** V.C.7
database registration, **1:** V.C.6
dispute resolution, **1:** V.C.9
notice, **1:** V.C.1
onward transfer agreements, **1:** V.C.8
privacy policies, **1:** V.C.2
retention of data, **1:** V.C.5
security, **1:** V.C.5

China
background checks, **2:** IV.A.1, IV.A.2
credit checks, **2:** IV.A.2.a
criminal records, **2:** IV.A.2.b
Email Services Procedures, Administration of, **3:** IV.B.1
health information, confidentiality of, **5:** IV.B
HIV/AIDS testing, **6:** IV.A
International Linkups of Computer Information Networks Tentative Provisions, Administration of, **3:** IV.B.1
Maintenance of Secrets in the International Networking of Computer Information Systems Provisions, Administration of, **3:** IV.B.1
medical examinations, **6:** IV.A
personnel records, access to, **7:** IV.A
Safe Production Law, **3:** IV.B.1
Safety and Protection of Computer Information Networks, Administrative Measure on, **3:** IV.B.1
Telecommunications Regulations, **3:** IV.B.1
work history, **2:** IV.A.2.c
workplace monitoring, general requirements for, **3:** IV.B.1

Civil Rights Act of 1964, Title VII, *4:* II.A.3

Code of Practice on Human Resource Management (Hong Kong)
employment-related data, transfer of, **1:** IV.B.6, IV.B.7
medical and health data, collection of, **2:** IV.B.1, **5:** IV.C
access requests, **7:** IV.B.1
applicants, **5:** IV.C.1
examination records, **6:** IV.B.1
existing employees, **5:** IV.C.2
sensitive information, **1:** IV.B.9.a
notice requirements, **1:** IV.B.1

Complaints
data security (Canada), **1:** V.B.2.i
HHS, to, **5:** II.A.1.l.iii.d
HIPAA violations, **5:** II.A.1.k.iv.e, II.A.1.k.xiii.a
Privacy Rules (U.S.), violations, **5:** II.A.1.k.iv.e, II.A.1.k.xiii.a

Computer Fraud and Abuse Act (CFAA, U.S.), *1:* I.B.2.a

Computer Processed Personal Data Protection Act (Taiwan), *1:* IV.F
access rights, **1:** IV.F.5
accuracy, **1:** IV.F.6
cease use, **1:** IV.F.6
consent, **1:** IV.F.2
cross-border limitations, **1:** IV.F.4
data retention, **1:** IV.F.7
license/database registration, **1:** IV.F.1

Computer Processed Personal Data Protection Act (Taiwan)—*cont'd*
limits on data transfers, ***1:*** IV.F.4
monitoring of employees, ***1:*** IV.F.8
penalties, ***1:*** IV.F.10
right to correct, ***1:*** IV.F.6
security, ***1:*** IV.F.9
use limitations, ***1:*** IV.F.3
Computer use, monitoring by employers, *3:* II.A.7, IV.D.2
Conditional job offers, medical examinations
ADA provisions, ***6:*** II.A.1.b.ii
EEOC definitions and, ***6:*** II.A.1.b.ii.a
standards for, ***6:*** II.A.1.b.ii.a
Confidentiality of Medical Information Act (California)
disclosures
authorized, ***5:*** II.A.3.a.ii.d
of genetic data, ***5:*** II.A.3.a.ii.j
of HIV/AIDS status, ***5:*** II.A.3.a.ii.k
of medical information, ***5:*** II.A.3.a.ii.c, II.A.3.a.ii.d
discrimination, prohibition on, ***5:*** II.A.3.a.ii.b
document destruction requirements, ***5:*** II.A.3.a.ii.g
employer compliance, ***5:*** II.A.3.a.ii
enforcement of rights, ***5:*** II.A.3.a.ii.n
health care providers acting as employers, ***5:*** II.A.3.a.ii.h
procedural safeguards, adoption of, ***5:*** II.A.3.a.ii.a
receipt of information, ***5:*** II.A.3.a.ii.e
right of access, ***5:*** II.A.3.a.ii.m
vendor relationships, effects on, ***5:*** II.A.3.a.ii.f
waivers, prohibition on, ***5:*** II.A.3.a.ii.l
Connecticut
drug testing of employees and job applicants, ***6:*** II.A.3.c.ii
email monitoring by employers, ***3:*** II.A.6.d
location-based surveillance restrictions, ***3:*** II.A.12
SSN privacy policy law, ***8:*** II.A.5.b.i
Constitutional protections
German Constitution, ***3:*** III.D.1, III.D.2
Korea, right to privacy, ***1:*** IV.D
political speech, ***4:*** II.A.2
state constitutions and privacy protections, ***1:*** I.C.1
California, ***6:*** II.A.3.c.i
Taiwan, right to privacy, ***1:*** IV.F, ***3:*** IV.G.1
U.S. *See* United States
Consumer Credit. *See* Credit reports
Consumer Credit Reporting Agencies Act (California), *1:* I.C.2.c, ***2:*** II.A.6.a
Consumer reporting agencies, employer coordination with, *9:* II.A.8.a
Controlled substances. *See* Alcohol; Drug testing of applicants and employees
Convictions. *See* Background checks and investigations
Cooperation Within Companies Act (Finland), *3:* III.B.1
COPPA (Children's Online Privacy Protection Act of 1998, U.S.), *1:* I.B.1.d
Court filings
SSN Protection Laws, exceptions, ***8:*** II.A.4.a
Credit reports
California Consumer Credit Reporting Agencies Act, ***1:*** I.C.2.c, ***2:*** II.A.6.a
China, ***2:*** IV.A.2.a
Fair and Accurate Credit Transactions Act of 2003 (FACTA), ***1:*** I.B.1.c.ii
France, ***2:*** III.B.7.a
Germany, ***2:*** III.C.7.a
Hong Kong, ***2:*** III.C.4.a
Korea, ***1:*** IV.D
United Kingdom, ***2:*** III.E.7.a
United States. *See* Fair Credit Reporting Act (FCRA)
Crimes, reporting of, *5:* II.A.1.k.xiii.b
Criminal convictions. *See* Background checks and investigations
Cross-border transfers and data security
Argentina, ***1:*** V.A.6
Chile, ***1:*** V.C.7

Directive 95/46/EC. *See* Directive 95/46/EC
Korea, ***1:*** IV.D.5
Taiwan, ***1:*** IV.F.4

D

Data classification systems, *10:* III.B
Data processors, contracts with, *1:* III.C.6, V.B.2.d
Data Protection Act (France)
email and Internet monitoring, ***3:*** III.C.1
notice requirements, ***2:*** III.B.4
telephone calls, monitoring of by employers, ***3:*** III.C.2
use restrictions, ***2:*** III.B.6
video surveillance by employers, ***3:*** III.E.3
Data Protection Act (UK)
email and Internet monitoring, ***3:*** III.E.1
telephone calls, monitoring, ***3:*** III.E.2
video surveillance, ***3:*** III.E.3
Data Protection in Electronic Communications Act (Finland), *3:* III.B.1
Data Protection in Working Life Act (Finland), *1:* III.A, ***3:*** III.B.1
Data Protection Law (Norway), *9:* III.B
Data security
ADA, ***1:*** I.B.1.b.i
Argentina. *See* Argentina and data security
Australia. *See* Australia
California, ***1:*** I.C.2.a, I.C.2.b, I.C.2.c, I.C.3.a
Canada. *See* Canada
CFAA, ***1:*** I.B.2.a
children's information, ***1:*** I.B.1.d
Chile. *See* Chile and data security
consumer report information, ***1:*** I.B.1.c, I.C.2.c
COPPA, ***1:*** I.B.1.d
database registration. *See* Database registration
Directive 95/46/EC. *See* Directive 95/46/EC (European Union)
ECPA, ***1:*** I.B.2.b
European Union. *See* European Union
FACTA, ***1:*** I.B.1.c.ii
FCRA, ***1:*** I.B.1.c.i
financial information, ***1:*** I.B.1.a, I.C.2.a
Financial Privacy Rule (U.S.), ***1:*** I.B.1.a.i
Finland, ***1:*** III.A
Freedom of Information Act, ***1:*** I
FTC Act, ***1:*** I.B.3.a
GLBA, ***1:*** I.B.1.a
global overview, ***1:*** I.A
health information, ***1:*** I.B.1.b, I.C.2.b
HIPAA. *See* Health Insurance Portability and Accountability Act of 1996
historical traditions, ***1:*** I
Hong Kong. *See* Hong Kong
information security programs. *See* Information security programs
Japan. *See* Japan
Korea. *See* Korea
New Zealand. *See* New Zealand
Ohio, ***1:*** I.C.4
Privacy Rules. *See* Privacy Rules
retention issues. *See* Retention issues
Security Rules. *See* Security Rules
South America, ***1:*** V
state constitutions, ***1:*** I.C.1
state laws, ***1:*** I.C
consumer report information, ***1:*** I.C.2.c
employee monitoring, ***1:*** I.C.3.d
financial information, ***1:*** I.C.2.a
health information, ***1:*** I.C.2.b
mini-FTC Acts, ***1:*** I.C.4
reasonable security procedures and practices, ***1:*** I.C.3.a
security breach notification, ***1:*** I.C.3.b
Social Security Number laws, ***1:*** I.C.3.c
unfair or deceptive acts or practices, ***1:*** I.C.4
Taiwan. *See* Taiwan
United Kingdom, ***1:*** III.A
U.S. Constitution, ***1:*** I
Database registration
Argentina, ***1:*** V.A.5
Canada, ***1:*** V.B.2.c
Chile, ***1:*** V.C.6

Database registration—*cont'd*
European Union, ***1:*** III.C.7
Taiwan, ***1:*** IV.F.1
Deceased individuals
health information relating to, ***5:*** II.A.1.k.x
Defamation claims, ***7:*** II.A.10
Delaware
email, surveillance of by employers, ***3:*** II.A.6.e
Destruction of records
information security programs, ***10:*** III.I
medical (California), ***5:*** II.A.3.a.ii.g
Directive 95/46/EC (European Union)
access rights, ***1:*** III.C.4
cross-border restrictions
adequate data protection, defined, ***1:*** III.D.1
adequate safeguards, defined, ***1:*** III.D.3
exemptions, ***1:*** III.D.4
Safe Harbor Framework, ***1:*** III.D.2
data processors, contracts with, ***1:*** III.C.6
email monitoring by employers, ***3:*** III.A.1
legal bases for processing personal information, ***1:*** III.C.1
legislative framework, ***1:*** III.B
notice requirements, ***1:*** III.C.3
objection rights, ***1:*** III.C.5
registration obligations, ***1:*** III.C.7
requirements, ***2:*** III
sensitive data, collection of, ***1:*** III.C.2
Standard Clauses, ***1:*** III.D.3
telephone calls, monitoring of by employers, ***3:*** III.A.2
video surveillance by employers, ***3:*** III.A.3
Disabilities
Hong Kong Disability Discrimination Ordinance, ***2:*** IV.B.1
inquiries
impermissible, ***6:*** II.A.2.b
permissible, ***6:*** II.A.2.a
United Kingdom Disability Discrimination Act (1995), ***2:*** III.E.1
United States. *See* Americans With Disabilities Act (ADA)
voluntary disclosure, inquiries following, ***6:*** II.A.2.c
Disclosures of information
accounting of nonroutine, right to, ***5:*** II.A.1.l.iii
authorized
California law, ***5:*** II.A.3.a.ii.d
Chile, ***1:*** V.C.4
consent, ***5:*** II.A.1.k.xiv
consequences for, ***7:*** II.A.6
disabilities, ***6:*** II.A.2.c
employee's identifying information, ***8:*** II.A.3.f
to family members, ***5:*** II.A.1.k.xi
to friends, ***5:*** II.A.1.k.xi
genetic data, California law, ***5:*** II.A.3.a.ii.j
HIV/AIDS status
New York law, ***5:*** II.A.3.b.v
of medical information
California law, ***5:*** II.A.3.a.ii.c
minors and, ***5:*** II.A.1.k.xii
notice of security breaches. *See* Security breach notifications
personnel records, ***7:*** II.A.4, II.A.5
security breaches. *See* Security breaches
voluntary restrictions on, ***5:*** II.A.1.l.iii.b
Discrimination
disabled persons. *See* Disabilities
Family Status Discrimination Ordinance (Hong Kong), ***2:*** IV.B.1
genetic information, collection of, ***6:*** II.A.4.a
Race Relations Act (UK, 1976), ***2:*** III.E.1
sex. *See* Sex discrimination
Sexual Orientation Regulations (UK, 2003), ***2:*** III.E.1
Title VII, Civil Rights Act of 1964 (U.S.), ***4:*** II.A.3
union membership or affiliation ***4:*** II.A.1, II.A.1.a, II.A.1.b
Dispute resolution
Argentina, ***1:*** V.A.8

Chile, ***1:*** V.C.9
Drinking. *See* Alcohol
Driver's license numbers
as personal information, ***9:*** II.A.3
Driver's Privacy Protection Act (U.S), ***9:*** II.A.9.a
Drug rehabilitation programs, participation in, ***4:*** II.A.7
Drug testing of applicants and employees, ***6:*** II.A.3
Belgium, ***6:*** III.A.2
Brazil, ***6:*** II.B.2
California, ***6:*** II.A.3.c.i
Canada, ***6:*** II.C.2
Connecticut, ***6:*** II.A.3.c.ii
current illegal drug use, inquiries about, ***6:*** II.A.3.a
France, ***6:*** III.B
Germany, ***6:*** III.C
Hong Kong, ***6:*** IV.B.2
Iowa, ***6:*** II.A.3.c.iii
Italy, ***6:*** III.D.2
Japan, ***6:*** IV.C.2
Korea, ***6:*** IV.D.2
Maine, ***6:*** II.A.3.c.iv
Mexico, ***6:*** II.D.2
Minnesota, ***6:*** II.A.3.c.iv
Oklahoma, ***6:*** II.A.3.c.v
past alcohol use, inquiries about, ***6:*** II.A.3.b
past illegal drug use, inquiries about, ***6:*** II.A.3.b
state laws, ***6:*** II.A.3.c
United Kingdom, ***6:*** III.E
Vermont, ***6:*** II.A.3.c.vi
Dubai International Financial Center Authority privacy law, ***9:*** IV.A

E

E-SIGN Act (Electronic Signatures in Global and National Commerce Act, U.S.), ***9:*** II.A.7
ECPA. *See* Electronic Communications Privacy Act (U.S.)
EEOC. *See* Equal Employment Opportunity Commission (EEOC) enforcement
Electronic Communications Data Protection Act (Finland), ***3:*** III.B.2
Electronic Communications Directive (European Union), ***9:*** III.A
Electronic Communications Privacy Act (ECPA, U.S.), ***3:*** II
business extension exception, ***3:*** II.A.3.b.ii
email, surveillance of, ***3:*** II.A.6.a
employer's rights or property, surveillance to protect, ***3:*** II.A.3.c
exceptions, ***1:*** I.B.2.b, ***3:*** II.A.3.b.ii
permitted surveillance, ***3:*** II.A.3.b.i, II.A.3.b.ii
prior consent, interceptions with, ***3:*** II.A.3.b.i
prohibited surveillance, ***3:*** II.A.3.a
telephone calls, surveillance of, ***3:*** II.A.1, II.A.3
Electronic notice of security breaches, ***9:*** II.A.7, II.A.7.b
Electronic Signatures in Global and National Commerce Act (E-SIGN Act, U.S.), ***9:*** II.A.7
Electronic transmission of SSNs, ***8:*** II.A.3.b
Email and Internet monitoring by employers
Australia, ***3:*** IV.A.1, IV.A.2
California, ***3:*** II.A.6.b
China, ***3:*** IV.B.1
Connecticut, ***3:*** II.A.6.d
Delaware, ***3:*** II.A.6.e
Electronic Communications Privacy Act (ECPA), ***3:*** II.A.6.a
European Union, ***3:*** III.A.1
federal law, ***3:*** II.A.6.a
Finland, ***3:*** III.B.1
France, ***3:*** III.C.1
Germany, ***3:*** III.D.1
Korea, ***3:*** IV.E.1
New South Wales, ***3:*** IV.A.2
New York, ***3:*** II.A.6.c
New Zealand, ***3:*** IV.F.1
Taiwan, ***3:*** IV.G.2
United Kingdom, ***3:*** III.E.1

Email Services Procedures Administration (China), *3:* IV.B.1
Employee Monitoring Guidelines (Hong Kong), ***1:*** IV.B.11
Employee Polygraph Protection Act (EPPA, U.S.), ***6:*** II.A.4.d.i, II.A.4.d.ii
Employee Retirement Income Security Act (ERISA, U.S.)
employee welfare benefit plans, ***5:*** II.A.1.b.iii
enforcement rights, ***5:*** II.A.1.m.iv
health plan classifications, ***5:*** II.A.1.k.i.b
SSNs and, ***8:*** II.A.8
Employees
background checks. *See* Background checks and investigations
health information regarding. *See* health information, confidentiality of
medical examinations of. *See* Medical examinations of applicants and employees
monitoring of. *See* Monitoring and surveillance by employers
off-duty conduct of. *See* Off-duty conduct of employees
personal information, acquisition of, ***9:*** II.A.4.c
personnel records. *See* Personnel records
training
in data security, ***10:*** III.E
in privacy matters, ***5:*** II.A.1.k.iv.b
Employment Equality Regulations (UK, 2003)
age, ***2:*** III.E.1
religion or belief, ***2:*** III.E.1
sexual orientation, ***2:*** III.E.1
Employment Practices Code (UK), ***1:*** III.A, ***2:*** III.E.2
Employment Practices Data Protection Code (UK), ***3:*** III.E.1, III.E.3
Employment Security Law (Japan)
background checks, restrictions on, ***2:*** IV.C.1.b
consent requirements, ***2:*** IV.C.1.c
Employment verification. *See* Work history questions in background checks
Encryption of data, ***10:*** III.H
EPPA. *See* Employee Polygraph Protection Act (U.S.)
Equal Employment Opportunity Commission (EEOC) enforcement
current illegal drug use, inquiries about, ***6:*** II.A.3.a
disability-related inquiries by employer, ***6:*** II.A.2.b
employees, medical examinations of, ***6:*** II.A.1.c
job offers, medical examinations, ***6:*** II.A.1.b.ii.a
medical examinations, defined, ***6:*** II.A.1.a
past illegal drug or alcohol use, inquiries about, ***6:*** II.A.3.b
ERISA. *See* Employee Retirement Income Security Act (U.S.)
European Union. *See also names of individual countries*
background checks and investigations, ***2:*** III, Exh. 2.5
data security, ***1:*** III.A
access rights, ***1:*** III.C.4
adequate data protection, defined, ***1:*** III.D.1
binding corporate rules, ***1:*** III.D.3
consent, ***1:*** III.C.1
contracts, approval of, ***1:*** III.D.3
cross-border restrictions, ***1:*** III.D
data processors, contracts with, ***1:*** III.C.6
employer policy formulation, ***1:*** III.E
exemptions, ***1:*** III.D.4
implementation legislation, ***Exh.*** 1.3
information, processing of, ***1:*** III.C
introduction, ***1:*** III.A
legal bases for processing personal information, ***1:*** III.C.1
notice requirements, ***1:*** III.C.3

onward transfer agreements, *1:* III.D.2, ***Exh.*** 1.3
registration obligations, *1:* III.C.7
right to object, *1:* III.C.5
Safe Harbor Privacy Principles, ***Exh.*** 1.1
sensitive data, *1:* III.C.2
statutes, *1:* III.B
U.S. Safe Harbor Framework, *1:* III.D.2
Directive 95/46/EC. *See* Directive 95/46/EC (European Union)
Electronic Communications Directive, *9:* III.A
email and Internet monitoring by employers, *3:* III.A.1
health information, confidentiality of, *5:* III
personnel records, access to, *7:* III.A
security breach notification laws, *9:* III.A
telephone calls, monitoring of by employers, *3:* III.A.2
video surveillance by employers, *3:* III.A.3
Works Councils, *3:* III.A.4

Executive Order 13224 (U.S.), *9:* II.A.9.a

Expunged convictions and background checks, *2:* II.A.8.a

External risks to data security, *10:* III.C

F

Fair and Accurate Credit Transactions Act of 2003 (FACTA, U.S.), *1:* I.B.1.c.ii

Fair Credit Reporting Act (FCRA, U.S.), *1:* I.B.1.c.i, *9:* II.A.9.a
access and correction rights, *2:* II.A.4
adverse actions, notice requirements, *2:* II.A.2.b
sample notices, ***Exh.*** 2.2, ***Exh.*** 2.3
authorization, sample, ***Exh.*** 2.1
background checks and investigations, *2:* II.A.1, II.A.3, II.A.7
consumer reporting agencies, defined, *2:* II.A.1.a
consumer reports, defined, *2:* II.A.1.b
disposal of background information, *2:* II.A.11
employer liability, *2:* II.A.5
exemptions from, *2:* II.A.2.c
notice and consent requirements, *2:* II.A.2.a

Family Status Discrimination Ordinance (Hong Kong), *2:* IV.B.1

FAX transmissions of SSNs, *8:* II.A.3.b

FCRA. *See* Fair Credit Reporting Act (U.S.)

Federal Driver's Privacy Protection Act (U.S.), *9:* II.A.9.a

Federal Trade Commission Act (FTC Act, U.S.), *1:* I.B.3.a

Federal Trade Commission (FTC)
information security programs, *10:* II

Fees for access to personnel records
France, *7:* III.B.2
Germany, *7:* III.C.2
Hong Kong, *7:* IV.B.5
United Kingdom, *7:* III.D.2

Financial Information Privacy Act (California), *1:* I.C.2.a

Financial Privacy Act (U.S.), *1:* I.B.1.a.i

Financial Transactions With Real Name and Guarantee of Secrecy Act of 1997 (Korea), *1:* IV.D

Fingerprinting, *2:* II.A.8.c

Finland
Cooperation Within Companies Act, *3:* III.B.1
Data Protection in Electronic Communications Act, *3:* III.B.1
Data Protection in Working Life Act, *1:* III.A, *3:* III.B.1
Electronic Communications Data Protection Act, *3:* III.B.2
email and Internet monitoring by employers, *3:* III.B.1
telephone calls, monitoring by employers, *3:* III.B.2
video surveillance by employers, *3:* III.B.3

Fitness for duty evaluations, *6:* II.A.1.c.iii

France
background checks and investigations, ***Exh.*** 2.5
access and correction, ***2:*** III.B.5
character questions, ***2:*** III.B.7.e
credit reports, ***2:*** III.B.7.a
criminal records, ***2:*** III.B.7.b
Data Protection Bill, ***2:*** III.B.1, III.B.4, III.B.6
references, ***2:*** III.B.7.d
reputation, ***2:*** III.B.7.e
requirements, ***2:*** III.B.2, III.B.4
sensitive data, ***2:*** III.B.3
statutes, ***2:*** III.B.1
use restrictions, ***2:*** III.B.6
work history, ***2:*** III.B.7.c
biometric data, collection of, ***6:*** III.B
Data Protection Act, ***3:*** III.C–III.C.3
drug and alcohol testing, ***6:*** III.B
genetic testing, ***6:*** III.B
health information, confidentiality of, ***5:*** III.A
fee and consultation terms, ***5:*** III.A.2
subject access requests, ***5:*** III.A.1, III.A.3
HIV/AIDS status, ***6:*** III.B
monitoring and surveillance by employers
email and Internet, ***3:*** III.C.1
telephone calls, ***3:*** III.C.2
video surveillance, ***3:*** III.C.3
personnel records, access to
denials of requests, ***7:*** III.B.3
fees for, ***7:*** III.B.2
subject matter, ***7:*** III.B.1
Works Councils, ***2:*** III.B.2, ***3:*** III.C.1
Fraternization of employees
United Kingdom, ***4:*** III.B.4
United States, ***4:*** II.A.4, II.A.4.a–II.A.4.c
Freedom of Information Act (U.S.), ***1:*** I
French Data Protection Act, ***6:*** III.B
FTC Act (Federal Trade Commission Act, U.S.), ***1:*** I.B.3.a
FTC (Federal Trade Commission)
information security programs, ***10:*** II

G

General Act on Equal Treatment (Germany), ***2:*** III.C.1, III.C.6
Genetic Information Nondiscrimination Act of 2008 (GINA), ***6:*** II.A.4.a
collection restrictions, ***6:*** II.A.4.a.i
confidentiality, ***6:*** II.A.4.a.iii
protection against discrimination, ***6:*** II.A.4.a.ii
Genetic testing of employees and job applicants
France, ***6:*** III.B
Germany, ***6:*** III.C
Hong Kong, ***6:*** IV.B.2
Japan, ***6:*** IV.C.2
United Kingdom, ***6:*** III.E
United States
collection of genetic information, nondiscrimination, ***6:*** II.A.4.a
state laws, ***6:*** II.A.4.b
Germany
background checks and investigations, ***Exh.*** 2.5
access and correction rights, ***2:*** III.C.5
character questions, ***2:*** III.C.7.e
credit reports, ***2:*** III.C.7.a
criminal records, ***2:*** III.C.7.b
general requirements, ***2:*** III.C.2
notice requirements, ***2:*** III.C.4
references, ***2:*** III.C.7.d
reputation, ***2:*** III.C.7.e
sensitive data, ***2:*** III.C.3
statutes, ***2:*** III.C.1
use restrictions, ***2:*** III.C.6
work history, ***2:*** III.C.7.c
Basic Act, ***2:*** III.C.1
Central Registry Act, ***2:*** III.C.1
Data Protection Act, ***2:*** III.C.1, III.C.2, ***3:*** III.D.1, III.D.3
drug testing, ***6:*** III.C
General Act on Equal Treatment, ***2:*** III.C.1, III.C.6

genetic testing, ***6:*** III.C
government identity numbers, use of, ***8:*** III.B
Grundgesetz (German Constitution), ***3:*** III.D.1, III.D.2
health information, confidentiality of, ***5:*** III.B
HIV/AIDS testing, ***6:*** III.C
monitoring and surveillance by employers
email and Internet, ***3:*** III.D.1
telephone calls, ***3:*** III.D.2
video surveillance, ***3:*** III.D.3
personnel records, access to
denials of requests, ***7:*** III.C.3
fees for, ***7:*** III.C.2
subject matter, ***7:*** III.C.1
Telecommunication Act, ***3:*** III.D.1
Telemedia Act, ***3:*** III.D.1
Works Council Act, ***3:*** III.D.1
GINA. *See* Genetic Information Nondiscrimination Act of 2008
GLBA. *See* Gramm-Leach-Bliley Act (U.S.)
Government identity numbers. *See also* Social Security Numbers (SSNs)
Australia, ***8:*** IV.A
Belgium, ***8:*** III.A
Brazil, ***8:*** II.B
Canada, ***8:*** II.C
Germany, ***8:*** III.B
Hong Kong
employment applicants, ***8:*** IV.B.1
existing employees, ***8:*** IV.B.2
protections, ***1:*** IV.B.9, ***8:*** IV.B
Italy, ***8:*** III.C
Japan, ***8:*** IV.C
Korea, ***8:*** IV.D
Mexico, ***8:*** II.D
New Zealand, ***8:*** IV.E
overview, ***8:*** I
United Kingdom, ***8:*** III.D
Gramm-Leach-Bliley Act (GLBA, U.S.), ***1:*** I.B.1.a, ***9:*** II.A.9, II.A.9.a
information security programs, ***10:*** II
Group health plans, ***5:*** II.A.1.b.iii
Grundgesetz (German Constitution), ***3:*** III.D.1, III.D.2

H

Health and Human Services, U.S. Department of (HHS)
complaints to, ***5:*** II.A.1.l.iii.d
compliance investigations by, ***5:*** II.A.1.m.ii, II.A.1.m.v
Office of Civil Rights, ***5:*** II.A.1.m.i
Health information, confidentiality of, ***Ch.*** 5
ADA. *See* Americans With Disabilities Act (ADA)
Australia, ***5:*** IV.A
Health Records (Privacy and Access) Act (1997) (ACT), ***5:*** IV.A.2
New South Wales Health Records and Information Privacy Act (2002), ***5:*** IV.A.1
Victoria's Health Records Act (2001), ***5:*** IV.A.3
China, ***5:*** IV.B
ERISA. *See* Employee Retirement Income Security Act (ERISA, U.S.)
European Union, ***5:*** III
France, ***5:*** III.A
fee and consultation terms, ***5:*** III.A.2
subject access requests, ***5:*** III.A.3
genetic information, ***6:*** II.A.4.a.iii
Germany, ***5:*** III.B
HIPAA. *See* Health Insurance Portability and Accountability Act of 1996 (U.S.)
Hong Kong, ***5:*** IV.C
Japan, ***1:*** IV.C, ***5:*** IV.D
Korea, ***1:*** IV.D
New York Public Health Law, confidentiality of medical records under, ***5:*** II.A.3.b.i
New Zealand, ***5:*** IV.E
overview, ***5:*** I
as personal information, ***9:*** II.A.3
in personnel records, ***7:*** II.A.9
Privacy Rules. *See* Privacy Rules (U.S.)
state rules, ***5:*** II.A.3
United Kingdom, ***5:*** III.C

Health information, confidentiality of—*cont'd*
United States, ***5:*** II.A. *See* also Health Insurance Portability and Accountability Act of 1996 (HIPAA, U.S.)
Health Information in Employment Management
Points to Consider when Handling (Japan), ***1:*** IV.C
Health Information Privacy Code (New Zealand), *5:* IV.E
Health Insurance Portability and Accountability Act of 1996 (HIPAA, U.S.), *5:* II.A.1
access, right of, ***5:*** II.A.1.l.i
accounting of nonroutine disclosures, right to, ***5:*** II.A.1.l.iii
amendments/corrections, right to request, ***5:*** II.A.1.l.ii
authorizations, ***5:*** II.A.1.k.xv
benefit plan administration, ***5:*** II.A.1.k.ii.a
business associate agreements, ***5:*** II.A.1.k.vii.a, II.A.1.k.vii.b
business associates, defined, ***5:*** II.A.1.a
complaints, ***5:*** II.A.1.k.iv.e, II.A.1.k.xiii.a
compliance responsibilities, ***5:*** II.A.1.k.i, II.A.1.k.i.c
confidential communications, ***5:*** II.A.1.l.iii.c
consents to disclosure, ***5:*** II.A.1.k.xiv
contact person, appointment of, ***5:*** II.A.1.k.iv.a
covered entities, ***5:*** II.A.1.b
crimes, reporting of, ***5:*** II.A.1.k.xiii.b
de-identification of health information, ***5:*** II.A.1.k.ix
deceased individuals, health information relating to, ***5:*** II.A.1.k.x
enforcement, ***5:*** II.A.1.m.i, II.A.1.m.v
family members, disclosures to, ***5:*** II.A.1.k.xi
friends, disclosures to, ***5:*** II.A.1.k.xi
group health plans, defined, ***5:*** II.A.1.b.iii
health care, defined, ***5:*** II.A.1.c
health care operations, defined, ***5:*** II.A.1.d
health care providers, defined, ***5:*** II.A.1.b.i
health information, defined, ***5:*** II.A.1.e
health plans
classifications of, ***5:*** II.A.1.k.i.b
defined, ***5:*** II.A.1.b.ii
employers, distinguished from, ***5:*** II.A.1.k.i.a
HHS. *See* Health and Human Services, U.S. Department of
implementation deadlines, ***5:*** II.A.1.k.viii
individual privacy rights, ***5:*** II.A.1.l.i–II.A.1.l.iii
individual rights, ***5:*** II.A.1.k.vi
individually identifiable health information, defined, ***5:*** II.A.1.f
information sharing, ***5:*** II.A.1.k.ii.b
marketing, ***5:*** II.A.1.k.xv.b
"minimum necessary" policies, ***5:*** II.A.1.k.iv.d
minors, disclosures relating to, ***5:*** II.A.1.k.xii
mitigation, duty of, ***5:*** II.A.1.k.iv.g
notice of privacy practices, ***5:*** II.A.1.k.iv.j, II.A.1.l.iii.a
participant advocacy, ***5:*** II.A.1.k.ii.c
payment, defined, ***5:*** II.A.1.g
plan amendments, ***5:*** II.A.1.k.v
plan compliance requirements, ***5:*** II.A.1.k.iii
policies and procedures, adoption and documentation of, ***5:*** II.A.1.k.iv.i
privacy rules. *See* Privacy Rules (U.S.)
privacy training for workforce, ***5:*** II.A.1.k.iv.b
private enforcement rights, ***5:*** II.A.1.m.iv
procedural safeguards, implementation of, ***5:*** II.A.1.k.iv.c
protected health information, defined, ***5:*** II.A.1.h
psychotherapy notes, ***5:*** II.A.1.k.xv.a
retaliation, ***5:*** II.A.1.k.iv.h
rules. *See* Privacy rules (U.S.); Security Rules (U.S.)
sanctions, ***5:*** II.A.1.k.iv.f, II.A.1.m.iii
security breach exemptions, ***9:*** II.A.9.a

state laws, impact of, *5:* II.A.1.k.xvi
treatment, defined, *5:* II.A.1.i
voluntary restrictions on disclosure, *5:* II.A.1.l.iii.b
waiver, *5:* II.A.1.k.iv.h

Health Records (Privacy and Access) Act (ACT, 1997), *5:* IV.A.2

HHS. *See* Health and Human Services, U.S. Department of (HHS)

HIPAA. *See* Health Insurance Portability and Accountability Act of 1996 (U.S.)

HIV/AIDS testing of employees and job applicants, *6:* II.A.4.c
California, *5:* II.A.3.a.ii.k
China, *6:* IV.A
France, *6:* III.B
Germany, *6:* III.C
Japan, *6:* IV.C.2
New York, *5:* II.A.3.b.v

Hong Kong
background checks and investigations
access, *2:* IV.B.4
credit reports, *2:* IV.B.4.a
criminal records, *2:* IV.B.4.b
employment applicants, general requirements for, *2:* IV.B.2
existing employees, general requirements for, *2:* IV.B.3
references, *2:* IV.B.4.d
statutes, *2:* IV.B.1
work history, *2:* IV.B.4.c
Code of Practice on Human Resource Management. *See* Code of Practice on Human Resource Management (Hong Kong)
data security
access and correction requirements, *1:* IV.B.3
accuracy requirements, *1:* IV.B.4
consent, *1:* IV.B.2
data transfers, *1:* IV.B.6, IV.B.7
employees, monitoring of, *1:* IV.B.11
job references, *1:* IV.B.8
medical and health data, *1:* IV.B.9.a
notice, *1:* IV.B.1
penalties, *1:* IV.B.12
retention of data, *1:* IV.B.5
security requirements, *1:* IV.B.10
Disability Discrimination Ordinance, *2:* IV.B.1
drug testing, *6:* IV.B.2
Family Status Discrimination Ordinance, *2:* IV.B.1
genetic testing, *6:* IV.B.2
government identity numbers, use of
employment applicants, *8:* IV.B.1
existing employees, *8:* IV.B.2
protections, *1:* IV.B.9, *8:* IV.B
health information, confidentiality of, *5:* IV.C
HR Code. *See* Code of Practice on Human Resource Management (Hong Kong)
identity cards. *See* Hong Kong Identity Cards, use of
IT Practitioners on Personal Data Handling, Recommended Procedures for, *1:* IV.B.10
medical examinations of applicants and employees, *6:* IV.B.1
moonlighting, *4:* III.B.1
Personal Data (Privacy) Ordinance. *See* Personal Data (Privacy) Ordinance (Hong Kong)
personnel records, access to
fees for, *7:* IV.B.5
general exemptions, *7:* IV.B.4
personal references exemptions, *7:* IV.B.3
relevant process exemptions, *7:* IV.B.2
requests, *7:* IV.B.1
Privacy Guidelines: Monitoring and Personal Data Privacy at Work, *1:* IV.2, *3:* IV.C
Rehabilitation of Offenders Ordinance, *2:* IV.B.1
Sex Discrimination Ordinance, *2:* IV.B.1
union membership or affiliation, *4:* III.B.2
workplace surveillance, *3:* IV.C

Hong Kong Identity Cards, use of
employment applicants, *8:* IV.B.1
existing employees, *8:* IV.B.2
protections, *1:* IV.B.9, *8:* IV.B

Human Rights Act (UK, 1998), *2:* III.E.1, III.E.2

I

Illiteracy programs, participation in, ***4:*** II.A.8
Information brokers and security breach notification laws, ***9:*** II.A.2.a
Information security programs, ***Ch.*** 10. *See also* Data security
access controls, ***10:*** III.F
physical access, ***10:*** III.G
technical controls, ***10:*** III.H
audits of, internal, ***10:*** III.L
confidentiality, levels of, ***10:*** III.F
coordinators of, ***10:*** III.D
data classification systems, ***10:*** III.B
destruction of data, ***10:*** III.I
employees, training of, ***10:*** III.E
encryption of data, ***10:*** III.H
external risks, ***10:*** III.C
internal risks, ***10:*** III.C
introduction, ***10:*** I
Massachusetts regulation. *See* Massachusetts Program Rule
overview of laws and regulations, ***10:*** II
passwords, ***10:*** III.H
personal information, ***10:*** III.H
physical access controls, ***10:*** III.G
protection steps, ***10:*** III.B
responses to security breaches, documentation of, ***10:*** III.J
retention of data, ***10:*** III.I
review of, internal, ***10:*** III.L
risk assessments, ***10:*** III.C
Safeguards Rule (FTC), ***10:*** II
service providers, ***10:*** III.K
statutory requirements, ***10:*** II
technical controls, ***10:*** III.H
vendors, provision of data to, ***10:*** III.K
written, ***10:*** III.B, III.E
Information sharing, ***5:*** II.A.1.k.ii.b
Inquiries related to physical or mental condition, ***6:*** II.A.2
drug and alcohol use, ***6:*** II.A.3
impermissible, ***6:*** II.A.2.b
legally restricted, examples, ***Exh.*** 6.2
permissible, ***6:*** II.A.2.a
timing of, under ADA, ***Exh.*** 6.1
Internal risks to data security, ***10:*** III.C
International Linkups of Computer Information Networks Tentative Provisions Administration (China), ***3:*** IV.B.1
Internet monitoring. *See* Email and Internet monitoring by employers
Invasion of privacy, ***3:*** II.A.15.a, II.A.15.b
Invasion of Privacy Act (California), ***3:*** II.A.13
Investigative Consumer Reporting Agencies Act (California), ***1:*** I.C.2.c, ***2:*** II.A.2.a.ii, II.A.6.a
Iowa
drug testing of employees and job applicants, ***6:*** II.A.3.c.iii
IT Practitioners on Personal Data Handling, Recommended Procedures for (Hong Kong), ***1:*** IV.B.10
Italy
background checks and investigations, ***2:*** III.D.1
drug testing, ***6:*** III.D.2
employment verification requests, ***2:*** III.D.2
medical examinations, ***6:*** III.D.1
personal identification information, ***8:*** III.C

J

Japan
alcohol testing, ***6:*** IV.C.2
background checks and investigations
information acquired after employment, ***2:*** IV.C.1.d
references, ***2:*** IV.C.1.c
restrictions on, ***2:*** IV.C.1.a, IV.C.1.b
sensitive data, prohibitions on collection of, ***2:*** IV.C.1.e
statutes, ***2:*** IV.C.1
computer use, monitoring of by employers, ***3:*** IV.D.2
data security, ***1:*** IV.C
access and correction rights, ***1:*** IV.C.9
breach notice, ***1:*** IV.C.2
consent, ***1:*** IV.C.4

employees, monitoring of, *1:* IV.C.10
labor unions, notice to, *1:* IV.C.3
notice, *1:* IV.C.1
security, *1:* IV.C.7
sensitive information, *1:* IV.C.8
service providers, supervision of, *1:* IV.C.6
third parties, sharing of employee information with, *1:* IV.C.5
drug testing, *6:* IV.C.2
Employment Security Law, *2:* IV.C.1, IV.C.1.b, IV.C.1.c
genetic testing, *6:* IV.C.2
government identity numbers, use of, *8:* IV.C
Guidelines for the Protection of Personal Information in the Economic and Industrial Areas, *4:* IV.C.2
health information
confidentiality of, *5:* IV.D
Points to Consider when Handling Health Information in Employment Management, *1:* IV.C
information access controls, *10:* III.F
Labor Standards Law, *4:* IV.C.1
Labor Union Law, *4:* IV.C.2
medical examinations, *6:* IV.C.1
mental health information, confidentiality of, *5:* IV.D.1
METI Guidelines. *See* Ministry of Economy, Trade and Industry (METI) Guidelines (Japan)
monitoring of employees, general requirements for, *3:* IV.D.1
moonlighting, prohibiting employees from, *4:* IV.C.1
Personal Information in Employment Management. *See* Personal Information in Employment Management, Guidelines for the Appropriate Handling of (Japan)
personnel records, access requests, *7:* IV.C.1
political activities, employee participation in, *4:* IV.C.3, IV.C.4
prohibited tests, *6:* IV.C.2
Protection of Personal Information in the Economic and Industrial Areas, Guidelines for, *4:* IV.C.2
Protection of Personal Information Law. *See* Protection of Personal Information Law (PIPL, Japan)
security breach notification laws, *9:* V.B
union activities of employees, monitoring, *4:* IV.C.2
Job applicants. *See* Applicants for jobs
Job references. *See* References

K

Korea
background checks, *2:* IV.D.1
constitutional right to privacy, *1:* IV.D
credit information, *1:* IV.D
data security
access and correction rights, *1:* IV.D.4
breach notification, *1:* IV.D.9
consent, *1:* IV.D.3
cross-border requirements, *1:* IV.D.5
data retention, *1:* IV.D.8
notice, *1:* IV.D.1
onward transfer agreements, *1:* IV.D.7
penalties, *1:* IV.D.10
privacy policies, *1:* IV.D.2
security, *1:* IV.D.6
service providers, supervision of, *1:* IV.D.7
surveillance and monitoring of employees, *1:* IV.D.11
drug testing, *6:* IV.D.2
email, monitoring of by employers, *3:* IV.E.1
employment verification requests, *2:* IV.D.2
Financial Transactions with Real Name and Guarantee of Secrecy Act of 1997, *1:* IV.D
government identity numbers, use of, *8:* IV.D
Labor Standards Act, *1:* IV.D.8
medical examinations, *6:* IV.D.1
Medical Service Act of 1973, *1:* IV.D

Korea—*cont'd*
- Pharmaceutical Affairs Act of 1997, *1:* IV.D
- Promotion of Information and Communications Network Utilization and Information Protection Act. *See* Promotion of Information and Communications Network Utilization and Information Protection Act
- Protection of Communications Secret Law of 1993, *1:* IV.D, IV.D.11, *3:* IV.E.1
- Telecommunications Business Act of 1991, *1:* IV.D
- Use and Protection of Credit Information Act of 1995, *1:* IV.D
- Video Camera Privacy Guidelines, *3:* IV.E.2
- video surveillance by employers, *3:* IV.E.2

L

Labor Management Relations Act (LMRA, U.S.), *3:* II.A.20
Labor Standards Act (Korea), *1:* IV.D.8
Labor Standards Law (Japan), *4:* IV.C.1
Labor Union Law (Japan), *4:* IV.C.2
Labor unions. *See* Unions
Lie detector examinations of employees and job applicants, *6:* II.A.4.d
- EPPA provisions, *6:* II.A.4.d.i
- state restrictions, *6:* II.A.4.d.ii

Literacy programs, participation in, *4:* II.A.8
LMRA (Labor Management Relations Act, U.S.), *3:* II.A.20

M

Mail
- email. *See* Email and Internet monitoring by employers
- monitoring of by employers, *3:* II.A.25
- security breaches, notification by, *9:* II.A.7
- SSNs, documents containing, *8:* II.A.3.a

Maine
- drug testing of employees and job applicants, *6:* II.A.3.c.iv

Maintenance of Secrets in the International Networking of Computer Information Systems Provisions Administration (China), *3:* IV.B.1
Massachusetts Program Rule, *1:* I.C.3.a, *10:* I, II
- access controls, *10:* III.F, III.G
- coordinators, *10:* III.D
- destruction of data, *10:* III.I
- employee training, *10:* III.E
- internal audits and reviews, *10:* III.L
- personal information, *10:* III.A
- physical access controls, *10:* III.G
- retention of data, *10:* III.I
- risk assessments, *10:* III.C
- service providers, *10:* III.K
- technical security controls, *10:* III.H
- written program, *10:* III.B

Media notification of security breaches, *9:* II.A.7.b
Medical examinations of applicants and employees, *Ch.* 6
- ADA provisions, *6:* II.A.1
  - after conditional job offer, *6:* II.A.1.b.ii
  - physical agility tests, *6:* II.A.1.a.iii
  - prior to job offer, *6:* II.A.1.b.i
- Belgium, *6:* III.A.1
- Brazil, *6:* II.B.1
- Canada, *6:* II.C.1
- China, *6:* IV.A
- defined, *6:* II.A.1.a
- EEOC enforcement, *6:* II.A.1.a
  - employee medical examinations, *6:* II.A.1.c.i
- EPPA provisions, *6:* II.A.4.d.i
- fitness for duty evaluations, *6:* II.A.1.c.iii
- genetic information
  - collection of, nondiscrimination, *6:* II.A.4.a
  - testing, state laws, *6:* II.A.4.b
- HIV/AIDS testing, *6:* II.A.4.c
- Hong Kong, *6:* IV.B.1

inquiries related to physical or mental condition, *6:* II.A.2
drug and alcohol use, *6:* II.A.3
impermissible, *6:* II.A.2.b
legally restricted, examples, ***Exh.*** 6.2
permissible, *6:* II.A.2.a
timing of, under ADA, ***Exh.*** 6.1
Italy, *6:* III.D.1
Japan, *6:* IV.C.1, IV.C.2
of job applicants, *6:* II.A.1.b, II.A.1.b.i
after conditional job offer, *6:* II.A.1.b.ii
Korea, *6:* IV.D.1
Mexico, *6:* II.D.1
necessity, showing, *6:* II.A.1.c.ii
overview, *6:* I
personality assessments as, *6:* II.A.1.a.ii
physical agility tests as, *6:* II.A.1.a.iii
psychological examinations as, *6:* II.A.1.a.i
state laws
genetic testing, *6:* II.A.4.b
HIV/AIDS testing, *6:* II.A.4.c
lie detector and polygraph tests, *6:* II.A.4.d.ii
United Kingdom, *6:* III.E
unlawful, *6:* II.A.1.d
voluntary disclosure of disabilities, following, *6:* II.A.2.c
Medical information. *See* Health information, confidentiality of
Medical Service Act of 1973 (Korea), *1:* IV.D
Mental health information, confidentiality of
inquiries. *See* Inquiries related to physical or mental condition
Japan, *5:* IV.D.1
Mexico
background checks, *2:* II.D.1
drug testing, *6:* II.D.2
employment verification requests, *2:* II.D.2
medical examinations, *6:* II.D.1
national identification numbers, *8:* II.D
Michigan
SSNs, use restrictions
privacy policy law, *8:* II.A.5.a.i
verifications and investigations, exceptions, *8:* II.A.4.b
Ministry of Economy, Trade and Industry (METI) Guidelines (Japan)
health information, collection of, *1:* IV.C.7
personal information, collection of, *1:* IV.C
security breaches, notice of, *1:* IV.C.2, *9:* V.B
third parties, sharing information with, *1:* IV.C.5
workplace surveillance, *3:* IV.D.1
Minnesota
drug testing of employees and job applicants, *6:* II.A.3.c.iv
Minors
disclosures of information, *5:* II.A.1.k.xii
Mitigation, duty of, *5:* II.A.1.k.iv.g
Monitoring and surveillance by employers, *Ch.* 3
amplifying or recording devices, use of, *3:* II.A.13
auditory surveillance, *3:* II.A.11
Australia, *3:* IV.A.1–IV.A.3
California. *See* California
China, *3:* IV.B.1
computer use, surveillance of, *3:* II.A.7
Connecticut, *3:* II.A.6.d, II.A.12
Delaware, *3:* II.A.6.e
duty to monitor, *3:* II.A.8
ECPA. *See* Electronic Communications Privacy Act (U.S.)
email, surveillance of, *3:* II.A.6
California, *3:* II.A.6.b
Connecticut, *3:* II.A.6.d
Delaware, *3:* II.A.6.e
federal law, *3:* II.A.6.a
New York, *3:* II.A.6.c
European Union, *3:* III.A.1–III.A.4
Finland, *3:* III.B.1–III.B.3
Fourth Amendment, *3:* II.A.16
France, *3:* III.C.1–III.C.3
Germany, *3:* III.D.1–III.D.3
Hong Kong, *3:* IV.C

Monitoring and surveillance by employers—*cont'd*
invasion of privacy claims, ***3:*** II.A.15, II.A.15.a, II.A.15.b
Japan, ***3:*** IV.D, IV.D.1, IV.D.2
Korea, ***3:*** IV.E.1, IV.E.2
LMRA, ***3:*** II.A.20
location-based restrictions, ***3:*** II.A.12
New York. *See* New York
New Zealand, ***3:*** IV.F.1, IV.F.2
NLRA, ***3:*** II.A.11, II.A.20
notice of surveillance, ***3:*** II.A.15.b
overview, ***3:*** I
pre-monitoring steps, ***3:*** V
privacy expectations, ***3:*** II.A.18
public-sector employment, surveillance in, ***3:*** II.A.16, II.A.17–II.A.19
SCA, ***3:*** II.A.6.a
state laws, ***3:*** II.A.1
Taiwan, ***3:*** IV.G.1, IV.G.2
telephone calls, monitoring of, ***3:*** II.A.1, II.A.3
Title III (U.S.), ***3:*** II.A.19
undercover investigators, ***3:*** II.A.14
unionized workplaces, surveillance in, ***3:*** II.A.20, II.A.21, II.A.22
United Kingdom, ***3:*** III.E.1–III.E.3
United States, ***3:*** II, II.A
video surveillance, ***3:*** II.A.17, II.A.22, III.A.3, III.C.3
visual surveillance, ***3:*** II.A.11
workplace searches, ***3:*** II.A
"competing nonprivacy interests" defense, ***3:*** II.A.23.b
intrusiveness, limiting, ***3:*** II.A.27
invasions of privacy interests, ***3:*** II.A.23.a.iii
liability limitation, steps for, ***3:*** II.A.26
postal mail received by employees, ***3:*** II.A.25
privacy expectations, ***3:*** II.A.23.a.ii, II.A.24
privacy interests, ***3:*** II.A.23.a.i
private-sector employers, ***3:*** II.A.23
public-sector employers, ***3:*** II.A.24, II.A.24.b
reasonable privacy expectations, setting of, ***3:*** II.A.26

Moonlighting
China, ***4:*** IV.A.1
Hong Kong, ***4:*** III.B.1
Japan, ***4:*** IV.C.1
United Kingdom, ***4:*** III.B.5
United States, ***4:*** II.A.5

N

Names as personal information, ***9:*** II.A.3
National identification numbers. *See* Government identity numbers
National Insurance Numbers (UK), ***8:*** III.D
National Labor Relations Act (NLRA, U.S.), ***4:*** II.A.1, II.A.1.a, II.A.1.b
National Privacy Principals (Australia), ***1:*** IV.A.3
Networks, information protection on. *See also information by country on computer data*
China, ***3:*** IV.B.1
Korea. *See* Promotion of Information and Communications Network Utilization and Information Protection Act (Korea)
New Mexico
SSN privacy policy law, ***8:*** II.A.5.a.ii
New South Wales Health Records and Information Privacy Act (Australia, 2002), ***5:*** IV.A.1
New York
background checks and investigations
fingerprinting, ***2:*** II.A.8.c
prior convictions, employer inquiries regarding, ***2:*** II.A.8.b, II.A.8.b.i, II.A.8.b.ii
by vendors, ***2:*** II.A.6.b
government employees, privacy rights of, ***5:*** II.A.3.b.iii
HIV/AIDS status
confidentiality of, ***5:*** II.A.3.b.v.a
unlawful disclosure, ***5:*** II.A.3.b.v.b
identifying information of employees, disclosure of, ***8:*** II.A.3.f
information security programs, ***10:*** II
monitoring and surveillance by employers

amplifying or recording devices used in workplace surveillance, *3:* II.A.13
email, surveillance of by employers, *3:* II.A.6.c
location-based restrictions on, *3:* II.A.12
postal mail received by employees, employer searches of, *3:* II.A.25
telephone calls, monitoring of by employers, *3:* II.A.5
of union activities, *3:* II.A.21
on-site medical facilities, *5:* II.A.3.b.ii
employee access to information, *5:* II.A.3.b.ii.b
medical ethics and employer instructions, conflicts between, *5:* II.A.3.b.ii.a
patient information, access to, *5:* II.A.3.b.i
political campaigns, employee participation in, *4:* II.A.2.a
Public Health Law §18
confidentiality of medical records under, *5:* II.A.3.b.i.a
violations, *5:* II.A.3.b.i.b
SSNs, use restrictions, *8:* II.A.2
court filings, exceptions, *8:* II.A.4.a
privacy policy law, *8:* II.A.5.a.iii
workers' compensation law, *5:* II.A.3.b.iv

New Zealand
data security
access and correction, *1:* IV.E.4
collection and use limitations, *1:* IV.E.1
data accuracy, *1:* IV.E.5
data retention, *1:* IV.E.3, IV.E.6
notice, *1:* IV.E.2
unique identifiers, restrictions on use of, *1:* IV.E.7
government identity numbers, use of, *8:* IV.E
health information, confidentiality of, *5:* IV.E
Health Information Privacy Code, *5:* IV.E
Privacy Act. *See* Privacy Act (New Zealand, 1993)
security breach notifications, *9:* V.C
contents of notice, *9:* V.C.3
personal information covered, *9:* V.C.1
risk assessments, *9:* V.C.2
timing of, *9:* V.C.3
workplace surveillance
email, monitoring of, *3:* IV.F.1
video surveillance, *3:* IV.F.2

NLRA. *See* National Labor Relations Act (U.S.)

Norway
security breach notification, *9:* III.B

Notice of security breaches. *See* Security breach notifications

Notice of surveillance, *3:* II.A.15.b

O

Occupational Health and Safety Act (OSHA, U.S.), *7:* II.A.2

Occupational Health and Safety Law (Japan), *6:* IV.C.1

Occupational health and safety records, employee access to, *7:* II.A.2

OCR (Office of Civil Rights), *5:* II.A.1.m.i

Off-duty conduct of employees, *Ch.* 4
alcohol, use of, *4:* II.A.6.a
alcohol rehabilitation programs, participation in, *4:* II.A.7
Asia, *4:* IV
California, *4:* II.A.2.b
China, *4:* IV.A
Civil Rights Act of 1964, *4:* II.A.3
co-workers, relationships between, *4:* II.A.4.b
drug rehabilitation programs, participation in, *4:* II.A.7
Europe, *4:* III
fraternization
United Kingdom, *4:* III.B.4
United States, *4:* II.A.4, II.A.4.a–II.A.4.c
illiteracy programs, participation in, *4:* II.A.8
Japan, *4:* IV.C
lawful off-duty activities, participation in, *4:* II.A.9
legal substances, use of, *4:* II.A.6

Off-duty conduct of employees—*cont'd*
literacy programs, participation in, ***4:*** II.A.8
managers and nonmanagers, relationships between, ***4:*** II.A.4.a
moonlighting. *See* Moonlighting
New York, ***4:*** II.A.2.a
NLRA. *See* National Labor Relations Act (U.S.)
non-employees, employee relationships with, ***4:*** II.A.4.c
outside employment. *See* Moonlighting
overview, ***4:*** I
political activities
United Kingdom, ***4:*** III.B.2
United States, ***4:*** II.A.2.a, II.A.2.b
protected conduct, ***Exh.*** 4.1
religious activities
United Kingdom, ***4:*** III.B.3
United States, ***4:*** II.A.3
romantic relationships
United Kingdom, ***4:*** III.B.4
United States, ***4:*** II.A.4, II.A.4.a–II.A.4.c
state laws, ***4:*** II.A.6.a, II.A.6.b, II.A.7–4.10
tobacco, use of, ***4:*** II.A.6, II.A.6.b
union membership or affiliation
China, ***4:*** IV.A.2
Hong Kong, ***4:*** III.B.2
United Kingdom, ***4:*** III.B.2
United States, ***4:*** II.A.1, II.A.1.a, II.A.1.b
United Kingdom, ***4:*** III.B
Office of Civil rights (OCR, U.S.), ***5:*** II.A.1.m.i
Ohio
unfair or deceptive acts or practices, ***1:*** I.C.4
Oklahoma
drug testing of employees and job applicants, ***6:*** II.A.3.c.v
Omnibus Crime Control and Safe Streets Act of 1968 (Title III, U.S.), ***3:*** II.A.19
On-site medical facilities
New York, patient health records, ***5:*** II.A.3.b.ii
Ontario
Personal Health Information Protection Act, ***1:*** V.B.3, ***9:*** II.B.5
Onward transfer agreements
Argentina, ***1:*** V.A.7
Australia, ***1:*** IV.A.3
Chile, ***1:*** V.C.8
European Union, ***1:*** III.D.2, ***Exh.*** 1.3
Korea, ***1:*** IV.D.7
OSHA (Occupational Health and Safety Act, U.S.), ***7:*** II.A.2
Outside employment. *See* Moonlighting

P

Paper records and security breaches, ***9:*** II.A.2.b
Passwords
as personal information, ***9:*** II.A.3
security controls, ***10:*** III.H
PATRIOT Act (U.S.), ***9:*** II.A.9.a
Penalties for misuse of data
Australia, ***1:*** IV.A.4
HIPAA, ***5:*** II.A.1.k.iv.f, II.A.1.m.iii
Hong Kong, ***1:*** IV.B.12
Korea, ***1:*** IV.D.10
Taiwan, ***1:*** IV.F.10
Personal Data (Privacy) Ordinance (Hong Kong)
access and correction requirements, ***1:*** IV.B.3
background checks, ***2:*** IV.B.1
email and Internet monitoring by employers, ***3:*** IV.C
employees, monitoring of, ***1:*** IV.B.11
government identity numbers, use of, ***8:*** IV.B
health information, collection of, ***1:*** IV.B.9.a, ***5:*** IV.C, ***6:*** IV.B.1, IV.B.2
penalties, ***1:*** IV.B.12
personal data
access requests, ***7:*** IV.B.1
collection of, ***1:*** IV.B
relevant process exemptions, ***7:*** IV.B.2
retention of data, ***1:*** IV.B.5
security requirements, ***1:*** IV.B.10
transfer of data, ***1:*** IV.B.7

video surveillance by employers, *3:* IV.C

Personal Data Protection Act (Argentina), *1:* V.A
- access and correction, ***1:*** V.A.3
- consent, ***1:*** V.A.2
- cross-border transfers, ***1:*** V.A.6
- database registration, ***1:*** V.A.5
- dispute resolution, ***1:*** V.A.8
- notice, ***1:*** V.A.1
- onward transfer agreements, ***1:*** V.A.7
- security and data retention, ***1:*** V.A.4
- use limitations, ***1:*** V.A.2

Personal Health Information Protection Act (PHIPA, Ontario), *1:* V.B.3, ***9:*** II.B.5

Personal information
- access codes as, ***9:*** II.A.3
- account numbers as, ***9:*** II.A.3
- Argentina. *See* Argentina and data security
- Australia, ***9:*** V.A.1
- British Columbia, ***1:*** V.B.3
- California, ***9:*** II.A.1, II.A.3, II.A.3.a
- Canada. *See* Canada
- Chile. *See* Chile and data security
- China. *See* China
- defined, ***9:*** II.A.3
- employees, acquisition by, ***9:*** II.A.4.c
- encryption of, ***10:*** III.H
- European Union. *See* European Union
- Finland. *See* Finland
- France. *See* France
- Germany. *See* Germany
- Hong Kong. *See* Hong Kong
- Japan. *See* Japan; Personal Information in Employment Management, Guidelines for the Appropriate Handling of (Japan)
- Korea. *See* Korea
- medical information as, ***9:*** II.A.3
- names, as, ***9:*** II.A.3
- New South Wales, ***5:*** IV.A.1
- New York. *See* New York
- New Zealand, ***9:*** V.C.1
- Ontario, ***1:*** V.B.3
- passwords as, ***9:*** II.A.3
- publicly available information, exceptions, ***9:*** II.A.3.a
- Quebec, ***1:*** V.B.3
- SSNs as, ***9:*** II.A.3
- State Identification Card numbers as, ***9:*** II.A.3
- unauthorized acquisition of, ***9:*** II.A.4.a, II.A.4.b
- United Kingdom. *See* United Kingdom

Personal Information in Employment Management, Guidelines for the Appropriate Handling of (Japan)
- employee consent, ***1:*** IV.C.4
- labor unions, notice to, ***1:*** IV.C.3
- Minister of Health, Labor and Welfare and, ***1:*** IV.C
- notice requirements, ***1:*** IV.C.1
- security measures required, ***1:*** IV.C.7

Personal Information Protection Act (British Columbia), *1:* V.B.3

Personal Information Protection and Electronic Documents Act (PIPEDA, Canada), *1:* V.B.1, V.B.2
- access, ***1:*** V.B.2.g
- audits, ***1:*** V.B.2.f
- complaint handling, ***1:*** V.B.2.i
- consent, ***1:*** V.B.2.b
- cross-border transfers, ***1:*** V.B.2.h
- data processing contracts, ***1:*** V.B.2.d
- data retention, ***1:*** V.B.2.k
- database registration, ***1:*** V.B.5
- notice, ***1:*** V.B.2.a
- policies and practices, implementation of, ***1:*** V.B.2.f
- privacy officers, designation of, ***1:*** V.B.2.e
- security, ***1:*** V.B.2.j
- security breach notification provisions, ***9:*** II.B

Personal Information Protection Law (Japan). *See* Protection of Personal Information Law (PIPL, Japan)

Personality assessments of employees and applicants, *6:* II.A.1.a.ii

Personnel records, *Ch.* 7
- China, ***7:*** IV.A
- consequences for improper disclosure, ***7:*** II.A.6
- defamation and, ***7:*** II.A.10
- defined, ***7:*** II.A.1.a

Personnel records—*cont'd*
employee access rights, ***7:*** I, II.A.1
European Union, ***7:*** III.A
explanatory statements, addition of, ***7:*** II.A.3
France, ***7:*** III.B
Germany, ***7:*** III.C
Hong Kong. *See* Hong Kong
Japan, ***7:*** IV.C.1
medical information, ***7:*** II.A.9
occupational health and safety records, ***7:*** II.A.2
security breaches, notification requirements for, ***7:*** II.A.8
SSNs, restrictions on use of, ***7:*** II.A.7, II.A.8, ***8:*** II.A.4.c
state laws
defamation and other legal claims, ***7:*** II.A.10
disclosure to third parties, consent of employee, ***7:*** II.A.4
employee rights, ***7:*** II.A.1
subpoenas, notice to employee, ***7:*** II.A.5
subpoenas for, ***7:*** II.A.5
third-party access, consent required for, ***7:*** II.A.4
United Kingdom, ***7:*** III.D
Pharmaceutical Affairs Act of 1997 (Korea), *1:* IV.D
PHIPA. *See* Personal Health Information Protection Act (Ontario)
Physical agility tests of employees and applicants, *6:* II.A.1.a.iii
PIPEDA. *See* Personal Information Protection and Electronic Documents Act (Canada)
PIPL. *See* Protection of Personal Information Law (PIPL, Japan)
Political activities, off-duty participation in, *4:* II.A.2.a, II.A.2.b
United Kingdom, ***4:*** III.B.2
Polygraph examinations of employees and job applicants, *6:* II.A.4.d
EPPA provisions, ***6:*** II.A.4.d.i
state restrictions, ***6:*** II.A.4.d.ii
Prior convictions and background checks. *See* Background checks and investigations
Privacy Act (Australia, 1988)
Employee Records Exemption, ***1:*** IV.A.2, ***5:*** IV.A
government identity numbers, collection and use of, ***8:*** IV.A
National Privacy Principals and, ***1:*** IV.A.3
requirements of, ***1:*** IV.A.1, ***5:*** IV.A
security breach notifications, ***9:*** V.A
workplace monitoring and surveillance, ***3:*** IV.A.1
Privacy Act (New Zealand, 1993)
access and correction, ***1:*** IV.E.4
collection and use limitations, ***1:*** IV.E.1
data accuracy, ***1:*** IV.E.5
data retention, ***1:*** IV.E.6
email, monitoring of by employers, ***3:*** IV.F.1
health information, ***5:*** IV.E
notice, ***1:*** IV.E.2
security and data retention, ***1:*** IV.E.3, IV.E.6
security breach notifications, ***9:*** V.C
unique identifiers, restrictions on use of, ***1:*** IV.E.7, ***8:*** IV.E
Privacy Guidelines: Monitoring and Personal Data Privacy at Work (Hong Kong), *1:* IV.2, ***3:*** IV.C
Privacy officers, designation of, *1:* V.B.2.e
Privacy Rules (U.S.)
access, right of, ***5:*** II.A.1.l.i
accounting of nonroutine disclosures, right to, ***5:*** II.A.1.l.iii
amendments/corrections, right to request, ***5:*** II.A.1.l.ii
authorizations, ***5:*** II.A.1.k.xv
benefit plan administration, ***5:*** II.A.1.k.ii.a
business associate agreements, ***5:*** II.A.1.k.vii.a
business associates, defined, ***5:*** II.A.1.a
complaints, ***5:*** II.A.1.k.iv.e, II.A.1.k.xiii.a
compliance responsibilities, ***5:*** II.A.1.k.i, II.A.1.k.i.c, II.A.1.k.iii

confidential communications, *5:* II.A.1.l.iii.c
consents to disclosure, *5:* II.A.1.k.xiv
contact person, appointment of, *5:* II.A.1.k.iv.a
covered entities, *5:* II.A.1.b
crimes, reporting of, *5:* II.A.1.k.xiii.b
de-identification of health information, *5:* II.A.1.k.ix
deceased individuals, health information relating to, *5:* II.A.1.k.x
enforcement, responsibility for, *5:* II.A.1.m.i
enforcement approach of HHS, *5:* II.A.1.m.v
exemptions, *9:* II.A.9.a
family members, disclosures to, *5:* II.A.1.k.xi
friends, disclosures to, *5:* II.A.1.k.xi
group health plans, defined, *5:* II.A.1.b.iii
health care, defined, *5:* II.A.1.c
health care operations, defined, *5:* II.A.1.d
health care providers, defined, *5:* II.A.1.b.i
health information, defined, *5:* II.A.1.e
health plans
  classifications of, *5:* II.A.1.k.i.b
  defined, *5:* II.A.1.b.ii
  employers, distinguished from, *5:* II.A.1.k.i.a
implementation deadlines, *5:* II.A.1.k.viii
individual privacy rights, *5:* II.A.1.k.vi, II.A.1.l.i, II.A.1.l.ii, II.A.1.l.iii
individually identifiable health information, defined, *5:* II.A.1.f
information sharing, *5:* II.A.1.k.ii.b
marketing, *5:* II.A.1.k.xv.b
"minimum necessary" policies, *5:* II.A.1.k.iv.d
minors, disclosures relating to, *5:* II.A.1.k.xii
mitigation, duty of, *5:* II.A.1.k.iv.g
notice of privacy practices, *5:* II.A.1.k.iv.j, II.A.1.l.iii.a
overview, *5:* II.A.1.j
participant advocacy, *5:* II.A.1.k.ii.c
payment, defined, *5:* II.A.1.g
plan amendments, *5:* II.A.1.k.v
policies and procedures, adoption and documentation of, *5:* II.A.1.k.iv.i
privacy training for workforce, *5:* II.A.1.k.iv.b
private enforcement rights, *5:* II.A.1.m.iv
procedural safeguards, implementation of, *5:* II.A.1.k.iv.c
protected health information, defined, *5:* II.A.1.h
psychotherapy notes, *5:* II.A.1.k.xv.a
retaliation, *5:* II.A.1.k.iv.h
sanctions, *5:* II.A.1.k.iv.f, II.A.1.m.iii
state laws, impact of, *5:* II.A.1.k.xvi
treatment, defined, *5:* II.A.1.i
voluntary restrictions on disclosure, *5:* II.A.1.l.iii.b
waiver, *5:* II.A.1.k.iv.h

Promotion of Information and Communications Network Utilization and Information Protection Act (Korea)
applicability, *1:* IV.D
cross-border requirements, *1:* IV.D.5
email, monitoring by employers, *1:* IV.D.11, *3:* IV.E.1
penalties, *1:* IV.D.10
privacy policies and, *1:* IV.D.2
security measures, *1:* IV.D.6

Protection and Monitoring of Communications Statute (Taiwan), *3:* IV.G.2

Protection of Communications Secret Law of 1993 (Korea), *1:* IV.D, IV.D.11, *3:* IV.E.1

Protection of Personal Information in the Economic and Industrial Areas, Guidelines for (Japan), *4:* IV.C.2

Protection of Personal Information Law (PIPL, Japan)
access and correction rights, *1:* IV.C.9
health information, *5:* IV.D
job applicants, *2:* IV.C.1, IV.C.1.a
notice, *1:* IV.C.1, IV.C.6
personal information, collection of, *1:* IV.C

Protection of Personal Information Law (PIPL, Japan)—*cont'd*
security, ***1:*** IV.C.7
breaches, notification requirements, ***9:*** V.B
Protection of Private Life Law (Chile), ***1:*** V.C
collection, use, and disclosure, limitations on, ***1:*** V.C.4
consent, ***1:*** V.C.3
cross-border limitations, ***1:*** V.C.7
data retention, ***1:*** V.C.5
database registration, ***1:*** V.C.6
dispute resolution, ***1:*** V.C.9
notice, ***1:*** V.C.1
onward transfer agreements, ***1:*** V.C.8
privacy policies, ***1:*** V.C.2
security, ***1:*** V.C.5
Psychological examinations of employees and applicants, ***6:*** II.A.1.a.i
Publicly available information
as personal information, ***9:*** II.A.3.a
Puerto Rico
SSN Protection Law, ***8:*** II.A.6

Q

Quebec
Protection of Personal Information in the Private Sector Act, ***1:*** V.B.3

R

Race Relations Act (UK, 1976), ***2:*** III.E.1
Reasonable privacy expectations, ***3:*** II.A.26
Records
health. *See* Health information, confidentiality of
personal. *See* Personal information
personnel. *See* Personnel records
References
defamation and, ***7:*** II.A.10
France, ***2:*** III.B.7.d
Germany, ***2:*** III.C.7.d
Hong Kong, ***1:*** IV.B.8, ***2:*** IV.B.4.d, ***7:*** IV.B.3
Japan, ***2:*** IV.C.1.c
United Kingdom, ***2:*** III.E.7.d
Registration. *See* Database registration
Regulation of Investigatory Powers Act (UK, 2000), ***3:*** III.E.1
Rehabilitation of Offenders Act (UK, 1974), ***2:*** III.E.1, III.E.7.b
Rehabilitation of Offenders Ordinance (Hong Kong), ***2:*** IV.B.1
Rehabilitation programs
employee participation in, ***4:*** II.A.7
Relevant process exemptions
personnel records (Hong Kong), ***7:*** IV.B.2
Religious activities of employees
Japan, ***4:*** IV.C.4
United Kingdom, ***4:*** III.B.3
United States, ***4:*** II.A.3
Reputation questions in background checks
France, ***2:*** III.B.7.e
Germany, ***2:*** III.C.7.e
United Kingdom, ***2:*** III.E.7.e
Resident Registration Act (Korea), ***8:*** IV.D
Responses to security breaches
documentation of, ***10:*** III.J
plans, ***9:*** II.A
Retaliation, ***5:*** II.A.1.k.iv.h
Retention issues
Argentina, ***1:*** V.A.4
Canada, ***1:*** V.B.2.k
Chile, ***1:*** V.C.5
Hong Kong, ***1:*** IV.B.5
information security programs, ***10:*** III.I
Korea, ***1:*** IV.D.8
New Zealand, ***1:*** IV.E.3, IV.E.6
Taiwan, ***1:*** IV.F.7
Risk assessments, ***10:*** III.C
information security programs and, ***10:*** III.C
security breaches
Australia, ***9:*** V.A.2
Canada, ***9:*** II.B.2
New Zealand, ***9:*** V.C.2
United Kingdom, ***9:*** III.C
Risk-based notification triggers for security breaches, ***9:*** II.A.4.b
Romantic relationships of employees, ***4:*** II.A.4, II.A.4.a–II.A.4.c

S

Safe Harbor Privacy Principles, *Exh.* 1.1
Safe harbors and security breaches, *9:* II.A.9
Safe Production Law (China), *3:* IV.B.1
Safeguards Rule (FTC), *1:* I.B.1.a.ii, *10:* II
Safety and Protection of Computer Information Networks, Administrative Measure on (China), *3:* IV.B.1
Sanctions. *See* Penalties for misuse of data
SCA (Stored Communications Act, U.S.), *3:* II.A.6.a
Sealed convictions
  background checks, *2:* II.A.8.a
Searches in the workplace, *3:* II.A
  "competing nonprivacy interests" defense, *3:* II.A.23.b
  intrusiveness, limiting, *3:* II.A.27
  invasions of privacy interests, *3:* II.A.23.a.iii
  liability limitation, steps for, *3:* II.A.23.a.iii
  postal mail received by employees, *3:* II.A.25
  privacy expectations, *3:* II.A.23.a.ii, II.A.24
  privacy interests, *3:* II.A.23.a.i
  private-sector employers, *3:* II.A.23
  public-sector employers, *3:* II.A.24
    legitimate interests of, *3:* II.A.24.b
  reasonable privacy expectations, setting of, *3:* II.A.26
Security breach notifications, *Ch.* 9
  Australia, *9:* V.A
  authorities, notification of, *9:* II.A.6
    Canada, *9:* II.B.3
  California. *See* California
  Canada, *9:* II.B
  consumer reporting agencies, coordination with, *9:* II.A.8.a
  contents of notice, *9:* II.A.8
    Australia, *9:* V.A.3
    Canada, *9:* II.B.3
    New Zealand, *9:* V.C.3
  covered entities, *9:* II.A.2.a
  covered information, *9:* II.A.3
  Data Protection Law (Norway), *9:* III.B
  E-SIGN Act (U.S.), *9:* II.A.7
  Electronic Communications Directive (European Union), *9:* III.A
  European Union, *9:* III.A
  exemptions, *9:* II.A.9.a
  GLBA, *9:* II.A.9, II.A.9.a
  information brokers, application to, *9:* II.A.2.a
  introduction, *9:* II.A.1
  Japan, *9:* V.B
  law enforcement investigations, delays for, *9:* II.A.5.b
  methods of notification
    Canada, *9:* II.B.3
    United States, *9:* II.A.7, II.A.7.b
  New Zealand, *9:* V.C
  Norway, *9:* III.B
  notification triggers
    employee exceptions, *9:* II.A.4.c
    risk-based, *9:* II.A.4.b
    unauthorized acquisition, *9:* II.A.4.a
  paper records, *9:* II.A.2.b
  personal information, defined, *9:* II.A.3. *See* also Personal information
  PHIPA requirements, *9:* II.B.5
  publicly available information, exceptions for, *9:* II.A.3.a
  response plans, development of, *9:* II.A
  risk assessments
    Australia, *9:* V.A.2
    New Zealand, *9:* V.C.2
  safe harbors, *9:* II.A.9
  scope and coverage of, *9:* II.A.2
  state laws, *1:* I.C.3.b, *9:* II.A.1
    California. *See* California
    summary of, *9: Exh.* 9.1
  substitute notice
    methods of, *9:* II.A.7.b
    thresholds for, *9:* II.A.7.a
  timing requirements
    Australia, *9:* V.A.3
    Canada, *9:* II.B.3
    delays for law enforcement investigation, *9:* II.A.5.b
    generally, *9:* II.A.5.a

Security breach notifications—*cont'd*
New Zealand, ***9:*** V.C.3
unauthorized acquisition, ***9:*** II.A.4.a
United Arab Emirates, ***9:*** IV.A
United Kingdom, ***9:*** III.C
United States, ***9:*** II.A
Security breaches, *9:* II.A
notification of. *See* Security breach notifications
passwords, ***10:*** III.H
personnel records and, ***7:*** II.A.8
response plans, development of, ***9:*** II.A
Social Security numbers, ***10:*** III.H
Security Rules (U.S.)
electronic health information, coverage of, ***1:*** I.B.1.b.i, ***5:*** II.A.1.n
employer compliance issues, ***5:*** II.A.1.n.i
individual rights, ***5:*** II.A.1.n.ii
Security Safeguard Act (California), *1:* I.C.3.a
Sensitive data, collection of
directive 95/46/EC (European Union), ***1:*** III.C.2
European Union, ***1:*** III.C.2
France, ***2:*** III.B.3
Germany, ***2:*** III.C.3
Japan, ***2:*** IV.C.1.e
United Kingdom, ***2:*** III.E.3
Service providers, oversight of, *10:* III.K
Sex discrimination
Hong Kong, ***2:*** IV.B.1
Title VII, Civil Rights Act of 1964 (U.S.), ***4:*** II.A.3
United Kingdom, ***2:*** III.E.1
Sex Discrimination Act (UK, 1975), *2:* III.E.1
Sex Discrimination Ordinance (Hong Kong), *2:* IV.B.1
Sexual Orientation Regulations (UK, 2003), *2:* III.E.1
Social insurance numbers (Canada), *8:* II.C
Social Security Numbers (SSNs), *8:* II.A. *See also* Government identity numbers
account numbers, as, ***8:*** II.A.3.d
Alaska, restrictions on collection and use of, ***8:*** II.A.3.e
business privacy policy requirements, ***8:*** II.A.5
internal policies, ***8:*** II.A.5.a
California. *See* California
collection of, ***8:*** II.A.3.e
Connecticut privacy policy law, ***8:*** II.A.5.b.i
court filings, privacy exceptions, ***8:*** II.A.4.a
electronic transmission of, ***8:*** II.A.3.b
employee's identifying information, disclosure of, ***8:*** II.A.3.f
employment records, ***8:*** II.A.4.c
enforcement and administration, ***8:*** II.A.7
federal legislation, ***8:*** II.A
investigations, privacy exceptions, ***8:*** II.A.4.b
mailing documents containing, ***8:*** II.A.3.a
Michigan, ***8:*** II.A.4.b
privacy policy law, ***8:*** II.A.5.a.i
New Mexico privacy policy law, ***8:*** II.A.5.a.ii
New York, use restrictions
Court filings, exceptions, ***8:*** II.A.4.a
privacy policy law, ***8:*** II.A.5.a.iii
overview, ***8:*** I
as personal information, ***9:*** II.A.3
in personnel records, ***7:*** II.A.7, II.A.8
privacy policy laws, ***8:*** II.A.5
external policies, ***8:*** II.A.5.b
internal policies, ***8:*** II.A.5.a
Protection Laws (state), ***8:*** II.A
application to employers, ***8:*** II.A.1
employers, compliance, ***8:*** II.A.8
enforcement and administration, ***8:*** II.A.7
exceptions, ***8:*** II.A.4
prohibited activities, ***8:*** II.A.3
summary of, Exh. 8.1
types of information covered, ***8:*** II.A.2
Puerto Rico protection law, ***8:*** II.A.6
sale of, ***8:*** II.A.3.c
security breaches and, ***10:*** III.H

South Carolina, use restrictions, *8:* II.A.4.c
Texas privacy policy law, *8:* II.A.5.b.ii
verifications, privacy exceptions, *8:* II.A.4.b

South Carolina
SSNs, use restrictions, *8:* II.A.4.c

Spam Act (Australia, 2003), *3:* IV.A.2

SSNs. *See* Social Security Numbers (SSNs)

Standard Clauses (European Union), *1:* III.D.3

State Identification Card numbers as personal information, *9:* II.A.3

State laws. *See also names of individual states*
alcohol, off-duty use by employees, *4:* II.A.6.a
arrests, employer inquiries regarding, *2:* II.A.8.a
background checks and investigations, *2:* II.A.2.a.ii, II.A.5, II.A.6
disposal of, *2:* II.A.12
drug testing of employees and job applicants, *6:* II.A.3.c
genetic testing of employees and job applicants, *6:* II.A.4.b
HIV/AIDS testing of employees and job applicants, *6:* II.A.4.c
information security programs, *10:* I, II
lie detector examinations of employees and job applicants, *6:* II.A.4.d.ii
off-duty activities of employees, *4:* II.A.9
personnel records
consent for disclosure to third parties, *7:* II.A.4
defamation claims, *7:* II.A.10
employee examination of, *7:* II.A.1
explanatory statements, employees' addition of, *7:* II.A.3
subpoena of, notice to employee, *7:* II.A.5
sealed or expunged convictions, employer inquiries regarding, *2:* II.A.8.a
security breach notification, *9:* II.A.1. *See* also Security breach notifications
smoking, off-duty by employees, *4:* II.A.6.b
SSN Protection Laws. *See* Social Security Numbers
telephone calls, monitoring of by employers, *3:* II.A.1

Stored Communications Act (SCA, U.S.), *3:* II.A.6.a

Subpoenas for personnel records, *7:* II.A.5

Substitute notice of security breaches, *9:* II.A.7.a, II.A.7.b

Surveillance. *See* Monitoring and surveillance by employers; Video surveillance by employers

T

Taiwan
Computer Processed Personal Data Protection Act, *1:* IV.F
constitutional right to privacy, *1:* IV.F, *3:* IV.G.1
data security
access rights, *1:* IV.F.5
accuracy, *1:* IV.F.6
cease use, *1:* IV.F.6
consent, *1:* IV.F.2
corrections, rights to, *1:* IV.F.6
cross-border limitations, *1:* IV.F.4
data retention, *1:* IV.F.7
license/database registration, *1:* IV.F.1
limits on data transfers, *1:* IV.F.4
monitoring of employees, *1:* IV.F.8
penalties, *1:* IV.F.10
security, *1:* IV.F.9
use limitations, *1:* IV.F.3
email, monitoring of by employers, *3:* IV.G.2
Statute Governing the Protection and Monitoring of Communications, *3:* IV.G.2
workplace monitoring, general requirements for, *3:* IV.G.1

Telecommunication Act (Germany), *3:* III.D.1

Telecommunications Business Act of 1991 (Korea), *1:* IV.D

Telecommunications (Lawful Business Practice) Regulations (UK, 2000), *3:* III.E.1
Telemedia Act (Germany), *3:* III.D.1
Telephone calls
monitoring of by employers, *3:* II.A.1, II.A.3
California, *3:* II.A.4
European Union, *3:* III.A.2
Finland, *3:* III.B.2
France, *3:* III.C.2
Germany, *3:* III.D.2
New York, *3:* II.A.5
United Kingdom, *3:* III.E.2
security breaches, notification by, *9:* II.A.7
Texas
background checks and investigations, *2:* II.A.12
SSN privacy policy law, *8:* II.A.5.b.ii
Third parties
Japan, cross-border vs. third-party transfers in, *1:* IV.C.5
onward transfer of data to. *See* Onward transfer agreements
personnel records and, *7:* II.A.4, II.A.5
Title III (Omnibus Crime Control and Safe Streets Act of 1968, U.S.), *3:* II.A.19
Title VII, Civil Rights Act of 1964 (U.S.), *4:* II.A.3
Tobacco
off-duty use of by employees, *4:* II.A.6
Training of employees
in data security, *10:* III.E
in privacy matters, *5:* II.A.1.k.iv.b

U

Unauthorized acquisition of personal information, *9:* II.A.4.a, II.A.4.b
Undercover investigators, *3:* II.A.14
Unfair or deceptive acts or practices, *1:* I.C.4
Unions
data security, *1:* IV.C.3
Japan, *4:* IV.C.2
New York, *3:* II.A.22
off-duty conduct of employees
China, *4:* IV.A.2
Hong Kong, *4:* III.B.2
United Kingdom, *4:* III.B.1
United States, *4:* II.A.1, II.A.1.a, II.A.1.b
workplace surveillance by employers, *3:* II.A.20–II.A.22
United Arab Emirates
security breach notifications, *9:* IV.A
United Kingdom (UK)
background checks and investigations
access and correction rights, *2:* III.E.5
character questions, *2:* III.E.7.e
credit reports, *2:* III.E.7.a
criminal records, *2:* III.E.7.b
general requirements, *2:* III.E.2
notice requirements, *2:* III.E.4
references, *2:* III.E.7.d
reputation, *2:* III.E.7.e
sensitive data, *2:* III.E.3
statutes, *2:* III.E.1
use restrictions, *2:* III.E.6
work history, *2:* III.E.7.c
Data Protection Act
email and Internet monitoring, *3:* III.E.1
telephone calls, monitoring, *3:* III.E.2
video surveillance, *3:* III.E.3
Disability Discrimination Act (1995), *2:* III.E.1
drug testing, *6:* III.E
email and Internet monitoring by employers, *3:* III.E.1
employment equality
Age Regulations (2003), *2:* III.E.1
Race Relations Act (1976), *2:* III.E.1
Religion or Belief Regulations (2003), *2:* III.E.1
Sex Discrimination Act (1975), *2:* III.E.1
Sexual Orientation Regulations (2003), *2:* III.E.1
Employment Practices Code, *1:* III.A, *2:* III.E.2
Employment Practices Data Protection Code, *3:* III.E.1–III.E.3
fraternization of employees, *4:* III.B.4
genetic testing, *6:* III.E

health information, confidentiality of, *5:* III.C
Human Rights Act (1998), *2:* III.E.1, III.E.2
medical examinations, *6:* III.E
moonlighting or outside employment, *4:* III.B.5
National Insurance Numbers, *8:* III.D
off-duty conduct of employees, *4:* III.B
personnel records, access to
denials of requests, *7:* III.D.3
fees for, *7:* III.D.2
subject matter, *7:* III.D.1
political activities, off-duty, *4:* III.B.2
Regulation of Investigatory Powers Act (2000), *3:* III.E.1
Rehabilitation of Offenders Act (1974), *2:* III.E.1
religious activities, off-duty, *4:* III.B.3
security breach notifications, *9:* III.C
Telecommunications (Lawful Business Practice) Regulations (2000), *3:* III.E.1
telephone calls, employers monitoring of, *3:* III.E.2
union membership, *4:* III.B.1
video surveillance by employers, *3:* III.E.3
United States
constitutional privacy protections, *1:* I
Financial Privacy Rule, *1:* I.B.1.a.i
Fourth Amendment, *3:* II.A.16, II.A.18
Privacy Rules. *See* Privacy Rules (U.S.)
Security Rules. *See* Security Rules (U.S.)
statutes. *See* name of Act
USA PATRIOT Act, *9:* II.A.9.a
Use and Protection of Credit Information Act of 1995 (Korea), *1:* IV.D

V

Vendors
background checks and investigations by, *2:* II.A.1, II.A.6, II.A.6.a, II.A.6.b
provision of data to, *10:* III.K
Vermont
drug testing of employees and job applicants, *6:* II.A.3.c.vi
Victoria Health Records Act (Australia, 2001), *5:* IV.A.3
Video Camera Privacy Guidelines (Korea), *3:* IV.E.2
Video surveillance by employers
Australia, *3:* IV.A.3
Data Protection Act (France), *3:* III.C.3
Data Protection Act (Germany), *3:* III.D.3
European Union, *3:* III.A.3
Finland, *3:* III.B.3
France, *3:* III.C.3
Germany, *3:* III.D.3
intrusiveness of, *3:* II.A.17
Korea, *3:* IV.E.2
Korea, Video Camera Privacy Guidelines, *3:* IV.E.2
New South Wales, Workplace Surveillance Act, *3:* IV.A.3
New Zealand, *3:* IV.F.2
notice of, *3:* II.A.15.b
unionized settings, *3:* II.A.22
United Kingdom, *3:* III.E.3

W

Waivers, *5:* II.A.1.k.iv.h
California, Confidentiality of Medical Information Act, *5:* II.A.3.a.ii
Work history questions in background checks
Belgium, *2:* III.A.2
Brazil, *2:* II.B.2
Canada, *2:* II.C.2
China, *2:* IV.A.2.c
France, *2:* III.B.7.c
Germany, *2:* III.C.7.c
Hong Kong, *2:* IV.B.4.c
Italy, *2:* III.D.2
Korea, *2:* IV.D.2
Mexico, *2:* II.D.2
United Kingdom, *2:* III.E.7.c
Workers' compensation laws
New York, *5:* II.A.3.b.iv

Workplace Email, Web Browsing and Privacy Guidelines (Australia), ***3:*** IV.A.1, IV.A.2
email, monitoring of by employers, ***3:*** IV.A.2
video surveillance by employers, ***3:*** IV.A.3
workplace monitoring, general requirements for, ***3:*** IV.A.1
Works Council Act (Germany), ***3:*** III.D.1
Works Councils
European Union, ***3:*** III.A.4
France, ***2:*** III.B.2, ***3:*** III.C.1
Germany, ***3:*** III.D.1